PRINCIPLES OF MICROECONOMICS

SEVENTH EDITION

Principles of Microeconomics

EDWIN MANSFIELD

DIRECTOR / CENTER FOR ECONOMICS AND TECHNOLOGY / UNIVERSITY OF PENNSYLVANIA

SEVENTH EDITION

W • W • NORTON & COMPANY   *NEW YORK • LONDON*

To Edward Deering Mansfield (1801–1880)
and his brother-in-law Charles Davies (1798–1876)
neither of whom should be held responsible
for the views expressed here.

Printed in the United States of America.

The text of this book is composed in Garamond Light, with the display set in Futura Book Bold.
Composition by TSI Graphics. Manufacturing by Arcata Hawkins.

Library of Congress Cataloging-in-Publication Data

Mansfield, Edwin.
    Principles of microeconomics/Edwin Mansfield. —7th ed.
        p. cm.
    Includes index.
    1. Microeconomics.   I. Title.
    HB172.M363 1992
    338.5—dc20   91-42863

ISBN 0-393-96175-3

W. W. Norton & Company, Inc., 500 Fifth Avenue, New York, N.Y. 10110
W. W. Norton & Company Ltd., 10 Coptic Street, London WCIA 1PU

2 3 4 5 6 7 8 9 0

CONTENTS

PART TWO CONSUMER BEHAVIOR AND BUSINESS DECISION MAKING

PART THREE   MARKET STRUCTURE AND ANTITRUST POLICY

PART FOUR   DISTRIBUTION OF INCOME

PART FIVE   GOVERNMENT AND THE ECONOMY

PART SIX   INTERNATIONAL TRADE AND ALTERNATIVE ECONOMIC SYSTEMS

BARRIERS

ONE FIRM

NO SUBSTIT.

PREFACE

Textbooks, like firms and economies, do not change at a constant rate; instead, some revisions are minor, while others are extensive and fundamental. This seventh edition, while it shares the same objectives as its predecessor, is a very substantial departure from it. Some of the major changes are briefly described below.

1. *New oligopoly chapter with emphasis on game theory.* The coverage of game theory has been expanded greatly, with sections on the Prisoners' Dilemma, tit-for-tat, non-credible threats, entry deterrence, and other topics; the coverage is unusually full, but nonetheless is readily accessible to the average student.

2. *New treatments of principal-agent problems, asymmetric information, education as a signaling device, diversification, and the capital asset pricing model.* In Chapters 6, 13, 14, there are discussions of these important new microeconomic concepts and techniques; these discussions are integrated with other relevant and related materials, not walled off in a separate chapter.

3. *Much more coverage of the major changes that have occurred in Eastern Europe (and the Soviet Union and China).* Beginning in Chapter 3, there is a prominent discussion of the historic economic changes in Poland and elsewhere in Eastern Europe. In Chapter 19, the treatments of the (recently disintegrated) Soviet Union and China have been thoroughly revised.

4. *Improved organization.* Many chapters have been moved to improve the organization of the book. The introductory discussion of the business firm has been moved to Chapter 6, and the chapters on government spending, taxation, and the environment have been moved to Chapters 16 and 17.

Based on the positive reaction of both students and instructors to the sections on central economic problems in the previous edition, each two or more pages long, this feature has been maintained and refined. Three of the new multipage inserts on *Central Economic Issues* are new: (1) How to Make the Transition from Communism to Capitalism: The Case of Poland, (2) Medical Care: Can Economic Analysis Be Used? and (3) What Should Be Done about Global Warming? These new features should be of great use in whetting the interests of students and in helping them to thread their way through complex contemporary issues.

As in previous editions, the boxed inserts and examples are designed to make economics more relevant and interesting to students. Some of the new boxed inserts are: (1) Toting up the Costs of the War against Saddam Hussein, (2) How Asymmetric Information Affects the Market for Used Cars, (3) Using Diversification to Reduce Risk, (4) The Principal-Agent Problem, (5) The Coca-Cola Company and the Price of Inputs, (6) Diversifiable Risk, Nondiversifiable Risk, and the Capital Asset Pricing Model, and (7) Why the Tennessee Valley Authority? These inserts take up a wide variety of topics of current interest, as well as a number of new theoretical topics. They are very important in showing how economics can be used to help solve a host of major problems. Also, three of the boxed examples are new: (1) The Costs of a Small Machine Shop, (2) Economies of Scale in Cable Television, and (3) What Will Be on the Covers of *Newsweek* and *Time?*

Most textbooks do not encourage the student to get involved in the subject. They simply lay out the material, leaving the student to absorb it passively. In previous editions, I have invited students to *do* economics in order to understand it better. Scores of examples were provided, each describing a real (or realistic) situation and then calling on the student to work through the solution. Also, in each chapter there were two problem sets, both designated "Test Yourself" that enabled students to check their comprehension of what they had just read. The reaction of instructors and students was very favorable, and the emphasis on doing economics is maintained in this Seventh Edition.

All of the empirical and policy-oriented chapters have been updated. Since a text should reflect current conditions and concerns, the government policies in all the major economic areas—fiscal, monetary, incomes, farm, energy, environmental, antitrust, and international—are reviewed in depth. The latest data available have been incorporated in the tables, diagrams, and discussions, while revisions in sections on a variety of other topics have brought them into line with current developments.

As supplements to this text, I have prepared both a book of readings and a study guide containing problems and exercises. The book of readings is *Principles of Microeconomics: Readings, Issues, and Cases,* Fourth Edition. It provides a substantial set of supplementary articles, carefully correlated with the text for instructors who want to introduce their students to the writings of major contemporary economists. It is designed to acquaint the student with a wide range of economic analysis, spanning the spectrum from the classics to the present-day radicals. The emphasis, as in the text, is on integrating theory, measurement, and applications.

The *Study Guide*, Seventh Edition, contains, in addition to problems, review questions, and tests, a large number of cases that require the student to work with quantitative material in applying concepts to practical situations. Both students and instructors have reported that such cases are important in motivating students and illuminating economic theory.

An *Instructor's Manual* has been prepared by Michael Claudon of Middlebury College to accompany the text. A *Test Item File*, prepared by Herbert Gishlick of Rider College, is available both in printed form and on computer disk. *Transparency Masters* are also available to instructors who adopt the text.

Finally, it is a pleasure to acknowledge the debts that I owe to the many teachers at various colleges and universities who have commented in detail on various parts of the manuscript. The first, second, and third editions benefited greatly from the advice I received from the following distinguished economists, none of whom is responsible, of course, for the outcome: Wallace Atherton, California State University at Long Beach; Bela Balassa, Johns Hopkins; Robert Baldwin, University of Wisconsin (Madison); Arthur Benavie, North Carolina; Lee Biggs, Montgomery College; Donald Billings, Boise State; William Branson, Princeton; Martin Bronfenbrenner, Duke; Edward Budd, Penn State; Phillip Burstein, Purdue; Wade Chio, U.S. Air Force Academy; Michael Claudon, Middlebury; Warren Coates, Federal Reserve; Richard Cooper, Harvard; Alan Deardorff, Michigan; William Desvousges, Missouri (Rolla); F. Trenery Dolbear, Brandeis; Robert Dorfman, Harvard; James Duesenberry, Harvard; William

Dugger, North Texas State University; Richard Easterlin, University of Southern California; Jonathan Eaton, Princeton; David Fand, Wayne State; Judith Fernandez, University of California (Berkeley); David Gay, University of Arkansas; Howard A. Gilbert, South Dakota State University; Gerald Goldstein, Northwestern; Robert Gordon, Northwestern; Edward Gramlich, Michigan; Herschel Grossman, Brown; William Gunther, Alabama; Jerry Gustafson, Beloit; Judith Herman, Queens College; Alan Heston, University of Pennsylvania; Albert Hirschman, Harvard; Ronald Jones, Rochester; John Kareken, Minnesota; Ann Krueger, Duke; Robert Kuenne, Princeton; Simon Kuznets, Harvard; William Leonard, St. Joseph's; Richard Levin, Yale; Raymond Lubitz, Columbia and the Federal Reserve; John F. MacDonald, Illinois (Chicago Circle); Sherman Maisel, University of California (Berkeley); Leonard Martin, Cleveland State University; Thomas Mayer, University of California (Davis); William McEachern, University of Connecticut; Joseph McKinney, Baylor; Edward McNertney, Texas Christian University; Steven Morrison, University of California (Berkeley); John Murphy, Canisius; Arthur Okun, Brookings Institution; Lloyd Orr, Indiana; R. D. Peterson, Markenomics Associates (Fort Collins); E. Dwight Phaup, Union College; Roger Ransom, University of California (Berkeley); Charles Ratliff, Davidson College; Albert Rees, Sloan Foundation; Edward Renshaw, State University of New York (Albany); Anthony Romeo, Unilever; Vernon Ruttan, Minnesota; Warren St. James, Nassau County Community College; Steven Sacks, University of Connecticut; Allen Sanderson, William and Mary; David Schulze, Florida, Edward Shapiro, University of Toledo; William Shugart, Arizona; Paul Sommers, Middlebury; Nicolas Spulber, Indiana; Charles Tone, Swarthmore; Richard Sutch, University of California (Berkeley); Frank Tansey, City University of New York; Michael Taussig, Rutgers; Thomas Tidrick, Clayton Junior College; Fred Westfield, Vanderbilt; Simon Whitney, Iona College; William Whitney, University of Pennsylvania; and Harold Williams, Kent State University.

Among the teachers who contributed comments and suggestions for the changes in subsequent editions are: Werner Baer, University of Illinois; Willie Belton, Georgia Institute of Technology; Don Billings, Linfield College; Steven Cunningham, University of Connecticut; Eric Engen, UCLA; Carl Enomoto, New Mexico State University; Edwin Fujii, University of Hawaii; Otis Gilley, University of Texas; Herbert Gishlick, Rider College; Marvin E. Goodstein, University of the South; Clyde A. Haulman, William and Mary; Marc Hayford, Loyola; Bruce Herrick, Washington and Lee; William Keeton, Yale; Michael Knetter, Dartmouth; Stuart Lynn, Assumption College; Thomas Maloy, Muskegon Community College; Walter Misiolek, Alabama; Edward Montgomery, Michigan State; Jennifer Roback, Yale; Newton Robinson, Alfred University; Leonard Schifrin, William and Mary; Thomas Shea, Springfield College; Calvin D. Siebert, Iowa; and Robert Withington, Jr., State University of New York.

I would like to thank Elisabeth Allison of Harvard University and Nariman Behravesh of Oxford Economics USA for contributing the inserts that appear (over their initials) in various chapters, and Catherine Wick and W. Drake McFeely of W. W. Norton for their efficient handling of the publishing end of the work. As always, my wife, Lucile, has contributed an enormous amount to the completion of this book.

Philadelphia, 1991   E.M.

PART ONE

INTRODUCTION TO ECONOMICS

ECONOMIC PROBLEMS AND ANALYSIS

GEORGE BERNARD SHAW, the great playwright, once said, "The only time my education was interrupted was when I was in school." Fortunately, economics, if properly presented, can contribute mightily to your education—and you can learn it without leaving school. Let's look at a sample of the major problems economists deal with; you'll find that each of them could have a big effect on your own life.

ECONOMIC PROBLEMS: A SAMPLER

Unemployment and Inflation

The history of the American economy is for the most part a story of growth. Our output—the amount of goods and services we produce annually—has grown rapidly over the years, giving us a standard of living that could not have been imagined a century ago. For example, output per person in the United States was about $22,000 in 1990; in 1900, it was much, much smaller. Nonetheless, the growth of output has not been steady or uninterrupted; instead, our output has tended to fluctuate and so has unemployment. In periods when output has fallen, thousands, even millions, of people have been thrown out of work. In the Great Depression of the 1930s over 20 percent of the labor force was unemployed (see Figure 1.1). Even in 1992, layoffs occurred in many areas.

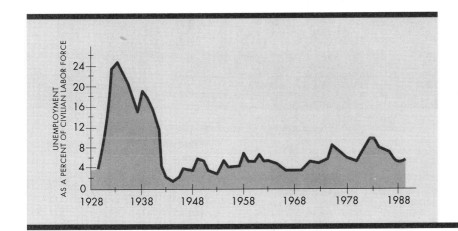

Figure 1.1
Unemployment Rates, United States, 1929–90
The unemployment rate has varied substantially from year to year. In the Great Depression, it reached a high of over 24 percent. In late 1990, it was about 6 percent.

The first of our sample of economic problems is: *What determines the extent of unemployment in the American economy, and what can be done to reduce it?* This problem is complicated by a related phenomenon: The level of prices may rise when we reduce the level of unemployment. In other words, inflation may occur. Thus the problem is not only to curb unemployment, but to do this without producing an inflation so ruinous to the nation's economic health that the cure proves more dangerous than the ailment. Consequently, another major accompanying question is: *What determines the rate of inflation, and how can it be reduced?* As Figure 1.2 shows, we have experienced considerable inflation since 1929; the dollar has lost over four-fifths of its purchasing power during the past forty years alone. Moreover, in the 1970s and early 1980s, our economy often was bedeviled by "stagflation": a combination of high unemployment and high inflation.

During the past 50 years, economists have learned a great deal about the factors that determine the extent of unemployment and inflation.

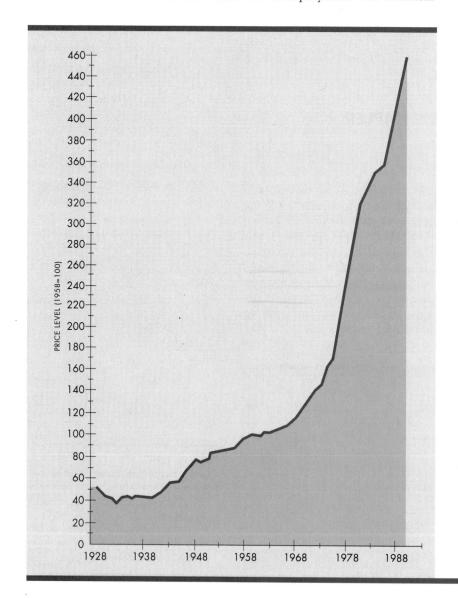

Figure 1.2
Changes in Price Level, United States, 1929–90
The price level has increased steadily since the 1930s, and is now over five times as high as it was in 1950.

Nonetheless, this topic remains the center of a great deal of controversy. Any responsible citizen needs to know what economists have learned—and to be aware of the differences of opinion among leading economists on this score. To understand many of the central political issues of the day, and to vote intelligently, this knowledge is essential. Also, to understand the fallacies in many apparently simple remedies for the complex economic problems in this area, you need to know some economics.

Economics is divided into two parts: microeconomics and macroeconomics. **Microeconomics** *deals with the economic behavior of individual units like consumers, firms, and resource owners, while* **macroeconomics** *deals with the behavior of economic aggregates like national output, the price level, and the level of unemployment.* This volume is concerned primarily with microeconomics, but since one must know some macroeconomics to understand microeconomics, we include some macroeconomics as well. However, the economic problem cited in this section is too purely macroeconomic in nature to be taken up in detail here. For a more intensive discussion of this sort of problem, see the companion volume to this one, *Principles of Macroeconomics*.

U.S. Competitiveness in World Markets and the Productivity Slowdown

During recent decades, American manufacturers have been experiencing increased difficulty in competing with their rivals in Japan, Germany, and elsewhere. In industries like steel, machine tools, consumer electronics, and autos, American firms, once world leaders, are confronted with foreign producers that can produce at lower cost than they can. Our second example of an economic problem is: *Why are American firms finding it so difficult to compete, and how can their competitiveness be enhanced?*

One factor that is relevant in this regard is the recent history of labor productivity in the United States. **Labor productivity** is defined as the amount of output that can be obtained per hour of labor. All nations are interested in increasing labor productivity, since it is intimately related to a nation's standard of living. Many factors, including new technologies like microelectronics and biotechnology, influence the rate of increase of labor productivity.

Historically, labor productivity has increased relatively rapidly in the United States; but beginning in the late 1960s, U.S. labor productivity rose at a slower pace. At first, it was unclear whether this slowdown was only temporary, but during the 1970s the situation got worse, not better. Between 1977 and 1980, labor productivity in the United States actually declined. (In other words, less was produced per hour of labor in 1980 than in 1977!) During the 1980s, productivity growth picked up, but was still below what it was in the 1960s. (And again in 1989 and 1990, labor productivity fell.)

Many observers regard this productivity slowdown as being partly responsible for the decline of American competitiveness. If so, this leads us to a further set of questions: *What determines the rate of increase of labor productivity? Why has this productivity slowdown occurred in the United States? What measures can and should be adopted to cope with it?* Economics provides a considerable amount of information on this score. Not only does economics tell us a good deal about the broad factors influencing national productivity levels; in addition, it provides rules and principles that are useful in increasing the productivity and efficiency of individual firms (and government agencies).

The Economic Ferment in Eastern Europe

While the United States has its share of economic troubles, it is regarded with envy by most of the world. One of the most startling developments of the 1990s has been the movement of the East European countries like Poland and Czechoslovakia away from central planning and toward capitalism. Under capitalism, individual firms make their own decisions concerning what to produce and how to produce it. This is in marked contrast to centrally planned economies where these decisions are made by planners in government agencies.

To make the transition from central planning to a more capitalistic system, factories owned by the state have been sold to private organizations and individuals, and governments have loosened their control over the prices of goods and services. In 1990, price controls were reported to have been removed in Poland and East Germany virtually overnight. In Czechoslovakia, the administration of Vaclav Havel asked the nation's Parliament to approve a strategy of rapid price decontrol. These are enormous and fundamental changes that have surprised even the most knowledgeable observers.

Our third example of an economic problem is: *What are the advantages of a capitalistic system? What do these countries hope to achieve by adopting such a system?* In 1990, it was obvious to practically any Russian citizen that the Russian economy was in trouble. Food was scarce, output was declining, and the price level was rising. According to the available estimates, Russian workers had to labor a great deal longer than Americans to obtain television sets or beef. But what made some Russian leaders believe that their country would be better off if it embraced capitalism, which for decades had been its arch foe?

It is important to recognize that the American brand of capitalism is built on the idea that firms should compete with one another. Thus the producers of steel, automobiles, oil, toothpicks, and other goods are expected to set their prices independently and not to collude. Certain acts of Congress, often referred to as the antitrust laws, make it illegal for firms to get together and set the price of a product. This leads to another question: *Why is competition of this sort socially desirable?* Of course, one reason why Americans have traditionally favored competition over collusion, and relatively small firms over giant ones, is that they have mistrusted the concentration of economic power, and obviously, this mistrust was based on both political and economic considerations. But beyond this, you should know when competition generally benefits society, and when it does not. Economists have devoted a huge amount of time and effort to help answer this question.

The Elimination of Poverty

As pointed out by Philip Wicksteed, a prominent twentieth-century British economist, "A man can be neither a saint, nor a lover, nor a poet, unless he has comparatively recently had something to eat." Although relatively few people in the United States lack food desperately, about 32 million American people, approximately 13 percent of the population of

The Berlin Wall comes down, November 11, 1989

the United States, live in what is officially designated as **poverty.** These people have frequently been called invisible in a nation where the average yearly income per family is about $35,000; but the poor are invisible only to those who shut their eyes, since they exist in ghettos in the wealthiest American cities like New York, Chicago, and Los Angeles, as well as near Main Street in thousands of small towns. They can also be found in areas where industry has come and gone, as in the former coal-mining towns of Pennsylvania and West Virginia, and in areas where decades of farming have depleted the soil.

Table 1.1 shows the distribution of income in the United States in 1989. Clearly, there are very substantial differences among families in income level. You as a citizen and a human being need to understand the social mechanisms underlying the distribution of income, both in the United States and in other countries, and how reasonable and just they are. Our fourth economic problem is: *Why does poverty exist in the world today, and what can be done to abolish it?* To help the poor effectively, we must understand the causes of poverty.

Since poverty is intimately bound up with our racial problems and the decay of our cities, the success or failure of measures designed to eradicate poverty may also help us determine whether we can achieve a society where equality of opportunity is more than a slogan and where people do not have to escape to the suburbs to enjoy green space and fresh air. Nor does the economist's concern with poverty stop at our shoreline. One of the biggest problems of the world today is the plight of the poor countries of Asia, Africa, and Latin America—the so-called less developed countries. The industrialized countries of the world, like the United States, Western Europe, and Japan, are really just rich little islands surrounded by seas of poverty. Over half of the world's population lives in countries where per capita income is less than $5,000 per year. These countries lack equipment, technology, and education; sometimes (but by no means always) they also suffer from overpopulation. Economists have devoted considerable attention to the problems of the less developed countries, and to developing techniques to assist them.

Table 1.1
Percentage Distribution of Households, by Annual Money Income, United States, 1989

MONEY INCOME (DOLLARS)	PERCENT OF ALL HOUSEHOLDS
Under 5,000	5
5,000 – 9,999	10
10,000 – 14,999	10
15,000 – 24,999	18
25,000 – 34,999	16
35,000 – 49,999	17
50,000 – 74,999	15
75,000 – 99,999	5
100,000 and over	4
Total	100

Source: U.S. Bureau of the Census.

WHAT IS ECONOMICS?

Human Wants and Resources

According to one standard definition, *economics is concerned with the way resources are allocated among alternative uses to satisfy human wants.* This definition is fine, but it does not mean much unless we define what is meant by *human wants* and by *resources.* What do these terms mean?

Human wants are things, services, goods, and circumstances that people desire. Wants vary greatly among individuals and over time for the same individual. Some people like sports, others like books; some want to travel, others want to putter in the yard. An individual's desire for a particular good during a particular period of time is not infinite, but, in the aggregate, human wants seem to be insatiable. Besides the basic desires for food, shelter, and clothing, which must be fulfilled to some extent if the human organism is to maintain its existence, wants stem from cultural factors. For example, society, often helped along by advertising and other devices to modify tastes, promotes certain images of "the good life," which frequently entails owning an expensive car and living in a $200,000 house in the suburbs.

Resources are the things or services used to produce goods which then can be used to satisfy wants. *Economic resources* are scarce, while *free resources,* such as air, are so abundant that they can be obtained without charge. The test of whether a resource is an economic resource or a free resource is price: economic resources command a nonzero price, but free resources do not. The number of free resources is actually quite limited. For instance, although the earth contains a huge amount of water, it is not a free resource to the typical urban or suburban home owner, who must pay a local water authority for providing and maintaining his or her water supply. In a world where all resources were free, there would be no economic problem, since all wants could be satisfied.

Economic resources can be classified into three categories, each of which is described below:

1. LAND. A shorthand expression for natural resources, land includes minerals as well as plots of ground. Clearly, land is an important and valuable resource in both agriculture and industry. Think of the fertile soil of Iowa or Kansas, from which are obtained such abundant crops. Or consider Manhattan island, which supports the skyscrapers, shops, and theaters in the heart of New York. In addition, land is an important part of our environment, and it provides enjoyment above and beyond its contribution to agricultural and industrial output.

2. LABOR. Human efforts, both physical and mental, are included in the category of labor. Thus, when you study for a final examination or make out an income tax return, this is as much labor as if you were to dig a ditch. In 1992, over 100 million people were employed (or looking for work) in the United States. This vast labor supply is, of course, an extremely important resource, without which our nation could not maintain its current output level.

3. CAPITAL. Buildings, equipment, inventories, and other nonhuman producible resources that contribute to the production, marketing, and distribution of goods and services all fall within the economist's definition of capital. Examples are machine tools and warehouses; but not all types of capital are big or bulky: for example, a hand calculator, or a pencil for that matter, is a type of capital. American workers have an enormous amount of capital to work with. Think of the oil refineries in New Jersey and Philadelphia, the electronics plants in Silicon Valley and Texas, the aircraft plants in Washington and Georgia, and the host of additional types of capital we have and use in this country. Without this capital, the nation's output level would be a great deal less than it is.

Technology and Choice

As pointed out above, economics is concerned with the way resources are allocated among alternative uses to satisfy human wants. An important determinant of the extent to which human wants can be satisfied from the amount of resources at hand is technology. *Technology* is society's pool of knowledge concerning the industrial arts. It includes the knowledge of engineers, scientists, artisans, managers, and others concerning how goods and services can be produced. For example, it in-

Land

Labor

cludes the best existing knowledge regarding the ways in which an automobile plant or a synthetic rubber plant should be designed and operated. The level of technology sets limits on the amount and types of goods and services that can be derived from a given amount of resources.

To see this, suppose that engineers and artisans do not know how an automobile can be produced with less than 500 hours of labor being used in its manufacture. Clearly, this sets limits on the number of automobiles that can be produced with the available labor force. Or suppose that scientists and engineers do not know how to produce a ton of synthetic rubber with less than a certain amount of capital being used in its manufacture. This sets limits on the amount of synthetic rubber that can be produced with the available quantity of capital.

Given the existing technology, the fact that resources are scarce means that only a limited amount of goods and services can be produced from them. In other words, the capacity to produce goods and services is limited—*far more limited than human wants*. Thus there arises the necessity for **choice.** Somehow or other, a choice must be made as to how the available resources will be used (or if they will be used at all). And somehow a choice must be made as to how the output produced from these resources will be distributed among the population.

Economics is concerned with how such choices are made. Economists have spent a great deal of time, energy, and talent trying to determine how such choices *are* made in various circumstances, and how they *should* be made. Indeed, as we shall see in the next section, the basic questions that economics deals with are problems of choice of this sort. Note that these problems of choice go beyond the problems of particular individuals in choosing how to allocate their resources; they are problems of social choice.

Capital

Central Questions in Economics

Economists are particularly concerned with four basic questions regarding the working of any economic system—ours or any other. These questions are: (1) What determines what (and how much) is produced? (2) What determines how it is produced? (3) What determines how the society's output is distributed among the members? (4) What determines the rate at which the society's per capita income will grow? These questions lie at the core of economics, because they are directed at the most fundamental characteristics of economic systems. And as stressed in the previous section, they are problems of choice.

To illustrate the nature and basic importance of these questions, suppose that, because of war or natural catastrophe, your town is isolated from the adjoining territory. No longer is it possible for the town's inhabitants to leave, or for people or goods to enter. (Lest you regard this as fanciful, it is perhaps worthwhile to note that Leningrad—now St. Petersburg, once again—was under siege in World War II for over two years.) In this situation, you and your fellow townspeople must somehow resolve each of these questions. You must decide what goods and services will be produced, how each will be produced, who will receive what, and how much provision there will be for increased output in the future.

In a situation of this sort, your very survival will depend on how effectively you answer these questions. If a decision is made to produce too much clothing and too little food, some of the townspeople may starve. If a decision is made to produce wheat from soil that is inappropriate for wheat, but excellent for potatoes, much the same result may occur. If a decision is made to allot practically all of the town's output to friends and political cronies of the mayor, those who oppose him or her may have a very rough time. And if a decision is made to eat, drink, and be merry today, and not to worry about tomorrow, life may be very meager in the days ahead.

Because we are considering a relatively small and isolated population, the importance of these questions may seem more obvious than in a huge country like the United States, which is constantly communicating, trading, and interacting with the rest of the world. But the truth is that these questions are every bit as important to the United States as to the isolated town. And, for this reason, it is important that we understand how these decisions are made, and whether they are being made effectively. Just as in the hypothetical case of the isolated town, your survival depends on these decisions—but in the United States the situation isn't hypothetical!

TEST YOURSELF

1. Explain why each of the following resources is or is not capital: (a) iron ore in Minnesota that is still in the ground; (b) a Boeing 747 airplane operated by American Airlines; (c) a Chrysler dealer's inventory of unsold cars; (d) a telephone used by the University of Oklahoma.

2. Alfred Marshall, the great British economist, defined economics as follows: "Economics is a study of men as they live and move and think in the ordinary business of life. But it concerns itself chiefly with those motives which affect, most powerfully and most steadily, man's conduct *in the business part of life*. . . . [The] steadiest motive to ordinary business work is the desire for the pay which is the material reward of work." Does this definition encompass all of the examples of economic analysis and problems contained so far in this chapter?

3. C. J. Blank and E. Rosinski of Mobil Research and Development Corporation invented a new type of catalyst which enables all refiners to save an estimated 200 million barrels of crude oil per year. Has this invention altered the technology of the oil refining industry? Has it changed the amount of goods and services that can be derived from a given amount of resources? Were resources used to obtain this invention? If so, what types of resources were used?

4. We described four basic questions that any economic system must answer. Which of these questions is involved in each of the following specific problems: (a) Should the United States use natural gas to produce ammonia? (b) Should taxes on the poor be lower? (c) Should American consumers save more? (d) Should more of our nation's industry be used to produce food?

OPPORTUNITY COST: A FUNDAMENTAL CONCEPT

In previous sections, we have emphasized that economics is concerned with the way resources are allocated among alternative uses to satisfy human wants. To help determine how resources should be allocated, economists often use the concept of ***opportunity cost.*** We turn now to an introductory discussion of this concept, which should help to acquaint you with how it is used.

Since a specific case is more interesting than abstract discussion, let's return to the case of the town that is isolated from the adjoining territory because of a war or natural catastrophe. Suppose that you are a member of the town council that is organized to determine how the town's resources should be utilized. To keep things simple, suppose that only two goods—food and clothing—can be produced. (This is an innocuous assumption that allows us to strip the problem to its essentials.) You must somehow figure out how much of each good should be produced. How can you go about solving the problem?

Clearly, the first step toward a solution is to list the various resources contained within the town. Using the technology available to the townspeople, each of these resources can be used to produce either food or clothing. Some of these resources are much more effective at producing one good than the other. For example, a tailor probably is better able to produce clothing than to produce food. But nonetheless most resources can be adapted to produce either good. For example, a tailor can be put to work on a farm, even though he or she may not be very good at farming.

After listing the various available resources and having determined how effective each is at producing food or clothing, the next step is to see how much food the town could produce per year, if it produced nothing but food, and how much clothing it could produce per year, if it produced nothing but clothing. Also, you should determine, if various amounts of food are produced per year, the maximum amount of clothing that the town can produce per year. For example, if the town produces 100 tons of food per year, what is the maximum amount of clothing it can produce per year? If the town produces 200 tons of food per year, what is the maximum amount of clothing it can produce per year? And so on.

Having carried out this step, suppose that the results are as shown in Table 1.2. According to this table, the town can produce (at most) 200 tons of clothing per year if it produces nothing but clothing (possibility A). Or it can produce (at most) 400 tons of food per year if it produces nothing but food (possibility E). Other possible combinations (labeled B, C, and D) of food and clothing output are specified in Table 1.2.

The data in Table 1.2 put in bold relief the basic problem of choice facing you and the other members of the town council. Because the town's resources are limited, the town can only produce limited amounts of each good. There is no way, for example, that the town can produce 200 tons of clothing per year and 200 tons of food per year. This is beyond the capacity of the town's resources. If the town wants to produce 200 tons of clothing, it can produce no food—which is hardly a pleasant prospect. And if the town wants to produce 200 tons of food, it can produce 150 (not 200) tons of clothing per year.

More Food Means Less Clothing

A very important fact illustrated by Table 1.2 is that, whenever the town increases its production of one good, it must cut back its production of the other good. For example, if the town increases its production of food from 100 to 200 tons per year, it must cut back its production of clothing from 180 to 150 tons per year. Thus *the cost to the town of increasing its*

Table 1.2
Combinations of Output of Food and Clothing That the Town Can Produce per Year

POSSIBILITY	AMOUNT OF FOOD PRODUCED PER YEAR (TONS)	AMOUNT OF CLOTHING PRODUCED PER YEAR (TONS)
A	0	200
B	100	180
C	200	150
D	300	100
E	400	0

TOTING UP THE COSTS OF THE WAR AGAINST SADDAM HUSSEIN

In late 1990 and early 1991, the United States and its allies were engaged in a full-scale war against Iraq. A half million soldiers and their equipment were transported to the Persian Gulf and maintained there. Thousands of missiles were used in the hostilities. According to the Bush administration, the cost of the war to the Pentagon was about $50 billion, but was this the cost to the United States? Absolutely not.

Because the allies pledged to contribute $53.9 billion to the United States to help pay for the war, the United States may more than recoup the Pentagon's expenses. Moreover, this is particularly likely since the Bush administration's cost estimate of $50 billion may have been too high. For example, the Pentagon seems to have overestimated the effects of the war on the price of oil—and hence on its fuel bills.

Further, many of the weapons lost in the war may really have been redundant. At the beginning of hostilities, the United States had 267,000 TOW anti-tank missiles, 428,000 multi-launch rocket systems, 5,000 Patriot missiles, and over 2,000 Tomahawk cruise missiles. This huge inventory of weapons was built up during the days when Russia and its allies were regarded as a much more dangerous threat than in the early 1990s. Many observers have questioned whether Congress would ever be willing to replace many of the weapons lost in the war.

On the other hand, many of the costs of the war are much more subtle than indicated by a simple listing of the expenses of the Pentagon. According to many economists, including Alan Greenspan, the chairman of the Federal Reserve, the war helped to bring about the reduction in national output and the increase in unemployment that occurred in the

United States in late 1990 and early 1991. (Why? Because it raised oil prices and reduced consumer and business confidence in the future.) If Greenspan is right, it is obvious that, even if the United States is paid in full by its allies for the expenses incurred by the Pentagon, the war may nonetheless have been costly.

Here, as in so many other areas, the concept of opportunity cost is of fundamental importance. To determine the actual cost of the war to the United States, you must try to determine what the United States really gave up by engaging in this war. Clearly, the actual cost was quite different from the amount the Pentagon spent.

food output from 100 to 200 tons per year is that it must reduce its cloth-ing output from 180 to 150 tons per year.

Economists refer to this cost as **opportunity cost** (or **alternative cost**): it is one of the most fundamental concepts in economics. *The op-portunity cost of using resources in a certain way is the value of what these resources could have produced if they had been used in the best al-ternative way.* In this case, the opportunity cost of the extra 100 tons of food per year is the 30 tons of clothing per year that must be forgone. This is what the town must give up in order to get the extra 100 tons of food. Why is opportunity cost so important? Because for you and the other members of the town council to determine which combination of food and clothing is best, you should compare the value of increases in food output with the opportunity costs of such increases.

For example, suppose that the town council is considering whether or not to increase food output from 100 to 200 tons per year. To decide this question, the council should compare the value of the extra 100 tons of food with the opportunity cost of the extra food (which is the 30 tons of clothing that must be given up). If the town council feels that the extra 100 tons of food are worth more to the town's welfare than the 30 tons of clothing that are given up, the extra food should be produced. Otherwise it should not be produced.

PARKS AND OPPORTUNITY COSTS.   As we have just seen, the concept of op-portunity cost can be used to help solve the hypothetical problem of the town council described above. Used in a similar way, the concept of op-portunity cost can throw significant light on many important real prob-lems as well. For example, suppose that a bill is presented to Congress to set aside certain wilderness areas as national parks. At first glance, it may appear that such a step entails no cost to society, since the land is not being utilized and the resources required to designate the areas as na-tional parks are trivial. But using the concept of opportunity cost, it is clear that this step may have very substantial costs to society. For in-stance, if these lands are made part of the national parks system, the min-erals, timber, and other natural resources contained within the areas cannot be extracted nor can the lands be used as sites for factories or processing plants. As pointed out above, the opportunity cost of using re-sources in one way is the value of what these resources could have pro-duced had they been used in the best alternative way. Suppose that if these lands are not turned into national parks, their most valuable alter-native use is for development of copper mines which would produce benefits amounting to $25 million per year to society. Then the actual cost to society of using these lands as parks is $25 million per year, since this is the amount that society is giving up when it uses them in this way (rather than selecting the most valuable alternative). Thus, whether these lands should be used as parks depends on whether the society believes that it is worth $25 million or more to do so.

The concept of opportunity cost is very important in analyzing per-sonal, managerial, and judicial issues, as well as questions involving gov-ernment policy. Example 1.1 shows how this concept can be applied to determine the true costs to a student of going to college. Example 1.2 in-dicates how this concept was used in a legal case to assess damages. Like the examples in subsequent chapters, they should be studied carefully.

THE IMPACT OF ECONOMICS ON SOCIETY

Economics has influenced generations of statesmen, philosophers, and ordinary citizens, and has played a significant role in shaping our society today.

Adam Smith, Father of Modern Economics

To illustrate the importance of economic ideas, let's consider some of the precepts of Adam Smith (1723–90), the man who is often called the father of modern economics. Much of his masterpiece *The Wealth of Nations* seems trite today, because it has been absorbed so thoroughly into modern thought, but it was not trite when it was written. On the contrary, Smith's ideas were revolutionary. *He was among the first to describe how a free, competitive economy can function—without central planning or government interference—to allocate resources efficiently. He recognized the virtues of the "invisible hand" that leads the private interest of firms and individuals toward socially desirable ends, and he was properly suspicious of firms that are sheltered from competition, since he recognized the potentially undesirable effects on resource allocation.*

In addition, Smith—with the dire poverty of his times staring him in the face—was interested in the forces that determined the evolution of the economy—that is, the forces determining the rate of growth of average income per person. Although Smith did not approve of avarice, he felt that saving was good because it enabled society to invest in machinery and other forms of capital. Accumulating more and more capital would, according to Smith, allow output to grow. In addition, he emphasized the importance of increased specialization and division of labor in bringing about economic progress. By specializing, people can concentrate on the tasks they do best, with the result that society's total output is raised.

All in all, Smith's views were relatively optimistic, in keeping with the intellectual climate of his time—the era of Voltaire, Diderot, Franklin, and Jefferson, the age of the Enlightenment, when men believed so strongly in rationality. Leave markets alone, said Smith, and beware of firms with too much economic power and government meddling. If this is done, there is no reason why considerable economic progress cannot be achieved. Smith's work has been modified and extended in a variety of ways in the past 200 years. Some of his ideas have been challenged and, in some cases, discarded. But his influence on modern society has been enormous.

The Influence of Economics Today

Turning from Adam Smith's day to the present, economics continues to have an enormous influence over the shape of our society. Economics, and economists, play an extremely important part in the formulation of public policy. Skim through the articles in a daily newspaper. Chances are that you will find a report of an economist testifying before Congress, perhaps on the costs and benefits of a program to reduce unemployment among black teenagers in the Bedford-Stuyvesant area of New York City, or on the steps to be taken to make American goods more competitive with those of Japan or Germany. Still another economist may crop up on

Paul Volcker, former chairman of the Federal Reserve, before a congressional committee

EXAMPLE 1.1 HOW MUCH DOES IT COST TO GO TO COLLEGE?

According to the College Board, the average college student incurred the following annual costs in 1990–91:

	PRIVATE COLLEGE	PUBLIC COLLEGE
	(DOLLARS)	
Tuition and fees	9,400	1,800
Meals, room, books, travel, and other expenses	5,900	5,200
Total	15,300	7,000

(a) Is $15,300 the total cost to the student of a year at a private college? (*Hint:* Are there opportunity costs?) (b) John Martin is a 40-year-old executive; James Miller is an 18-year-old with no job experience. They are both full-time students. Although both must pay the same costs (given above), the true cost to Martin is more than the true cost to Miller. Why? (c) Is $1,800 the total cost to the typical public college of a student's going there for a year? (d) Is $15,300 the total cost to society of a student's going to a private college for a year?

Solution

(a) No, the true cost of going to college is considerably in excess of the out-of-pocket expenses because one can obtain wages by working rather than attending classes and studying. In other words, the time spent in school has opportunity costs, since it could be devoted to a job rather than to education. For example, if the student could earn $8,000 during a school year if he or she worked rather than going to college, the true total annual cost of a college education is $15,300 + $8,000 = $23,300. (b) Martin can earn much more than Miller if, rather than going to school, he were to work. Thus the opportunity cost of his time spent in school is greater than for Miller. (c) No. Tuition and fees cover only part of the public college's costs; the rest are covered by government support, alumni contributions, and other payments. (d) No. The cost to society equals the value to society of the resources used to teach, house, feed, and maintain the student, as well as the opportunity cost to society of his or her time. Although it is not easy to pin down all of the social costs, they clearly do not equal $15,300.

the editorial page, discussing the pros and cons of various proposed ways to reduce the federal deficit.

Economics and economists play a key role at the highest levels of our government. The president, whether a Democrat or a Republican, relies heavily on his economic advisers in making the decisions that help to shape the future of the country. In Congress, too, economics plays a major role. Economists are frequent witnesses before congressional committees, staff members for the committees, and advisers to individual representatives and senators. Many congressional committees focus largely on economic matters. For example, in 1991, many members of Congress spent large chunks of their time wrestling with budgetary and tax questions.

Perhaps the most dramatic evidence of the importance of economics in the formulation of public policy is provided during presidential elections, like that in 1992 (or the 1988 election that pitted George Bush against Michael Dukakis). Each candidate—with his or her own cadre of

ADAM SMITH ON THE "INVISIBLE HAND"

Adam Smith (1723–90) lived during the Industrial Revolution and was one of the first scholars to understand many of the central mechanisms of a free, or unplanned, economy. Much of his life was spent as professor of moral philosophy at the University of Glasgow in Scotland. In 1759, he published *The Theory of Moral Sentiments,* which established him as one of Britain's foremost philosophers; but this was not the book for which he is famous today. His masterpiece, published in 1776 (while the American colonists were brewing rebellion), was *The Wealth of Nations,* a long encyclopedic book twelve years in the writing. It was not an instant success, but the laurels it eventually won undoubtedly compensated for its early neglect.

One of Smith's central contentions was that firms and individuals, by pursuing their own objectives, often will promote the general welfare. In a famous passage, he stated that:

``It is only for the sake of profit that any man employs [his] capital in the support of industry, and he will always, therefore, endeavor to employ it in the support of that industry of which the produce is likely to be of greatest value, or to exchange the greatest quantity either of money or of other goods. But the annual revenue of every society is always precisely equal to the exchangeable value of the whole annual produce of its industry, or rather is precisely the same thing with that exchangeable value. As every individual, therefore, endeavors as much as he can both to employ his capital in the support of domestic industry, and so to direct that industry that its produce may be of the greatest value, every individual necessarily labors to render the annual revenue of the society as great as he can: He generally, indeed, neither intends to promote the public interest, nor knows how much he is promoting it. . . . He intends only his own security; and by directing that industry in such a manner as its produce may be of the greatest value, he intends only his own gain, and *he is in this, as in many other cases, led by an invisible hand to promote an end which was no part of his intention.* Nor is it always the worse for the society that it was no part of it. *By pursuing his own interest he frequently promotes that of the society more effectually than when he really intends to promote it.* I have never known much good done by those who affected to trade for the public good. It is an affectation, indeed, not very common among merchants, and very few words need be employed in dissuading them from it. . . ."[1]

[1] Adam Smith, *The Wealth of Nations,* London: George Routledge, 1900, p. 345. Originally published in 1776. (Italics added.)

economic advisers supplying ideas and reports—stakes out a position on the major economic issues of the day. This position can be of crucial importance in determining victory or defeat, and you, the citizen, must know some economics to understand whether a candidate is talking sense or nonsense (or merely evading an issue). For example, if a candidate promises to increase government expenditures, lower taxes, and reduce the federal deficit, you can be pretty certain that he is talking through his hat. This may not be obvious to you now, but it should be later on.

Also, economics and economists play an extremely important role in private decision making. Their role in the decision-making process in business firms is particularly great, since many of the nation's larger corporations hire professional economists to forecast their sales, reduce their costs, increase their efficiency, negotiate with labor and government, and carry out a host of other tasks. Judging from the fancy salaries business economists are paid, the firms seem to think they can deliver the goods, and in fact, the available evidence seems to indicate that they do provide important guidance to firms in many areas of their operations.

Positive Economics versus Normative Economics

Before concluding this chapter, it is essential that we recognize the distinction between positive economics and normative economics. ***Positive economics*** *contains descriptive statements, propositions, and predictions about the world.* For instance, an economic theory may predict that the price of copper will increase by $.01 a pound if income per person in the United States rises by 10 percent; this is positive economics. Positive economics tells us only what will happen under certain circumstances. It says nothing about whether the results are good or bad—or about what we should do. ***Normative economics,*** *on the other hand, makes statements about what ought to be, or about what a person, organization, or nation ought to do.* For instance, a theory might say that Chile should introduce new technology more quickly in many of its copper mines; this is normative economics.

Clearly, positive economics and normative economics must be treated differently. Positive economics is science in the ordinary sense of the word: Propositions in positive economics can be tested by an appeal to the facts. In a nonexperimental science like economics, however, it is sometimes difficult to get the facts you need to test particular propositions. For example, if income per person in the United States does not rise by 10 percent, it may be difficult to tell what the effect of such an increase would be on the price of copper. Moreover, even if per capita income does increase by this amount, it may be difficult to separate the effect of the increase in income per person on the price of copper from the effect of other factors. But nonetheless, we can, in principle, test propositions in positive economics by an appeal to the facts.

In normative economics, this is not the case. *In normative economics, the results you get depend on your values or preferences.* For example, if you believe that reducing unemployment is more important than maintaining the purchasing power of the dollar, you will get one answer to certain questions; whereas if you believe that maintaining the purchasing power of the dollar is more important than reducing unemployment, you are likely to get a different answer to the same questions. This is not at all strange. After all, if people desire different things (which is another way of saying that they have different values), they may well make different

EXAMPLE 1.2   THE ASSESSMENT OF DAMAGES

In a well-known legal case, the United States was sued by O'Brien Bros., Inc., the owner of a Brooklyn-bound barge that was sunk by a U.S. Navy tug that collided with the barge. O'Brien Bros. received damages stemming from the collision. The calculation of the damages was turned over to a commissioner, who found them to be as follows:

	DOLLARS
Costs of raising the wreck	7,732.21
Repairs	43,245.22
Compensation for loss of earnings from the barge during the time it was unavailable for work	6,620.25
Miscellaneous costs	3,423.91
Total	61,021.59

(a) Why should O'Brien Bros. be compensated for the loss of earnings? It did not pay out $6,620.25 to anyone. Why should it receive this amount in damages? (b) The United States appealed the decision. Government attorneys introduced evidence that a similar barge could have been built new for $33,000. Does this mean that the damages should have been $33,000? (c) Suppose that O'Brien Bros. could have bought a similar barge for $25,000 and that its forgone earnings during the time elapsing from the sinking of the old barge to the availability of the new barge was $5,000. If the sunk barge would cause no problems either to O'Brien Bros. or anyone else, should it have been raised and repaired? (d) Suppose that O'Brien Bros. could have obtained $8,500 for the wreck (for scrap metal, salvageable parts, and so forth), if it was raised? Should it have been raised?

Solution

(a) If the barge had not been sunk, O'Brien Bros. would have earned this amount. It is the opportunity cost of the barge's being sunk. (b) No. The barge that was sunk may have been worth less than $33,000, since it was not new. On the other hand, the figure of $33,000 takes no account of lost earnings in the time interval until the barge was replaced. (c) No. The cost of raising and repairing it exceeded the cost of buying a similar barge. (d) Yes, because the amount that could be obtained for the wreck would exceed the cost of raising it.*

* For further description of this case, see "O'Brien Bros., Inc. v. The Helen B. Moran et al." in R. Byrns and G. Stone, Jr., *An Economics Casebook: Applications from the Law*, Santa Monica: Goodyear, 1980.

---

decisions and advocate different policies. It would be strange if they did not.

This book will spend a lot of time on the principles of positive economics—the principles and propositions concerning the workings of the economic system about which practically all economists tend to agree. Normative economics will also be treated, since we must discuss questions of policy—and all policy discussions involve individual preferences, not solely hard facts. In these discussions, we shall try to indicate how the conclusions depend on one's values. Then you can let your own values be your guide. The purpose of this book is not to convert you to a particular set of values. It is to teach you how to obtain better solutions to economic problems, whatever set of values you may have.

TEST YOURSELF

1. In a famous passage from The Wealth of Nations, Adam Smith said that: "It is the maxim of every prudent master of a family, never to make at home what it will cost him more to make than to buy." Suppose that Mrs. Harris spends an hour preparing a meal. She is a psychologist in private practice and can obtain $50 per hour for her services. What is the cost to the Harris family of her preparing this meal? Explain.

2. "Resources are scarce and once a decision is made to use them for one purpose, they are no longer available for another. One opportunity cost of reading [an] . . . article, for example, is not simultaneously being able to read [another article]." Explain, and relate to the question of how a student should allocate his or her time among various course assignments.

3. Suppose that it costs a college student $1,000 per year more for room and board than if he or she works (and lives at home). If this assumption is correct, why is this amount, rather than the full cost of room and board, the proper amount to use in Example 1.1?

4. On the basis of positive economics alone, which of the following statements can be determined to be true or false? (a) The tax cut of 1981 reduced unemployment in the United States by 3 percentage points. (b) The tax cut was timed improperly. (c) The tax cut was a less equitable way of reducing unemployment than a program whereby the unemployed were hired by the government to perform important social functions.

SUMMARY

1. According to one standard definition, economics is concerned with the way resources are allocated among alternative uses to satisfy human wants. A resource is a thing or service used to produce goods (or services) which can satisfy wants. Not all resources are scarce. Free resources, such as air, are so abundant that they can be obtained without charge.

2. Those resources that are scarce are called economic resources. The test of whether a resource is an economic resource or a free resource is price: economic resources command a nonzero price but free resources do not. Economists often classify economic resources into three categories: land, labor, and capital.

3. Since economic resources are scarce, only a limited amount of goods and services can be produced from them, and there arises the necessity for choice. For example, if an isolated town has a certain amount of resources, it must choose how much of each good it will produce from these resources. If it increases the amount produced of one good, it must reduce the amount produced of another good.

4. The opportunity cost (or alternative cost) of using a resource to increase the production of one good is the value of what the resource could have produced had it been used in the best alternative way. To illustrate the use of the concept of opportunity cost, which is one of the most important in economics, we discussed the cases of public parks and a college education.

5. Economists are particularly concerned with four basic questions regarding the working of any economic system, ours or any other. These questions are (1) What determines what (and how much) is produced? (2) What determines how it is produced? (3) What determines how the society's output is distributed among the members? (4) What determines the rate at which the society's per capita income will grow?

6. Economists often distinguish between positive economics and normative economics. Positive economics contains descriptive statements, propositions, and predictions about the world; whereas normative economics contains statements about what ought to be, or about what a person, organization, or nation ought to do.

7. In normative economics, the results you get depend on your basic values and preferences; in positive economics, the results are testable, at least in principle, by an appeal to the facts.

CONCEPTS FOR REVIEW

Unemployment	Resources	Technology
Inflation	Economic resources	Choice
Labor productivity	Free resources	Opportunity cost
Poverty	Land	Alternative cost
Economics	Labor	Positive economics
Human wants	Capital	Normative economics

ECONOMIC MODELS AND CAPITALISM, AMERICAN-STYLE

THE UNITED STATES, LIKE all other nations, is beset by many economic problems. As pointed out in Chapter 1, the early 1990s were a period when the competitiveness and efficiency of many American industries were questioned, and in late 1990 the unemployment rate rose. Also, there were problems in controlling the federal deficit and in bringing our exports and imports into balance. Yet, despite these problems, the American economy is among the most prosperous in the world. The average American family has plenty of food, clothing, housing, appliances, and luxuries of many kinds. The tremendous strength and vitality of the American economy should be recognized, as well as its shortcomings. Nothing is gained by overlooking either the successes or the faults of our system.

As a first step toward understanding why we are so well off in some respects and so lacking in others, we need to understand how our economy works. Of course, this is a big task. Indeed, you could say that this whole book is devoted to discussing this subject. So we will not try to present a detailed picture of the operation of the American economy at this point. All we will do now is give a preliminary sketch, a basic blueprint of what an economic system must do and how our mixed capitalistic system works.

First, however, we must provide a brief description of the role of model building in economics, since this will introduce you to the methods used by economists. Without such an introduction to economic methodology, it would be difficult, if not impossible, for you to understand fully much of the material that follows in this and succeeding chapters. Only after these preliminary matters are covered will we be able to turn to a discussion of the tasks of an economic system and the way our economy functions.

THE METHODOLOGY OF ECONOMICS

Model Building in Economics

Like other types of scientific analysis, economics is based on the formulation of **models.** *A model is a theory. It is composed of a number of assumptions from which conclusions—or predictions—are deduced.* An astronomer who wants to formulate a model of the solar system might represent each planet by a point in space and assume that each would change position in accord with certain mathematical equations. Based on this model, the astronomer might predict when an eclipse would occur, or estimate the probability of a planetary collision. The economist proceeds along similar lines when setting forth a model of economic behavior.

There are several important points to be noted concerning models:

1. TO BE USEFUL, A MODEL MUST SIMPLIFY THE REAL SITUATION. The assumptions made by a model need not be exact replicas of reality. If they were, the model would be too complicated to use. The basic reasons for using a model is that the real world is so complex that masses of detail often obscure underlying patterns. The economist faces the familiar problem of seeing the forest as distinct from just the trees. Other scientists must do the same; physicists work with simplified models of atoms, just as economists work with simplified models of markets. However, this does not mean that *all* models are good or useful. A model may be so oversimplified and distorted that it is utterly useless. The trick is to construct a model so that irrelevant and unimportant considerations and variables are neglected, but the major factors—those that seriously affect the phenomena the model is designed to predict—are included.

2. THE PURPOSE OF A MODEL IS TO MAKE PREDICTIONS ABOUT THE REAL WORLD; AND IN MANY RESPECTS THE MOST IMPORTANT TEST OF A MODEL IS HOW WELL IT PREDICTS. In this sense, a model that predicts the price of copper within plus or minus $.01 a pound is better than a model that predicts it within plus or minus $.02 a pound. Of course, this does not mean that a model is useless if it cannot predict very accurately. We do not always need a very accurate prediction. For example, a road map is a model that can be used to make predictions about the route a driver should take to get to a particular destination. Sometimes, a very crude map is good enough to get you where you want to go, but such a map would not, for instance, serve the hiker who needs to know the characteristics of the terrain through which he plans to walk. How detailed a map you need depends on where you are going and how you want to get there.

3. A PERSON WHO WANTS TO PREDICT THE OUTCOME OF A PARTICULAR EVENT WILL BE FORCED TO USE THE MODEL THAT PREDICTS BEST, EVEN IF THIS MODEL DOES NOT PREDICT VERY WELL. The choice is not between a model and no model; it is between one model and another. After all, a person who must make a forecast will use the most accurate device available—and any such device is a model of some sort. Consequently, when economists make simplifying assumptions and derive conclusions that are only approximately true, it is somewhat beside the point to complain that the assumptions are simpler than reality or that the predictions are not always accurate. This may be true, but if the predictions based on the economists' model are better than those obtained on the basis of other models, their model must, and will, be used until something better comes along. Thus, if a model can predict the price of copper to within plus or minus $.01 per pound, and no other model can do better, this model will be used even if those interested in the predictions bewail the model's limitations and wish it could be improved.

Economic Measurement

To utilize and test their models, economists need facts of many sorts. For example, suppose that an economist constructs a model which predicts

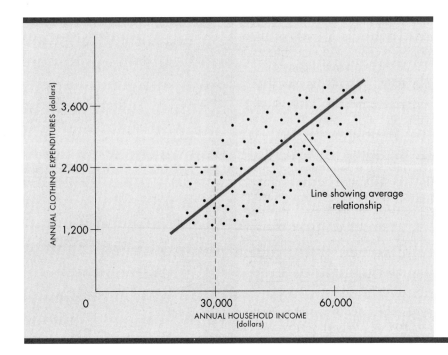

ANNUAL CLOTHING EXPENDITURES (dollars)

3,600

2,400

1,200

0

30,000

60,000

ANNUAL HOUSEHOLD INCOME
(dollars)

Line showing average
relationship

**Figure 2.1
Relationship between Annual
Clothing Expenditures and
Annual Household Income**
Each family is represented by a
dot. The line shows the average
relationship. The line does not fit
all families exactly, since all the
points do not fall on it. The line
does, however, show average
clothing expenditure for each income level.

that a household's annual clothing expenditure tends to increase by $60 when its income increases by $1,000. To see whether this model is correct, he or she must gather data concerning the incomes and clothing expenditures of a large number of households and study the relationship between them. Suppose that Figure 2.1 shows the relationship the economist finds. The line represents an average relationship between household income and household clothing expenditure. Judging by Figure 2.1, his or her model is reasonably accurate, at least for households with incomes between $30,000 and $60,000 per year.[1]

Measurements like those in Figure 2.1 enable economists to *quantify* their models; in other words, they enable them to construct models that predict *how much* effect one variable has on another. The economist above has shown that a $1,000 increase in a household's income results, on the average, in a $60 increase in clothing expenditures. Notice how much more useful this specific relationship is than simply saying that with more income, a person will tend to buy more clothes. You do not need an economist to tell you that.

GRAPHS AND RELATIONSHIPS

To conclude our brief discussion of economic methodology, we must describe the construction and interpretation of graphs, such as Figure 2.1, which economists use to present data and relationships. Such graphs are used repeatedly throughout this book, and it is essential that the following three points be understood:

[1] It is worth noting that, although it is useful to see how well a model would have fit the historical facts, this is no substitute for seeing how well it will predict the future. As a distinguished mentor of mine once observed. "It's a darned poor person who can't predict the past."

1. A graph has a horizontal axis and a vertical axis, each of which has a scale of numerical values. For example, in Figure 2.1, the horizontal axis shows a household's annual income, and the vertical axis shows the annual amount spent by the household on clothing. The intersection of the two axes is called the origin and is the point where both the variable measured along the horizontal axis and the variable measured along the vertical axis are zero. In Figure 2.1, the origin is at the lower lefthand corner of the figure, labeled "0."

2. To show the relationship between two variables, one can plot the value of one variable against the value of the other variable. Thus, in Figure 2.1, each family is represented by a dot. For example, the colored dot is in the position shown in Figure 2.1 because it represents a family whose income was $30,000 and whose clothing expenditure was $2,400. Clearly, the line showing the average relationship does not fit all the families exactly, since all the points do not fall on the line. This line does, however, give the average clothing expenditure for each level of income: it is an average relationship.

3. The relationship between two variables is *direct* if, as in Figure 2.1, the line of average relationship is upward sloping. In other words, if the variable measured along the vertical axis tends to increase (decrease) in response to increases (decreases) in the variable measured along the horizontal axis, the relationship is direct. On the other hand, if the line of average relationship is downward sloping, as in Figure 2.2, the relationship is *inverse*. In other words, if the variable measured along the vertical axis tends to decrease (increase) in response to increases (decreases) in the variable measured along the horizontal axis, the relationship is inverse.

To illustrate how one can graph a relationship between two variables, consider Table 2.1, which shows the amount of tennis balls demanded in a particular market at various prices. Putting price on the vertical axis and quantity demanded on the horizontal axis, one can plot each combination of price and quantity in this table as a point on a graph; and that is precisely what has been done in Figure 2.2 (points *A* to *E*).

Table 2.1
Quantity of Tennis Balls Demanded in a Particular Market at Various Prices

PRICE OF A TENNIS BALL (DOLLARS)	QUANTITY OF TENNIS BALLS DEMANDED (MILLIONS)
1.50	1
1.20	2
0.90	3
0.60	4
0.30	6

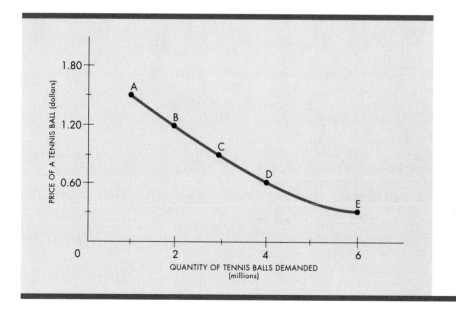

Figure 2.2
Relationship between Quantity Demanded and Price of Tennis Balls (as shown in Table 2.1)

OF AN ECONOMIC SYSTEM

scussed the nature and quantification of economic models, we
turn to the primary purpose of this chapter, which is to provide
liminary sketch of what an economic system must do and how our
xed capitalistic system works. In this section, we describe what an economic system—*ours or any other*—must do. Basically, as we saw in
Chapter 1, there are four tasks that any economic system must perform:

**1. AN ECONOMIC SYSTEM MUST DETERMINE THE LEVEL AND COMPOSITION OF SOCI-
ETY'S OUTPUT.** That is, it must answer questions like: To what extent
should society's resources be used to produce new aircraft carriers and
missiles? To what extent should they be used to produce sewage plants to
reduce water pollution? To what extent should they be used to produce
low-cost housing for the poor? Pause for a moment to think about how
important—and how vast—this function is. Most people simply take for
granted that somehow it is decided what we as a society are going to produce, and far too few people really think about the social mechanisms
that determine the answers to such questions.

**2. AN ECONOMIC SYSTEM MUST DETERMINE HOW EACH GOOD AND SERVICE IS TO BE
PRODUCED.** Given existing technology, a society's resources can be used
in various ways. Should the skilled labor in Birmingham, Alabama, be
used to produce cotton or steel? Should a particular machine tool be used
to produce aircraft or automobiles? The way questions of this sort are answered will determine the way each good and service is produced. In
other words, it will determine which resources are used to produce which
goods and services. If this function is performed badly, society's resources
are put to the wrong uses, resulting in less output than if this function is
performed well.

**3. AN ECONOMIC SYSTEM MUST DETERMINE HOW THE GOODS AND SERVICES THAT
ARE PRODUCED ARE TO BE DISTRIBUTED AMONG THE MEMBERS OF SOCIETY.** In
other words, how much of each type of good and service should each
person receive? Should there be a considerable amount of income inequality, the rich receiving much more than the poor? Or should incomes
be relatively equal? Take your own case. Somehow or other, the economic system determines how much income you will receive. In our economic system, your income depends on your skills, the property you
own, how hard you work, and prevailing prices, as we shall see in succeeding chapters. But in other economic systems, your income might depend on quite different factors. This function of the economic system has
generated, and will continue to generate, heated controversy. Some people favor a relatively egalitarian society where the amount received by
one family varies little from that received by another family of the same
size. Other people favor a society where the amount a family or person
receives can vary a great deal. Few people favor a thoroughly egalitarian
society, if for no other reason than that some differences in income are required to stimulate workers to do certain types of work.

**4. AN ECONOMIC SYSTEM MUST DETERMINE THE RATE OF GROWTH OF PER CAPITA
INCOME.** An adequate growth rate has come to be regarded as an important economic goal, particularly in the less developed countries of Africa,
Asia, and Latin America. There is very strong pressure in these countries
for changes in technology, the adoption of superior techniques, increases
in the stock of capital resources, and better and more extensive education

and training of the labor force. These are viewed as some of the major ways to promote the growth of per capita income.

TEST YOURSELF

1. Suppose that the quantity of corn demanded annually by American consumers at each price of corn is as follows:

PRICE (DOLLARS PER BUSHEL)	QUANTITY OF CORN (MILLIONS OF BUSHELS)
1	2.0
2	1.0
3	0.5
4	0.4

How much will farmers receive for their corn crop if it is 2 million bushels? If it is 1 million bushels? If you owned all of the farms producing corn, would you produce 2 million bushels? Why, or why not?

2. Plot the relationship between price and quantity demanded in Question 1 on a graph. Is the relationship direct or inverse? Based on your graph, estimate how much corn is likely to be demanded if the price is (a) $1.50, (b) $2.50, and (c) $3.50.

3. Suppose that Americans begin to take up tennis in much larger numbers. Will the curve in Figure 2.2 shift? If so, will it shift to the right or to the left? Explain.

4. Suppose that you wanted to construct a model to explain and predict the breakfast food that your neighbor will choose tomorrow. What factors would you include? How well do you think you could predict?

THE ECONOMIC SYSTEM: A SIMPLE INTRODUCTORY MODEL

The Production Possibilities Curve and the Determination of What Is Produced

We've seen that economists use models to throw light on economic problems. At this point, let's try our hand at constructing a simple model to illuminate the basic functions any economic system, ours included, must perform. To keep things simple, suppose that society produces only two goods, food and tractors. This, of course, is unrealistic, but, as we've seen, a model does not have to be realistic to be useful. Here, by assuming that there are only two goods, we eliminate a lot of unnecessary complexity and lay bare the essentials. In addition, we suppose that society has at its disposal a certain amount of resources, and that this amount is fixed for the duration of the period in question. This assumption is quite realistic. So long as the period is relatively short, the amount of a society's resources is relatively fixed (except, of course, under unusual circumstances, such as if a country annexes additional land). Finally, we suppose as well that society's technology is fixed. So long as the period is relatively short, this assumption too is realistic.

Under these circumstances, it is possible to figure out the various amounts of food and tractors that society can produce. Specifically, we can proceed as in Chapter 1, where we determined the amounts of food and clothing that an isolated town could produce. Let's begin with how many tractors society can produce if all resources are devoted to tractor production. According to Table 2.2, the answer is 15 million tractors.

Next, let's consider the opposite extreme, where society devotes all its resources to food production. According to Table 2.2, it can produce 12 million tons of food in this case. Next, let's consider cases where both products are being produced. Such cases are represented by possibilities B to F in the table. As emphasized in Chapter 1, the more of one good that is produced, the less of the other good that can be produced. Why? Because to produce more of one good, resources must be taken away from the production of the other good, lessening the amount of the other good produced.

Figure 2.3 shows how we can use a graph to show the various production possibilities society can attain. It is merely a different way of presenting the data in Table 2.2; the output of food is plotted on the horizontal axis and the output of tractors on the vertical axis. The curve in Figure 2.3, which shows the various combinations of output of food and tractors that society can produce, is called a **production possibilities curve.**

The production possibilities curve sheds considerable light on the economic tasks facing any society. It shows the various production possibilities open to society. According to Figure 2.3, society can choose to produce 4 million tons of food and 12 million tractors (point *C*), or 6 million tons of food and 10 million tractors (point *D*), but it cannot choose to produce 6 million tons of food and 12 million tractors (point *H*). Point *H* is inaccessible with this society's resources and technology. Perhaps it will become accessible if the society's resources increase or if its technology improves, but for the present, point *H* is out of reach.

If resources are fully and efficiently utilized, *the first function of any economic system—to determine the level and composition of society's output—is really a problem of determining at what point along the production possibilities curve society should be.* Should society choose point *A*, *B*, *C*, *D*, *E*, *F*, or *G*? In making this choice, one thing is obvious from the production possibilities curve: *you cannot get more of one good without giving up some of the other good.* In other words, you cannot escape the problem of choice. So long as resources are limited and technology is less

Table 2.2
Alternative Combinations of Outputs of Food and Tractors That Can Be Produced

POSSIBILITY	FOOD (MILLIONS OF TONS)	TRACTORS (MILLIONS)
A	0	15
B	2	14
C	4	12
D	6	10
E	8	7
F	10	4
G	12	0

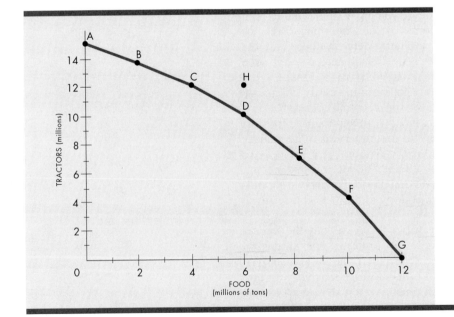

FOOD (millions of tons)

Figure 2.3
Production Possibilities Curve
This curve shows the various combinations of tractors and food that can be produced efficiently with given resources and technology. Point *H* is unattainable.

EXAMPLE 2.1 HAY AND GRAIN IN IOWA

According to studies carried out at Iowa State University, the following combinations of grain and hay could be produced from 100 acres of land in a particular part of Iowa:

NUMBER OF ACRES DEVOTED TO EACH USE		TOTAL PRODUCTION (POUNDS)	
HAY	GRAIN	GRAIN	HAY
0	100	224,000	0
25	75	212,920	89,600
33	67	166,194	96,400

That is, if all 100 acres were devoted to grain, 224,000 pounds of grain could be produced; if 75 of the 100 acres were devoted to grain, 212,920 pounds of grain and 89,600 pounds of hay could be produced; and so on.

(a) If a 100-acre farm in this part of Iowa was producing 212,920 pounds of grain and 89,600 pounds of hay, what was the approximate cost of increasing its production of grain by 1 pound? (b) Suppose that the profit to be made from a pound of grain was five times the profit to be made from a pound of hay, and that the owner of this farm claimed that, because this was the case, he should produce no hay. Would he be correct? (c) Suppose that, if hay production was increased from zero to about 100,000 pounds, the production of grain *increased*, not *decreased* (because hay contributed elements to the soil needed in the production of grain). Under these circumstances, would the slope of the production possibilities curve be negative at all points? Would it be rational for a farmer to produce no hay? (d) Would the production possibilities curve for a farm of this sort be the same now as in the 1940s?

Solution

(a) If it increased its grain output by 11,080 pounds (from 212,920 to 224,000 pounds), it had to reduce its hay output by 89,600 pounds. Thus an extra pound of grain output cost the farm about $89,600 \div 11,080$, or 8.09 pounds of hay. (b) No. If he produced 212,920 pounds of grain, and 89,600 pounds of hay, his profits would be larger than if he produced no hay, because the profit from the extra 89,600 pounds of hay was greater than the profit from the 11,080 pounds of grain forgone. (c) No. No, because by producing up to 100,000 pounds of hay, the farmer increased the output of grain too. (d) No, because of changes in technology.

than magic, you must reckon with the fact (emphasized in Chapter 1) that more of one thing means less of another. The old saw that you don't "get something for nothing" is hackneyed but true, so long as resources are fully and efficiently utilized.

The Law of Increasing Cost

In the previous section, we stressed that an increased output of one good (say, food) means a decreased output of the other good (say, tractors). This amounts to saying (in the language of Chapter 1) that the opportunity cost of producing more food is the output of tractors that must be forgone. In this section, we go a step further; we point out that, *as more and more of a good is produced, the production of yet another unit of this good is likely to entail a larger and larger opportunity cost* and we explain why this is true.

This so-called law of increasing cost can be demonstrated in Figure 2.3. As more and more food is produced, the cost of increasing food output by 2 million tons increases. To see this, note that the *first* 2 million tons of food cost 1 million tractors (because this is the amount that tractor output must be reduced if food output increases from 0 to 2 million tons). The *second* 2 million tons of food cost 2 million tractors (because this is the that tractor output must be reduced if food output increases from [mi]llion tons). Skipping to the *sixth* 2 million tons of food, the cost [of a]dditional food output is 4 million tractors (because this is the amount that tractor output must be reduced if food output increases from 10 to 12 million tons). Clearly, the more food that is already being produced, the greater the cost of producing an additional 2 million tons.

Why is this the case? Basically, it is because resources are not as effective in producing one good as in producing the other. When society only produces a small amount of food, it can use in food production those resources that are well suited to producing food and not so well suited to producing tractors. But as society produces more and more food, it tends to run out of such resources, and must absorb into food production those resources that are less suited to producing food and better suited to producing tractors. To increase food output by 2 million tons with the latter type of resources, a greater reduction must occur in tractor output than when the 2-million-ton increase in food output occurred with the resources that were well suited to food production (and not so well suited to producing tractors). Thus the cost of producing an additional 2 million tons of food tends to increase as more food is already being produced.

This law of increasing cost explains why a production possibilities curve has the shape shown in Figure 2.3. <u>That is, it explains why the production possibilities curve has the "bowed out" shape</u> (rather than the "bowed in" shape) indicated in Figure 2.4. <u>Because the cost of increasing food output by a certain amount increases as more of it is already produced, the production possibilities curve tends to fall more steeply as one moves from left to right along the horizontal axis—which explains why the production possibilities curve has the "bowed out" shape.</u>

The Production Possibilities Curve and the Determination of How Goods Are Produced

Let's turn now to the second basic function of any economic system: to determine how each good and service should be produced. In Table 2.2, we assumed implicitly that society's resources would be fully utilized and that the available technology would be applied in a way that would get the most out of the available resources. In other words, we assumed that the firms making food and tractors were as efficient as possible and that there was no unemployment of resources. But if there is widespread unemployment of people and machines, will society still be able to choose a point on the production possibilities curve? Clearly, the answer is no. Since society is not using all of its resources, it will not be able to produce as much as if it used them all. <u>Thus, *if there is less than full employment of resources, society will have to settle for points inside the production possibilities curve.*</u> For example, the best society may be able to do under these circumstances is to attain point *K* in Figure 2.5. *K* is a less desirable point than *C* or *D*—but that is the price of unemployment.

Suppose, on the other hand, that there is full employment of resources but that firms are inefficient. Perhaps they promote relatives of the boss, regardless of their ability; perhaps the managers are lazy or not much interested in efficiency; or perhaps the workers like to take long coffee breaks and are unwilling to work hard. Whatever the reason, will society still be able to choose a point on the production possibilities curve? Again, the answer is no. Since society is not getting as much as it could out of its resources, it will not be able to produce as much as it would if its resources were used efficiently. Thus, <u>*if resources are used inefficiently, so-*</u>

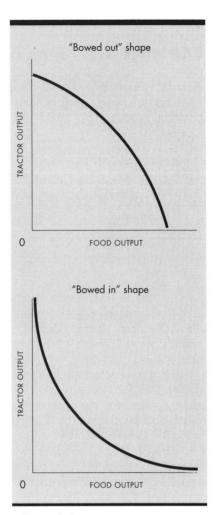

Figure 2.4
Shape of the Production Possibilities Curve
So long as the law of increasing cost holds true, the production possibilities curve will have the shape at the top ("bowed out"), *not* the shape at the bottom ("bowed in").

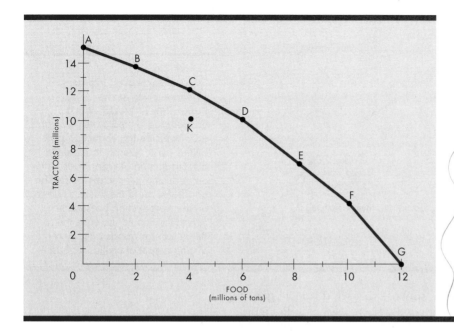

Figure 2.5
Production Possibilities Curve
This curve, like Figure 2.3, shows
the various combinations of tractors and food that can be produced efficiently with given
resources and technology. Point K
is less desirable than points C or
D, because less output is produced
at this point. But because of unemployment or inefficiency, society
may wind up at point K.

ciety will have to settle for points inside the production possibilities curve.
Perhaps in these circumstances, too, the best society can do may be point
K in Figure 2.5. The difference between this less desirable position and
positions on the production possibilities curve is the price of inefficiency.

At this point, it should be obvious that our model at least partially answers the question of how each good and service should be produced.
The answer is to *produce each good and service in such a way that you
wind up on the production possibilities curve, not on a point inside it.* Of
course, this is easier said than done, but at least our model indicates a
couple of villains to watch out for: unemployment of resources and inefficiency. When these villains are present, we can be sure that society is not
on the production possibilities curve.

If there is unemployment or inefficiency, society may be able to increase its output of one good without producing less of another good.
Otherwise this cannot be done, as long as technology and the quantity of
resources are fixed. Thus the old saw is wrong, and it is possible to "get
something for nothing" when society is inside the production possibilities
curve. Society need not give up anything—in the way of production of
other goods—to increase the production of this good under these circumstances.

For example, consider the sequence of events in two different countries at the beginning of World War II. In the Soviet Union, the war effort
meant a substantial decrease in the standard of living on the home front.
Resources had to be diverted from the production of civilian goods to the
production of military goods, and the war struck a severe blow at the living standards of the civilian population. In the United States, however, it
was possible to increase the production of military goods without making
such a dent in the living standards of the civilian population. How was
this possible? The United States at the beginning of World War II was still
struggling to emerge from the Great Depression, and several million people were still unemployed. The Soviet Union, however, was suffering no
such unemployment. Thus we could increase the production of both guns
and butter, whereas they could not.

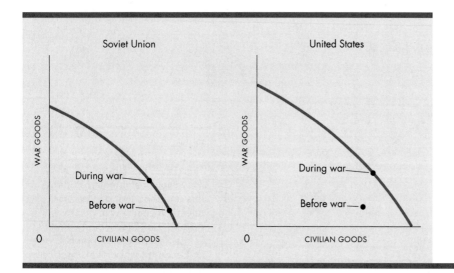

Figure 2.6
Effect of Increased Production of War Goods at the Beginning of World War II
Because the United States was at a point inside its production possibilities curve, we could increase our production of war goods without reducing production of civilian goods. Because the Russians were on their production possibilities curve, they could increase their output of war goods only by reducing output of civilian goods.

To put this comparison in a diagram, suppose that we divide all goods into two classes: war goods and civilian goods. Then, as shown in Figure 2.6, *we were inside our production possibilities curve at the beginning of the war, while the Soviets were not.*

The Production Possibilities Curve, Income Distribution, and Growth

Let's return now to the case where our economy produces food and tractors. The third basic function of any economic system is to distribute the goods and services that are produced among the members of society. Each point on the production possibilities curve in Figure 2.5 represents society's total pie, but to deal with the third function, we must know how the pie is divided up among society's members. Since the production possibilities curve does not tell us this, it cannot shed light on this third function.

Fortunately, the production possibilities curve is of more use in analyzing the fourth basic function of any economic system: to determine the society's rate of growth of per capita income. Suppose that the society in Figure 2.5 invests a considerable amount of its resources in developing improved processes and products. It might establish agricultural experiment stations to improve farming techniques and industrial research laboratories to improve tractor designs. As shown in Figure 2.7, the production possibilities curve will be pushed outward. This will be the result of improved technology, enabling more food and/or more tractors to be produced from the same amount of resources. Thus one way for an economy to increase its output—and its per capita income—may be to invest in research and development.

Another way is by devoting more of its resources to the production of capital goods rather than consumers' goods. **Capital goods** consist of plant and equipment that are used to make other goods; **consumers' goods** are items that consumers purchase like clothing, food, and drink. Since capital goods are themselves resources, a society that chooses to produce lots of capital goods and few consumers' goods will push out its production possibilities curve much farther than a society that chooses to produce lots of consumers' goods and few capital goods.

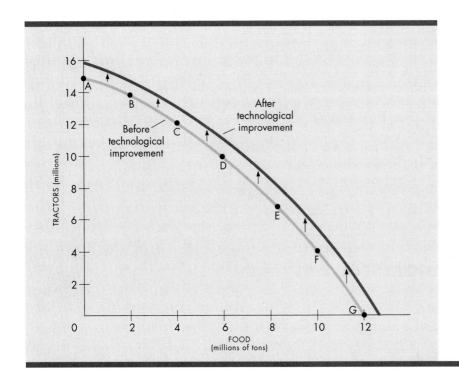

Figure 2.7
Effect of Improvement in Technology on Production Possibilities Curve
An improvement in technology results in an outward shift of the production possibilities curve.

To illustrate this point, consider our simple society that produces food and tractors. The more tractors (and the less food) this society produces, the more tractors it will have in the next period; and the more tractors it has in the next period, the more of both goods—food and tractors—it will be able to produce then. Thus the more tractors (and the less food) this society produces, the farther out it will push its production possibili-

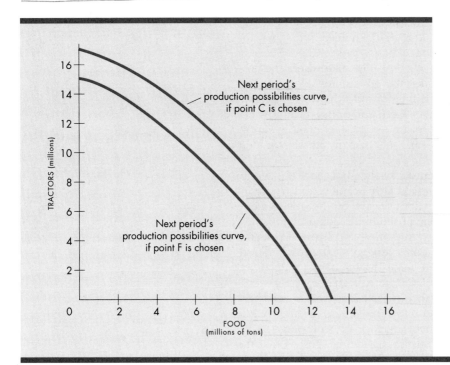

Figure 2.8
Effect of Increase in Capital Goods on Production Possibilities Curve
An increase in the amount of capital goods results in an outward shift of the production possibilities curve. The choice of point C means the production of more capital goods than the choice of point F.

ties curve—and the greater the increase in output (and per capita income) that it will achieve in the next period. If this society chooses point *F* (shown in Figures 2.7, 2.5, or 2.3), the effect will be entirely different than if it chooses point *C*. If it chooses point *F*, it produces 4 million tractors, which we assume to be the number of tractors worn out each year. Thus, if it chooses point *F*, it adds nothing to its stock of tractors; it merely replaces those that wear out. Since it has no more tractors in the next period than in the current period, the production possibilities curve does not shift out at all if point *F* is chosen. On the other hand, if point *C* is chosen, the society produces 12 million tractors, which means that it has 8 million additional tractors at the beginning of the next period. Thus, as shown in Figure 2.8, the production possibilities curve is pushed outward. By producing more capital goods (and less consumers' goods) our society has increased its production possibilities and its per capita income.

CAPITALISM: AN ECONOMIC SYSTEM

What Is Capitalism?

In previous sections we have discussed the basic tasks that any economic system must perform. Now we must look at how our own economic system performs these tasks. The particular kind of economic system adopted by the United States is **capitalism.** Capitalism is one of those terms that is frequently used but seldom defined, and even less frequently understood. Its operation is complex, but its principal characteristics can be lumped into four major categories.

1. PRIVATE OWNERSHIP OF CAPITAL.   Under capitalism you or I can buy the tools of production. We can own factories, equipment, inventories, and other forms of capital. In a capitalistic system, somebody owns each piece of capital—and receives the income from it. Each piece of equipment has some sort of legal instrument indicating to whom it belongs. (If it belongs to a corporation, its owners basically are the stockholders who own the corporation). Moreover, each piece of capital has a market value. This system is in marked contrast to a communist or socialist state where the government owns the capital. In these states, the government decides how much and what kinds of capital goods will be produced; it owns the capital goods; and it receives and distributes the income they produce. For example, in China, no one can buy or put up a new steel plant; it simply isn't allowed. (As noted above, in the early 1990s many Russian leaders favored moving toward capitalism.)

    The United States is basically a capitalistic system, but there are certain areas where the government, not individuals, owns capital, and where individual property rights are limited in various ways by the government. The government owns much of the tooling used in the defense industries; it owns dams and the Tennessee Valley Authority; and it owns research laboratories in such diverse fields as atomic energy, space exploration, and health. Further, the government determines how much of a deceased person's assets can go to his or her heirs. (The rest goes to the government in the form of estate and inheritance taxes.) Also, the government can make a person sell his or her property to allow a road or other public project to be built. There are many such limitations on property rights. Ours is basically a capitalistic system, but it must be recognized that the government's role is important.

THE ROLE OF SAVING IN THE INDUSTRIAL REVOLUTION AND JAPANESE ECONOMIC GROWTH

One of the most remarkable developments in human history was the Industrial Revolution. Until the middle of the eighteenth century, industry (as distinct from agriculture or commerce) played a small role in the economies of Europe or America. But during the late eighteenth and early nineteenth centuries a host of important technological innovations, such as James Watt's steam engine and Richard Arkwright's spinning jenny, made possible a very rapid growth in the output of industrial goods (like textiles and pig iron). And accompanying this growth of industrial output was the advent of the factory—a social and economic institution that is taken for granted today, but which was largely unknown prior to the Industrial Revolution.

The Industrial Revolution was characterized by major improvements in technology and by large increases in the amount of capital resources available to society. Both the improvements in technology and the additional capital resulted in an outward shift in the production possibilities curve in England, where the Industrial Revolution first took hold. (See Figure 2.7 and 2.8). Due to this shift, the standard of living in England, as measured by per capita income (total income divided by population), grew at an unprecedented rate. As the Industrial Revolution spread, this rise in living standards occurred too on the European continent and in the United States; it remained one of the lasting effects of industrialization.

As stressed above, the Industrial Revolution was characterized by considerable increases in capital. How did England (and other countries) bring about this increase in capital? By saving and investing. In other words, the English people had to set aside some of their resources and say in effect, "These resources will *not* be used to satisfy the current needs of our population for food, clothing, and other forms of consumption. Instead, they will be used to produce capital—factories, machines, equipment, railroads, and canals—which will increase our future productive capacity." Much more will be said about this saving process in subsequent chapters. For now, the essential point is that this saving process was one of the necessary conditions that made possible the Industrial Revolution.

Turning from the Industrial Revolution to the present, one of the reasons for Japan's remarkable increase in output during the period since World War II has been the very high Japanese savings rate. In the period during the 1960s and early 1970s when output in Japan was growing at about 10 percent per year, the Japanese were saving about 25 percent of their income. Like the English during the Industrial Revolution, the Japanese said in effect: "These resources will be used for factories, equipment, and other forms of investment, not for consumption." The result was an outward shift of the production possibilities curve, as in Figure 2.8.

2. FREEDOM OF CHOICE AND ENTERPRISE. Another important characteristic of capitalism is freedom of choice and freedom of enterprise. ***Freedom of choice*** means that consumers are free to buy what they please and reject what they please; that laborers are free to work where, when, and if they please; and that investors are free to invest in whatever property they please. By ***freedom of enterprise***, we mean that firms are free to enter whatever markets they please, obtain resources in whatever ways they can, and organize their affairs as best they can. Needless to say, this does not mean that firms can run roughshod over consumers and workers. Even the strongest champions of capitalism are quick to admit that the government must set "rules of the game" to prevent firms from engaging in sharp or unfair practices. But granting such limitations, the name of the game under capitalism is economic freedom.

Freedom to do what? Under capitalism, individuals and firms are free to pursue their own self-interest. Put in today's idiom, each individual or firm can do his, her, or its own thing. However, it is important to note that this freedom is circumscribed by one's financial resources. Consumers in a capitalistic system can buy practically anything they like—if they have the money to pay for it. Similarly, workers can work wherever or whenever they please—if they don't mind the wages. And a firm can run its business as it likes—if it remains solvent. Thus an important regulator of economic activity under capitalism is the pattern of income and prices that emerges in the marketplace.

3. COMPETITION. Still another important characteristic of capitalism is ***competition***. Firms compete with one another for sales. Under perfect competition, there are a large number of firms producing each product; indeed, there are so many that no firm controls the product's price. Because of this competition, firms are forced to jump to the tune of the consumer. If a firm doesn't produce what consumers want—at a price at least as low as other firms are charging—it will lose sales to other firms. Eventually, unless it mends its ways, such a firm will go out of business. Of course, in real-life American markets, the number of producers is not always so large that no firm has any control over price. (Much more will be said about this below.) But in the purest form of capitalism, such imperfections do not exist. Also, lest you think that competition under capitalism is confined to producers, it must be remembered that owners of resources also compete. They are expected to offer their resources—including labor—to the buyer who gives them the best deal, and buyers of resources and products are supposed to compete openly and freely.

4. RELIANCE UPON MARKETS. Finally, another very important characteristic of capitalism is its reliance upon markets. *Under pure capitalism, the market—the free market—plays a central role.* Firms and individuals buy and sell products and resources in competitive markets. Some firms and individuals make money and prosper; others lose money and fail. Each firm or individual is allowed freedom to pursue its or his or her interests in the marketplace; the government guards against shady and dishonest dealings. Such is the nature of the economic system under pure capitalism.

How Does Capitalism Perform the Four Basic Economic Tasks?

The ***price system*** lies at the heart of any capitalist economy. In a purely capitalist economy, it is used to carry out the four basic economic functions discussed above. The price system is a way to organize an economy. Under such a system, every commodity and every service, including labor, has a price. We all receive money for what we sell, including labor, and we use this money to buy the goods and services we want. If more is wanted of a certain good, the price of this good tends to rise; if less is wanted, the price of the good tends to fall. Producers base their production decisions on the prices of commodities and inputs. Thus increases in a commodity's price generally tend to increase the amount of it produced, and decreases generally tend to decrease the amount produced. In this way, firms' output decisions are brought into balance with consumers' desires.

The very important question of how the price system performs the basic economic functions we discussed above will be answered in some detail in the next chapter. All we can do here is provide a preliminary sketch.

1. HOW DOES THE PRICE SYSTEM DETERMINE WHAT SOCIETY WILL PRODUCE? In a substantially capitalistic economy, such as ours, consumers choose the amount of each good that they want, and producers act in accord with these decisions. The importance consumers attach to a good is indicated by the price they are willing to pay for it. Of course, the principle of **consumer sovereignty**—producers dancing to the tune of consumers' tastes—should not be viewed as always and completely true, since producers do attempt to manipulate the tastes of consumers through advertising and other devices, but it is certainly a reasonable first approximation.

2. HOW DOES THE PRICE SYSTEM DETERMINE HOW EACH GOOD AND SERVICE WILL BE PRODUCED? Prices indicate the desires of workers and the relative value of various types of materials and equipment as well as the desires of consumers. For examples, if plumbers are scarce relative to the demand for them, their price in the labor market—their wage—will be bid up, and they will tend to be used only in the places where they are productive enough so that their employers can afford to pay them the higher wages. The forces that push firms toward actually carrying out the proper decisions are profits and losses. Profits are the carrot and losses are the stick used to eliminate the less efficient and less alert firms and to increase the more efficient and the more alert.

3. HOW DOES THE PRICE SYSTEM DETERMINE HOW MUCH IN THE WAY OF GOODS AND SERVICES EACH MEMBER OF THE SOCIETY IS TO RECEIVE? In general, an individual's income depends largely on the quantities of resources of various kinds that he or she owns and the prices he or she gets for them. For example, if a man both works and rents out farm land he owns, his income is the number of hours he works per year times his hourly wage rate plus the number of acres of land he owns times the annual rental per acre. Thus the distribution of income depends on the way resource ownership—including talent, intelligence, training, work habits, and, yes, even character—is distributed among the population. Also, to be candid, it depends on just plain luck.

4. HOW DOES THE PRICE SYSTEM DETERMINE THE NATION'S RATE OF GROWTH OF PER CAPITA INCOME? A nation's rate of growth of per capita income depends on the rate of growth of its resources and the rate of increase of the efficiency with which they are used. In our economy, the rate at which labor and capital resources are increased is motivated, at least in part, through

Trade plays an important role in capitalism, as we have seen. Why do individuals trade with one another? Consider the hypothetical case of Jane Barrister, a lawyer, divorced with two children. The Barrister family, like practically all families, trades continually with other families and with business firms. Since Ms. Barrister is a lawyer, she trades her legal services for money which she uses to buy the food, clothing, housing, and other goods and services her family wants. Why does the Barrister family do this? What advantages does it receive through trade? Why doesn't it attempt to be self-sufficient?

To see why the Barrister family prefers to opt for trade rather than self-sufficiency, let's compare the current situation—where Ms. Barrister specializes in the production of legal services and trades the money she receives for other goods and services— with the situation of self-sufficiency. In the latter case, the Barristers would have to provide their own transportation, telephone service, foodstuffs, clothing, and a host of other things. Ms. Barrister is a lawyer—a well-trained, valuable, productive member of the community. But if she were to try her hand at making automobiles—or even bicycles— she might be a total loss. Thus, if the Barrister family attempted to be self-sufficient, it might be unable to provide many of the goods it now enjoys.

Trade permits specialization, and specialization increases output. In our hypothetical case, it is obvious that, because she can trade with other families and with firms, Ms. Barrister can specialize in doing what she is good at—practicing law. Consequently, she can be more productive than if she were forced to be a Jane-of-all-trades, as she would have to be if she could not trade with others.

Let's turn now from individuals to nations. Basically, the same reasons exist for trade among nations as for trade among individuals. Because the United States can trade with other nations, it can specialize in the goods and services it produces particularly well. Then it can trade them for goods that other countries are especially good at producing. Thus both we and our trading partners benefit.

Some countries have more and better resources of

An immigration lawyer conferring with her client before a court hearing

certain types than others. Saudi Arabia has oil, Canada has timber, Japan has a skilled labor force, and so on. _International differences in resource endowments, and in the relative quantity of various types of human and nonhuman resources, are important bases for specialization_. Consider countries with lots of fertile soil, little capital, and much unskilled labor. They are likely to find it advantageous to produce agricultural goods, while countries with poor soil, much capital, and highly skilled labor will probably do better to produce capital-intensive, high-technology goods. We must recognize, however, that the bases for specialization do not remain fixed over time. Instead, as technology and the resource endowments of various countries change, the pattern of international specialization changes as well. For instance, the United States specialized more in raw materials and foodstuffs a century ago than it does now.

Surprising as it may seem, even if one country is able to produce everything more cheaply than another country, it still is likely that they both can benefit from specialization and trade. This proposition, known as *the law of comparative advantage,* will be discussed at length in Chapter 18. To illustrate why this law is valid, consider Jane Barrister and her friend, Ann Jones. Suppose that Jane is ten times as good at legal work and twice as good at typing as Ann. Should Jane do both legal work and typing? By no means. She should hire Ann to do the typing. Why? Because she earns so much more by specializing in law that it pays her to turn the typing over to Ann.

While Ann is half as good a typist as Jane, she is only a tenth as good a lawyer. Thus, by doing the typing, she is engaged in the type of work where she is best *comparatively.* Similarly, by doing the legal work, Jane is engaged in the type of work where she is best *comparatively.* (Recall that she is ten times as good a lawyer as Ann but only twice as good a typist.) If each does the type of work where she has a comparative advantage, both can benefit. This is true for countries as well as for individuals. Even if one country is more efficient than another in the production of everything, both countries can improve their lot by specializing in the production of the things where they have a comparative advantage.

the price system. Higher wages for more skilled work are an incentive for an individual to undergo further education and training. Capital accumulation occurs in response to the expectation of profit. Increases in efficiency, due in considerable measure to the advance of technology, are also stimulated by the price system.

OUR MIXED CAPITALIST SYSTEM

Since the days of Adam Smith, economists have been fascinated by the features of a purely capitalistic economic system — an economy that relies entirely on the price system. Smith, and many generations of economists since, have gone to great pains to explain that in such an economic system, *the price system, although it is not controlled by any person or small group, results in economic order, not chaos.* The basic economic tasks any economy must perform can, as we have said, be carried out in such an economic system by the price system. It is an effective means of coordinating economic activity through decentralized decision making based on information disseminated through prices and related data.

But does this mean that the American economy is purely capitalistic? As we have noted repeatedly, the answer is no. A purely capitalistic system is a useful model of reality, not a description of our economy as it exists now or existed in the past. It is useful because a purely capitalistic economy is, for some purposes, a reasonably close fit to our own. However, this does not mean that such a model is useful for all purposes. Many American markets are not perfectly competitive and never will be; they are dominated by a few producers or buyers who can influence price and thus distort the workings of the price system. Moreover, *the American economy is a mixed capitalistic economy, an economy where both government and private decisions are important.* The role of the government in American economic activity is very large indeed. Although it is essential to understand the workings of a purely capitalistic system, any model that omits the government entirely cannot purport to be adequate for the analysis of many major present-day economic issues.

To create a more balanced picture of the workings of the American economy, we must recognize that, although the price system plays an extremely important role, it is not permitted to solve all of the basic economic problems of our society. Consumer sovereignty does not extend—and cannot realistically be extended—to all areas of society. For example, certain public services cannot be left to private enterprise. The provision of fire protection, the operation of schools, and the development of weapons systems are examples of areas where we rely on political decision making, not the price system alone. Moreover, with regard to the consumption of commodities like drugs, society imposes limits on the decisions of individuals.

In addition, certain consequences of the price system are, by general agreement, unacceptable. Reliance on the price system alone does not ensure a just or equitable or optimal distribution of income. It is possible, for example, that one person will have money to burn while another person will live in degrading poverty. Consequently, society empowers the government to modify the distribution of income by imposing taxes that take more from the rich than the poor, and by welfare programs that try to keep the poor from reaching the point where they lack decent food, adequate clothing, or shelter. Besides providing public services and maintaining certain minimum income standards, the government also carries out a variety of regulatory functions. Industries do not police the actions of their constituent firms, so it falls to the government to establish laws that impose limits on the economic behavior of firms. For example, these laws say that firms must not misrepresent their products, that child labor must not be employed, and that firms must not collude and form monopolies to interfere with the proper functioning of the price system. In this way, the government tries, with varying degrees of effectiveness, to establish the "rules of the game"—the limits within which the economic behavior of firms (and consumers) should lie.

TEST YOURSELF

1. Suppose that a society's production possibilities curve is as follows:

| | OUTPUT(PER YEAR) | |
POSSIBILITY	FOOD (MILLIONS OF TONS)	TRACTORS (MILLIONS)
A	0	30
B	4	28
C	8	24
D	12	20
E	16	14
F	20	8
G	24	0

(a) Is it possible for the society to produce 30 million tons of food per year? (b) Can it produce 30 million tractors per year? (c) Suppose this society produces 20 million tons of food and 6 million tractors per year. Is it operating on the production possibilities curve? If not, what factors might account for this?

2. Plot the production possibilities curve in Question 1 on a graph. At what point along the horizontal axis does the curve cut the axis? At what point along the vertical axis does the curve cut the axis?

3. Suppose that, because of important technological improvements, the society in Question 1 can double its production of tractors at each level of food production. If so, is this society on its new production possibilities curve if it produces 20 million tons of food and 16 million tractors? Plot the new production possibilities curve. At what point along the horizontal axis does the new curve cut the axis? At what point along the vertical axis does it cut the axis?

4. "[Some people] . . . fail to realize that the price system is, and ought to be, a method of coercion. . . . The very term 'rationing by the purse' illustrates the point. Economists defend such forms of rationing, but they have to do so primarily in terms of its efficiency and its fairness." Comment.

5. "The great advantage of the [price system] . . . is that it permits wide diversity. It is, in political terms, a system of proportional representation. Each man can vote, as it were, for the color of tie he wants and get it; he does not have to see what color the majority wants and then, if he is in the minority, submit." Comment.

SUMMARY

1. The methodology used by economists is much the same as that used in any other kind of scientific analysis. The basic procedure is the formulation and testing of models.

2. A model must in general simplify and abstract from the real world. Its purpose is to make predictions, and in many respects the most important test of a model is how well it predicts. To test and quantify their models, economists gather data and utilize various statistical techniques.

3. The production possibilities curve, which shows the various production possibilities a society can attain, is useful in indicating the nature of the economic tasks any society faces.

4. Society has to recognize that it cannot get more of one good without giving up some of another good, if resources are fully and efficiently used. However, if they are not fully and efficiently used, society will have to settle for points inside the production possibilities curve—and it will be possible to obtain more of one good without giving up some of another good.

5. The task of determining how each good and service should be produced is, to a considerable extent, a problem of keeping society on its production possibilities curve, rather than at points inside the curve. The production possibilities curve does not tell us anything about the distribution of income, but it does indicate various ways that a society can promote growth in per capita income.

6. The American economy is a capitalistic economy, an economic system in which there is private ownership of capital, freedom of choice, freedom of enterprise, competition, and reliance upon markets.

7. Under pure capitalism, the price system is used to perform the four basic economic tasks. Although it is not controlled by any person or small group, the price system results in order, not chaos.

8. A purely capitalistic system is a useful model of reality, not a description of our economy as it exists now or in the past. The American economy is a mixed capitalistic economy, in which both government and private decisions are important.

CONCEPTS FOR REVIEW

Model	**Capitalism**	**Competition**
Production possibilities curve	**Freedom of choice**	**Price system**
Capital goods	**Freedom of enterprise**	**Consumer sovereignty**
Consumers' goods		

THE PRICE SYSTEM

IN THE EARLY 1990S, POLAND adopted an ambitious plan to make the transition from communism to capitalism, a step that would have seemed utterly impossible only a few years before. This plan called for the transfer of industry from government to private hands, and for reliance on market prices. As we shall see in this chapter, economists played a major role in the formulation of this plan, which in effect called for Poland to adopt the price system.

This chapter takes up the nature and functions of the price system, as well as some applications of our theoretical results to real-life problems. For example, we show how the price system determines the quantity produced of a commodity like wheat, and how the pricing policies of the Broadway theater have hurt show business in a variety of ways. These applications, like the fascinating case of Poland, help to illustrate the basic theory and indicate its usefulness.

The Polish parliament building in Warsaw

CONSUMERS, FIRMS, AND MARKETS

We begin by describing and discussing consumers and firms, the basic building blocks that make up the private, or nongovernmental, sector of the economy.

CONSUMERS.   Sometimes—for example, when a person buys a beer on a warm day—the consumer is an individual. In other cases—for example, when a family buys a new car—the consumer may be an entire household. **Consumers** purchase the goods and services that are the ultimate products of the economic system. When a man buys tickets to a ball game, he is a consumer; when he buys himself a Coke at the game, he is a consumer; and when he buys his wife a book on baseball for their twentieth wedding anniversary, he is a consumer.

FIRMS.   There are over 10 million firms in the United States. About nine-tenths of the goods and services produced in this country are produced by firms. (The rest are provided by government and not-for-profit institutions like universities and hospitals.) A **firm** is an organization that produces a good or service for sale. In contrast to not-for-profit organizations, firms attempt to make a profit. It is obvious that our economy is centered around the activities of firms.

MARKETS.   Consumers and firms come together in a market. The concept of a market is not quite as straightforward as it may seem, since most markets are not well defined geographically or physically. For example, the New York Stock Exchange is an atypical market because it is located principally in a particular building. For present purposes, a ***market*** can be defined as a group of firms and individuals that are in touch with each other in order to buy or sell some good. Of course, not every person in a market has to be in contact with every other person in the market. A person or firm is part of a market even if it is in contact with only a subset of the other persons or firms in the market.

Markets vary enormously in their size and procedures. For some goods like toothpaste, most people who have their own teeth (and are interested in keeping them) are members of the same market; while for other goods like Picasso paintings, only a few dealers, collectors, and museums in certain parts of the world may be members of the market. And for still other goods, like lemonade sold by neighborhood children for a nickel a glass at a sidewalk stand, only people who walk by the stand—and are brave enough to drink the stuff—are members of the market. Basically, however, all markets consist primarily of buyers and sellers, although third parties like brokers and agents may be present as well.

Markets also vary in the extent to which they are dominated by a few large buyers or sellers. For example, in the United States, there was for many years only one producer of aluminum. This firm, the Aluminum Company of America, had great power in the market for aluminum. In contrast, the number of buyers and sellers in some other markets is so large that no single buyer or seller has any power over the price of the product. This is true in various agricultural markets, for example. When a market for a product contains so many buyers and sellers that none of them can influence the price, economists call the market ***perfectly competitive.*** In these introductory chapters, we make the simplifying assumption that markets are perfectly competitive. We will relax that assumption later.

THE DEMAND SIDE OF A MARKET

Every market has a demand side and a supply side. *The **demand** side can be represented by a **market demand curve,** which shows the amount of the commodity buyers would like to purchase at various prices.* Consider Figure 3.1, which shows the demand curve for wheat in the American market during the early 1990s.[1] The figure shows that about 2.4 billion bushels of wheat will be demanded annually if the farm price is $2.80 per bushel, about 2.5 billion bushels will be demanded annually if the farm price is $2.40 per bushel, and about 2.6 billion bushels will be demanded annually if the farm price is $2.00 per bushel. The total demand for wheat is of several types: to produce bread and other food products for domestic use, as well as for feed use, for export purposes, and for industrial uses. The demand curve in Figure 3.1 shows the total demand—including all these components—at each price. Any demand curve pertains to a particular period of time, and the shape and position of the demand curve depend on the length of this period.

Take a good look at the demand curve for wheat in Figure 3.1. This simple, innocent-looking curve influences a great many people's lives.

[1] I am indebted to officials of the U.S. Department of Agriculture for providing me with this information. Of course, these estimates are only rough approximations, but they are good enough for present purposes.

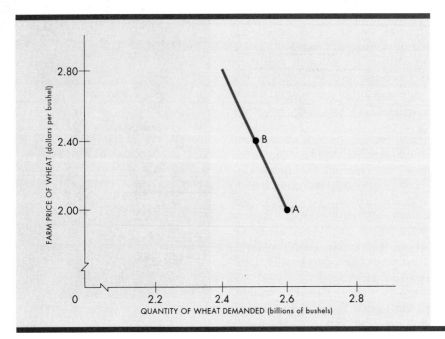

After all, wheat is the principal grain used for direct human consumption in the United States. To states like Kansas, North Dakota, Oklahoma, Montana, Washington, Nebraska, Texas, Illinois, Indiana, and Ohio, wheat is a mighty important cash crop. Note that the demand curve for wheat slopes downward to the right. In other words, the quantity of wheat demanded increases as the price falls. This is true of the demand curve for most commodities: they almost always slope downward to the right. This makes sense; one would expect increases in a good's price to result in a smaller quantity demanded.

Any demand curve is based on the assumption that the tastes, incomes, and number of consumers, as well as the prices of other commodities, are held constant. Changes in any of these factors are likely to shift the position of a commodity's demand curve, as indicated below.

CONSUMER TASTES. If consumers show an increasing preference for a product, the demand curve will shift to the right; that is, at each price, consumers will desire to buy more than previously. On the other hand, if consumers show a decreasing preference for a product, the demand curve will shift to the left, since, at each price, consumers will desire to buy less than previously. Take wheat. If consumers become convinced that foods containing wheat prolong life and promote happiness, the demand curve may shift, as shown in Figure 3.2; and the greater the shift in preferences, the larger the shift in the demand curve.

INCOME LEVEL OF CONSUMERS. For some types of products, the demand curve shifts to the right if per capita income increases; whereas for other types of commodities, the demand curve shifts to the left if per capita income rises. Economists can explain why some goods fall into one category and other goods fall into the other, but, at present, this need not concern us. All that is important here is that changes in per capita income affect the demand curve, the size and direction of this effect varying from product to product. In the case of wheat, a 10 percent increase in per

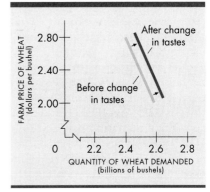

Figure 3.2
Effect of Increased Preference for Wheat on Market Demand Curve
An increased preference for wheat would shift the demand curve to the right.

capita income would probably have a relatively small effect on the demand curve, as shown in Figure 3.3.

NUMBER OF CONSUMERS IN THE MARKET. Compare Austria's demand for wheat with the United States'. Austria is a small country with a population of less than 8 million; the United States is a huge country with a population of over 200 million. Clearly, at a given price of wheat, the quantity demanded by American consumers will greatly exceed the quantity demanded by Austrian consumers, as shown in Figure 3.4. Even if consumer tastes, income, and other factors were held constant, this would still be true simply because the United States has so many more consumers in the relevant market.[2]

LEVEL OF OTHER PRICES. A commodity's demand curve can be shifted by a change in the price of other commodities. Whether an increase in the price of good B will shift the demand curve for good A to the right or the left depends on the relationship between the two goods. If they are substitutes, such an increase will shift the demand curve for good A to the right. Consider the case of corn and wheat. If the price of corn goes up, more wheat will be demanded since it will be profitable to substitute wheat for corn. If the price of corn drops, less wheat will be demanded since it will be profitable to substitute corn for wheat. Thus, as shown in Figure 3.5, increases in the price of corn will shift the demand curve for wheat to the right, and decreases in the price of corn will shift it to the left.[3]

The Distinction between Changes in Demand and Changes in the Quantity Demanded

It is essential to distinguish between a *shift in a commodity's demand curve* and a change in the *quantity demanded of the commodity*. A shift in a commodity's demand curve is a change in the *relationship* between price and quantity demanded. Figures 3.2, 3.3, and 3.5 show cases where such a change occurs. A change in the quantity demanded of a commodity may occur even if *no* shift occurs in the commodity's demand curve. For example, in Figure 3.1, if the price of wheat increases from $2.00 to $2.40 per bushel, the quantity demanded falls from 2.6 to 2.5 billion bushels. This change in the quantity demanded is due to a *movement along* the demand curve (from point *A* to point *B* in Figure 3.1), not to a *shift* in the demand curve.

When economists refer to an *increase in demand,* they mean a *rightward shift* in the demand curve. Thus Figures 3.2, 3.3, and 3.5 show increases in demand for wheat. When economists refer to a *decrease in demand,* they mean a *leftward shift* in the demand curve. An increase in demand for a commodity is not the same as an increase in the quantity demanded of the commodity. In Figure 3.1, the quantity demanded of wheat increases if the price falls from $2.40 to $2.00 per bushel, but this is

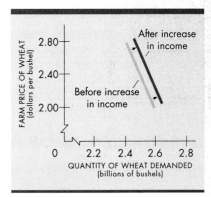

Figure 3.3
Effect of Increase in Income on Market Demand Curve for Wheat
An increase in income would shift the demand curve for wheat to the right, but only slightly.

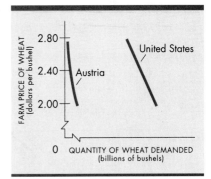

Figure 3.4
Market Demand Curve for Wheat, Austria and the United States
Since the United States has far more consumers than Austria, the demand curve in the United States is far to the right of Austria's.

[2] Note that no figures are given along the horizontal axis in Figure 3.4. This is because we do not have reasonably precise estimates of the demand curve in Austria. Nonetheless, the hypothetical demand curves in Figure 3.4 are close enough to the mark for present purposes.
[3] If goods A and B are complements, an increase in the price of good B will shift the demand curve for good A to the left. Thus an increase in the price of gin is likely to shift the demand curve for tonic to the left. Why? Because gin and tonic tend to be used together. The increase in gin's price will reduce the quantity of gin demanded, which in turn will reduce the amount of tonic that will be demanded at each price of tonic.

not due to an increase in demand, since there is no rightward shift of the demand curve. Similarly, a decrease in demand for a commodity is not the same as a decrease in the quantity demanded of the commodity. In Figure 3.1, the quantity demanded of wheat *decreases* if the price rises from $2.00 to $2.40 per bushel, but this is not due to a decrease in demand, since there is no leftward shift of the demand curve.

THE SUPPLY SIDE OF A MARKET

So much for our first look at demand. What about the other side of the market: supply? *The **supply** side of a market can be represented by a **market supply curve** that shows the amount of the commodity sellers would offer at various prices.* Let's continue with the case of wheat. Figure 3.6 shows the supply curve for wheat in the United States in the early 1990s, based on estimates made informally by government experts.[4] According to the figure, about 2.3 billion bushels of wheat would be supplied if the farm price were $2.00 per bushel, about 2.5 billion bushels if the farm price were $2.40 per bushel, and about 2.7 billion bushels if the farm price were $2.80 per bushel.

Look carefully at the supply curve shown in Figure 3.6. Although it looks innocuous enough, it summarizes the potential behavior of thousands of American wheat farmers—and their behavior plays an important role in determining the prosperity of many states and communities. Note that the supply curve for wheat slopes upward to the right. In other words, the quantity of wheat supplied increases as the price increases. This seems plausible, since increases in price give a greater incentive for farms to produce wheat and offer it for sale. Empirical studies indicate that the supply curves for a great many commodities share this characteristic of sloping upward to the right.

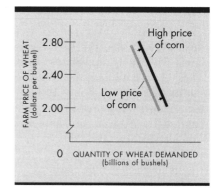

Figure 3.5
Effect of Price of Corn on Market Demand Curve for Wheat
Price increases for corn will shift the demand curve for wheat to the right.

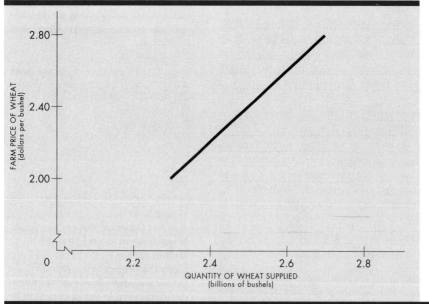

Figure 3.6
Market Supply Curve for Wheat, Early 1990s
The curve shows the amount of wheat sellers would supply at various prices. At $2.80 per bushel, about 17 percent more wheat would be supplied than at $2.00 per bushel.

[4] Officials of the U.S. Department of Agriculture provided me with these estimates. Although rough approximations, they are good enough for present purposes.

Any supply curve is based on the assumption that technology and input prices are held constant. Changes in these factors are likely to shift the position of a commodity's supply curve, as indicated below.

TECHNOLOGY. Recall that technology was defined in Chapter 1 as society's pool of knowledge concerning the industrial arts. As technology progresses, it becomes possible to produce commodities more cheaply, so that firms often are willing to supply a given amount at a lower price than formerly. Thus technological change often causes the supply curve to shift to the right. This certainly has occurred in the case of wheat, as shown in Figure 3.7. There have been many important technological changes in wheat production, ranging from advances in tractors to the development of improved varieties, like semi-dwarf wheats.

INPUT PRICES. The supply curve for a commodity is affected by the prices of the resources (labor, capital, and land) used to produce it. Decreases in the price of these inputs make it possible to produce commodities more cheaply, so that firms may be willing to supply a given amount at a lower price than they formerly would. Thus decreases in the price of inputs may cause the supply curve to shift to the right. On the other hand, increases in the price of inputs may cause it to shift to the left. For example, if the wage rates of farm labor increase, the supply curve for wheat may shift to the left, as shown in Figure 3.8.

An *increase in supply* is defined to be a *rightward shift* in the supply curve; a *decrease in supply* is defined to be a *leftward shift* in the supply curve. A change in supply should be distinguished from a change in the quantity supplied. In Figure 3.6, the quantity supplied of wheat will increase from 2.3 to 2.5 billion bushels if the price increases from $2.00 to $2.40 per bushel, but this is not due to an increase in supply, since there is no rightward shift of the supply curve in Figure 3.6.

EQUILIBRIUM PRICE

The two sides of a market, demand and supply, interact to determine the price of a commodity. Recall from the previous chapter that prices in a capitalistic system are important determinants of what is produced, how it is produced, who receives it, and how rapidly per capita income grows. It behooves us, therefore, to look carefully at how prices themselves are determined in a capitalist system. As a first step toward describing this process, we must define the equilibrium price of a product.

An **equilibrium** is a situation where there is no tendency for change: in other words, it is a situation that can persist. Thus an **equilibrium price** is a price that can be maintained. Any price that is not an equilibrium price cannot be maintained for long, since there are basic forces at work to stimulate a change in price.

For example, consider the wheat market. Let's put both the demand curve for wheat (in Figure 3.1) and the supply curve for wheat (in Figure 3.6) together in the same diagram. The result, shown in Figure 3.9, will help us determine the equilibrium price of wheat.

We begin by seeing what would happen if various prices were established in the market. For example, if the price were $2.80 per bushel, the demand curve indicates that 2.4 billion bushels of wheat would be demanded, while the supply curve indicates that 2.7 billion bushels would be supplied. Thus, if the price were $2.80 a bushel, there would be a mis-

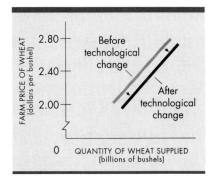

Figure 3.7
Effect of Technological Change on Market Supply Curve for Wheat
Improvements in technology often shift the supply curve to the right.

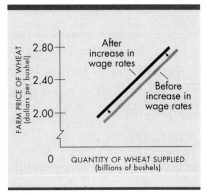

Figure 3.8
Effect of Increase in Farm Wage Rates on Market Supply Curve for Wheat
An increase in the wage rate might shift the supply curve to the left.

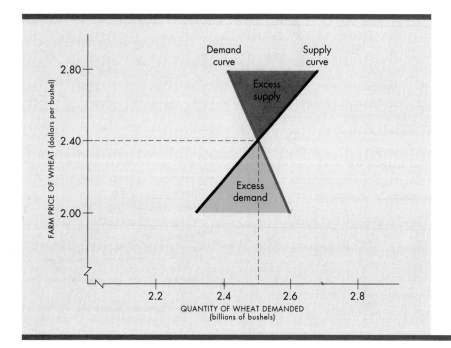

Figure 3.9
Determination of the Equilibrium Price of Wheat, Early 1990s
The equilibrium price is $2.40 per bushel, and the equilibrium quantity is 2.5 billion bushels. At a price of $2.80 per bushel, there would be an excess supply of 300 million bushels. At a price of $2.00 per bushel, there would be an excess demand of 300 million bushels.

match between the quantity supplied and the quantity demanded per year, since the rate at which wheat is supplied would be greater than the rate at which it is demanded. Specifically, as shown in Figure 3.9, there would be an *excess supply* of 300 million bushels. Under these circumstances, some of the wheat supplied by farmers could not be sold, and, as inventories of wheat built up, suppliers would tend to cut their prices in order to get rid of unwanted inventories. Thus a price of $2.80 per bushel would not be maintained for long—and for this reason $2.80 per bushel is not an equilibrium price.

If the price were $2.00 per bushel, on the other hand, the demand curve indicates that 2.6 billion bushels would be demanded, while the supply curve indicates that 2.3 billion bushels would be supplied. Again we find a mismatch between the quantity supplied and the quantity demanded per year, since the rate at which wheat is supplied would be less than the rate at which it is demanded. Specifically, as shown in Figure 3.9, there would be an *excess demand* of 300 million bushels. Under these circumstances, some of the consumers who want wheat at this price would have to be turned away empty-handed. There would be a shortage. And given this shortage, suppliers would find it profitable to increase the price, and competition among buyers would bid the price up. Thus a price of $2.00 per bushel could not be maintained for long—so $2.00 per bushel is not an equilibrium price.

Under these circumstances, the equilibrium price must be the price where the quantity demanded equals the quantity supplied. Obviously, this is the only price at which there is no mismatch between the quantity demanded and the quantity supplied; and consequently the only price that can be maintained for long. In Figure 3.9, the price at which the quantity supplied equals the quantity demanded is $2.40 per bushel, the price where the demand curve intersects the supply curve. Thus $2.40 per bushel is the equilibrium price of wheat under the circumstances visualized in Figure 3.9, and 2.5 billion bushels is the equilibrium quantity.

ACTUAL PRICE

The price that counts in the real world, however, is the ***actual price,*** not the equilibrium price, and it is the actual price that we set out to explain. In general, economists simply assume that the actual price will approximate the equilibrium price, which seems reasonable enough, since the basic forces at work tend to push the actual price toward the equilibrium price. Thus, if conditions remain fairly stable for a time, the actual price should move toward the equilibrium price.

To see that this is the case, consider the market for wheat, as described in Figure 3.9. What if the price somehow is set at $2.80 per bushel? As we

---

EXAMPLE 3.1 HOW THE ORANGE MARKET WORKS

In recent years, many oranges grown in California and Arizona have been provided to cattle for feed or given away to juicing plants. An 11-member committee of farmers and shippers establishes the number and size of oranges that can be sold. Anyone selling oranges without the committee's permission can face civil and criminal prosecution by the Department of Justice. Although some industry representatives claim that the oranges held off the market are too small to be sold, it is reported that the industry's figures show that some of these oranges are as large as those sent to market.

(a) In the absence of government intervention, suppose that the demand and supply curves for oranges would be as shown below:

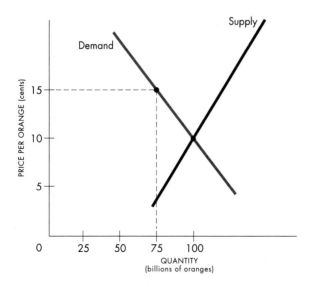

What would be the equilibrium price under these circumstances? (b) If the committee says that the quantity of oranges that can be sold must be 25 percent less than what would be sold in a free market, what will be the equilibrium price? (c) Under the committee's edict, will the growers receive more or less for their crop than under the free market? How much more or less? (d) How are consumers affected by the committee's edict?

Solution

(a) 10 cents per orange. (b) In a free market, 100 billion oranges would be sold. If this quantity is reduced by 25 percent, only 75 billion oranges can be sold. Based on the demand curve, this amount can be sold for 15 cents per orange. Thus this will be the price. (c) Under the committee's edict, growers will sell 75 billion oranges at 15 cents each, so they will receive $11.25 billion. Under the free market, they will sell 100 billion oranges at 10 cents each, so they will receive $10 billion. Thus they will receive $1.25 billion more under the committee's edict than under the free market. (d) They consume fewer oranges and pay more for those they do consume.

saw in the previous section, there is downward pressure on the price of wheat under these conditions. Suppose the price, responding to this pressure, falls to $2.70. Comparing the quantity demanded with the quantity supplied at $2.70, we find that there is still downward pressure on price, since the quantity supplied exceeds the quantity demanded at $2.70. The price, responding to this pressure, may fall to $2.60, but comparing the quantity demanded with the quantity supplied at this price, we find that there is still a downward pressure on price, since the quantity supplied exceeds the quantity demanded at $2.60.

So long as the actual price exceeds the equilibrium price, there will be a downward pressure on price. Similarly, so long as the actual price is less than the equilibrium price, there will be an upward pressure on price. Thus there is always a tendency for the actual price to move toward the equilibrium price. But it should not be assumed that this movement is always rapid. Sometimes it takes a long time for the actual price to get close to the equilibrium price. Sometimes the actual price never gets to the equilibrium price because by the time it gets close, the equilibrium price changes (because of shifts in either the demand curve or the supply curve or both). All that safely can be said is that the actual price will move toward the equilibrium price. But of course this information is of great value, both theoretically and practically. For many purposes, all that is needed is a correct prediction of the direction in which the price will move.

TEST YOURSELF

1. Assume that the market for electric toasters is competitive and that the quantity supplied per year depends as follows on the price of a toaster:

PRICE OF A TOASTER (DOLLARS)	NUMBER OF TOASTERS SUPPLIED (MILLIONS)
12	4.0
14	5.0
16	5.5
18	6.0
20	6.3

Plot the supply curve for toasters. Is this a direct or inverse relationship? Are supply curves generally direct or inverse relationships?

2. Suppose that the quantity of toasters demanded per year depends as follows on the price of a toaster:

PRICE OF A TOASTER (DOLLARS)	NUMBERS OF TOASTERS DEMANDED (MILLIONS)
12	7.0
14	6.5
16	6.2
18	6.0
20	5.8

Plot the demand curve for toasters. If the price is $14, will there be an excess demand of toasters? If the price is $20, will there be an excess demand? What is the equilibrium price of a toaster? What is the equilibrium quantity? (Use the data in Question 1.)

3. Suppose that the government imposes a price ceiling on toasters. In particular, suppose that it decrees that a toaster cannot sell for more than $14. Will the quantity supplied equal the quantity demanded? What sorts of devices may come into being to allocate the available supply of toasters to consumers? What problems will the government encounter in keeping the price at $14? What social purposes, if any, might such a price ceiling serve? (Use the data in Questions 1 and 2.)

4. Suppose that the government imposes a price floor on toasters. In particular, suppose that it decrees that a toaster cannot sell for less than $20. Will the quantity supplied equal the quantity demanded? How will the resulting supply of toasters be taken off the market? What problems will the government encounter in keeping the price at $20? What social purposes, if any, might such a price floor serve? (Use the data above.)

5. If the demand curve for butter is $Q_D = 20 - 4P$

(where Q_D is the quantity demanded and P is the price of butter) and the supply curve for butter is $Q_S = 2P$ (where Q_S is the quantity supplied), what is the equi- equilibrium price? What is the equilibrium quantity? (Both Q_D and Q_S are measured in millions of pounds, and price is measured in dollars per pound.)

THE EFFECTS OF SHIFTS IN THE DEMAND CURVE

Heraclitus, the ancient Greek philosopher, said you cannot step in the same stream twice: everything changes, sooner or later. One need not be a disciple of Heraclitus to recognize that demand curves shift. Indeed, we have already seen that demand curves shift in response to changes in tastes, income, population, and prices of other products, and that supply curves shift in response to changes in technology and input prices. Any supply-and-demand diagram like Figure 3.9 is essentially a snapshot of the situation during a particular period of time. The results in Figure 3.9 are limited to a particular period because the demand and supply curves in the figure, like any demand and supply curves, pertain only to a certain period.

What happens to the equilibrium price of a product when its demand curve changes? This is an important question because it sheds a good deal of light on how the price system works. Suppose that consumer tastes shift in favor of foods containing wheat, causing the demand curve for wheat to shift *to the right,* as shown in Figure 3.10. It is not hard to see the effect on the equilibrium price of wheat. Before the shift, the equilib-

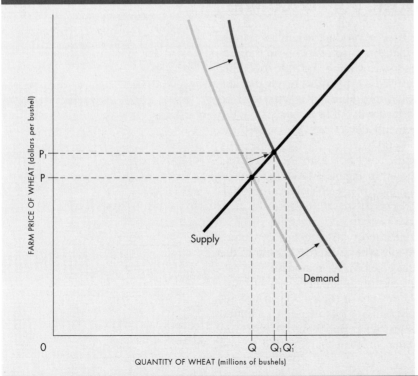

Figure 3.10
Effect on the Equilibrium Price of a Shift to the Right of the Market Demand Curve
This shift of the demand curve to the right results in an increase in the equilibrium price from OP to OP_1 and an increase in the equilibrium quantity from OQ to OQ_1.

rium price is *OP*. But when the demand curve shifts to the right, a shortage develops at this price.[5] Consequently, suppliers raise their prices. After some testing of market reactions and trial-and-error adjustments, the price will tend to settle at OP_1, the new equilibrium price, and quantity will tend to settle at OQ_1.

On the other hand, suppose that consumer demand for wheat products falls off, perhaps because of a great drop in the price of corn products. The demand for wheat now shifts *to the left*, as shown in Figure 3.11. What will be the effect on the equilibrium price of wheat? Clearly, the equilibrium price falls to OP_2, where the new demand curve intersects the supply curve.

In general, *a shift to the right in the demand curve results in an increase in the equilibrium price, and a shift to the left in the demand curve results in a decrease in the equilibrium price*. This is the lesson of Figures 3.10 and 3.11. Of course, this conclusion depends on the assumption that the supply curve slopes upward to the right, but, as we noted in a previous section, this assumption is generally true.

At this point, since all of this is theory, you may be wondering how well this theory works in practice. In 1972 and 1973, there was a vivid demonstration of the accuracy of this model in various agricultural markets, including wheat. Because of poor harvests abroad and greatly increased foreign demand for American wheat, the demand curve for wheat shifted markedly to the right. What happened to the price of wheat? In accord with our model, the price increased spectacularly, from about $1.35 a bushel in the early summer of 1972 to over $4.00 a year later. Anyone who witnessed this phenomenon could not help but be impressed by the usefulness of this model.

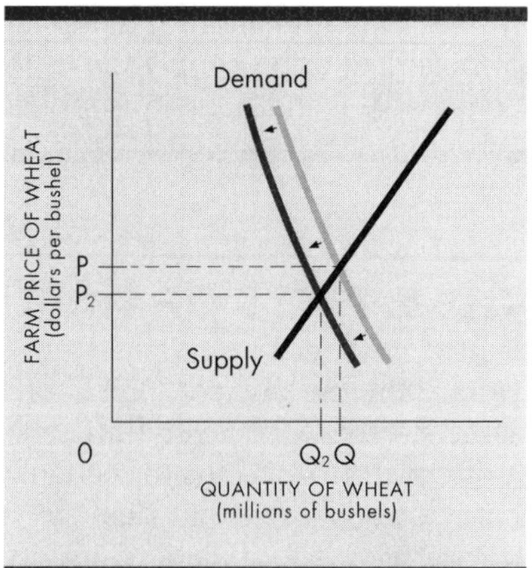

Figure 3.11
Effect on the Equilibrium Price of a Shift to the Left of the Market Demand Curve
This shift of the demand curve to the left results in a decrease in the equilibrium price from *OP* to OP_2 and a decrease in the equilibrium quantity from *OQ* to OQ_2.

THE EFFECTS OF SHIFTS IN THE SUPPLY CURVE

What happens to the equilibrium price of a product when its supply curve changes? For example, suppose that, because of technological advances in wheat production, wheat farmers are willing and able to supply more wheat at a given price than they used to, with the result that the supply curve shifts *to the right*, as shown in Figure 3.12. What will be the effect on the equilibrium price? Clearly, it will fall from *OP* (where the original supply curve intersects the demand curve) to OP_3 (where the new supply curve intersects the demand curve).

On the other hand, suppose the weather is poor, with the result that the supply curve shifts *to the left*, as shown in Figure 3.12. What will be the effect? The equilibrium price will increase from *OP* (where the original supply curve intersects the demand curve) to OP_4 (where the new supply curve intersects the demand curve).

In 1990, law enforcement officers concerned with narcotics consumption in the United States were shown vividly what a shift to the left in the supply curve of a commodity will do. Because of poor marijuana harvests in the United States, as well as the destruction or interception of marijuana by federal agents (for example, 90 percent of Hawaii's crop was reported to be destroyed), the supply curve for marijuana shifted dramatically to the left. The result was just what our theory would predict: a big jump in the price of marijuana. In some parts of the United

[5] This shortage is equal to $OQ'_1 - OQ$ in Figure 3.10.

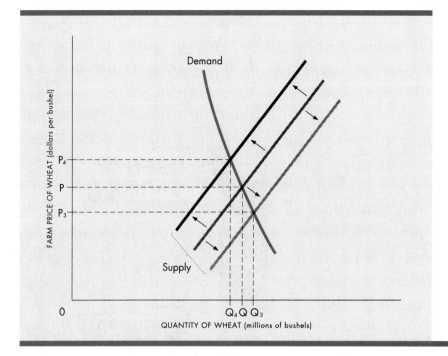

FARM PRICE OF WHEAT (dollars per bushel)

Demand

P_4

P

P_3

Supply

0    $Q_4 Q Q_3$

QUANTITY OF WHEAT (millions of bushels)

Figure 3.12
Effects on the Equilibrium
Price of Shifts in the Market
Supply Curve
The shift of the supply curve to the right results in a decrease in the equilibrium price from OP to OP_3. The shift of the supply curve to the left increases the equilibrium price from OP to OP_4.

States, marijuana sold in 1990 for $2,000 per pound, up from about $1,200 a year before.

In general, *a shift to the right in the supply curve results in a decrease in the equilibrium price, and a shift to the left in the supply curve results in an increase in the equilibrium price*. Of course, this conclusion depends on the assumption that the demand curve slopes downward to the right, but, as we noted in a previous section, this assumption is generally true.

HOW THE PRICE SYSTEM DETERMINES WHAT IS PRODUCED

Having described how prices are determined in free markets, we can now describe somewhat more fully how the price system goes about performing the four basic tasks that face any economic system. Let's begin by considering the determination of what society will produce: How does the price system carry out this task? Consumers indicate what goods and services they want in the marketplace, and producers try to meet these wants. More specifically, the demand curve for a product shows how much of that product consumers want at various prices. If consumers don't want much of it at a certain price, its demand curve will indicate that fact by being positioned close to the vertical axis at that price. In other words, the demand curve will show that, at this price for the product, the amount consumers will buy is small. On the other hand, if consumers want lots of the product at this price, its demand curve will be far from the vertical axis.

A product's demand curve is an important determinant of how much firms will produce of the product, since it indicates the amount of the product that will be demanded at each price. From the point of view of

HOW ASYMMETRIC INFORMATION AFFECTS THE MARKET FOR USED CARS

In some markets, like the market for used cars, buyers and sellers do not have the same information. Suppose that you are selling a used car. Given that you have operated the car for a while (and paid the bills for repairs and other expenses), you have a pretty good idea of the car's virtues and defects. If it is a lemon (that is, a defective car), you know it. On the other hand, if you are thinking of buying such a used car, you are likely to know little about how it will perform. Unless you have a considerable amount of detailed knowledge concerning automobiles, you can easily be fooled.

Thus there is an asymmetry of information, in the sense that sellers have more information than buyers about the quality of the product. This asymmetry of information influences how the market for used cars works. To see that this is the case, suppose for simplicity that all new cars are good or defective, that after a person buys a new car, he or she finds out whether it is good or defective, and that, if this car is offered for sale (as a used car), a potential buyer will not be able to determine (before buying it) whether it is good or defective.

Because the buyer of a used car cannot tell the difference between a good car and a defective car, both good and defective used cars must sell for the same price. Obviously, this price must be below the price of a new car. Otherwise, it would pay to purchase a new car, find out whether it is defective, and (if it turns out to be defective) sell it and purchase another new car. Unless the price of a used car is below the price of a new one, there would be no demand for used cars.

Defective cars—that is, lemons—are likely to constitute a large proportion of the used cars offered for sale. If a person owns a good used car, he or she will be unlikely to offer it for sale because the equilibrium price of a used car is relatively low. And since defective used cars may constitute a large number of the used cars offered for sale, potential buyers— wary of buying a lemon—are even more inclined to offer relatively low prices for used cars.

Perhaps the most important point to note is the following: *The buyer of a used car would be willing to pay more than the equilibrium price if he or she were sure of getting a good one, and the seller of a good used car would be happy to agree to such a transaction. But the asymmetry of information—the fact that the seller knows whether the used car is defective or good, but the buyer does not—makes it hard for such trades to occur.* How do sellers of used cars try to deal with this situation? They attempt in various ways to *signal* potential purchasers that their car is good. They provide information about the car, they encourage the potential purchaser to have his or her experts inspect it before purchase, and they offer free service contracts or money-back guarantees.[1]

---

[1] For a famous article on this topic, see G. Akerlof, "The Market for Lemons," *Quarterly Journal of Economics,* August 1970.

the producers, the demand curve indicates the amount they can sell at each price. In a capitalist economy, firms are in business to make money. Thus the manufacturers of any product will turn it out only if the amount of money they receive from consumers exceeds the cost of putting the product on the market. Acting in accord with the profit motive, firms are led to produce what the consumers desire. As we have seen, if consumers' tastes shift in favor of foods containing wheat, the demand curve for wheat will shift to the right, which will result in an increase in the price of wheat. This increase will stimulate farmers to produce more wheat. For example, when the demand curve shifts to the right in Figure 3.10, the equilibrium quantity produced increases from OQ to OQ_1. Given the shift in the demand curve, it is profitable for firms to step up their production. Acting in their own self-interest, they are led to make production decisions geared to the wants of the consumers.

Thus the price system uses the self-interest of the producers to get them to produce what consumers want. Consumers register what they want in the marketplace by their purchasing decisions—shown by their demand curves. Producers can make more money by responding to consumer wants than by ignoring them. Consequently, they are led to produce goods and services consumers want—and for which they are willing to pay enough to cover the producers' costs. Note that costs as well as demand determine what will be produced, and that producers are not forced by anyone to do anything. They can produce air conditioners for Eskimos if they like—and if they are prepared to absorb the losses. The price system uses prices to communicate the relevant signals to producers, and metes out the penalties and rewards in the form of losses or profits.

HOW THE PRICE SYSTEM DETERMINES HOW GOODS ARE PRODUCED

Next, consider how society determines how each good and service is produced. How does the price system carry out this task? The price of each resource gives producers an indication of how scarce this resource is, and how valuable it is in other uses. Clearly, firms should produce goods and services at minimum cost. Suppose that there are two ways of producing tables: Technique A and Technique B. Technique A requires 4 hours of labor and $10 worth of wood per table, whereas Technique B requires 5 hours of labor and $8 worth of wood. If the price of an hour of labor is $5, Technique A should be used since a table costs $30 with this technique, as opposed to $33 with Technique B.[6] In other words, Technique A uses fewer resources per table.

The price system nudges producers to opt for Technique A rather than Technique B through profits and losses. If each table commands a price of $45, then by using Technique A, producers make a profit of $45 – $30 = $15 per table. If they use Technique B, they make a profit of $45 – $33 = $12 per table. Thus producers, if they maximize profit, will be led to adopt Technique A. Their desire for profit leads them to adopt the techniques that will enable society to get the most out of its resources. No one commands firms to use particular techniques. Washington officials do not order steel plants to substitute the basic oxygen process for open

[6] To obtain these figures, note that the cost with Technique A is 4 hours times $5 plus $10, or $30, while the cost with Technique B is 5 hours times $5 plus $8, or $33.

hearths, or petroleum refineries to substitute catalytic cracking for thermal cracking. It is all done through the impersonal marketplace.

You should not, however, get the idea that the price system operates with kid gloves. Suppose all firms producing tables used Technique B until this past year, when Technique A was developed: in other words, Technique A is based on a new technology. Given this technological change, the supply curve for tables will shift to the right, as we have seen, and the price of a table will fall. Suppose it drops to $32. If some firm insists on sticking with Technique B, it will lose money at the rate of $1 a table; and as these losses mount, the firm's owners will become increasingly uncomfortable. The firm will either switch to Technique A or go bankrupt. The price system leans awfully hard on producers who try to ignore its signals.

HOW THE PRICE SYSTEM DETERMINES WHO GETS WHAT

Let's turn now to how society's output will be distributed among the people: How does the price system carry out this task? How much people receive in goods and services depends on their money income, which in turn is determined under the price system by the amount of various resources that they own and by the price of each resource. Thus, under the price system, each person's income is determined in the marketplace: the person comes to the marketplace with certain resources to sell, and his or her income depends on how much he or she can get for them.

The question of who gets what is solved at two levels by the price system. Consider an individual product—for example, the tables discussed in the previous section. For the individual product, the question of who gets what is solved by the equality of quantity demanded and quantity supplied. If the price of these tables is at its equilibrium level, the quantity demanded will equal the quantity supplied. Consumers who are willing and able to pay the equilibrium price (or more) get the tables, while those who are unwilling or unable to pay it do not get them. It is just as simple—and as impersonal—as that. It doesn't matter whether you are a nice guy or a scoundrel, or whether you are a connoisseur of tables or someone who doesn't know good workmanship from poor workmanship: all that matters is whether you are able and willing to pay the equilibrium price.

Next, consider the question of who gets what at a somewhat more fundamental level. After all, whether a consumer is able and willing to pay the equilibrium price for a good depends on his or her money income. Thus the super-rich can pay the equilibrium price for an astonishing variety of things, whereas those in abject poverty can scrape up the equilibrium price for very little. As we have already seen, a consumer's money income depends on the amount of resources of various kinds that he or she owns and the price that he or she can get for them. Some people have lots of resources: they are endowed with skill and intelligence and industry, or they have lots of capital or land. Other people have little in the way of resources. Moreover, some people have resources that command a high price, while others have resources that are of little monetary value. The result is that, under the price system, some consumers get a lot more of society's output than do other consumers.

HOW THE PRICE SYSTEM DETERMINES THE RATE OF ECONOMIC GROWTH

Let's turn now to the task of determining a society's rate of growth of per capita income. How does the price system do this? As pointed out in the previous chapter, a nation's rate of increase of per capita income depends on the rate of growth of its resources and the rate of increase of the efficiency with which they are used. First, consider the rate of growth of society's resources. The price system influences the amount society invests in educating, training, and upgrading its labor resources. To a considerable extent, the amount invested in such resource-augmenting activities is determined by the profitability of such investments, which is determined in turn by the pattern of prices.

Next, consider the rate of increase of the efficiency with which a society's resources are used. Clearly, this factor depends heavily on the rate of technological change. If technology is advancing at a rapid rate, it should be possible to get more and more out of a society's resources. But if technology is advancing rather slowly, it is likely to be difficult to get much more out of them. The price system affects the rate of technological change in a variety of ways: it influences the profitability of investing in research and development, the profitability of introducing new processes and products into commercial practice, and the profitability of accepting technological change—as well as the losses involved in spurning it.

The price system establishes strong incentives for firms to introduce new technology. Any firm that can find a cheaper way to produce an existing product, or a way to produce a better product, will have a profitable jump on its competitors. Until its competitors can do the same thing, this firm can reap higher profits than it otherwise could. Of course, these higher profits will eventually be competed away, as other firms begin to imitate this firm's innovation. But lots of money can be made in the period during which this firm has a lead over its competitors. These profits are an important incentive for the introduction of new technology.

TWO CASE STUDIES

The Price System in Action behind Enemy Lines

The real story of a World War II prisoner-of-war camp affords an excellent view of the price system in action. Just as certain elementary forms of life illustrate important biological principles in a simple way, so the economic organization of a prisoner-of-war camp is an elementary form of economic system that illustrates certain important economic principles simply and well. What made the camp's economic system so elementary was the fact that no goods were produced there. All commodities were provided by the country running the camp, by the Red Cross, and by other outside donors. Each prisoner received an equal amount of food and supplies—canned milk, jam, butter, cookies, cigarettes, and so on. In addition, private parcels of clothing, cigarettes, and other supplies were received, with different prisoners, of course, receiving different quantities. Because no goods were produced in the prisoner-of-war camp, the first two tasks of an economic system (What will be produced? How will it be produced?) were not relevant; neither was the fourth task (What provision is to be made for growth?)

HOW TO MAKE THE TRANSITION FROM COMMUNISM TO CAPITALISM: THE CASE OF POLAND

The price system seems to be gaining adherents throughout the world. After decades of criticizing capitalism, the governments of many communist countries, particularly in Eastern Europe, have begun to talk seriously about abandoning central planning and turning to the price system. Unquestionably, this is one of the most dramatic and significant economic developments of the 1990s. Practically everyone— including the most sophisticated observers—has been struck by how quickly the movement toward economic reform has progressed in some of these countries.

Poland is at the vanguard of this movement. At the beginning of 1990, Poland adopted a bold and controversial plan to make the transition from communism to capitalism. Specifically, this plan called for the transfer of industry from government to private hands, for an end to government subsidies, and for reliance on market prices. Also, in contrast to earlier days, bankruptcy and unemployment would now be tolerated. Unlike other East European countries, Poland jumped into capitalism like a child enters a swimming pool—feet first. Critics said this economic plan was "cold turkey" or "shock treatment."

Why are Poland and its East European neighbors abandoning central planning? As the Council of Economic Advisers has pointed out,

> A fundamental distinguishing feature of centrally planned economies is that state authorities, not private citizens, own and control most of the means of production. Instead of allocating resources through markets that establish prices based on supplies and demands, the state authorities generally formulate detailed plans for inputs and outputs. Coordinating this process properly requires an immense amount of information, making it exceedingly difficult for a centralized system of managers to allocate scarce resources according to what people want, or to respond to changes in demands, supplies and technologies. The lack of private ownership implies that individuals have little stake in improving resource allocation. Of course, the population as a whole would gain if resources were used to produce goods and services they valued more highly.
>
> Although the operation of centrally planned systems

Jeffrey Sachs

is very complex, a simple polar example illustrates key issues. Consider an enterprise producing shirts. In a centrally planned economy, planners would typically determine the amounts of cloth, dye, thread, and other inputs the enterprise would receive and the source and price of each input. Workers would be assigned to the enterprise, and often allocated to particular tasks. The plan would also set targets for output of each type of shirt and determine the final prices to households.

The contrast with a market economy is striking. In a centrally planned economy, prices of labor, goods, and services do not adjust to reflect supplies and demands, and production decisions are not motivated by profitability. Unlike a market system, producers typically have no leeway to reduce prices or production when inventories accumulate or to raise prices or production as inventories decline—even if consumers form long queues. The enterprise does not base hiring decisions on its assessment of needs and worker quality, nor does it choose where to purchase inputs so as to minimize production costs. Furthermore, state-owned enterprises are allocated the credit needed to finance operations through a centralized banking system. Most centrally planned economies have never developed laws to deal with bankruptcies, because enterprises are typically bailed out if costs exceed revenues. Consider the implications for U.S. firm behavior if the Federal Government promised to mail a check to cover the losses of every business that lost money. Such a system severely weakens the incentives for producers to use resources efficiently.

Because individuals in centrally planned economies own few of the factories or other productive assets, individuals have little incentive to respond to market signals about resource scarcity, even if such signals exist. Instead, the central planning system puts a premium on meeting output targets. The lack of private ownership also provides little incentive for innovation or quality control. New firms cannot simply enter the market to take advantage of better management or new ideas.[1]

Given these problems, Poland has decided to abandon central planning and to adopt the price system. In many respects, this is an unprecedented experiment. Although the world has plenty of experience with the functioning of a price system, very little is known about how to get a price system started. In the case of Poland, the government's "cold turkey" program, devised in considerable part by Harvard's Jeffrey Sachs, has undoubtedly caused pain. Critics point to the fact that substantial unemployment has occurred, that inflation has been very serious, and that living standards have fallen. Because of the huge increase in food prices, working families in early 1990 spent over half of their income on food. (See Table 1.) Some assert that the treatment may be as bad as the ailment.

But Sachs and others argue that a gradual transition from central planning will not work. In his view, "A step-by-step approach can't work for very good and deep and solid economic, financial, and political reasons. You get trapped in a mass of contradictions. You have to go far beyond simply decentralizing the economy. You have to go all the way to embracing a full market economy with private ownership, free international trade, and prices set according to supply and demand."[2]

Not all economists and politicians agree. Thus, Mikhail Gorbachev, president of the Soviet Union (prior to its disintegration in 1991), decided in 1990 not to emulate the Polish model. Instead, he proposed a gradual transition to a "regulated market

Lech Walesa, president of Poland

economy." Criticizing the proponents of a quick transition, he said, "They want to take a gamble. [They say that] everything should be thrown open tomorrow. Let market conditions be put in place everywhere. Let's have free enterprise and give the green light to all forms of ownership, private ownership. Let everything be private. Let us sell the land, everything. I cannot support such ideas, no matter how decisive and revolutionary they might appear. These are irresponsible ideas, irresponsible."[3]

Will Poland's bold new program work? It is a safe

Table 1 Percentage of Workers' Incomes Spent on Various Items, 1989 and 1990

ITEM	1989	1990
Food	38	52
Clothing	21	12
Rent	11	11
Energy	3	3
Entertainment	10	7
Transportation	6	6
Health Care	4	3
Other	7	6
Total	100	100

Source: New York Times, July 29, 1990.

[1] *Economic Report of the President,* Washington, D.C.: Government Printing Office, 1990, pp. 227–28.
[2] "The Debt Offensive," *Philadelphia Inquirer,* May 6, 1990.

[3] "How Gorbachev Rejected Plan to "Shock Treat" the Economy," *New York Times,* May 14, 1990.

bet that the price system by itself will not be a cure for all of Poland's economic ills. Poland's output per capita is only about one-fourth of that in the United States. It lacks modern equipment and sophisticated managers, among other things. According to the Joint Economic Committee of Congress, economic performance and living standards in Poland may decline in the near term as a result of this program.[4] But in the longer term, there is reason to believe that the price system will enable Poland to raise its standard of living.

Probing Deeper

1. Why does the coordination of the process of allocating resources in a centrally planned economy require "an immense amount of information"?

2. Why does the lack of private ownership of capital in a centrally planned economy imply "that individuals have little stake in improving resource allocation"?

3. Why does the lack of private ownership provide "little incentive for innovation or quality control"?

4. In 1990, Poland tried to sell a dozen large state enterprises to private groups, but failed. What are some of the problems in auctioning off enterprises of this sort?

5. Why do economists feel that it is a good idea to end government subsidies of enterprises?

6. Why has Poland decided that bankruptcy and unemployment should be tolerated? Aren't they to be avoided?

[4] "Jobless to Soar in a Free-Market East," New York Times, May 17, 1990.

All that did matter in this elementary economic system was the third task: to determine who would consume the various available goods. At first blush, the answer may seem obvious: each prisoner would consume the goods he received from the detaining country, the Red Cross, and private packages. But this assumes that prisoners would not trade goods back and forth ("I'll swap you a cigarette for some milk"), which is clearly unrealistic. After all, some prisoners smoked cigarettes, others did not; some liked jam and didn't like canned beef, others liked canned beef and didn't like jam. Thus there was bound to be exchange of this sort, and the real question is in what way and on what terms such exchange took place.

How did the prisoners go about exchanging goods? According to one observer, the process developed as follows:

> Starting with simple direct barter, such as a nonsmoker giving a smoker friend his cigarette issue in exchange for a chocolate ration, more complex exchanges soon became an accepted custom. . . . Within a week or two, as the volume of trade grew, rough scales of exchange values came into existence. [Some prisoners], who had at first exchanged tinned beef for practically any other foodstuff, began to insist on jam and margarine. It was realized that a tin of jam was worth one-half pound of margarine plus something else, that a cigarette issue was worth several chocolate issues, and a tin of diced carrots was worth practically nothing. . . . By the end of the month, there was a lively trade in all commodities and their relative values were well known, and expressed not in terms of one another—one didn't quote [jam] in terms of sugar—but in terms of cigarettes. The cigarette became the standard of value.[7]

Thus the prisoners used the price system to solve the problem of allocating the available supply of goods among consumers. A market developed for each good. This market had, of course, both a demand and a supply side. Each good had its price but this price was quoted in

[7] R. A. Radford, "The Economic Organization of a P.O.W. Camp," reprinted in E. Mansfield, *Principle of Microeconomics: Readings, Issues, and Cases,* 4th ed., New York: Norton, 1983.

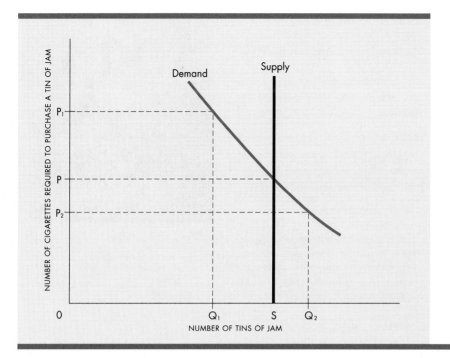

Figure 3.13
Determinants of Equilibrium Price of a Tin of Jam (in terms of cigarettes) in a P.O.W. Camp
The market supply for jam is fixed at OS tins. Thus the equilibrium price of a tin of jam is OP cigarettes. If the price were OP_1, OQ_1 tins would be demanded; if the price were OP_2, OQ_2 tins would be demanded.

cigarettes, not dollars and cents. These markets were not started in a self-conscious, deliberate way. No one said, "Let's adopt the price system to allocate available supplies," or "Let's vote on whether or not to adopt the price system." Instead, the system just evolved . . . and it worked.

To see how the supply of a particular good—jam, say—was allocated, look at Figure 3.13, which shows the market supply curve for jam. In the short run, this supply was fixed, so this supply curve is a vertical line. Figure 3.13 also provides the market demand curve for jam, which shows the amount of jam the prisoners wanted to consume at various prices of jam—expressed in terms of cigarettes. For example, the prisoners wanted OQ_1 tins of jam when a tin of jam cost OP_1 cigarettes, and OQ_2 tins of jam when a tin of jam cost OP_2 cigarettes. For the quantity demanded to equal the available supply, the price of a tin of jam had to be OP cigarettes; one tin of jam had to exchange for OP cigarettes. At this price, the available supply of jam was rationed, without resort to fights among prisoners or intervention by the prison authorities. Those prisoners who could and would pay the price had the jam and there were just enough such consumers to exhaust the available supply. Moreover, this held true for each of the other goods (including cigarettes) as well.

The Price System in Action on the Great White Way

It is a long way from a prisoner-of-war camp to the Broadway theater, but economics, like any good tool of analysis, applies to a very wide variety of problems. In this section, we discuss the theater's pricing problems and the role of the price system in helping to solve these problems. Prices for tickets to Broadway shows are established at levels that are much the same whether the show is a success or a flop. An orchestra ticket to *Kelly* (which managed to hold out for one performance before closing) cost about as much as an orchestra ticket to such hits as *Les Misérables* or *The Phantom of the Opera*. And once a play opens, the price of a ticket remains much the same whether the play is greeted with universal praise or with discontented critics and customers.

Because of these pricing methods, the Broadway theater has been beset for many years by serious problems. Here they are described by two veteran observers of the Broadway stage:

> For centuries the sale of theater tickets has brought on corruption and confusion. When there are more buyers than sellers, a black market results. The so-called "retail" price, the price printed on the ticket, becomes meaningless. Speculation doubles, triples, or quadruples the "real" as opposed to the "legal" asking price. A smash hit on Broadway means "ice"—the difference between the real and legal prices—a well-hidden but substantial cash flow that is divided among shadowy middlemen. Ticket scandals break out in New York as regularly as the flu. The scenario is familiar. A play opens and becomes a superhit. Tickets become difficult, then impossible, to obtain. There are letters to the newspapers. . . . Shocking corruption is discovered. Someone . . . is convicted of overcharging and accepting illegal gratuities. Someone may even go to jail. The black market, valiantly scotched, *never stops for a single moment*.[8]

Besides enriching crooked box-office workers and managers, as well as other shadowy elements of society, the black market for theater tickets has the additional undesirable effect of excluding the authors, composers, directors, and stars of the play from participation in the premium revenue. Almost all of these people receive a percentage of the play's revenues; and if the revenues at the box office are less than what customers pay for their seats (because of "ice"), these people receive less than they would if no black market existed. The amount of "ice" can be substantial. For example, Rodgers and Hammerstein estimated that, at one performance of their play, *South Pacific,* the public probably paid about $25,000 for tickets with a face value of $7,000, the amount turned in at the box office.

To focus on the problem here, let's look at the market for tickets to a particular performance of *A Chorus Line* (Broadway's longest-running show) when it was at the height of its popularity. Since the supply of tickets to a given performance of this play is fixed, the market supply curve, shown in Figure 3.14, is a vertical line at the quantity of tickets corresponding to the capacity of the theater. The price set officially on a ticket was about $30. But because the show was enormously popular, the market demand curve was *D* in Figure 3.14, and the equilibrium price for a ticket was $60.[9]

Figure 3.14 makes the nature of the problem apparent: at the official price of $30, the quantity of tickets demanded is much greater than the quantity supplied. Supply and demand don't match. Obviously, there is an incentive for people to buy the tickets from the box office at $30 and sell them at the higher prices customers are willing to pay. There is also an incentive for box-office workers to sell them surreptitiously at higher prices and turn in only $30. The price system cannot play the role it did in the prisoner-of-war camp for jam and other goods. It cannot act as an effective rationing device because, to do so, the price of tickets would have to increase to its equilibrium level, $60.

---

[8] S. Little and A. Cantor, *The Playmakers,* New York: Norton, 1970, p. 220.
[9] This figure is only a rough estimate, but it is good enough for present purposes.

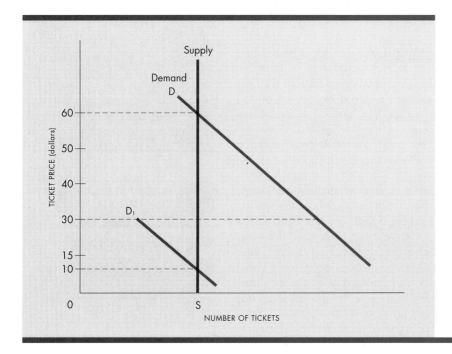

Figure 3.14
Equilibrium Price for Tickets to
A Chorus Line
The market supply for tickets is fixed at OS per performance. If the demand curve is D, the equilibrium price of a ticket is $60. (If the demand curve is D_1, the equilibrium price is $10.) If the demand curve is D and the price of a ticket is $30, the quantity of tickets demanded will far exceed the quantity supplied.

Many theater experts believe that the solution to Broadway's pricing problems lies in allowing the price system to work more effectively by permitting ticket prices to vary depending on a show's popularity. For example, the official ticket price would have been allowed to rise to $60 for *A Chorus Line*. On the other hand, if *A Chorus Line* had been much less popular and its market demand curve had been D_1 in Figure 3.14, its official ticket price would have been allowed to fall to $10. In this way, the black market for tickets would be eliminated, since the equilibrium price—which equates supply and demand—would be the official price. "Ice" would also be eliminated, since there would be no difference between the official and the actual price paid, and the people responsible for the show would receive its full receipts, not share them with crooked box-office workers and illegal operators.[10]

PRICE CEILINGS AND PRICE SUPPORTS

During national emergencies, the government sometimes puts a lid on prices, not allowing them to reach their equilibrium levels. For example, during World War II, the government did not allow the prices of various foodstuffs to rise to their equilibrium levels, because it felt that this would have been inequitable (and highly unpopular). Under such circumstances, the quantity demanded of a product exceeds the quantity supplied. In other words, the situation is like that in Figure 3.14, where the quantity of tickets demanded for *A Chorus Line* exceeded the quantity supplied at a price of $30. There is a shortage.

[10] Steps have been taken toward somewhat greater price flexibility for Broadway shows. For example, in the mid-1970s, a booth was established in Times Square where tickets to some shows were on sale at (approximately) half of the official ticket price. In this way, a show was enabled to cut its price, if it was unable to fill the theater at the official ticket price. Apparently, this has worked quite well, both for the producers of the shows and the theatergoing public.

Since the price system is not allowed to perform its rationing function, some formal system of rationing or allocating the available supply of the product may be required. Thus, in World War II, families were issued ration coupons which determined how much they could buy of various commodities. And in the 1970s, when the Organization of Petroleum Exporting Countries cut back oil production and reduced exports of oil to the United States, there was serious talk that gasoline and oil might be rationed in a similar way. Such rationing schemes may be justified in emergencies (of reasonably short duration), but they can result eventually in serious distortions, since prices are not allowed to do the job normally expected of them.

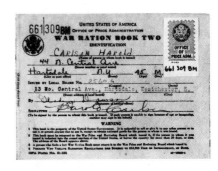

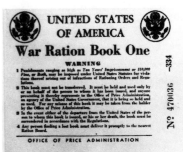

Ration coupons from World War II

To illustrate the sorts of problems that can arise when price ceilings are imposed, consider the rent ceilings that exist on some apartments in New York City. Originally imposed to prevent dwelling costs from soaring during World War II, these ceilings have been defended on the ground that they help the poor, at least in the short run. Although this may be so, they have also resulted in a shortage of housing in New York City. Because they have pushed the price of housing below the equilibrium price, less housing has been supplied than has been demanded. The depressed price of housing has discouraged investors from building new housing, and has made it unprofitable for some owners of existing housing to maintain their buildings. Thus, although it would be socially desirable to channel more resources into New York housing, the rent ceilings have prevented this from occurring.

Government authorities may also impose price floors—or price supports, as they often are called. These floors are generally defended on the ground that they enable the producers of the good in question to make a better living. For example, the federal government has imposed price supports on a wide range of agricultural commodities, the purpose being to increase farm incomes. Just as in the case in Figure 3.14 where the demand curve is D_1 and where a price floor of $30 exists, the result is that the quantity supplied exceeds the quantity demanded at the support price. Thus there is a surplus of the commodity—and, in the case of agricultural commodities, the government has had to buy up and store these surpluses. As in the case of a price ceiling, the result is that the price system is not allowed to do the job expected of it.

Whether price ceilings or floors are socially desirable depends on whether the loss in social efficiency resulting from them is exceeded by the gain in equity they achieve. As indicated above, their purpose is to help or protect particular parts of the population which would be treated inequitably by the unfettered price system. Since one person's view of what is equitable differs from another person's, this is an area of considerable controversy. More will be said about both price ceilings and floors in subsequent chapters, particularly Chapters 4 and 16.

THE CIRCULAR FLOWS OF MONEY AND PRODUCTS

So far we have been concerned largely with the workings of a single market—the market for wheat or tables or jam or tickets to *A Chorus Line*. But how do all of the various markets fit together? This is a very important question. Perhaps the best way to begin answering it is to distinguish

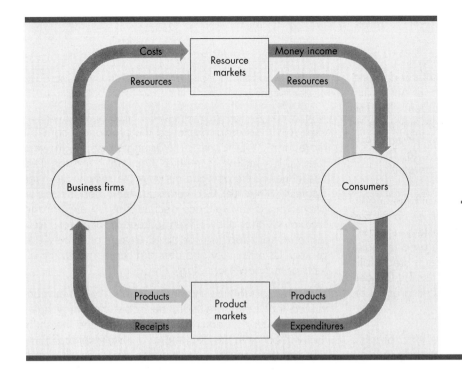

Figure 3.15
The Circular Flows of Money and Products
In product markets, consumers exchange money for products and firms exchange products for money. In resource markets, consumers exchange resources for money and firms exchange money for resources.

between product markets and resource markets. As their names indicate, ***product markets*** *are markets where products are bought and sold; and* ***resource markets*** *are markets where resources are bought and sold.* Let's first consider product markets. As shown in Figure 3.15, firms provide products to consumers in product markets, and receive money in return. The money the firms receive is their receipts; to consumers, on the other hand, it represents their expenditures.

Next, let's consider resource markets. Figure 3.15 shows that consumers provide resources—including labor—to firms in resource markets, and they receive money in return. The money the consumers receive is their income; to firms, on the other hand, it represents their costs. Note that the flow of resources and products in Figure 3.15 is counterclockwise: that is, *consumers provide resources to firms which in turn provide goods and services to consumers.* On the other hand, the flow of money in Figure 3.15 is clockwise: that is, *firms pay money for resources to consumers who in turn use the money to buy goods and services from the firms.* Both flows—that of resources and products, and that of money—go on simultaneously and repeatedly.

So long as consumers spend all their income, the flow of money income from firms to consumers is exactly equal to the flow of expenditure from consumers to firms. Thus these circular flows, like Ole' Man River, just keep rolling along. As a first approximation, this is a perfectly good model. But as we pointed out in Chapter 1, capitalist economies have experienced periods of widespread unemployment and severe inflation that this model cannot explain. Also, note that our simple economy in Figure 3.15 has no government sector. Under pure capitalism, the government would play a limited role in the economic system, but in the mixed capitalistic system we have in the United States, the government plays an important role indeed.

TEST YOURSELF

1. Will each of the following tend to shift the demand curve for toasters to the right, to the left, or not at all? (a) Consumer incomes rise by 20 percent. (b) The price of bread falls by 10 percent. (c) The price of electricity increases by 5 percent. (d) Medical reports indicate that toast prevents heart attacks. (e) The cost of producing a toaster increases by 10 percent.

2. Will each of the following tend to shift the supply curve for toasters to the right, to the left, or not at all? (a) The wage of workers producing toasters increases by 5 percent. (b) The price of the metal used to make toasters falls by 10 percent. (c) The price of bread falls by 10 percent. (d) Consumer incomes rise by 20 percent. (e) New technology makes toaster production much more efficient.

3. If both the demand and supply curve for a product shift to the right, can one predict whether the product's equilibrium price will increase or decrease? Can one predict whether its equilibrium quantity will increase or decrease?

4. In 1987, apple growers in the state of Washington expected their crop to exceed the previous record by more than 25 percent. (a) Washington apple growers spent $1.5 million to market their fruit overseas. Did this influence the demand curve or the supply curve for apples? Why? (b) Growers said their best hope for preventing a severe price decline was a new storage technology that allows them to keep apples fresh tasting and fresh looking for up to a year after they are picked. Using supply and demand curves, show the effects of this new technology on price.

5. Suppose that the American public becomes convinced that beets are more desirable than they have been, and string beans are less so. Describe the shifts that will occur in the demand and supply curves in the relevant markets, and the mechanisms that will signal and trigger a redeployment of resources.

SUMMARY

1. There are two sides of every market: the demand side and the supply side. The demand side can be represented by the market demand curve, which almost always slopes downward to the right and whose location depends on consumer tastes, the number and income of consumers, and the prices of other commodities.

2. The supply side of the market can be represented by the market supply curve, which generally slopes upward to the right and whose location depends on technology and resource prices.

3. The equilibrium price and equilibrium quantity of the commodity are given by the intersection of the market demand and supply curves. If conditions remain reasonably stable for a time, the actual price and quantity should move close to the equilibrium price and quantity.

4. Changes in the position and shape of the demand curve—in response to changes in consumer tastes, income, population, and prices of other commodities—result in changes in the equilibrium price and equilibrium output of a product. Similarly, changes in the position and shape of the supply curve—in response to changes in technology and resource prices, among other things—also result in changes in the equilibrium price and equilibrium output of a product.

5. To determine what goods and services society will produce, the price system sets up incentives for firms to produce what consumers want. To the extent that they produce what consumers want and are willing to pay for, firms reap profits; to the extent that they don't, they experience losses.

6. The price system sets up strong incentives for firms to produce goods at minimum cost. These incentives take the form of profits for firms that minimize costs and losses for firms that operate with relatively high costs.

7. To determine who gets what, the price system results in each person's receiving an income that depends on the quantity of resources he or she owns and the prices that they command.

8. The price system establishes incentives for activities that result in increases in a society's per capita income. For example, it influences the amount of new capital goods produced, as well as the amount society spends on educating its labor force and improving its technology.

9. There are circular flows of money and products in a capitalist economy. In product markets, firms provide products to consumers and receive money in return. In resource markets, consumers provide resources to firms, and receive money in return.

CONCEPTS FOR REVIEW

Consumers

Firms

Markets

Perfect competition

Demand

Market demand curve

Supply

Market supply curve

Equilibrium

Equilibrium price

Actual Price

Product market

Resource market

P A R T   T W O

CONSUMER BEHAVIOR AND BUSINESS DECISION MAKING

MARKET DEMAND AND PRICE ELASTICITY

IN OCTOBER 1990, APPLE COMPUTER launched a new product, the Macintosh Classic, which sold very well. In other words, market demand for the Classic was high. In a capitalist economy, market demand is a fundamental determinant of what is produced and how. It is no exaggeration to say that firms spend enormous time and effort trying to cater to, estimate, and influence market demand.

In this chapter, we discuss the factors influencing the market demand curve for a commodity, as well as the measurement of market demand curves and their role in decision making by private business firms and government agencies. We consider questions like: How can we measure market demand curves? How sensitive is the quantity demanded of various products to changes in price? What factors underlie the market demand curve for a commodity? These are important questions, from both a theoretical and a practical point of view.

MARKET DEMAND CURVES

Let's review what a market demand curve is. We saw in Chapter 3 that a commodity's market demand curve shows how much of the commodity will be purchased during a particular period of time at various prices. Figure 4.1 ought to be familiar; it is the ***market demand curve*** for wheat in the early 1990s, which figured prominently in our discussion of the price system in Chapter 3. Among other things, it shows that during the early 1990s about 2.6 billion bushels of American wheat would have been purchased per year if the price was $2.00 per bushel, that about 2.5 billion bushels would have been purchased per year if the price was $2.40 per bushel, and that about 2.4 billion bushels would have been purchased if the price was $2.80 per bushel.

Since the market demand curve reflects what consumers want and are willing to pay for, when the market demand curve for wheat shifts upward to the right, this indicates that consumers want more wheat at the existing price. On the other hand, when the curve shifts downward to the left, this indicates that consumers want less wheat at the existing price. Such shifts in the market demand curve for a commodity trigger changes in the behavior of the commodity's producers. When the market demand curve shifts upward to the right, the price of wheat will tend to rise, thus inducing farmers to produce more wheat, because they will find that, given the price increase, their profits will increase if they raise their out-

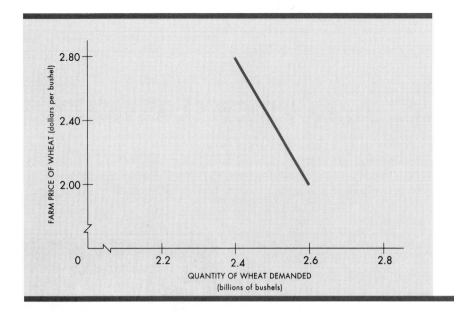

Figure 4.1
Market Demand Curve for Wheat, Early 1990s
This curve shows how much wheat would be purchased per year at various prices.

put levels. The same process occurs in other parts of the economy. Shifts in the demand curve reflecting the fact that consumers want more (less) of a commodity set in motion a sequence of events leading to more (less) production of the commodity.

Measuring Market Demand Curves

To be of practical use, market demand curves must be based on careful measurements. Let's look briefly at some of the techniques used to estimate the market demand curve for particular commodities. At first glance, a quick and easy way to estimate the demand curve might seem to be interviewing consumers about their buying habits and intentions. However, although more subtle variants of this approach sometimes may pay off, simply asking people how much they would buy of a certain commodity at particular prices does not usually seem very useful, since off-the-cuff answers to such questions are rarely very accurate. Thus marketing researchers and econometricians interested in measuring market demand curves have been forced to use more complex procedures.

One such procedure is the ***direct market experiment.*** Although the designs of such experiments vary greatly and are often quite complicated, the basic idea is simple—to see the effects on the quantity demanded of actual variations in the price of the product. (Researchers attempt to hold other market factors constant or to take into account whatever changes may occur.) The Parker Pen Company conducted an experiment to estimate the demand curve for their ink, Quink. They increased the price from $.15 to $.25 in four cities, and found that the quantity demanded was quite insensitive to the price. Experiments like this are frequently made to try to estimate a product's market demand curve.

Still another technique is to use statistical methods to estimate demand curves from historical data on price and quantity purchased of the commodity. For example, one might plot the price of slingshots in various periods in the past against the quantity sold, as shown in Figure 4.2. Judging from the results, curve *D* in Figure 4.2 seems a reasonable ap-

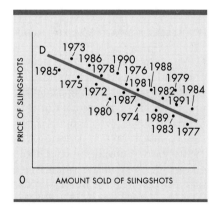

Figure 4.2
Estimated Demand Curve for Slingshots
One very crude way to estimate the market demand curve is to plot the amount sold of a commodity in each year against its price in that year, and draw a curve that seems to fit the points reasonably well. However, this technique is generally too crude to be reliable.

proximation to the demand curve. Although this simple analysis provides some insight into how statistical methods are used to estimate demand curves from historical data, it is a vast oversimplification. For one thing, the market demand curve may have shifted over time, so that curve D is not a proper estimate. Fortunately, modern statistical techniques recognize this possibility and allow us to estimate the position and shape of this curve (at each point in time) in spite of it.

Hundreds, perhaps thousands, of studies have been made to estimate the demand curves for particular commodities. In view of the importance of the results for decision making, this is not surprising. To illustrate the role played by such studies in the formulation of public policy, let's consider the following case involving the Boston and Maine Railroad.

Railroad Transportation in Metropolitan Boston: A Case Study

When the Boston and Maine Railroad wanted to discontinue passenger commuter service into Boston (because it felt such service was unprofitable), the Mass Transportation Commission of Massachusetts contracted with the Boston and Maine to establish a demonstration project to estimate the effect of lowering fares on the quantity of commuter tickets sold. The Boston and Maine was requested not to file a petition for the discontinuance of commuter service into Boston until after the experiment. During the experiment, which lasted about a year, fares were reduced about 28 percent on the average. The result was, of course, an increase in the number of tickets sold. However, the more important thing to the railroad and the commission was the *extent* to which the fare cut would increase the number of tickets sold. *How great* would be the resulting increase in the number of tickets sold? This was the important question because to increase the railroad's profits, a fare cut had to increase the railroad's revenues more than it increased its costs. And unless the price cut increased the number of tickets sold by a greater percentage than the reduction in price, it would not increase the railroad's revenues at all.

A comparison of the Boston and Maine's commuter revenues showed that this large fare reduction resulted in only a 0.6 percent increase in the railroad's revenues. Thus the price reduction increased the railroad's revenues by little or nothing. Since the reduction in fares increased the railroad's costs—because it was more costly to handle the larger volume of traffic—and increased its revenues scarcely at all, it did not increase the railroad's profits. Thus, after the experiment, the Boston and Maine decided to continue with its petition to terminate commuter service. (Eventually, however, public subsidies were instituted to keep the service going.)

This is a fairly typical example of a direct market experiment designed to obtain information on relevant aspects of a market demand curve. Note the problems experiments of this sort must face. First, *the experiment can be very costly if it alienates customers or reduces the firm's profits*. Second, *it is difficult to hold other relevant variables constant*. For example, the effect of price changes was mixed up, to some extent, with the effect of increased service in the Boston and Maine case. Third, *it is hard to conduct an experiment of this sort over a long enough period to estimate long-run effects*. Thus, in the Boston and Maine case, the effect of the fare reduction on the number of tickets sold might have been much greater if the

EXAMPLE 4.1   SPECULATION AND THE DEMAND CURVE

In many markets speculators buy and sell, hoping to make money in the process. Suppose that the demand and supply curves for corn this year and next year are as shown below. Speculators, seeing that the price of corn is likely to rise (from OA to OH), decide to buy corn this year and sell it next year. Thus, including the speculators, the demand curve shifts to the right this year, and the supply curve shifts to the right next year, as shown below:

Solution

(a) Yes. Without the speculators, much less corn would be consumed next year than this year. With them, consumption of corn is relatively constant. (b) Yes. The value (price times quantity) of the corn sold this year is increased considerably (from area $OABS_0$ to area $OCES_0$). The value of the corn sold next year does not change very much, based on the diagram. (It is area

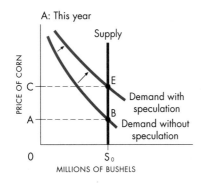

A: This year

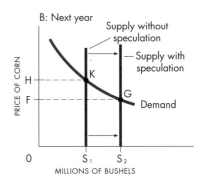

B: Next year

(a) In this case, do speculators even out the consumption of corn over time, thus avoiding famine-feast cycles? (b) In this case, do speculators raise the total value of the corn sold in the two periods? (c) In this case, speculators guessed correctly that the price of corn would rise. If they guess incorrectly, can they make more uneven the consumption of corn over time? (d) Once speculation is included in the analysis, does the demand curve for a product depend on its expected future price?

$OHKS_1$ without speculation and area $OFGS_2$ with speculation.) Thus the total value of the corn sold in the two periods is raised. (c) Yes. (d) Yes. If there is a general feeling that the price of a product is going to increase substantially, the demand curve for this product may shift to the right.

experiment had lasted longer. Nonetheless, despite these problems, experiments of this sort can produce useful evidence on the location and shape of a product's market demand curve. They are an important supplement to statistical analysis of historical data to estimate market demand curves.

THE PRICE ELASTICITY OF DEMAND

The quantity demanded of some commodities, like beef in Figure 4.3, is fairly sensitive to changes in the commodity's price. That is, changes in price result in significant changes in quantity demanded. On the other hand, the quantity demanded of other commodities, like cotton in Figure

4.3, is very insensitive to changes in the price. Large changes in price result in small changes in the quantity demanded.

To promote unambiguous discussion of this subject, we must have some measure of the sensitivity of quantity demanded to changes in price. The measure customarily used for this purpose is the **price elasticity of demand**, *defined as the percentage change in quantity demanded resulting from a 1 percent change in price.*[1] For example, suppose that a 1 percent reduction in the price of slingshots results in a 2 percent increase in quantity demanded. Then, using this definition, the price elasticity of demand for slingshots is 2. (Convention dictates that we give the elasticity a positive sign even though the change in price is negative and the change in quantity demanded is positive.) The price elasticity of demand is likely to vary from one point to another on the market demand curve. For example, the price elasticity of demand for slingshots may be higher when a slingshot costs $1.00 than when it costs $0.25.

Note that the price elasticity of demand is expressed in terms of *relative*—i.e., proportional or percentage—changes in price and quantity demanded, not *absolute* changes in price and quantity demanded. Thus, in studying the slingshot market, we looked at the *percentage* change in quantity demanded resulting from a 1 *percent* change in price. This is because absolute changes depend on the units in which price and quantity are measured. Suppose that a reduction in the price of good Y from $100 to $99 results in an increase in the quantity demanded from 200 to 210 pounds per month. If price is measured in dollars, the quantity demanded of good Y seems quite sensitive to price changes, since a decrease in price of "1" results in an increase in quantity demanded of "10." On the other hand, if price is measured in cents, the quantity demanded of good Y seems quite insensitive to price changes, since a decrease in price of "100" results in an increase in quantity demanded of "10." By using relative changes, we do not encounter this problem. Relative changes do not depend on the units of measurement. Thus the percentage reduction in the price of good Y is 1 percent, regardless of whether price is measured in dollars or cents. And the percentage increase in the quantity demanded of good Y is 5 percent, regardless of whether it is measured in pounds or tons.

Calculating the Price Elasticity of Demand

The price elasticity of demand is a very important concept and one that economists use often, so it is worthwhile to spend some time explaining exactly how it is computed. Suppose that you have a table showing various points on a market demand curve. For example, Table 4.1 shows the quantity of wheat demanded at various prices, as estimated by Professor Karl Fox of Iowa State University during the early 1960s.[2] Given these data, how do you go about computing the price elasticity of demand for wheat? Since the price elasticity of demand for any product generally

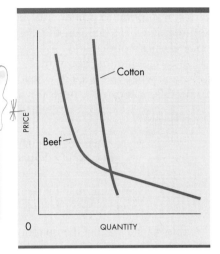

Figure 4.3
Market Demand Curves, Beef and Cotton
The quantity demanded of beef is much more sensitive to price than is the quantity demanded of cotton.

Table 4.1
Market Demand for Wheat, Early 1960s

FARM PRICE OF WHEAT (DOLLARS PER BUSHEL)	QUANTITY OF WHEAT DEMANDED (MILLIONS OF BUSHELS)
1.00	1,500
1.20	1,300
1.40	1,100
1.60	900
1.80	800
2.00	700
2.20	675

Source: K. Fox, V. Ruttan, and L. Witt, *Farming, Farmers, and Markets for Farm Goods.* New York: Committee for Economic Development, 1962.

---

[1] What if price does not change by 1 percent? Then the price elasticity of demand is defined as the *percentage change in quantity demanded divided by the percentage change in price.* This definition will be used in the next section. Put in terms of symbols, the price elasticity of demand equals $\dfrac{-\Delta Q}{\Delta P} \times \dfrac{P}{Q}$, where P is price, ΔP is the change in price, Q is quantity demanded, and ΔQ is the change in the quantity demanded.

[2] Note that Table 4.1 pertains to the early 1960s whereas Figure 4.1 pertains to the early 1990s. Consequently, the demand curves are quite different, as you can see.

varies from point to point on its market demand curve, you must first determine at what point on the demand curve you want to measure the price elasticity of demand.

Let us assume that you want to estimate the price elasticity of demand for wheat when the price of wheat is between $2.00 and $2.20 per bushel. To do this, you can use the following formula:

price elasticity =

$$\frac{\text{percentage change}}{\text{in quantity demanded}} \div \frac{\text{percentage change}}{\text{in price}} =$$

$$\frac{\text{change in quantity demanded}}{\text{original quantity demanded}} \div \frac{\text{change in price}}{\text{original price}}.$$

Table 4.1 shows that the quantity demanded equals 700 million bushels when the price is $2.00, and that it equals 675 million bushels when the price is $2.20. But should we use $2.00 and 700 million bushels as the original price and quantity? Or should we use $2.20 and 675 million bushels as the original price and quantity? If we choose the former,

price elasticity =

$$-\frac{675 - 700}{700} \div \frac{2.20 - 2.00}{2.00} = .36.$$

The price elasticity of demand is estimated to be .36. (The minus sign at the beginning of this equation is due to the fact, noted above, that convention dictates that the elasticity be given a positive sign.)

But we could just as well have used $2.20 and 675 million bushels as the original price and quantity. If this had been our choice, the answer would be

price elasticity =

$$-\frac{700 - 675}{675} \div \frac{2.00 - 2.20}{2.20} = .41,$$

which is somewhat different from the answer we got in the previous paragraph.

To get around this difficulty, the generally accepted procedure is to use the average values of price and quantity as the original price and quantity. In other words, we use as an estimate of the price elasticity of demand:

price elasticity =

$$\frac{\text{change in quantity demanded}}{\text{sum of quantities}/2} \div \frac{\text{change in price}}{\text{sum of prices}/2}.$$

This is the so-called **arc elasticity of demand.** In the specific case we are considering, the arc elasticity is

price elasticity =

$$-\frac{(675 - 700)}{\left(\frac{675 + 700}{2}\right)} \div \frac{2.20 - 2.00}{\left(\frac{2.20 + 2.00}{2}\right)} = .38.$$

This is the answer to our problem.

DETERMINANTS OF THE PRICE ELASTICITY OF DEMAND

Many studies have been made of the price elasticity of demand for particular commodities, Table 4.2 reproduces the results of some of them. Note the substantial differences among products. For example, the estimated price elasticity of demand for women's hats is about 3.00, while for cotton it is only about 0.12. Think for a few minutes about these results, and try to figure out why these differences exist. If you rack your brains for a while, chances are that you will agree that the following factors are important determinants of whether the price elasticity of demand is high or low.

NUMBER AND CLOSENESS OF AVAILABLE SUBSTITUTES. *If a commodity has many close substitutes, its demand is likely to be highly elastic,* i.e., the price elasticity is likely to be high. If the price of the product increases, a large proportion of its buyers will turn to the close substitutes that are available. If its price decreases, a great many buyers of substitutes will switch to this product. Naturally, the closeness of the substitutes depends on how narrowly the commodity is defined. In general, one would expect that, as the definition of the product becomes narrower and more specific, the product has more close substitutes and its price elasticity of demand is higher. Thus the demand for a particular brand of oil is more price elastic than the overall demand for oil, and the demand for oil is more price elastic than the demand for fuel as a whole. If a commodity is defined so that it has perfect substitutes, its price elasticity of demand approaches infinity. Thus, if one farmer's wheat is exactly like that grown by other farmers and if the farmer raises the price slightly (to a point above the market level), the farmer's sales will be reduced to nothing.

IMPORTANCE IN CONSUMERS' BUDGETS. It is often asserted that the price elasticity of demand for a commodity is likely to depend on the importance of the commodity in consumers' budgets. The elasticity of demand for commodities like pepper and salt may be quite low. Typical consumers spend a very small portion of their income on pepper and salt, and the quantity they demand may not be influenced much by changes in price within a reasonable range. However, although a tendency of this sort is often hypothesized, there is no guarantee that it always exists.

LENGTH OF THE PERIOD. Every market demand curve pertains, you will recall, to a certain time interval. In general, *demand is likely to be more sensitive to price over a long period than over a short one.* The longer the period, the easier it is for consumers and business firms to substitute one good for another. If, for example, the price of oil should decline relative to other fuels, oil consumption in the month after the price decline would probably increase very little. But over a period of several years, people would have an opportunity to take account of the price decline in choosing the type of fuel to be used in new and renovated houses and businesses. In the longer period of several years, the price decline would have a greater effect on the consumption of oil than in the shorter period of one month.[3]

---

[3] For durable goods like automobiles, the price elasticity of demand may be smaller over a long period than a short one. If the price of autos increases, the quantity demanded is likely to fall substantially because many people will postpone buying a new car. But as time goes on, the quantity of autos demanded will tend to rise as old autos wear out.

Table 4.2
Estimated Price Elasticities of Demand for Selected Commodities, United States

COMMODITY	PRICE ELASTICITY
Women's hats	3.00
Gasoline	0.30
Sugar	0.31
Corn	0.49
Cotton	0.12
Hay	0.43
Potatoes	0.31
Oats	0.56
Barley	0.39
Buckwheat	0.99
Refrigerators	1.40
Airline travel	2.40
Radio and TV sets	1.20
Legal services	0.50
Pleasure boats	1.30
Canned tomatoes	2.50
Newspapers	0.10
Tires	0.60
Beef	0.92
Shoes	0.40

In 1905 the average automobile produced in the United States cost more than the average Datsun seventy years later. Many of the firms in the auto industry were warmed-over buggy makers who handcrafted rich men's toys. But change was in the air. *Motor Age,* the industry's first trade magazine, prophesied that "the simple car is the car of the future—. A golden opportunity awaits some bold manufacturer of a simple car."

It remained for Henry Ford, the son of a Wisconsin farmer, to translate these words into a car—the Model T. Ford, commenting on his rural youth, declared, "It was life on the farm that drove me into devising ways and means to better transportation." Turning from the kid glove and checkbook set, he saw the potential market—at the right price—for car sales in the agricultural community.

The Model T was introduced in 1909. A few numbers indicate its phenomenal progress.

Henry Ford in his first automobile, 1903

YEAR	PRICE (DOLLARS)	CARS SOLD
1909	900	58,022
1914	440	472,350
1916	360	730,041

However, all good things come to an end. By the twenties, Ford's unwillingness to alter the Model T in any fashion (cosmetic or mechanical), as well as increased competition from other manufacturers, and the development of trade-in and installment buying (which reduced the price elasticity of demand for automobiles) brought the Model T to an end. But the record profits of the Ford Motor Company between 1910 and 1920 vindicated Henry Ford in his belief that "it is better to sell a large number of cars at a reasonably small margin than to sell fewer cars at a larger margin of profit. Bear in mind that when you reduce the price of the car without reducing the quality you increase the possible number of purchases. There are many men who will pay $360 for a car who would not pay $440. I figure that on the $360 basis we can increase the sales to 800,000 cars for the year—less profit on each car, but more cars, more employment of labor and in the end, we get all the profit we ought to make." Needless to say, price reductions do not always result in higher profits. But in his appraisal of the auto market between 1910 and 1920, Henry Ford seemed right.

E.A.

PRICE ELASTICITY AND TOTAL MONEY EXPENDITURE

Many important decisions hinge on the price elasticity of demand for a commodity. In this section, we show how the price elasticity of demand determines the effect of a price change on the total amount spent on a commodity. As a first step, we must define three terms: price elastic, price inelastic, and unitary elasticity. The demand for a commodity is **price elastic** if the price elasticity of demand is *greater than* 1. The demand for a commodity is **price inelastic** if the price elasticity of demand is *less than* 1. And the demand for a commodity is of **unitary elasticity** if the price elasticity of demand *equals* 1. As indicated below, the effect of a price change on the total amount spent on a commodity depends on whether the demand for the commodity is price elastic, price inelastic, or of unitary elasticity. Let's consider each case.

Case 1: Demand Is Price Elastic

In this case, if the price of the commodity is *reduced,* the total amount spent on the commodity will *increase.* To see why, suppose that the price elasticity of demand for compact discs is 2 and that the price of the compact discs is reduced by 1 percent. Because the price elasticity of demand is 2, the 1 percent reduction in price results in a 2 percent increase in quantity of compact discs demanded. Since the total amount spent on compact discs equals the quantity demanded times the price, the 1 percent reduction in price will be more than offset by the 2 percent increase in quantity demanded. The result of the price cut will be an increase in the total amount spent on compact discs.

On the other hand, if the price of the commodity is *increased,* the total amount spent on the commodity will *fall.* For example, if the price of compact discs is raised by 1 percent, this will reduce the quantity demanded by 2 percent. The 2 percent reduction in the quantity demanded will more than offset the 1 percent increase in price, the result being a decrease in the total amount spent on compact discs.

Case 2: Demand Is Price Inelastic

In this case, if the price is *reduced,* the total amount spent on the commodity will *decrease.* To see why, suppose that the price elasticity of demand for corn is 0.5 and the price of corn is reduced by 1 percent. Because the price elasticity of demand is 0.5, the 1 percent price reduction results in a ½ percent increase in the quantity demanded of corn. Since the total amount spent on corn equals the quantity demanded times the price, the ½ percent increase in the quantity demanded will be more than offset by the 1 percent reduction in price. The result of the price cut will be a decrease in the total amount spent on corn.

On the other hand, if the price of the commodity is *increased,* the total amount spent on the commodity will *increase.* For example, if the price of corn is raised by 1 percent, this will reduce quantity demanded by ½ percent. The 1 percent price increase will more than offset the ½ percent reduction in quantity demanded, the result being an increase in the total amount spent on corn.

Table 4.3
Effect of an Increase or Decrease in the Price of a Commodity on the Total Expenditure on the Commodity

COMMODITY'S PRICE ELASTICITY OF DEMAND	EFFECT ON TOTAL EXPENDITURE OF:	
	PRICE DECREASE	PRICE INCREASE
Price elastic (which means that elasticity is greater than 1)	Increase	Decrease
Price inelastic (which means that elasticity is less than 1)	Decrease	Increase
Unitary elasticity (which means that elasticity equals 1)	No change	No change

Case 3: Demand Is of Unitary Elasticity

In this case, a price increase or decrease results in no difference in the total amount spent on the commodity. Why? Because a price decrease (increase) of a certain percentage always results in a quantity increase (decrease) of the same percentage, so that the product of the price and quantity is unaffected.

Table 4.3 summarizes the results of this section. It should help you review our findings.

TEST YOURSELF

1. Professor Kenneth Warner of the University of Michigan has estimated that a 10 percent increase in the price of cigarettes results in a 4 percent decline in the quantity of cigarettes consumed. For teenagers, he estimated that a 10 percent price increase results in a 14 percent decline in cigarette consumption. Based on his estimates, what is the price elasticity of demand for cigarettes? Among teenagers, what is the price elasticity of demand? Why is the price elasticity different among teenagers than for the public as a whole?

2. Suppose that each of the four corners of an intersection contains a gas station, and that the gasoline is essentially the same. Do you think that the price elasticity of demand for each station's gasoline is above or below 1? Why? Do you think that it is less than or greater than the price elasticity of demand for all gasoline in the U.S.?

3. The Bugsbane Music Box Company is convinced that an increase in its price will reduce the total amount of money spent on its product. Can you tell from this whether the demand for its product is price elastic or price inelastic?

4. Suppose that the relationship between the price of aluminum and the quantity of aluminum demanded is as follows:

PRICE (DOLLARS)	QUANTITY
1	8
2	7
3	6
4	5
5	4

What is the arc elasticity of demand when price is between $1 and $2? Between $4 and $5?

THE FARM PROBLEM AND THE PRICE ELASTICITY OF DEMAND

To illustrate the importance of the price elasticity of demand, let's consider American agriculture. One of the most difficult problems for farmers is that, under a free market, farm incomes vary enormously between good times and bad, the variation being much greater than for nonfarm incomes. This is so because farm prices vary a great deal between good times and bad, whereas farm output is much more stable than industrial output. Why is agriculture like this?

The answer lies in considerable part with the price elasticity of demand for farm products. Food is a necessity with few good substitutes. Thus we would expect the demand for farm products to be price inelastic. And as Table 4.2 suggests, this expectation is borne out by the facts. Given that the demand curve for farm products is price inelastic—and that the quantity supplied of farm products is also relatively insensitive to price—it follows that relatively small shifts in either the supply curve or the demand curve result in big changes in price. This is why farm prices are so unsta-

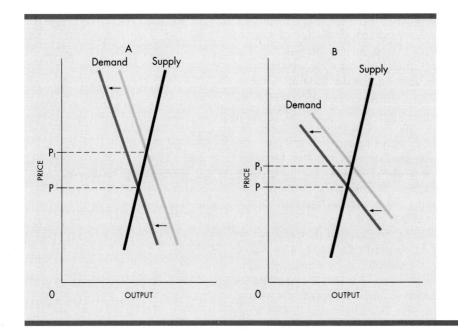

Figure 4.4
Instability of Farm Prices and Incomes
Because the demand curve in panel A is much less elastic than in panel B, a small shift in the demand curve has a much bigger impact on price in panel A than in panel B.

ble. Panel A of Figure 4.4 shows a market where the demand curve is much more inelastic than in panel B. As you can see, a small shift to the left in the demand curve results in a much larger drop in price in panel A than in panel B.

Price Elasticity and the Brannan Plan

This is not the only role the price elasticity of demand plays in our farm problems. Many other questions involve it. Consider the plan proposed after World War II by Charles Brannan who served as President Truman's secretary of agriculture. The plan was later supported in somewhat modified form by Ezra Taft Benson, secretary of agriculture in the Eisenhower administration. But it drew fire from many farmers, and not until 1973, after nearly three decades of controversy, was the plan approved by Congress.

According to the **Brannan plan,** a floor is established under the price received by farmers. Suppose that the market price is below this target level. If the target level is $3 in Figure 4.5, and if the output that farmers can grow (without violating government restrictions) is OQ_3, this plan lets the competitive market alone, so that the output of OQ_3 is sold at a price of $2. Then according to this plan, the government issues subsidy checks to farmers to cover the difference between the market price ($2) and the target price ($3).

The cost to the Treasury under the Brannan plan is ($3 − $2) × OQ_3. Why? Because the Treasury pays a subsidy of ($3 − $2) per bushel, and OQ_3 bushels are grown; thus the total subsidy is ($3 − $2) × OQ_3. Before the Brannan plan was adopted, the government supported the price at $3, and bought the amount—$(OQ_3 − OQ_2)$—that private buyers would not purchase at that price. The cost to the Treasury under this system is $3 × $(OQ_3 − OQ_2)$. Why? Because the Treasury buys $(OQ_3 − OQ_2)$ bushels at $3 per bushel.

An important question is: Will the cost to the U.S. Treasury under the

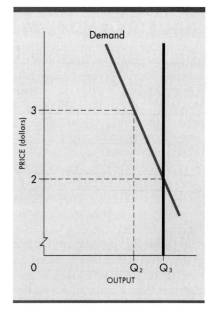

Figure 4.5
Effect of the Brannan Plan
Under the Brannan plan, the competitive market would be let alone, so that, if output were OQ_3, the price would be $2. Then the government would pay farmers the difference between this price and the target price, $3.

Brannan plan be greater than under the previous system? The answer can be shown to depend on the price elasticity of demand. As demonstrated in footnote 4, the cost under the Brannan plan is greater than under the previous system [4] if $2 \times OQ_3 < \$3 \times OQ_2$. But since $2 \times OQ_3$ is the total money expenditure at a price of $2 and $3 \times OQ_2$ is the total money expenditure at a price of $3, it follows from the previous section that $2 \times OQ_3$ will be less than $3 \times OQ_2$ if the price elasticity of demand is less than 1. (Why? Because the total amount spent on a commodity will be less at a lower price [such as $2] than at a higher price [such as $3] if demand is price inelastic.) Thus, since the elasticity of demand for farm products is in fact less than 1, the cost to the Treasury will be greater under the Brannan plan than under a system whereby the price is supported at $3, with the government clearing the market of the farm products not purchased by the private sector at that price.[5]

Our purpose here is not to decide whether the Brannan plan is good or bad. To make such a decision, we would have to take account of many factors besides the cost to the Treasury. (In Chapter 16, a detailed examination of our nation's farm programs is provided.) Instead, our point is that the price elasticity of demand is an important concept in discussing the effects of the Brannan plan, just as in discussing the instability of farm income and prices. Moreover, as we shall see in subsequent sections, the price elasticity of demand is equally as important in problems concerning the industrial sector of the economy as in problems concerning agriculture.

INDUSTRY AND FIRM DEMAND CURVES

Up to this point, we have been dealing with the market demand curve for a commodity. *The market demand curve for a commodity is not the same as the market demand curve for the output of a single firm that produces the commodity, unless, of course, the industry is composed of only a single firm.* If the industry is composed of more than one firm, as is usually the case, the demand curve for the output of each firm producing the commodity will usually be quite different from the demand curve for the commodity. The demand curve for the output of Farmer Brown's wheat is quite different from the market demand curve for wheat.

In particular, the demand curve for the output of a particular firm is generally more price elastic than the market demand curve for the commodity, because the products of other firms in the industry are close substitutes for the product of this firm. As pointed out earlier, products with many close substitutes have relatively high price elasticities of demand.

If there are many, many firms selling a homogeneous product, the individual firm's demand curve becomes *horizontal,* or essentially so. To see this, suppose that 100,000 firms sell a particular commodity and that each of these firms is of equal size. If any one of these firms were to triple

[4] The cost to the government under the Brannan plan is $(\$3 - \$2) \times OQ_3 = \$3 \times OQ_3 - \$2 \times OQ_3$, while the cost under the other system is $3 \times (OQ_3 - OQ_2) = \$3 \times OQ_3 - \$3 \times OQ_2$. Thus the difference in cost between the Brannan plan and the other system is $3 \times OQ_2 - \$2 \times OQ_3$, which means that the cost under the Brannan plan would be greater than under the other system if $2 \times OQ_3 < \$3 \times OQ_2$.

[5] Note that this result does not depend on our choice of $3 as the target price and of $2 as the market price. Regardless of what the target price and market price may be, this result will hold, if the price elasticity of demand is less than 1.

its output and sales, the total industry output would change by only .002 percent—too small a change to have any perceptible effect on the price of the commodity. Consequently, each firm can act as if variations in its output—within the range of its capabilities—will have no real impact on market price. In other words, the demand curve facing the individual firm is horizontal, as in Figure 4.6.

INCOME ELASTICITY OF DEMAND

So far this chapter has dealt almost exclusively with the effect of a commodity's price on the quantity demanded of it in the market. But price is not, of course, the only factor that influences the quantity demanded of the commodity. Another important factor is the level of money income among the consumers in the market. The sensitivity of the quantity demanded to the total money income of all of the consumers in the market is measured by the *income elasticity of demand, which is defined as the percentage change in the quantity demanded resulting from a 1 percent increase in total money income (all prices being held constant)*.

A commodity's income elasticity of demand may be positive or negative. For many commodities, increases in income result in increases in the amount demanded. Such commodities, like steak or caviar, have positive income elasticities of demand. For other commodities, increases in income result in decreases in the amount demanded. These commodities, like margarine and poor grades of vegetables, have negative income elasticities of demand. However, be careful to note that the income elasticity of demand of a commodity is likely to vary with the level of income under consideration. For example, if only families at the lowest income levels are considered, the income elasticity of demand for margarine may be positive.

Luxury items tend to have higher income elasticities of demand than necessities. Indeed, one way to define luxuries and necessities is to say that luxuries are commodities with high income elasticities of demand, and necessities are commodities with low income elasticities of demand.

Empirical Studies

Many studies have been made to estimate the income elasticity of demand for particular commodities, since, like the price elasticity of demand, it is of great importance to decision makers. In making long-term forecasts of industry sales, for example, firms must take the income elasticity of demand into account. Thus, if the income elasticity of demand for a product is high, and if incomes increase considerably during the next 20 years, the product's sales will tend to increase greatly during that period. On the other hand, if the income elasticity of demand for a product is close to zero, one would expect the product's sales not to increase very much on account of such increases in income.

To illustrate the findings of empirical studies in this area, consider the following results: The income elasticity of demand has been estimated, according to one well-known study, to be 0.37 for eggs, 0.34 for cheese, 0.42 for butter, 1.00 for liquor, −0.20 for margarine, 0.07 for milk and cream, and 1.48 for restaurant consumption of food. Certainly, these estimates seem reasonable. One would expect the income elasticity of demand to be negative for margarine, because consumers tend to view mar-

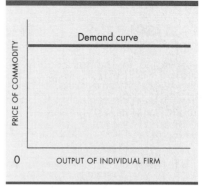

Figure 4.6
Demand Curve for Output of an Individual Firm: The Case of a Great Many Sellers of a Homogeneous Commodity
If there are many firms selling a homogeneous product, the demand curve facing an individual firm is horizontal.

EXAMPLE 4.2   THE DEMAND FOR "SUDS"

According to Thomas Fogarty and Kenneth Elzinga, the price elasticity of demand for beer in the United States is about 0.8, and the income elasticity of demand for beer is about 0.4.

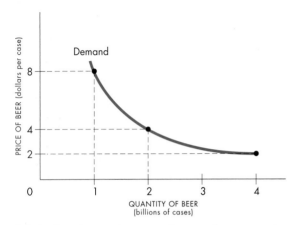

(a) Is the demand curve shown above consistent with their findings? Why, or why not? (b) If the price of a case of beer increases, will this result in an increase or decrease in the amount of money spent per year on beer? (c) If consumer income increases by 15 percent, while the price of beer remains constant, what will be the effect on the amount of money spent per year on beer? (d) Holding the prices of other goods and income constant, do you think that the market demand curve for beer varies from month to month? From state to state? If so, why? (e) If Budweiser lowers the price of its beer by 1 percent, can it expect to increase the quantity it sells by 0.8 percent? Why, or why not? (f) A number of years ago, Budweiser was selling for 58 cents per case more than its rivals in the St. Louis market and had 12 percent of the market. About a year later, Budweiser sold its beer at the same price as its rivals and had 39 percent of the market. Suppose that other brewers held their price constant at $2 per case during this period, and that the total amount of beer sold in this market was constant during this period. What was the price elasticity of demand for Budweiser beer in this market?

Solution

(a) No. According to this demand curve, the price elasticity of demand for beer is 1, since the amount spent on beer is the same ($8 billion) regardless of the price. (b) Increase. (c) It will increase by about 6 percent. (d) Yes, because of differences among months and states in temperature, tastes, and other factors. (e) No. Because Budweiser is only one firm in the market, the percentage increase in the quantity it sells is likely to be greater than 0.8 percent, if other firms hold their price constant. (f) —($.39X − .12X$)/$.255X$ ÷ ($2.00 − $2.58)/$2.29 = 4.2. (X is the total amount of beer sold in this market then.)

garine as an inferior good, and as their incomes rise, they tend to switch from margarine to butter. Also, it is not surprising that the income elasticity of demand for milk and cream is close to zero, since people tend to view milk and cream as necessities, particularly for children. In addition, it is quite reasonable that the income elasticity of demand for liquor and restaurant consumption of food is higher than for the other commodities. Liquor and restaurant meals tend to be luxury items for most people.

CROSS ELASTICITY OF DEMAND

Besides the price of the commodity and the level of total money income—the factors discussed primarily in previous sections of this chapter—the quantity demanded of a commodity also depends on the prices of other commodities. Suppose the price of butter is held constant. The amount of butter demanded will be influenced by the price of margarine.

The **cross elasticity of demand,** *defined as the percentage change in the quantity demanded of one commodity resulting from a 1 percent change in the price of another commodity, is used to measure the sensitivity of the former commodity's quantity demanded to changes in the latter commodity's price.*

Pairs of commodities are classified as **substitutes** or **complements,** depending on the sign of the cross elasticity of demand. *If the cross elasticity of demand is positive, two commodities are substitutes.* Butter and margarine are substitutes because a decrease in the price of butter will result in a decrease in the quantity demanded of margarine—many margarine eaters really prefer the "higher-priced spread." *On the other hand, if the cross elasticity of demand is negative, two commodities are complements.* For example, gin and tonic may be complements since a decrease in the price of gin may increase the quantity demanded of tonic. The reduction in the price of gin will increase the quantity demanded of gin, thus increasing the quantity demanded of tonic since gin and tonic tend to be used together.

Many studies have been made of the cross elasticity of demand for various pairs of commodities. After all, it frequently is very important to know how a change in the price of one commodity will affect the sales of another commodity. For example, what would be the effect of a 1 percent increase in the price of pork on the quantity demanded of beef? According to one study, the effect would be a .28 percent increase in the quantity demanded of beef—since this study estimates that the cross elasticity of demand for these two commodities is 0.28. What effect would a 1 percent increase in the price of butter have on the quantity demanded of margarine? According to the same study, the effect would be a .81 percent increase in the quantity demanded of margarine—since this study estimates that the cross elasticity of demand for these two commodities is 0.81.

TEST YOURSELF

1. Is each of the following statements true, partly true, or false? Explain. (a) If a good's income elasticity of demand is less than one, an increase in the price of the good will increase the amount spent on it. (b) The income elasticity of demand will have the same sign regardless of the level of income at which it is measured. (c) If Mr. Miller spends all of his income on steak (regardless of his income or the price of steak), Mr. Miller's cross elasticity of demand between steak and any other good is zero.

2. What is the sign of the cross elasticity of demand for each of the following pairs of commodities: (a) tea and coffee, (b) tennis rackets and tennis balls, (c) whiskey and gin, (d) fishing licenses and fishing poles, (e) nylon rugs and wool rugs?

3. On page 72, we saw the quantity of Model T's sold increased from about 472,000 to about 730,000 when its price was reduced from $440 in 1914 to $360 in 1916. How can this fact be reconciled with recent studies which indicate that the price elasticity of demand for automobiles is about 1.2 to 1.5?

4. According to the U.S. Department of Agriculture, the income elasticity of demand for coffee is about 0.23. If incomes rose by 1 percent, what effect would this have on the quantity demanded of coffee?

SUMMARY

1. The market demand curve, which is the relationship between the price of a commodity and the amount of the commodity demanded in the market, is one of the most important and frequently used concepts in economics. The shape and position of a product's market demand curve depend on consumers' tastes, consumer incomes, the price of other goods, and the number of consumers in the market.

2. The market demand curve for a commodity is not the same as the demand curve for the output of a single firm that produces the commodity, unless the industry is composed of only one firm. In general, the demand curve for the output of a single firm will be more elastic than the market demand curve for the commodity. Indeed, if there are many firms selling a homogeneous commodity, the individual firm's demand curve becomes horizontal.

3. There are many techniques for measuring demand curves, such as interview studies, direct experiments, and the statistical analysis of historical data.

4. The price elasticity of demand, defined as the percentage change in quantity demanded resulting from a 1 percent change in price, measures the sensitivity of the amount demanded to changes in price. Whether a price increase results in an increase or decrease in the total amount spent on a commodity depends on the price elasticity of demand.

5. The income elasticity of demand, defined as the percentage change in quantity demanded resulting from a 1 percent increase in total money income, measures the sensitivity of the amount demanded to changes in total income. Luxury items are generally assumed to have higher income elasticities of demand than necessities.

6. The cross elasticity of demand, defined as the percentage change in the quantity demanded resulting from a 1 percent change in the price of another commodity, measures the sensitivity of the amount demanded to changes in the price of another commodity. If the cross elasticity of demand is positive, two commodities are substitutes; if it is negative, they are complements.

CONCEPTS FOR REVIEW

Market demand curve	**Price elastic**	**Income elasticity of demand**
Direct market experiment	**Price inelastic**	**Cross elasticity of demand**
Price elasticity of demand	**Unitary elasticity**	**Substitute**
Arc elasticity of demand	**Brannan plan**	**Complement**

GETTING BEHIND THE DEMAND CURVE: CONSUMER BEHAVIOR

CRATE & BARREL, A SELLER OF moderately priced tableware, experienced sales during the 1990 Christmas season that were over 14 percent higher than the year before. Apparently, this was due to many consumers who, feeling the financial pinch of the recession that occurred then, decided to buy moderately priced items. To a considerable extent consumers, voting with their pocketbooks, are the masters of our economic system. No wonder, then, that economists spend much of their time describing and analyzing how consumers act. In this chapter, we present the basic model economists use to analyze consumer behavior.

Product display in a Crate & Barrel store

CONSUMER EXPENDITURES

The Martins of Jacksonville

Since we are concerned here with consumer behavior, perhaps the best way to begin is to look at the behavior of a particular consumer. It is hard to find any consumer who is "typical." There are hundreds of millions of consumers in the United States, and they vary enormously. Nonetheless, it is instructive to look at how a particular American family—the Martins of Jacksonville, Florida[1]—spends its money. The Martins are about 40 years old, are both married for the second time, and have three children (by his first marriage). They own their own home, and both work. Mr. Martin is a computer programmer, and Mrs. Martin is a product manager at American Transtech. Together the Martins make about $66,000 a year.

How do the Martins spend their money? For most consumers, we cannot answer this question with any accuracy, because the people in question simply do not tell anyone what they do with their money. But because the Martins and their buying habits were scrutinized in an article in a national magazine, it is possible to describe quite accurately where their money goes. As shown in Table 5.1, the Martins, who own their own home, spend about $1,000 a month—about 18 percent of their income—on housing. In addition, they spend about $300 a month—about 5 percent of their income—on food and drink. Also, they spend about $700 a month—about 13 percent of their income—on child support and education.

In addition, as shown in Table 5.1, the Martins spend about $700 a

---

[1] This case study comes from a national magazine. The name of the family has been changed, but the facts are real.

Table 5.1
Monthly Spending Pattern of Mr. and Mrs. Martin of Jacksonville, Florida

ITEM	AMOUNT (DOLLARS)	PERCENT OF INCOME
Housing	1,000	18
Food and drink	300	5
Child support and education	700	13
Entertainment and clothing	700	13
Medical, dental, and insurance expenses	200	4
Transportation	200	4
Other expenditures	800	15
Taxes and saving	1,600	29
Monthly income	5,500	100[a]

[a] Because of rounding errors, the percentages do not sum to 100.

month—about 13 percent of their income—on entertainment and clothing. Medical, dental, and insurance expenses consume about $200 a month—about 4 percent of income; another $200 a month—again, about 4 percent of their income—is spent on transportation. Finally, the Martins allocate about $800 a month—about 15 percent of their income—to other expenditures, and about $1,600 a month—about 29 percent of their income—to taxes and savings.

This, in a nutshell, is how the Martins spend their money. The Martins exchange their resources—mostly labor—in the resource markets for $66,000 a year. They take this money into the product markets and spend about three-fourths of it for the goods and services described above. The remaining one-fourth of their income goes for taxes and saving. The Martins, like practically every family, keep a watchful eye on where their money goes and what they are getting in exchange for their labor and other resources. As stressed in Chapter 2, the basic purpose of our economic system is to satisfy the wants of consumers.

AGGREGATE DATA FOR THE UNITED STATES

How does the way that the Martins spend their money compare with consumer behavior in general? In Table 5.2, we provide data on how all consumers allocated their aggregate income in 1990. These data tell us much more about the typical behavior of American consumers than our case study of the Martins. Note first of all that American households paid about 15 percent of their income in taxes. In addition, American households saved about 4 percent of their income. In other words, they refrained from spending 4 percent of their income on goods and services; instead, they put this amount into stocks, bonds, bank accounts, or other such channels for saving. Also, about 2 percent of their income went for interest payments to banks and other institutions from which they had borrowed money.

American consumers spent the remaining 79 percent of their income on goods and services. Table 5.2 makes it clear that they allocated much of their expenditures to housing, food and drink, and transportation.

Table 5.2
Allocation of Income by U.S. Households, 1990

	PERCENT OF TOTAL[a]
Personal taxes	15
Personal saving	4
Interest payments	2
Consumption expenditures	
Autos and parts	5
Furniture and household equipment	4
Other durable goods	2
Food and drink	13
Clothing and shoes	5
Gasoline and oil	2
Other nondurable goods	6
Housing	12
Household operations	5
Transportation	3
Medical costs	10
Other services	13
Total income	100

[a] Because of rounding errors, figures do not sum to total.
Source: Survey of Current Business, January 1991.

Spending on housing, household operations, and furniture and other durable household equipment accounted for about 21 percent of American consumers' total income. Spending on food and beverages accounted for about 13 percent of total income. Spending on automobiles and parts, gasoline and oil, and other transportation accounted for about 10 percent of total income. Thus taxes, savings, housing, food and drink, and transportation accounted for about two-thirds of the total income of all households in the United States.

The data in Table 5.2 make it obvious that the Martin family is not very typical of American consumers. For example, it spends a much larger percentage of its income on entertainment and education than do consumers as a whole. To some degree, this is because the Martins are more affluent than most American families, but this is only part of the reason. To a large extent, it simply reflects the fact that people want different things. Looking around you, you see considerable diversity in the way consumers spend their money. Take your own family as an example. It is a good bet that your family spends its money quite differently than the nation as a whole. If your parents like to live in a big house, your family may spend much more than the average on housing. Or if they like to go to sports events, their expenditures on such entertainment may be much higher than average.

A MODEL OF CONSUMER BEHAVIOR

Why do consumers spend their money the way they do? The economist answers this question with the aid of a **model of consumer behavior,** which is useful both for analysis and for decision making. To construct this model, the economist obviously must consider the tastes of the consumer. As Henry Adams put it, "Everyone carries his own inch-rule of taste, and amuses himself by applying it, triumphantly, wherever he travels." Certainly one would expect that the amount a consumer purchases of a particular commodity is influenced by his or her tastes. Some people like beef, others like pork. Some people like the opera, others would trade a ticket to hear Luciano Pavarotti for a ticket to the Dallas Cowboys game any day of the week. Three assumptions, which seem reasonable for most purposes, underlie the economist's model of consumer preferences.

1. We assume that *consumers, when confronted with two alternative market baskets, can decide whether they prefer the first to the second, the second to the first, or whether they are indifferent between them.* For example, suppose Mrs. Martin is confronted with a choice between a market basket containing 3 chocolate bars and a ticket to the movies and another market basket containing 2 chocolate bars and a record of the Tabernacle Choir singing Chopin's Minute Waltz. Despite the rather bizarre composition of these two market baskets, we assume that she can somehow decide whether she prefers the first market basket to the second, the second market basket to the first, or whether she is indifferent between them.

2. We assume that *the consumer's preferences are transitive.* The meaning of transitive in this context is simple enough. Suppose that Mrs. Martin prefers an ounce of Chanel No. 5 perfume to an ounce of Blue Grass perfume, and that she prefers an ounce of Blue Grass perfume to an ounce of Sortilège perfume. Then, if her preferences are transitive, she must prefer an ounce of Chanel No. 5 perfume to an ounce of Sortilège perfume.

Alfred Marshall (1842–1924) played a major role in the construction of consumer demand theories, and was a pioneer in many other areas of economics as well. His *Principles of Economics* (1890), which had eight editions, was a leading economics text for many years.

The reason for this assumption is clear. If the consumer's preferences were not transitive, the consumer would have inconsistent or contradictory preferences. Although some people may have preferences that are not transitive, this assumption seems to be a reasonable first approximation—for the noninstitutionalized part of the population at least.

3. We assume that *the consumer always prefers more of a commodity to less.* For example, if one market basket contains 3 bars of soap and 2 monkey wrenches and a second contains 3 bars of soap and 3 monkey wrenches, it is assumed that the second market basket is preferred to the first. To a large extent, this assumption is justified by the definition of a commodity as something the consumer desires.[2] This does not mean that certain things are not a nuisance. If one market basket contains 3 bars of soap and 2 rattlesnakes, we would not be at all surprised if the consumer did *not* prefer this market basket to one containing 3 bars of soap and no rattlesnakes. But to such a consumer, a rattlesnake would not be desired—and thus would not be a commodity. Instead, the absence of a rattlesnake would be desired—and would be a commodity.

Total Utility

In Chapter 2, we pointed out that a model, to be useful, must omit many unimportant factors, concentrate on the basic factors at work, and simplify in order to illuminate. So that we focus on the important factors at work here, let's assume that there are only two goods, food and clothing. This is an innocuous assumption, since the results we shall obtain can be generalized to include cases where any number of goods exists. For simplicity, food is measured in pounds, and clothing is measured in number of pieces of clothing.

Consider Mrs. Martin, making choices for her family. Undoubtedly, she regards certain market baskets—that is, certain combinations of food and clothing (the only commodities)—to be more desirable than others. She certainly regards 2 pounds of food and 1 piece of clothing to be more desirable than 1 pound of food and 1 piece of clothing. For simplicity, suppose that it is possible to measure the amount of satisfaction that she gets from each market basket by its utility. A *utility* is a number that represents the level of satisfaction that the consumer derives from a particular market basket. For example, the utility attached to the market basket containing 2 pounds of food and 1 piece of clothing may be 10 utils, and the utility attached to the market basket containing 1 pound of food and 1 piece of clothing may be 6 utils. (A util is the traditional unit in which utility is expressed.)

Marginal Utility

It is important to distinguish between total utility and marginal utility. The total utility of a market basket is the number described in the previous paragraph, whereas *the marginal utility measures the additional satisfaction derived from an additional unit of a commodity.* To see how marginal utility is obtained, let's take a close look at Table 5.3. The total

---

[2] An individual's desire for a particular good during a particular period of time is not infinite but in the aggregate human wants seem to be insatiable. Besides the basic desires for food, shelter, and clothing, which must be fulfilled to some extent if the human organism is to survive, wants arise from cultural factors. Advertising and the emulation of social leaders stimulate and extend a person's wants.

Table 5.3
Total Utility and Marginal Utility Derived by the Martins from Consuming Various Amounts of Food per Day[a]

POUNDS OF FOOD	TOTAL UTILITY	MARGINAL UTILITY
0	0	3 (=3–0)
1	3	4 (=7–3)
2	7	2 (=9–7)
3	9	1 (=10–9)
4	10	

[a] This table assumes that no clothing is consumed. If a nonzero amount of clothing is consumed, the figures in this table will probably be altered since the marginal utility of a certain amount of food is likely to depend on the amount of clothing consumed.

utility the Martin family derives from the consumption of various amounts of food is given in the middle column of this table. (For simplicity, we assume for the moment that the Martins consume only food.) The marginal utility, shown in the right-hand column, is the extra utility derived from each amount of food over and above the utility derived from 1 less pound of food. Thus it equals the difference between the total utility of a certain amount of food and the total utility of 1 less pound of food.

For example, as shown in Table 5.3, the *total* utility of 3 pounds of food is 9 utils, which is a measure of the total amount of satisfaction that the Martins get from this much food. In contrast, the *marginal* utility of 3 pounds of food is the extra utility obtained from the third pound of food—that is, the total utility of 3 pounds of food less the total utility of 2 pounds of food. Specifically, as shown in Table 5.3, it is 2 utils. Similarly, the *total* utility of 2 pounds of food is 7 utils, which is a measure of the total amount of satisfaction that the Martins get from this much food. In contrast, the *marginal* utility of 2 pounds of food is the extra utility from the second pound of food—that is, the total utility of 2 pounds of food less the total utility of 1 pound of food. Specifically, as shown in Table 5.3, it is 4 utils.

The Law of Diminishing Marginal Utility

Economists generally assume that, as a person consumes more and more of a particular commodity, there is, beyond some point, a decline in the extra satisfaction derived from the last unit of the commodity consumed. For example, if the Martins consume 2 pounds of food in a particular period of time, it may be just enough to meet their basic physical needs. If they consume 3 pounds of food in the same period of time, the third pound of food is likely to yield less satisfaction than the second. If they consume 4 pounds of food in the same period of time, the fourth pound of food is likely to yield less satisfaction than the third. And so on.

This assumption or hypothesis is often called the **law of diminishing marginal utility.** This law states that, *as a person consumes more and more of a given commodity (the consumption of other commodities being held constant), the marginal utility of the commodity eventually will tend to decline*. The figures concerning the Martin family in Table 5.3 are in accord with this law, as shown in Figure 5.1, which plots the marginal utility of food against the amount consumed. Once the consumption of food exceeds about 1 1/2 pounds, the marginal utility of food declines.

THE EQUILIBRIUM MARKET BASKET

Preferences alone do not determine the consumer's actions. *Besides knowing the consumer's preferences, we must also know his or her income and the prices of commodities to predict which market basket he or she will buy.* The consumer's money income is the amount of money he or she can spend per unit of time. A consumer's choice of a market basket is constrained by the size of his or her money income. For example, although Mr. Martin may regard a Hickey Freeman as his favorite suit, he may not buy it because he may have insufficient funds (as the bankers delicately put it). Also, the market basket the consumer chooses is influenced by the prices of commodities. If the Hickey Freeman suit were offered by a discount store at $100, rather than its list price of $850, Mr. Martin might purchase it after all.

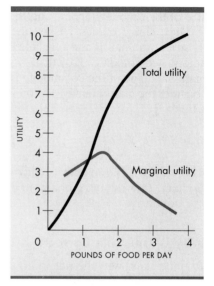

Figure 5.1
Total and Marginal Utility from Food Consumption, Martin Family
The marginal utility of the first pound of food (which, according to Table 5.3, equals 3 utils) is plotted at the midpoint between 0 and 1 pounds of food. The marginal utility of the second pound of food (which, according to Table 5.3, equals 4 utils) is plotted at the midpoint between 1 and 2 pounds of food. The marginal-utility curve connects these and other points showing the marginal utility of various amounts of food consumed.

Beyond some point, the marginal utility curve of any commodity would be expected to fall, according to the law of diminishing marginal utility (which states that, as a person consumes more and more of a given commodity, the marginal utility of the commodity eventually will tend to decline). In the case shown here, the marginal utility curve falls when the Martin family's consumption of food exceeds about 1 1/2 pounds per day.

Given the consumer's tastes, economists assume that he or she attempts to maximize utility. In other words, _consumers are assumed to be rational in the sense that they choose the market basket—or more generally, the course of action—that is most to their liking_. As previously noted, consumers cannot choose whatever market basket they please. Instead, they must maximize their utility subject to the constraints imposed by the size of their money income and the nature of commodity prices.

The optimal market basket, the one that maximizes utility subject to these constraints, is the one where the consumer's income is allocated among commodities so that, for every commodity purchased, the marginal utility of the commodity is proportional to its price. For example, consider the Martin family. For them, the optimal market basket is the one where

$$\frac{MU_F}{P_F} = \frac{MU_C}{P_C} \tag{5.1}$$

where MU_F is the marginal utility of food, MU_C is the marginal utility of clothing, P_F is the price of a pound of food, and P_C is the price of a piece of clothing.

Why Is This Rule Correct?

To understand why the rule in Equation (5.1) is correct, it is convenient to begin by pointing out that $MU_F \div P_F$ is the marginal utility of the _last dollar's worth_ of food and that $MU_C \div P_C$ is the marginal utility of the _last dollar's worth_ of clothing. To see why this is so, take the case of food. Since MU_F is the extra utility of the _last pound_ of food bought, and since P_F is the price of this _last pound_, the extra utility of the _last dollar's worth_ of food must be $MU_F \div P_F$. For example, if the last pound of food results in an extra utility of 4 utils and this pound costs \$2, then the extra utility from the last dollar's worth of food must be $4 \div 2$, or 2 utils. In other words, the marginal utility of the last dollar's worth of food is 2 utils.

Since $MU_F \div P_F$ is the marginal utility of the last dollar's worth of food and $MU_C \div P_C$ is the marginal utility of the last dollar's worth of clothing, what Equation (5.1) really says is that _the rational consumer will choose a market basket where the marginal utility of the last dollar spent on all commodities purchased is the same_. To see why this must be so, consider the numerical example in Table 5.4, which shows the marginal utility the Martins derive from various amounts of food and clothing. Rather than measuring food and clothing in physical units, we measure them in Table 5.4 in terms of the amount of money spent on them.

Given the information in Table 5.4, how much of each commodity should Mrs. Martin buy if her money income is only \$4 (a ridiculous assumption but one that will help to make our point)? Clearly, the first dollar she spends should be on food since it will yield her a marginal utility of 20. The second dollar she spends should also be on food since a second dollar's worth of food has a marginal utility of 16. (Thus the total utility derived from the \$2 of expenditure is $20 + 16 = 36$.)[3] The marginal utility of the third dollar is 12 if it is spent on more food—and 12 too if it is spent on clothing. Suppose that she chooses more food. (The total util-

---

[3] Since the marginal utility is the extra utility obtained from each dollar spent, the total utility from the total expenditure must be the sum of the marginal utilities of the individual dollars of expenditure.

**Table 5.4
Marginal Utility Derived by the Martins from Various Quantities of Food and Clothing**

| COMMODITY | DOLLARS WORTH | | | | |
	1	2	3	4	5
	MARGINAL UTILITY (UTILS)				
Food	20	16	12	10	7
Clothing	12	10	7	5	3

ity derived from the $3 of expenditure is 20 + 16 + 12 = 48.) What about the final dollar? Its marginal utility is 10 if it is spent on more food and 12 if it is spent on clothing; thus she will spend it on clothing. (The total utility derived from all $4 of expenditure is then 20 + 16 + 12 + 12 = 60.)

Thus Mrs. Martin, if she is rational, will allocate $3 of her income to food and $1 to clothing. This is the ***equilibrium market basket,*** the market basket that maximizes consumer satisfaction. The important thing to note is that this market basket demonstrates the principle set forth earlier in Equation (5.1). As shown in Table 5.4, the marginal utility derived from the last dollar spent on food is equal to the marginal utility derived from the last dollar spent on clothing. (Both are 12.) Thus this market basket has the characteristic described above: the marginal utility of the last dollar spent on all commodities purchased is the same. In the next section, we show that this will always be the case for market baskets that maximize the consumer's utility. If it were not true, the consumer could obtain a higher level of utility by changing the composition of his or her market basket.

Further Proof of the Budget Allocation Rule

In the previous section, we stated the proposition that the consumer, to maximize utility, will choose a market basket where the marginal utility of the last dollar spent on all commodities purchased is the same. In this section, we show that, if this budget allocation rule is not followed, the consumer cannot be maximizing utility. This is offered as further proof of the proposition in the previous section. For simplicity, we assume that the consumer buys only two commodities, food and clothing.

Suppose that the marginal utility of the last dollar spent on food is 5 utils whereas the marginal utility of the last dollar spent on clothing is 3 utils. The consumer is not maximizing utility, because spending $1 more on food will increase total utility by 5 utils,[4] and spending $1 less on clothing will reduce total utility by 3 utils. Thus the transfer of $1 of expenditure from clothing to food will increase total utility by 2 utils— which means that the consumer currently isn't maximizing utility. More generally, a transfer of expenditure from clothing to food will always increase a consumer's utility so long as the marginal utility of the last dollar spent on food exceeds the marginal utility of the last dollar spent on clothing. Thus *the consumer will not be maximizing utility if the marginal utility of the last dollar spent on food exceeds the marginal utility of the last dollar spent on clothing.*

Suppose that the situation is reversed, the marginal utility of the last dollar spent on food being 3 utils and the marginal utility of the last dollar spent on clothing being 5 utils. The consumer is not maximizing utility, because spending $1 more on clothing will increase total utility by 5 utils,[5] and spending $1 less on food will reduce total utility by 3 utils. Thus the transfer of $1 of expenditure from food to clothing will result in a net increase of utility of 2 utils—which means that the consumer currently isn't maximizing utility. More generally, a transfer of expenditure from food to clothing will always increase total utility so long as the

[4] We assume here that the extra utility from an *extra* dollar spent on food equals the extra utility from the *last* dollar spent on food. This is an innocuous assumption.
[5] We assume here that the extra utility from an *extra* dollar spent on clothing equals the extra utility from the *last* dollar spent on clothing. This, like the assumption in footnote 4, is innocuous.

EXAMPLE 5.1   THE DIAMOND-WATER PARADOX

In 1991, flawless diamonds frequently sold for over $10,000 per carat, while water sold for about 2 cents per hundred gallons. For centuries, people have been fascinated by this fact. Diamonds, after all, are hardly essential to life, whereas water *is* essential. How is it, then, that people are willing to buy diamonds at a price that seems so much higher than that of water? Suppose that the typical consumer's marginal utility curves for diamonds and water are as shown below:

carat of diamonds will be 500,000 times as great as the marginal utility of a hundred gallons of water? (d) Describe in your own words why people are willing to buy diamonds at a price that seems so much higher than that of water.

Solution

(a) No. If the consumer is maximizing utility, the

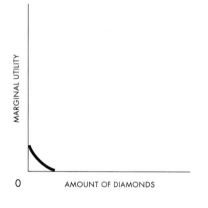

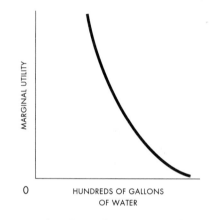

(a) If the price per carat of a diamond is 500,000 times as great as the price per hundred gallons of water, and if the consumer buys both diamonds and water, does it follow that the total utility that the consumer receives from the diamonds is 500,000 times as great as the total utility received from the water? (b) Does it follow that the marginal utility of a carat of diamonds is 500,000 times as great as the marginal utility of a hundred gallons of water? (c) If the consumer buys a great deal of water and practically no diamonds, is it possible that the marginal utility of a

marginal utility of a carat of diamonds must be 500,000 times as great as the *marginal* utility of a hundred gallons of water. But there is no reason to believe that this is true of the *total* utilities. (b) Yes. (c) Yes. (d) They buy practically no diamonds and very large quantities of water. The marginal utility of diamonds is so much higher than the marginal utility of water that the marginal utility of the last dollar spent on diamonds is equal to the marginal utility of the last dollar spent on water.

---

marginal utility of the last dollar spent on clothing exceeds the marginal utility of the last dollar spent on food. Thus *the consumer will not be maximizing utility if the marginal utility of the last dollar spent on clothing exceeds the marginal utility of the last dollar spent on food.*

In the previous paragraph, we showed that the consumer will *not* be maximizing utility if the marginal utility of the last dollar spent on food *is less than* the marginal utility of the last dollar spent on clothing. In the paragraph before last, we showed that the consumer will *not* be maximizing utility if the marginal utility of the last dollar spent on food *exceeds* the marginal utility of the last dollar spent on clothing. It follows that the consumer will be maximizing utility only when the marginal utility of the last dollar spent on food *equals* the marginal utility of the last dollar spent on clothing. This is what we set out to prove.

TEST YOURSELF

1. Suppose that the total utility attached by Ms. Johnson to various quantities of hamburgers consumed (per day) is as follows:

NUMBERS OF HAMBURGERS	TOTAL UTILITY (UTILS)
0	0
1	5
2	12
3	15
4	17
5	18

Between 3 and 4 hamburgers, what is the marginal utility of a hamburger? Between 4 and 5 hamburgers, what is the marginal utility of a hamburger? Do these results conform to the law of diminishing marginal utility?

2. If Ms. Johnson is maximizing her satisfaction, and if the marginal utility of a hot dog is twice that of a bottle of beer, what must the price of a hot dog be if (a) the price of a bottle of beer is $.75, (b) the price of a bottle of beer is $1? (Assume that Ms. Johnson consumes both beer and hot dogs.)

3. "A good's price is related to its marginal utility, not its total utility. Thus a good like water or air may be cheap, even though its total utility is high." Comment and evaluate.

4. If the marginal utility of one good is 3 and its price is $1, while the marginal utility of another good is 6 and its price is $3, is the consumer maximizing his or her satisfaction, given that he or she is consuming both goods? Why, or why not?

THE CONSUMER'S DEMAND CURVE

In analyzing consumer behavior, economists often use the concept of an **_individual demand curve._** Like the market demand curve (discussed at length in Chapter 4), the individual demand curve is the relationship between the quantity demanded of a good and the good's price. But whereas the market demand curve shows the quantity demanded in the _entire market_ at various prices, the individual demand curve shows the quantity demanded by a _particular consumer_ at various prices. Applying the theory of consumer behavior presented earlier in this chapter, one can derive a particular consumer's demand curve for a particular good. To see how this can be done, let's turn to Mrs. Martin and show how we can derive the relationship between the price of food and the amount of food she will buy per week.

Assuming that food and clothing are the only goods, that Mrs. Martin's weekly income is $400, and that the price of clothing is $40 per piece of clothing, we confront Mrs. Martin with a variety of prices of food. First, we confront her with a price of $1 per pound of food. How much food will she buy? Next, we confront her with a price of $2 per pound of food. How much food will she buy? The theory of consumer behavior shows how, under each of these sets of circumstances, she will allocate her income between food and clothing. (From Equation (5.1), we know that she will choose an allocation where the marginal utility of the last dollar spent on food will equal the marginal utility of the last dollar spent on clothing.) Suppose that she will buy 200 pounds of food when the price is $1 per pound, and 100 pounds of food when the price is $2 per pound. These are two points on Mrs. Martin's individual demand curve for food—those corresponding to prices of $1 and $2 per pound. Figure 5.2 shows these two points, _X_ and _Y._

It is no trick to obtain more points on her individual demand curve for

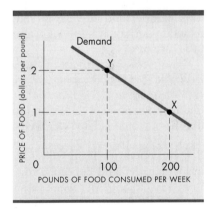

Figure 5.2
Mrs. Martin's Individual Demand Curve for Food
The consumer's individual demand curve for a commodity shows the amount of the commodity the consumer will buy at various prices. (Point _X_ and _Y_ on Mrs. Martin's individual demand curve for food are derived in Figure 5.13.)

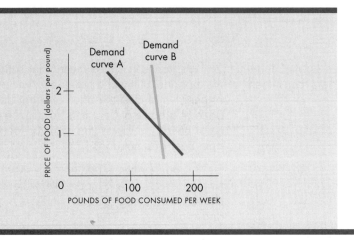

food. All that we have to do is confront her with other prices of food, and
see how much food she buys at each price. Plotting the amount of food
she buys against the price, we obtain new points on her individual demand curve for food. Connecting up all these points, we get her complete
individual demand curve for food, shown in Figure 5.2.

Factors Influencing the Demand Curve

*The location and shape of an individual demand curve depend on the
tastes of the consumer.* For example, if Mrs. Martin values food so much
that she is determined to maintain her family's consumption of this commodity regardless of its price, her individual demand curve for food may
look like demand curve *B* in Figure 5.3. But if she is less determined to
maintain her family's food consumption, it may look like demand curve *A*
in Figure 5.3.

*Besides the consumer's tastes, other factors determining the location
and shape of the consumer's individual demand curve are the income of
the consumer and the prices of other goods.* For example, Mrs. Martin's individual demand curve for food in Figure 5.2 is based on the assumption
that her income is $400 per week and that the price of a piece of cloth-
ing is $40. If her income or the price of clothing changes, her individual
demand curve for food will change as well. Figure 5.4 shows how her
individual demand curve for food may change if her income increases
from $300 to $500 per week (assuming that the price of a piece of clothing remains fixed at $40). Figure 5.5 shows how her individual demand
curve for food may change if the price of a piece of clothing increases
from $40 to $50 (assuming that her income remains constant at $500 per
week).

In Chapter 3, we learned the importance of distinguishing between
changes in the quantity demanded and *changes in demand.* This is just as
true for individual consumers as for the market as a whole. The shifts in
Mrs. Martin's demand curve for food shown in Figures 5.4 and 5.5 are
changes in demand. In other words, they are changes in the relationship
between the quantity demanded and price. Even if there is no change in
demand—that is, even if there is no shift in the demand curve—the
quantity demanded may change because of a change in price. For exam-

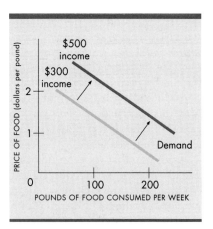

Figure 5.4
**Effect of a Change in Income
(from $300 to $500 per Week)
on Mrs. Martin's Individual Demand Curve for Food**
If Mrs. Martin's income increases
from $300 to $500 per week (and
if the price of a piece of clothing
remains at $40), her demand
curve will shift upward and to the
right.

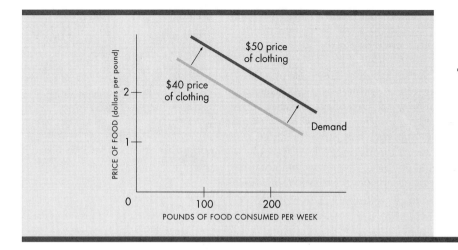

Figure 5.5
Effect of a Change in the Price of a Piece of Clothing (from $40 to $50) on Mrs. Martin's Individual Demand Curve for Food
If the price of a piece of clothing increases from $40 to $50 (and if her income remains at $500 per week), her demand curve for food will shift upward and to the right.

ple, in Figure 5.2, the quantity of food demanded by Mrs. Martin increases from 100 to 200 pounds per week if the price of food declines from $2 to $1 per pound. Yet Mrs. Martin's demand curve for food is unchanged in Figure 5.2, so there is no increase in demand. Instead, there has been a *movement along* Mrs. Martin's demand curve from point *Y* to point *X*. The quantity of food demanded by Mrs. Martin has changed even though her demand for food has *not* changed.

WHY DO INDIVIDUAL DEMAND CURVES GENERALLY SLOPE DOWNWARD?[6]

Individual demand curves almost always slope downward to the right. That is, consumers almost always respond to an increase in a commodity's price by reducing the amount of it they consume. Or, put the other way around, a commodity's price almost always must be reduced to persuade the consumer to buy more of it. One way to explain this fact is by an appeal to the law of diminishing marginal utility, which (as we've seen) states that, as a person consumes more and more of a particular commodity, the commodity's marginal utility declines. *Since the marginal utility—the extra utility derived from an extra unit of the commodity— declines, the price the consumer is willing to pay for an extra unit of the commodity must decline too.* This explanation relies on the assumption that marginal utility is measurable. Another way to explain the same thing makes no such assumption. According to this explanation, an increase in a commodity's price has two kinds of effects on the consumer—a substitution effect and an income effect.

Substitution Effect

*If the price of a commodity increases, the **substitution effect** of this price increase is the change in the quantity demanded of the commodity result-*

---

[6] This section is optional. Some instructors may want to skip it. The reader can go to the next section without losing the thread of the argument.

ing from the commodity's becoming more expensive relative to other commodities, if the consumer's level of utility is held constant. Suppose that the price of chicken increases. Because of this price increase, the consumer may not be able to achieve as high a level of utility as he or she achieved before the price increase. Nonetheless, let's see what effect the price increase would have on the amount of chicken consumed by the consumer, *even if his or her level of utility were unchanged.* This effect is the substitution effect. *The substitution effect of a price increase always is a reduction in the quantity demanded of the commodity.* Suppose the price of chicken increases, while other prices and the consumer's level of utility are held constant. Because chicken becomes more expensive relative to other goods, the consumer will substitute other goods for chicken. Thus the substitution effect would be a *reduction* in the quantity demanded of chicken.

Income Effect

If the price of a commodity increases, the consumer's level of utility may be reduced, as pointed out above. *The **income effect** of the price increase is the change in the quantity demanded of the commodity due to this change in the consumer's utility level.* If an increase in the price of chicken cuts the consumer's level of utility by a particular amount, which in turn reduces the quantity of chicken demanded by the consumer, this reduction in the quantity demanded is the income effect. *The income ef-*

EXAMPLE 5.2   MEAT AND CONSUMER'S SURPLUS

It is important to recognize that consumers generally would be willing to pay more than in fact they pay for a particular good. Suppose that a consumer's demand curve for meat is as shown below, and that the price of a pound of meat is $2.

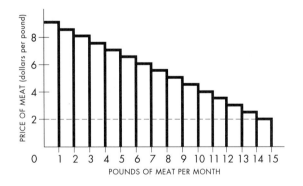

(a) What is the maximum amount that the consumer would pay for the first pound of meat per month? By how much does this exceed the actual price? (b) What

is the maximum amount that the consumer would pay for the second pound of meat per month? By how much does this exceed the actual price? (c) What is the maximum amount that the consumer would pay for the 15 pounds of meat consumed per month? By how much does this exceed the actual amount paid? (d) Returning to Example 5.1, do you think that the actual amount paid for water is much less than the maximum amount that would be paid? Does this help to explain the diamond-water paradox?

Solution

(a) $9. $7. (b) $8.50. $6.50. (c) $82.50. $52.50. (d) Yes. Yes, the actual amount paid for water is not a good indicator of the importance to the consumer (that is, the total utility) of water, since the actual amount paid is much less than the maximum amount that would be paid for it. *Economists use the term, **consumer's surplus,** to mean the difference between the maximum amount that the consumer would pay and what he or she actually pays.* For example, the consumer's surplus for the first pound of meat is $7.

---

fect of a price increase can be either a reduction or increase in the quantity demanded. For some commodities, like steak and probably chicken, a reduction in the consumer's utility level will result in the consumer's demanding *less* of them; thus the income effect of a price increase is a *reduction* in the quantity demanded of these commodities. For other commodities like margarine and poorer grades of food products, a reduction in the consumer's utility level may result in the consumer's demanding *more* of them; thus the income effect of a price increase is an *increase* in the quantity demanded of these commodities.

The Total Effect of a Price Increase

The *total* effect of a price increase is the *sum* of the income effect and the substitution effect. That is, the total change in the quantity demanded is the change in the quantity demanded due to the change in the consumer's utility level (the income effect) plus the change in the quantity demanded that would have occurred even if the consumer's utility level had not changed (the substitution effect). If (as is frequently the case) the income effect of a price increase is a reduction in the quantity demanded, the demand curve must slope downward. Why? Because both the income effect and the substitution effect are reductions in the quantity demanded, so the total effect of a price increase must be a reduction in the quantity demanded. Even if the income effect of a price increase is an increase in the quantity demanded, the demand curve may slope downward. Why? Because the increase in the quantity demanded due to the income effect may be more than offset by the substitution effect, which is always a reduction in the quantity demanded. Thus the demand curve will slope upward only in those *rare* cases where the income effect is an increase in the quantity demanded and where the income effect is big enough to offset the substitution effect.

DERIVING THE MARKET DEMAND CURVE

In previous sections, we have described how each consumer's individual demand curve for a commodity can be derived, given the consumer's tastes and income, as well as the prices of other commodities. Suppose that we have obtained the individual demand curve for each of the consumers in the market. How can these individual demand curves be used to derive the market demand curve?

The answer is simple. *To derive the market demand curve, we obtain the horizontal sum of all the individual demand curves.* In other words, to find the total quantity demanded in the market at a certain price, we add up the quantities demanded by the individual consumers at that price.

Table 5.5 shows the individual demand curves for food of four families: the Walters, Joneses, Smiths, and Kleins. For simplicity, suppose that these four families constitute the entire market for food. (This assumption can easily be relaxed; it just makes things simple.) Then the market demand curve for food is shown in the last column of Table 5.5. Figure 5.6 shows the families' individual demand curves for food, as well as the resulting market demand curve. To illustrate how the market demand

Table 5.5
Individual Demand Curves and Market Demand Curve for Food

PRICE OF FOOD (DOLLARS PER POUND)	JONES	KLEIN	INDIVIDUAL DEMAND SMITH (HUNDREDS OF POUNDS PER MONTH)	WALTER	MARKET DEMAND
1.00	50.0	45.0	5.0	2.0	102
1.20	43.0	44.0	4.2	1.8	93
1.40	36.0	43.0	3.4	1.6	84
1.60	30.0	42.0	2.6	1.4	76
1.80	25.0	41.4	2.4	1.2	70
2.00	20.0	41.0	2.0	1.0	64

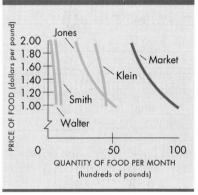

Figure 5.6
Individual Demand Curves and Market Demand Curve for Food
The market demand curve is the horizontal sum of all the individual demand curves.

curve is derived from the individual demand curves, suppose that the price of food is $1 per pound. Then the total quantity demanded in the market is 102 hundreds of pounds per month, since this is the sum of the quantities demanded at this price by the four families. (As shown in Table 5.5, this sum equals 50.0 + 45.0 + 5.0 + 2.0, or 102.)

Since individual demand curves for a commodity almost always slope downward to the right it follows that *market demand curves too almost always slope downward to the right*. (Why? Because, as stressed above, the market demand curve is the horizontal sum of all of the individual demand curves.) However, as emphasized in Chapter 4, the shape and location of the market demand curve vary greatly from commodity to commodity and from market to market. Market demand curves, like people, do not look alike.

TEST YOURSELF

1. Suppose that there are five people who are the only members of a particular market. The amount that each person will buy of the product in question (at each price) is shown below. Determine five points on the market demand curve for the product.

PRICE (DOLLARS)	FIRST PERSON	QUANTITY DEMANDED SECOND PERSON	THIRD PERSON	FOURTH PERSON	FIFTH PERSON
1	5	4	2	8	7
2	4	4	2	7	6
3	3	4	1	6	5
4	2	3	0	5	4
5	1	3	0	5	2

2. Some people judge the quality of a good by its price. If a consumer does this, how does it affect the

model presented in this chapter? (*Hint:* Is utility independent of price?)

3. Bill Thompson would be willing to pay 30 cents for the first apple he consumes per day and 24 cents for the second apple he consumes per day. The current price of an apple is 24 cents. How great is Bill Thompson's consumer's surplus? What does this number mean? How might such a number be used?

4. Mrs. Moriarty (the Professor's wife) learns that the price of turkey has fallen. (a) What is the substitution effect? Do you think that it will be positive or negative? Why? (b) What is the income effect? Do you think that it will be positive or negative? Why? (c) Do you think that the Moriarty family's demand curve for turkey slopes downward to the right? Why, or why not?

RECENT DEVELOPMENTS IN ECONOMICS: THE ROLE OF TIME IN CONSUMPTION DECISIONS

In recent years, economists, led by Gary Becker of the University of Chicago, have begun to view a household as similar to a firm, in the sense that a household uses inputs of various kinds to produce outputs, like meals or recreation. Some of the inputs that the household uses are food, chairs, tables, and beds, but another input of great importance is *time*. The consumer has only a limited amount of time, and this time limitation, as well as his or her limited income, must be taken into account in making decisions.

To illustrate the importance of time to the consumer, take the case of a haircut. The cost to the consumer of a haircut is not only the $8 he must pay the barber; it is also the value of the time it takes for the barber to cut his hair, and, often more important, the value of the time he must wait before the barber is free to begin to cut his hair. Similarly, the cost of a vacation in Florida is not just the amount of money that must be paid for air tickets, hotels, meals, and entertainment; it is also the value placed on the reduced amount of time available to engage in non-vacation activities.

How does the economist measure the value of the time that is used up in consuming a particular item like a vacation? By the opportunity cost of the time. Thus the value of the time spent on the Florida vacation is the value of that time in its best alternative use. For example, if the consumer could have used this time to earn $100 a day, and if this would have been the best alternative use of this time to the consumer, then the value of the time spent on this vacation is $100 per day to this consumer.

Some economists have calculated the elasticity of demand for particular services with respect to the time they consume. In other words, they have estimated the percentage reduction in quantity demanded resulting from a 1 percent increase in the time taken by the service. For example, Jan Acton of

Gary Becker

the RAND Corporation studied the relationship between the number of visits to free sources of medical care by Brooklyn residents and the length of time, on the average, that such residents had to spend traveling and waiting for service. He found that a 1 percent increase in travel time was associated with slightly less than a 1 percent fall in number of visits.

Of course, the value of time is not the same for all people. For example, the alternative cost of time to a teenager is generally lower than for an adult. This helps to explain the fact that teenagers frequently are more willing than adults to wait in line for tickets to various kinds of sports and musical events. Further, it has been suggested that the rise of fast-food chains has been due to an increase in the opportunity cost of time. Because of the increase in wage rates, there has been a rise in the value of time, according to this argument.

SUMMARY

1. The amount of a particular commodity a consumer purchases is clearly influenced by his or her preferences. The model of consumer behavior assumes that the consumer's preferences are transitive and that commodities are defined so that more of them is preferred to less.

2. Utility is a number that represents the level of satisfaction derived by the consumer from a particular market basket. Market baskets with higher utilities are preferred over market baskets with lower utilities.

3. The model of consumer behavior recognizes that preferences alone do not determine the consumer's actions. The choices open to the consumer are dictated by the size of his or her money income and the nature of commodity prices. These factors, as well as the consumer's preferences, determine his or her choice.

4. If the consumer maximizes utility, his or her income is allocated among commodities so that, for every commodity purchased, the marginal utility of the commodity is proportional to its price. In other words, the marginal utility of the last dollar spent on each commodity is made equal for all commodities purchased.

5. The individual demand curve shows the quantity of a good demanded by a particular consumer at various prices of the good. The individual demand curve for practically all goods slopes downward to the right. Its location depends on the consumer's income and tastes and the prices of other goods.

6. To derive the market demand curve, we obtain the horizontal sum of all the individual demand curves of the people in the market. Since individual demand curves for a commodity almost always slope downward to the right, it follows that market demand curves too almost always slope downward to the right.

CONCEPTS FOR REVIEW

Model of consumer
  behavior

Utility

Marginal utility

Law of diminishing
  marginal utility

Equilibrium market
  basket

Individual demand curve

Substitution effect

Consumer's surplus

Income effect

*Indifference curve

*Budget line

* This concept is presented in the Appendix to this chapter.

APPENDIX: HOW INDIFFERENCE CURVES CAN BE USED TO ANALYZE CONSUMER BEHAVIOR

In this Appendix, we show how the theory of consumer behavior can be used in cases where one is not willing to assume that marginal utility is measurable. Generally, it is exceedingly difficult to formulate meaningful measures of a person's extra satisfaction from an extra amount of a particular good. We shall show that the theory remains useful even if such measures cannot be obtained. Once again, we assume for simplicity that there are only two goods, food and clothing, since this allows us to use simple two-dimensional diagrams to illustrate the model. Since there are only

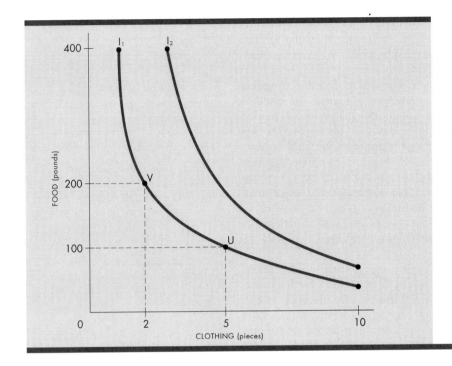

Figure 5.7
Two of Mrs. Martin's Indifference Curves
I_1 and I_2 are two of Mrs. Martin's indifference curves. Each shows market baskets that are equally desirable to Mrs. Martin. For example, she is indifferent between 200 pounds of food and 2 pieces of clothing (point V) and 100 pounds of food and 5 pieces of clothing (point U).

these two commodities, we can represent every possible combination of goods purchased by a consumer by a point in Figure 5.7, which measures the amount of food purchased along the vertical axis and the amount of clothing purchased along the horizontal axis.

Indifference Curves

An **indifference curve** contains points representing market baskets among which the consumer is indifferent. To illustrate, consider Mrs. Martin, making choices for her family. Certain market baskets—that is, certain combinations of food and clothing (the only commodities)—will be equally desirable for her. For example, she may be indifferent between a market basket containing 100 pounds of food and 5 pieces of clothing and a market basket containing 200 pounds of food and 2 pieces of clothing. These two market baskets can be represented by two points, U and V, in Figure 5.7. In addition, other market baskets—each of which can be represented by a point in Figure 5.7—are just as desirable to Mrs. Martin as those represented by points U and V. If we connect all of these points, we get a curve that represents market baskets that are equally desirable to the consumer. In our case, Mrs. Martin is indifferent among all of the market baskets represented by points on curve I_1 in Figure 5.7. I_1 is therefore called an indifference curve.

There are three important things to note about any consumer's indifference curves:

1. *Any consumer has lots of indifference curves, not just one.* If Mrs. Martin is indifferent among all the market baskets represented by points on I_2 in Figure 5.7, I_2 is another of her indifference curves. Moreover, one thing is certain. She prefers any market basket on I_2 to any market basket on I_1, since I_2 includes market baskets with as much clothing and more food (or as much food and more clothing) than the market baskets

on I_1. (Remember that commodities are defined so that more of them is preferred to less.) Consequently, it must always be true that market baskets on higher indifference curves like I_2 must be preferred to market baskets on lower indifference curves like I_1.

2. *Every indifference curve must slope downward to the right,* to reflect the fact that commodities are defined so that more of them is preferred to less. If one market basket has more of one commodity than a second market basket, it must have less of the other commodity than the second market basket—assuming that the two market baskets are to yield equal satisfaction to the consumer. You can prove this to yourself. Suppose that you have a choice between two snacks and that you are indifferent between them. One snack consists of 1 piece of apple pie and 2 glasses of milk. The other consists of 2 pieces of apple pie and a certain number of glasses of milk. If you prefer more apple pie to less, and if you prefer more milk to less, can the number of glasses of milk in the latter snack be as large as 2? Clearly, the answer is no.

3. *Indifference curves cannot intersect.* If they did, this would contradict the assumption that more of a commodity is preferred to less. For example, suppose that I_1 and I_2 in Figure 5.8 are two indifference curves and that they intersect. If this is the case, the market basket represented by point D is equivalent in the eyes of the consumer to the one represented by point E, since both are on indifference curve I_1. Moreover, the market basket represented by point F is equivalent in the eyes of the consumer to the one represented by point E, since both are on indifference curve I_2. And this means that the market basket represented by point F must be equivalent in the eyes of the consumer to the one represented by point D. (Remember that consumer preferences are assumed to be transitive!) But this is impossible because market basket F contains the same amount of food and 6 more pieces of clothing than does market basket D. Since more of a commodity is preferred to less, market basket F must be preferred to market basket D.

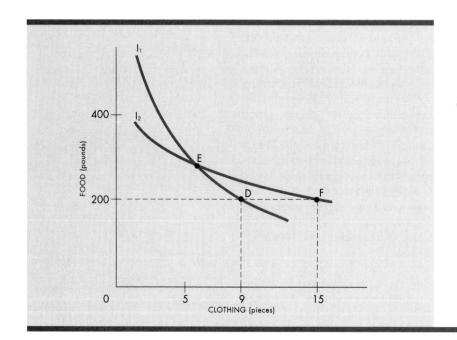

Figure 5.8
Intersecting Indifference Curves: A Contradiction
Indifference curves cannot intersect. If they did, the consumer would be indifferent between D and E, since both are on indifference curve I_1; and between F and E, since both are on indifference curve I_2. But this implies that he or she must be indifferent between D and F, which is impossible since F contains the same amount of food and 6 more pieces of clothing than D.

Indifference Curves and Utility

To continue building this new version of our model of consumer behavior, we need to return to the concept of utility. Since all market baskets on a particular indifference curve yield the same satisfaction to the consumer, they all must have the same utility. For example, all market baskets on indifference curve I_1 in Figure 5.7 must have the same utility. Moreover, market baskets on higher indifference curves must have higher utilities than market baskets on lower indifference curves. For example, all market baskets on indifference curve I_2 in Figure 5.7 must have higher utilities than market baskets on indifference curve I_1.

Given a group of indifference curves for a certain consumer, it is easy to establish an index of the utility obtained from any market basket by this consumer. *All that we have to do is attach a number to each indifference curve, this number being larger for higher indifference curves than for lower indifference curves. The utility index for any market basket is then the number attached to the indifference curve on which this market basket is located.* The resulting utility index shows at a glance which market baskets the consumer will pick over other market baskets. The rational consumer will, of course, try to pick the market basket that maximizes this index of utility.

Note that this utility index is not unique. Any set of numbers that increases as one goes from successively lower to higher indifference curves will constitute a suitable set of indices. Thus no assumption is made that we can obtain a meaningful measure of marginal utility. But it is possible to construct a utility index of this sort, so long as the three basic assumptions underlying the theory of consumer demand (described in the earlier section on "A Model of Consumer Behavior") are met.

The Budget Line

The consumer wants to maximize his or her utility, which means that he or she wants to achieve the highest possible indifference curve. But whether or not a particular indifference curve is attainable depends on the consumer's money income and on commodity prices. Exactly what constraints are imposed on the consumer by the size of his or her money income and the nature of commodity prices? To make things concrete, let's return to Mrs. Martin. Suppose that her total income is $400 per week, and that she can spend this amount only on two commodities, food and clothing. Needless to say, it is unrealistic to assume that there are only two commodities in existence, but, to repeat what was said earlier, this makes it easier to present the model, and the results can easily be generalized to cases where more than two commodities exist. (Also, the assumption that her income is $400 is arbitrary, but this assumption can readily be relaxed.)

Given these conditions, the answer to how much of each commodity Mrs. Martin can buy depends on the price of a pound of food and the price of a piece of clothing. Suppose the price of a pound of food is $1 and the price of a piece of clothing is $40. Then if she spent all of her income on food, she could buy 400 pounds of food per week. On the other hand, if she spent all of her income on clothing, she could buy 10 pieces of clothing per week. Or she could, if she wished, buy some food and some clothing. There are a large number of combinations of amounts of

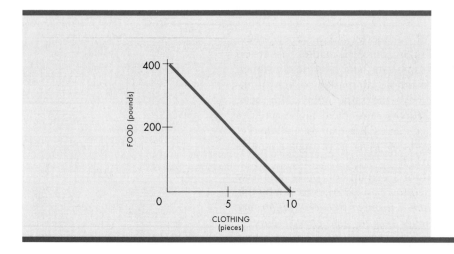

food and clothing that she could buy, and each such combination can be
represented by a point on the line in Figure 5.9. This line is called her
budget line. *A consumer's* **budget line** *shows the market baskets that he or
she can purchase, given the consumer's income and prevailing market
prices.*

The consumer's budget line will shift if changes occur in the consumer's money income or in commodity prices. In particular, an increase
in money income means that the budget line rises, and a decrease in
money income means that the budget line falls. This is illustrated in Figure 5.10, which shows Mrs. Martin's budget line at money incomes of
$200, $400, and $600 per week. As you can see, her budget line moves
upward as her income rises.

Commodity prices too affect the budget line. A decrease in a commodity's price causes the budget line to cut this commodity's axis at a point
farther from the origin. Figure 5.11 shows Mrs. Martin's budget line when
the price of a pound of food is $1 and when it is $2. You can see that the
budget line cuts the vertical, or food, axis farther from the origin when the
price of food is $1 per pound.

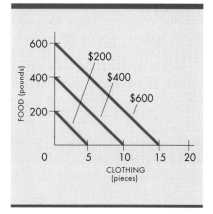

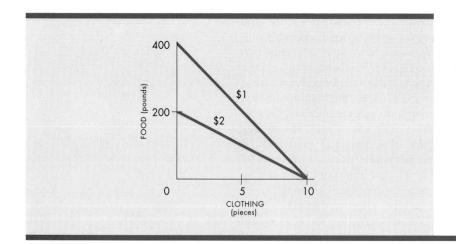

The Equilibrium Market Basket

With information on the consumer's indifference curves and budget line, we are in a position to determine the consumer's equilibrium market basket—the market basket that, among all those that the consumer can purchase, yields the maximum utility. The first step is to combine the indifference curves with the budget line on the same graph. Figure 5.12 brings together Mrs. Martin's indifference curves (from Figure 5.7) and her budget line (Figure 5.9). Given the information assembled in Figure 5.12, it is a simple matter to determine her equilibrium market basket. *Her indifference curves show what she wants:* specifically, she wants to attain the highest possible indifference curve. Thus, she would rather be on indifference curve I_2 than on indifference curve I_1, and on indifference curve I_3 than on indifference curve I_2. But, as we have pointed out repeatedly, she cannot choose any market basket she likes. *The budget line shows which market baskets her income and commodity prices permit her to buy.* Thus she must choose some market basket on her budget line.

Consequently, *the consumer's choice boils down to choosing that market basket on the budget line that is on the highest indifference curve. This is the equilibrium market basket.* For example, Mrs. Martin's equilibrium market basket is clearly at point G in Figure 5.12; it consists of 200 pounds of food and 5 pieces of clothing per week. This is her equilibrium market basket because any other market basket on the budget line is on a lower indifference curve than point G is. But will the consumer choose this market basket? Admittedly, it may take some time and fumbling for the consumer to find out that this is the best market basket for him or her under the circumstances. Consumers, after all, do make mistakes. But they also learn, and eventually one would expect a consumer to come very close to acting in the predicted way.

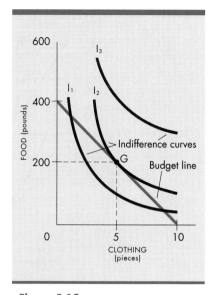

Figure 5.12
Mrs. Martin's Equilibrium Market Basket
Mrs. Martin's equilibrium market basket is at point G, containing 200 pounds of food and 5 pieces of clothing. This is the point on her budget line that is on the highest indifference curve, I_2, she can attain.

Deriving the Individual Demand Curve

Finally, we show how indifference curves can be used to derive the consumer's demand curve. In particular, let's return to the case of Mrs. Martin, and show how her demand curve for food can be derived.

Assuming that food and clothing are the only goods, that Mrs. Martin's weekly income is $400, and that the price of clothing is $40 per piece of clothing, Mrs. Martin's budget line is budget line 1 in Figure 5.13, when the price of food is $1 per pound. Thus, as we saw in Figure 5.2, Mrs. Martin will buy 200 pounds of food per week under these conditions.

If, however, the price of food increases to $2 per pound, her income and the price of clothing remaining constant, her budget line will be budget line 2 in Figure 5.13, and she will attain her highest indifference curve, I_1, by choosing the market basket corresponding to point U, a market basket containing 100 pounds of food per week. Thus, if the price of food is $2 per pound, she will buy 100 pounds of food per week.

We have derived two points on Mrs. Martin's individual demand curve for food—those corresponding to prices of $1 and $2 per pound. Figure 5.2 shows these two points, X and Y. To obtain more points on her individual demand curve for food, all we have to do is assume a particular price of food, construct the budget line corresponding to this price (holding her income and the price of clothing constant), and find the market basket on this budget line that is on her highest indifference curve. Plot-

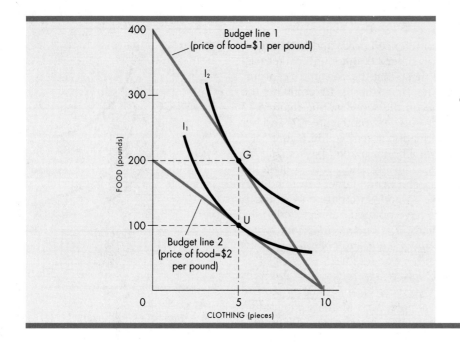

Figure 5.13
Effect of Change in Price of Food on Mrs. Martin's Equilibrium Market Basket
If the price of a pound of food is $1, Mrs. Martin's budget line is such that her equilibrium market basket is at point G, where she buys 200 pounds of food per week. If the price of a pound of food is $2, Mrs. Martin's budget line is such that her equilibrium market basket is at point U, where she buys 100 pounds of food per week.

ting the amount of food in this market basket against the assumed price of food, we obtain a new point on her individual demand curve for food. Connecting up all these points, we get her complete individual demand curve for food, shown in Figure 5.2.

A GUIDED TOUR OF THE BUSINESS FIRM

IT IS HARD TO OVERSTATE the importance of business firms in the American economy. They produce the bulk of our goods and services, hire most of the nation's workers, and issue stocks and bonds that represent a large percentage of the nation's wealth. Judged by any yardstick—even less complimentary ones like the responsibility for environmental pollution—business firms are an extremely important part of the American economy. In this chapter, we discuss the various types of business firms, such as proprietorships and corporations. Then we describe the various types of securities—common stock, bonds, and so forth—issued by firms, and discuss the workings of the stock market. Next, we take up the motivation and structure of firms, as well as their technology. Finally, we provide some essential elements of accounting. This material is a necessary introduction to the workings of the business enterprise, absolutely essential to anyone who works for, manages, or invests in a firm.

THE IBM CORPORATION: A CASE STUDY

To begin with, let's look in some detail at one of America's biggest firms: the IBM Corporation. A description of its history and vicissitudes should give you a better feel for what firms do and the sorts of problems they face.

IBM world headquarters

Electronic Computers: Coming from Behind

The IBM Corporation operated under the strong leadership of Thomas Watson, Sr., until his death in 1956. Watson joined the Computing-Tabulating-Recording Corporation in 1914, and renamed it International Business Machines in 1924. The firm became a very successful and fast-growing office-equipment company. In the late 1940s and early 1950s, the first electronic computers were developed, but IBM did not then appreciate the commercial potential of such equipment. According to Watson's son:

> During these really earth-shaking developments in the accounting machine industry, IBM slept soundly. We had put the first electronically-operated punched card calculator on the market in 1947. We clearly knew that electronic computing even in those days was so fast that the machine waited 9/10 of every card cycle for the mechanical portions of the machine to feed the next card. In spite of this, we didn't jump to the obvious conclusion that if we could feed data

more rapidly, we could increase speeds by 900 percent. Remington Rand and Univac drew this conclusion and were off to the races.

Finally we awoke and began to act. We took one of our most competent operating executives with a reputation for fearlessness and competence and put him in charge of all phases of the development of an IBM large-scale electronic computer. He and we were successful.

How did we come from behind? First, we had enough cash to carry loads of engineering, research, and production, which were heavy. Second, we had a sales force which enabled us to tailor our machine very closely to the market. Finally, and most important, we had good company morale. All concerned realized that this was a mutual challenge to us as an industry leader. We had to respond with all that we had to win, and we did.[1]

Snow White and the Seven Dwarfs

Although IBM was a slow starter, it soon became the dominant producer of electronic computers. By 1956, it had over 80 percent of the market. According to many observers, its success was due particularly to its marketing skills. In the 1960s, it became known as Snow White, while its rivals—Burroughs, Univac, NCR, Control Data, Honeywell, GE, and RCA—were referred to as the Seven Dwarfs. In the 1970s, after GE and RCA left the computer industry, only five dwarfs remained.

On January 17, 1969, the federal government brought a massive antitrust case against IBM, accusing it of monopolistic practices. The case went on for thirteen years. According to IBM's former chairman, Frank Cary, "The suit was a tremendous cloud that was over the company. . . . It couldn't help influencing us in a whole variety of ways. Ending it lifted a huge burden from management's shoulders." In January 1982, the Justice Department dropped the case, saying that it was "without merit."

After the settlement of the case, IBM proceeded to sell aggressively and to enter new markets. Some observers worried that it was becoming too big and powerful; others felt that it had plenty of competition from the Japanese, among others.

The IBM Personal Computer

One of IBM's most dramatic moves in the early 1980s was its entrance into the personal computer market. The job of overseeing the development of IBM's personal computer (PC) was entrusted to a twelve-member group, which worked for about a year on the project. The group broke with tradition by making the PC's technical specifications available to other firms, thus allowing outsiders to write software and make peripheral equipment for the PC that would extend its appeal. Within a few months after its introduction, the IBM PC was setting the standard for the industry. By 1983, IBM had garnered about 28 percent of the market for personal computers.

However, IBM is not invincible. During the mid-1980s, it was rocked by competition from Digital Equipment Corporation and imitators of its PCs, among others. From 1986 to 1988, it fought back by streamlining management, speeding up product introductions, and cutting spending where possible. In the first quarter of 1991, its earnings plunged by about 50 percent. While it attributed this to the recession, some analysts cited delays in introducing new products as another factor.

The first IBM personal computer

---

[1] T. Belden and M. Belden. *The Lengthening Shadow: The Life of Thomas J. Watson,* Boston: Little, Brown, 1962.

AMERICAN FIRMS, BIG AND SMALL

IBM is an economic colossus—a huge organization with over 300,000 employees. Of course it is not typical of American business firms. If we broaden our focus to take in the entire population of business firms in the United States, the first thing we note is their tremendous number; according to government statistics, there are over 10 million. The vast majority of these firms, as one would expect, are very small. There are lots of grocery stores, gas stations, auto dealers, drugstores, clothing shops, restaurants, and so on. You see hundreds of them as you walk along practically any downtown city street. But these small firms, although numerous, do not control the bulk of the nation's productive capacity. The several hundred largest firms have great economic power, measured by their sales, assets, employment, or other such indices. The small firms tend to be weak and short-lived. Although some prosper, many small firms go out of business after only a few years of existence.

PROPRIETORSHIPS

Most of the nation's business firms are proprietorships. A proprietorship is a legal form of business organization—the most common form and also the simplest. Specifically, a ***proprietorship*** is a firm owned by a single individual. For example, the corner drugstore may well be one. If so, it has a single owner—say, Bill Randolph. He hires the people he needs to wait on customers, deliver orders, do the bookkeeping, and so forth. He borrows, if he can, whatever money he feels he needs. He reaps the profits, or incurs the losses. All his personal assets—his house, his furniture, his car—can be taken by creditors to meet the drugstore's bills; that is, he has unlimited liability for the debts of the business.

PROS. What Lincoln said about the common man or woman applies as well to proprietorships: God must love them, or He wouldn't have created so many of them. If proprietorships didn't have advantages over other legal forms of business organization under many sorts of circumstances, there wouldn't be so many of them. What are these advantages? First, *owners of proprietorships have complete control over their businesses.* They don't have to negotiate with partners or other co-owners. They are the boss—and the only boss. Anyone who has been in a position of complete authority knows the joy it can bring. Many proprietors treasure this feeling of independence. Second, *a proprietorship is easy and inexpensive to establish:* all you have to do is hang out your shingle and announce you are in business. This too is a great advantage.

CONS. But proprietorships have important disadvantages as well—and for this reason, they are seldom found in many important industries. One disadvantage is that *it is difficult for a proprietor to put together enough financial resources to enter industries like automobiles, steel, or computers.* No one in the world has enough money to establish, by himself or herself, a firm of IBM's present size. Another disadvantage is that *proprietors are liable for all of the debts of the firm.* If their business fails, their personal assets can be taken by their creditors, and they can be completely wiped out.

PARTNERSHIPS

A ***partnership*** is somewhat more complicated than a proprietorship. As its name implies, it is a form of business organization where two or more people agree to own and conduct a business. Each partner agrees to contribute some proportion of the capital and labor used by the business, and to receive some proportion of the profits or losses. There are a variety of types of partnerships. In some cases, one or more of the partners may be "silent partners," who put up some of the money, but have little or nothing to do with the operations of the firm. The partnership is a common form of business organization in some industries and professions, like the law.

PROS. A partnership has certain advantages. Like a proprietorship, *it can be established without great expense or legal red tape.* (However, if you ever go into a partnership with someone, you would be well advised to have a good lawyer draw up a written agreement establishing such things as the salaries of each partner and how profits are to be shared.) In addition, a partnership can avoid some of the problems involved in a proprietorship. *It can usually put together more financial resources and specialized know-how than a proprietorship*—and this can be an important advantage.

CONS. But the partnership also has certain drawbacks. First, *each partner is liable without limit for the bills of the firm.* For example, even if one partner of a law firm has only a 30 percent share of the firm, he or she may be called upon to pay all the firm's debts if the other partners cannot do so. Second, *there is some red tape in keeping a partnership in existence.* Whenever a partner dies or withdraws, or whenever a new partner is admitted, a new partnership must be established. Third, like the proprietorship, *the partnership is not a very effective way to obtain the large amounts of capital required for some modern industries.* A modern automobile plant may cost $500 million, and not many partnerships could assemble that much capital. For these reasons, as well as others discussed in the next section, the corporation has become the dominant form of business organization.

CORPORATIONS

A far more complicated form of business organization than either the proprietorship or partnership, the ***corporation*** is a fictitious legal person, separate and distinct from its owners. A corporation is formed by having lawyers draw up the necessary papers stating (in general terms) what sorts of activities the owners of the corporation intend to engage in. The owners of the corporation are the stockholders. ***Stock,*** pieces of paper signifying ownership of the corporation, is issued to the owners, generally in exchange for their cash. Ordinarily, each ***share*** of stock gives its owner one vote. The corporation's ***board of directors,*** which is responsible for setting overall policy for the firm, is elected by the stockholders. The firm's owners can, if they are dissatisfied with the company's policies or think they have better opportunities elsewhere, sell their stock to someone else, assuming, of course, that they can find a buyer.

PROS. The corporation has many advantages over the partnership or proprietorship. In particular, *each of the corporation's owners has limited,*

not unlimited, liability. If I decide to become one of the owners of IBM and if a share of IBM stock sells for $110 a share, I can buy ten shares of IBM stock for $1,100. And I can be sure that, if IBM falls on hard times, I cannot lose more than the $1,100 I paid for the stock. There is no way that I can be assessed beyond this. Moreover, *the corporation, unlike the partnership or proprietorship, has unlimited life.* If several stockholders want to withdraw from the firm, they simply sell their stock. The corporation goes on, although the identity of the owners changes. For these reasons, *the corporation is clearly a better device for raising large sums of money than the partnership or proprietorship.* This is an enormous advantage of the corporation, particularly in industries like automobiles and steel, which could not otherwise finance their operations.

CONS. Without question, the corporation is a very important social invention. It permits people to assemble the large quantities of capital required for efficient production in many industries. Without limited liability and the other advantages of the corporation, it is doubtful that the opportunities and benefits of large-scale production could have been reaped. However, this does not mean that the corporate form will work for all firms. In many cases, a firm requires only a modest amount of capital, and there is no reason to go to the extra trouble and expense of establishing a corporation. Moreover, one disadvantage of the corporation is **double taxation of income,** since corporations pay income taxes—and the tax rate is often about one-third of every extra dollar earned. Thus every dollar earned by a corporation and distributed to stockholders is taxed twice by the federal government—once when it is counted as income by the corporation, and once when the remainder is counted as income by the stockholders.

CORPORATE SECURITIES

The corporation raises money by issuing various kinds of securities; of these, three kinds—common stock, preferred stock, and bonds—are particularly significant. Each of these types of securities is important to the workings of the corporation and to the public's investment decisions.

COMMON STOCK. *Common stock* is the ordinary certificate of ownership of the corporation. Holders of common stock are owners of the firm. They share in the firm's profits—if there are any profits. At frequent intervals, the board of directors of the firm may declare a dividend of so much per share for the common stockholders. For example, the common stockholders of IBM received dividends of $4.84 per share in 1990. **Dividends** are thus the income the owners of common stock receive. (In addition, of course, common stockholders may make money by selling their stock for more than they paid for it; such income is called **capital gains.**) Common stock is generally regarded as more risky than preferred stock or bonds, for reasons that will be explained.

PREFERRED STOCK. *Preferred stock* is a special kind of certificate of ownership that pays at most a stated dividend. For example, consider the General Motors Corporation, the huge auto maker. Owners of one type of General Motors preferred stock receive $5 a share per year, as long as the firm makes enough to pay this dividend. To protect the owners of preferred stock, it is stipulated that no dividends can be paid on the common stock unless the dividends on the preferred stock are paid in full. Since

BUYING AND SELLING COMMON STOCKS

Over 30 million Americans own common stocks, which indicates that you don't have to be wealthy to be an investor. Suppose that you are interested in buying IBM stock. To determine its current price, you need only look at the financial pages of any major newspaper. For example, on April 2, 1991, the *Wall Street Journal* showed the following information concerning IBM common stock:

| 52-week | | | | Sales | | | | Net |
High	Low	Stock	Div	100s	High	Low	Last	Change
139 ¾	96 ¼	IBM	4.84	14230	114 ¼	111 ⅞	112 ¼	−1 ⅝

Reading from left to right, $139.75 and $96.25 are the highest and lowest prices of IBM stock in the previous year, and $4.84 is the level of IBM's dividends in the previous year. The last five figures show the number of shares sold (1,423,000), the highest price (114.25), the lowest price (111.87 ½), and the final price (112.25) of a share on the previous day, as well as the change in the price from the day before (down $1.62 ½ per share).

To determine whether IBM common stock is a good buy, you would be well advised to look at IBM's recent earnings record and to obtain as much information as you can concerning the firm's earning prospects. This is because, as a firm's earnings (per share of common stock) go up, the price of its stock tends to go up too. Some economists and business analysts have gone so far as to publish formulas by which one can determine, on the basis of forecasts of what a firm's earnings will be, how much the stock is worth. They believe that one should buy if the current price of the stock is below this measure of the stock's intrinsic value and sell if the price is above it.

In contrast, other economists believe that the movement of stock prices has more to do with psychology than with financial valuation of this sort. As John Maynard Keynes put it, "[Most persons] are concerned, not with what an investment is really worth to a man who buys it 'for keeps,' but with what the market will value it at, under the influence of mass psychology, three months or a year hence. . . . For it

is not sensible to pay 25 for an investment of which you believe the prospective yields to justify a value of 30, if you also believe that the market will value it at 20 three months hence." As Princeton's Burton Malkiel observes, "This theory might . . . be called the 'greater-fool theory.' It's perfectly all right to pay three times what a stock is worth as long as later on you can find some innocent to pay five times what it's worth."[1]

There is no simple, foolproof way to determine whether IBM common stock is a good buy. Since even the most astute traders on Wall Street frequently do no better than one could do by buying the Dow-Jones average, you would do well to approach the stock market with caution. More than one economic savant has lost his or her shirt.

[1] B. Malkiel, *A Random Walk down Wall Street*, 5th ed., New York: Norton, 1990, p. 32.

the common stockholders cannot receive their dividends unless the preferred stock's dividends have been paid, common stock is obviously more risky than preferred stock. But by the same token, the amount preferred stockholders have to gain if the company prospers is less than the amount common stockholders have to gain, since however high its profits may be, the firm will pay only the stated dividend—for example, $5 per share per year in the case of General Motors—to the owners of preferred stock.

BONDS. Bonds are quite different from both common and preferred stocks. *Bonds* are debts of the firm; in other words, they are IOUs issued by the firm. In contrast to stockholders, the bondholders are not owners of a firm: they are its creditors, and receive interest, not dividends. Specifically, a bond is a certificate bearing the firm's promise to pay the interest every six months until the bond matures, at which time the firm also promises to pay the bondholders the principal (the amount they lent the firm) as well. Often bonds are sold in $1,000 denominations. For example, one type of bond issued by IBM is a 9 3/8 percent bond, due in 2004. The owner of each such bond receives $93.75 per year in interest, and IBM promises to pay him or her the principal of $1,000 when the bond falls due in 2004. A firm must pay the interest on the bonds and the principal when it is due, or it can be declared bankrupt. In other words, the bondholders are legally entitled to receive what is due them before the stockholders can get anything.

Thus, from the point of view of the investor, bonds are generally considered less risky than preferred stock, and preferred stocks are considered less risky than common stock. But we have ignored another fact: inflation. The tendency for the price level in the United States to increase over time has meant that bondholders have been paid off with dollars that were worth less than those they lent. For this reason, together with the fact that owners of common stocks reaped substantial capital gains during the 1960s and early 1970s, many investors tended to favor common stocks. Indeed, during the 1960s, a "cult of equities" developed; these were the years when it appeared that stock prices were headed only one way—even higher. It became very fashionable to buy common stock. But in the middle 1970s, the public's infatuation with common stocks seemed to fade, as stock prices fell; and the 1980s and early 1990s have seen considerable variation in stock prices. To understand why the value of stocks can gyrate so considerably, it is necessary to look briefly at the workings of the stock market.

THE STOCK MARKET

In general, large corporations do not sell stock directly to the investor. Instead, the investor buys stock on the stock market. Two major stock exchanges in the United States are the New York Stock Exchange and the American Stock Exchange, both in New York City. On these and similar exchanges in other cities, the common stocks of thousands of corporations are bought and sold.

PRICE FLUCTUATIONS. The price of each common stock fluctuates from day to day, indeed from minute to minute. Basically, the factors responsible for these price fluctuations are the shifts in the demand curve and supply curve for each kind of common stock. For example, if a strike breaks out

at a General Motors plant, this may cause the demand curve for General Motors stock to shift downward to the left, since the strike is liable to mean lower profits for General Motors. Because of this downward, or leftward, shift in the demand curve, the price of General Motors common stock will tend to fall, as in fact happened during a recent United Auto Workers strike.

THE GREAT CRASH. When stock prices tumble substantially, old investors think back to the Great Crash of 1929. The 1920s witnessed a feverish interest in investing in the stock market. Along with raccoon coats, Stutz Bearcats, and the Charleston, common stocks were the rage. Both the professionals on Wall Street and the neophytes on Main Street bought common stocks and more common stocks. Naturally, as the demand curves for common stocks shifted upward to the right, their prices rose, thus whetting the appetites of investors for still more common stocks. This upward spiral continued until 1929, when the bubble burst. Suddenly the prices of common stocks fell precipitously—and continued to drop during the early 1930s. The most famous average of industrial stock prices, the Dow-Jones average, fell from 381 in 1929 to 41 in 1933. Many investors, large and small, were wiped out.

STOCKS COME BACK. The Great Crash made investors wary of common stocks for many years. But by the 1960s confidence in them was fully restored, and there certainly was no tendency for investors to shy away from them. In the 1970s and 1980s, the stock market remained a major outlet for savings. However, this does not mean that stock prices did not fluctuate. On October 19, 1987, the Dow-Jones average of stock prices fell by about 20 percent, the largest loss on a single day in history. Dubbed Black Monday by journalists, this day saw 600 million shares of stock change hands, as investors lost about $500 billion, at least on paper. This crash illustrated vividly and painfully what sensible observers knew all along: the stock market goes up and it goes down. During 1986, the stock market increased dramatically (by over 23 percent); in late 1987, investors lost a substantial proportion of these gains.

Judging from historical experience, the public's taste for common stocks seems to be justified. Studies show that, during the course of a lifetime, the typical investor would have done better to invest in common stocks than in the best-quality bonds, because stock prices have tended to rise. This tended to apply in a great many cases, even for investors who lived through the Great Crash. And it has certainly been borne out over the past 50 years. Thus, although common stocks are riskier in some respects than bonds or preferred stocks, they seem to have performed better, on the average, at least in recent times.

Making Money on Stocks

During periods when the average of stock prices is going up, such as the 1920s and much of the 1950s and 1960s (as well as in more recent bull markets), it is relatively easy to be a financial wizard, whether by luck or calculation. A much more exacting test of your financial acumen is how well you can pick which stocks will outperform the averages. If you can predict that increases will occur in a certain firm's profits, and if other people don't predict the same thing, you may be able to pass this test. However, the sobering truth is that "playing the stock market" is much more an art than a science. The stock market is affected by psychological

Stocks are a risky investment; that is, you cannot be at all sure of how much money you will make or lose on them. *One way that professional investors reduce risk is by diversification: they invest in a number of stocks, and avoid putting all of their eggs in a single basket.* To see how diversification can reduce risk, consider the following simple example. Suppose that you can buy stock in only two firms, an overcoat manufacturer and a sportswear producer. If next year's weather is mild, stock in the sportswear producer will earn 20 cents per dollar invested, while stock in the overcoat manufacturer will earn nothing. If next year's weather is not mild, stock in the overcoat manufacturer will earn 20 cents per dollar invested, while stock in the sportswear producer will earn nothing.

Based on previous experience, there is a 50-50 chance that next year will be mild—and a 50-50 chance that it will not be mild. *Thus an investment in either one of these stocks is quite risky.* For example, if you buy stock in the overcoat manufacturer, there is a 50-50 chance that you will receive 20 cents per dollar invested, since this is the chance that the weather will not be mild. On the other hand, there is also a 50-50 chance that you will receive nothing, since this is the chance that the weather will be mild.

A simple and effective way to reduce this risk is to diversify. Rather than buying only one stock or the other, suppose that you put half of your money into each stock. *After diversifying in this way, you can be sure of getting 10 cents per dollar invested.* Why? Because if next year is not mild, you will receive 20 cents per dollar invested from your overcoat stock and nothing from your sportswear stock; thus your return from both stocks combined is 10 cents per dollar invested. Similarly, if next year is mild, you will receive 20 cents per dollar invested from your sportswear stock and nothing from your overcoat stock; thus your return from both stocks combined is 10 cents per dollar invested.

The reason why risk is eliminated through diversification is that the stocks of the two firms are affected differently by different weather conditions. Since the one firm's stock always does well when the other firm's stock does poorly, diversification can, as we have seen, do away with risk. But this is a very unusual situation. Ordinarily, it is possible to reduce, but not eliminate, risk through diversification. This is because there generally is not a simple inverse relationship (like that assumed above) between the returns from various firms' stocks.

In recent decades, economists have devoted considerable attention to financial topics of this sort. In 1990, three American economists—Harry Markowitz, Merton Miller, and William Sharpe—received the Nobel Prize in economics for their work in this area.

Harry Markowitz

Merton Miller

William F. Sharpe

as well as economic considerations. Moreover, when you try to spot stocks that will increase in price, you are pitting your knowledge and experience against those of skilled professionals with big research staffs and with friends and acquaintances working for the companies in question. And even these professionals can do surprisingly poorly at times.

Do economists have a nose for good investments? John Maynard Keynes was an extremely successful speculator who made millions of dollars. Other economists have been far less successful. Certainly, a knowledge of basic economics is not sufficient to enable you to make money on the stock market, but insofar as the market reflects economic realities, a knowledge of basic economics should be helpful.

THE GIANT CORPORATION

Much of the trading on the stock market centers around the relatively small number of giant corporations that control a very substantial percentage of the total assets and employment in the American economy. And well it might, for the largest 100 manufacturing corporations control about half of this country's manufacturing assets. These firms have tremendous economic and political power. They include the giant automobile manufacturers (General Motors, Ford), the big oil firms (Exxon, Amoco, Mobil, Chevron, Atlantic-Richfield), the big computer and office machinery producers (IBM, Hewlett Packard, Xerox), the leading tobacco firms (American Brands, RJR Nabisco, Philip Morris), the electrical equipment producers (General Electric, Westinghouse), and many others.

Management

Usually, the president is the chief operations officer in the firm, although sometimes the chairman of the board of directors fills this role. As for the board of directors, some members are chosen for their reputations and contacts, while others are chosen for their knowledge of the firm, the industry, or some profession or specialty.

The board generally contains at least one representative of the financial community, and a university president or former government official is often included to show that the firm is responsive to broad social issues. Members of IBM's board include Harold Brown, a former secretary of defense, and Nanneri Keohane, president of Wellesley College.

The board of directors is concerned with overall policy. Since it meets only a few times a year, it seldom becomes involved in day-to-day decisions; and it usually goes along with management's policies, so long as management retains the board's confidence.

Separation of Ownership from Control

An interesting and important feature of the large corporation is the fact that it is owned by many people, practically all of whom have little or no detailed information about the firm's operations. The owners of IBM number over 800,000, but most of them know relatively little about what is going on in the firm. Moreover, because of the wide diffusion of ownership, working control of a large corporation can often be maintained by a group with only one-fifth or less of all the voting stock. The result is a *sep-*

aration of ownership from control. In other words, the owners control the firm in only a limited and somewhat sporadic sense.

So long as a firm's management is not obviously incompetent or corrupt, it is difficult for insurgent stockholders to remove the management from office. Most stockholders do not go to the annual meetings to vote for members of the firm's board of directors. Instead, they receive *proxies,* which, if returned, permit the management to exercise their votes. Usually enough shareholders mail in their proxies to give management the votes it needs to elect a friendly board of directors. In recent years, the Securities and Exchange Commission, which oversees and regulates the financial markets, has attempted to make the giant corporations more democratic by enabling insurgent groups to gain access to mailing lists of stockholders and so forth. But there is still a noteworthy and widespread separation of ownership from control.

TEST YOURSELF

1. The Exxon Corporation built a new olefins plant (costing $500 million) in Baytown, Texas. Is this plant a firm? Why or why not? Do you think that a proprietorship would be likely to build and own such a plant? Why, or why not?

2. Assume that a partnership wanted to enter the automobile industry. What problems would such a legal form of organization impose upon the potential entrants? Are any of the Big Three in the U.S. automobile industry (General Motors, Ford, and Chrysler) partnerships?

3. Explain why each of the following statements is true or false. (a) The University of Texas is a firm. (b) Massachusetts General Hospital is a firm. (c) A firm must be owned by more than one person. (d) The owner of a firm must participate in its management.

4. On April 1, 1991, the common stock of Exxon Corporation closed at $57.50 per share. What effect would each of the following have on its price? (a) A marked increase in the demand for gasoline. (b) A prolonged strike at a major Exxon refinery. (c) Price ceilings on gas and oil.

5. Explain why bondholders do not vote for a corporation's board of directors and why common stockholders are not guaranteed a particular dividend rate.

MOTIVATION OF THE FIRM

What determines the behavior of the business firm? As a first approximation, *economists usually assume that firms attempt to maximize profits,* which are defined as the difference between the firm's revenue and its costs. In other words, economists generally assume that firms try to make as much money as possible. This assumption certainly does not seem unreasonable; most business executives appear to be interested in making money. Nonetheless, the assumption of profit maximization oversimplifies the situation. Although business executives certainly want profits, they are interested in other things as well. Some firms claim that they want to promote better cultural activities or better racial relations in their community. At a less lofty level, other firms say that their aim is to increase their share of the market. Whether or not one takes these self-proclaimed goals very seriously, it is clear that firms are not interested *only* in making money—

often for the same reason that Dr. Johnson gave for not becoming a philosopher: "because cheerfulness keeps breaking in."[2]

INTRAFIRM POLITICS.   In a large corporation, there are some fairly obvious reasons why firms may not maximize profits. Various groups within such firms develop their own party lines, and intrafirm politics is an important part of the process determining firm behavior. Whereas in a small firm it may be fairly accurate to regard the goals of the firm as being the goals of the proprietor, in the large corporation the decision on the goals of the firm is a matter of politics, with various groups within the organization struggling for power. In addition, because of the separation of ownership from control, top management usually has a great deal of freedom as long as it seems to be performing reasonably well. Under these circumstances, the behavior of the firm may be dictated in part by the interests of the management group, resulting in higher salaries, more perquisites, and a bigger staff for their own benefit than would otherwise be the case.

RISK AND UNCERTAINTY.   Also, in a world full of risk and uncertainty, it is difficult to know exactly what profit maximization means, since the firm cannot be sure that a certain level of profit will result from a certain action. Instead, the best the firm can do is to estimate that a certain probability distribution of profit levels will result from a certain action. Under these circumstances, the firm may choose less risky actions even though they have a lower expectation of very high profits than other actions. In a world where ruin is ruinous, this may be perfectly rational policy.

Profit Maximization Is the Standard Assumption

Nonetheless, profit maximization remains the standard assumption in economics. As we agreed in our discussion of model building in Chapter 2, to be useful, models need not be exact replicas of reality. Economic models based on profit maximization have been very useful indeed. For one thing, they help to show how the price system functions. For another, in the real world, they suggest how a firm should operate if it wants to make as much money as possible. Even if a firm does not want to maximize profit, these theories can be utilized. For example, they can show how much profit the firm is forgoing by taking certain courses of action. In recent years, the theory of the profit-maximizing firm has been studied more and more for the sake of determining profit-maximizing rules of business behavior.

TECHNOLOGY, INPUTS, AND THE PRODUCTION FUNCTION

The decisions a firm should make in order to maximize its profits are determined by the current state of technology. Technology, it will be recalled from Chapter 1, is the sum total of society's knowledge concerning the industrial arts. Just as consumers are limited by their income, firms are limited by the current state of technology. If the current state of technol-

---

[2] This quote is taken from R. Solow, "The New Industrial State, or Son of Affluence," *The Public Interest*, Fall 1967. Since footnotes are so often used to cite dreary material, it seems worthwhile to use them occasionally to cite humor as well.

THE PRINCIPAL-AGENT PROBLEM

Although economists generally assume as a first approximation that firms maximize profit, they realize that this does not always occur. One factor that can interfere with profit maximization is the so-called principal-agent problem. In a large corporation, the managers very seldom own the firm. Instead, a firm's managers are agents who work for the firm's owners, who are the principals. *The principal-agent problem is that the managers may pursue their own objectives, even though this decreases the profits of the owners.*

Consider William Moran, a manager and part-owner of the Media Company. If he were the sole owner of this firm, an extra dollar of benefits (large staff, company-paid travel, and so on) that he receives from the firm would reduce his profits by one dollar. That is, the cost of these benefits would come entirely out of his own pocket. However, if he were to own only one-fifth of the firm, an extra dollar of benefits would reduce his profits by only 20 cents. Hence, only one-fifth of the cost of these benefits would come out of his pocket.

William Moran is likely to increase the amount of benefits he receives if the cost to him of a dollar's worth of benefits is 20 cents rather than a dollar. Since the other owners pick up four-fifths of the bill, why not take an extra "business" trip to Acapulco or the Riviera? If he had to pay the full cost, he would settle for a vacation in the Catskills, but since he only pays 20 percent of the full cost, he finds it worthwhile to take the extra "business" trip.

If a manager is not an owner or part-owner of the firm, this problem becomes even more serious. Because the cost of the benefits he or she receives is borne entirely by the owners, the manager has an incentive to increase these benefits very substantially. Since the owners of the firm find it hard to distinguish between those benefits that bolster profits and those that do not do so, the manager has some leeway. However, if the manager tries to cheat the owners in too blatant a fashion, the owners may fire the manager.

Recognizing the existence of this principal-agent problem, people avoid investing in a firm where managers behave in this way. If no one is willing to invest and if the managers have to put up their own funds to finance the business, they will be much less

likely to take "business" trips to Acapulco or the Riviera (or even the Catskills). Conceivably, owners could make managers sign contracts making the managers responsible for paying for the excessive benefits they receive, but since this would make it necessary for the owners to monitor the managers' activities in minute detail (and would cause enormous ill-will among the managers), it would not be a practical solution.

To deal with this problem, firms often establish contracts that give the managers an incentive to reduce such benefits and to pursue objectives that are reasonably close to profit maximization. Thus the firm's owners might give the managers a financial stake in the success of the firm. Many corporations have adopted stock-option plans, whereby managers can purchase shares of common stock at less than market price. These plans give managers an incentive to promote the firm's profits and to act in accord with the owners' interests. There is some evidence that these plans do have an effect. For example, according to one recent study, if managers own between 5 and 20 percent of a firm, the firm is likely to perform better (in terms of profitability) than if they own less than 5 percent.[1]

[1] R. Morck, A. Shleifer, and R. Vishny, "Management Ownership and Corporate Performance: An Empirical Analysis," *Journal of Financial Economics*, March 1988.

ogy is such that we do not know how to produce more than 40 bushels of corn per year from an acre of land if 2 workers are hired, then this is as much as the firm can produce from this combination of land and labor. In making its decisions, the firm must take this into account.

Inputs

In constructing a model of the profit-maximizing firm, economists must somehow represent the state of technology and include it in their model. As a first step toward this end, we must define an **input.** Perhaps the simplest definition of an input is that it is anything the firm uses in its production process. Some of the inputs of a farm producing corn might be seed, land, labor, water, fertilizer, various types of machinery, as well as the time of the people managing the farm.

Production Function

Having defined an input, we can now describe how economists represent the state of technology. The basic concept economists use for this purpose is the production function.

For any commodity, *the **production function** is the relationship between the quantities of various inputs used per period of time and the maximum quantity of the commodity that can be produced per period of time.* More specifically, the production function is a table, a graph, or an equation showing the maximum output rate that can be achieved from any specified set of usage rates of inputs. The production function summarizes the characteristics of existing technology at a given point in time. It reflects the technological constraints the firm must reckon with.

To see more clearly what we mean by a production function, consider the Milwaukee Machine Company, a hypothetical machine shop that produces a simple metal part. Suppose that we are dealing with a period of time that is so short that the firm's basic plant and equipment cannot be altered. For simplicity, suppose that the only input whose quantity can be altered in this period is the amount of labor used by the machine shop. Suppose that the firm collects data showing the relationship between the quantity of its output and the quantity of labor it uses. This relationship, given in Table 6.1, is the firm's production function. It shows that, when 1 worker is employed, 100 parts are produced per month; when 2 workers are employed, 210 parts are produced per month; and so on. Information concerning a firm's production function is often obtained from the firm's engineers, as well as its artisans and technicians. Much more will be said about production functions in later chapters. All that we want to do here is to introduce the concept of the production function.

Table 6.1
Production Function, Milwaukee Machine Company

QUANTITY OF LABOR USED PER MONTH (NUMBER OF WORKERS EMPLOYED)	OUTPUT PER MONTH (NUMBER OF PARTS)
0	0
1	100
2	210
3	315
4	415
5	500

ELEMENTS OF ACCOUNTING: THE FIRM'S BALANCE SHEET

Having touched on the firm's technology, we must return to the motivation of the firm. In a previous section, we stated that economists generally assume that firms attempt to maximize profits. Viewed as a first approximation, this assumption does not seem too hard to swallow, but exactly what do we mean by profit? This is an important question, of interest to business executives and investors as well as to economists. The account-

HAS THE UNITED STATES LOST ITS TECHNOLOGICAL EDGE?

Although it is very difficult to measure international differences in technological levels, the available evidence suggests that the United States long has been a leader in technology. Scattered impressionistic evidence indicates that this was true in many fields before 1850. After 1850, the available quantitative evidence indicates that productivity was higher in the United States than in Europe, that the United States had a strong export position in technically progressive industries, and that Europeans tended to imitate American techniques. The existence of such a gap in the nineteenth century would not be surprising, since this was a heyday of American invention. (Among the key American inventions of the period was the system of interchangeable parts.) Needless to say, the United States did not lead in all fields, but it appears that we held a technological lead in many important parts of manufacturing.

After World War II, there was a widespread feeling that this technological gap widened, due in part to the wartime devastation of many countries in Europe and elsewhere. In the 1960s, Europeans expressed considerable concern over the technology gap. They asserted that superior know-how stemming from scientific and technical achievements in the United States had allowed American companies to obtain large shares of European markets in fields like aircraft, space equipment, computers, and other electronic products. In 1966, Italy's foreign minister Amintore Fanfani went so far as to call for a "technological Marshall Plan" to speed the flow of American technology across the Atlantic. In response to this concern, the Organization for Economic Cooperation and Development (OECD) made a large study of the nature and causes of the technology gap. It concluded that a large gap existed in computers and some electronic components, but that no general or fundamental gap existed in pharmaceuticals, bulk plastics, iron and steel, machine tools (other than numerically controlled machine tools), nonferrous metals (other than tantalum and titanium), and scientific instruments (other than electronic test and measuring instruments). Thus the OECD studies indicated that the American technological lead was greatest in relatively research-intensive sectors of the economy.

The factors responsible for these technological

Bell Laboratories headquarters in Murray Hill, NJ

gaps were difficult to sort out and measure. A host of factors—the social climate, the educational system, the scientific community, the amount and quality of industrial research, the nature of domestic markets, the quality of management, and government policies, among others—influence a country's technological position. According to the OECD studies, the size and homogeneity of the American market was an important factor, but not a decisive one. Also, the large size of American firms was another factor, but not a decisive one. In addition, the large government expenditures on research and development (R and D) in the United States played an important role. Also, according to the OECD studies, a very important factor was that American firms had a significant lead in the techniques of management, including the management of R and D and the coupling of R and D with marketing and production.[1]

During the past twenty years, the U.S. technological lead has been reduced in a great many areas. Frequently, this lead no longer exists at all. The following table shows the difference between the annual rate of growth of output per hour of labor in the United States and in other major industrial nations during 1950–85. Clearly, productivity increased much more rapidly in practically all these other countries than in the United States. In industries like

[1] E. Mansfield et al., *Technology Transfer, Productivity, and Economic Policy,* New York: Norton, 1982.

steel and automobiles, the United States has yielded the technological lead to others, notably the Japanese. Even in relatively new industries born largely in the United States, such as semiconductors, many fault the American industries for lagging behind the Japanese.

Confronted with this trend, the federal government under both Democratic and Republican administrations has tried to establish appropriate policies. During President Reagan's administration, Congress established a 25 percent (later reduced to 20 percent) incremental tax credit for R and D. That is, a firm could reduce its income tax liability by an amount equal to 25 percent of the difference between its current R and D expenditure and the average amount of its R and D expenditure in the previous three years. The available evidence suggests that this R and D tax credit has had only a limited effect on industrial R and D spending, but it does appear to have increased it somewhat.

The Bush administration, like its predecessor, has avoided subsidizing specific new technologies. In the words of President Bush's Council of Economic Advisers, "The private sector has inherent advantages over government in identifying potentially useful new technologies. Private decisions are disciplined by careful market evaluations of their prospects. Government decisions, in contrast, are often influenced by noneconomic objectives and based on information supplied by self-interested parties, without regard to taxpayers' cost. Governments in the United States and elsewhere have shown themselves to be less able than private businesses to pick specific technologies that will be commercially successful."[2]

Nonetheless, in response to pressure from Congress and from within the administration itself, the Bush administration began in 1991 to move in the direction of subsidizing civilian R and D. The White House Office of Science and Technology Policy published a list of critical technologies for industry. Recommendations were made that defense R and D be cut, and that civilian R and D be expanded. The emphasis seemed to be on technologies that would be applicable in a variety of areas and that were in a pre-competitive stage. It will take many years to determine what, if anything, will come out of this ferment.

Part of America's problem seems to be due to its apparent inability to match the Japanese as quick and effective users of technologies developed elsewhere. American firms, long accustomed to leading the world, do not monitor, imitate, and build on the technological advances of their rivals (here and abroad) as quickly and cheaply as do the Japanese. However, for innovations based on technologies developed largely within the innovating firm, there is no evidence that the Japanese can develop and introduce a new product or process more quickly or cheaply than the Americans.

Difference between Annual Growth Rate of Manufacturing Output per Hour of Labor in Selected Foreign Countries and in the United States

COUNTRY	1950–57	1957–66	1966–73	1973–79	1979–85
(DIFFERENCE FROM THE UNITED STATES, IN PERCENTAGE POINTS)					
West Germany	4.8	3.3	3.0	2.8	0.2
France	2.2	3.2	3.6	3.5	0.9
Italy	3.6	3.6	4.1	1.9	0.8
Japan	7.5	5.2	8.3	4.0	2.5
United Kingdom	−0.8	0.5	2.2	0.2	0.9
China	1.4	1.3	2.2	0.8	−1.4

Source: Panel on Technology and Employment, Technology and Employment, Washington, D.C.: National Academy Press, 1987, p. 83.

Probing Deeper

1. How can one tell whether the United States does, or does not, have a technological lead in a particular industry?

2. What factors determine whether the United States has such a lead?

3. What difference does it make to the American people if the United States loses whatever lead it had in a particular industry?

4. If it is true that the United States is losing its technological lead in a particular industry, why should the government intervene? (Can't the private sector be counted on to take the appropriate measures?)

5. Is the fact that an industry is in trouble, or that it is declining, or that it has difficulty competing with foreign firms an adequate justification for additional investment in R and D in this industry?

6. Are there advantages as well as disadvantages resulting from the reduction of America's technological lead? If so, what are they?

[2] Economic Report of the President, 1990, p. 117.

ing profession provides the basic figures that are reported in the newspapers and in a firm's annual reports to its stockholders. If IBM reports that it made a particular amount last year, this figure is provided by IBM's accountants. How do the accountants obtain this figure? What are its limitations?

Basically, accounting concepts are built around two very important statements: the balance sheet and the income statement. A *firm's **balance sheet*** *shows the nature of its assets, tangible and intangible, at a certain point in time.*

Left-Hand Side of the Balance Sheet

Let us return to the Milwaukee Machine Company. Its balance sheet might be as shown in Table 6.2. The left-hand side of the balance sheet shows the assets of the firm as of December 31, 1991. **Current assets** are assets that will be converted into cash relatively quickly (generally within a year), whereas **fixed assets** generally will not be liquidated quickly. The firm has $20,000 in cash, $120,000 in inventory, $160,000 in equipment, and $180,000 in buildings. At first glance, these figures may seem more accurate than they are likely to be. It is very difficult to know how to value various assets. For example, should they be valued at what the firm paid for them, or at what it would cost to replace them? More will be said about these problems below.

Table 6.2
Balance Sheet, Milwaukee Machine Company, as of December 31,1991

ASSETS (DOLLARS)		LIABILITIES AND NET WORTH (DOLLARS)	
Current assets		Current liabilities	
Cash	20,000	Accounts payable	20,000
Inventory	120,000	Notes payable	40,000
Fixed assets		Long-term liabilities	
Equipment	160,000	Bonds	160,000
Buildings	180,000		
		Net worth	
		Preferred stock	100,000
		Common stock	100,000
		Retained earnings	60,000
Total	480,000	Total	480,000

Right-Hand Side of the Balance Sheet

The right-hand side of the firm's balance sheet shows the claims by creditors on the firm's assets and the value of the firm's ownership. In Table 6.2, the Milwaukee Machine Company has total liabilities—or debts—of $220,000. There is $60,000 in **current liabilities,** which come due in less than a year; and $160,000 in **long-term liabilities,** which come due in a year or more. Specifically, there is $20,000 in **accounts payable,** which are bills owed for goods and services that the firm bought; $40,000 in **notes payable,** short-term notes owed to banks, finance companies, or other creditors; and $160,000 in **bonds payable,** or bonds outstanding.

Left-Hand Side = Right-Hand Side

The difference between the value of a firm's assets and the value of its liabilities is its **net worth,** which is the value of the firm's owners' claims against the firm's assets. In other words, the value of the firm to its owners is the total value of its assets less the value of the debts owed by the firm. Since

total value of assets – total liabilities = net worth,

it follows that

total value of assets = total liabilities + net worth.

That is, *the sum of the items on the left-hand side of the balance sheet must equal the sum of the items on the right-hand side.* This, of course, must be true because of the way we define net worth.

In the case of the Milwaukee Machine Company, the firm's net worth—the difference between its assets and its liabilities—is $260,000. Specifically, there is $100,000 worth of preferred stock and $100,000 worth of common stock; there is also $60,000 in retained earnings. **Retained earnings** is the total amount of profit that the stockholders have reinvested in the business. In other words, the stockholders of the Milwaukee Machine Company have reinvested $60,000 of their profits in the business. Rather than withdrawing this sum as dividends, they have kept it invested in the firm.

THE FIRM'S INCOME STATEMENT

*A firm's **income statement** shows its sales during a particular period, its costs incurred in connection with these sales, and its profits during this period.* Table 6.3 shows the Milwaukee Machine Company's income statement during the period January 1, 1992, to December 31, 1992. Sales during this period were $240,000. The cost of manufacturing the items made during this period was $110,000 which includes $30,000 for materials, $40,000 for labor, $34,000 for depreciation (discussed below), and $6,000 for miscellaneous operating expenses.

However, because the firm has reduced its inventory from $120,000 to $110,000 during the period, the cost of manufacturing the items *made* during the period does not equal the cost of manufacturing the items *sold* during the period. To find the *cost of goods sold*—which is the amount that logically should be deducted from sales to get the profits made from the sale of these goods—we must add the decrease in the value of inventory to the total manufacturing cost. (Why? Because the firm sold more items than it produced during this period. Thus the cost of the items it sold equals the cost of the items it produced during this period plus the cost of the items it sold from its inventory. Since the cost of the items it sold from its inventory equals the decrease in the value of its inventory, the cost of the items it sold equals the cost of the items it produced during this period plus the decrease in inventory.) Putting it another way, we must add the beginning inventory and subtract the closing inventory, as shown in Table 6.3. The resulting figure for cost of goods sold is $120,000.

But manufacturing costs are not the only costs the firm incurs. To estimate the firm's profits, we must also deduct from sales its selling and ad-

Table 6.3
Income Statement, Milwaukee Machine Company,
January 1, 1992, to December 31, 1992 (dollars)

Net sales		240,000
Manufacturing cost of goods sold		120,000
Materials	30,000	
Labor	40,000	
Depreciation	34,000	
Miscellaneous operating costs	6,000	
Total	110,000	
Plus beginning inventory	120,000	
Less closing inventory	−110,000	
Adjusted total	120,000	
Selling and administrative costs		20,000
Fixed interest charges and state and		
local taxes		10,000
Net earnings before income taxes		90,000
Corporation income taxes		40,000
Net earnings after taxes		50,000
Dividends on preferred stock		4,000
Net profits of common stockholders		46,000
Dividends paid on common stock		20,000
Addition to retained earnings		26,000

ministrative expenses, its interest charges, and its state and local taxes, as well as its federal income taxes. Table 6.3 shows that the Milwaukee Machine Company's after-tax earnings during 1992 were $50,000. This is the amount left for the owners of the business. The income statement also shows what the owners do with what is left. Table 6.3 shows that the Milwaukee Machine Company used $4,000 to pay dividends to holders of preferred stock. When this was done, the holders of common stock were free to distribute some of the profits to themselves. According to Table 6.3, they distributed $20,000 to themselves in dividends on the common stock, and plowed the rest—$26,000—back into the business as retained earnings.

Depreciation

Before leaving the income statement, we should explain one element of manufacturing cost—***depreciation.*** While the other elements of manufacturing cost are self-explanatory, this one is not. The idea behind depreciation is that the buildings and equipment will not last forever; eventually they will have to be replaced. Clearly, it would be foolish to charge the entire cost of replacing them to the year when they are replaced. Instead, a better picture of the firm's true profitability will be drawn if the cost of replacing them is spread gradually over the life of buildings and equipment, thus recognizing that each year's output has a hand in wearing them out. One frequently used technique is so-called ***straight-line depreciation,*** which spreads the cost of buildings and equipment (less their scrap value) evenly over their life. Thus, if the Milwaukee Machine Company buys a piece of equipment for $20,000 and if it is expected to last ten years (its scrap value being zero), it would charge depreciation of $2,000 per year for this machine (for ten years after its purchase). The

$34,000 charge for depreciation in Table 6.3 is the sum of such charges. Clearly, this is only a rough way to estimate the true depreciation charges, but it is good enough for many purposes.

Economic versus Accounting Profits

The previous section described the nature of profit, as defined by accountants. This is the concept on which practically all published figures in business reports are based. But economists define profits somewhat differently.

To economists, profit is the amount that a firm's owners receive over and above what they could make from the capital and labor they provide, if this capital and labor were used outside the firm. In this way, the opportunity costs of their capital and labor are taken into account. Also,

---

EXAMPLE 6.1   HOW TO DEPRECIATE A BASEBALL CLUB

Suppose that you decide to buy the Philadelphia Phillies for $80 million. There are some important tax advantages you should understand. According to Bill Veeck, former owner of the Chicago White Sox, "It is almost impossible not to make money on a baseball club when you are buying it new, because, unless you are inordinately successful, you pay no income tax." In particular, half of the purchase price of the team can be regarded as the cost of the players, which are depreciable assets like machinery or breeding cattle. Suppose that you regard 5 years as being the "useful life" of the players, and that you use straight-line depreciation.

(a) How much depreciation (of the players) can you deduct from the Phillies' receipts each year to figure your profits? (b) Suppose that you pay $10 million in cash and borrow the remaining $70 million to pay for the Phillies. If you pay 10 percent interest, how much interest expense do you deduct from the Phillies' receipts each year to figure your profits? (c) Suppose that this year the Phillies' receipts equal $44 million and their operating expenses (excluding depreciation of the players and the interest on your loan) equal $30 million. Must you pay any income tax? (Assume that you have no income from sources other than the Phillies.)

Solution

(a) Since the cost of the players can be regarded as one-half of the purchase price of the team, it equals one-half of $80 million, or $40 million. Since the life of the players is 5 years, annual depreciation equals $40 million divided by 5, or $8 million. (b) $70 million times 10 percent, or $7 million. (c) Your income from the Phillies is as follows:

Earnings(before depreciation and interest)	$14 million
Less depreciation	−8 million
Less interest	−7 million
	−$1 million

Since you incurred a loss (because of the depreciation of the players), you pay no income tax.

---

economists do not assume that the firm attempts to maximize the current, short-run profits measured by the accountant. Instead they assume that the firm will attempt to maximize the sum of profits over a long period of time.[3]

Suppose that the owners of the Milwaukee Machine Company, who receive profits but no salary or wages, put in long hours for which they could receive $30,000 in 1992 if they worked for someone else. Also suppose that if they invested their capital somewhere other than in this firm, they could obtain a return of $22,000 on it in 1992. Under these circumstances, economists would say that the firm's after-tax profits in 1992 were $50,000 − $30,000 − $22,000, or − $2,000, rather than the $50,000 shown in Table 6.3. In other words, the economists' concept of profit includes only what the owners make above and beyond what their labor and capital employed in the business could have earned elsewhere. In this case, that amount is negative.

EXAMPLE 6.2   HOW MUCH DOES A HOT DOG VENDOR MAKE?

Louie Stathopoulos sells hot dogs out of a steel cart under an umbrella in the Wall Street area in New York City. On a sunny day, he sells the following numbers of hot dogs, sodas, knishes, and sausages per day, his price and cost per unit being shown below.

ITEM	NUMBER SOLD	PRICE	COST
Hot Dog	125	$1	36¢
Soda	75	60¢	33¢
Knish	20	75¢	33¢
Sausage	10	$1	40¢

He pays $40 per day for ice, $3 for propane, $13 for rent, and $2 for insurance. His cart cost $4,500, and will have to be replaced after about 1,000 days of use.[*]
(a) What are Mr. Stathopoulos's total sales on a sunny day? (b) What is his total cost, including depreciation? (c) What is his accounting profit? (d) He works from 6 A.M. to 9 P.M. on a sunny day. If he could earn $4 per hour at another job, is he earning an economic profit? (e) If it rains, he sells about 70 percent less than the above amounts. Does he earn a positive economic profit on a rainy day?

Solution

(a) $125 \times \$1 + 75 \times 60¢ + 20 \times 75¢ + 10 \times \$1 =$ $195. (b) $125 \times 36¢ + 75 \times 33¢ + 20 \times 33¢ + 10 \times 40¢ + \$58$ (for ice, propane, rent, and insurance) + $4.50 (for straight-line depreciation of his cart) = $142.85. (c) $195 − $142.85 = $52.15. (d) Working 15 hours per day, he could earn $15 \times \$4$, or $60, at another job. Thus he is not earning an economic profit. (e) No, since he will earn even less per hour of work than on a sunny day.

[*] These are actual figures for Mr. Stathopoulos's business. See "Selling the Sidewalk Frank," *New York Times*, July 26, 1987.

---

[3] The profits earned at various points in time should be *discounted* before being added together, but, for simplicity's sake, we neglect this point here. For some relevant discussion, see Chapter 14.

To a considerable extent, the differences between the concepts used by the accountant and the economist reflect the difference in their functions. The accountant is concerned with controlling the firm's day-to-day operations, detecting fraud or embezzlement, satisfying tax and other laws, and producing records for various interested groups. On the other hand, the economist is concerned primarily with decision making and rational choice among prospective alternatives. Although the figures published on profits almost always conform to the accountant's, not the economist's, concept, the economist's concept is the more relevant one for many kinds of decisions. (And this, of course, is recognized by sophisticated accountants.) For example, suppose the owners of the Milwaukee Machine Company are trying to decide whether they should continue in business. If they are interested in making as much money as possible, the answer depends on the firm's profits as measured by the economist, not the accountant. If the firm's economic profits are greater than (or equal to) zero, the firm should continue in existence; otherwise, it should not. Thus the Milwaukee Machine Company should not stay in existence if 1992 is a good indicator of its future profitability.

TEST YOURSELF

1. Which of the following are inputs in the steel industry? (a) coke, (b) iron ore, (c) labor, (d) land, (e) capital, (f) water, (g) oxygen, (h) food eaten by Bethlehem Steel's workers.

2. Changes in the tax law have allowed firms to depreciate assets more quickly. For example, they can depreciate some types of assets over 3 years, rather than 5 years. If a firm depreciates an asset more quickly, will its accounting profits in the first year after it buys the asset be increased or decreased?

3. Suppose that a firm's balance sheet is as follows:

ASSETS (DOLLARS)		LIABILITIES AND NET WORTH (DOLLARS)	
Current assets		Current liabilities	
Cash	200,000	Accounts payable	100,000
Inventory	300,000	Notes payable	_____
Fixed assets		Long-term liabilities	
Equipment	_____	Bonds	400,000
Buildings	800,000		
		Net worth	400,000
Total	2,000,000	Total	_____

Fill in the three blanks. What is the total amount that the firm owes? How much have the owners contributed? What is the difference between current assets and fixed assets?

4. Suppose that a firm's accounting profits for 1992 are $20,000. The firm is a proprietorship, and the owner worked 500 hours managing the business during 1992, for which she received no compensation other than the profits. If she could have gotten $10 an hour working for someone else, how much were her economic profits during 1992? Suppose that she also contributed $50,000 in capital to the firm, and that she could have obtained 6 percent interest on this capital if she had invested it elsewhere. In this case, how much were her economic profits?

SUMMARY

1. There are three principal types of business firms: proprietorships, partnerships, and corporations. The corporation has many advantages over the other two—limited liability, unlimited life, and greater ability to raise large sums of money. Nonetheless, because the corporation also has disadvantages, many firms are not corporations.

2. The corporation raises money by issuing various kinds of securities, of which three kinds—common stock, preferred stock, and bonds—are particularly important.

3. A relatively small number of giant corporations control a very substantial proportion of the total assets and employment in the American economy. In the large corporation, ownership and control tend to be separated.

4. As a first approximation, economists generally assume that firms attempt to maximize profits. In large part, this is because it is a close enough approximation to reality for many of the most important purposes of economics. Also, economists are interested in the theory of the profit-maximizing firm because it provides rules of behavior for firms that do want to maximize profits.

5. To summarize the characteristics of existing technology at a given point in time, the economist uses the concept of the production function, which shows the maximum output rate of a given commodity that can be achieved from any specified set of usage rates of inputs.

6. Accounting concepts are built around two very important statements: the balance sheet and the income statement. The balance sheet shows the nature of the firm's assets and liabilities at a given point in time. The difference between its assets and its liabilities is its net worth, which is the value of the firm's owners' claims against its assets.

7. A firm's income statement shows its sales during a particular period, its costs incurred in connection with these sales, and its profits during the period.

8. Economists define profits somewhat differently than accountants do. In defining profit, economists deduct the amount the owners could receive from the capital and labor they provide, if this capital and labor were used outside the firm. Also, economists are interested in longer periods than those to which accounting statements apply. Although the profit figures that are published almost always conform to the accountant's concept, the economist's concept is the more relevant one for many kinds of decisions.

CONCEPTS FOR REVIEW

Proprietorship	Dividends	Balance sheet
Partnership	Preferred stock	Current assets
Corporation	Bonds	Fixed assets
Board of directors	Profits	Net worth
Double taxation of income	Input	Income statement
Common stock	Production function	Depreciation

OPTIMAL INPUT DECISIONS BY BUSINESS FIRMS

FIRMS MUST CONSTANTLY TRY to determine whether they are using the most appropriate techniques. Take the steel industry. In 1991, Weirton and National Steel decided to use continuous casting, which transforms molten metal directly into slabs, to make all their steel. Nucor Corporation uses continuous casting to produce steel slabs 2 inches thick, cutting energy costs by 20–40 percent and slashing labor hours per ton of output in half. No decision a firm makes is more important than its choice of production technique.

In this chapter, we shall take a closer look at the decision-making process within the firm. Our discussion builds on the previous chapter, which dealt with the organization, motivation, and technology of the firm. We look in more detail at the firm's technology, and focus particular attention on the following central question: If a firm attempts to maximize profits, what production technique—that is, what combination of inputs—should it choose to produce a particular quantity of output? Two points should be noted at the outset. First, when finding the optimal input combination, we take as given the quantity of output that the firm will produce. In subsequent chapters, we shall discuss how the firm should choose this quantity. Second, just as one purpose of Chapters 4 and 5 was to show how a product's market demand curve can be derived, so an important purpose of Chapters 7 through 9 is to show how a product's market supply curve can be derived. In this chapter, we present some of the concepts and findings that are required for this purpose.

THE PRODUCTION FUNCTION REVISITED

If the Bethlehem Steel Corporation decides to produce a certain quantity of steel, it can do so in many ways. It can use open-hearth furnaces, or basic oxygen furnaces, or electric furnaces; it can use various types of iron ore; and it can use various types of coke. Which of these many ways will maximize Bethlehem Steel's profits? The management of Bethlehem Steel—and every business firm—devotes considerable time and energy to answering this kind of question. Let's restate it in the economist's terms. Given that a firm is going to produce a certain quantity of output, what production technique—i.e., what combination of inputs—should it choose to maximize its profits?

As a first step toward answering this question, it is wise to review the concept of the production function, taken up in the previous chapter. As you will recall, *the **production function** shows the most output that existing technology permits the firm to extract from each quantity of inputs.* Consider the hypothetical case of a wheat farm with 1 acre of land. The relationship between the amount of labor used per year by this farm and the farm's output is shown in Table 7.1. This is the farm's production function. It shows that the farm can produce 30 bushels of wheat per year if 1 unit of labor is used, 70 bushels of wheat per year if 2 units of labor are used, and so on.

The production function summarizes the characteristics of existing technology at a given point in time; it shows the technological constraints that a firm must reckon with. Like it or not, the most that the wheat farm in Table 7.1 can produce, if it uses 2 units of labor, is 70 bushels per year. This is the best that existing technology permits. Perhaps future advances in technology will permit such a farm (with 2 units of labor) to produce more than 70 bushels per year, but this presently cannot be done.

A Crude-Oil Pipeline: A Case Study

To illustrate what a production function looks like in a real case, let's consider a crude-oil pipeline that transports petroleum from oil fields and storage areas over hundreds of miles to major urban and industrial centers. We begin by noting that the output of such a pipeline is the amount of oil carried per day, and that the two principal inputs are the diameter of the pipeline and the horsepower applied to the oil carried. Both inputs are important. The bigger the diameter of the pipe, the more oil the pipeline can carry, holding constant the horsepower applied. And the greater the horsepower applied, the more oil the pipeline can carry, holding constant the diameter of the pipeline.

The production function shows the maximum output rate that can be derived from each combination of input rates. Thus, in this case, the production function shows the maximum amount of oil carried per day as a function of the pipeline's diameter and the amount of horsepower applied. On the basis of engineering estimates, one can derive the production function for crude-oil pipelines. Leslie Cookenboo of the Exxon Corporation derived such a production function, assuming that the pipeline carries Mid-Continent crude, has ¼-inch pipe throughout the lines, has lines 1,000 miles in length with a 5 percent terrain variation, and no net gravity flow in the line.[1] Some of his results are shown in Table 7.2. For example, the production function shows that if the diameter of the pipeline is 22 inches and the horsepower is 40,000, the pipeline can carry 215,000 barrels per day. Certainly, any firm operating a pipeline or considering the construction of one is vitally interested in such information. The production function plays a strategic role in the decision making of any firm.

TYPES OF INPUTS

As pointed out in the previous chapter, an input is anything that the firm uses in its production process. In analyzing production processes, we

[1] L. Cookenboo, "Production Functions and Cost Functions: A Case Study," in E. Mansfield (ed.), *Managerial Economics and Operations Research,* 5th ed., New York: Norton, 1987.

Table 7.1
Relationship between Labor Input and Output on 1-Acre Wheat Farm

NUMBER OF UNITS OF LABOR	BUSHELS OF WHEAT PRODUCED PER YEAR
0	0
1	30
2	70
3	100
4	125
5	145

Table 7.2
Production Function, Crude-Oil Pipeline

LINE DIAMETER (INCHES)	HORSEPOWER (THOUSANDS)				
	20	30	40	50	60
	Output rate (thousands of barrels per day)				
14	70	90	95	100	104
18	115	140	155	165	170
22	160	190	215	235	250
26	220	255	290	320	340

suppose that all inputs can be classified into two categories: fixed and variable.

A **fixed input** *is one whose quantity cannot change during the period of time under consideration*. This period will vary. It may be six months in one case, six years in another case. Among the most important inputs often included as fixed are the firm's plant and equipment—that is, its factory and office buildings, its machinery, its tooling, and its transportation facilities. In the simple example of the wheat farm in Table 7.1, land is a fixed input since its quantity is assumed to be fixed at 1 acre.

A **variable input** *is one whose quantity can be changed during the relevant period*. It is generally possible to increase or decrease the number of workers engaged in a particular activity (although this is not always the case, since they may have long-term contracts). Similarly, it frequently is possible to alter the amount of raw material that is used. In the case of the wheat farm in Table 7.1, labor clearly is a variable input since its quantity can be varied from 0 to 5 units.

THE SHORT RUN AND THE LONG RUN

Whether an input is considered variable or fixed depends on the length of the period under consideration. The longer the period, the more inputs are variable, not fixed. Although the length of the period varies from case to case, economists have found it very useful to focus special attention on two time periods: the short run and the long run. *The* **short run** *is defined as the period of time in which at least one of the firm's inputs is fixed*. More specifically, since the firm's plant and equipment are among the most difficult inputs to change quickly, *the short run is generally understood to mean the length of time during which the firm's plant and equipment are fixed*. On the other hand, *the* **long run** *is that period of time in which all inputs are variable*. In the long run, the firm can make a complete adjustment to any change in its environment.

To illustrate the distinction between the short run and the long run, let's consider the General Motors Corporation. Any period of time during which GM's plant and equipment cannot be altered freely is the short run. A period of one year is certainly a case of the short run, because in a year GM could not vary the quantity of its plant and equipment. It takes longer than a year to construct an automotive plant, or to alter an existing plant to produce a new kind of automobile. For example, the tooling phase of the model changeover cycle has often taken about 2 years. Also, because some of its existing contracts with suppliers and workers extend for more than a year, GM cannot vary all its inputs in a year without violating these contracts. On the other hand, any period of time during which GM can vary the quantity of all inputs is the long run. A period of 50 years is certainly a case of the long run. Whether a shorter period of time—10 years, say—is a long-run situation depends on the problem at hand. If all the relevant inputs can be varied, it is a long-run situation; if not, it is a short-run situation.

A useful way to look at the long run is to consider it a *planning horizon*. While operating in the short run, the firm must continually be planning ahead and deciding its strategy in the long run. Its decisions concerning the long run determine the sort of short-run position the firm will occupy in the future. Before a firm makes the decision to add a new type of product to its line, the firm is in a long-run situation (with regard

General Motors headquarters

to the new product), since it can choose among a wide variety of types and sizes of equipment to produce the new product. But once the investment is made, the firm is confronted with a short-run situation, since the type and size of equipment is, to a considerable extent, frozen.

AVERAGE PRODUCT OF AN INPUT

In order to determine which production technique—that is, which combination of inputs—a firm should use, it is necessary to define the average product and marginal product of an input. *The **average product** of an input is the firm's total output divided by the amount of input used to produce this amount of output.* The average product of an input can be calculated from the production function. Consider the wheat farm in Table 7.1. The average product of labor is 30 bushels per unit of labor when 1 unit of labor is used, 35 bushels per unit of labor when 2 units are used, 33⅓ bushels per unit of labor when 3 units are used, and so forth.

MARGINAL PRODUCT OF AN INPUT

As the amount of labor used on the farm increases, so does the farm's output, but the amount of extra output from the addition of an extra unit of labor varies depending on how much labor is already being used. The extra output from the addition of the first unit of labor is 30 − 0 = 30 bushels per unit of labor. The extra output due to the addition of the second unit of labor is 70 − 30 = 40 bushels per unit of labor. And the extra output from the addition of the fifth unit of labor is 145 − 125 = 20 bushels per unit of labor. *The **marginal product** of an input is the addition to total output due to the addition of the last unit of input, the quantity of other inputs used being held constant.* Thus the marginal product of labor is 30 bushels when between 0 and 1 units of labor are used, 40 bushels when between 1 and 2 units of labor are used, and so on.

The concept of marginal product is analogous to that of marginal utility, which we discussed in Chapter 5. Recall that marginal utility is the extra utility resulting from an additional unit of a commodity. Substitute "output" for "utility" and "an input" for "a commodity" in the previous sentence, and you get a perfectly valid definition of marginal product. Economics is chock full of marginal "thises" and marginal "thats," and it is important that you become aware of their general family traits.

Table 7.3 shows the average and marginal products of labor at various levels of utilization of labor; Figure 7.1 shows the same thing graphically. The data in both Table 7.3 and Figure 7.1 concerning the average and marginal products of labor are derived from the production function. Given the production function, shown in Table 7.1 and reproduced in Table 7.3, the average and marginal products at each level of utilization of labor can be determined in the way we have indicated.

In Figure 7.1, as in the case of most production processes, the average product of the variable input—labor in this case—rises, reaches a maximum, and then falls. The marginal product of labor also rises, reaches a maximum, and falls. This too is typical of many production processes. Why do average product and marginal product behave in this way? Because of the law of diminishing marginal returns, to which we now turn.

Table 7.3
Average and Marginal Products of Labor, 1-Acre Wheat Farm

NUMBER OF UNITS OF LABOR	TOTAL OUTPUT (BUSHELS PER YEAR)	MARGINAL PRODUCT (BUSHELS PER UNIT OF LABOR)	AVERAGE PRODUCT (BUSHELS PER UNIT OF LABOR)
0	0		—
1	30	30	30
2	70	40	35
3	100	30	33⅓
4	125	25	31¼
5	145	20	29

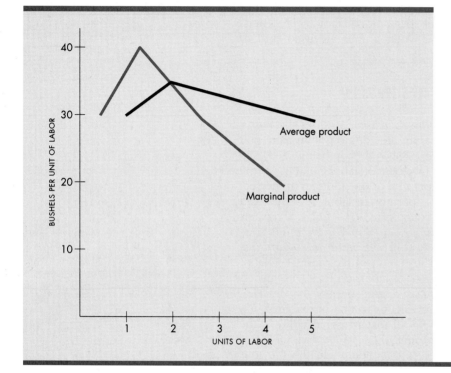

Figure 7.1
Average and Marginal Products of Labor, 1-Acre Wheat Farm
The marginal product of the first unit of labor (which, according to Table 7.3, equals 30 bushels per unit of labor) is plotted at the midpoint between 0 and 1 units of labor. The marginal product of the second unit of labor is plotted at the midpoint between 1 and 2 units of labor. The marginal product curve connects these and other points showing the marginal product of various amounts of labor.

The average product curve shows the average product of labor when various amounts of labor are used. As the graph shows, both the average product and the marginal product of labor rise, reach a maximum, and then fall.

THE LAW OF DIMINISHING MARGINAL RETURNS

Perhaps the best-known—and certainly one of the least understood—laws of economics is the so-called **law of diminishing marginal returns.** Put in a single sentence, this law states that *if equal increments of an input are added, the quantities of other inputs being held constant, the resulting increments of product will decrease beyond some point;* that is, the marginal product of the input will diminish.

Suppose that a small factory that manufactures a metal automobile component has eight machine tools. If this firm hires only one or two workers, total output and output per worker will be quite low. These workers will have a number of quite different tasks to perform, and the advantages of specialization will be sacrificed. Workers will spend considerable time switching from one machine to another, and many of the eight machine tools will be idle much of the time. What happens as the firm increases its work force? As more and more workers are added, the marginal product (that is, the extra product) of each will tend to rise, as the work force grows to the point where it can man the fixed amount of equipment effectively. However, if the firm continues to increase the number of workers, the marginal product of a worker will eventually begin to decrease. Why? Because workers will have to wait in line to use the fixed number of machine tools, and because the extra workers will have to be assigned to less and less important tasks: Eventually, if enough workers are hired (and utilized within the plant), they may get in each other's way to such an extent that production may grind to a halt.

Returning to the wheat farm discussed in the previous section, Table 7.3 shows that the law of diminishing marginal returns applies in this case too. The third column of this table indicates that, beyond 2 units of labor, the marginal product of labor falls. Certainly, it seems entirely reasonable that, as more and more of a variable input (in this case, labor) is combined with a fixed amount of another input (in this case, land), the additional output to be derived from an additional unit of the variable input will eventually decrease. In the case of a 1-acre wheat farm, one would expect that, as more and more labor is added, the extra workers' functions eventually would become less and less important and productive.

The law of diminishing marginal returns plays a major part in determining the firm's optimal input combination and the shape of the firm's cost functions, as we shall see in this and the next chapter. To prevent misunderstanding and confusion, several points about this law should be stressed. First, *it is assumed that technology remains fixed*. If technology changes, the law of diminishing marginal returns cannot predict the effect of an additional unit of input. Second, *at least one input must be fixed in*

EXAMPLE 7.1   PRODUCTION THEORY IN THE MILKING SHED

According to the U.S. Department of Agriculture, the relationship between a cow's total output of milk and the amount of grain it is fed is as follows:

AMOUNT OF GRAIN (POUNDS)	AMOUNT OF MILK (POUNDS)
1,200	5,917
1,800	7,250
2,400	8,379
3,000	9,371

Forage input is assumed to be fixed at 6,500 pounds of hay.

(a) What is the average product of grain when each amount is used? (b) Should a milk producer feed a cow the amount of grain that will maximize its aver-

age product? Why, or why not? (c) What is the marginal product of grain when between 1,200 and 1,800 pounds are fed; when between 1,800 and 2,400 pounds are fed; and when between 2,400 and 3,000 pounds are fed? (d) Does this production function exhibit diminishing marginal returns?

Solution

(a) At 1,200 pounds, it is 4.93; at 1,800 pounds, it is 4.03; at 2,400 pounds, it is 3.49; and at 3,000 pounds, it is 3.12 pounds of milk per pound of grain. (b) No, because this generally will not maximize profit, as we shall see in subsequent discussions. (c) 2.22, 1.88, and 1.65 pounds of milk per pound of grain. (d) Yes. The marginal product of grain decreases as more of it is used.

quantity, since the law of diminishing marginal returns is not applicable to cases where there is a proportional increase in all inputs. Third, *it must be possible to vary the proportions in which the various inputs are utilized.* This is generally possible in industry and agriculture.

TEST YOURSELF

1. Suppose that a firm has the following production function:

HOURS OF LABOR PER YEAR (THOUSANDS)	OUTPUT PER YEAR (THOUSANDS)
0	0
1	2
2	8
3	12
4	14
5	15

Plot on a graph the marginal product of labor at various levels of utilization of labor.

2. Using the data in Question 1, plot the average product of labor at various levels of utilization of labor.

3. A tool and die shop has three types of inputs: labor, machines, and materials. It cannot obtain additional machines in less than 6 months. In the next month, do you think that labor is a fixed or variable input? Do you think that machines are a fixed or variable input? Explain.

4. The tool and die shop in Question 3 expands its use of all three types of inputs. The owner of the shop worries that by doing so the firm may encounter diminishing marginal returns. Is this a legitimate concern? Why, or why not?

THE OPTIMAL INPUT DECISION

Now we are in a position to answer the question posed at the beginning of this chapter: Given that a firm is going to produce a particular quantity of output, what production technique—i.e., what combination of inputs—should it choose to maximize profits? Note first that if the firm maximizes its profits, it must minimize the cost of producing this quantity of output. This seems obvious enough. But what combination of inputs (that will produce the required quantity of output) will minimize the firm's costs?

A firm will minimize cost by combining inputs in such a way that the marginal product of a dollar's worth of any one input equals the marginal product of a dollar's worth of any other input used. Another way to say the same thing is: *The firm will minimize cost by combining inputs in such a way that, for every input used, the marginal product of the input is proportional to its price.* Why does this say the same thing? Because the marginal product of a dollar's worth of an input equals the marginal product of the input divided by its price. If the marginal product of a unit of labor is 40 units of output, and if the price of labor is $8,000 per unit, the marginal product of a dollar's worth of labor is 40 ÷ 8,000 = .005 units of output. Thus, if the firm is combining inputs so that the marginal product of a dollar's worth of any one input equals the marginal product of a dollar's worth of any other input used, it must at the same time be combining inputs so that, for every input used, the marginal product of the input is proportional to its price.

Consider the wheat farm cited above. Suppose that the farm can vary the amount of labor it uses. Table 7.4 shows the marginal product of each input when various combinations of inputs (all combinations being able

Table 7.4
Determination of Optimal Input Combination

| AMOUNT OF INPUT USED | | MARGINAL PRODUCT | | MARGINAL PRODUCT ÷ PRICE OF INPUT | | TOTAL COSTS |
LABOR (UNITS)	LAND (ACRES)	LABOR	LAND	LABOR	LAND	(DOLLARS)
0.5	7.0	50	5	50 ÷ 8,000	5 ÷ 2,000	18,000
1.0	4.1	40	10	40 ÷ 8,000	10 ÷ 2,000	16,200
1.5	3.0	30	30	30 ÷ 8,000	30 ÷ 2,000	18,000
2.5	2.0	20	50	20 ÷ 8,000	50 ÷ 2,000	24,000

to produce the specified quantity of output) are used. Suppose that the price of labor is $8,000 per unit and that the annual price of using land is $2,000 per acre. (We assume that the firm takes the prices of inputs as given and that it can buy all it wants of the inputs at these prices.) For each combination of inputs, Table 7.4 shows the marginal product of each input divided by its price. Based on our rule, the optimal input combination is 4.1 acres of land and 1 unit of labor, since this is the only combination (capable of producing the required output) where the marginal product of labor divided by the price of labor equals the marginal product of land divided by the price of land. (See Table 7.4.)

Is this rule correct? Does it really result in a least-cost combination of inputs? Let's look at the cost of the various input combinations in Table 7.4. The first combination (0.5 units of labor and 7 acres of land) costs $18,000; the second combination (1.0 units of labor and 4.1 acres of land) costs $16,200; and so on. An examination of the total cost of each input combination shows that the input combination chosen by our rule—1.0 units of labor and 4.1 acres of land—is indeed the least-cost input combination, the one for the profit-maximizing firm to use.

A MORE GENERAL PROOF OF THE RULE

One example really does not prove that the rule results in minimum costs; it only demonstrates that it does so in this particular case. In this section, we prove that this rule generally is valid. To do so, we show that, if this rule is violated (and the firm combines inputs so that the marginal product of a dollar's worth of one input does *not* equal the marginal product of a dollar's worth of some other input used), the firm is not minimizing its costs. Specifically, we take the case of the wheat farm, and proceed in two steps. (1) We show that if the marginal product of a dollar's worth of labor is *greater* than the marginal product of a dollar's worth of land, the firm is not minimizing costs. (2) We show that if the marginal product of a dollar's worth of labor is *less* than the marginal product of a dollar's worth of land, the firm is not minimizing costs.

Suppose that *the marginal product of a dollar's worth of labor is greater than the marginal product of a dollar's worth of land*. Since the marginal product of a dollar's worth of labor is greater than the marginal product of a dollar's worth of land, it must follow that the wheat farm can increase its output, *without increasing its costs,* if it substitutes a dollar's worth of labor for a dollar's worth of land. Suppose that the marginal product of a dollar's worth of labor is 2 bushels of wheat, whereas the marginal product of a dollar's worth of land is 1 bushel of wheat. Then, if it substitutes a

HOW TO MAKE MONEY IN REAL ESTATE BY LOGIC ALONE

One of the most common errors made by decision makers is that they do not ignore sunk costs. What is a sunk cost? It is a cost that has been incurred in the past and that cannot be altered or affected by any action the decision maker can take. For example, suppose that a real estate investor signs an agreement to buy a lot. The purchase price is $20,000. He makes a $5,000 down payment and will pay the remaining $15,000 in six months. Under the terms of the agreement, he will not secure title to the lot until he has paid the entire $20,000. If he fails to make the remaining payment of $15,000, the agreement states that he will lose his down payment, but he is not liable for the unpaid balance.

After buying this lot, and making the $5,000 down payment, the real estate investor travels to another city where he finds a lot which is just as desirable from his point of view as the one he has bought. Because the real estate market in this city is depressed, the price of this lot is $14,000. The real estate investor wishes that he had seen this lot before purchasing the other one, but feels that there is nothing he can do. He only wants one such lot and, if he were to back out of the purchase agreement he signed, he would lose $5,000. Clearly, he doesn't want to incur such a loss!

But the real estate investor is committing a cardinal sin: he is not ignoring a sunk cost. Regardless of

which lot he purchases, he loses the $5,000. Thus the $5,000 is a sunk cost. The real question is whether he will pay an *additional* $15,000 for the lot on which he has paid the down payment or whether he will pay an *additional* $14,000 for the lot he has seen more recently. Put in this way, there is no doubt about the proper course of action: he should ignore the $5,000 sunk cost, and buy the lot for $14,000. In this way, the total cost (including the sunk cost) is $19,000, which is less than the price of the lot he originally intended to purchase.

---

dollar's worth of labor for a dollar's worth of land, the wheat farm can increase its output by 1 bushel of wheat without increasing its costs. (Why? Because the addition of an extra dollar's worth of labor increases output by 2 bushels, while the subtraction of the dollar's worth of land reduces output by 1 bushel—and the net effect is an increase in output of 1 bushel.) Thus, since the firm can increase its output without increasing its costs, it must be able to reduce its costs, if it maintains the same output. In other words, it must not be minimizing its costs.

Suppose that *the marginal product of a dollar's worth of labor is less than the marginal product of a dollar's worth of land.* Since the marginal product of a dollar's worth of labor is less than the marginal product of a dollar's worth of land, it must follow that the wheat farm can increase its output, *without increasing its costs,* if it substitutes a dollar's worth of land for a dollar's worth of labor. Suppose that the marginal product of a dollar's worth of labor is 1 bushel of wheat, whereas the marginal product of a dollar's worth of land is 2 bushels of wheat. Then, if it substitutes a dollar's worth of land for a dollar's worth of labor, the wheat farm can increase its output by 1 bushel of wheat without increasing its costs. (Why? Because the addition of an extra dollar's worth of land increases output by 2 bushels, while the subtraction of a dollar's worth of labor reduces output by 1 bushel—and the net effect is an increase in output of 1 bushel.) Thus, since the firm can increase its output without increasing its costs, it must be able to reduce its costs, if it maintains the same output. In other words, it must not be minimizing its costs.

Since the firm is not minimizing the cost of producing its current output when the marginal product of a dollar's worth of labor is greater than, or less than, that of a dollar's worth of land, it must be true that *the firm is minimizing its cost only when the marginal product of a dollar's worth of labor equals that of a dollar's worth of land.* This is what we set out to prove.

PRODUCING KANSAS CORN: A CASE STUDY

If by now you wonder about the practical payoff from this sort of analysis, consider how a distinguished agricultural economist, Earl Heady of Iowa State University, used these methods to help farmers make better production decisions. Table 7.5 shows the various amounts of land and fertilizer that will produce 82.6 bushels of corn on Kansas Verdigras soil. As you can see, this amount of corn can be produced if 1.19 acres of land and no fertilizer are used, or if 1.11 acres of land and 20 pounds of fertilizer are used, or if .99 acres of land and 60 pounds of fertilizer are used, and so forth.

The third column of Table 7.5 shows the ratio of the marginal product of a pound of fertilizer to the marginal product of an acre of land, when each of these input combinations is used. For example, when 1.19 acres of land and no fertilizer are used, this ratio equals .0045. Based on the rule discussed in previous sections, a firm, if it minimizes costs, must set this ratio equal to the ratio of the price of a pound of fertilizer to the price of an acre of land. Why? Because the rule discussed above stipulates that the firm should choose an input combination so that

$$\frac{\text{marginal product of fertilizer}}{\text{price of fertilizer}} = \frac{\text{marginal product of land}}{\text{price of land}}.$$

So if we multiply both sides of this equation by the price of fertilizer, and divide both sides by the marginal product of land, we get

$$\frac{\text{marginal product of fertilizer}}{\text{marginal product of land}} = \frac{\text{price of fertilizer}}{\text{price of land}}.$$

Thus, to minimize costs, a firm should set the ratio in the third column of Table 7.5 equal to the ratio of the price of fertilizer to the price of land.

Heady and his coworkers, having obtained the results in Table 7.5, used this technique to determine the optimal input combination farmers should use to minimize their costs.[2] The optimal input combination de-

---

[2] It is assumed that a certain amount of labor is used, this amount being proportional to the number of acres of land.

Table 7.5
Combinations of Fertilizer and Land Required to Produce 82.6 Bushels of Corn, and Ratio of Marginal Products at Each Such Combination

AMOUNT OF INPUT USED		MARGINAL PRODUCT OF FERTILIZER ÷ MARGINAL PRODUCT OF LAND
FERTILIZER (POUNDS)	LAND (ACRES)	
0	1.19	.0045
20	1.11	.0038
40	1.04	.0030
60	0.99	.0019
80	0.96	.0010
100	0.95	.0003

THE COCA-COLA COMPANY AND THE PRICES OF INPUTS

In 1985 the Coca-Cola company made a well-publicized change in its formula for Coke. The company touted the change with a huge marketing campaign. In fact, the formula for Coke had been quietly changed six years earlier.

Because of worldwide shortages, the price of beet and cane sugar jumped from 19 cents per pound in September 1978 to 26 cents per pound in January 1979. While such a price hike does not dramatically affect most sugar buyers, for Coke it was catastrophic. A change of 1 cent per pound in sugar prices can cause a $20 million swing in Coke's operating profits. The bottling empire is America's largest sugar buyer, taking a million tons per year or about 10 percent of all the sugar sold in the United States.

Because of the efficiencies of corn production in this country, a sweetener made by refining corn into sugar makes high-fructose corn sweeteners about 10 percent cheaper than beet and cane sugar when prices are normal. By using a 55 percent fructose sweetener, Coca-Cola can realize substantial cost savings, particularly when sugar prices are abnormally high. Coke publicly announced the switch to corn sweeteners in January 1979, but other than sugar producers and traders, no one seemed to notice. Eight months later, 7-Up followed suit and decided to increase its use of corn sweeteners, and Pepsi also considered such a move.

The response of the soft drink companies to the high price of sugar is typical of any firm faced with a high-priced input. Firms try to reduce the use of expensive inputs in order to maintain profits or to avoid having to raise the price of their products (and risk losing sales to competitors). The higher the price of an input, the more incentive there is for a profit-maximizing firm to conserve on its use of that input.

N.B.

pends on the price of land and the price of fertilizer. Suppose that a pound of fertilizer costs .003 times as much as an acre of land. Under these circumstances, the minimum-cost input combination would be 40 pounds of fertilizer and 1.04 acres of land—since, as shown in Table 7.5, this is the input combination where the ratio of the marginal product of fertilizer to the marginal product of land is .003. No matter what the ratio of the price of fertilizer to the price of land may be, the least-cost input combination can be derived this way.

Such results are of considerable practical value to farmers. Moreover, the same kind of analysis can be used by organizations in other sectors of the economy. not just agriculture. Studies of how the Defense Department could reduce its costs have utilized concepts and techniques of essentially this sort. In a more peaceful vein, this same kind of analysis has been used in various kinds of manufacturing firms. For example, steel firms have made many such studies to determine least-cost ways to produce steel, and auto firms have made similar studies to reduce their costs.

TEST YOURSELF

1. Suppose that a cost-minimizing firm in a perfectly competitive market uses two inputs: labor and capital. If the marginal product of capital is twice the marginal product of labor, and if the price of a unit of labor is $4, what must be the price of a unit of capital?

2. In Figure 7.1 the marginal product of labor equals its average product when the latter is a maximum. Do you think that this is generally the case? Why, or why not? (*Hint:* if the marginal product of an extra amount of labor exceeds the average product, will the average product increase? If it is less than the average product, will the average product decrease?)

3. A firm uses two inputs: capital and labor. The firm's chief engineer says that its output depends in the following way on the amount of labor and capital it uses:

$$Q = 3L + 4C,$$

where Q is the number of units of output produced per day, L is the number of units of labor used per day, and C is the amount of capital used per day. Does this relationship seem sensible? Why, or why not?

4. In the previous problem, suppose that the price of using a unit of labor per day is $50 and the price of using a unit of capital per day is $100. What is the optimal input combination for the firm, if the relationship in the previous problem is valid? Does this seem reasonable? Why, or why not?

SUMMARY

1. Inputs can be classified into two categories: fixed and variable. A fixed input is one whose quantity cannot be changed during the period of time under consideration. A variable input is one whose quantity can be changed during the relevant period.

2. Whether an input is considered variable or fixed depends on the length of the period under consideration. The longer the period, the more inputs are variable, not fixed. The short run is defined as the period of time in which some of the firm's inputs (generally its plant and equipment) are fixed. The long run is the period of time in which all inputs are variable.

3. The average product of an input is the firm's total output divided by the amount of input used to produce this amount of output. The marginal product of an input is the addition to total output due to the addition of the last unit of input, the quantity of other inputs used being held constant.

4. The law of diminishing marginal returns states that if equal increments of an input are added (and the quantities of other inputs are held constant), the resulting increments of product will decrease beyond some point; that is, the marginal product of the input will diminish.

5. To minimize its costs, a firm must choose its input combination so that the marginal product of a dollar's worth of any one input equals the marginal product of a dollar's worth of any other input used. Put differently, the firm should combine inputs so that, for every input used, the marginal product of the input is proportional to its price.

CONCEPTS FOR REVIEW

Production function

Fixed input

Variable input

*** Isoquant**

Short run

Long run

Average product

***Isocost curve**

Marginal product

Law of diminishing marginal returns

---

* This concept is presented in the Appendix to this chapter.

APPENDIX: ISOQUANTS, ISOCOST CURVES, AND THE OPTIMAL INPUT COMBINATION

In this Appendix, we present a somewhat different way of finding a firm's optimal input combination. This approach is based on the use of isoquants and isocost curves.

Isoquants

In the case of a crude-oil pipeline, a given amount of oil can be carried per day either by using a large diameter of pipe and relatively small horsepower or by using a smaller diameter of pipe and greater horsepower. Similar opportunities to vary inputs to achieve a given output rate exist in practically all industries. To describe these opportunities, economists use the concept of an isoquant. An ***isoquant*** *is a curve showing all possible efficient combinations of inputs capable of producing a certain quantity of output.* An *inefficient* combination of inputs is one that includes more of at least one input, and as much as other inputs, as some other combination of inputs that can produce the same quantity of output. Inefficient combinations cannot minimize costs or maximize profits. On a wheat farm, it may be possible to produce 1 unit of output with 2 units of land and 3 units of labor. It may also be possible to produce 1 unit of output with 3 units of land and 3 units of labor. The second input combination—which is inefficient—cannot be the least-cost input combination, so long as land has a *positive* price. Only *efficient* input combinations are worth bothering with in the present circumstances, and they alone are included in an isoquant.

There is an isoquant pertaining to each level of production. Figure 7.2 shows some isoquants for a wheat farm. These isoquants show the various combinations of inputs that can produce 100, 200, and 300 bushels of wheat per period of time. Consider the isoquant for 100 bushels of wheat per period of time. According to this isoquant, the farm can attain this output rate if OL_1 units of labor and OD_1 units of land are used per period of time. Alternatively, this output rate can be attained with OL_2 units of labor and OD_2 units of land—or OL_3 units of labor and OD_3 units of land—per period of time.

The shape and position of a firm's isoquants are derived from the firm's production function. Indeed, one way to represent the firm's production function is by showing its isoquants. Thus the firm's isoquants, like its production function, show the firm's technological possibilities—the various efficient input-output combinations that can be achieved with existing technology. The shape of an isoquant is typically like that shown in Figure 7.2; that is, it slopes downward to the right, but *its slope becomes less and less steep.*

To illustrate what isoquants in an actual firm look like, consider once again our crude-oil pipeline. Figure 7.3 shows the isoquants corresponding to 100,000, 200,000, and 300,000 barrels of crude oil carried per day. For example, the isoquant corresponding to 100,000 barrels per day shows all the combinations of line diameter and horsepower that permit a pipeline to carry 100,000 barrels per day (for 1,000 miles). Note that each of these isoquants slopes downward to the right. Moreover, comparing these isoquants with Table 7.2, you can readily see that, if Table 7.2 contained more detailed data on the production function, it would be simple to derive the isoquants from the data regarding the production func-

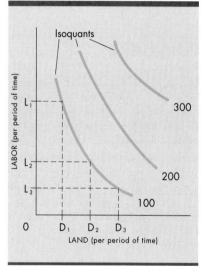

Figure 7.2
Isoquants, Wheat Farm
An isoquant shows all possible efficient combinations of inputs capable of producing a certain quantity of output. These isoquants show the various combinations of inputs that can produce 100, 200, and 300 bushels of wheat per period of time. For example, 100 bushels of wheat can be produced with OL_1 units of labor and OD_1 units of land, with OL_2 units of labor and OD_2 units of land, or with OL_3 units of labor and OD_3 units of land.

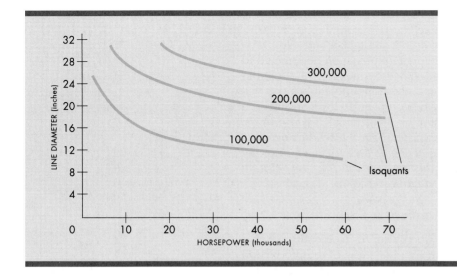

Figure 7.3
Isoquants for 100,000, 200,000 and 300,000 Barrels of Crude Oil Carried per Day, Crude-Oil Pipeline
This graph shows the isoquants in an actual case. Note that they are shaped as economic theory would predict.

tion in Table 7.2. How? By determining from this more detailed version of Table 7.2 the various input combinations that can produce each output rate. For example, to derive the isoquant corresponding to 100,000 barrels of crude oil carried per day, one could determine from such a table the various input combinations that can produce this output rate.

Isocost Curves and the Optimal Input Decision

To determine the combination of inputs that will minimize the firm's costs, one can use the isoquant concept. All input combinations that can efficiently produce the specified level of output can be represented by the isoquant corresponding to this level of output. For example, the isoquant in Figure 7.4 shows all the input combinations a wheat farm can use to produce a certain amount of wheat. The optimal input combination must lie on this isoquant, but where? A simple way to determine the optimal input combination is to draw a number of *isocost curves,* as shown in Figure 7.4. *Each isocost curve shows the input combinations the firm can obtain for a given expenditure.* Consider the isocost curves corresponding to expenditures of $12,000, $16,200, and $20,000, shown in Figure 7.4.

In Figure 7.4 the price of labor is $8,000 per unit, and the annual price of using land is $2,000 per acre. Given the price of each input, it is a simple matter to draw each isocost curve. Take the case of the isocost curve corresponding to annual expenditures of $12,000. If this expenditure were devoted entirely to labor, 1½ units of labor could be hired. Thus this isocost curve must cut the horizontal axis in Figure 7.4 at 1½ units of labor. Similarly, if this expenditure were devoted entirely to land, 6 acres of land could be hired. Thus this isocost curve must cut the vertical axis at 6 acres of land. Finally, if we connect the point where the isocost curve cuts the vertical axis to the point where it cuts the horizontal axis, we obtain the entire isocost curve.

Given both the isoquant and the isocost curves, one can readily determine the input combination that will minimize the firm's costs. This input combination corresponds to *that point on the isoquant that lies on the lowest isocost curve*—in other words, point A in Figure 7.4. Input combinations on lower isocost curves (like that corresponding to $12,000) that lie

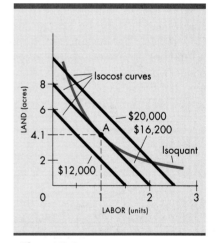

Figure 7.4
Least-Cost Input Combination
The least-cost input combination is at point A, where 4.1 acres of land and 1 unit of labor are used. The isoquant shows all input combinations that can be used to produce the required amount of wheat, and the isocost curves show the input combinations costing $12,000, $16,200, and $20,000, respectively.

below *A* are cheaper than *A*, but cannot produce the desired output. Input combinations on isocost curves (like that corresponding to $20,000) that lie above *A* will produce the desired output at a higher cost than *A*.

What is the relationship between the input combination determined in this way and the input combination determined by means of the rule described on page 132? Reassuringly enough, these input combinations will always be the same, since the rule described on page 132 will always give the same answer as the geometric technique. In general, *if you find the combination of inputs where the marginal product of a dollar's worth of any one input equals the marginal product of a dollar's worth of any other input used, this will give you the same answer as if you find the point on the isoquant that lies on the lowest isocost curve.*

Finding the Optimal Input Combination: A Case Study

To illustrate the use of isoquants and isocost curves to identify optimal input combinations, let's go back to Earl Heady's study of the production of corn, discussed on page 135. Figure 7.5 shows an isoquant that Heady and his coworkers estimated from the production of corn on Kansas Verdigras soil. This isoquant shows the amounts of land and fertilizer that will produce 82.6 bushels of corn. It indicates that this amount of corn can be produced if 1.19 acres of land and no fertilizer are used, or if 1.11 acres of land and 20 pounds of fertilizer are used, or if .99 acres of land and 60 pounds of fertilizer are used, and so forth. (The same data are shown in Table 7.5.)

After estimating isoquants of this sort, Heady and his coworkers derived the optimal input combination farmers should use to minimize their costs. Suppose that a pound of fertilizer costs .003 times as much as an acre of land. Then the isocost curves would be as shown in Figure 7.5. Under these circumstances, the minimum-cost combination would be 40 pounds of fertilizer and 1.04 acres of land. (This finding agrees with the results obtained on page 136, where we took up this same case.) No matter what the ratio of the price of fertilizer to the price of land may be, the least-cost input combination can be derived this way.

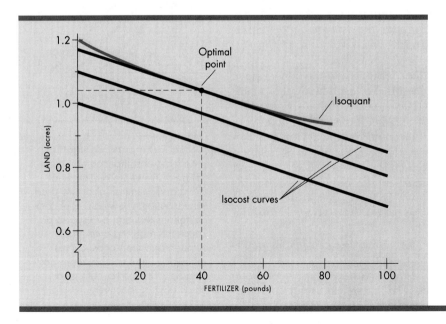

**Figure 7.5
Isoquant for the Production of 82.6 Bushels of Corn in Kansas**
This graph shows how economic analysis has been used to help farmers make better production decisions. Given the assumed conditions, the optimal input combination would be 40 pounds of fertilizer and 1.04 acres of land.

COST ANALYSIS

WELL OVER 10 MILLION people subscribe to cable television. An important question facing both government officials and the cable operators themselves is whether it is efficient for more than one firm to provide cable television in a particular city. Does the cost per subscriber of providing cable television go down markedly as a firm gains more and more subscribers? If so, it is less costly for a single firm to provide cable television than to have two or more firms share the market. But since this single firm would have substantial power over the price it charges subscribers, some have argued that, if costs go down markedly, this single firm should be regulated in various ways by government agencies.

This example illustrates the major role played by a firm's costs in many issues facing the government and the public at large—as well, of course, as the firms themselves. In this chapter, we discuss the nature of costs, describe the various cost functions of the firm, and indicate some of the ways that these cost functions can be measured and used. Among the major questions taken up are: What do we mean by a firm's costs? How do various types of costs vary with the firm's output rate? Of what significance or use are the relationships between a firm's output and its various types of cost? These questions are of the utmost importance, both for the managers of a firm and for society as a whole.

WHAT ARE COSTS?

The previous chapter discussed how we can determine the input combination that minimizes costs. But what do we mean by costs?

Although this question may seem foolishly simple, it is in fact tricky. *Fundamentally, the cost of a certain course of action is the value of the best alternative course of action that could have been adopted instead.* The cost of producing automobiles is the value of the goods and services that could be obtained from the resources used currently in automobile production if these resources were no longer used to produce automobiles. In general, the costs of inputs to a firm are their values in their most valuable alternative uses. As we pointed out in Chapter 1, this is the so-called **opportunity cost,** or **alternative cost** doctrine.

Suppose that a firm's owner devotes 50 hours a week to the firm's business, and that, because he is the owner, he pays himself no salary.

According to the usual rules of accounting, as we saw in Chapter 6, the costs of his labor are not included in the firm's income statement. But according to the economist's opportunity cost doctrine, the cost of his labor is by no means zero! Instead, this cost equals whatever amount he could obtain if he worked 50 hours a week for someone else. Both economists and sophisticated accountants agree that opportunity costs are the relevant costs for many types of problems, and that failure to use the proper concept of cost can result in serious mistakes.

Costs for the individual firm are the necessary payments to the owners of resources to get them to provide these resources to the firm. To obtain these resources as inputs, the firm must bid them away from alternative uses. The payments made to the owners of these resources may be either explicit or implicit costs. If a payment is made to a supplier, laborer, or some other resource owner besides the firm's owner, this is an explicit cost, which is paid for in an explicit way. But if a resource is owned by the firm's owner, there may be no explicit payment for it, as in the case of the labor of the owner who paid himself no salary. *The costs of such owner-supplied resources are called* ***implicit costs.*** As we stressed above, such implicit costs equal what these resources could bring if they were used in their most valuable alternative employments. And the firm's profits (or losses), as defined by the economist, are the difference between the firm's revenues and its total costs, both explicit and implicit.

SHORT-RUN COST FUNCTIONS

In the previous chapter, we showed how to determine the least-cost combination of inputs to produce any quantity of output. With this information at our disposal, it is easy to determine the minimum cost of producing each quantity of output. *Knowing the (minimum) cost of producing each quantity of output, we can define and measure the firm's* ***cost functions,*** *which show how various types of costs are related to the firm's output.* A firm's cost functions will vary, depending on whether they are based on the short or long run. In the short run, the firm cannot vary the quantities of plant and equipment it uses. These are the firm's fixed inputs, and they determine the scale of its operations.

Total Fixed Cost

Three kinds of costs are important in the short run—total fixed cost, total variable cost, and total cost. ***Total fixed cost*** *is the total expenditure per period of time by the firm for fixed inputs.* Since the quantity of the fixed inputs is unvarying (by definition), the total fixed cost will be the same whatever the firm's level of output. Among the firm's fixed costs in the short run are property taxes and interest on bonds issued in the past. If the firm has contracts with suppliers and workers that cannot be renegotiated (without dire consequences) in the short run, the expenses involved in meeting these contracts are also fixed costs.

To inject a whimsical note into a subject not otherwise noted for its amusement value, consider a hypothetical firm—the Bugsbane Music Box Company. This firm produces a high-priced line of music boxes that, when opened, play your favorite aria, show tune, or hymn, and emit a deadly gas that kills all insects, rodents, or pests—and, alas, occasionally

Table 8.1
Fixed, Variable, and Total Costs, Bugsbane Music Box Company

NUMBER OF MUSIC BOXES PRODUCED PER DAY	TOTAL FIXED COST	TOTAL VARIABLE COST (DOLLARS)	TOTAL COST
0	300	0	300
1	300	60	360
2	300	110	410
3	300	160	460
4	300	200	500
5	300	260	560
6	300	360	660
7	300	510	810
8	300	710	1,010
9	300	1,060	1,360

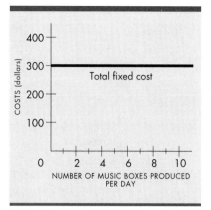

Figure 8.1
Total Fixed Cost, Bugsbane Music Box Company
The total fixed cost function is always a horizontal line, since fixed costs do not vary with output.

a frail Chihuahua—within a 50-foot radius. Table 8.1 shows that Bugsbane's fixed costs are $300 per day; the firm's total fixed cost function is shown in Figure 8.1.

Total Variable Cost

Total variable cost is the firm's total expenditure on variable inputs per period of time. Since higher output rates require greater utilization of variable inputs, they mean a higher total variable cost. Thus, if Bugsbane increases its daily production of music boxes, it must increase the amount it spends per day on metal (for the components), wood (for the outside of the boxes), labor (for the assembly of the boxes), and other variable inputs. Table 8.1 shows Bugsbane's total variable costs at various output rates; Figure 8.2 shows the firm's total variable cost function.

Up to the output rate of 4 music boxes per day, total variable cost increases at a decreasing rate; beyond that output rate, total variable cost increases at an increasing rate. It is important to understand that this characteristic of the total variable cost function results from the operation of the law of diminishing marginal returns. At small output rates, increases in the utilization of variable inputs may bring about increases in their productivity, causing total variable cost to increase with output, but at a decreasing rate. Beyond a point, however, there are diminishing marginal returns from the variable input, with the result that total variable costs increase at an increasing rate.

Total Cost

Total cost is the sum of total fixed cost and total variable cost. Thus, to obtain the Bugsbane Company's total cost at a given output, we need only add its total fixed cost and its total variable cost at that output. The result is shown in Table 8.1, and the corresponding total cost function is shown in Figure 8.3. Since the total cost function and the total variable cost function differ by only a constant amount (equal to total fixed cost), they have the same shape, as shown in Figure 8.4, which brings together all three of the total cost functions (or cost curves as they are often called).

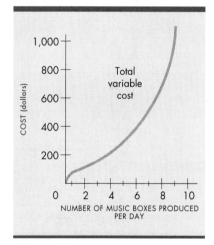

Figure 8.2
Total Variable Cost, Bugsbane Music Box Company
Total variable cost is the total expenditure per period of time on variable inputs. Due to the law of diminishing marginal returns, total variable cost increases first at a decreasing rate, then at an increasing rate.

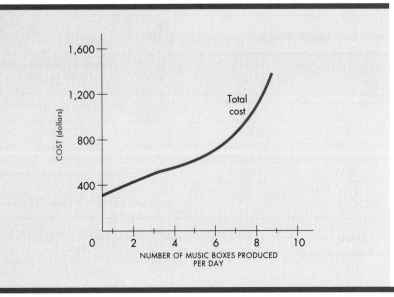

Figure 8.3
Total Cost, Bugsbane Music Box Company
Total cost is the sum of total fixed cost and total variable cost. It has the same shape as the total variable cost curve, since they differ by only a constant amount (equal to total fixed cost).

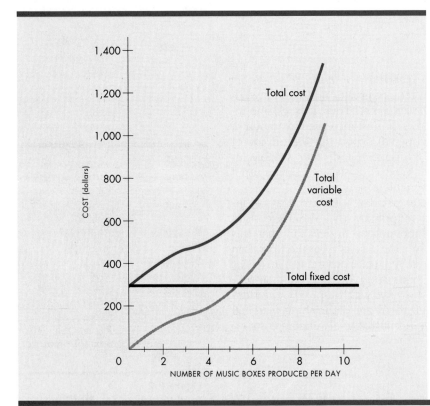

Figure 8.4
Fixed, Variable, and Total Costs, Bugsbane Music Box Company
All three cost functions, presented in Figures 8.1–8.3, are brought back for a curtain call.

AVERAGE COST IN THE SHORT RUN

The president of Bugsbane unquestionably cares about the average cost of a music box as well as the total cost incurred; so do economists. *Average cost tells you how much a product costs per unit of output.* There are three average cost functions, one corresponding to each of the three total cost functions.

Table 8.2
Average Fixed Cost, Average Variable Cost, and Average Total Cost, Bugsbane Music Box Company

NUMBER OF MUSIC BOXES PRODUCED PER DAY	AVERAGE FIXED COST	AVERAGE VARIABLE COST (DOLLARS)	AVERAGE TOTAL COST
1	300(= 300 ÷ 1)	60(= 60 ÷ 1)	360(= 360 ÷ 1)
2	150(= 300 ÷ 2)	55(= 110 ÷ 2)	205(= 410 ÷ 2)
3	100(= 300 ÷ 3)	53(= 160 ÷ 3)	153(= 460 ÷ 3)
4	75(= 300 ÷ 4)	50(= 200 ÷ 4)	125(= 500 ÷ 4)
5	60(= 300 ÷ 5)	52(= 260 ÷ 5)	112(= 560 ÷ 5)
6	50(= 300 ÷ 6)	60(= 360 ÷ 6)	110(= 660 ÷ 6)
7	43(= 300 ÷ 7)	73(= 510 ÷ 7)	116(= 810 ÷ 7)
8	38(= 300 ÷ 8)	89(= 710 ÷ 8)	126(= 1010 ÷ 8)
9	33(= 300 ÷ 9)	118(= 1060 ÷ 9)	151(= 1360 ÷ 9)

Average Fixed Cost

Let's begin with ***average fixed cost***, *which is simply the total fixed cost divided by the firm's output.* Table 8.2 and Figure 8.5 show the average fixed cost function for the Bugsbane Music Box Company. Average fixed cost must decline with increases in output, since it equals a constant— total fixed cost—divided by the output rate.

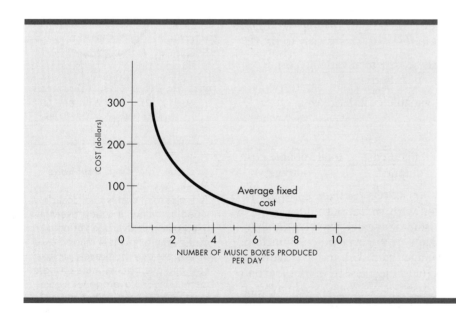

Figure 8.5
Average Fixed Cost, Bugsbane Music Box Company
Average fixed cost is total fixed cost divided by the firm's output. Since it equals a constant (total fixed cost) divided by the output rate, it must decline with increases in output.

Average Variable Cost

The next type of average cost is ***average variable cost,*** *which is total variable cost divided by output.* For Bugsbane, the average variable cost function is shown in Table 8.2 and Figure 8.6. At first, increases in the output rate result in decreases in average variable cost, but beyond a point, they result in higher average variable cost. This is because the law of diminishing marginal returns is in operation. As more and more of the variable inputs are utilized, the extra output they produce declines be-

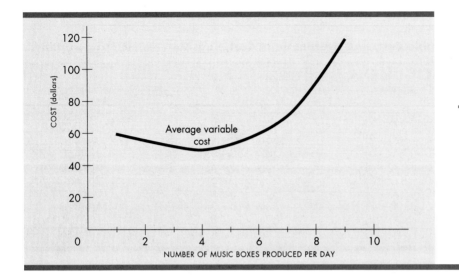

Figure 8.6
Average Variable Cost, Bugsbane Music Box Company
Average variable cost is total variable cost divided by the firm's ouput. Beyond a point (in this case, 4 music boxes per day), average variable cost rises with increases in output because of the law of diminishing marginal returns.

yond some point, so that the amount spent on variable input per unit of output tends to increase.

Average Total Cost

The third type of average cost is **_average total cost, which is total cost divided by output_**. For Bugsbane, the average total cost function is shown in Table 8.2 and Figure 8.7. At any level of output, _average total cost equals average fixed cost plus average variable cost_. This is easy to prove:

$$\text{average total cost} = \frac{\text{total cost}}{\text{output}} = \frac{\text{total fixed cost} + \text{total variable cost}}{\text{output}}$$

since total cost = total fixed cost + total variable cost. Moreover,

$$\frac{\text{total fixed cost} + \text{total variable cost}}{\text{output}} =$$

$$\frac{\text{total fixed cost}}{\text{output}} + \frac{\text{total variable cost}}{\text{output}}$$

and the right-hand side of this equation equals average fixed cost plus average variable cost. Thus we have proved what we set out to prove.

The fact that average total cost is the sum of average fixed cost and average variable cost helps explain the shape of the average cost function. If, as the output rate goes up, both average fixed cost and average variable cost decrease, average total cost must decrease too. But beyond some point, average total cost must increase because increases in average variable cost eventually more than offset decreases in average fixed cost. However, average total cost achieves its minimum after average variable cost, because the increases in average variable cost are for a time more than offset by decreases in average fixed cost. All the average cost functions are shown in Figure 8.9 on page 148.

MARGINAL COST IN THE SHORT RUN

No one can really understand the operations of a business firm without understanding the concept of **_marginal cost, the addition to total cost re-_**

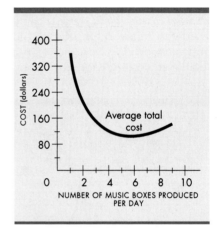

Figure 8.7
Average Total Cost, Bugsbane Music Box Company
Average total cost is total cost divided by output. It equals average fixed cost plus average variable cost. When output is 4 music boxes or less per day, both average fixed cost and average variable cost are decreasing, so average total cost must _decrease_ too. When output is 5 or 6 music boxes per day, average total cost _decreases_ because the fall in average fixed cost more than offsets the rise in average variable cost. When output exceeds 6 music boxes per day, the rise in average variable cost more than offsets the fall in average fixed cost, so average total cost increases.

Table 8.3
Calculation of Marginal Cost, Bugsbane Music Box Company

NUMBER OF MUSIC BOXES PRODUCED PER DAY	TOTAL COST (DOLLARS)	MARGINAL COST
0	300	
1	360	60(=360 – 300)
2	410	50(=410 – 360)
3	460	50(=460 – 410)
4	500	40(=500 – 460)
5	560	60(=560 – 500)
6	660	100(=660 – 560)
7	810	150(=810 – 660)
8	1,010	200(=1,010 – 810)
9	1,360	350(=1,360 – 1,010)

sulting from the addition of the last unit of output. To see how marginal cost is calculated, look at Table 8.3, which shows the total cost function of the Bugsbane Music Box Company. When output is between 0 and 1 music box per day, the firm's marginal cost is $60, since this is the *extra cost* of producing the first music box per day. In other words, $60 equals marginal cost in this situation because it is the difference between the total cost of producing 1 music box per day ($360) and the total cost of producing 0 music boxes per day ($300).

In general, marginal cost will vary depending on the firm's output level. Thus Table 8.3 shows that at Bugsbane marginal cost is $50 when the firm produces between 1 and 2 music boxes per day, $100 when the firm produces between 5 and 6 music boxes per day, and $350 when the firm produces between 8 and 9 music boxes per day. Table 8.3—and Figure 8.8, which shows the marginal cost function graphically—indicates that marginal cost, after decreasing with increases in output at low output levels, increases with further increases in output. In other words, *beyond some point it becomes more and more costly for the firm to produce yet another unit of output.*

Increasing Marginal Cost and Diminishing Returns

The reason why marginal cost increases beyond some output level is to be found in the law of diminishing marginal returns. *If (beyond some point) increases in variable inputs result in less and less extra output, it follows that a larger and larger quantity of variable inputs must be added to produce an extra unit of output. Thus the cost of producing an extra unit of output must increase.*

To illustrate how diminishing marginal returns result in increasing marginal cost, let's return for a moment to the wheat farm in Tables 7.1 and 7.3. (For convenience, the data regarding this farm are reproduced in Table 8.4.) If it is producing 70 bushels of wheat, it requires an extra 1/30 unit of labor to produce an extra bushel—since Table 8.4 shows that the marginal product of a unit of labor is 30 bushels. But if it is producing 100 bushels of wheat, an extra 1/25 unit of labor is needed to produce an extra bushel, since Table 8.4 shows that the marginal product of a unit of labor is 25 bushels. Thus more of the variable input (specifically, 1/25 unit of labor rather than 1/30 unit of labor) is required to produce an

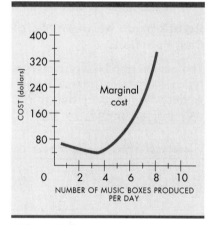

Figure 8.8
Marginal Cost, Bugsbane Music Box Company
Marginal cost is the addition to total cost arising from the addition of the last unit of output. The marginal cost of the first unit of output (which, according to Table 8.3, is $60) is plotted at the midpoint between 0 and 1 units of output. The marginal cost of the second unit of output is plotted at the midpoint between 1 and 2 units of output. The marginal cost function connects these and other points showing the marginal cost of various amounts of output. Beyond a point (in this case, between 3 and 4 music boxes per day), marginal cost increases because of the law of diminishing marginal returns.

Table 8.4
Average and Marginal Products of Labor, 1-Acre Wheat Farm

NUMBER OF UNITS OF LABOR	TOTAL OUTPUT	MARGINAL PRODUCT (BUSHELS PER UNIT OF LABOR)	AVERAGE PRODUCT
0	0		—
		30	
1	30		30
		40	
2	70		35
		30	
3	100		33⅓
		25	
4	125		31¼
		20	
5	145		29

extra bushel of wheat. And *since more and more of the variable input is required to produce an extra unit of output, the cost of producing an extra unit of output increases as output rises.*

Relationship between Marginal Cost and Average Cost Functions

The relationship between the marginal cost function and the average cost functions must be noted. Figure 8.9 shows the marginal cost curve together with the three average cost curves. *The marginal cost curve intersects both the average variable cost curve and the average total cost curve*

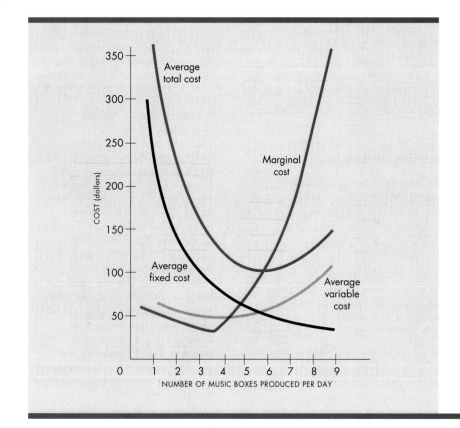

Figure 8.9
Average Fixed Cost, Average Variable Cost, Average Total Cost, and Marginal Cost, Bugsbane Music Box Company
All of the curves presented in Figures 8.5–8.8 are brought together for review. Note that the marginal cost curve intersects both the average variable cost curve and the average total cost curve at their minimum points.

at their minimum points. The reason for this is simple. If the extra cost of a unit of output is greater (less) than the average cost of the units of output already produced, the addition of the extra unit of output clearly must raise (lower) the average cost of production. Thus, if marginal cost is greater (less) than average cost, average cost must be rising (falling). And if this is so, average cost can be a minimum only when it equals marginal cost. (The same reasoning holds for both average total cost and average variable cost, and for the short and long runs.)

$MC > AC \Rightarrow AC \uparrow$

To make sure that you understand this point, consider the following numerical example. Suppose that the average total cost of producing 4 units of output is $10, and that the marginal cost of the fifth unit of output is less than $10. Will the average total cost be less for 5 units of output than for 4 units? It will be less, because the fifth unit's cost will pull down the average. On the other hand, if the marginal cost of the fifth unit of output had been greater than $10, the average total cost for 5 units of output would have been greater than for 4 units of output, because the fifth unit's cost would pull up the average. Thus *average total cost will fall when it is above marginal cost, and it will rise when it is below marginal cost.* Consequently, *when it is a minimum, average total cost must equal marginal cost*, as shown in Figure 8.9.

EXAMPLE 8.1   THE COSTS OF A SMALL MACHINE SHOP

A machine shop has the following relationship between cost and output:

OUTPUT (THOUSANDS OF UNITS OF OUTPUT PER YEAR)	TOTAL FIXED COST (DOLLARS PER YEAR)	TOTAL VARIABLE COST (DOLLARS PER YEAR)
0	64,000	0
400	64,000	20,000
440	64,000	23,000
480	64,000	27,000
520	64,000	32,000

(a) Included in the fixed cost is $5,600 in interest on the owner's investment in the machine shop. If the owner owns the shop completely (and does not have to pay interest to anyone else), should this item still be included? (b) Suppose that the owner and his wife do all the work, and that the opportunity cost of their labor is the same, regardless of the shop's output. Is their labor cost a fixed or variable cost? (c) What is the marginal cost of a unit of output when output is between 480 and 520 thousands of units per year? (d) At which of the above output levels is average total cost a minimum? Is this the output that the owner should choose?

Solution

(a) Yes, because if he sold this shop, he could lend out the proceeds and get $5,600 in interest. Thus this is the opportunity cost of the owner's investment in the shop. (b) It is a fixed cost. (c) ($32,000 – $27,000) ÷ 40,000 = 12.5 cents. (d) 520 thousand units. In general, as we shall see in the following chapter, the owner, wanting to maximize profit, should not choose the output in the short run that minimizes average total cost.

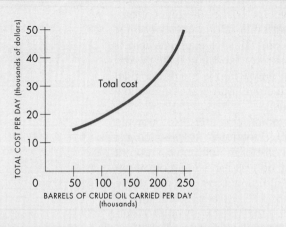

SHORT-RUN COST FUNCTIONS OF A CRUDE-OIL PIPELINE: A CASE STUDY

Cost functions are not academic toys, but eminently practical analytical devices that play a major role in decision making by business executives and government agencies. To illustrate the nature and use of short-run cost functions, we will take up the real-world case of crude-oil pipelines where we left off (in the previous chapter). In the short run, it is reasonable to assume that the diameter of a pipeline is fixed. Given the production function in Table 7.2, it is easy to figure out the total cost of carrying various amounts of oil per day, with a pipeline of a given diameter. In other words, we assume that the company that owns the pipeline can vary the horsepower by varying the number and type of pumping stations, but that the diameter of the pipeline is fixed.[1] Under these circumstances, if the diameter of the pipeline is 18 inches, what will the pipeline's cost functions look like?

Figures 8.10 and 8.11 answer this question. Figure 8.10 shows the ***total cost function*** for an 18-inch pipeline—the total daily cost of operating it, given that it carries various amounts of crude oil per day. If the pipeline carries 200,000 barrels of oil per day, the total daily cost is $33,000; if the amount of oil is increased to 250,000 barrels per day, the total daily cost rises to $48,000.

Figure 8.11 shows the ***average total cost function*** for an 18-inch pipeline—the total daily cost per barrel for the pipeline, given that it carries various amounts of crude oil per day. According to Figure 8.11, the total daily cost per barrel for this pipeline to carry 200,000 barrels per day is $.16 ½, and the total daily cost per barrel for it to carry 250,000 barrels per days is $.19 ⅕. Figure 8.11 also shows the ***marginal cost function*** for such a pipeline—the additional daily cost of carrying an extra barrel of crude oil per day. When this pipeline is carrying 200,000 barrels per day, the marginal cost runs to about $.23.

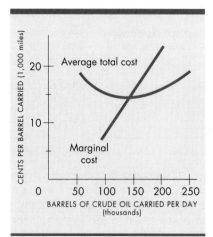

[1] Because the number and type of pumping stations must be altered, Leslie Cookenboo refers to this as the "intermediate run." See Cookenboo, *op. cit.*

To the operators of the pipeline, a knowledge of these cost functions can mean the difference between profit and loss. For example, suppose that the operators of a particular 18-inch pipeline are thinking about increasing the amount of oil the pipeline will carry per day. Specifically, suppose that the pipeline can now carry 200,000 barrels per day and that the operators are thinking about adding enough horsepower so that it can carry 250,000 barrels per day. Suppose that, according to the best estimates available, the pipeline can get $5 million in additional revenue each year if it carries the additional 50,000 barrels per day. Should the operators increase in this way the amount of oil the pipeline can carry?

If they want to increase profits, they should decide against this increase in the amount of horsepower. According to the total cost function in Figure 8.10, the pipeline's daily costs would increase by $15,000 per day if horsepower were increased so that 250,000, rather than 200,000 barrels of oil could be carried per day, while the extra oil carried would increase daily revenues by $5 million ÷ 365, or about $14,000 per day. Thus the extra costs would exceed the extra revenue, which means that the pipeline's profit would be reduced by increasing the amount of horsepower. In making decisions of this sort (and they must make them repeatedly!), managers must rely heavily on information about the relevant cost functions.

TEST YOURSELF

1. Suppose that a firm's short-run total cost function is as follows:

OUTPUT(NUMBER OF UNITS PER YEAR)	TOTAL COST PER YEAR (DOLLARS)
0	20,000
1	20,100
2	20,200
3	20,300
4	20,500
5	20,800

What are the firm's total fixed costs? What are its total variable costs when it produces 4 units per year?

2. In Question 1, what is the firm's marginal cost when between 4 and 5 units are produced per year? Does marginal cost increase beyond some output level?

3. In Question 1, what is the firm's average cost when it produces 1 unit per year? 2 units per year? 3 units per year? 4 units per year? 5 units per year?

4. Fill in the blanks below:

TOTAL OUTPUT	TOTAL FIXED COST	TOTAL VARIABLE COST	AVERAGE TOTAL COST (DOLLARS)	AVERAGE FIXED COST	AVERAGE VARIABLE COST
0	500	—			
1	—	20	—	—	—
2	—	—	300	—	—
3	—	—	—	—	133⅓
4	—	1,100	—	—	—

5. In Question 4, does marginal cost increase with increases in output? Explain.

LONG-RUN COST FUNCTIONS

The Long-Run Average Cost Function

We have held to the last one additional kind of cost function that plays a very important role in economic analysis. This is the firm's **long-run average cost function,** which shows the minimum average cost of produc-

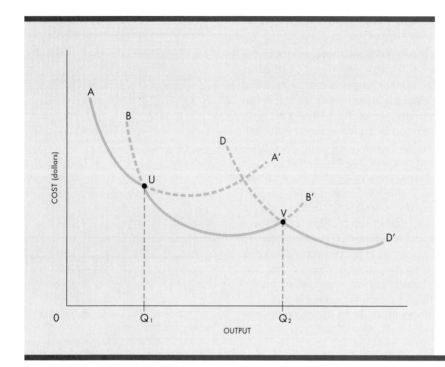

Figure 8.12
Short-Run Average Cost
Curves and Long-Run Average
Cost Curve
The short-run average total cost
functions for three plants—small,
medium, and large—are *AA'*, *BB'*,
and *DD'*. The long-run average
cost function is *AUVD'*, if these are
the only three types of plants that
can be built.

ing each output level when any desired type or scale of plant can be built.
Unlike the cost functions discussed in the previous sections, this cost
function pertains to the long run—*to a period long enough so that all inputs are variable and none is fixed.* As pointed out in the previous chapter, a useful way to look at the long run is to consider it a *planning
horizon.* The firm must continually be planning ahead and trying to decide its strategy in the long run.

Suppose a firm can build plants of three sizes—small, medium, and
large. The short-run average total cost functions corresponding to these
plants are *AA'*, *BB'*, and *DD'* in Figure 8.12. If the firm is still in the planning stage of plant construction, it can choose whichever plant has the
lowest costs. Consequently, the firm will choose the small plant if it believes its output rate will be smaller than OQ_1, the medium plant if it believes its output rate will be above OQ_1, but below OQ_2, and the large
plant if it believes that its output rate will be above OQ_2. Thus the long-
run average cost curve is *AUVD'*. And if, as is generally the case, there are
many possible types of plants, the long-run average cost curve looks like
LL' in Figure 8.13. (Only a few of the short-run average cost curves are
shown in Figure 8.13.)

The usefulness of the long-run average cost function can be illustrated
by the familiar case of crude-oil pipelines. Figure 8.14 shows the long-run
average cost function for these pipelines, as well as selected short-run average cost functions (corresponding to diameters of 8, 10, 12, 14, 16, 18,
20, 24, 26, 30, and 32 inches). Note that long-run average cost—that is,
cost per barrel—decreases as more and more oil is carried per day, at
least up to 400,000 barrels per day. Thus it appears that costs are reduced
when the greatest possible quantities of oil are transported in large-diam-
eter pipelines.

This fact is important in evaluating the effects of various kinds of mar-

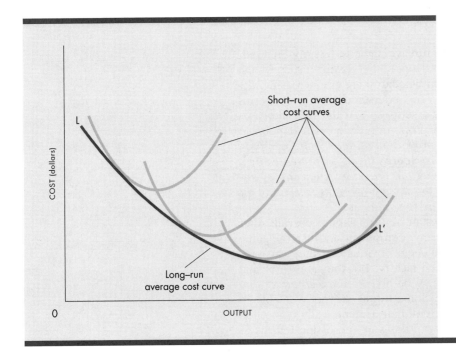

Figure 8.13
Long-Run Average Cost Curve
If many possible types of plants can be built, the long-run average cost function is *LL'*.

ket structure in the pipeline industry. *If long-run average costs decrease with increases in output up to an output representing all, or nearly all, of the market, it is wasteful to force competition in such an industry, since costs would be greater if the industry output were divided among a number of firms than if it were produced by only one or two firms.* More will be said on this score in Chapter 10.

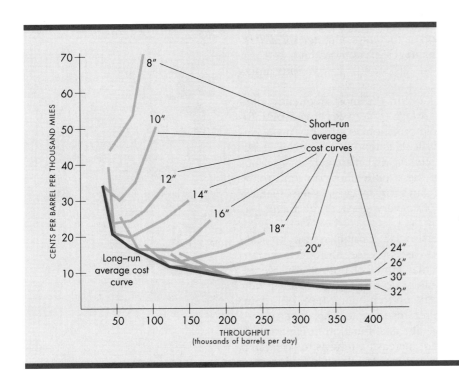

Figure 8.14
Costs per Barrel of Operating Crude-Oil Trunk Pipeline
This graph shows the long-run average cost curve (and the relevant short-run average cost curves) in an actual case. Note that in this range at least, long-run average cost decreases as output increases.

RETURNS TO SCALE

What determines the shape of the long-run average cost function in a particular industry? Its shape must depend upon the characteristics of the production function—specifically, upon whether there are increasing, decreasing, or constant returns to scale. To understand what these terms mean, consider a long-run situation and suppose that the firm increases the amount of all inputs by the same proportion. What will happen to output? *If output increases by a larger proportion than each of the inputs, this is a case of **increasing returns to scale**. If output increases by a smaller proportion than each of the inputs, this is a case of **decreasing returns to scale**. If output increases by the same proportion as each of the inputs, this is a case of **constant returns to scale***.

At first glance it may seem that constant returns should prevail: After all, if two factories are built with the same equipment and use the same type and number of workers, it would seem obvious that they can produce twice as much output as one such factory. But things are not that simple. If a firm doubles its scale, it may be able *to use techniques that could not be used at the smaller scale.* Some inputs are not available in small units; for example, we cannot install half a numerically controlled machine tool. Because of indivisibilities of this sort, increasing returns to scale may occur. Thus, although one could double a firm's size by simply building two small factories, this may be inefficient. One large factory may be more efficient than two smaller factories of the same total capacity because it is large enough to use certain techniques and inputs that the smaller factories cannot use.

Another reason for increasing returns to scale stems from certain *geometrical relations.* For example, since the volume of a box that is $3 \times 3 \times 3$ feet is 27 times as great as the volume of a box that is $1 \times 1 \times 1$ foot, the former box can carry 27 times as much as the latter box. But since the area of the six sides of the $3 \times 3 \times 3$-foot box is 54 square feet and the area of the six sides of the $1 \times 1 \times 1$-foot box is 6 square feet, the former box only requires 9 times as much wood as the latter. Greater *specialization* also can result in increasing returns to scale. As more men and machines are used, it is possible to subdivide tasks and allow various inputs to specialize.

Decreasing returns to scale can also occur; the most frequently cited reason is *the difficulty of coordinating a large enterprise.* It can be difficult even in a small firm to obtain the information required to make important decisions; in a large firm, the difficulties tend to be greater. It can be difficult even in a small firm to be certain that management's wishes are being carried out; in a larger firm these difficulties too tend to be greater. Although the advantages of a large organization seem to have captured the public fancy, there are often very great disadvantages as well.

Whether there are increasing, decreasing, or constant returns to scale in a particular situation must be settled case by case. Moreover, the answer is likely to depend on the particular range of output considered. There frequently are increasing returns to scale up to some level of output, then perhaps constant returns to scale up to a higher level of output, beyond which there may be decreasing returns to scale. This pattern is responsible for the *U*-shaped long-run average cost function in Figure 8.13. At relatively small output levels, there are increasing returns to scale, and long-run average cost decreases as output rises. At relatively high output

EXAMPLE 8.2 ECONOMIES OF SCALE IN CABLE TELEVISION?

According to a study reported to the U.S. House of Representatives, the long-run average cost function of a firm providing cable television to households is as follows:

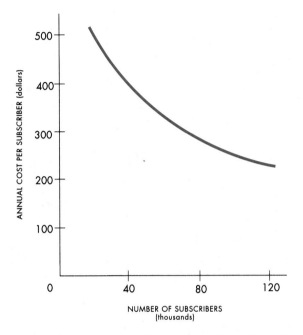

(a) Do there appear to be **economies of scale** in the cable television business? In other words, does long-run average cost fall with increases in output? (b)

If so, why do you think that this is the case? (c) According to the authors of this study, long-run marginal cost in this business tends to be less than long-run average cost. Is this true? If so, why? (d) Would you expect that a large number of firms would provide cable television in a particular city? Why, or why not?

Solution

(a) Yes. Long-run average costs fall as the number of subscribers (a rough measure of output) increases. (b) A firm providing cable television must invest in a substantial amount of equipment—satellite dishes, towers, antennas, and cable distribution facilities—before it can service its first customer. The investment required to service additional customers is minor compared to this initial investment. Thus, in the long run (when any desired type or scale of plant can be built), the average cost of servicing a subscriber goes down as the number of subscribers goes up. (c) It is true because (as pointed out on page 149) if average cost decreases with increased output, marginal cost must be less than average cost. (d) No. Because there are economies of scale, one would expect that many communities would have only one firm providing cable television—and this in fact is true.[*]

[*]For further discussion, see J. Gomez-Ibanez and J. Kalt, eds., *Cases in Microeconomics*, Englewood Cliffs, N.J.: Prentice Hall, 1990.

---

levels, there are decreasing returns to scale, and long-run average cost increases as output rises.

As we shall see in the following section, this *U*-shaped pattern is not found in all industries. Within the range covered by the available data, there is little or no evidence in many industries that long-run average cost increases as output rises. But this may be because the data do not cover a wide enough range. Eventually, one would expect long-run average cost to rise because of problems of coordination, increased red tape, and reduced flexibility. Firms as large as General Motors or IBM are continually bedeviled by the very real difficulties of enormous size.

MEASUREMENT AND APPLICATION OF COST FUNCTIONS

Measurement of Cost Functions

Countless studies have been made to estimate cost functions in particular firms and industries. Many of these have been based on the relationship

CAN AMERICAN FIRMS COMPETE?

The 1980s were a very bruising decade for many American manufacturers. Whereas 20 years ago, American firms were regarded, both here and abroad, as models of efficiency, they have been twitted recently of growing fat and lazy. As *Business Week* put it, "While the Japanese were developing remarkably higher standards for a whole host of products, from consumer electronics to cars and machine tools, many U.S. managers were smugly dozing at the switch."[1] As evidence, the critics point to the fact that plants in the United States have been having a very difficult time producing goods of comparable quality at as low a cost as their foreign rivals.

To illustrate, consider the important case of automobiles. According to the National Research Council, the Japanese could produce a small car and ship it to the United States at an overall cost that was $700–$1,500 below the production cost of American producers. Obviously, this is an enormous difference. Moreover, the Japanese cars tended to be of higher quality. Even in 1987, after American firms had taken numerous steps to improve quality, the number of problems reported by owners of new cars was about 35 percent greater for American than Japanese cars.[2]

The following is a brief summary of the reasons for this Japanese cost and quality advantage, according to an influential report by the National Research Council:

> Popular accounts of the emergence of Japanese producers as first-rate, worldwide competitors tend to emphasize the impact of new automation technology (e.g., robotics), strong support of the central government (i.e., "Japan, Inc."), and influence of Japanese culture (i.e., a dedicated work force). There is no doubt that these factors have played some role. Yet, it is our view that the sources of the Japanese advantage are not to be found in such factors. Rather, they are rooted in a commitment to manufacturing excellence and a strategy that uses manufacturing as a competitive weapon.
>
> The key to Japan's lead . . . appears to be the interaction of the material control system, maintenance practices, and employee involvement. The key to the

material control system is the concept of "just in time" production. Often called "Kanban" (after the production cards or tickets used to trigger production), the system is designed so that materials, parts, and components used at a given step in production are produced or delivered just before they are needed. Thus, stages in the process (including suppliers) are tightly coupled, with very little work-in-process inventory. Suppliers must therefore make frequent deliveries of parts, and lot sizes must be small to accommodate product variety.

It is the Japanese view that reduction of decoupling inventory exposes "the real problems"—waste of time and materials, imbalance in operations, defective parts, equipment operating improperly, and so forth. ([The table on the facing page] provides comparative data on inventory levels. These data show that dramatically less inventory is used by Japanese firms in the production of automobiles. This is true whether one looks at the process as a whole or at specific plants.)

With smaller buffer stocks the production system will simply not work if there are frequent or lengthy breakdowns. Thus, the just-in-time approach exposes opportunities for reducing waste and solving problems, while at the same time creating pressure for maximizing uptime and minimizing defects. Maintenance programs, preventive and scheduled, are therefore pursued vigorously. Plants operate with only two shifts, and equip-

[1]"The Push for Quality," *Business Week,* June 8, 1987, p.131.
[2]Ibid., p. 139.

ment is maintained during nonproduction time. The result is a much lower rate of machine failure and breakdown.

Pressure for defect elimination is reflected in relationships with suppliers and in work practices on the line. "Just in time" production does not allow for extensive inspection of incoming parts. Suppliers must, therefore, achieve highly demanding quality levels, consistently and reliably. The major Japanese manufacturers work closely with outside vendors to make sure that responsibility for quality is felt and acted upon at the source of product. This same approach—quality control at the source—is used in production on the line, where workers have the authority to stop the operation if they spot defects or other production problems. Worker-initiated line stops are central to the concept of Jidoka: making problems visible to everyone's eye and stopping the line if trouble occurs; all thoughts, methods, and tools to avoid stops are Jidoka.

The basic thrust of the Kanban system and the concept of Jidoka are to eliminate waste, expose problems, and conserve resources. This is not simply a different technique of controlling production, but a very different way of managing the production process. It is clear that these systems interact with other factors in our list of productivity determinants. Separating their effects from the effects of quality systems and job structure, for example, is somewhat arbitrary. The Kanban-Jidoka system uses fewer inspectors, and its success requires broader and deeper jobs. . . .

Indeed, it appears that job structure plays an important role in explaining observed productivity differentials. We have already noted two features of the Japanese system (maintenance practices and Jidoka) in which jobs are designed to involve workers in a variety of tasks. The effects of structure, and the differences in management style and practices that go with it (fewer layers of management, more managing from the bottom up), extend to other aspects of production. Quality circles or "small group involvement activities" deal with such questions as layout, process methods, and automation. Such involvement appears to be an important factor in obtaining relatively high levels of commitment and motivation.

The nature of worker-management relations in Japan is further suggested by much lower levels of unexcused absence than that found in the United States. . . . In general, absenteeism influences costs, not only through redundant labor but also through fringe costs of the absent group as well as indirect effects such as scrap, reduced learning, and so forth. It appears that absenteeism may actually account for as much as 10–12 percent of the cost gap.

. . . [It] is clear that work-force management must be a significant factor in explaining the Japanese cost advantage. Likewise, an attempt to explain quality differences would certainly accord a major influence to the work force and its management. It seems evident,

Inventory Comparisons—U.S. and Japan

LEVEL/PROCESS	JAPAN	UNITED STATES
1. *Plant and Process Inventories* Assembly plant component inventories (equivalent units of production)		
Heaters	1 hour	5 days
Radiators	2 hours	5 days
Brake drums	1.5 hours	3 days
Front-wheel-drive transfer case in process parts storage by operation (number of parts)		
Mill	7	240
Drill	11	200
Ream and chamfer	13	196
Drill	24	205
Mill, washer, test	10	40
Assemble	6	96
Finish	7	87
Total	79	1064
2. *Company Inventories* Work in process inventories per vehicle		
1979	$80.2	$536.5
1980	$74.2	$584.3
Work in process turns[a]		
1979	40.0	12.1
1980	46.1	13.4

[a] Defined as cost of goods sold divided by work in process inventories.
Source: 1.—Industry sources (data provided by panel members); 2.—Annual reports for representative producers.

therefore, that in concert with different systems of production management and control, the work force plays a central role in the Japanese competitive advantage.[3]

Probing Deeper

1. Do all firms, like the Japanese, use manufacturing as a "competitive weapon"? What other sorts of "competitive weapons" exist?

2. The table shows that inventory levels have tended to be lower in Japanese than in American

[3] National Research Council, "The Japanese Cost and Quality Advantages in the Auto Industry," in E. Mansfield, ed., *Managerial Economics and Operations Research*, 5th ed., New York: Norton, 1987, pp. 34, 39–42.

over time between cost and output. Figure 8.15 shows the total costs of a hypothetical firm in various years plotted against the firm's output in these years. Based on the data, a reasonable approximation to the firm's total cost function might be the curve that is drawn in Figure 8.15. However, there are a number of difficulties in this simple procedure. For one thing, the firm's cost function may not have remained fixed throughout this period. For another, accounting data on costs may not be as accurate as one would like.[2] For these and other reasons, economists and statisticians have devised more sophisticated techniques to estimate cost functions.

To illustrate the sorts of results that have been obtained, Figure 8.16 shows the total cost function, average total cost function, and marginal cost function for a leather belt shop. Note that the total cost function appears linear, that is, a straight line, in the relevant range.

These results were obtained over 40 years ago by one of the pioneers in this field, Joel Dean of Columbia University. Since that time, a great deal of evidence has been amassed on the shape of the cost functions of individual firms and industries. Two findings are particularly worth noting. First, *within the range of observed data, the long-run average cost*

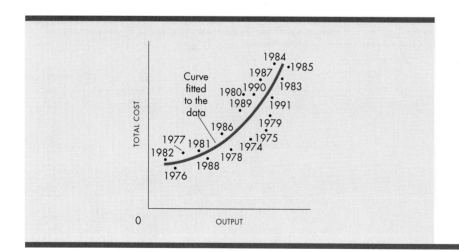

Figure 8.15
Relationship between Total Cost and Output: Time Series for a Particular Firm
One very crude way to estimate the total cost curve is to plot total cost in each year against total output in that year, and draw a curve, like the one shown in the diagram, that fits the points reasonably well. However, this technique is generally too crude to be reliable.

[2] Some of the difficulties are that the depreciation of an asset is often determined by the tax laws rather than economic criteria, many inputs are valued at historical, rather than opportunity cost, and accountants sometimes use arbitrary allocations of overhead and joint costs.

curve in many industries seems to be L-shaped (as in Figure 8.17), *not U-shaped* (as in Figure 8.13). That is, there is little or no evidence that it turns upward, rather than remains horizontal, at high output levels. As pointed out in the previous section, this may be due in part to the limited range of the data. Second, *many empirical studies indicate that marginal cost in the short run tends to be constant in the relevant output range.* However, this really does not contradict our assertions in previous sections, because the data used in these studies often do not cover periods when the firm was operating at peak capacity.

Break-Even Charts

Estimated cost functions are used in a variety of ways by firms and government agencies. As an illustration, consider **break-even charts**. To construct a break-even chart, *the firm's total revenue must be plotted on the same chart with its total cost function.* It is generally assumed that the price the firm receives for its product will not be influenced by the amount it sells, so that total revenue is proportional to output. Thus the total revenue curve is a straight line through the origin. Also, it is generally assumed that the firm's average variable cost and marginal cost are constant *in the relevant output range,* meaning that the firm's total cost function is also assumed to be a straight line.

Panel A of Figure 8.18 shows the break-even chart for an actual cable manufacturing firm. The sales price of each unit of its output was $200. The firm's fixed costs were $50,000 per month and its average variable cost per unit of output was $20. The break-even chart shows the monthly profit or loss that will result from each sales level. Panel A (Figure 8.18) shows that the firm would have lost $14,000 per month if it had sold 200 units per month. On the other hand, it would have made a profit of $22,000 per month if it had sold 400 units per month. The chart also shows the **break-even point,** *the output level that must be reached if the firm is to avoid losses.* In panel A, the break-even point is 278 units of output per month.

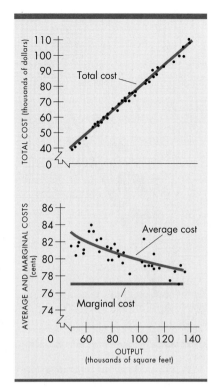

Figure 8.16
Total, Average, and Marginal Cost Functions of a Leather Belt Shop
This graph shows the short-run total, average, and marginal cost curves in an actual case. Note that marginal cost is constant in this case, but the data pertain only to a limited range of output levels.

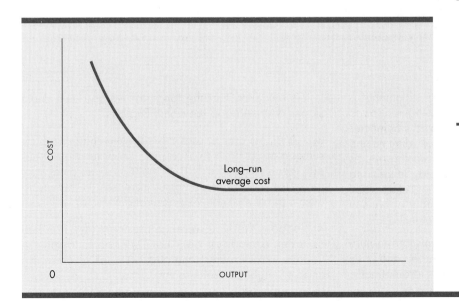

Figure 8.17
Apparent Shape of Many Long-Run Average Cost Curves
Within the range of observed data, there is little or no evidence in many industries that the long-run average cost curve turns upward, rather than remains horizontal, at high output levels. But the range of observed data is limited.

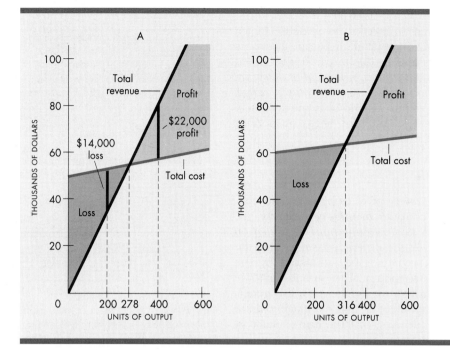

Figure 8 .18
Break-Even Chart, Cable Manufacturing Firm
In panels A and B, the sales price of each unit of output is $200. In panel A, the firm's fixed costs are $50,000 per month, and its average variable cost per unit of output is $20. In panel B, the firm's fixed costs are $60,000 per month, and its average variable cost per unit of output is $10. In panel A, the firm's break-even point is 278 units of output per month, whereas in panel B it is 316 units of output per month.

Break-even charts are used very extensively by firms and other groups to estimate the effect of the sales rate on costs, receipts, and profits. A firm may use a break-even chart to determine the effect on profits of a projected increase in sales, or how many units of a particular product it must sell in order to break even. For instance, the cable manufacturing firm wanted to find out, among other things, how its break-even point would be affected if it installed new equipment that would increase its fixed costs to $60,000 per month and reduce its average variable cost to $10. Panel B of Figure 8.18 shows that, under these circumstances, the firm's break-even point would be 316, rather than 278, units of output per month. This information is, of course, of considerable value to the firm. It means that if the firm installs the new equipment, it must sell at least 316 units of output per month to stay in the black.

TEST YOURSELF

1. Explain why each of the following statements is true, partly true, or false. (a) "Decreasing returns to scale occur when increased scale allows efficiencies of various sorts." (b) "The law of diminishing marginal returns is inconsistent with increasing returns to scale." (c) "John Maynard Keynes said, 'In the long run we are all dead.' He was right. What is important for the determination of the optimal number of firms in an industry is the short-run average cost function."

2. As the electronics industry has grown more mature and new technologies have been developed, the costs of many electronic products have fallen dramatically. Is this evidence that the long-run average cost curve slopes downward to the right? Explain.

3. A business analyst uses a break-even chart which assumes that her firm's total cost is a linear function of output (as in Figure 8.18). If the firm's marginal cost increases sharply as its output increases, is this break-even chart likely to be very accurate? Why, or why not?

4. Suppose that you were the president of a firm that operates a crude-oil pipeline. Describe in detail the various ways in which the cost functions given in this chapter might be useful to you.

SUMMARY

1. The cost of a certain course of action is the value of the best alternative course of action that could have been pursued instead. This is the doctrine of opportunity, or alternative, cost.

2. Three kinds of total cost functions are important in the short run—total fixed cost, total variable cost, and total cost. In addition, there are three kinds of average cost functions (corresponding to each of the total cost functions)—average fixed cost, average variable cost, and average total cost.

3. Marginal cost—the addition to total cost due to the addition of the last unit of output—is of enormous significance in the firm's decision making process. Because of the law of diminishing marginal returns, marginal cost tends to increase beyond some output level.

4. The firm's long-run average cost curve shows the minimum average cost of producing each output level when any desired type or scale of plant can be built. The shape of the long-run average cost curve is determined in part by whether there are increasing, decreasing, or constant returns to scale.

5. Suppose that a firm increases the amount of all inputs by the same percentage. If output increases by more than this percentage, this is a case of increasing returns to scale. If output increases by less than this percentage, this is a case of decreasing returns to scale. If output increases by this percentage, this is a case of constant returns to scale.

6. If long-run average costs decrease with increases in output up to an output representing all, or nearly all, of the market, it is wasteful to force competition in such an industry, since costs would be greater if the industry output were divided among a number of firms than if it were produced by only one or two firms.

7. Cost functions play a very important practical role in economics and management. There have been countless studies to estimate cost functions in particular firms and industries, based on engineering and accounting data.

8. Cost functions can be used to help solve important sorts of managerial problems, as well as problems of public policy. We have shown how estimates of cost functions have been used to construct break-even charts, commonly employed by firms to promote better decisions.

CONCEPTS FOR REVIEW

Opportunity cost

Alternative cost

Implicit cost

Cost functions

Total fixed cost

Total variable cost

Total cost

Average fixed cost

Average variable cost

Average total cost

Marginal cost

Total cost function

Average total cost function

Marginal cost function

Long-run average cost function

Increasing returns to scale

Decreasing returns to scale

Constant returns to scale

Break-even chart

Break-even point

Economies of scale

PART THREE

MARKET STRUCTURE AND ANTITRUST POLICY

PERFECT COMPETITION

EVEN A COUNTRY AS RICH as the United States cannot afford to waste resources, particularly when much of the world is hungry. One of the important determinants of how a society's resources are used is how its markets are organized. Thus, if the market for wheat contained few sellers rather than many, it would certainly use resources quite differently. Or if 20 firms, rather than one, provided local telephone service in Chicago, resources would be used differently. Economists do not have any simple formulas that will eliminate all social waste. But based on existing models and evidence, they believe that some forms of market organization tend to minimize social waste, whereas other forms seem to promote it.

In this chapter, we examine the way resources are allocated and prices are set under *perfect competition.* This type of market organization—or market structure, as it is often called—is a polar case which seldom, if ever, occurs in a pure form in the real world. But it is an extremely useful model that sheds much light on a market structure's effects on resource allocation. Anyone who wants to understand how markets work in a capitalistic economy—or why our public policies toward business are what they are—must understand perfect competition, as well as the other market structures taken up in the next two chapters.

MARKET STRUCTURE AND ECONOMIC PERFORMANCE

Many economists have come to the conclusion, based on their studies of the workings of markets, that certain kinds of market organization are better, from society's point of view, than others. This is a much stronger statement than merely saying, as we did in the previous section, that market structure influences market behavior. This statement is based on some set of values and preferences, explicit or implicit, and on certain economic models that predict that "better" behavior is more likely if markets are organized in certain ways than in other ways. Although there is considerable controversy on this score, many economists believe that, from society's point of view, market structures should be as close as possible to perfect competition (for reasons given in the next three chapters).

Economists have generally found it useful to classify markets into four broad types: *perfect competition, monopoly, monopolistic competition,* and *oligopoly.* Each of these terms describes a particular type of

Table 9.1
Types of Market Structure

MARKET STRUCTURE	EXAMPLES	NUMBER OF PRODUCERS	TYPE OF PRODUCT	POWER OF FIRM OVER PRICE	BARRIERS TO ENTRY	NONPRICE COMPETITION
Perfect competition	Parts of agriculture are reasonably close	Many	Standardized	None	Low	None
Monopolistic competition	Retail trade	Many	Differentiated	Some	Low	Advertising and product differentiation
Oligopoly	Autos, steel, machinery	Few	Standardized or differentiated	Some	High	Advertising and product differentiation
Monopoly	Public utilities	One	Unique product	Considerable	Very high	Advertising

market structure or organization. Table 9.1 provides a capsule description of each of these types. Before looking in detail at each of them, we must go over this table to see how these market structures differ.

NUMBER OF FIRMS. The economist's classification of market structures is based to an important extent on the number of firms in the industry that supplies the product. In perfect competition and monopolistic competition, there are *many* sellers, each of which produces only a small part of the industry's output. In monopoly, on the other hand, the industry consists of only a *single* seller. Oligopoly is an intermediate case where there are a *few* sellers. Thus Consolidated Edison, if it is the only supplier of electricity in a particular market, is a monopoly. And since there is only a small number of computer manufacturers, the market for computers is an oligopoly.

CONTROL OVER PRICE. Market structures differ considerably in the extent to which an individual firm has control over price. A firm under perfect competition has *no control* over price. For example, a wheat farm (which is close to being a perfectly competitive firm) has no control over the price of wheat. On the other hand, a monopolist is likely to have *considerable control* over price. Thus, in the absence of public regulation, Consolidated Edison would have considerable control over the price of electricity in New York City. A firm under monopolistic competition or oligopoly is likely to have *more* control over price than a perfectly competitive firm and *less* control over price than a monopolist.

TYPE OF PRODUCT. These market structures also differ in the extent to which the firms in an industry produce standardized (that is, identical) products. Firms in a perfectly competitive market all produce *identical* products. Thus Farmer Brown's corn is essentially the same as Farmer Smith's. In a monopolistic competitive industry like dress manufacturing, firms produce *somewhat different* products. One firm's dresses differ in style and quality from another firm's dresses. In an oligopolistic industry, firms *sometimes,* but not always, produce identical products. And in a monopolistic industry, there can be *no difference* among firms in their products, since there is only one firm.

BARRIERS TO ENTRY. The ease with which firms can enter the industry differs from one market structure to another. In perfect competition, barriers to entry are *low.* Thus only a small investment is required to enter many parts of agriculture. Similarly, there are *low* barriers to entry in monopolistic competition. But in oligopolies such as autos and steel, there tend to be *very considerable* barriers to entry because it is so expensive to build an auto or steel plant (and for many other reasons too). In monopoly, entry is blocked; once entry occurs, the monopolist is an ex-monopolist.

NONPRICE COMPETITION. These market structures also differ in the extent to which firms compete on the basis of advertising and differences in product characteristics, rather than price. In perfect competition, there is *no* nonprice competition. In monopolistic competition, there is *considerable emphasis* on nonprice competition. Thus dress manufacturers compete by trying to develop better styles and by advertising their product lines. Oligopolies also tend to rely *heavily* on nonprice competition. For example, auto firms try to increase their sales by building better and more attractive cars and by advertising. Monopolists also engage in advertising, although this advertising is not directed at reducing the sales of other firms in the industry, since no other firms exist.

Table 9.1 provides a useful summary of some of the key characteristics of each market structure. Before proceeding further, study it carefully.

PERFECT COMPETITION

When business executives speak of a highly competitive market, they often mean one in which each firm is keenly aware of its rivalry with a few others and in which advertising, styling, packaging, and other such commercial weapons are used to attract business away from them. In contrast, the basic feature of the economist's definition of perfect competition is its *impersonality.* Because there are so many firms in the industry, no firm views another as a competitor, any more than one small tobacco farmer views another small tobacco farmer as a competitor. A market is perfectly competitive if it satisfies the following three conditions.

HOMOGENEITY OF PRODUCT. The first condition is that *the product of any one seller must be the same as the product of any other seller.* This condition ensures that buyers do not care from which seller they purchase the goods, so long as the price is the same. This condition is met in many markets. As pointed out in the previous section, Farmer Brown's corn is likely to be essentially the same as Farmer Smith's.

MANY BUYERS AND SELLERS. The second condition is that there must be a large number of buyers and sellers. *Each participant in the market, whether buyer or seller, must be so small in relation to the entire market that he or she cannot affect the product's price.* That is, all buyers and sellers must be "price takers," not "price makers." As we know from Chapter 4, a firm under perfect competition faces a *horizontal demand curve,* since variations in its output—within the range of its capabilities—will have no effect on market price.

MOBILITY OF RESOURCES. The third condition is that *all resources must be able to switch readily from one use to another, and consumers, firms, and* resource owners must have complete knowledge of all relevant economic and technological data.

No industry in the real world, now or in the past, satisfies all these conditions completely; thus no industry is perfectly competitive. Some agricultural markets may be reasonably close, but even they do not meet all the requirements. But this does not mean that it is useless to study the behavior of a perfectly competitive market. The conclusions derived from the model of perfect competition have proved very helpful in explaining and predicting behavior in the real world. Indeed, as we shall see, they have permitted a reasonably accurate view of resource allocation in many important segments of our economy.

THE OUTPUT OF THE FIRM

What determines the output rate in the short run of a perfectly competitive firm? Since the firm is perfectly competitive, it cannot affect the price of its product, and it can sell any amount it wants at this price. Since we are concerned with the short run, the firm can expand or contract its output rate by increasing or decreasing its utilization of its variable, but not its fixed, inputs. The situation in the long run will be reserved for a later section.

What Is the Profit at Each Output Rate?

To see how a firm determines its output rate, suppose that your aunt dies and leaves you her business, the Allegro Piano Company. Once you take over the business, your first problem is to decide how many pianos (each of which has a price of $1,000) the firm should produce per week. Having a good deal of economic intuition, you instruct your accountants to estimate the company's *total revenue* (defined as price times output) and total costs (as well as fixed and variable costs) at various output levels. They estimate the firm's total revenue at various output rates and its total cost function (as well as its total fixed cost function and total variable cost function), with the results shown in Table 9.2. Subtracting the total cost at a given output rate from the total revenue at this output rate, you obtain

Table 9.2
Costs and Revenues, Allegro Piano Company

Total Revenue − Total cost = Total profit

OUTPUT PER WEEK (PIANOS)	PRICE	TOTAL REVENUE (PRICE X OUTPUT)	TOTAL FIXED COST (DOLLARS)	TOTAL VARIABLE COST	TOTAL COST	TOTAL PROFIT
0	1,000	0	1,000	0	1,000	−1,000
1	1,000	1,000	1,000	200	1,200	− 200
2	1,000	2,000	1,000	300	1,300	700
3	1,000	3,000	1,000	500	1,500	1,500
4	1,000	4,000	1,000	1,000	2,000	2,000
5	1,000	5,000	1,000	2,000	3,000	2,000
6	1,000	6,000	1,000	3,200	4,200	1,800
7	1,000	7,000	1,000	4,500	5,500	1,500
8	1,000	8,000	1,000	7,200	8,200	− 200

the total profit at each output rate, which is shown in the last column of Table 9.2.

Finding the Maximum-Profit Output Rate

As the output rate increases from 0 to 4 pianos per week, the total profit *rises*. As the output rate increases from 5 to 8 pianos per week, the total profit *falls*. Thus the *maximum* profit is achieved at an output rate between 4 and 5 pianos per week.[1] (Without more detailed data, one cannot tell precisely where the maximum occurs, but this is close enough for present purposes.) Since the maximum profit is obtained at an output of between 4 and 5 pianos per week, this is the output rate you choose.

Figure 9.1 gives a somewhat more vivid picture of the firm's situation by plotting the relationship between total revenue and total cost, on the one hand, and output on the other. At each output rate, the vertical distance between the total revenue curve and the total cost curve is the amount of profit the firm earns. Below an output rate of about 1 piano per week and above a rate of about 8 pianos per week, the total revenue curve lies *below* the total cost curve, indicating that profits are negative—that is, there are losses. Both Table 9.2 and Figure 9.1 show that the output rate that will maximize the firm's profits is between 4 and 5 pianos per week. At this output rate, the firm will make a profit of over $2,000 per week, which is more than it can make at any other output rate.

There is an alternative way to analyze the firm's situation. Rather than

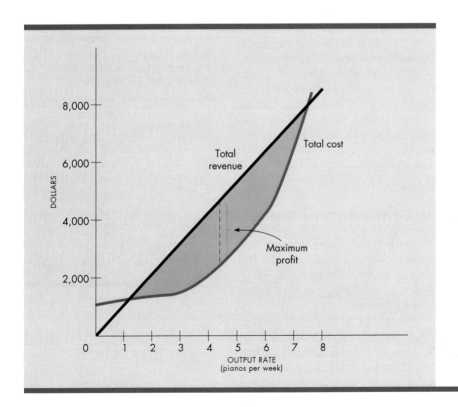

Figure 9.1
Costs, Revenues, and Profits, Allegro Piano Company
Profit equals the vertical distance between the total revenue curve and the total cost curve. This distance is maximized when the output rate is between 4 and 5 pianos per week. At this output rate, profit (measured by the vertical distance) is somewhat more than $2,000.

---

[1] This assumes that the output rate can be varied continuously and that there is a single maximum. These are innocuous assumptions.

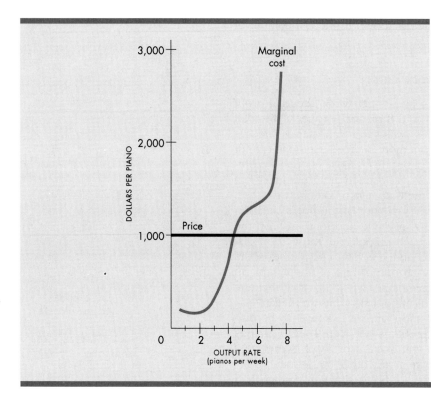

looking at total revenue and total cost, let's look at price and marginal cost. Table 9.3 and Figure 9.2 show the product price and marginal cost of each output rate. It turns out that the maximum profit is achieved at the output rate where price equals marginal cost. In other words, both Table 9.3 and Figure 9.2 indicate that price equals marginal cost at the profit-maximizing output rate of between 4 and 5 pianos per week. This raises a question. Will price usually equal marginal cost at the profit-maximizing output rate, or is this merely a coincidence?

The Golden Rule of Output Determination

Readers familiar with television scripts and detective stories will have recognized that the question just posed can only be answered in one way without ruining the plot. The equality of marginal cost and price at the profit-maximizing output rate is no mere coincidence. It will usually be true if the firm takes the price of its product as given. Indeed, the Golden Rule of Output Determination for a perfectly competitive firm is: *Choose the output rate at which marginal cost is equal to price.*

To determine the profit-maximizing output rate of a firm, compare the extra revenue with the extra cost of each additional unit of output. If the extra revenue (which equals price in the case of perfect competition) is greater than the extra cost (which equals marginal cost), the extra unit should be produced; otherwise, it should not be produced. For example, let's reconsider the Allegro Piano Company. Should this firm produce the first piano? Yes, because (according to Table 9.3) the extra revenue ($1,000) exceeds the extra cost ($200). Should it produce a second piano? Yes, because the extra revenue ($1,000) exceeds the extra cost ($100).

Table 9.3
Marginal Cost and Price, Allegro Piano Company

OUTPUT PER WEEK (PIANOS)	MARGINAL COST (DOLLARS)	PRICE
0		1,000
1	200	1,000
2	100	1,000
3	200	1,000
4	500	1,000
5	1,000	1,000
6	1,200	1,000
7	1,300	1,000
8	2,700	1,000

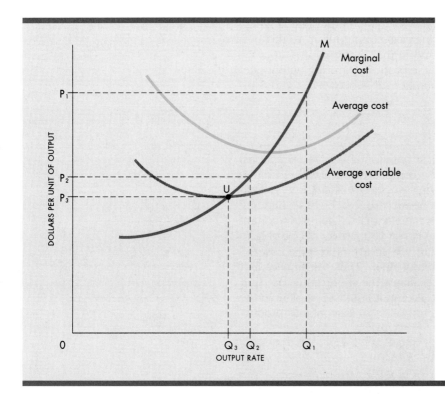

Figure 9.3
Short-Run Average and Marginal Cost Curves
If price is OP_1, the profit-maximizing output rate is OQ_1. If price is OP_2, the profit-maximizing output rate is OQ_2, even though the firm will incur a loss. If the price is below OP_3, the firm will discontinue production. (Note that, regardless of what the price is, the demand curve facing the firm is a horizontal line at this price.)

Should it produce a sixth piano? No, because the extra revenue ($1,000) is less than the extra cost ($1,200).

To prove that a perfectly competitive firm will maximize profit by producing the output where price equals marginal cost, consider Figure 9.3, which shows a typical short-run marginal cost function. Suppose that the price is OP_1. At any output rate less than OQ_1, price is greater than marginal cost.[2] This means that increases in output will increase the firm's profits since they will add more to total revenues than to total costs. Why? Because, as we have seen, an extra unit of output adds an amount equal to price to total revenue and an amount equal to marginal cost to total cost. Thus, since price exceeds marginal cost, an extra unit of output adds more to total revenue than to total cost.

At any output rate above OQ_1, price is less than marginal cost. This means that decreases in output will increase the firm's profits since they will subtract more from total costs than from total revenue. This happens because one less unit of output subtracts an amount equal to price from total revenue and an amount equal to marginal cost from total cost. Thus, since price is less than marginal cost, one less unit of output subtracts more from total cost than from total revenue. (Such a case occurs when the Allegro Piano Company is producing 7 pianos per week. As shown in Table 9.3, the extra cost of producing the seventh piano is $1,300, while the extra revenue it brings in is $1,000. So it pays the Allegro Piano Company to produce less than 7 pianos per week.)

Since increases in output will increase profits if output is less than OQ_1, and decreases in output will increase profits if output is greater than OQ_1,

[2] Except perhaps for an irrelevant range where marginal cost decreases with increases in output.

it follows that profits must be maximized at OQ_1, the output rate at which price equals marginal cost. After all, if increases in output up to this output (OQ_1) result in increases in profit and further increases in output result in decreases in profit, OQ_1 must be the profit-maximizing output rate. For the Allegro Piano Company, this output rate is between 4 and 5 pianos per week, as we saw above.

Does It Pay to Be a Dropout?

All rules—even the Golden Rule we just mentioned—have exceptions. Under some circumstances, the perfectly competitive firm will not maximize its profits if it sets marginal cost equal to price. Instead, it will maximize profits only if it becomes an economic dropout by discontinuing production. Let's demonstrate that this is indeed a fact. The first important point is that even if the firm is doing the best it can, it may not be able to earn a profit. If the price is OP_2 in Figure 9.3, short-run average cost exceeds the price, OP_2, at all possible output rates. Thus the firm cannot earn a profit whatever output it produces. Since the short run is too short for the firm to alter the scale of its plant, it cannot liquidate its plant in the short run. Its only choice is to produce at a loss or discontinue production.

Under what conditions will the firm produce at a loss, and under what conditions will it discontinue production? *If there is an output rate where price exceeds average variable cost, it will pay the firm to produce, even though price does not cover average total cost. If there is no such output rate, the firm is better off to produce nothing at all.* This is true because even if the firm produces nothing, it must pay its fixed cost. Thus, if the loss resulting from production is less than the firm's fixed cost, the firm is better off producing than not producing. On the other hand, if the loss resulting from production is greater than the firm's fixed cost, the firm is better off not to produce.

In other words, *the firm will find it advantageous to produce if total losses are less than total fixed cost.* Since

$$\text{total losses} = \text{total cost} - \text{total revenue},$$

this will be the case if

$$\text{total cost} - \text{total revenue} < \text{total fixed cost}.$$

If we subtract total fixed cost from both sides of this inequality, and if we add total revenue to both sides, we find that the firm is better off to produce if

$$\text{total cost} - \text{total fixed cost} < \text{total revenue}.$$

Dividing each side of this inequality by output (and recognizing that total revenue = price × output), we find that the firm is better off to produce if

$$\text{average variable cost} < \text{price},$$

since average variable cost equals average total cost minus average fixed cost.

Once again, we have proved what we set out to prove—that the firm will maximize profits by producing *nothing* if there is no output rate at which price exceeds average variable cost. If such an output rate does exist, the Golden Rule applies: The firm will set its output rate at the point where marginal cost equals price.

Dropping Out: Illustrative Cases

To illustrate the conditions under which it pays a firm to drop out, suppose that the cost functions of the Allegro Piano Company are as shown in Table 9.4. In this case, there exists no output rate such that average variable cost is less than price—which, you will recall, is $1,000 per piano. Thus, according to the results of the last paragraphs, the Allegro Piano Company should discontinue production under these conditions. The wisdom of this course of action is shown by the last column of Table 9.4, which demonstrates that the profit-maximizing—or, what amounts to the same thing, the loss-minimizing—output rate is zero.

Sometimes, as in the present case, the best thing to produce is nothing. The situation is analogous to the common experience of leaving a movie after the first ten minutes indicate that it is not going to be a good one, even though the admission price is not refundable. One ignores the fixed costs (the admission price) and, finding that the variable cost (the pleasure gained from activities that would be forgone by seeing the rest of the show) is going to exceed the benefits of staying, one leaves.

Table 9.4
Costs and Revenues, Allegro Piano Company

$\rightarrow TR-TC$

OUTPUT PER WEEK (PIANOS)	PRICE	TOTAL REVENUE	TOTAL FIXED COST	TOTAL VARIABLE COST (DOLLARS)	AVERAGE VARIABLE COST	TOTAL COST	TOTAL PROFIT
0	1,000	0	1,000	0	—	1,000	–1,000
1	1,000	1,000	1,000	1,200	1,200	2,200	–1,200
2	1,000	2,000	1,000	2,600	1,300	3,600	–1,600
3	1,000	3,000	1,000	4,200	1,400	5,200	–2,200
4	1,000	4,000	1,000	6,000	1,500	7,000	–3,000
5	1,000	5,000	1,000	8,000	1,600	9,000	–4,000
6	1,000	6,000	1,000	10,200	1,700	11,200	–5,200
7	1,000	7,000	1,000	12,600	1,800	13,600	–6,600
8	1,000	8,000	1,000	15,200	1,900	16,200	–8,200

Several years ago, some sour cherry producers left cherries on their trees unpicked for essentially this reason. A warm spring created a bumper crop so big that the prices dropped sharply. For some producers, average variable costs exceeded price at all possible output levels. The consequence, as our theory would predict, was that producers began to close down. For example, in western New York, some cherry growers considered "bulldozing their orchards and going out of business," in the words of a Williamson, New York, farmer.

THE MARKET SUPPLY CURVE

In Chapter 3, we described some of the factors underlying a commodity's market supply curve, but we could not go into much detail. Now we can, because our Golden Rule of Output Determination underlies the market supply curve. As a first step, let's derive the ***firm's supply curve,*** which shows how much the firm will want to produce at each price.

The Firm's Supply Curve

Since the firm takes the price of its product as given (and can sell all it wants at that price), we know from the previous sections that the firm will choose the output level at which price equals marginal cost. Or if the price is below the firm's average variable cost curve at every output level, the firm will produce nothing. These results are all we need to determine the firm's supply curve.

Suppose that the firm's short-run cost curves are as shown in Figure 9.3. The marginal cost curve must intersect the average variable cost curve at the latter's minimum point, U. If the price of the product is less than OP_3, the firm will produce nothing, because there is no output level where price exceeds average variable cost. If the price of the product exceeds OP_3, the firm will set its output rate at the point where price equals marginal cost. Thus, if the price is OP_1, the firm will produce OQ_1; if the price is OP_2, the firm will produce OQ_2; and so forth. Consequently, *the firm's supply curve is exactly the same as the firm's marginal cost curve for prices above the minimum value of average variable cost (OP_3).* For prices at or below the minimum value of average variable cost, the firm's supply curve corresponds to the price axis, the desire to supply at these prices being uniformly zero. Thus the firm's supply curve is OP_3UM.

DERIVING THE MARKET SUPPLY CURVE

Our next step is to derive the market supply curve from the supply curves of the individual firms. If one assumption holds, the ***market supply curve*** *can be regarded as the horizontal summation of the supply curves of all the firms producing the product.* If there were 3 firms in the industry and their supply curves were as shown in Figure 9.4, the market supply curve would be the horizontal summation of their 3 supply curves. Thus,

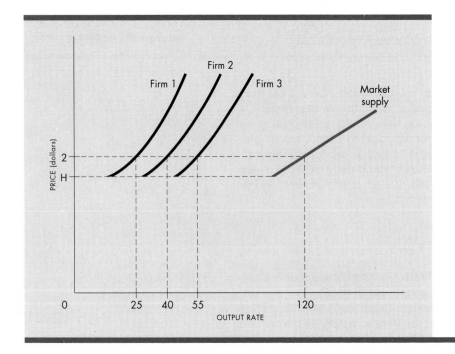

Figure 9.4
Horizontal Summation of Short-Run Supply Curves of Firms
If each of the three firms' supply curves is as shown here (and if each firm supplies nothing if the price is below *OH*), the market supply curve is the horizontal summation of the firms' supply curves, assuming that input prices are not influenced by the output of the industry. If the price is $2, firm 1 will supply 25 units, firm 2 will supply 40 units, and firm 3 will supply 55 units; thus, the total amount supplied is 120 units.

EXAMPLE 9.1   HOW MUCH MERCURY DO WE HAVE?

According to the U.S. Bureau of Mines, the quantity of mercury reserves in the United States at selected price levels of mercury is as follows:

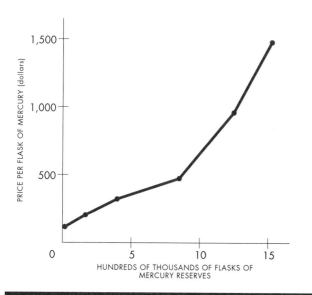

(a) Is this the supply curve for mercury? Why, or why not? (b) Does this curve show how much mercury will be supplied per period of time? (c) Why is the quantity of reserves sensitive to price? (d) Does it appear that, as price increases, beyond some point increasing price begins to lose its power to elicit substantially larger supplies? Is this reasonable? Why, or why not?

Solution

(a) No. This curve shows how much mercury will be available (not produced) at various prices. (b) No. (c) Because, at higher mercury prices, it becomes profitable to obtain mercury from relatively high-cost sources; whereas at lower mercury prices this is not the case. (d) Yes. This is reasonable because beyond some point it becomes increasingly expensive to find and obtain an extra flask of mercury.

since these 3 supply curves show that firm 1 would supply 25 units of output at a price of $2 per unit, that firm 2 would supply 40 units at this price, and that firm 3 would supply 55 units at this price, the market supply curve shows that 120 units of output will be supplied if the price is $2 per unit. Why? Because the market supply curve shows the *total* amount of the product that all of the firms together would supply at this price—and 25 + 40 + 55 = 120. If there were only 3 firms, the market would not be perfectly competitive, but we can ignore this inconsistency. Figure 9.4 is designed to illustrate the fact that the market supply curve is the horizontal summation of the firm supply curves, at least under one important assumption.

The assumption underlying this construction of the short-run market supply curve is that *increases or decreases in output by all firms simultaneously do not affect input prices*. This is a convenient simplification, but it is not always true. Although changes in the output of one firm alone often cannot affect input prices, the simultaneous expansion or contraction of output by all firms may well alter input prices, so that the individual firm's cost curves—and supply curve—will shift. For instance, an expansion of the whole industry may bid up the price of certain inputs, with the result that the cost curves of the individual firms will be pushed upward. In the aerospace industry, a sudden expansion of the industry might well increase the price of certain inputs like the services of aerospace scientists and engineers.

If, contrary to the assumption underlying Figure 9.4, input prices *are* increased by the expansion of the industry, one can still derive the short-run market supply curve by seeing how much the industry will supply in the short run at each price of the product. But it is incorrect to assume that the market supply curve is the horizontal summation of the firm supply curves. More will be said in the chapter Appendix about the effects of industry output on input prices.

Determinants of the Location and Shape of the Market Supply Curve

Based on the preceding discussion, we now can identify the basic determinants of the location and shape of a commodity's short-run market supply curve. If increases or decreases in output by all firms do not affect input prices, the short-run market supply curve is the horizontal summation of the firm supply curves. Thus its location and shape are derived from the location and shapes of the marginal cost curves of the firms in the industry, since these marginal cost curves determine the firm supply curves. From previous chapters, we know that the location and shape of each marginal cost curve depend on *the size of the firm's plants, the level of input prices, and the state of technology* in particular. Thus these factors play a major role in determining the location and shape of the market supply curve. Also, its location and shape in the short run are determined by the *number of firms* in the industry. The market supply curve in Figure 9.4 would be located farther to the right if there were more firms in the industry. In addition, its location and shape are determined by *the effect of industry output on input prices.*

The short-run market supply curve generally slopes upward and to the right because marginal cost curves (in the relevant range) generally slope upward to the right. If industry output does not affect input prices, the market supply curve is the horizontal sum of the firms' marginal cost curves (in the range where they are rising). Consequently, since each of the marginal cost curves slopes upward and to the right (in this range), this is also true of their horizontal sum, the short-run market supply curve.

TEST YOURSELF

1. Suppose that the total costs of a perfectly competitive firm are as follows:

OUTPUT RATE	TOTAL COST (DOLLARS)
0	40
1	60
2	90
3	130
4	180
5	240

If the price of the product is $50, what output rate should the firm choose?

2. Suppose that the firm in Question 1 experienced an increase of $30 in its fixed costs. Plot its new total cost function. What effect will this increase in its fixed costs have on the output it will choose?

3. After the increase in fixed costs described in Question 2, what does the firm's marginal cost curve look like? Plot it on a graph. Does it differ from what it was before the increase in fixed costs? Why, or why not?

4. After the increase in fixed costs described in Question 2, what output rate would the firm choose if the price of its product were $40? $50? $60? $70?

THE PRICE ELASTICITY OF SUPPLY

Market supply curves vary in their shape. For some commodities, the quantity supplied is very sensitive to changes in the commodity's price. For others, the quantity supplied is not at all sensitive to changes in price. To measure the sensitivity of quantity supplied to changes in price, economists use the **price elasticity of supply,** *which is defined as the percentage change in quantity supplied resulting from a 1 percent change in price*. Suppose that a 1 percent reduction in the price of slingshots results in a 1.5 percent reduction in the quantity supplied. Then the price elasticity of supply for slingshots (in the neighborhood of the existing price) is 1.5. The price elasticity of supply is likely to vary from one point to another on the market supply curve. Thus the price elasticity of supply for slingshots may be higher when the price of a slingshot is $2 than when it is $1.

The same factors that influence the location and shape of the market supply curve also determine the price elasticity of supply. But to these factors previously mentioned—the number of plants, input prices, and the nature of technology, among others—another important factor should be added—the length of the time period to which the supply curve pertains. *Market supply curves, like market demand curves, tend to be more price elastic if the time period is long rather than short*. Consider the market for watermelons. If we are dealing with a very short period—a few hours or a day—the supply of watermelons may be fixed, as shown in Figure 9.5. That is, the market supply curve may be perfectly inelastic, the price elasticity of supply being zero, because the period is too short to grow any more watermelons or transport any more watermelons into the market.

Suppose now that we lengthen the period of time to a year or so. In this period, farmers can alter the size of their watermelon crop in response to variations in price. Thus the price elasticity of supply will be higher than in the very short period of a few hours or a day. In this longer period, the price elasticity of supply has been estimated to be about .30; and the supply curve may be as shown in Figure 9.5.

Finally, suppose that we lengthen the period further—to 10 years. In this period, farmers will take land out of watermelon production or put

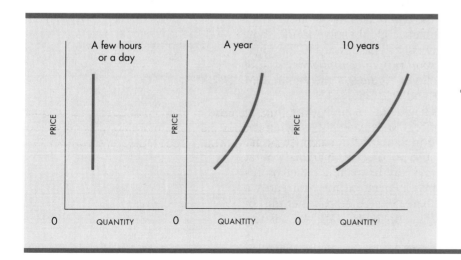

Figure 9.5
Market Supply Curves for Watermelons, Periods of Varying Length
The left-hand panel shows the market supply curve in a period of a few hours or a day. The middle panel refers to a year or so. The right-hand panel refers to 10 years.

land into watermelon production. Indeed, they can make all reasonable adjustments to changes in price. So the price elasticity of supply will be higher than in a period of a year or so—and much higher than in a period of a few hours or a day. The supply curve may be as shown in Figure 9.5.

PRICE AND OUTPUT: THE MARKET PERIOD

How much of a particular product will be produced if the market is perfectly competitive, and what will the price be? The answers depend on the length of the time period. To begin with, let's consider the relatively short period of time when the supply of the relevant good is *fixed*. This period of time is called the **market period.** In the market period, as in the short and long runs, the price of a good in a perfectly competitive market is determined by the market demand and market supply curves. However, in the market period, the market supply curve is a vertical line, as shown in Figure 9.6.

Thus, in the market period, output is unaffected by price. In Figure 9.6, output is OQ—and regardless of price, it cannot be changed. The equilibrium price depends on the position of the demand curve. Price is OP_1 if the demand curve is A, and OP_2 if the demand curve is B.

The role of the price as a rationing device is particularly obvious in the market period, where this is the major function of price. Consumers who are willing to pay a relatively high price get some of the product; others do without. The allocation of jam in the prisoner-of-war camp and the allocation of tickets to *A Chorus Line*, both taken up in Chapter 3, are among the examples you have encountered earlier of how price rations output in the market period. These cases can be regarded as taking place in the market period because the supply is fixed in each case.

PRICE AND OUTPUT: THE SHORT RUN

Let's turn now to the short run, the period during which each firm's plant and equipment are fixed. What determines the price and output of a good in a perfectly competitive market in the short run? The answer once again is the market demand and market supply curves. However, the position and shape of these curves will generally be different in the short run than in the market period. In particular, the market supply curve in the short run will not be a vertical line; it will generally slope upward to the right, as in panel B of Figure 9.7. Thus, *in the short run, price influences, as well as rations, the amount supplied.* In panel B of Figure 9.7, the equilibrium price and output in the short run are OP and OQ.

Panel A of Figure 9.7 shows the behavior of an individual firm in short-run equilibrium. Since OP is the price, the demand curve facing the firm is a horizontal line at OP, as shown in panel A. To maximize profit, the firm produces an output of Oq, because price equals marginal cost at this output. In short-run equilibrium, firms may be making either profits or losses. In the particular case described in panel A, the firm earns a profit equal to the shaded area shown there. Since the profit per unit of output equals CP, total profit equals CP multiplied by Oq, which is this shaded area.

Taken together, the two panels in Figure 9.7 bring out the following

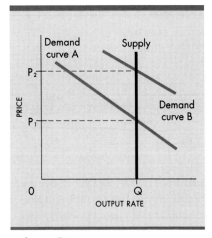

Figure 9.6
Price Determination in the Market Period
In the market period, supply is fixed at OQ. Equilibrium price is OP_1 if the demand curve is demand curve A, and OP_2 if the demand curve is demand curve B.

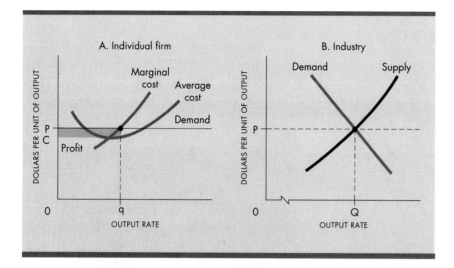

A. Individual firm

DOLLARS PER UNIT OF OUTPUT

Marginal cost
Average cost
Demand
P
C
Profit

0   q
OUTPUT RATE

B. Industry

DOLLARS PER UNIT OF OUTPUT

Demand   Supply
P

0   Q
OUTPUT RATE

Figure 9.7
Short-Run Competitive Equilibrium
In the short run, equilibrium price is OP, and the equilibrium output of the industry is OQ, since (as shown in panel B) the industry demand and supply curves intersect at this price and output. The demand curve facing the individual firm is a horizontal line at OP (as shown in panel A). Each firm produces Oq units of the product, since this is the output that maximizes its profits. The output of the industry (OQ) is the sum of the outputs (Oq) of the individual firms. In short-run equilibrium, firms may be making either profits or losses. In this particular case, the individual firm earns a profit equal to the shaded area in panel A. (Why? Because the profit *per unit of output* equals the price [OP] minus average cost [OC], or the vertical distance CP. To obtain the firm's *total profit*, this distance must be multiplied by the firm's output [Oq], the result being the shaded area.) If firms were making losses rather than profits, the demand curve confronting each firm would intersect the marginal cost curve at a point below (rather than above) the average cost curve.

important point. To the *individual* firm, the price of the product is taken as given. If the price is OP, the firm in panel A reacts to this price by setting an output rate of Oq units. It cannot alter the price; it can only react to it. But *as a group* the reactions of the firms are a major determinant of the price of the product. The supply curve in panel B shows the total amount that the entire group of firms will supply at each price. It summarizes the reactions of the firms to various levels of the price. Put briefly, the equilibrium price is viewed by the individual firm as being beyond its control; yet the supply decisions of all firms taken as a group are a basic determinant of the equilibrium price.

PRICE AND OUTPUT: THE LONG RUN

In the long run, what determines the output and price of a good in a perfectly competitive market? In the long run, a firm can change its plant size, which means that established firms may *leave* an industry if it has below-average profits, or that new firms may *enter* an industry with above-average profits. Suppose that textile firms can earn up to (but no more than) a 15 percent rate of return by investing their resources in other industries. If they can earn only 12 percent by keeping these resources invested in the textile industry, they will leave the textile industry. On the other hand, if a rate of return of 18 percent can be earned by investing in the textile industry, firms in other industries, attracted by this relatively high return, will enter the textile industry.

Equilibrium: Zero Economic Profit

Equilibrium is achieved in the long run when enough firms—no more, no less—are in the industry so that **economic profits**—*defined as the excess of a firm's profits over what it could make in other industries*—*are zero*. This condition is necessary for long-run equilibrium because, as we have seen, new firms will enter the industry if there are economic profits, and existing firms will leave if there are economic losses. This process of entry and exit is the key to long-run equilibrium. It is discussed repeatedly in this and subsequent sections.

RECENT DEVELOPMENTS IN ECONOMICS: LABORATORY EXPERIMENTATION

In the past decade or two, economists have begun to use laboratory experiments to understand better how markets work. In an experimental market, the subjects (often college students) trade a commodity (e.g., a scrap of paper) that has no intrinsic value. Buyers make a profit by purchasing the commodity from sellers and reselling it to the experimenter. For example, the rules of the experiment may state that the experimenter will redeem the first unit of the commodity for $2.00, the second unit for $1.50, the third unit for $1.00, and so on. Sellers make a profit by buying units from the experimenter and selling them to the buyers. For example, the experimenter may provide the seller with the first unit of the commodity for $0.25, the second unit for $0.75, the third unit for $1.00, and so on.

The way in which the market is organized varies from experiment to experiment. Frequently, they are organized as double auctions, which are characterized by public bids to buy units of the commodity and public offers to sell units of it. Any participant is free to accept whatever terms he or she wants. Typically, bids are made verbally. An auctioneer, when hearing a bid or offer, writes it on the blackboard. The last bid and offer remain standing until accepted, cancelled, or replaced.

Based on the work of Caltech's Charles Plott, Arizona's Vernon Smith, and other leaders in this new field, auctions of this type tend to converge to the competitive equilibrium even with relatively few traders. In other words, if one constructs a market demand curve (based on the amount of the commodity that each buyer will purchase at a given price in order to maximize profit) and a market supply curve (based on the amount of the commodity that each seller will sell at a given price in order to maximize profit), the actual price in the experiment gen-

Charles Plott

erally moves toward the level at which the market demand curve intersects the market supply curve.

This, of course, is an interesting test of the basic model considered in this chapter, which seems to come through with flying colors. Laboratory experiments have also been carried out to test and extend the models of monopoly, monopolistic competition, and oligopoly discussed in succeeding chapters. Without question, such experiments have been and will be useful in a variety of ways. However, as the leading experimenters are quick to point out, one must be very careful in extrapolating behavior from a very simple laboratory setting to a complex industrial environment. The real world is, of course, a lot more complicated than these simple experiments.

Note that the existence of economic profits or losses in an industry brings about a shift in the industry's short-run supply curve. If there are economic profits, new firms will enter the industry, and so shift the short-run supply curve to the right. On the other hand, if there are economic losses in the industry (i.e., if the industry's profits are less than could be obtained elsewhere), existing firms will leave the industry, causing the short-run supply curve to shift to the left. Only if economic profits are zero will the number of firms in the industry—and the industry's short-run supply curve—be stable. Putting this equilibrium condition another way, *the long-run equilibrium position of the firm is at the point where its long-run average costs (i.e., average total costs) equal price.* If price exceeds average total costs, economic profits are being earned; and if price is less than average total costs, economic losses are being incurred.

Equilibrium: Maximum Economic Profit

Going a step further, *long-run equilibrium requires that price equal the lowest value of long-run average total costs.* In other words, firms must be producing at the *minimum point* on their long-run average cost curves, because to maximize their profits they must operate where price equals long-run marginal costs,[3] and at the same time they also have to operate where price equals long-run average cost. But if both these conditions are satisfied, long-run marginal cost must equal long-run average cost—since both equal price. And we know that long-run marginal cost equals long-run average cost only at the point at which long-run average cost is a minimum.[4] Consequently, if long-run marginal cost equals long-run average cost, the firm must be producing at the minimum point on the long-run average cost curve.

This equilibrium position is illustrated in Figure 9.8. When all adjust-

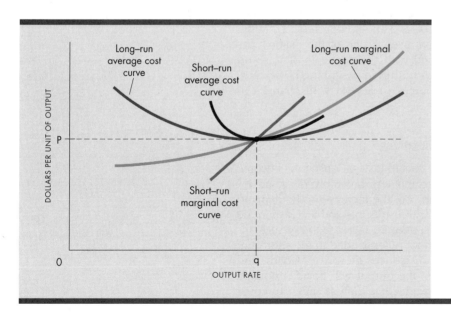

Figure 9.8
Long-Run Equilibrium of a Perfectly Competitive Firm
In long-run equilibrium, output is *Oq* and the firm's plant corresponds to the short-run average and marginal cost curves shown here. At *Oq*, long-run marginal cost equals short-run marginal cost equals price; also, long-run average cost equals short-run average cost equals price. These conditions ensure that the firm is maximizing profits and that economic profits are zero.

---

[3] The reasons why marginal cost must be equal to price, if profits are to be maximized, are given in earlier sections of this chapter.
[4] The previous discussion of this point on p. 149 concerned short-run cost functions, but the argument applies just as well to long-run cost functions.

ments are made, price equals *OP*. The equilibrium output of the firm is *Oq*, and its plant corresponds to the short-run average and marginal cost curves in Figure 9.8. At this output and with this plant, long-run marginal cost equals short-run marginal cost equals price. This ensures that the firm is maximizing profit. Also, long-run average cost equals short-run average cost equals price. This ensures that economic profits are zero. Since the long-run marginal cost and long-run average cost must be equal, the firm is producing at the minimum point on its long-run average cost curve.

To illustrate the process of entry and exit in an industry that has approximated perfect competition, let's consider the bituminous coal industry. Entry into this industry has been relatively easy, but exit has been relatively difficult, for at least two reasons. First, it is costly to shut down a mine and reopen it later. Second, because of corrosion and water damage, it is hard to shut down a mine for longer than two years unless it is to be abandoned entirely. For these reasons, mines tend to stay open and produce even though short-term losses are incurred. In the period before World War II, the demand for coal fell substantially, but while the industry suffered substantial losses, mines were slow to close down. Nonetheless, the competitive process had its way. Slowly, but surely, the number of mines fell markedly in response to these losses. Thus, despite the barriers to rapid exit, firms eventually left the industry, just as the model would predict.

THE ALLOCATION OF RESOURCES UNDER PERFECT COMPETITION: A MORE DETAILED VIEW

At this point, it is instructive to describe the process by which a perfectly competitive economy—one composed of perfectly competitive industries—would allocate resources. In Chapters 2 and 3, we stressed that the allocation of resources among alternative uses is one of the major functions of any economic system. Equipped with the concepts of this and previous chapters, we can now go much further in describing how a perfectly competitive economy shifts resources in accord with changes in tastes, technology, and other factors.

Consumers Turn from Corn to Wheat

To be specific, suppose that a change occurs in tastes. Consumers become more favorably disposed toward wheat and less favorably disposed toward corn than in the past.[5] In the short run, the increase in the demand for wheat increases the price of wheat, and results in some increase in the output of wheat. However, the output cannot be increased very substantially because the industry's capacity cannot be expanded in the short run. Similarly, the fall in the demand for corn reduces the price of corn, and results in some reduction in output. But the output will not be curtailed greatly because firms will continue to produce as long as they can cover variable costs.

[5] Since we assume here that the markets for wheat and corn are perfectly competitive, it is also assumed that there is no government intervention in these markets.

Prices Signal Resource Reallocation

The change in the relative prices of wheat and corn tells producers that a reallocation of resources is called for. Because of the increase in the price of wheat and the decrease in the price of corn, wheat producers are earning economic profits and corn producers are showing economic losses. This will trigger a new deployment of resources. If some variable inputs in corn production can be used as effectively in the production of wheat, they may be switched from corn production to wheat production. Even if no variable inputs are used in both wheat and corn production, adjustments can be made in various interrelated markets, with the result that wheat production gains resources and corn production loses resources. When short-run equilibrium is attained in both the wheat and corn industries, the reallocation of resources is not yet complete since there has not been enough time for producers to build new capacity or liquidate old capacity. In particular, neither industry is operating at minimum average cost. The wheat producers are operating at greater than the output level where average cost is a minimum; and the corn producers are operating at less than this level.

Effects in the Long Run

What will happen in the long run? The shift in consumer demand from corn to wheat will result in greater adjustments in production and smaller adjustments in price than in the short run. In the long run, existing firms can leave corn production and new firms can enter wheat production. Because of short-run economic losses in corn production, some corn land and related equipment will be allowed to run down, and some firms engaged in corn production will be liquidated. As firms leave corn production, the supply curve shifts to the left, causing the price to rise above its short-run level. The transfer of resources out of corn production will stop when the price has increased, and costs have decreased, to the point where losses are avoided.

While corn production is losing resources, wheat production is gaining them. The prospect of positive economic profits in wheat production will cause new firms to enter the industry. The increased demand for inputs will raise input prices and cost curves in wheat production, and the price of wheat will be depressed by the movement to the right of the supply curve because of the entry of new firms. Entry ceases when economic profits are no longer being earned. At this point, when long-run equilibrium is achieved, more resources will be used in the industry than were used in the short run. (Note that, if corn land and equipment can be converted to the production of wheat, some of the "entry" may occur through existing farmers' shifting of their crop mix toward wheat and away from corn.)

Finally, long-run equilibrium is established in both industries, and the reallocation of resources is complete. It is important to note that this reallocation can affect industries other than wheat and corn. If corn land and equipment can be easily adapted to the production of wheat, corn producers can simply change to wheat production. If not, the resources used in corn production are converted to some use other than wheat, and the resources that enter wheat production come from some use other than corn production.

EXAMPLE 9.2   HOW MANY APPLES SHOULD BE PRODUCED?

Suppose that the demand and supply curves for apples are as shown below:

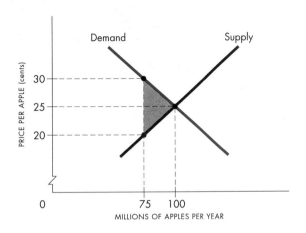

(a) If 75 million apples are produced per year, how much would an additional apple cost to produce? How much would an additional apple be worth to consumers? (b) Under these circumstances, is it socially worthwhile to increase apple production? Why, or why not? (c) If 100 million apples are produced per year, how much would an additional apple cost to produce? How much would an additional apple be worth to consumers? (d) If 100 million apples are produced, is it socially worthwhile to increase apple production? Explain. (e) How great is the loss to society if 75 million, rather than 100 million, apples are produced?

Solution

(a) 20 cents, since the supply curve shows marginal cost. 30 cents, because the demand curve shows the maximum amount consumers would pay for an extra apple. (b) Yes, because the extra social cost of producing an extra apple is less than the extra social benefit from doing so. Consumers would be glad to pay producers to produce extra apples. (c) 25 cents. 25 cents. (d) No, since the extra social cost of producing an extra apple is no less than the maximum amount that consumers would pay for an extra apple. If private benefits and costs do not differ from social benefits and costs, 100 million apples is the optimal output level. It would not be socially worthwhile to exceed or fall short of it. (e) The vertical distance from the demand curve to the supply curve is the difference between the social benefit and the social cost of an *extra* apple. (For example, if 75 million apples are produced, the social benefit of an extra apple exceeds its social cost by 30 – 20 = 10 cents.) Thus the difference between the social benefit and social cost of the *extra 25 million apples* equals the sum of these vertical distances for all of the extra apples. This sum equals the shaded area in the above diagram, which amounts to 25 million × 5 cents = $1.25 million. This is the loss to society.

BITUMINOUS COAL: A CASE STUDY

To illustrate how resources are allocated in the long run, we will look in more detail at the bituminous coal industry. Although it does not have all the characteristics of a perfectly competitive industry, it has had enough of them so that the perfectly competitive model has predicted many aspects of its behavior reasonably well. From the turn of the century until about 1923, the bituminous coal industry expanded rapidly. Between 1903 and 1923, the price of coal increased from $1.24 to $2.68 per ton, in considerable part because of the marked upward shift to the right of the demand curve for coal, an important fuel in this period of general industrial growth. In addition, the high prices of the period were sometimes the result of temporary shortages caused by strikes and insufficient railroad transportation. Thus temporary upward shifts to the left of the supply curve for coal, as well as shifts of the demand curve, were responsible for the increases in price.

Given the very high coal prices of 1917–23, coal mining was very profitable. Indeed, after-tax income in 1920 was about 20 percent of invested capital for all bituminous coal companies—and much higher for particular companies. These high profits signaled that more resources should be invested in the industry. And just as the perfectly competitive model would predict, more resources were invested; the number of bituminous coal firms increased by over 130 percent in nine key states between 1903 and 1923, and the industry's capacity grew by over 50 percent between 1913 and 1923.

Unfortunately, the demand for coal dropped considerably from 1923 to 1933, plunging the industry into a severe economic crisis. The downward shift to the left of the demand curve for coal during the early 1930s was due in considerable part to the fall in national output during the Great Depression. It was accompanied by a marked decrease in the price of coal. From $2.68 in 1923, the price per ton fell to $1.34 in 1933. Needless to say, this tremendous drop meant losses for bituminous coal producers. Indeed, in every year between 1925 and 1940, the bituminous coal industry as a whole showed losses.

These economic losses signaled that resources should be withdrawn from the bituminous coal industry and used elsewhere in the economy where they could be more valuably employed. And as the perfectly competitive model would predict, resources were in fact taken out of bituminous coal. Between 1923 and 1933, there was a reduction of over 40 percent in the number of coal companies operating in nine key states. And the industry's capacity fell by almost 40 percent between 1923 and 1933. Despite the difficulties in exit that we described in a previous section, the competitive process had its way. Its signals were heeded. Consequently, the industry began to move closer and closer to a position of long-run equilibrium, and although the industry remained on the nation's sick list, it began to show much smaller losses. By the onset of World War II, many of the basic adjustments had occurred.

In the postwar period, many important changes have taken place in the bituminous coal industry. Strip mining has become much more important relative to underground mining. The federal government has passed new legislation setting stricter safety requirements for coal. The energy crisis of the 1970s focused new attention on our great coal resources. But from the point of view of the present chapter, perhaps the most interesting development is the increased dominance of the industry by relatively few large firms—and the fact that many big coal companies have been purchased by the major oil firms. About half of the country's 10 biggest coal companies were bought up during the 1960s. Some observers worry that the bituminous coal industry, which tended to be relatively competitive in the past, may be less so in the future.

TEST YOURSELF

1. If the price elasticity of supply for corn is about 0.1 in the short run, as estimated by Marc Nerlove of the University of Pennsylvania, a 1 percent increase in the price of corn would have approximately what impact on the quantity supplied?

2. In Example 9.2, suppose that 125 million apples are produced per year. Under these circumstances, is it socially desirable to reduce apple production? Explain.

3. Suppose that the demand curve for onions is $P = 10 - 3Q$, where P is the price of a pound of onions and Q is the quantity demanded (in millions of pounds). If the supply of onions in the market period is 3⅙ million pounds, what is the equilibrium price of onions in the market period? What does the supply curve for onions look like in the market period?

4. In the short run, suppose that the demand curve for onions is as given in Question 3, and that the supply curve is $P = Q/3$. What is the equilibrium price of onions in the short run? What does the supply curve of onions look like in the short run?

SUMMARY

1. Economists generally classify markets into four types—perfect competition, monopoly, monopolistic competition, and oligopoly. Perfect competition requires that the product of any seller be the same as the product of any other seller, that no buyer or seller be able to influence the price of the product, and that resources be able to switch readily from one use to another.

2. If it maximizes profit, a perfectly competitive firm should set its output rate in the short run at the level where marginal cost equals price, so long as price exceeds average variable cost. If there is no output rate at which price exceeds average variable cost, the firm should discontinue production.

3. The firm's supply curve coincides with its marginal cost curve for prices exceeding the minimum value of average variable cost. For prices that are less than or equal to the minimum value of average variable cost, the firm's supply curve coincides with the price axis.

4. As a first approximation, the market supply curve can be viewed as the horizontal summation of the supply curves of all the firms producing the product. This assumes that increases or decreases in output by all firms simultaneously do not affect input prices.

5. The market supply curve of a product is determined by the size of the firms' plants, the level of input prices, the nature of technology, and the other factors determining the shape of the firms' marginal cost curves, as well as by the effect of changes in the industry output on input prices and by the number of firms producing the product.

6. The sensitivity of the quantity supplied to changes in price is measured by the price elasticity of supply, defined as the percentage change in quantity supplied resulting from a 1 percent change in price. In general, the price elasticity of supply is greater if the time interval is long rather than short.

7. Price and output under perfect competition are determined by the intersection of the market supply and demand curves. In the market period, supply is fixed; thus price plays the role of the allocating device. In the short run, price influences as well as rations the amount supplied.

8. In the long run, equilibrium is achieved under perfect competition when enough firms—no more, no less—are in the industry so that economic profits are eliminated. In other words, the long-run equilibrium position of the firm is at the point where its long-run average cost equals price. But since price must also equal marginal cost (to maximize profit), it follows that the firm must be operating at the minimum point on the long-run average cost curve.

9. In a perfectly competitive economy, prices are the signals that are used to guide the reallocation of resources in response to changes in consumer tastes, technology, and other factors.

CONCEPTS FOR REVIEW

Perfect competition
Monopoly
Monopolistic competition
***Constant cost industry**

Oligopoly
Firm's supply curve
Market supply curve
***Increasing cost industry**

Price elasticity of supply
Market period
Economic profits
***Decreasing cost industry**

* This concept is presented in the Appendix to this chapter.

APPENDIX: CONSTANT, INCREASING, AND DECREASING COST INDUSTRIES

Perfectly competitive industries can be categorized into three types—constant cost industries, increasing cost industries, and decreasing cost industries.

Constant Cost Industries

*In a **constant cost industry** an expansion of output does not result in a change in input prices.* Figure 9.9 shows the long-run equilibrium in a constant cost industry. Panel A shows the short- and long-run cost curves of a typical firm in the industry. Panel B shows the demand and supply curves for the industry as a whole. It is assumed that the industry is in long-run equilibrium, with the result that the price line is tangent to the long-run (and short-run) average cost curve at its minimum point. The price is *OP*.

Let's assume that the demand curve shifts upward and to the right, as shown in panel B. In the short run, with the number of firms fixed, the

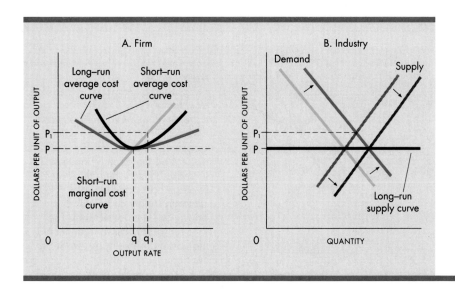

Figure 9.9
Long-Run Equilibrium: Constant Cost Industry
If the demand curve shifts upward and to the right, the price will increase in the short run from *OP* to *OP*$_1$. Each firm will expand output from *Oq* to *Oq*$_1$, and entry will occur, thus shifting the supply curve downward and to the right. The long-run supply curve in a constant cost industry is horizontal.

price of the product will rise from OP to OP_1; each firm will expand output from Oq to Oq_1; and each firm will be making economic profits since OP_1 exceeds the short-run average costs of the firm at Oq_1. The consequence is that firms will enter the industry and shift the short-run supply curve to the right. In a constant cost industry, the entrance of the new firms does not affect the costs of the existing firms. The inputs used by this industry are used by many other industries as well, and the appearance of the new firms in this industry does not bid up the price of inputs (and consequently raise the costs of existing firms). In the long run, the price settles back to OP, the level of (minimum) long-run average cost. Thus *a constant cost industry has a horizontal long-run supply curve.* Since output can be varied by varying the number of firms producing Oq units at an average cost of OP, the long-run supply curve is horizontal at OP.

Increasing Cost Industries

Most economists seem to regard increasing, not constant, cost industries as the most prevalent of the three types. *An **increasing cost industry** is one where the price of inputs increases with the amount the industry uses.* The situation in such an industry is shown in Figure 9.10. The original conditions are the same as those in Figure 9.9, and we suppose again that the demand curve shifts upward and to the right, with the result that the price of the product increases and firms earn economic profits, thus attracting new entrants. More and more inputs are required by the industry, and in an increasing cost industry the price of inputs increases with the amount the industry uses. Consequently, the cost of inputs increases for the established firms as well as the new entrants. The long-run average cost curve of each firm is pushed up, as shown in panel A. The short-run supply curve shifts downward and to the right, as shown in panel B. Thus the new equilibrium price is OP_2 and each firm produces Oq_2 units. *An increasing cost industry has a positively sloped long-run supply curve,* as shown in Figure 9.10. That is, after long-run equilibrium is achieved, increases in output require increases in the price of the product.

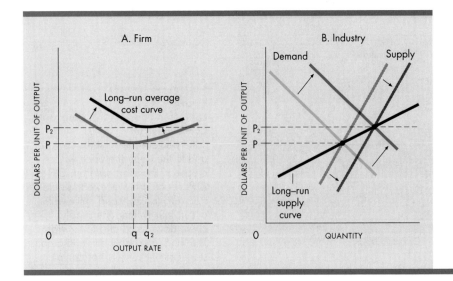

Figure 9.10
Long-Run Equilibrium: Increasing Cost Industry
If the demand curve shifts upward and to the right, the price will increase in the short run. Entry will occur, and the price of inputs will increase, thus pushing the long-run average cost curve upward. The short-run supply curve will shift downward and to the right. The long-run supply curve in an increasing cost industry slopes upward to the right.

Decreasing Cost Industry

Decreasing cost industries are the most unusual situation, although quite young industries may sometimes fall into this category. *In a **decreasing cost industry,** the expansion of the industry results in a decrease in the costs of the established firms.*[6] Thus *a decreasing cost industry has a negatively sloped long-run supply curve.* That is, after long-run equilibrium is reached, increases in output are accompanied by decreases in price.

Whether an industry is a constant cost industry, an increasing cost industry, or a decreasing cost industry is an empirical question that must be settled case by case. In trying to determine whether a particular industry is an increasing or constant cost industry, one important consideration is whether or not it is a relatively large user of certain inputs. Because the automobile industry uses a great deal of the nation's steel, an expansion of the automobile industry might well cause an increase in the price of steel; but an expansion of the paper-clip industry, which uses very little of the nation's steel, would be unlikely to raise the price of steel.

---

[6] Certain *external economies,* which are cost reductions that occur when an industry expands, may be responsible for the existence of decreasing cost industries. An example of such an external economy is an improvement in transportation that is due to the expansion of an industry and that reduces the costs of each firm in the industry.

MONOPOLY AND ITS REGULATION

AT THE OPPOSITE EXTREME from perfect competition is monopoly. Under a monopolistic market structure, what sorts of behavior can we expect? How much of the product will be produced, and at what level will its price be set? What are the social disadvantages of monopoly? In what ways have government commissions attempted to regulate industries whose market structures approximate monopoly? These are some of the major questions dealt with in this chapter.

To begin with, recall what is meant by **monopoly:** *a market where there exists one, and only one, seller.* Monopoly, like perfect competition, seldom corresponds more than approximately to conditions in real industries, but it is a very useful model. In several respects, monopoly and perfect competition stand as polar opposites. The firm in a perfectly competitive market has so many rivals that competition becomes entirely impersonal. The firm is a price taker, an inconspicuous seller in a sea of inconspicuous sellers. Under monopoly, on the other hand, the firm has no direct competitors at all; it is the sole supplier.

However, even the monopolist is affected by certain indirect and potential forms of competition. Suppose a firm managed to obtain a monopoly on wheat production. It would have to worry about competition from corn and other agricultural commodities that could be substituted for wheat. Moreover, the wheat monopolist would also have to take into account the possibility that new firms might arise to challenge its monopoly if it attempted to extract conspicuously high profits. Thus even the monopolist is subject to some restraint imposed by competitive forces.

CAUSES OF MONOPOLY

There are many reasons why monopolies, or market structures that closely approximate monopoly, may arise.

PATENTS. A firm may acquire a monopoly over the production of a good by having patents on the product or on certain basic processes used in its production. The patent laws of the United States give an inventor the exclusive right to make a certain product or to use a certain process for 17 years. The purpose of the patent system is to encourage invention and innovation and to discourage industrial secrecy. Many firms with monopoly power achieved it in considerable part through patents. For example, the United Shoe Machinery Company became the sole supplier of certain important kinds of shoemaking equipment through control of basic patents. United Shoe was free to dominate the market until 1954, when, after prosecution under the antitrust laws, the firm was ordered to license its patents. And in 1968, when this remedy seemed insufficient, a divestiture program was agreed upon.

CONTROL OF INPUT. A firm may become a monopolist by obtaining control over the entire supply of a basic input required to manufacture a product. The International Nickel Company of Canada controls about nine-tenths of the proven nickel reserves in the world. Since it is hard to produce nickel without nickel, the International Nickel Company obviously has a strong monopoly position. Similarly, the Aluminum Company of America (Alcoa) kept its dominant position for a long time by controlling practically all the sources of bauxite, the ore used to make aluminum. However, as we shall see in Chapter 12, Alcoa's monopoly was broken in 1945 when the Supreme Court decided that Alcoa's control of practically all the industry's output violated the antitrust laws.

GOVERNMENT ACTION. A firm may become a monopolist because it is awarded a market franchise by a government agency. The government may give a particular firm the franchise to sell a particular product in a public facility. Or it may give a particular company the right to provide a service, such as telephone service, to people in a particular area. In exchange for this right, the firm agrees to allow the government to regulate certain aspects of its operation. The form of regulation does not matter here; the important point for now is that the monopoly is created by the government.

DECLINING COST OF PRODUCTION. A firm may become a monopolist because the average costs of producing the product reach a minimum at an output rate that is large enough to satisfy the entire market (at a price that is profitable). In a case like this, a firm obviously has an incentive to expand until it produces all the market wants of the good. (Its costs fall as it continues to expand.) Thus competition cannot be maintained in this case. If there are a number of firms in the industry, the result is likely to be economic warfare—and the survival of a single victor, the monopolist.[1]

Cases where costs behave like this are called **_natural monopolies._** When an industry is a natural monopoly, the public often insists that its behavior be regulated by the government. For example, electric power is an industry where there seem to be great economies of scale—and thus decreasing average costs. Fuel consumed per kilowatt hour is lower in larger power generating units, and there are economies in combining generating units at a single site. Because of these factors, there has been little attempt to force competition in the industry, since it would be wasteful. Instead, as we describe later, the market for electric power in a particular area tends to be a regulated monopoly.[2]

The likelihood that the long-run average cost curve will decrease up to a point that satisfies the entire market depends on the size of the market. The smaller the market, the more likely it is. In Figure 10.1, the industry is a natural monopoly if the demand curve is _A,_ but not if it is _B._ In a large

[1] Note that economies of scale are different from the external economies discussed in note 6 of the previous chapter. The individual firm has no control over external economies.
[2] However, it is worth noting that technological developments in this industry may permit more competition in the future.

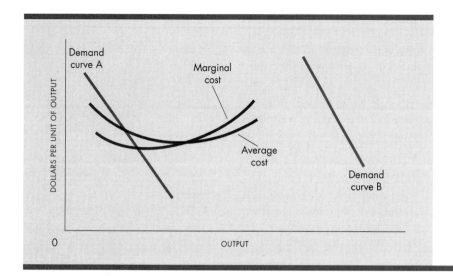

Figure 10.1
Natural Monopoly
The industry is a natural monopoly if the demand curve is *A*, but not if it is *B*.

market like the United States, it is much less likely that an industry will be a natural monopoly than in a small market like Belgium or Denmark. One of the advantages claimed for the reduction in trade barriers among West European countries in 1992 was that it would create a larger market that could support more efficient production and more competitive industries. For now, the important point to recognize is that, just as stagnant marshes are the breeding ground for mosquitos, so small, insulated markets are the breeding ground for monopoly.

DEMAND CURVE AND MARGINAL REVENUE UNDER MONOPOLY

Before we can make any statements about the behavior of a monopolistic market, we must point out certain important characteristics of the demand curve facing the monopolist. Since the monopolist is the only seller of the commodity, the demand curve it faces is the market demand curve for the product. Since the market demand curve is almost always downward-sloping to the right, the monopolist's demand curve must also be downward-sloping to the right. This is quite different from perfect competition, where the firm's demand curve is horizontal. To illustrate the situation faced by a monopolist, consider the hypothetical case in Table 10.1. The price at which each quantity (shown in column 1) can be sold by the monopolist is shown in column 2. The firm's **total revenue**—its total dollar sales volume—is shown in column 3. Obviously, column 3 is the product of the first two columns. Column 4 contains the firm's **marginal revenue,** *defined as the addition to total revenue attributable to the addition of one unit to sales*. (Thus, if *R(q)* is total revenue when *q* units are sold and *R(q−1)* is total revenue when (*q−1*) units are sold, the marginal revenue between *q* units and (*q−1*) units is *R(q) − R(q−1)*.)

Marginal revenue is very important to the monopolist. We can estimate it from the figures in the first three columns of Table 10.1. The marginal revenue between 1 and 2 units of output per day is $180 − $100, or $80; the marginal revenue between 2 and 3 units of output per day is $240 − $180, or $60; the marginal revenue between 3 and 4 units of output per

Table 10.1
Demand and Revenue of a Monopolist

QUANTITY	PRICE	TOTAL REVENUE (DOLLARS)	MARGINAL REVENUE
1	100	100	80
2	90	180	60
3	80	240	40
4	70	280	20
5	60	300	0
6	50	300	−20
7	40	280	−40
8	30	240	

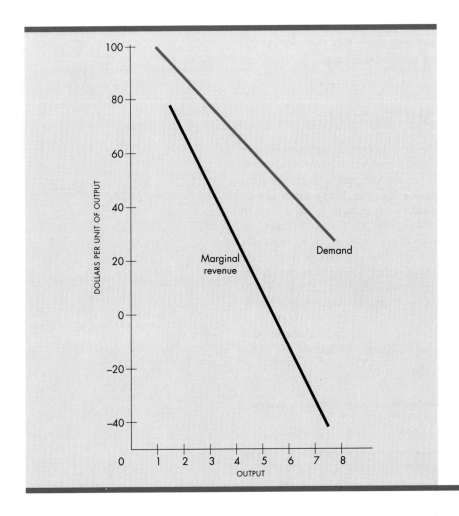

Figure 10.2
Marginal Revenue and
Demand Curves
The demand curve comes from Table 10.1. Each value of marginal revenue is plotted at the midpoint of the range of output to which it pertains. Since the demand curve is downward-sloping, marginal revenue is always less than price, for reasons discussed in the text. Note that the value of marginal revenue is related to the price elasticity of demand. At outputs where demand is price elastic, marginal revenue is *positive*; at outputs where it is price inelastic, marginal revenue is *negative*; and at outputs where it is of unitary elasticity, marginal revenue is *zero*.

day is $280 − $240, or $40; and so on. The results are shown in column 4 of the table (and are plotted in Figure 10.2). Note that marginal revenue is analogous to marginal cost (and marginal utility and marginal product, for that matter). Recall that marginal cost is the extra cost resulting from an extra unit of production. Substitute "revenue" for "cost" and "sales" for "production" in the previous sentence, and what do you get? A perfectly acceptable definition of marginal revenue.

Marginal revenue will always be less than price if the firm's demand curve is downward-sloping (as it is under monopoly and other market structures that are not perfectly competitive). In Table 10.1, the extra revenue from the second unit of output is $80 whereas the price of this unit is $90. *The basic reason is that the firm must reduce the price of all units of output, not just the extra unit, in order to sell the extra unit.* Thus, in Table 10.1, the extra revenue from the second unit of output is $80 because, while the price of the second unit is $90, the price of the first unit must be reduced by $10 in order to sell the second unit. Thus the extra revenue (that is, marginal revenue) from selling the second unit of output is $90 − $10, or $80, which is less than the price of the second unit.

Similarly, the marginal revenue from selling the third unit of output ($60, according to Table 10.1) is less than the price at which the third unit can be sold ($80, according to Table 10.1). Why? Because, to sell the third unit of output, the price of the first two units of output must be reduced by $10 each (that is, from $90 to $80). Thus the extra revenue (that is, marginal revenue) from selling the third unit is not $80, but $80 less the $20 reduction in the amount received for the first two units.

PRICE AND OUTPUT: THE SHORT RUN

We are now in a position to determine how output and price behave under monopoly. If the monopolist is free to maximize its profits, it will choose the price and output rate at which the difference between total revenue and total cost is greatest. Suppose that the firm's costs are as shown in Table 10.2 and that the demand curve it faces is as shown in Table 10.1. Based on the data in these two tables, the firm can calculate the profit that it will make at each output rate. To do so, it subtracts its total cost from its total revenue, as shown in Table 10.3. What output rate will maximize the firm's profit? According to Table 10.3, profit *rises* as its output rate increases from 1 to 3 units per day, and profit *falls* as its output rate increases from 4 to 8 units per day. Thus the *maximum* profit is achieved at an output rate between 3 and 4 units per day.[3] (Without more detailed data, one cannot tell precisely where the maximum occurs, but this is close enough for present purposes.) Figure 10.3 shows the same thing graphically.

Table 10.2
Costs of a Monopolist

QUANTITY	TOTAL VARIABLE COST	TOTAL FIXED COST (DOLLARS)	TOTAL COST	MARGINAL COST
0	0	100	100	
1	40	100	140	40
2	70	100	170	30
3	110	100	210	40
4	150	100	250	40
5	200	100	300	50
6	260	100	360	60
7	350	100	450	90
8	450	100	550	100

Table 10.3
Profits of a Monopolist

QUANTITY	TOTAL REVENUE	TOTAL COST	TOTAL PROFIT
		(DOLLARS)	
1	100	140	−40
2	180	170	10
3	240	210	30
4	280	250	30
5	300	300	0
6	300	360	−60
7	280	450	−170
8	240	550	−310

What price will the monopolist charge? To maximize its profit, it must charge the price that results in its selling the profit-maximizing output, which in this case is between 3 and 4 units per day. Thus, according to Table 10.1, it must charge between $70 and $80 per unit. Why? Because if it charges $70, it will sell 4 units per day; and if it charges $80, it will sell 3 units per day. Consequently, to sell the profit-maximizing output of between 3 and 4 units per day, it must charge a price of between $70 and $80 per unit.

[3] This assumes that the output rate can vary continuously and that there is a single maximum. These are innocuous assumptions.

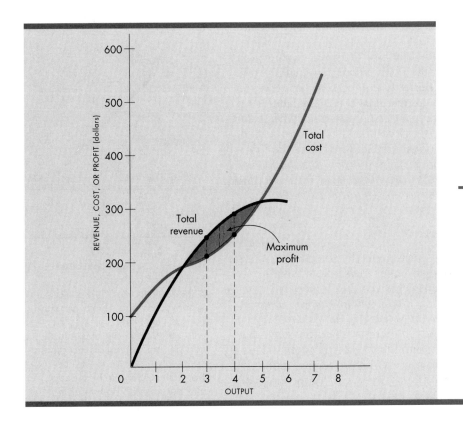

Figure 10.3
Total Revenue, Cost, and Profit of a Monopolist
The output rate that will maximize the firm's profit is between 3 and 4 units per day. At this output rate, profit (which equals the vertical distance between the total revenue and total cost curves) is over $30 per day. Based on the demand curve for its product (shown in Table 10.1), the firm must set a price of between $70 and $80 to sell between 3 and 4 units per day.

The Golden Rule of Output Determination

In Chapter 9, we set forth the Golden Rule of Output Determination for a perfectly competitive firm. We can now formulate a Golden Rule of Output Determination for a monopolist: *set the output rate at the point where marginal revenue equals marginal cost.* Table 10.4 and Figure 10.4 show that this rule results in a maximum profit in this example. It is evident from Table 10.4 that marginal revenue equals marginal cost at the profit-maximizing output of between 3 and 4 units per day. Figure 10.4 shows the same thing graphically.

Why is this rule generally a necessary condition for profit maximization? At any output rate at which marginal revenue *exceeds* marginal cost, profit can be increased by *increasing* output, since the extra revenue will exceed the extra cost. At any output rate at which marginal revenue is *less than* marginal cost, profit can be increased by *reducing* output, since the decrease in cost will exceed the decrease in revenue. Thus, since profit will *not* be a maximum when marginal revenue exceeds marginal cost or falls short of marginal cost, *it must be a maximum only when marginal revenue equals marginal cost.*

The Monopolist's Equilibrium Position

Figure 10.5 shows the equilibrium position of a monopolist in the short run. Short-run equilibrium will occur at the output, *OQ*, where the marginal cost curve intersects the marginal revenue curve (the curve that shows the firm's marginal revenue at each output level). And if the monopolist is to sell *OQ* units per period of time, the demand curve shows

Table 10.4
Marginal Cost and Marginal Revenue of a Monopolist

QUANTITY	TOTAL PROFIT	MARGINAL COST	MARGINAL REVENUE
		(DOLLARS)	
1	−40		80
		30	
2	10		60
		40	
3	30		40
		40	
4	30		20
		50	
5	0		0
		60	
6	−60		−20
		90	
7	−170		−40
		100	
8	−310		

that it must set a price of *OP*. Thus the equilibrium output and price are *OQ* and *OP*, respectively.

It is interesting to compare the Golden Rule of Output Determination for a monopolist (set the output rate at the point where marginal revenue equals marginal cost) with that for a perfectly competitive firm (set the output rate at the point where price equals marginal cost). The latter is really the same as the former because, *for a perfectly competitive firm, price equals marginal revenue.* Since the perfectly competitive firm can sell all it wants at the market price, each additional unit sold increases the firm's total revenue by the amount of the price. Thus, *for both the monopolist and the perfectly competitive firm, profits are maximized by setting the output rate at the point where marginal revenue equals marginal cost.*

When Will a Monopolist Shut Down?

From the previous chapter, we know that perfectly competitive firms sometimes find it preferable to shut down rather than follow this rule. Is this true for monopolists as well? The answer is yes. *Just as perfectly competitive firms will discontinue production if they will lose more money by producing than by shutting down, so monopolists will do the same thing, and for the same reasons.* In other words, if there is no output such that price exceeds average variable cost, monopolists, like perfect competitors, will discontinue production. This makes sense. If by producing, monopolists incur greater losses than their fixed costs, they will "drop out," i.e., produce nothing.

Two Misconceptions

Finally, note two misconceptions concerning monopoly behavior. First, it is sometimes said that monopolists will charge "as high a price as they can get." This is nonsense. The monopolist in Table 10.1 could charge a higher price than $70 to $80, but to do so would be foolish since it would

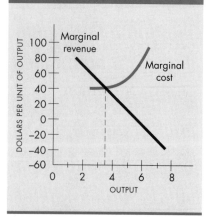

Figure 10.4
Marginal Cost and Marginal Revenue of a Monopolist
At the profit-maximizing output rate of between 3 and 4 units per day, marginal cost (which is $40 between an output rate of 3 and 4 units per period) equals marginal revenue (which also is $40 between an output rate of 3 and 4 units per period). Both marginal cost and marginal revenue are plotted at the midpoints of the ranges of output to which they pertain. (See Figures 8.8 and 10.2.)

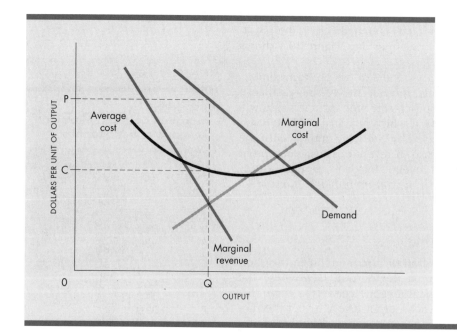

Figure 10.5
Equilibrium Position of a Monopolist
The monopolist sets its output rate at *OQ*, where the marginal revenue curve intersects the marginal cost curve. At this output, price must be *OP*. And profit per unit of output equals *CP*, since average cost equals *OC*.

result in lower profits. Second, it is sometimes said that monopolists will seek to maximize their profit per unit of output. This too is nonsense, since monopolists are interested in their total profits and their return on capital, not on the profit per unit of output. Rational monopolists will not sacrifice their total profits to increase their profit per unit of output.

PRICE AND OUTPUT: THE LONG RUN

In contrast to the situation under perfect competition, the long-run equilibrium of a monopolistic industry may not be marked by the absence of economic profits. If a monopolist earns a short-run economic profit, it will not be confronted in the long run with competitors, unless the industry ceases to be a monopoly. The entrance of additional firms into the industry is incompatible with the existence of monopoly. Thus the long-run equilibrium of an industry under monopoly may be characterized by economic profits.

On the other hand, if the monopolist incurs a short-run economic loss, it will be forced to look for other, more profitable uses for its resources. One possibility is that the firm's existing plant is not optimal and that it can earn economic profits by appropriate alterations to its scale and characteristics. If so, the firm will make these alterations in the long run and remain in the industry. However, *if there is no scale of plant that will enable the firm to avoid economic losses, it will leave the industry in the long run*. The mere fact of having a monopoly over the production of a certain commodity does not mean that the firm must be profitable. A monopoly over the production of cut-glass spittoons would be unlikely to catapult a firm into financial glory—or even allow it to avoid losses.

PERFECT COMPETITION AND MONOPOLY: A COMPARISON

At the beginning of the previous chapter, we said that a market's structure would be likely to affect the behavior of the market; in other words, a market's structure would influence how much was produced and the price that would be set. If we could perform an experiment in which an industry was first operated under conditions of perfect competition and then under conditions of monopoly (assuming that the demand for the industry's product and the industry's cost functions would be the same in either case),[4] we would find that the equilibrium price and output would differ under the two sets of conditions.

Higher Price and Less Output under Monopoly

Specifically, if the product demand curve and the industry's cost functions are the same, *the output of a perfectly competitive industry tends to be greater and the price tends to be lower than under monopoly*. We see this in Figure 10.6, which shows the industry's demand and supply curves, if it is perfectly competitive. Since price and output under perfect competition are given by the intersection of the demand and supply curves, OQ_C is

[4] However, the cost and demand curves need not be the same. For example, the monopolist may spend money on advertising, thus shifting the demand curve. It should be recognized that the assumption that they are the same is stronger than it appears at first glance.

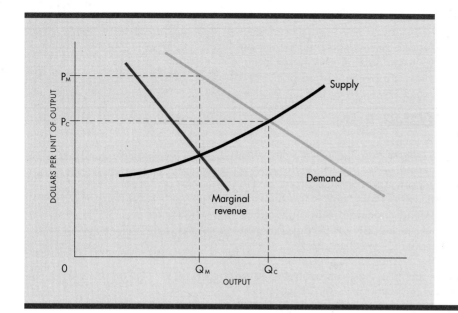

Figure 10.6
Comparison of Long-Run Equilibria: Perfect Competition and Monopoly
Under perfect competition, OQ_C is the industry output and OP_C is the price. Under monopoly, OQ_M is the industry output, OP_M is the price. Clearly, output is higher and price is lower under perfect competition than under monopoly.

the industry output and OP_C is the price. But what if all of the competitive firms are bought up by a single firm, which operates as a pure monopolist? Under these conditions, what formerly was the industry's supply curve is now the monopolist's marginal cost curve.[5] And what formerly was the industry's demand curve is now the monopolist's demand curve. Since the monopolist chooses the output where marginal cost equals marginal revenue, the industry output will be OQ_M and the price will be OP_M. Clearly, OQ_M is less than OQ_C, and OP_M is greater than OP_C — which is what we set out to prove.

Of course, all this is theory. But there is plenty of evidence that monopolists restrict output and charge higher prices than under competition. Take the case of tungsten carbide, which sold for $50 per pound until a monopoly was established in 1927 by General Electric. Then the price went to between $225 and $453 per pound, until the monopoly was broken by the antitrust laws in 1945. The price then dropped back to between $27 and $45 per pound.[6] This case was extreme, but by no means unique. For centuries people have observed that when monopolies are formed, output tends to be restricted, and price tends to be driven up.

Monopoly and Resource Allocation

Moreover, it has long been felt that the allocation of resources under perfect competition is socially more desirable than under monopoly. Society

[5] The monopolist will operate the various plants that would be independent under perfect competition as branches of a single firm. The marginal cost curve of a multiplant monopoly is the horizontal sum of the marginal cost curves of the individual plants. (To see why, suppose that a monopoly has two plants, A and B. The total amount that the monopoly can produce at a particular marginal cost is the sum of (1) the amount plant A can produce at this marginal cost, and (2) the amount plant B can produce at this marginal cost.) From the previous chapter, we know that this is also the supply curve of the industry if the plants are operated as separate firms under perfect competition.

[6] W. Adams, *The Structure of American Industry,* 5th ed., New York: Macmillan, 1977, p. 485.

might be better off if more resources were devoted to producing the monopolized good in Figure 10.6, and if the competitive, not the monopolistic, output were produced. For example, in the *Wealth of Nations,* published about 200 years ago, Adam Smith stressed that when competitive forces are thwarted by "the great engine . . . of monopoly," the tendency for resources to be used "as nearly as possible in the proportion which is most agreeable to the interest of the whole society" is thwarted as well.

Why do many economists believe that the allocation of resources under perfect competition is more socially desirable than that under monopoly? This is not a simple question, and like most hard questions can be answered at various levels of sophistication. Put most simply, many economists believe that firms under perfect competition are induced to produce quantities of goods that are more in line with consumer desires, and that firms under perfect competition are induced to use the least costly methods of production. In the following section, we shall indicate in detail why they believe that these things are true. In Chapter 12 (and in Appendix C), we provide a much more complete discussion of the pros and cons of monopoly and competition.

EXAMPLE 10.1   ANOTHER NEWSPAPER FOR HAVERHILL?

In Haverhill, Massachusetts, one newspaper had been published for over a century. Then, another newspaper was founded. In the Haverhill market, suppose that the market demand curve for the town's newspapers, and the demand curve facing each newspaper, were as shown below. Also, each newspaper's cost curves and marginal revenue curve are given below. (Note: In this special case, the firm's demand curve is the same as a monopolist's marginal revenue curve.)

(a) If both firms stay in business, how much will each lose? (b) If only one of them stays in business,

can it make a profit? How big a profit? (c) Is this a case of natural monopoly? (d) If entry by one firm may drive the other out of business, is this illegal?

Solution

(a) Each firm will produce OQ_0 newspapers, since this is the output where marginal revenue equals marginal cost. To sell this output, each sets a price of OA, since this is the price on the firm's demand curve corresponding to the sale of OQ_0 newspapers. At an output of OQ_0 newspapers, each firm's average total cost equals OE. Thus it loses $(OE - OA)$ cents per newspaper sold, and since it sells OQ_0 newspapers per year, its total annual loss is $OQ_0 \times (OE - OA)$ cents. (b) The monopolist will produce OQ_1 newspapers, since this is the output where its marginal revenue equals marginal cost. (Recall that in this case the firm's demand curve is the same as the monopolist's marginal revenue curve.) To sell this output, it must charge a price equal to OC cents per newspaper. Since its average total cost is OB cents per newspaper, it makes a profit of $(OC - OB)$ cents per newspaper sold, and its total annual profit is $OQ_1 \times (OC - OB)$ cents. (c) Yes. (d) This question was taken to court by these newspapers. The decision was that it was not illegal.

TEST YOURSELF

1. If you were the president of a firm that has a monopoly on a certain product, would you choose an output level where demand for the product was price inelastic? Explain.

2. Suppose that a monopolist's demand curve is as follows:

QUANTITY DEMANDED (PER YEAR)	PRICE (DOLLARS)
8	1,000
7	2,000
6	3,000
5	4,000
4	5,000
3	6,000
2	7,000
1	8,000

Plot the firm's marginal revenue curve.

3. Suppose that the monopolist in Question 2 has fixed costs of $10,000 and an average variable cost of $4,000. The average variable cost is the same for outputs of 1 to 10 units per year. What output rate will the firm choose? What price will it set?

4. Plot the marginal cost curve of the firm in Question 3. Where does this curve intersect the marginal revenue curve you drew in Question 2?

5. Suppose that the firm in Question 3 experienced a 50 percent increase in both its fixed and average variable costs. If the demand curve in Question 2 remains valid, what effect will this cost increase have on the output rate and price that the firm will choose?

THE CASE AGAINST MONOPOLY

Many people oppose monopolies on the grounds that they "gouge" the consumers by charging a higher price than would otherwise exist—a price that can be sustained only because monopolists artificially limit the supply. In other words, these people claim that monopolists reap higher profits than would be possible under perfect competition and that these profits are at the expense of consumers, who pay higher prices than under perfect competition. Is their claim accurate? As we have just seen, a monopolist will reap higher profits than under perfect competition and consumers will pay higher prices under monopoly than under perfect competition. But is this bad?

To the extent that the monopolist is rich and the consumers are poor, we are likely to answer yes. Also, to the extent that the monopolist is less deserving than the consumers, we are likely to answer the same thing. But suppose the monopolist is a selfless philanthropist who gives to the poor. Is monopoly still socially undesirable? The answer remains yes, because *monopoly imposes a burden on society by misallocating resources. In the presence of monopoly, the price system cannot be relied on to direct the allocation of resources to their most efficient use.*

The Misallocation of Resources

To see more precisely how monopoly interferes with the proper functioning of the price system, suppose that all industries other than the shoe industry are perfectly competitive. The shoe industry, however, has been monopolized. How does this cause a misallocation of resources? Under fairly general circumstances, a good's price can be taken as a measure of the social value of an extra unit of the good. Thus, if the price of a pair of socks is $1, the value to the consumer of an extra pair of socks can be taken to be $1. Moreover, under fairly general circumstances, a good's marginal cost can be taken as a measure of the cost to society of an extra unit of the good. Thus, if the marginal cost of a pair of shoes is $30, the cost to society of producing an extra pair of shoes can be taken to be $30.

In perfectly competitive industries, price is set equal to marginal cost, as we saw in Chapter 9. Thus each of the competitive industries produces up to the point where the social value of an extra unit of the good (which equals price) is set equal to the cost to society of producing an extra unit of the good (which equals marginal cost). This is the amount each of these industries should produce—the output rate that will result in an optimal allocation of resources.

Why Is the Competitive Output Optimal?

To see that this is the optimal output rate, consider what happens when an industry produces up to the point where the social value of an extra unit of the good is *more* than the cost to society of producing an extra unit. This isn't the socially optimal output rate because a one-unit increase in the output rate will increase the social value of output by more than the social cost of production, which means that it will increase social welfare. Thus, since a one-unit increase in the output rate will increase social welfare, the existing output rate cannot be optimal. (Recall Example 9.2.)

Next, consider what happens when an industry produces up to the point where the social value of an extra unit of the good is *less* than the cost to society of producing the extra unit. This isn't the socially optimal output rate because a one-unit decrease in the output rate will decrease the social value of output by less than the social cost of production, which means that it will increase social welfare. Thus, since a one-unit decrease in the output rate will increase social welfare, the existing output rate cannot be optimal.

Putting together the results of the previous two paragraphs, it follows that the socially optimal output rate must be at the point where the social value of an extra unit of the good *equals* the social cost of producing an extra unit of the good. Why? Because if the output rate is not optimal when the social value of an extra unit of the good exceeds or falls short of the cost to society of producing the extra unit, it must be optimal only when the two are equal.

The Monopolist Produces Too Little

Now let's return to the shoe industry—the sole monopolist.[7] Is the shoe industry producing the optimal amount of shoes? The answer is no. Like any monopolist, it produces at the point where marginal revenue equals marginal cost. Thus, since marginal revenue is *less* than price (as was proved above), the monopolist produces at a point where price is *greater* than marginal cost. Consequently, *the monopolistic industry produces at a point where the social value of an extra unit of the good (which equals price) is greater than the cost to society of producing the extra unit (which equals marginal cost)*. As we saw in a previous paragraph, this means that the monopolist's output rate is too small. A one-unit increase in the output of shoes will increase the social value of output by more than the

---

[7] Are puns really the lowest form of humor?

social cost of production. (The situation is similar to that in Example 9.2 when 75 million apples are produced.)

In summary, *monopoly results in a misallocation of resources since too little is produced of the monopolized good.* Here lies the economist's principal complaint against monopoly: it results in a misallocation of resources. Too little is produced of the monopolized good. Society is less well off—in terms of its own tastes and potentialities—than it could be. The price system, which would not lead to, or tolerate, such waste if all industries were perfectly competitive, is not allowed to perform as it should. (These inefficiencies caused by monopoly are described further and in more detail in Appendix C.)

Income Distribution, Efficiency, and Technological Change

Misallocation of resources is only part of the economist's brief against monopoly. As we have already pointed out, *monopoly redistributes income in favor of the monopolists.* In other words, monopolists can fatten their own purse by restricting their output and raising their price. Admittedly, there is no scientific way to prove that monopolists are less deserving than the rest of the population, but it is also pretty difficult to see why they are more deserving.

In addition, *since monopolists do not have to face direct competition, they are likely to be less diligent in controlling costs and in using resources efficiently.* As Sir John Hicks put it, "The best of all monopoly profits is a quiet life." Certainly we all dream at times of being able to take life easy. It would be strange if monopolists, having succeeded in insulating themselves from direct competition, did not take advantage of the opportunity—not open to firms in perfectly competitive markets—to relax a bit and worry less about pinching pennies. For this reason, economists fear that, to use Adam Smith's pungent phrase, "Monopoly . . . is a great enemy to good management."

Further, *it is often claimed that monopolists are slow to innovate and adopt new techniques and products.* This lethargy stems from the monopolist's freedom from direct competition. Innovation tends to be disruptive, while old ways, like old shoes, tend to be comfortable. The monopolist may be inclined, therefore, to stick with "time-honored" practices. Without question, competition is an important spur to innovation and to the rapid diffusion of innovations. But there are well-known arguments on the other side as well. Some economists argue that substantial monopoly power promotes innovation and technological change. Much more will be said on this score in Chapter 12.

PUBLIC REGULATION OF MONOPOLY

One way that society has attempted to reduce the harmful effects of monopoly is through **public regulation.** Suppose that the long-run cost curve in a particular industry is such that competition is not feasible. In such a case, society may permit a monopoly to be established. But a commission or some other public body is also established to regulate the monopoly's behavior. Among the many such regulatory commissions in the United States are the Federal Energy Regulatory Commission, the Federal Communications Commission, and the Interstate Commerce Commission. They regulate the behavior of firms with monopoly power in the

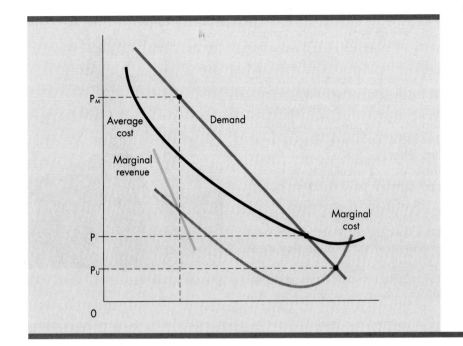

Figure 10.7
Regulation of Monopoly

The price established by a commission might be OP, where the demand curve intersects the average total cost curve. (Costs here include what the commission regards as a fair profit per unit of output.) In the absence of regulation, the monopolist would set a price of OP_M (because it would set its output at the point where marginal revenue equals marginal cost). Since OP is less than OP_M, regulation has reduced price in this instance, but not to the point where price equals marginal cost (as in perfect competition). For price to equal marginal cost, price would have to equal OP_u. (For a discussion of marginal-cost pricing, see the Appendix to this chapter.)

electric power, communication, transportation, and other industries. These industries are big as well as important, taking in about 10 percent of the national output. Thus we need to know how these commissions operate and make decisions on prices and other matters.

Regulatory commissions often set the price — or the maximum price — at the level at which it equals average total cost, including a "fair" rate of return on the firm's investment. In Figure 10.7, the price would be established by the commission at OP, where the demand curve intersects the average total cost curve (which includes what the commission regards as a fair profit per unit of output). Needless to say, there has been considerable controversy over what constitutes a fair rate of return. Frequently, commissions have settled on 8 to 10 percent. In addition, there has been a good deal of controversy over what should be included in the company's "investment" on which the fair rate of return is to be earned. A company's assets can be valued at **historical cost** or at **reproduction cost**—at what the company paid for them or at what it would cost to replace them. If the price level does not change much, these two approaches yield much the same answer. But if prices are rising—as they have been during most of the past 40 years—replacement cost will be greater than historical cost, with the result that the company will be allowed higher profits and rates if replacement cost is used. Most commissions now use historical cost.[8]

DOES REGULATION AFFECT PRICES?

The regulatory commissions and the principles they use have become extremely controversial. *Many observers feel that the commissions are lax,*

[8] The use of marginal-cost pricing by regulated industries is discussed in the Appendix to this chapter.

and that they tend to be captured by the industries they are supposed to regulate. Regulated industries, recognizing the power of such commissions, invest considerable time and money in attempts to influence the commissions. The public, on the other hand, often has only a foggy idea of what the commissions are doing, and of whether or not it is in the public interest. According to some critics like Ralph Nader, "Nobody seriously challenges the fact that the regulatory agencies have made an accommodation with the businesses they are supposed to regulate—and they've done so at the expense of the public." For these and other reasons, some economists believe that regulation has little effect on prices.

It is difficult to isolate and measure the effects of regulation on the average level of prices. Some well-known economists have conducted studies which suggest that regulation has made little or no difference in this regard. Nobel laureate George Stigler and Claire Friedland of the University of Chicago compared the levels of rates charged for electricity by regulated and unregulated electric power companies. They found that there was no significant difference between the average rates charged by the two sets of firms. Other economists challenge Stigler's and Friedland's interpretation of their factual findings, and much more research on this

George J. Stigler

EXAMPLE 10.2   PRICE DISCRIMINATION IN DENTISTRY

An isolated town of 5,000 inhabitants in the Rocky Mountains is looking for a dentist. To simplify matters, we divide the town's inhabitants into two categories: the rich and the poor. The demand curve for dental care among each type of inhabitant is shown below. Adding the two demand curves horizontally, we find that the total demand curve for dental care is *DAB*.

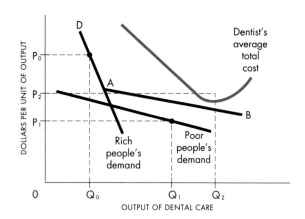

(a) If a dentist charges the same price to all inhabitants (rich or poor), can the dentist cover his or her average total costs? (b) If the dentist charges the rich a higher price than the poor, can the dentist cover his or her average total costs? (c) **Price discrimination** occurs when a producer sells the same commodity or service

at more than one price. Thus the dentist in (b) is engaging in price discrimination. In fact, do physicians and dentists engage in price discrimination? (d) In some instances, is it true that a good or service cannot be produced without price discrimination? (e) Is this always the case?

Solution

(a) No. The total demand curve lies below the average total cost curve. Thus, regardless of what output the dentist chooses, price would be less than average total cost. (b) Yes. If the dentist charges rich people a price of OP_O, he or she can sell OQ_O units of dental care to them. If he or she charges poor people a price of OP_1, he or she can sell OQ_1 units of dental care to them. Thus the total output, which equals OQ_2 brings an average price of OP_2, which is greater than average total cost. (c) Yes. (d) Yes, the situation depicted in the graph is an example. Without price discrimination, this dentist could not cover his or her costs. (e) No. It is important to note that price discrimination frequently occurs in situations where the good or service could be produced without it. Price discrimination is used in these situations to increase the profits of the producer. (From the point of view of society as a whole, price discrimination frequently is objectionable because it violates the conditions for optimal resource allocation described in Appendix C.)

topic is needed. Nonetheless, it seems fair to conclude that, although the simple model of the regulatory process presented in previous sections would predict that regulated prices would be lower, on the average, than unregulated prices (of the same item), the evidence in support of this prediction is much weaker than might be supposed.

Whether or not regulation has a significant effect on the *average* level of prices, it certainly has an effect on *particular* prices charged by regulated firms. In some cases, it has reduced the price of a product. There seems to be general agreement that the Federal Energy Regulatory Commission kept the price of natural gas (in interstate commerce) below what this price would have been during the 1970s in the absence of regulation. In other cases, it has increased the price of a product. Some observers believe that prior to the deregulation of the airlines in the late 1970s, the Civil Aeronautics Board (CAB) increased the airplane fare between New York and Washington. As evidence of this, they compared at that time this fare with the fare from San Francisco to Los Angeles, which was not subject to CAB regulation since the trip was entirely within California. Although the distance from San Francisco to Los Angeles is almost twice as great as that from New York to Washington, the fare from San Francisco to Los Angeles was less than that from New York to Washington.

Federal Energy Regulatory Committee headquarters, Washington, D.C.

THE DEREGULATION MOVEMENT: THE CASE OF THE AIRLINES

As pointed out above, considerable controversy has centered on the regulatory process, with many observers feeling that the commissions are lax and that they tend to be captured by the industries they are supposed to regulate. The regulatory process in a variety of industries, such as airlines, railroads, and trucking, has been criticized severely. For example, the Civil Aeronautics Board (CAB), which was established in 1938, and which regulated the prices charged by the interstate scheduled airlines as well as entry into the industry, was criticized during the 1970s for preventing price competition among airlines and for permitting little new entry. According to the General Accounting Office (a federal government agency), airline fares would have been 20 to 50 percent lower in the absence of CAB regulation.

In the late 1970s and early 1980s, there was a dramatic movement toward deregulation in the United States. A variety of industries, including airlines, railroads, trucking, and financial institutions, were affected. In the case of the airlines, the seeds for deregulation were sown in the 1970s with the appointment of Alfred Kahn, a Cornell economist, as chairman of the CAB. During the late 1970s, airlines were allowed to institute discount fares, and entry restrictions were relaxed. Eventually, Congress passed legislation that phased out the CAB's powers. The power to regulate routes terminated at the end of 1981, and the power to regulate rates terminated at the end of 1982.

During the late 1980s and early 1990s, the deregulation of the airlines became controversial, for at least two reasons. First, since deregulation brought lower fares, it also brought a rise in airline passenger traffic, which in turn helped to produce more congestion in airports and more delayed flights. Second, while deregulation initially stimulated an increase in the number of airlines, the airline industry subsequently became much

Alfred Kahn

more concentrated, as a number of firms merged. Thus Texas Air took over Eastern (and People Express) in 1986; and Northwest acquired Republic. In 1989, more than 90 percent of the domestic market was controlled by eight airlines. Deregulation was one of the factors blamed for this increase in concentration, which some observers regarded as excessive.

Nonetheless, there is no evidence that the airline industry is going to be regulated again. Economists point out that deregulation has raised the airline industry's efficiency by increasing the number of passengers per plane, encouraging the airlines to get more productivity out of their workers, and improving the match between types of equipment and types of market. Also, deregulation has resulted in the consumer's being offered a much greater variety of combinations of price and service quality. Most observers seem to conclude that, although deregulation has not been an unalloyed blessing, it has resulted in many economic advantages.

Long lines at an airport ticket counter

EFFECTS OF REGULATION ON EFFICIENCY

As previous chapters have stressed, competitive markets provide considerable incentives for a firm to increase its efficiency. Firms that are able to push their costs below those of their competitors reap higher profits than their competitors. As a simple illustration, suppose that firms A and B both have contracts to produce 100 airplanes, and that the price they will get for each airplane is $25,000. Firm A's management, which is diligent, imaginative, and innovative, gets the cost per airplane down to $10,000, and thus makes a healthy profit of $1,500,000. Firm B's management which is lazy, unimaginative, and dull, lets the cost per airplane rise to $30,000, and thus loses $500,000. Clearly, firm A is rewarded for its good performance, while firm B is penalized for its poor performance.

No Incentive for Efficiency

One of the primary purposes of regulators is to prevent a monopoly from earning excessive profits. The firm is allowed only a "fair" rate of return on its investment. One problem with this arrangement is that the firm is guaranteed this rate of return, regardless of how well it performs. If the regulators decide that the Sleepy Hollow Electric and Gas Company should receive a 10 percent rate of return on its investment, this is the rate of return it will receive regardless of whether the Sleepy Hollow Electric and Gas Company is managed well or poorly. Why is this a problem? Because unlike the competitive firms discussed in the previous paragraph, there is no incentive for the firm to increase its efficiency.

The available evidence indicates that, if a firm is guaranteed a fixed amount of profit for a job (regardless of how efficiently it does this job), the firm will tend to be less efficient than if the amount of profit it receives is directly related to its efficiency. The Department of Defense has found that, when it bought goods or services on a cost-plus-fixed-fee basis, these goods and services were not produced as cheaply as when it bought them in a competitive market. This is reasonable. It takes time, energy, and lots of trouble to make a firm more efficient. Why should a firm's managers bother to induce added efficiency if the firm's profits are the same, regardless of how efficient or inefficient it is?

Regulatory Lag and Incentive for Efficiency

The regulatory process is characterized by long delays. In many regulated industries, a proposed rate increase or decrease may be under consideration for months before a decision is made by the commission. In cases where such a price change is strongly contested, it may take years for the required hearings to occur before the commission and for appeals to be made subsequently to the courts. Such a delay between a proposed price change and its ultimate disposition is called a ***regulatory lag.*** Long regulatory lags are often criticized by those who would like the regulatory process to adapt more quickly to changing conditions and to provide more timely decisions. But one advantage of regulatory lags is that they result in some rewards for efficiency and penalties for inefficiency.

To see why this is so, consider a regulated company whose price is set so that the firm can earn a rate of return of 10 percent (which is what the commission regards as a "fair" rate of return). The firm develops and introduces some improved manufacturing processes which reduce the firm's costs, thus allowing it to earn 13 percent. If it takes 18 months for the commission to review the prices it approved before and to modify them to take account of the new (lower) cost levels, the firm earns a higher rate of return (13 percent rather than 10 percent) during these 18 months than if it had not developed and introduced the improved manufacturing processes. This is a reward for efficiency.

On the other hand, suppose that this firm makes several serious blunders which result in a substantial increase in its costs; thus the firm earns only a rate of return of 6 percent. If it takes 18 months for the commission to review the prices it set before and to modify them to take account of the changes in firms' cost levels, this firm earns a lower rate of return (6 percent rather than 10 percent) during these 18 months than if it had not made these blunders. This is a penalty for inefficiency.

Although regulatory lag does restore some of the incentives for efficiency (and some of the penalties for inefficiency), it would be a mistake to believe that it results in as strong a set of incentives as does competitive markets. One of the basic problems with regulation is that, *if a regulatory commission prevents a firm from earning higher-than-average profits, there may be relatively little incentive for the firm to increase its efficiency and innovate.*

TEST YOURSELF

1. Compare the long-run equilibrium of a perfectly competitive industry with that which would occur if all the firms were to be merged in a single monopolistic firm. Is there any reason for society to prefer one equilibrium over the other?

2. "No firm has a monopoly since every good competes to some extent with every other good. Thus there is no good that is completely sealed off from competition." Comment and evaluate.

3. "Firms with relatively high profits are bound to be monopolists. If they were competitive, the entry of new firms into the industry would drive economic profits down to zero. Thus the easiest and best way to determine whether a firm is a monopolist is to look at its profits." Comment and evaluate.

4. According to the Council of Economic Advisers, "although exit from an industry via bankruptcy is a normal characteristic of efficient competitive markets, the bankruptcy of a regulated firm tends to be viewed as a sign of regulatory failure." What problems are likely to result from this attitude?

SUMMARY

1. A pure monopoly is a market with one, and only one, seller. Monopolies may occur because of patents, control over basic inputs, and government action, as well as decreasing average costs up to the point where the market is satisfied.

2. If average costs reach their minimum at an output rate large enough to satisfy the entire market, perfect competition cannot be maintained; and the public often insists that the industry (a natural monopoly) be regulated by the government.

3. Since the monopolist is the only seller of the product, the demand curve facing the monopolist is the market demand curve, which slopes downward (rather than being horizontal as in perfect competition).

4. The unregulated monopolist will maximize profit by choosing the output where marginal cost equals marginal revenue, marginal revenue being defined as the addition to total revenue attributable to the addition of one unit to sales. This rule for output determination also holds under perfect competition, since price equals marginal revenue under perfect competition.

5. If monopolists cannot prevent losses from exceeding fixed costs, they, like perfect competitors, will discontinue production. In contrast to the case in perfect competition, the long-run equilibrium of a monopolistic industry may not be marked by the absence of economic profits.

6. The output of a monopoly tends to be smaller and the price tends to be higher than under perfect competition.

Economists tend to believe that society would be better off if more resources were devoted to the production of the good than under monopoly, the competitive output often being regarded as best.

7. One way that society has attempted to reduce the harmful effects of monopoly is through public regulation. Commissions often set price at the level at which it equals average total cost, including a "fair rate of return" on the firm's investment.

8. There has been a great deal of controversy over the practices of the regulatory commissions. Many economists have viewed them as lax or ill-conceived. In many areas, like transportation, they have been concerned as much with the regulation of competition as with the regulation of monopoly; and, according to many studies, their decisions have resulted in substantial costs and inefficiencies.

9. Regulatory commissions try to prevent a monopoly from earning excessive profits; the firm is allowed only a "fair rate of return" on its investment. One difficulty with this arrangement is that, since the firm is guaranteed this rate of return (regardless of how well or poorly it performs), there is no incentive for the firm to increase its efficiency. Although regulatory lag results in some incentives of this sort, they often are relatively weak.

10. In some industries (like airlines, trucking, and railroads), the late 1970s and early 1980s saw a strong movement toward deregulation. More recently, there have been fewer dramatic changes along this line.

CONCEPTS FOR REVIEW

Monopoly

Natural monopoly

Total revenue

Marginal revenue

Public regulation

Historical cost

*Marginal cost pricing

Reproduction cost

Price discrimination

Regulatory lag

* This concept is presented in the Appendix to this chapter.

APPENDIX: MARGINAL COST PRICING

In this and the previous chapter, we indicated that, under the assumptions made here, the conditions for optimal resource allocation are satisfied under perfect competition. (See Appendix C for a more detailed discussion of this point.) Economists interested in the functioning of planned, or socialist, economies have pointed out that a price system also could be used to increase social welfare in such economies. Also, it has been argued that government-owned enterprises and public utilities in capitalist economies should set price equal to marginal cost, just as perfectly competitive firms do. In this Appendix, we discuss marginal cost pricing, and how it might be used by government-owned or regulated monopolists, as well as by socialist economies.

Socialist Economies

It is often argued that rational economic organization could be achieved in a socialist economy that is decentralized, as well as under perfect competition. The socialist government might solve the system of equations that is solved automatically in a perfectly competitive economy, and obtain the prices that would prevail under perfect competition. Then the government might publish this price list, together with instructions for consumers to maximize their satisfaction and for producers to maximize profit. (Of course, the wording of the instructions to consumers might be a bit less heavy-handed than "Maximize your satisfaction!")

Under a socialist system of this sort, the government does not have to become involved in the intricate and detailed business of setting production targets for each plant. It need only compute the proper set of prices. In following the rules to maximize "profits," plant managers will choose the proper production levels. Thus decentralized decision making, rather than detailed centralized direction, could be used, thus reducing administrative costs and bureaucratic disadvantages—or so, at least, the theorists say.

Government-Owned or Regulated Monopolies

The prices the government would publish, like those prevailing in a perfectly competitive economy, would equal marginal cost. Many economists have recommended that government-owned enterprises in basically capitalist economies also adopt **_marginal cost pricing,_** i.e., that they set price equal to marginal cost. Taking the case of a bridge where the marginal cost (the extra cost involved in allowing an additional vehicle to cross) is zero, Harold Hotelling argued in a famous article that the socially optimal price for crossing the bridge is zero, and that its costs should be defrayed by general taxation. If a toll is charged, the conditions for optimal resource use are not met.[9]

Marginal cost pricing has fascinated economists during the fifty years that have elapsed since Hotelling's article, but there are a number of problems in the application of this idea. One of the most important is that if the firm's average costs decrease with increases in its scale of output (as is frequently the case in public utilities), it follows from the discussion in

---

[9] Harold Hotelling, "The General Welfare in Relation to Problems of Taxation and of Railway and Utility Rates," _Econometrica,_ 1938.

Chapter 8 that marginal cost must be less than average cost, with the consequence that the firm will not cover its costs if price is set equal to marginal cost.[10] This means that marginal cost pricing must be accompanied by some form of subsidy if the firm is to stay in operation—and the collection of the funds required for the payment of the subsidy may also violate the conditions for optimal resource allocation. This subsidy also means that there is a change in the income distribution favoring users of the firm's output and penalizing nonusers.

The Common Sense of Marginal Cost Pricing

To illustrate the reasoning that underlies marginal cost pricing, consider the case of water supplies. What determines the level at which the price of water should be set?

> Suppose that at a certain moment in time [consumers are willing to pay] $30 per unit. Then, if the community as a whole can acquire and transport another unit of water for say, $20, it would clearly be desirable to do so; in fact, any of the individual customers to whom the unit of water is worth $30 would be happy to pay the $20 cost, and none of the other members of the community would be made worse off thereby. We may say that, on efficiency grounds, additional units should be made available so long as any members of the community are willing to pay the additional or marginal costs incurred. . . . So the . . . rule is to make the price equal to marginal cost and equal for all customers.[11]

Unfortunately, it seems that water-pricing practices do not often conform to this rule. Some types of water users are commonly charged lower prices than other types of water users, although the marginal cost of the water is the same. According to a study carried out at the RAND Corporation,

> In Los Angeles, for example, there is an exceptionally low rate for irrigation use. Domestic, commercial, and industrial services are not distinguished as such, but they are differentially affected by the promotional volume rates. More serious, because much more common, is the system of block rates, with reductions [in price] for larger quantities used. . . . [This system leads] to wasteful use of water by large users, since small users would value the same marginal unit of water more highly if delivered to them. . . . The customer paying the lower price will on the margin be utilizing water for less valuable purposes than it could serve if transferred to the customer paying the higher price.

---

[10] Recall from Chapter 8 that an increase in output results in a reduction in average cost only when marginal cost is less than average cost. Since the firm's receipts will cover its costs only if price is at least equal to average cost, it follows that, under these circumstances, the firm cannot cover its costs if it sets price equal to marginal cost.

[11] Hirshleifer, Milliman, and DeHaven, "The Allocation of Water Supplies," in E. Mansfield (ed.), *Microeconomics: Selected Readings,* 4th ed., New York: Norton, 1982.

OLIGOPOLY, GAME THEORY, AND MONOPOLISTIC COMPETITION

CONSIDER THE COMPUTER, soap, electrical equipment, steel, oil, and motorcycle industries, all of which are taken up in this chapter. None of these industries is perfectly competitive or monopolistic. Although perfect competition and monopoly are very useful models that shed much valuable light on the behavior of markets, they are polar cases. Economists have developed other models that portray more realistically the behavior of many modern industries. Oligopoly models, with their emphasis on strategic behavior, have proved useful in analyzing industries like computers, oil and motorcycles. In these industries, there are few firms, and the rivalry among them has many of the characteristics of a game. Thus game theory has been utilized to study decision making by these firms.

In this chapter, we focus attention on theories of oligopoly and strategic behavior. Game theory, which has contributed a great deal in recent years to our understanding of these topics, is considered at length. In addition, we take up the theory of monopolistic competition, which helps to explain market behavior in such industries as retail trade. We examine how resources are allocated and prices are set under oligopoly and monopolistic competition. We also compare the behavior of oligopolistic and monopolistically competitive markets with the behavior of perfectly competitive and monopolistic markets.

OLIGOPOLY

Oligopoly (domination by a few firms) is a common and important market structure in the United States; many industries, like steel, automobiles, oil, and electrical equipment, are oligopolistic. An example of an oligopolist is IBM, described in Chapter 6. *The key characteristic of oligopoly is interdependence, actual and perceived, among firms*. Each oligopolist formulates its policies with an eye to their effect on its rivals. Since an oligopoly contains a small number of firms, any change in one firm's price or output influences the sales and profits of its competitors. Moreover, since there are only a few firms, each must recognize that changes in its own policies are likely to result in changes in the policies of its rivals as well.

What factors are responsible for oligopoly? First, in some industries, *low production costs cannot be achieved unless a firm is producing an output equal to a substantial portion of the total available market,* with the consequence that the number of firms will tend to be rather small. Second, *there may be economies of scale in sales promotion* in certain industries, and this too may promote oligopoly. Third, entry into some industries may be blocked by the requirement that a firm build and maintain a large, complicated, and expensive plant, or have access to patents or scarce raw materials. Only a few firms may be in a position to obtain all these necessary prerequisites for membership in the club.

AT&T switching station

Economies of Scale

To illustrate the effects of *economies of scale*, consider the market for central office switches. Central office switches are the main computers that run local telecommunications networks. Because it costs over $1 billion to develop a modern central office switch, no single European country is big enough to support such a development project. Switch manufacturers must compete in international markets to obtain the very large sales needed to reduce their average costs to the point where they can make a profit. Due to the great economies of scale in this industry, only a small number of firms can survive.[1]

The automobile industry is a good example of *economies of scale in sales promotion*. To be effective, advertising must often be carried out on a large scale, the result being that the advertising cost per unit of output decreases with increases in output, at least up to some point. Also, car buyers like to deal with firms with a large, dependable dealer network. Since it takes a lot of money to establish such a network, and since the better dealers are attracted by the more popular brands, the smaller automobile manufacturers are at a substantial disadvantage.

Barriers to Entry

In addition, the automobile industry offers a good example of *barriers to entry due to large financial requirements.* An automobile plant of minimum efficient size costs hundreds of millions of dollars to build and put into operation. This is an enormous amount of money, beyond the reach of practically all individuals. It takes the help of major financial interests and financial institutions to break into the automobile business. Since World War II, no new domestic firms have obtained a foothold in the American automobile industry.

The *availability of raw materials* can also be a barrier to entry. Such is the case in the steel industry, where a few big firms have most of the available iron ore, partly through foresight and partly because they were the only organizations that could afford to spend the vast sums required to obtain the ore. Also, *patents* can be a very big barrier to entry. The electric light industry is a famous example. General Electric was able to dominate the industry from 1892 to 1930 through the acquisition of the basic Edison patents and then the acquisition of patents on many of the improvements.

[1] J. Hausman, "Joint Ventures, Strategic Alliances, and Collaboration in Telecommunications," *Regulation*, Winter 1991.

COLLUSION AND CARTELS

In oligopolistic industries, collusion is much more likely than under perfect competition or monopolistic competition. ***Collusion*** *occurs when firms get together and agree on price and output.* Conditions in oligopolistic industries tend to promote collusion, since the number of firms is small and the firms recognize their interdependence. *The advantages of collusion to the firms seem obvious: increased profits, decreased uncertainty, and a better opportunity to prevent entry.* Not all collusion is disguised from the public or secret. In contrast to illicit collusion, a ***cartel*** is an open, formal collusive arrangement among firms. In many countries in Europe, cartels have been common and legally acceptable. In the United States, most collusive arrangements, whether secret or open cartels, were declared illegal by the Sherman Antitrust Act, which was passed in 1890, but this does not mean that such arrangements do not exist.

For example, consider the electrical equipment industry. Widespread collusion to fix prices occurred among American electrical equipment manufacturers during the 1950s, and when the collusion was uncovered a number of high executives were tried, convicted, and sent to jail. Moreover, collusion of this sort is not limited to a single industry—or a single country. Some cartels, like that in quinine in the early 1960s or in crude oil in the 1970s to 1990s, are international in scope.

PRICE AND OUTPUT OF A CARTEL

If a cartel is established to set a uniform price for a particular product, what price will it charge? As a first step, the cartel must estimate the marginal cost curve for the cartel as a whole. Then it must find the output where its marginal cost equals its marginal revenue, since this output maximizes the total profit of the cartel members. In Figure 11.1, this output is OQ. Thus, if it maximizes cartel profits, the cartel will choose a price of OP, which is the monopoly price. In short, *the cartel acts like a monopolist with a number of plants or divisions, each of which is a member firm.*

How will the cartel allocate sales among the member firms? If its aim is to maximize cartel profits, it will allocate sales to firms in such a way that the sum of the firms' costs is minimized. But this allocation is unlikely to occur in reality. The allocation process is a bargaining process, and firms with the most influence and the shrewdest negotiators are likely to receive the largest sales quotas, even though this decreases the total profits of the cartel. Moreover, high-cost firms are likely to receive larger sales quotas than would be the case if total cartel profits were maximized, since they would be unwilling otherwise to stay in the cartel. In practice, it appears that cartels often divide markets geographically or in accord with a firm's level of sales in the past.

The Electrical Conspiracy

To illustrate how firms collude, consider the electrical equipment manufacturers we mentioned above. During the 1950s, there was widespread collusion among about 30 firms selling turbine generators, switchgear, transformers, and other products with total sales of about $1.5 billion per

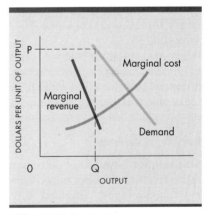

Figure 11.1
Price and Output of a Cartel
The marginal cost curve shows the marginal cost for the cartel as a whole. Based on the demand curve for the industry's product, the cartel can derive the marginal revenue curve. The output that maximizes the total profit of the cartel members is OQ. The corresponding price is OP.

year. Representatives of these firms got together and agreed upon prices for many products. The available evidence indicates that both prices and profits tended to be increased by the collusive agreements—or at least until the firms were prosecuted under the antitrust laws by the Department of Justice. The following statement by F. M. Scherer is a good description of some of the procedures used by these firms:

> Some of the most elaborate procedures were devised to handle switchgear pricing. As in the case of generators, book prices served as the initial departure point. Each seller agreed to quote book prices in sales to private buyers, and meetings were held regularly to compare calculations for forthcoming job quotations. Sealed-bid competitions sponsored by government agencies posed a different set of problems, and new methods were worked out to handle them. Through protracted negotiation, each seller was assigned a specific share of all sealed-bid business, e.g., General Electric's share of the high voltage switchgear field was set at 40.3 per cent in late 1958, and Allis-Chalmers' at 8.8 per cent. Participants then coordinated their bidding so that each firm was low bidder in just enough transactions to gain its predetermined share of the market. In the power switching equipment line, this was achieved for a while by dividing the United States into four quadrants, assigning four sellers to each quadrant, and letting the sellers in a quadrant rotate their bids. A "phases of the moon" system was used to allocate low-bidding privileges in the high voltage switchgear field, with a new seller assuming low-bidding priority every two weeks. The designated bidder subtracted a specified percentage margin from the book price to capture orders during its phase, while others added various margins to the book price. The result was an ostensibly random pattern of quotations, conveying the impression of independent pricing behavior.[2]

BARRIERS TO COLLUSION

The fact that oligopoly often can lead to collusion is not new. Nor is it newly understood. Back in 1776, Adam Smith warned that "people of the same trade seldom meet together even for merriment and diversion, but the conversation ends in a conspiracy against the public, or in some contrivance to raise prices." However, it must be borne in mind that collusive arrangements are often difficult to accomplish and maintain for long. In particular, there are several important barriers to collusion.

Legal Problems

The antitrust laws forbid outright collusion and price fixing. This does not mean that firms do not break those laws; witness the electrical equipment manufacturers just described. But the antitrust laws are an important obstacle to collusion.

Technical Problems

Collusion is often difficult to achieve and maintain because an oligopoly contains an unwieldy number of firms, or the product is quite heterogeneous, or the cost structures of the firms differ considerably. It is clear that a collusive agreement will be more difficult to achieve and maintain if there are a dozen oligopolists than if there are three or four. Moreover, if

---

[2] F. M. Scherer, *Industrial Market Structure and Economic Performance*, p. 160.

the products sold by the oligopolists differ substantially, it will probably be more difficult for them to find a common price strategy that will be acceptable to all. Similarly, if the firms' cost structures differ, it will be more difficult to get agreement, since the low-cost firms will be more inclined to cut price. For example, National Steel, after introducing low-cost continuous strip mills in the 1930s, became a price cutter in the steel industry.

Cheating

There is a constant temptation for oligopolists to cheat on any collusive agreement. If other firms stick to the agreement, any firm that cheats—by cutting its price below that agreed to under the collusive arrangement—can take a lot of business away from the other firms and increase its prof-

EXAMPLE 11.1   THE END OF THE COZY MILK OLIGOPOLY IN NEW YORK

On July 4, 1987, Governor Mario Cuomo of New York, together with the state legislature, put through a bill to terminate a half-century of restrictions on milk sales in the state. This bill ended rules that blocked milk dealers in one county from selling in another county, and that denied milk licenses to dealers whose entry into the state was deemed "destructive" to the New York market. Prior to the passage of the 1987 bill, five major dealers dominated the sale of milk in New York City. According to the *New York Times*, the old state rules were used by state administrators to deny licenses to potential entrants that might reduce price. What precipitated the 1987 bill rescinding these rules was the entrance of a New Jersey firm, Farmland Dairies, into the New York City market in December 1986, after a federal court gave it permission to begin deliveries in the city.

(a) After Farmland entered the New York City milk market, do you think that the price of milk changed? If so, how? (b) According to the state attorney general, Robert Abrams, the old rules "encouraged and facilitated" price fixing by the New York dairies. How did the old rules do this? (c) Farmland's president, Marc Goldman, said that Farmland's production costs were only several cents a gallon less than in New York; yet the price dropped between 30 and 71 cents per gallon in New York supermarkets after Farmland's entry. Why did the price drop by so much more than the cost differential? (d) Members of Local 584 of the teamsters charged that many of their milk truck drivers would lose their jobs because of deregulation of the milk industry. The Milk Industry Council, which represents milk dealers, said that many small milk dealers

would be put out of business. Doesn't this mean that it was socially unwise to enact the 1987 bill?*

Solution

(a) Yes. The retail cost of a gallon of milk fell from $2.42 to $1.98, saving consumers about $100 million a year. (b) They kept out entrants, and helped keep only a few dairies in existence. (c) Because the profit margin—the difference between price and unit production cost—was reduced. (d) No. Consumers gained because of the lower price. The gains to consumers are likely to have exceeded the losses to the existing dealers and their employees.

* For further discussion, see "Albany Set to End Milk Rules." *New York Times*, July 4, 1987.

its substantially, at least in the short run. This temptation is particularly great when an industry's sales are depressed and its profits are low. Every firm is hungry for business, and it is difficult to resist. Moreover, one firm may be driven to cheating because it hears that another firm is doing so, with the eventual result that the collusive agreement is torn apart.

To illustrate the problems of maintaining a collusive agreement, let's return to the electrical equipment manufacturers. As the *Wall Street Journal* summed it up,

> One of the great ironies of the conspiracies was that no matter how hard the participants schemed, no matter how friendly their meetings and communications might be, there was an innate tendency to compete. Someone was always violating the agreements to get more business and this continually called for new illegal plans. For example, price-cutting in sales of power switching equipment to government agencies was getting out of hand in late 1958. This led to the "quadrant" system of dividing markets [described in the previous section].

As one executive of General Electric complained, "No one was living up to the agreements and we . . . were being made suckers. On every job someone would cut our throat; we lost confidence in the group." Given that these agreements were illegal, it is remarkable that such a complaint was uttered with a straight face.

PRICE LEADERSHIP

In order to coordinate their behavior without outright collusion, some industries contain a ***price leader.*** It is quite common in oligopolistic industries for one or a few firms to set the price and for the rest to follow their lead. Two types of price leadership are the dominant-firm model and the barometric-firm model. *The **dominant-firm** model applies to cases where the industry has a single large dominant firm and a number of small firms.* The dominant firm sets the price for the industry, but it lets the small firms sell all they want at that price. *The **barometric-firm** model applies to cases where one firm usually is the first to make changes in price that are generally accepted by other firms in the industry.* The barometric firm may not be the largest, or most powerful, firm. Instead, it is a reasonably accurate interpreter of changes in basic cost and demand conditions in the industry as a whole. According to some authorities, barometric price leadership often occurs as a response to a period of violent price fluctuation in an industry, during which many firms suffer and greater stability is widely sought.

In the past, the steel industry was a good example of price leadership of the dominant-firm variety. The largest firm in the industry was U.S. Steel (now USX Corporation), which was formed in 1901 by the merger of a number of companies. Judge Elbert Gary, the first chairman of the board of U.S. Steel, sought the cooperation of the smaller firms in the industry. He inaugurated a series of so-called "Gary dinners," attended by all the major steel producers, which made declarations of industry policy on pricing and other matters. Since any formal pricing agreements would have been illegal, they made no such agreements. But, generally speaking, U.S. Steel set the pricing pattern and other firms followed. Moreover, this relationship continued long after Judge Gary had gone to his reward. According to Walter Adams of Michigan State University, U.S. Steel typi-

EXAMPLE 11.2 HOW OTHER SOURCES OF OIL INFLUENCE OPEC'S PRICE

The Organization of Petroleum Exporting Countries (OPEC) is a cartel that includes many of the world's leading oil producers, such as Saudi Arabia, Nigeria, Venezuela, Indonesia, and others. Nonetheless, OPEC does not supply all the world's oil. Important oil producers outside OPEC include the United States, Mexico, Canada, Britain, Norway, and Australia. Suppose that the supply curve for non-OPEC oil and the world demand curve for oil are as shown below:

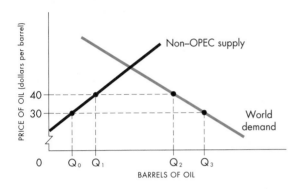

(a) If the price of oil is $30 per barrel, what is the quantity demanded of OPEC oil? (b) If the price of oil is $40 per barrel, what is the quantity demanded of OPEC oil? (c) From the above graph, how can we determine the demand curve for OPEC oil? (d) Given the demand curve for OPEC oil, how can we determine the price that would maximize OPEC's profit?

Solution

(a) $(OQ_3 - OQ_0)$ barrels of oil. (b) $(OQ_2 - OQ_1)$ barrels of oil. (c) To determine the quantity of OPEC oil demanded at each price, subtract the quantity of non-OPEC oil supplied at that price from the quantity of oil demanded in the world as a whole at that price. (d) Find the marginal revenue curve corresponding to the demand curve for OPEC oil, and determine the output at which this marginal revenue curve intersects OPEC's marginal cost curve. The profit-maximizing price is the one that results in OPEC's selling this quantity of output.

cally set the price "and the other companies follow in lockstep—both in their sales to private customers and in their secret bids on government contracts."[3]

NONPRICE COMPETITION

Oligopolists often compete aggressively through advertising and the development of new and different products. This is an important characteristic of oligopoly. In contrast to the case of perfect competition, ***nonprice competition*** plays a central role in oligopoly. It is worthwhile, therefore, to note a few salient points about the advertising and product development strategies of oligopolists.

Advertising

Advertising is a very big business. Tens of billions of dollars are spent on it in the United States. One important purpose of advertising is to convince the consumer that one firm's product is better than another's. In industries where there is less physical differentiation of the product, advertising expenditures often are larger than in industries where the product varies more. Thus the cigarette, liquor, and soap industries spend over

[3] W. Adams, *The Structure of American Industry*, New York: Macmillan, 1961, p. 168.

10 percent of their gross revenues (excluding excise taxes) on advertising whereas the automobile industry spends less than 1 percent of its gross revenues on advertising.

The social desirability of much of this advertising is debatable, and much debated. While advertising can serve an important purpose by keeping the consumer better informed, some advertising is more misleading than informative. Unfortunately, it is difficult to make reliable estimates of the extent to which oligopolists may be overinvesting, from society's point of view, in advertising.[4]

Product Development

The development of new and improved products is also a very big business in the United States. In 1991, industry spent over $78 billion on research and development. In many industries, R and D is a central part of oligopolistic competition. For example, a spectacular case occurred in the motorcycle industry in Japan in the early 1980s. Honda, the industry leader, was being pressed by Yamaha, a rival firm whose share of the market was rising. It responded by introducing 81 new motorcycle models within 18 months (and by cutting prices as well). In January 1983, Yamaha's president admitted defeat: "We cannot match Honda's product development and sales strength. . . . I would like to end the Honda-Yamaha war."

It is important to add, however, that much of industry's R and D is aimed at fairly minor improvements in products and processes. Moreover, a good deal of the engineering efforts of many important industries is aimed largely at style changes, not basic improvements in the product. A case in point is the automobile industry, which spends many billions of dollars per year to produce the model changes that are familiar to car buyers throughout the land.[5] From society's point of view, some observers question whether such huge expenditures are justifiable.

Perhaps the main reason why some oligopolists would rather compete through advertising and product differentiation than through price is that a firm's rivals can easily and quickly match a price reduction, whereas they may find it difficult to match a clever advertising campaign or an attractive product improvement. Eastman Kodak had to work over six years to develop the instant camera it introduced in 1976 to compete with Polaroid's instant camera. Thus many oligopolists tend to feel that they have a better chance of improving their long-run profits at the expense of their rivals in the arena of nonprice competition than by price cutting.

THE THEORY OF CONTESTABLE MARKETS

During the late 1970s and early 1980s, the theory of contestable markets was born. This theory has received considerable attention. Because it is so new, it is very difficult to predict how significant it will eventually turn out to be. But it has had enough influence to warrant discussion.

[4] See W. Comanor and T. Wilson, *Advertising and Market Power*, Cambridge: Harvard University Press, 1975.
[5] For example, see L. White, *The Automobile Industry Since 1945*, Cambridge, Mass.: Harvard University Press, 1971. Earlier data were presented by Frank Fisher, Zvi Griliches, and Carl Kaysen.

What is a **contestable market?** It is a market into which entry is absolutely free, *and exit is absolutely costless.* Any firm can leave the market without impediment, and can get back whatever costs it incurred in entering. *The key characteristic of a contestable market is its vulnerability to hit-and-run entry.* A firm can enter such a market, make a quick profit, and leave without cost, if this seems to be the most profitable course of action.

Just as a perfectly competitive market is only a model, so the same is true of a contestable market. Nonetheless, models of this sort can be very useful and suggestive. At least three characteristics of a contestable market are worth noting. First, it can be shown that *profits are zero in equilibrium in a contestable market.* If profits were positive, a firm could enter the market, undercut the price of the firm with profits, and make a profit, after which it could leave the market if this seemed desirable. Thus profits will be eroded by such price cutting until they are zero. This is true regardless of how few firms exist in the contestable market. Because each is subject to such hit-and-run tactics, profits are eliminated.

Second, the organization of a contestable market is efficient in the sense that *the average cost of production is as low as possible.* Again because of the possibility of hit-and-run entry, firms in such a market must maintain their costs at the lowest possible level in the long run. If they do not do so, more efficient firms will enter, undercut their price, and force them to reduce their costs or withdraw from the market.

Third, if a contestable market contains two or more sellers, *their prices, in equilibrium, must equal their marginal costs.* As pointed out in Chapter 10, there are fundamental reasons why economists favor markets in which price equals marginal cost. One reason why perfect competition is favored by so many economists is that price equals marginal cost. Thus it is very interesting that this desirable feature of perfect competition exists as well in contestable markets.

In the past, it has often been presumed that these three outcomes—zero profits, minimum cost, and price equal to marginal cost—would be very unlikely to occur when there are few sellers. The theory of contestable markets implies that this is not necessarily the case. However, many critics say that this theory is based on very unrealistic assumptions concerning entry and exit. In particular, they point out that entry often is not free and that exit seldom is costless.

TEST YOURSELF

1. Suppose that a cartel consists of four firms, each of which has a horizontal marginal cost curve. For each firm, marginal cost equals $4. Suppose that the marginal revenue curve for the cartel is $MR = 10 - 2Q$, where MR is marginal revenue (in dollars) and Q is the cartel's output per year (in thousands of units). What output rate will the cartel choose?

2. According to the Senate Subcommittee on Antitrust and Monopoly, "Some system of marketing quotas, whether overt or carefully hidden, must underlie any price-fixing agreement." Comment and evaluate.

3. Discuss the incentives that each firm in Question 1 would have to cheat on the collusive agreement described there.

4. Explain why the average cost of production will be as low as possible in a contestable market. What is the significance of this fact?

THE THEORY OF GAMES

As pointed out at the beginning of this chapter, the rivalry among oligopolists has many of the characteristics of a game. As in a game, in oligopoly each firm must take account of its rivals' reactions to its own actions. For this reason, an oligopolistic firm cannot tell what effect a change in its output will have on the price of its product and on its profits unless it can guess how its rivals will respond to the change. To understand game theory, you have to know what a ***game*** is. It is a competitive situation where two or more persons pursue their own interests and no person can dictate the outcome. Poker is a game, and so is a situation in which two firms are engaged in competitive advertising campaigns. A game is described in terms of its players, rules, payoffs, and information conditions. These elements are common to all conflict situations.

Definitions of Terms

More specifically, a ***player,*** whether a single person or an organization, is a decision-making unit. Each player has a certain amount of resources, and the ***rules of the game*** describe how these resources can be used. Thus the rules of poker indicate how bets can be made and which hands are better than others. A ***strategy*** is a complete specification of what a player will do under each contingency in the playing of the game. Thus a corporation president might tell her subordinates how she wants an advertising campaign to start, and what should be done at subsequent times in response to various actions of competing firms. The game's outcome clearly depends on each player's strategies. A player's ***payoff*** varies from game to game. It is win, lose, or draw in checkers, and various sums of money in poker.

A SIMPLE TWO-PERSON GAME

For simplicity we will restrict our attention to *two-person games*: those with only two players. The relevant features of a two-person game can be shown by constructing a ***payoff matrix***. To illustrate, consider the case of two big soap producers, Procter & Gamble and Lever Brothers. Suppose that these two firms are about to stage rival advertising campaigns and that each firm has a choice of strategies. Procter & Gamble can choose to concentrate on either television ads or magazine ads; Lever Brothers has the same choice. Table 11.1 shows what will happen to the

Table 11.1
Payoff Matrix: Procter & Gamble and Lever Brothers

POSSIBLE STRATEGIES FOR P & G	POSSIBLE STRATEGIES FOR LEVER BROTHERS	
	CONCENTRATE ON TV	CONCENTRATE ON MAGAZINES
Concentrate on TV	P & G's profit: $3 million Lever's profit: $2 million	P & G's profit: $4 million Lever's profit: $3 million
Concentrate on magazines	P & G's profit: $2 million Lever's profit: $3 million	P & G's profit: $3 million Lever's profit: $4 million

profits of each firm when each combination of strategies is chosen. If both firms concentrate on TV ads, Procter & Gamble gains $3 million and Lever Brothers gains $2 million. If Procter & Gamble concentrates on TV ads and Lever Brothers concentrates on magazine ads, Procter and Gamble gains $4 million and Lever Brothers gains $3 million. And so on.

Procter & Gamble's Viewpoint

Given the payoff matrix in Table 11.1, there is a definite optimal choice (called a **dominant strategy**) for each firm. To see that this is the case, let's begin by looking at the situation from Procter & Gamble's point of view. If Lever Brothers concentrates on TV ads, Procter & Gamble will make more money ($3 million rather than $2 million) if it concentrates on TV rather than magazines. If Lever Brothers concentrates on magazines, Procter & Gamble will make more money ($4 million rather than $3 million) if it concentrates on TV rather than magazines. Thus, regardless of the strategy chosen by Lever Brothers, Procter & Gamble will do best to concentrate on TV.

Lever Brothers' Viewpoint

Now let's look at the situation from the point of view of Lever Brothers. If Procter & Gamble concentrates on TV ads, Lever Brothers will make more money ($3 million rather than $2 million) if it concentrates on magazines rather than TV. If Procter & Gamble concentrates on magazines, Lever Brothers will make more money ($4 million rather than $3 million) if it concentrates on magazines rather than TV. Thus, regardless of the strategy chosen by Procter and Gamble, Lever Brothers will do best to concentrate on magazines.

The Solution of the Game

At this point, the solution of this game is clear. *Procter & Gamble will concentrate on TV ads and Lever Brothers will concentrate on magazine ads.* This is the best that either firm can do.

Noteworthy Features of This Game

Several points should be noted concerning this game. First, in this game, both players have a **dominant strategy**—a strategy that is its best choice regardless of what the other player does. Not all games have a dominant strategy for each player.

Second, in this game the best strategy for each player is the same regardless of whether the players choose their strategies simultaneously or whether one of the players goes first. For example, Procter & Gamble will choose to concentrate on TV regardless of whether it picks its strategy before, after or at the same time as Lever Brothers. As we shall see, this is not true for all games. In some games, a player's best strategy depends on the timing of the player's move.

THE PRISONERS' DILEMMA

The theory of games enables us to reach a deeper understanding of the conditions under which oligopolists are likely to cheat on a collusive

Table 11.2
Payoff Matrix: National Robot and Robotica, Inc.

POSSIBLE DECISIONS BY ROBOTICA	POSSIBLE DECISIONS BY NATIONAL ROBOT	
	STICK BY AGREEMENT	CHEAT
Stick by agreement	Robotica's profit: $6 million National's profit: $6 million	Robotica's profit: $3 million National's profit: $7 million
Cheat	Robotica's profit: $7 million National's profit: $3 million	Robotica's profit: $4 million National's profit: $4 million

agreement. Suppose that the only two producers of robots—National Robot and Robotica, Inc.—form a cartel. Each firm can either stick by the cartel agreement or cheat. There are four possible outcomes, depending on which decision each firm makes. They are shown in Table 11.2, which is the payoff matrix showing the profit levels of each firm, depending on the decisions made by both.

What should National do? If Robotica sticks by the agreement, it appears that the better strategy for National is to cheat, since National's profits will be greater than if it sticks by the agreement. If Robotica cheats, the better strategy for National seems to be to cheat as well, since National's profits will be higher than if it sticks by the agreement. Thus it appears that National *will choose the strategy of cheating, since regardless of which strategy Robotica adopts, National seems better off by cheating than by sticking by the agreement.* In other words, cheating seems to be the dominant strategy.

What should Robotica do? If National sticks by the agreement, the better strategy for Robotica seems to be to cheat, since Robotica's profits will be greater than if it sticks by the agreement. If National cheats, the better strategy for Robotica appears to be to cheat as well, since Robotica's profits will be higher than if it sticks by the agreement. Thus it seems that Robotica *will choose the strategy of cheating, since regardless of which strategy National adopts, Robotica is better off by cheating than by sticking by the agreement.* Again, cheating seems to be the dominant strategy.

Consequently, in this situation, it appears that both firms will cheat. However, it is important to note that National and Robotica, because they do not trust each other to stick by their agreement, wind up with lower profits than if they both were to stick by the agreement ($4 million versus $6 million).

The type of game considered in Table 11.2 is often called the **prisoners' dilemma** because it is similar to a situation where two persons are arrested after committing a crime. The police lock each person in a separate room and offer each the following deal. "If you confess while your partner does not confess, you will get a 2-year jail term, while he or she will get 12 years." Each person knows that if they both confess, each will get 10 years (not 12 years because they cooperated with the police). If neither confesses, each will get only 3 years because the evidence against them is weak. In such a case, each will be likely to confess, even though they will do worse than if they could bring themselves to trust each other.

EXAMPLE 11.3 WHAT WILL BE ON THE COVERS OF NEWSWEEK AND TIME?

Every week, *Time* and *Newsweek*, two leading news magazines, must each pick a story to emphasize on their covers. Suppose that there are two possibilities for next week's cover: a terrorist attack on a U.S. ambassador or a military agreement between the United States and China. Suppose that the editor of each magazine wants to maximize readership, and that the number of people reading each magazine depends as follows on which story is featured on the cover of each magazine:

	NEWSWEEK'S CHOICE	
TIME'S CHOICE	TERRORIST ATTACK	U.S.–CHINA AGREEMENT
Terrorist attack	Newsweek: 6 million readers Time: 10 million readers	Newsweek: 7 million readers Time: 9 million readers
U.S.–China agreement	Newsweek: 6 million readers Time: 9 million readers	Newsweek: 5 million readers Time: 8 million readers

a) Does *Time* have a dominant strategy? If so, what is it? (b) Does *Newsweek* have a dominant strategy? If so, what is it? (c) If you were *Newsweek*'s editor, what story would you expect *Time* to put on its cover? Why? (d) Given the answer to part (c), what choice would you make if you were the editor of *Newsweek*? (e) What do you think will be on the cover of each magazine? Why?

Solution

(a) Yes. Regardless of whether *Newsweek* has the terrorist attack or the U.S.–China agreement on its cover, *Time* has a higher readership if it exhibits the terrorist attack on its cover. (b) No. If *Time* has the terrorist attack on its cover, *Newsweek* will get more readers by putting the U.S.–China agreement on its cover. If *Time* has the U.S.–China agreement on its cover, *Newsweek* will get more readers by putting the terrorist attack on its cover. (c) *Time* would be expected to put the terrorist attack on its cover because this is its dominant strategy, as pointed out in the answer to part (a). (d) Given that *Time* would be expected to put the terrorist attack on its cover (since this is its dominant strategy), the editor of *Newsweek* would be expected to put the U.S.–China agreement on its cover, because this would produce a higher readership (7 million vs. 6 million). (e) Based on the foregoing analysis, *Time* would be expected to put the terrorist attack on its cover, and *Newsweek* would be expected to put the U.S.–China agreement on its cover.[*]

[*] For further discussion, see A. Dixit and B. Nalebuff, *Thinking Strategically*, New York: W. W. Norton, 1991.

The situation in Table 11.2 is similar because, if the two firms could trust each other, both would enjoy higher profits.

WHAT IF THE GAME IS REPEATED?

In some cases, a game is played only once; in others, it is repeated over and over. If National and Robotica must decide continually whether to cheat or not, the analysis in the previous section may not be correct. Suppose that National refuses to cheat the first time that it must make a decision and that it continues to stick by the agreement so long as Robotica does so. But if Robotica fails even once to cooperate, National will revert forever to the safe policy of cheating. Suppose that Robotica adopts exactly the same policy. What will be the result? Both firms will make a $6 million profit. If either one cheats, it will raise its profit to $7 million for a short period of time, but afterward its profit will fall permanently to $4 million because its rival will cheat as well. Consequently, if the game is repeated indefinitely, it will not be in the interest of either firm to cheat.[6]

Of course, this assumes that each firm can quickly detect whether the other firm is cheating. In fact, this may not be so easy. In some cases, trade associations have been authorized to collect detailed data regarding each firm's sales and prices. In this way, an attempt has been made to detect cheating quickly. The more promptly cheating is detected, the less profitable it tends to be.

Michigan's Robert Axelrod has argued that a good strategy for each player in a game of this sort is "*tit for tat*," which means that each player should do on this round whatever the other player did on the previous round. If National adopts a tit-for-tat strategy, it should abide by the agreement on the first round. If Robotica also abides by it, National should continue to do so, but once Robotica cheats, National should retaliate by cheating as well. Empirical studies suggest that some cartel members actually seem to have adopted tit-for-tat strategies in the past.

WHEN IS A THREAT CREDIBLE?

Oligopolists like General Motors or Ford often send signals to one another indicating their motives, intentions, and objectives. Some signals are threats. Suppose, for example, that the Medea Company learns that the Pocono Corporation, its principal rival, is about to lower its price. Medea may announce its intention of lowering its own price substantially, thus signaling to Pocono that it is willing to start a price war if Pocono carries out its price reduction. In addition, some of Medea's managers may see to it that this message gets transmitted indirectly to some of Pocono's managers.

However, not all threats are credible. For example, if the payoff matrix is as shown in Table 11.3, Medea's threat is not very credible. (For simplicity, we assume in Table 11.3 that price can be set at only two levels— "high" and "low.") If Pocono sets a high price, Medea makes $5 million if it sets a high price and $3 million if it sets a low price. If Pocono sets a low price, Medea loses $1 million if it sets a high price and $2 million if it sets a low price.

Table 11.3
Payoff Matrix: Medea Company and Pocono Corporation

POSSIBLE STRATEGIES FOR MEDEA	POSSIBLE STRATEGIES FOR POCONO	
	LOW PRICE	HIGH PRICE
Low Price	Medea's profit: –$2 million Pocono's profit: $2 million	Medea's profit: $3 million Pocono's profit: –$1 million
High Price	Medea's profit: –$1 million Pocono's profit: $6 million	Medea's profit: $5 million Pocono's profit: $4 million

---

[6] Stanford's D. Kreps, P. Milgrom, J. Roberts, and R. Wilson, among others, have carried out important research on this topic.

Hence, it certainly seems unlikely that Medea will carry out its threat to reduce its price to the low level, since, as we've just seen, Medea will make more (or lose less) money by keeping its price at the high level than by reducing it to the low level. This is true, regardless of whether Pocono reduces its price. Thus, if Pocono can be certain that Medea will do what maximizes its profit, it can regard Medea's threat as an idle gesture.

But things are not quite so simple. If Medea can convince Pocono that it will *not* do what maximizes its profit, it can make its threat credible. Thus, if it can convince Pocono that, if Pocono sets the low price, it will match it, *even though this reduces Medea's own profits*, Pocono may decide not to set the low price. Why? Because Pocono's profits are higher ($4 million versus $2 million) if it maintains a high price (and Medea does the same) than if Pocono sets a low price (and Medea does the same).

How can Medea convince Pocono that it will reduce its price, even though this seems to be irrational? For one thing, its managers may develop a reputation of doing what they say, "regardless of the costs." They may exhibit a well-publicized taste for facing down opponents and for refusing to back down, regardless of how crazy they may seem. Confronted with the "irrational" Medea Company, the Pocono Corporation may decide not to cut price. However, if Medea cannot convince Pocono of its "irrationality," Pocono will justifiably regard Medea's threat to reduce price as not being credible.

MAKING RESISTANCE CREDIBLE

Oligopolists generally try to discourage firms from entering their market. As we have seen in previous sections, the entry of new firms tends to decrease the profits of existing firms. Take the case of the Berwyn Corporation, which faces the threat of entry by the Roanoke Company. Table 11.4 shows the profits of each firm, depending on whether or not Roanoke enters the market and on whether or not Berwyn resists Roanoke's entry by cutting its price and increasing its output (thus reducing Roanoke's profits if it enters).[7]

Table 11.4
Payoff Matrix, before the Berwyn Corporation Makes Its Resistance Credible

POSSIBLE STRATEGIES FOR BERWYN CORPORATION	POSSIBLE STRATEGIES FOR ROANOKE COMPANY	
	ENTER	DO NOT ENTER[a]
Resist Entry	Berwyn's profit: $2 million Roanoke's profit: $4 million	Berwyn's profit: $4 million Roanoke's profit: $6 million
Do Not Resist Entry	Berwyn's profit: $3 million Roanoke's profit: $8 million	Berwyn's profit: $4 million Roanoke's profit: $6 million

[a] See footnote 7.

[7] If Roanoke does not enter the market, there is no difference between Berwyn's resisting and not resisting, since there is nothing to resist. Consequently, Berwyn's profit figures in Table 11.4 are the same regardless of which strategy Berwyn is assumed to pursue.

The first move in this game is up to Roanoke, which must decide whether or not to enter. If it enters, Berwyn must decide whether or not to resist. Given the payoff matrix in Table 11.4, Berwyn, if it is "rational," will not resist because its profits will be lower ($2 million rather than $3 million) if it resists than if it does not resist. Since Roanoke knows that this is the case, it will enter, since its profits will be higher ($8 million rather than $6 million) if it enters than if it does not enter. Needless to say, Berwyn may threaten to resist, but this threat is not credible (if Berwyn is "rational") because, as we have just seen, Berwyn would lower its profits by resisting.

To make this threat credible, Berwyn may alter the payoff matrix in Table 11.4. Suppose that it builds lots of excess production capacity so that, if Roanoke enters, it can increase its output enormously and push price down to the point where Roanoke will lose money. Since it is expensive to keep excess capacity on hand, Berwyn's profit if it does not resist entry is now lower than before it built the extra capacity. The new payoff matrix is shown in Table 11.5. Now if Roanoke enters, Berwyn's profits are higher ($1.5 million versus $1 million) if it resists Roanoke's entry than if it does not resist. Consequently, Berwyn's threat to resist becomes credible. Under these circumstances, Roanoke will not enter because its profits will be $7 million higher ($6 million rather than –$1 million) if it does not enter than if it enters.

Table 11.5
Payoff Matrix, after the Berwyn Corporation Makes Its Resistance Credible

POSSIBLE STRATEGIES FOR BERWYN CORPORATION	POSSIBLE STRATEGIES FOR ROANOKE COMPANY	
	ENTER	DO NOT ENTER[a]
Resist Entry	Berwyn's profit: $1.5 million Roanoke's profit: –$1 million	Berwyn's profit: $3 million Roanoke's profit: $6 million
Do Not Resist Entry	Berwyn's profit: $1 million Roanoke's profit: $8 million	Berwyn's profit: $3 million Roanoke's profit: $6 million

[a] See Footnote 7.

Note a very interesting fact about Berwyn's successful attempt to deter Roanoke from entering: *Berwyn has convinced Roanoke not to enter by reducing its own profits if it does not resist entry.* In this way, Berwyn has committed itself irrevocably to fight. If Roanoke enters, Berwyn is ready to fight (by raising output greatly and by pushing price down) and has an incentive to fight (because its profits are greater than if it does not fight). By committing itself in this way to resist entry, it has gained an advantage.

However, as pointed out in the previous section, there are other ways that Berwyn can convince Roanoke not to enter. If Berwyn has imposed enormous losses on every firm that has tried to enter in the past, and has a reputation for "irrational" opposition to entry, Roanoke may decide that it wants no part of a struggle with Berwyn. Consequently, Berwyn may find it worthwhile to foster such a reputation by hammering every entrant that appears, because the longer-term gains from the prevention of entry may exceed the short-term costs of these wars.

THE ADVANTAGES OF BEING FIRST

Wal-Mart merchandise on display

In many cases, the firm that makes the first move has a big advantage. Take the case of Wal-Mart stores, a chain of discount retail stores. Sam Walton, the company's founder, set up hundreds of such stores in small towns in the Southwest. Since the market in each such town was too small to support more than one discount store, his strategy was to be the first to do so. That is, he had a preemptive strategy—a strategy of establishing stores before his rivals did so.

Suppose that Wal-Mart and a rival firm are both considering the establishment of a discount store in a particular small town, and that the relevant payoff matrix is shown in Table 11.6. If Wal-Mart enters the town but its rival does not, Wal-Mart will make $10 million and its rival will make nothing. If its rival enters the town but Wal-Mart does not, its rival will make $10 million and Wal-Mart will make nothing. If both Wal-Mart and its rival enter the town, both will lose $5 million because the town is too small to support two discount stores.

How this game will turn out depends on which firm acts first. If Wal-Mart acts first, it can enter and be reasonably sure that its rival will not do the same (because its rival would lose $5 million if it entered). On the other hand, if its rival acts first, it can enter and be confident that Wal-Mart would not do so (because Wal-Mart would lose $5 million if it entered). In a case like this, the prize goes to the swift and the nimble. In oligopoly as in boxing, it often pays to be fast on your feet.

Table 11.6
Payoff Matrix: Wal-Mart and Its Rival

POSSIBLE STRATEGIES FOR WAL-MART STORES	POSSIBLE STRATEGIES FOR WAL-MART'S RIVAL	
	ENTER THE TOWN	DO NOT ENTER THE TOWN
Enter the Town	Wal-Mart's profit: –$5 million Rival's profit: –$5 million	Wal-Mart's profit: $10 million Rival's profit: zero
Do Not Enter the Town	Wal-Mart's profit: zero Rival's profit: $10 million	Wal-Mart's profit: zero Rival's profit: zero

COMPARISON OF OLIGOPOLY WITH PERFECT COMPETITION

We have seen that economists have constructed a number of types of models of oligopoly behavior—the cartel models, price leadership models, contestable market models, various game theoretic models, and others—but there is no agreement that any of these models is an adequate general representation of oligopoly behavior. For this reason, it is difficult to estimate the effects of an oligopolistic market structure on price, output, and profits. Nonetheless, if a perfectly competitive industry were turned overnight into an oligopoly, it is likely that changes would occur.

1. Price would probably be higher than under perfect competition. The difference between the oligopoly price and the perfectly competitive price will depend on the number of firms in the industry and the ease of entry. The larger the number of firms and the easier it is to enter the industry, the closer the oligopoly price will be to the perfectly competitive level.

2. If the demand curve is the same under oligopoly as under perfect competition, it also follows that *output will be less under oligopoly than under perfect competition.* However, it is not always reasonable to assume that the demand curve is the same in both cases, since the large expenditures for advertising and product differentiation incurred by some oligopolies may tend to shift the demand curve to the right. Consequently in some cases both price and output may tend to be higher under oligopoly than under perfect competition.

3. Oligopolistic industries tend to spend more on advertising, product differentiation, and style changes than do perfectly competitive industries. The use of some resources for these purposes is certainly worthwhile, since advertising provides buyers with information, and product differentiation allows greater freedom of choice. Whether oligopolies spend too much for these purposes is by no means obvious. However, there is a widespread feeling among economists, based largely on empirical studies (and hunch), that in some oligopolistic industries such expenditures have been expanded beyond socially optimal levels.

4. One might expect on the basis of the models presented in this chapter that the *profits earned by oligopolists would be higher, on the average, than the profits earned by perfectly competitive firms.* This conclusion is supported by some statistical evidence. In an early study, Joe Bain of the University of California found that firms in industries in which the largest few firms had a high proportion of total sales tended to have higher rates of return than firms in industries in which the largest few firms had a small proportion of total sales. Nonetheless, this is a controversial topic.[8]

MONOPOLISTIC COMPETITION

The key feature of **monopolistic competition** is **product differentiation.** In contrast to perfect competition, where all firms sell an identical product, firms under monopolistic competition sell somewhat different products. We are talking here about what sometimes may appear to be subtle differences—Macy's dresses as compared to Wanamaker's dresses, or McDonald's Big Mac versus Burger King's Whopper—but they are significant in economic analysis.

One sector of the economy where product differentiation occurs frequently is retail trade. Producers try to make their product a little different, by altering the product's physical make-up, the services they offer, and other such variables. Other differences—which may be spurious—are based on brand name, image making, advertising claims, etc. In this way, the producers have some monopoly power, but it usually is small, because the products of other firms are very similar.

In perfect competition, the firms included in an industry are easy to de-

---

[8] For some relevant discussion, see L. Weiss, "The Concentration-Profits Relationship and Antitrust," in H. Goldschmid, H. M. Mann, and J. F. Weston, *Industrial Concentration, The New Learning*, Boston: Little Brown, 1974.

termine because they all produce the same product. But if product differentiation exists, it is no longer easy to define an industry, since each firm produces a somewhat different product. Nevertheless, it may be useful to group together firms that produce similar products and call them a **product group.** We can formulate a product group called "toothpaste" or "toilet soap" or "chocolate bars." The process by which we combine firms into product groups is bound to be somewhat arbitrary, since there is no way to decide how close a pair of substitutes must be to belong to the same product group. But it is assumed that meaningful product groups can be established.

Besides product differentiation, other conditions must be met for an industry to qualify as a case of monopolistic competition. First, *there must be a large number of firms in the product group*. In other words, the product must be produced by perhaps 50 to 100 or more firms, with each firm's product a fairly close substitute for the products of the other firms in the product group. Second, *the number of firms in the product group must be large enough so that each firm expects its actions to go unheeded by its rivals and is unimpeded by possible retaliatory moves on their part*. If there is a large number of firms, this condition will normally be met. Third, *entry into the product group must be relatively easy, and there must be no collusion, such as price fixing or market sharing, among firms in the product group*. If there is a large number of firms, collusion generally is difficult, if not impossible.[9]

PRICE AND OUTPUT UNDER MONOPOLISTIC COMPETITION

Under monopolistic competition, what determines how much output a firm will produce, and what price it will charge? If each firm produces a somewhat different product, it follows that the demand curve facing each firm slopes downward to the right. That is, if the firm raises its price slightly it will lose some, but by no means all, of its customers to other firms. And if it lowers its price slightly, it will gain some, but by no means all, of it competitors' customers. This is in contrast to perfect competition, where the demand curve facing each firm is horizontal.

Figure 11.2 shows the short-run equilibrium of a monopolistically competitive firm. The firm in the short run will set its price at OP_0 and its output rate at OQ_0, since this combination of price and output will maximize its profits. We can be sure that this combination of price and output maximizes profit because marginal cost equals marginal revenue at this output rate. Economic profits will be earned because price, OP_0 exceeds average total costs, OC_0, at this output rate.

What will the equilibrium price and output be in the long run? One condition for long-run equilibrium is that *each firm be making no economic profits or losses,* since entry or exit of firms will occur otherwise — and entry and exit are incompatible with long-run equilibrium. Another condition for long-run equilibrium is that *each firm be maximizing its profits*. At what price and output will both these conditions be fulfilled?

[9] For the theory of monopolistic competition, we are indebted largely to Edward Chamberlin of Harvard University, whose path-breaking book on the subject first appeared in 1933. See E. Chamberlin *The Theory of Monopolistic Competition*, Cambridge, Mass.: Harvard University Press, 1933.

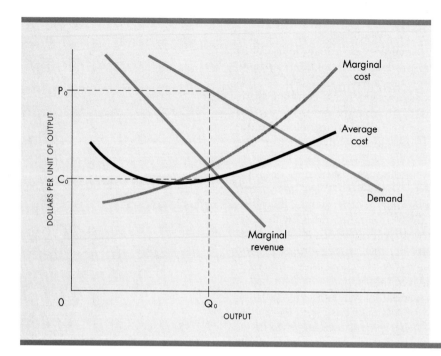

Figure 11.2
Short-Run Equilibrium:
Monopolistic Competition
The firm will set price at OP_0 and its output rate at OQ_0 since marginal cost equals marginal revenue at this output. It will earn a profit of C_0P_0 per unit of output.

Figure 11.3 shows that the long-run equilibrium is at a price of OP_1 and an output of OQ_1. The zero-economic-profit condition is met at this combination of price and output since the firm's average cost at this output equals the price, OP_1. And the profit-maximization condition is met since the marginal revenue curve intersects the marginal cost curve at this output rate.

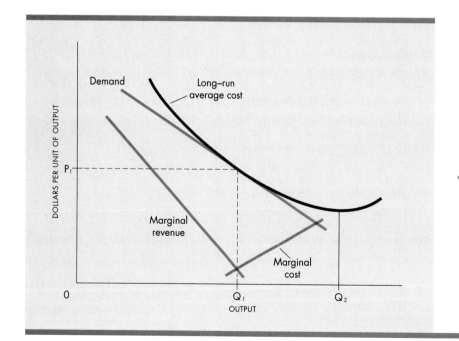

Figure 11.3
Long-Run Equilibrium:
Monopolistic Competition
The long-run equilibrium is at a price of OP_1 and an output of OQ_1. There are zero profits since long-run average cost equals price. Profits are being maximized since marginal cost equals marginal revenue at this output.

Excess Capacity and Product Diversity

A famous conclusion of the theory of monopolistic competition is that *a firm under this form of market organization will tend to operate with excess capacity.* In other words, the firm will construct a plant smaller than the minimum-cost size of plant and operate it at less than the minimum-cost rate of output. Why? Because, as shown in Figure 11.3, the long-run average cost curve must be tangent in long-run equilibrium to the demand curve. (This tangency condition insures that, if the firm produces the profit-maximizing output, it obtains a zero economic profit, in accord with the conditions for long-run equilibrium.) Thus, since the demand curve is *downward-sloping,* the long-run average cost curve must also be *downward-sloping* at the long-run equilibrium output rate. Consequently, the firm's output must be less than OQ_2, the output rate at which long-run average costs are minimized, since the long-run average cost curve slopes downward only at output rates less than OQ_2.

This is an interesting conclusion, since it suggests that monopolistically competitive industries will be overcrowded with firms. There may be too many firms (from society's point of view), each of which is smaller than required to minimize its unit costs. However, one must be careful to recognize that, if there were fewer firms, there would be less diversity of products. Whether the apparently excessive number of firms is really excessive (from society's viewpoint) depends on whether, if there were fewer firms, the reduction in unit costs would outweigh the loss to consumers due to less product diversity.

COMPARISONS WITH PERFECT COMPETITION AND MONOPOLY

Market structure is important because it influences market behavior. We need to know how the behavior of a monopolistically competitive industry differs from that of a perfectly competitive industry or a monopoly. Suppose that there exists a magician who can transform an industry's structure by a wave of a wand. (John D. Rockefeller was a real-life magician who transformed the structure of the oil industry in the late 1800s—but he seemed to favor mergers, mixed with some ungentlemanly tactics, over wands.) Suppose that the magician makes an industry monopolistically competitive, rather than perfectly competitive or monopolistic. What difference would it make in the behavior of the industry? Or, to take a less fanciful case, what difference would it make if government action or technological change resulted in such a change in an industry's market structure? It is difficult to say how the industry's behavior would be affected, because output would be heterogeneous in one case and homogeneous in the other, and its cost curves would probably vary with its organization. But many economists seem to believe that differences of the following kind can be expected.

1. The firm under monopolistic competition is likely to produce less, and charge a higher price, than under perfect competition. The demand curve confronting the monopolistic competitor slopes downward to the right. Consequently, as we saw in the previous chapter, marginal revenue must be less than price. Thus, under monopolistic competition, marginal cost must also be less than price, since marginal revenue must equal marginal cost at the firm's profit-maximizing output rate. But if marginal cost is less than price, the firm's output rate must be smaller—and the price higher—than if marginal cost equals price, which is the case under perfect competition. On the other hand, *relative to monopoly, monopolistically competitive firms are likely to have lower profits, greater output, and lower price.* The firms in a product group might obtain positive economic profits if they were to collude and behave as a monopolist. Such an increase in profits would benefit the producers. Consumers would be worse off because of the higher prices and smaller output of goods.

2. As noted in the previous section, *a firm under monopolistic competition may be somewhat inefficient because it tends to operate with excess capacity.* Each firm builds a smaller-than-minimum-cost plant and produces a smaller-than-minimum-cost output. More firms exist than if there were no excess capacity, resulting in some overcrowding of the industry. Inefficiencies of this sort would not be expected under perfect competition. However, these inefficiencies may not be very great, since the demand curve confronting the monopolistically competitive firm is likely to be highly elastic; and the more elastic it is, the less excess capacity the firm will have.

3. Firms under monopolistic competition will offer a wider variety of styles, brands, and qualities than firms under perfect competition. Moreover, they will spend much more on advertising and other selling expenses than a perfectly competitive firm would. Whether this product diversity is worth its cost is hard to say. Some economists are impressed by the apparent waste in monopolistic competition. They think it results in too many firms, too many brands, too much selling effort, and too much spurious product differentiation. But if the differences among products are real and are understood by consumers, the greater variety of alternatives available under monopolistic competition may be very valuable to consumers.[10]

TEST YOURSELF

1. In Table 11.1, suppose that Procter & Gamble's profit if it concentrates on TV and if Lever Brothers concentrates on magazines is $1 million, rather than $4 million. If the rest of the payoff matrix is unchanged, do Procter & Gamble and Lever Brothers still have dominant strategies? Explain.

2. Under the conditions given in Question 1, can Procter & Gamble predict what strategy Lever Brothers will adopt? (Hint: Does Lever Brothers have a dominant strategy?) If its prediction is correct, what strategy should Procter & Gamble choose?

3. In a previous section, it was asserted that, if the demand curve confronting a monopolistically competitive firm is highly elastic, the firm is likely to have less excess capacity than if it is relatively inelastic. Explain why this is true.

4. Explain how a firm's output and price are determined under monopolistic competition in (a) the short run and (b) the long run.

---

[10] Before leaving the subject of monopolistic competition, it should be recognized that Professor Chamberlin's theory has been subjected to considerable criticism. As a case in point, the definition of the product group is ambiguous. See G. Stigler, *Five Lectures on Economic Problems,* London: Longmans Green, 1949.

SUMMARY

1. Oligopoly is characterized by a small number of firms and a great deal of interdependence, actual and perceived, among them. Oligopoly is a common market structure in the United States.

2. Conditions in oligopolistic industries tend to promote collusion. A cartel is an open, formal, collusive arrangement. A profit-maximizing cartel will act like a monopolist with a number of plants or divisions, each of which is a member firm. In practice, it appears that the members of a cartel often divide markets geographically or in accord with each firm's level of sales in the past.

3. Price leadership is quite common in oligopolistic industries, one or a few firms apparently setting the price and the rest following their lead. Two types of price leadership are the dominant-firm model and the barometric-firm model.

4. A contestable market is a market where entry is absolutely free and where exit is absolutely costless. Under these stringent assumptions, it appears that there will be zero profits, minimum cost, and price equal to marginal cost.

5. Game theory is often used to analyze oligopolistic markets. For example, the prisoners' dilemma sheds light on the factors determining whether firms will cheat on a cartel agreement. We also showed how game theory can be employed to determine when a threat is credible, to indicate how to discourage entry, and to show the nature of first-mover advantages.

6. Relative to perfect competition, it seems likely that both price and profits will be higher under oligopoly. Moreover, oligopolistic industries will tend to spend more on advertising, product differentiation, and style changes than perfectly competitive industries.

7. Monopolistic competition occurs where there are many sellers whose products are somewhat different. The demand curve facing each firm slopes downward to the right. The conditions for long-run equilibrium are that each firm is maximizing profits and that economic profits are zero.

8. The firm under monopolistic competition is likely to produce less, and charge a higher price, than under perfect competition. Relative to pure monopoly, monopolistically competitive firms are likely to have lower profits, greater output, and lower prices. Firms under monopolistic competition will offer a wider variety of styles, brands, and qualities than will firms under perfect competition.

CONCEPTS FOR REVIEW

Oligopoly	**Dominant firm**	**Payoff matrix**
Economies of scale	**Barometric firm**	**Prisoner's dilemma**
Barriers to entry	**Nonprice competition**	**Tit for tat**
Collusion	**Contestable markets**	**Monopolistic competition**
Cartel	**Game theory**	**Dominant strategy**
Price leadership	**Strategy**	

INDUSTRIAL ORGANIZATION AND ANTITRUST POLICY

MONOPOLY AND MONOPOLIST have long been dirty words—or at least slightly derogatory ones. The public has tended to view monopolists with suspicion at least since Adam Smith's famous attack on monopolies in the eighteenth century. Smith preached and generations of economists since have taught that a monopolist charges a price in excess of the price that would prevail under perfect competition. For reasons given in Chapter 10, this is likely to result in a misallocation of society's resources. One way that society has attempted to deal with problems caused by monopoly is through public regulation, discussed in Chapter 10. Another way is through antitrust policy, discussed in the present chapter.

In this chapter we begin by discussing the case against oligopoly and monopolistic competition, after which we take up the defense of monopoly power made by some economists. Then, after describing the extent of industrial concentration in the United States, we discuss the nature, history, and effectiveness of antitrust policy in the United States, together with the problems in constructing standards for antitrust policy. Finally, we describe some laws in this country that restrict, rather than promote, competition.

THE CASE AGAINST OLIGOPOLY AND MONOPOLISTIC COMPETITION

COMPLAINTS AGAINST OLIGOPOLY. In Chapter 10, we discussed the case against monopoly. Although economists are more concerned about monopoly than about oligopoly or monopolistic competition, this does not mean that they give either oligopoly or monopolistic competition a clean bill of health. Even though oligopoly has aroused less public indignation and opposition than out-and-out monopoly, an oligopoly can obviously be just as deleterious to social welfare. After all, *if oligopolists engage in collusion, open or tacit, their behavior with regard to price and output may resemble a monopolist's*. Only if there is real competition among the oligopolists can we expect price to be pushed closer to marginal cost under oligopoly than under monopoly. If oligopolists "cooperate" and "maintain orderly markets," the amount of social waste may be no less than under monopoly.

COMPLAINTS AGAINST MONOPOLISTIC COMPETITION. Monopolistic competition can also be a socially wasteful form of market organization. As we saw in Chapter 11, monopolistically competitive markets may be characterized by overcrowding and excess capacity. In addition, price under monopolistic competition—as well as under monopoly and oligopoly—will exceed marginal cost, although the difference between price and marginal cost may be smaller than under monopoly or oligopoly. Thus monopolistic competition, like monopoly and oligopoly, results in a misallocation of resources. The argument leading to this conclusion is exactly like that given in Chapter 10 (and Appendix C) for monopoly. Also, monopolistic competition, as well as oligopoly, may allow waste arising from too much being spent (from society's point of view) on product differentiation, advertising, and other selling expenses. (On the other hand, the diversity of products may benefit consumers enough to offset these disadvantages of monopolistic competition, as pointed out in Chapter 11.)

THE BOTTOM LINE.   The moral is that many economists look with disfavor on serious departures from perfect competition, whether these departures are in the direction of monopoly, oligopoly, or monopolistic competition. Judged against the perfectly competitive model, all may lead to social waste and inefficiency. However, monopoly is generally presumed to be the greatest evil, with the result that economists usually look with most disfavor on markets dominated by one, or a very few, sellers—or buyers.[1]

THE DEFENSE OF MONOPOLY POWER

Joseph Schumpeter

Not all economists agree that monopoly power is a bad thing. On the contrary, some respected voices in the economics profession have been raised to praise monopoly, not bury it. In discussing the social problems due to monopoly in Chapter 10, we assumed that the rate of technological change is independent of an industry's market structure. Some economists like Joseph Schumpeter have challenged this assumption. *They assert that the rate of technological change is likely to be higher in an imperfectly competitive industry (i.e., monopoly, oligopoly, etc.) than in a perfectly competitive industry.* Since the rate of technological change affects productivity and living standards, in their view a perfectly competitive economy is likely to be inferior in a dynamic sense to an economy containing many imperfectly competitive industries.

ARGUMENTS AGAINST PERFECT COMPETITION.   These economists point out that firms under perfect competition have fewer resources to devote to research and experimentation than do firms under imperfect competition. Because profits are at a relatively low level, it is difficult for firms under perfect competition to support large expenditures on research and development. Moreover, they argue that unless a firm has sufficient control over the market to reap the rewards from an innovation, the introduction of the innovation may not be worthwhile. If competitors can imitate the innovation very quickly, the innovator may be unable to make any money from it.

REJOINDERS TO THE CRITICS.   Defenders of perfect competition retort that there is likely to be less pressure for firms in imperfect markets to introduce new techniques and products, since such firms have fewer competitors. Moreover, firms in imperfect markets are better able to drive out

[1] Monopsony, where a single buyer exists, is taken up in Chapter 13.

entrants who, uncommitted to present techniques, are likely to be relatively quick to adopt new ones. (Entrants, unlike established producers, have no vested interest in maintaining the demand for existing products and the profitability of existing equipment.) Also, there are advantages in having a large number of independent decision-making units. There is less chance that an important technological advance will be blocked by the faulty judgment of a few men or women.

It is very difficult to obtain evidence to help settle this question, if it is posed in this way, since perfect competition is a hypothetical construct that does not exist in the real world. However, it does seem unlikely that a perfectly competitive industry (if such an industry could be constructed) would be able in many areas of the economy to carry out the research and development required to promote a high rate of technological change. Moreover, if entry is free and rapid, firms in a perfectly competitive industry will have little motivation to innovate. Although the evidence is not at all clear-cut, at least this much can be granted the critics of perfect competition.

MONOPOLY POWER, BIG BUSINESS, AND TECHNOLOGICAL CHANGE

But some economists go much further than the assertion that a certain amount of market imperfection will promote a more rapid rate of technological change. *They say that an industry composed of or dominated by a few large companies is the best market structure for promoting rapid technological change.* Harvard's John Kenneth Galbraith has said that the "modern industry of a few large firms [is] an almost perfect instrument for inducing technical change."[2] And in some circles, it is accepted as an obvious fact that giant firms with their financial strength and well-equipped laboratories are absolutely necessary to maintain a rapid rate of technological change.

Suppose that, for a market of given size, we could replace the largest firms by a larger number of somewhat smaller firms—and thus reduce the extent to which the industry is dominated by the largest firms. Is there any evidence that this would decrease the rate of technological change, as is sometimes asserted? The evidence currently available is much more limited than one would like, but the available studies—based on detailed data concerning research expenditures, patents, important inventions and innovations, and the diffusion of innovations—do not indicate that such a decrease in industrial concentration would reduce the rate of technological change in most industries.

Specifically, the available studies do not show that total research and development expenditures in most industries would decrease if the largest firms were replaced by somewhat smaller ones. Nor do they indicate that the research and development expenditures carried out by the largest firms are generally more productive (or more ambitious or more risky) than those carried out by somewhat smaller firms. Moreover, they do not suggest that greater concentration of an industry results in a faster diffusion of innovations. However, if innovations require a large amount of capital, they do suggest that the substitution of a larger number of

---

[2] John Kenneth Galbraith, *American Capitalism,* Boston: Houghton Mifflin, 1952, p. 91.

smaller firms for a few large ones may lead to slower commercial intro-duction of the innovations.[3]

Thus, *contrary to the allegations of Galbraith and others, there is little evidence that industrial giants are needed in most industries to ensure rapid technological change and rapid utilization of new techniques.* This does not mean that industries composed only of small firms would neces-sarily be optimal for the promotion and diffusion of new techniques. On the contrary, there seem to be considerable advantages in a diversity of firm sizes. Complementarities and interdependencies exist among large and small firms. There is often a division of labor. Smaller firms may focus on areas requiring sophistication and flexibility and cater to specialized needs, while bigger firms concentrate on areas requiring large production, marketing, or technical resources. However, there is little evidence in most industries that firms considerably smaller than the biggest firms are not big enough for these purposes.

HOW MUCH MONOPOLY POWER IS OPTIMAL?

The discussion in previous sections makes it clear that the case against monopoly power is not open and shut. On the contrary, a certain amount of monopoly power is inevitable in practically all real-life situations, since perfect competition is a model that can only be approximated in real life. Moreover, a certain amount of monopoly power may be needed to pro-mote desirable technological change. The difficult problem is to deter-mine how much monopoly power is optimal under various circumstances (and how this power is to be measured). Some economists (like Gal-braith) are convinced that a great deal of monopoly power is both in-evitable and desirable. Others believe the opposite. And the economic arguments are not strong enough to resolve the differences of opinion.

CONCENTRATION OF ECONOMIC POWER

Some critics of monopoly power and big business are concerned with the centralization of power in the hands of a relatively few firms. Although this is only partly an economic matter, it is obviously relevant to public policy makers. Economic power in the United States is distributed very unevenly; a few hundred corporations control a very large share of the total assets of the nonfarm economy. Moreover, within particular indus-tries, there is considerable concentration of ownership and production, as we shall see in the next sections. This concentration of power has been viewed with concern by observers like A. A. Berle, who asserted that the largest several hundred firms "each with its own dominating pyramid within it—represent a concentration of power over economies which makes the medieval feudal system look like a Sunday School party. In sheer economic power this has gone far beyond anything we have yet seen."

It is important to note that this distrust of power leads to a distrust of giant firms, whether or not they have substantial monopoly power. Even

[3] Edwin Mansfield, Anthony Romeo, Mark Schwartz, David Teece, Samuel Wagner, and Peter Brach, *Technology Transfer, Productivity, and Economic Policy*, New York: Norton, 1982, and the references cited there.

if General Motors had little power over prices, it would still have considerable economic—and political—power because of its sheer size. Note too that a firm's size is not necessarily a good indicator of the extent of its monopoly power. A small grocery store in a remote community may be a monopolist, but a large merchandising firm with many rivals may have little monopoly power.

Let's look at the 100 biggest manufacturing firms in the United States. Recognizing that bigness is not the same as monopoly power, what percentage of the nation's assets do these firms control, and is this percentage increasing or decreasing over time? According to the latest available figures, the 100 largest manufacturing firms control over half of all manufacturing assets in the United States, and this percentage seems to have increased considerably since the end of World War II.

INDUSTRIAL CONCENTRATION IN THE UNITED STATES

Economists and policy makers are interested in market structure because it influences market performance. But how can one measure an industry's market structure? How can one tell how close an industry is to being a monopoly or a perfectly competitive industry?

The ***market concentration ratio,*** which shows the percentage of total sales or production accounted for by the 4 largest firms, is a measure of how concentrated an industry is. The higher the market concentration ratio, the more concentrated the industry is in a very few hands. Basing this measure on 4 firms is arbitrary. You can use 5, 6, 7, or any number of firms you like. But the figures issued by the government are generally based on 4 firms. Also, this measure has important limitations, discussed below.

Consider Table 12.1, which shows the market concentration ratios for selected industries. These ratios vary widely from industry to industry. At one extreme, the automobile industry is a tight oligopoly, with the concentration ratio about as high as it can get: 92 percent. At the other extreme, there is very little industrial concentration in the commercial printing industry; its concentration ratio is only 6 percent.

Most economists who have studied trends in industrial concentration seem to agree that remarkably little change has occurred in the past 70 years in the average level of concentration in the United States. Also, the available evidence seems to indicate that the levels of market concentration are lower in the United States than in other major industrialized countries, with the possible exception of Great Britain and Japan.

Finally, it is important to recognize that the concentration ratio is only a rough measure of an industry's market structure. Certainly, to provide a reasonably adequate description, it must be supplemented with data on the extent and type of product differentiation in the industry, as well as on barriers to entry. Moreover, even with these supplements, it is still a crude measure. (Among other things, it takes no account of competition from foreign suppliers.) Nonetheless, the concentration ratio has proved to be a valuable tool to economists.

**Table 12.1
Concentration Ratios in
Selected Manufacturing
Product Markets, 1982[a]**

INDUSTRY	MARKET SHARE OF 4 LARGEST FIRMS (PERCENT)
Automobiles	92
Photographic equipment	74
Tires	66
Aircraft	64
Blast furnaces and steel plants	42
Electronic computing equipment	43
Petroleum refining	28
Bread and cake	34
Pharmaceuticals	26
Radio and TV equipment	22
Newspapers	22
Commercial printing	6

[a]As of late 1991, these were the most recent data available.
Source: Statistical Abstract of the United States.

THE ANTITRUST LAWS

National policies are too ambiguous and rich in contradictions to be summarized neatly and concisely. Consequently, it would be misleading to say that the United States has adopted a policy of promoting competition and controlling monopoly. To a large extent, it certainly is true that "competition is our fundamental national policy," as the Supreme Court said in 1963. But it is also true that we have adopted many measures to promote monopoly and to limit competition, as we shall see in subsequent sections (and as has already been pointed out in Chapter 10). On balance, however, we probably have gone further in promoting competition than other major industrialized countries, and the principal pieces of legislation designed to further this objective are the ***antitrust laws.***

The Sherman Act

In 1890, the first antitrust law, the Sherman Act, was passed by Congress. Although the common law had long outlawed monopolistic practices, it appeared to many Americans in the closing years of the nineteenth century that legislation was required to discourage monopoly and to preserve and encourage competition. The formation of "trusts"—monopolistic combines that colluded to raise prices and restrict output—brought the matter to a head. The heart of the Sherman Act lies in the following two sections:

> Sec. 1. Every contract, combination in the form of trust or otherwise, or conspiracy, in restraint of trade or commerce among the several states or with foreign nations, is hereby declared to be illegal. Every person who shall make any such contract or engage in any such combination or conspiracy, shall be deemed guilty of a misdemeanor. . . .
> Sec. 2. Every person who shall monopolize, or attempt to monopolize or combine or conspire with any other person or persons, to monopolize any part of the trade or commerce among the several States, or with foreign nations shall be deemed guilty of a misdemeanor.

The Clayton Act

The first 20 years of experience with the Sherman Act were not very satisfying to its supporters. The ineffectiveness of the Sherman Act led in 1914 to passage by Congress of two additional laws—the Clayton Act and the Federal Trade Commission Act. The Clayton Act tried to be more specific than the Sherman Act in identifying certain practices that were illegal because they would "substantially lessen competition or tend to create a monopoly." In particular, the Clayton Act outlawed unjustified ***price discrimination,*** a practice whereby one buyer is charged more than another buyer for the same product. It also outlawed the use of a ***tying contract,*** which makes the buyers purchase other items to get the product they want. Further, it outlawed mergers that substantially lessen competition; but since it did not prohibit one firm's purchase of a competitor's plant and equipment, it really could not stop mergers. In 1950, this loophole was closed by the Celler-Kefauver Anti-Merger Act.

The Federal Trade Commission Act

The Federal Trade Commission Act was designed to prevent undesirable and unfair competitive practices. Specifically, it created a Federal Trade Commission to investigate unfair and predatory practices and to issue cease-and-desist orders. The act stated that "unfair methods of competition in commerce are hereby declared unlawful." However, the commission—composed of 5 commissioners, each appointed by the president for a term of 7 years—was given the unenviable task of defining exactly what was "unfair." Eventually, the courts took away much of the commission's power; but in 1938, the commission acquired the function of outlawing untrue and deceptive advertising. Also, the commission has authority to carry out economic investigations of the structure and conduct of American business.

THE ROLE OF THE COURTS

The antitrust laws, like any laws, are enforced in the courts. Typically, charges are brought against a firm or group of firms by the Antitrust Division of the Department of Justice, a trial is held, and a decision is reached by the judge. In key cases, appeals are made that eventually reach the Supreme Court. The real impact of the antitrust laws depends on how the courts interpret them. And the judicial interpretation of these laws has changed considerably over time.

The first major set of antitrust cases took place in 1911 when the Standard Oil Company and the American Tobacco Company were forced to give up a large share of their holdings of other companies. In these cases, the Supreme Court put forth and used the famous ***rule of reason***—that only unreasonable combinations in restraint of trade, not all trusts, required conviction under the Sherman Act. In 1920, the rule of reason was used by the Supreme Court in its finding that U.S. Steel had not violated the antitrust laws even though it had tried to monopolize the industry—since the Court said it had not succeeded. Moreover, U.S. Steel's large size and its potential monopoly power were ruled beside the point since "the law does not make mere size an offense. It . . . requires overt acts."

During the 1920s and 1930s the courts, including the conservative Supreme Court, interpreted the antitrust laws in such a way that they were as toothless as a new-born babe. Although Eastman Kodak and International Harvester controlled very substantial shares of their markets, the Court, using the rule of reason, found them innocent on the grounds that they had not built up their near-monopoly position through overt coercion or predatory practices. Moreover, the Court reiterated that mere size was not an offense, no matter how great the unexerted monopoly power might be.

In the late 1930s, this situation changed very greatly, with the prosecution of the Aluminum Company of America (Alcoa). This case, decided in 1945 (but begun in 1937), reversed the decisions in the *U.S. Steel* and *International Harvester* cases. Alcoa had achieved its 90 percent of the market by means that would have been considered "reasonable" in the earlier cases—keeping its price low enough to discourage entry, building capacity to take care of increases in the market, and so forth. (Recall our discussion of Alcoa in Chapter 10.) Nonetheless, the Court decided that Alcoa, because it controlled practically all the industry's output, violated

Alcoa headquarters

the antitrust laws. Thus, to a considerable extent, *the Court used market structure rather than market conduct as a test of legality*.

THE ROLE OF THE JUSTICE DEPARTMENT

The Justice Department, Washington, D.C.

The impact of the antitrust laws is determined by the vigor with which the Antitrust Division of the Justice Department prosecutes cases. If the Antitrust Division does not prosecute, the laws can have little effect. Like the judicial interpretation of the laws, the extent to which the Justice Department has prosecuted cases has varied from one period to another. Needless to say, the attitude of the political party in power has been an important determinant of how vigorously antitrust cases have been prosecuted. When the Sherman Act was first passed, it was of singularly little value. For example, President Grover Cleveland's attorney general did not agree with the law and would not prosecute under it. "Trust-busting" was truly a neglected art until President Theodore Roosevelt devoted his formidable energies to it. In 1903, he established the Antitrust Division of the Justice Department. Moreover, his administration started the major cases that led to the *Standard Oil, American Tobacco,* and *U.S. Steel* decisions.

Subsequently, there was a long lull in the prosecution of antitrust cases, reflecting the Supreme Court's rule-of-reason doctrine and a strong conservative tide in the nation. The lull continued for about 25 years, until 1937, when there was a significant upsurge in activity on the antitrust front. Led by Thurman Arnold, the Antitrust Division entered one of the most vigorous periods of antitrust enforcement to date. Arnold went after the glass, cigarette, cement, and other industries, the most important case being that against Alcoa. The Antitrust Division attempted in this period to reopen cases that were hopeless under the rule-of-reason doctrine. With the change in the composition of the Supreme Court, Arnold's activism turned out to be effective.

LANDMARK DECISIONS SINCE WORLD WAR II

The 1960s and 1970s generally were a period of vigorous antitrust activity, with at least five notable developments.

1. *One of the biggest cases in the history of antitrust occurred in 1961 when, as you will recall from the previous chapter, the major electrical equipment manufacturers were convicted of collusive price agreements.* Executives of General Electric, Westinghouse, and other firms in the industry admitted that they met secretly in hotels and communicated by mail in order to maintain prices, share the market, and eliminate competition. Some of the executives were sentenced to jail on criminal charges, and the firms had to pay large amounts to customers to make up for the overcharges. In particular, 1,800 triple damage suits against the firms resulted in payments estimated at between $400 and $600 million. Even the most zealous antitrusters will admit that this was no slap on the wrist!

2. *Following the enactment of the Celler-Kefauver Anti-Merger Act, horizontal mergers—mergers of firms making essentially the same good—became increasingly likely to run afoul of the antitrust laws.* In 1962, Chief Justice Earl Warren went so far as to say that a merger that resulted in a firm having 5 percent of the market might be undesirable. In the *Von's*

Grocery case in 1965, the Court disallowed a merger between two supermarkets that together had less than 8 percent of the Los Angeles market. (In this case, the Court emphasized the trend toward increasing concentration in grocery retailing in Los Angeles.) Also, vertical mergers—mergers of firms that supply or sell to one another—have been viewed with a jaundiced eye by the courts. For example, in the *Brown Shoe* case, the Supreme Court said that the merger of Brown with R. G. Kinney would mean that other shoe manufacturers would be frozen out of a substantial part of the retail shoe market.

3. *A leading problem confronting the Justice Department in the 1960s was conglomerate mergers—mergers of firms in unrelated industries.* Conglomerate firms like Litton Industries, International Telephone, and Ling-Temco-Vought were regarded very highly by investors during the 1960s. Inspired by their apparent success, other firms began to merge with firms in other industries in order to become conglomerates themselves. Supporters of these mergers claimed that they enabled weak companies to be revitalized by superior management, bigger research facilities, and so on. However, this merger movement was opposed by many other observers on the grounds that conglomerates were obtaining too much power in the economy. To some extent, this problem diminished in importance after the conglomerates began to show relatively disappointing earnings in the late 1960s. But the Justice Department continued to keep a watchful eye on conglomerate mergers. In 1967 it succeeded in preventing a conglomerate merger between Procter & Gamble, the big soap manufacturer, and Clorox, a maker of liquid bleach. And in 1971 it made some attempt to force ITT to divest itself of the Hartford Fire Insurance Company, but the case was dropped.

4. *In 1982, a government antitrust suit (begun in 1974) against the American Telephone and Telegraph Company (AT&T) was settled.* According to the settlement, AT&T divested itself of 22 companies that provide most of the nation's local telephone service, and kept its Long Lines division, Western Electric, and the Bell Laboratories. While many observers worried that one result was likely to be an increase in local telephone rates, there was also considerable feeling that, after the telephone industry was restructured in this way, AT&T would be a leaner and more dynamic firm. One immediate effect of this divestiture was a great deal of confusion among customers and costly adjustments within AT&T, but subsequently many observers believed that it was resulting in faster introduction of new technologies and services and lower long-distance phone rates.

5. *The Antitrust Division sued IBM Corporation under Section 2 of the Sherman Act in January 1969, thus starting one of the biggest and costliest antitrust cases in history.* The government charged that IBM held a monopoly and that the firm's 360 line of computers was introduced in 1965 in a way that eliminated competition. IBM's defense was that its market position stemmed from its innovative performance and economies of scale, that its pricing was competitive, and that its profit rate really had not been high. Once the trial began in 1975, it took the government almost three years to present its case. In early 1982, on the same day that it settled the antitrust case against AT&T, the Reagan administration dropped the IBM case. It said the case was "without merit and should be dismissed."

AT&T headquarters, Basking Ridge, NJ

THE GROWTH OF PRIVATE ANTITRUST SUITS

Recent decades have seen a great increase in the number of private antitrust suits. You may have thought that only governments can bring antitrust suits, but this is not true. Private parties can and do bring damage suits—and if they win, they get triple damages plus their reasonable costs. By the 1970s, the number of private antitrust cases (over 1,000 per year) far exceeded the number of government antitrust cases, and in some cases the judgments were very large. The growth of private antitrust suits has raised many questions. For one thing, firms have sometimes brought suit against their rivals, claiming that their rivals have violated the antitrust laws, when in fact this has not been true. Instead, their rivals have simply been more efficient and imaginative than these firms have been. Nonetheless, this legal ploy can be an effective way for an otherwise unsuccessful firm to try to strike back at its more successful rivals. Some people think that winners of antitrust suits should get less than triple damages; in this way, the incentive for such suits would decline.

THE WAVE OF CORPORATE TAKEOVERS DURING THE 1980S

To understand the nature of antitrust policy during the 1980s, you must know that there was a rash of merger activity in that decade. Among other examples, General Electric took over RCA, and Chevron took over Gulf Oil. In terms of the value of the acquired firms, the volume of acquisitions was unprecedented. Moreover, a distinguishing characteristic of this recent wave of mergers was the frequency with which the acquiring firm by-passed the target corporation's management and tried to purchase a controlling interest directly from the target's stockholders.

An intense debate has taken place concerning the social costs and benefits of this wave of takeovers. On the one hand, it is clear that mergers can have substantial economic benefits. For example, they can result in economies of scale, as well as the more appropriate valuation of particular resources. Even hostile takeovers can be good for the economy if a more efficient management replaces a less efficient one. But there is no assurance that a merger will necessarily be socially beneficial. Once taken over, some firms may operate less efficiently, not more so, than before.

F. M. Scherer and David Ravenscraft have used accounting data in an attempt to shed light on this question. They conclude that

> there is no evidence that the acquiring companies managed their acquired assets either clearly worse or clearly better than the average of the industries to which the acquiring lines belonged. This finding of "no significant change" is at odds with the hypothesis that takeovers increase efficiency and pre-tax profits. If the takeover premium was paid in the expectation of increased profitability, tenderers must have systematically overestimated their ability to manage the target firm's operations better than the prior incumbents.[4]

---

[4] F. M. Scherer, "Takeovers: Present and Future Dangers," *The Brookings Review*, Winter 1986, p. 18. Also, see W. Adams and J. Brock, "The New Learning and the Euthanasia of Antitrust," *California Law Review*, October 1986.

As would be expected, those who feel that the takeover wave has been beneficial have attacked these conclusions. Thus Douglas Ginsburg and John Robinson argue that accounting studies,

> particularly those that attempt to measure profitability, suffer from serious methodological problems that limit their relevance for policy purposes. For example, they do not take into account the real market values of acquired assets—only the accounting valuations, which may significantly understate their value. They generally encounter great difficulty in allocating beneficial externalities that the purchase may generate for the acquirer, such as a target's tax-loss carry-forward. Moreover, unlike the studies based on stock price data, accounting studies have not yielded consistent significant results. As a result, the interpretation and value of these studies is highly uncertain.[5]

ANTITRUST IN THE REAGAN AND BUSH YEARS

Antitrust policy changed in 1981 when President Reagan took office. His Antitrust Division believed that a fair number of activities that had been deemed antitrust violations in the past not only were legal, but also were beneficial to the economy. According to this view, business decisions should be free of antitrust interference unless they are unequivocally anticompetitive. Given the huge costs (about $1 billion to IBM, according to some estimates) of the IBM case, and the feeling among some economists that economies of scale were sometimes underestimated, it is not surprising that such a change in emphasis and direction occurred. But economists who favor an aggressive antitrust policy tended to regard this change with suspicion.

During the 1980s, antitrust officials felt that they should attack conspiracies to fix prices, but they were less concerned than their predecessors about many kinds of mergers.[6] (For example, little attention was paid to mergers between firms in different industries.) There was also more sympathy for the view that big firms often are more efficient than small ones, and that it is therefore a mistake to try to limit their growth. While some believe that antitrust enforcement was too lax, the Reagan administration argued that it was enforcing the laws in ways that advanced rather than hindered competition and consumer welfare.

In the Bush administration, there was more activity on the antitrust front. In 1990, the Justice Department filed suit against the American Institute of Architects charging that it unreasonably restrained price competition among architects. Also, it initiated an investigation into whether some leading colleges and universities had violated the antitrust laws. Further, the Federal Trade Commission complained that Capital Cities-ABC Inc. and the College Football Association had illegally conspired to limit the

---

[5] D. Ginsburg and J. Robinson, "The Case Against Federal Intervention in the Market for Corporate Control," *The Brookings Review,* Winter 1986, p. 13. Also, see A. Schleifer and R. Vishny, "The Takeover Wave of the 1980s," *Science,* August 17, 1990.

[6] In 1982, the Justice Department announced the following merger guidelines: (1) If the Herfindahl-Hirschman index (after the merger) is less than 1,000, the Justice Department is unlikely to challenge any merger. (2) If this index is between 1,000 and 1,800, a merger that changes the index by less than 100 points probably will not be challenged. (3) If this index is greater than 1,800, a merger that changes the index by less than 50 points will probably not be challenged. (The Herfindahl-Hirschmann index equals the sum of the squared market shares of the firms in the market. For example, if two firms exist in a market, and each firm has 50 percent of the market, this index equals $50^2 + 50^2 = 5,000$.)

number of football games shown on television. Many observers feel that the Bush administration focused more attention on the antitrust laws than did the Reagan administration.

TEST YOURSELF

1. "Perfect competition results in optimal efficiency and an optimal distribution of income. This is why the United States opts for a perfectly competitive economy." Comment and evaluate.

2. "The real impact of the antitrust laws depends on judicial interpretation." Comment and evaluate.

3. Suppose that an industry is composed of five firms. The market share of each firm is given in the table at right. What is the concentration ratio for this industry?

FIRM	MARKET SHARE (PERCENT)
A	10
B	10
C	20
D	25
E	35

4. Suppose that firm E loses half of its sales to firm C. If the sales of the other firms remain constant, what is the effect on the concentration ratio in Question 3?

STANDARDS FOR ANTITRUST POLICY

There are at least two fairly distinct approaches to antitrust policy. *The first looks primarily and directly at **market performance**—the industry's rate of technological change, efficiency, and profits, the conduct of individual firms, and so on.* Advocates of this approach argue that, in deciding antitrust cases, one should review in detail the performance of the firms in question to see how well they have served the economy. If they have served well they should not be held in violation of the antitrust laws simply because they have a large share of the market. This test, as it is usually advocated, relies heavily on an evaluation of the technological "progressiveness" and "dynamism" of the firms in question. Although this approach seems quite sensible, it has a number of disadvantages. In particular, it is very difficult to tell at present whether a particular industry's performance is "good" or "bad." Economists simply do not have the sorts of measuring rods that would be required to obtain reasonably accurate and well-accepted readings on an industry's performance. In view of the vagueness of the criteria and the practical realities of the antitrust environment, adopting this approach would probably invite nonenforcement of the laws.

*The second approach emphasizes the importance of an industry's **market structure**—the number and size distribution of buyers and sellers in the market, the ease with which new firms can enter, and the extent of product differentiation.* According to this approach, one should look to market structure for evidence of undesirable monopolistic characteristics. The basic idea behind this approach, as the late George Stigler put it, is that "an industry which does not have a competitive structure will not have competitive behavior." This approach, too, has lots of critics. Many economists and lawyers feel that the relationship between market structure and market performance is so weak that it is a mistake to choose, more or less arbitrarily, some level of concentration and to say that, if concentration exceeds this level, market performance is likely to be undesirable.

THE EFFECTIVENESS OF ANTITRUST POLICY

How effective have the antitrust laws been? Obviously it is difficult to tell with any accuracy, since there is no way to carry out an experiment in which American history is rewritten to show what would have happened if the antitrust laws had not been on the books. Many experts seem to feel that the antitrust laws have not been as effective as they might—or should—have been, largely because they do not have sufficient public support and there is no politically powerful pressure group pushing for their enforcement.

But this does not mean that the antitrust laws have had no effect. As Edward Mason of Harvard University pointed out, their effectiveness is due "not so much to the contribution that particular judgments have made to the restoring of competition as it is to the fact that the consideration of whether or not a particular course of action may or may not be in violation of the antitrust acts is a persistent factor affecting business judgment, at least in large firms."[7] This same idea is summed up in the old saying that the ghost of Senator Sherman sits as an *ex officio* member of every firm's board of directors.

Some indication of the effects of our antitrust laws can perhaps be obtained by looking at experience in other countries, since Britain, Germany, and many other European countries (as well as Japan) took a very tolerant view of monopoly power for a long time. After World War II, there was pressure to break up some of the powerful combines in Germany and Japan, but this pressure has been somewhat relaxed more recently—although antitrust practices seem to be gaining ground in the European Common Market. Foreign experience seems to indicate that the antitrust laws have helped prevent American firms from adopting many restrictive and predatory practices common elsewhere.

THE PABST CASE: ANTITRUST IN ACTION

Perhaps the most effective way to learn certain things about the antitrust field is to try to decide an actual antitrust case. Suppose that, over the protests of the American Bar Association, you are appointed a district court judge and that your first job is to hear a case (actually brought by the government some years ago) to prevent Pabst Brewing Company from acquiring the Blatz Brewing Company. According to the government, the effect of this merger "may be substantially to lessen competition, or to tend to create a monopoly" in the production and sale of beer in the state of Wisconsin, the three-state area of Wisconsin, Illinois, and Michigan, and the United States.

A fundamental issue in any case of this sort is the definition of market and industry boundaries. Market boundaries must be broad enough to include all relevant competitors but not so broad as to include products that

PABST QUALITY.
IT'S A TRADITION THAT KEEPS
GROWING.

[7] Edward Mason, Preface to Carl Kaysen and Donald Turner, *Antitrust Policy* (and reprinted in E. Mansfield, *Monopoly Power and Economic Performance,* 4th ed. New York: Norton, 1978).

are not reasonable substitutes. The delineation of market and industry boundaries—in terms of "line of commerce" and "section of the country"—is bound to involve judgment, there being no simple, mechanical rule to settle it.

In the *Pabst* case, both the government and Pabst agreed "that the line of commerce involved the production, sale, and distribution of beer and that the continental United States is a relevant geographic market." However, there was disagreement over the government's use of Wisconsin and the three-state area of Wisconsin, Illinois, and Michigan as separate geographical markets. Pabst and Blatz claimed that there was no good reason to single out these particular areas as distinct markets. The government, on the other hand, claimed that they were distinct markets because the two firms competed most intensively in these areas. Pabst was the nation's eleventh largest seller of beer; its sales were 2.67 percent of the national market and about 11 percent of the sales in Wisconsin. Blatz was the nation's thirteenth largest seller of beer, its sales being 2.04 percent of the national market and about 13 percent of the sales in Wisconsin. Thus, *if you look at the smaller geographical area (Wisconsin and the three-state area), the two firms account for a substantial proportion of the market—about 24 percent in Wisconsin. But if you look at the national market as a whole, they account for a small proportion—less than 5 percent.*

As the district judge how should you decide the case? Should you agree with the government that Wisconsin and the three-state area are relevant markets? Or should you agree with Pabst and Blatz that they are not relevant markets in themselves, but just parts of a market? Moreover, if you agree with the government concerning the market definition, should you also agree that two firms with a total of 24 percent of Wisconsin sales should not be allowed to merge? Or if you agree with Pabst and Blatz concerning the market definition, should you allow a merger between two firms that together account for about 5 percent of the national market? It is a tough problem, isn't it? To demonstrate just how tough it is, the district judge decided one way, while the Supreme Court decided the other way. The district court, agreeing with Pabst and Blatz that Wisconsin and the three-state area should not be treated as distinct relevant areas, dismissed the government's complaint. But the district court's decision was reversed by the Supreme Court, which agreed with the government's position that the smaller areas should be treated as relevant, distinct markets.

The antitrust field is characterized by many complexities and uncertainties, as well as by legal and economic vagueness and ambiguity. This case illustrates how difficult it is even to decide what the relevant market is!

THE PATENT SYSTEM

In a previous section, we pointed out that our national economic policies are by no means free of contradiction. In particular, although many of our policies are designed to promote competition and limit monopoly, one should not assume that all of them are meant to promote these objectives. On the contrary, quixotic as it may seem, some are designed to do just the opposite—to restrict competition. Among the most important of these policies are our laws concerning patents, which grant inventors exclusive control over the use of their inventions for 17 years. That is, inventors are given a temporary monopoly over the use of their inventions.

The Pros

Since Congress passed the original patent act in 1790, the arguments used to justify the existence of the patent laws have not changed very much. First, *these laws are regarded as an important incentive to induce the inventor to put in the work required to produce an invention.* Particularly in the case of the individual inventor, it is claimed that patent protection is a strong incentive. Second, *patents are regarded as a necessary incentive to induce firms to carry out the further work and make the necessary investment in pilot plants and other items that are required to bring the invention to commercial use.* If an invention became public property when made, why should a firm incur the costs and risks involved in attempting to develop, debug, and perfect it? Another firm could watch, take no risks, and duplicate the process or product if it were successful. Third, it is argued that because of the patent laws, *inventions are disclosed earlier than otherwise, the consequence being that other inventions are facilitated by the earlier dissemination of the information.* The resulting situation is often contrasted with the intense secrecy about processes that characterized the medieval guilds and which undoubtedly retarded technological progress and economic growth.

The Cons

Not all economists agree that the patent system is beneficial. A patent represents a monopoly right, although, as many inventors can testify, it may be a very weak one. Critics of the patent system stress the social costs arising from the monopoly. After a new process or product has been discovered, it may cost very little for other persons who could make use of this knowledge to acquire it. The patent gives the inventor the right to charge a price for the use of the information, with the result that the knowledge is used less widely than is socially optimal. Critics also point out that patents have been used to create monopoly positions, which were sustained by other means after the original patents had expired. They cite as examples the aluminum, shoe machinery, and plate-glass industries. In addition, the cross-licensing of patents often has been used by firms as a vehicle for joint monopolistic exploitation of their market.

Critics also question the extent of the social gains arising from the system. They point out that the patent system was designed for the individual inventor, but that over the years most research and development has been institutionalized. They assert that patents are not really important as incentives to the large corporation, since it cannot afford to fall behind in the technological race, whether or not it receives a patent. Also, they say that because of long lead times, most of the innovative profits from many innovations can be captured before imitators have a chance to enter the market, whether or not the innovator is granted a patent. Finally, they claim that firms keep secret what inventions they can, and patent those they cannot.

These questions concerning the effects and desirability of the patent system have proven extremely difficult to settle. But most observers seem to agree that, despite its faults, it is hard to find a realistic substitute for the patent system.

OTHER POLICIES DESIGNED TO RESTRICT COMPETITION

The reasons why laws are enacted to restrict, rather than promote, competition are not difficult to understand. People want competition for the other guy, but not for themselves. Moreover, certain sectors of the economy seem to need help, and have the political muscle to get it—partly in the form of laws designed to take some of the competitive heat off them.

Robinson-Patman Act

A case of this sort is retail trade, where the small independent retailers felt threatened by the advent of the chain store. The chain stores were able to reduce the costs of distribution below those of the smaller retailers, with the result that the total number of grocery stores and drugstores fell considerably in the 1920s and 1930s. The small retailers charged that their smaller numbers were due to the predatory tactics of the chain stores. They took their charges to Congress and succeeded in getting the Robinson-Patman Act enacted in 1936.

The Robinson-Patman Act says that sellers must not discriminate in price among purchasers of similar grade and quality where the effect might be to drive competitors out of business. The act was aimed at preventing price discrimination in favor of chain stores that buy goods in large quantities. Most economists do not regard the Robinson-Patman Act with enthusiasm because it attempts to keep competitors in existence even if they are inefficient. (The social virtues of the competitive system do not lie in maintaining a lot of inefficient small businessmen in operation.) Moreover, most observers seem to believe that the act has had the effect of reducing the vigor of price competition in retail trade.

Miller-Tydings Act

Another law designed to limit competition in U.S. retail trade was the Miller-Tydings Act of 1937, which exempted from the antitrust laws the use of resale price maintenance agreements in states permitting such agreements. **Resale price maintenance agreements** permitted manufacturers of a trademarked or branded item to establish the retail price of the item by contracts with retailers. Moreover, the Miller-Tydings Act permitted the manufacturer to bind *all* retailers in a state to a contract simply by signing such a contract with *any one* of the retailers in the state. The result was to reduce the amount of price competition in retail trade. In 1975, Congress passed a bill nullifying such agreements.

Other Policies Limiting Competition

Finally, you should recognize that policies designed to limit competition are found in many other areas besides retail trade. Our national farm policies have been aimed at keeping the prices of agricultural products at a level exceeding what they would be under competition. In Chapter 13, we shall see that the government has promoted the growth of strong labor unions, which try to raise wages above competitive levels. In the field of international trade, the Webb-Pomerene Act of 1918 allowed American exporters to get together to form export trade associations,

EXAMPLE 12.1   RESALE PRICE MAINTENANCE AND COSMETICS

Until 1975, resale price maintenance agreements allowed manufacturers of a trademarked item to establish a floor under the retail price of the item. Suppose that the manufacturer of a cosmetic established OP as its minimum retail price, and that D_0 is the demand curve for this cosmetic at a particular drugstore. The drugstore's average costs are also shown in the diagram.

(a) Only the solid portion of demand curve D_0 is relevant to the drugstore. Why? (b) Can the drugstore make a profit on the sale of the cosmetic? (c) Will there be a change in the number of drugstores selling the cosmetic? What sort of a change? Why? (d) As changes occur in the number of drugstores selling the cosmetic, the demand curve eventually moves to D_1. Why? At this point, can a drugstore make a profit on the sale of the cosmetic?

Solution

(a) Because the drugstore cannot sell the cosmetic at a price less than OP without running afoul of the resale price maintenance agreements. (b) Yes. If it sells between OQ_0 and OQ_1 ounces of the cosmetic, the price it receives will exceed its average cost. (c) Yes. Because profits are made on this cosmetic, other stores will begin to sell it, the result being that the number of stores selling it will increase. (d) Because more and more stores sell the cosmetic, the total volume is spread more thinly among the stores. In other words, the demand curve facing a particular drugstore shifts to the left. When the demand curve reaches D_1, a drugstore can no longer make a profit from the sale of the cosmetic. Thus entry ceases.[*]

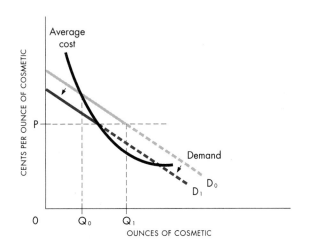

* For further discussion, see L. Weiss, Case Studies in American Industry, New York: Wiley, 1980.

---

which, according to some observers, may have tended to reduce competition. Even in the bituminous coal industry, which we looked at in some detail in Chapter 9, Congress passed the Bituminous Coal Act of 1937 to establish minimum prices and reduce "cutthroat" competition, though in 1943 the act was not renewed.

Thus it is erroneous to think that the United States has opted decisively for competition. On the contrary, although the antitrust laws are clearly designed to promote competition and limit monopoly, a number of other laws are designed to do just the opposite. In many of the industries where laws designed to restrict competition have been enacted—for example, agriculture, retail trade, and bituminous coal—the basic problem has been that too many people and too much capital were tied up in the industry. Economists generally believe that it would be wiser to encourage people and capital to leave these industries than to attempt to limit competition. (More will be said on this score in Chapter 16, where we discuss American farm policies.)

TEST YOURSELF

1. "The antitrust laws effectively protect the large business from social pressure or regulation by maintaining the myth that the market does the regulating instead." Do you agree? Why, or why not?

2. General Motors and Toyota are two of the world's largest auto manufacturers. Several years ago, they proposed a joint venture to assemble a small car in California. The Federal Trade Commission approved this joint venture. Why wasn't this venture in violation of the antitrust laws?

3. Chief Justice Hughes observed, "Good intentions will not save a plan otherwise objectionable, but knowledge of actual intent is an aid in the interpretation of facts and prediction of consequence." Relate this to the construction of standards for antitrust policy.

4. What are the arguments in favor of the patent system? What are the arguments against it? Is there currently considerable political support for the abolition of the patent system?

SUMMARY

1. A monopolistic industry produces too little of the monopolized good. Society is less well off than it could be. Oligopoly can be as bad as monopoly if oligopolists engage in collusion; and even if they don't collude, inefficiencies are likely to result. Monopolistic competition can also be a socially wasteful form of market organization.

2. In defense of monopoly power, some economists have asserted that the rate of technological change is likely to be greater in an imperfectly competitive industry than under perfect competition. It does seem unlikely that a perfectly competitive industry would be able—and have the incentive—to carry out the research and development required to promote a rapid rate of technological change in many sectors of the economy.

3. On the other hand, there is little evidence that giant firms are needed to ensure rapid technological change in a great many sectors of the economy. The technological contributions of smaller firms are much greater than is commonly recognized.

4. Economic power in the United States is distributed very unevenly; 100 corporations control about half the total manufacturing assets of the economy. Moreover, many individual industries are dominated by a few firms. This concentration of power is viewed with concern by some economists and lawyers.

5. In 1890, the Sherman Act was passed. It outlawed any contract, combination, or conspiracy in restraint of trade and made it illegal to monopolize or attempt to monopolize. In 1914, Congress passed the Clayton Act, and the Federal Trade Commission was created. A more recent antitrust development was the Celler-Kefauver Anti-Merger Act of 1950.

6. The real impact of the antitrust laws depends on the interpretation placed on these laws by the courts. In its early cases, the Supreme Court put forth and used the famous rule of reason—that only unreasonable combinations in restraint of trade, not all trusts, required conviction under the Sherman Act. The situation changed greatly in the 1940s when the Court decided that Alcoa, because it controlled practically all of the nation's aluminum output, was in violation of the antitrust laws.

7. In the Reagan administration, antitrust officials felt that they should attack conspiracies to fix prices, but they were much less concerned than their predecessors about many kinds of mergers, which took place in very large numbers during the 1980s. According to many observers, the Bush administration focused more attention on the antitrust laws than did the Reagan administration.

8. Many observers seem to feel that the antitrust laws have not been as effective as they might—or should—have been, largely because they do not have sufficient public support. At the same time, many feel that the evidence, although incomplete and unclear, suggests that the antitrust laws have had a nonnegligible effect on business behavior and markets.

9. Not all our laws are designed to promote competition and restrict monopoly. On the contrary, some laws are designed to do just the opposite. The patent system confers a temporary monopoly on inventors. And the Robinson-Patman Act and many other laws have been designed to restrict competition. The truth is that, despite some protests to the contrary, our nation is by no means fully committed to promoting competition and preventing monopoly.

CONCEPTS FOR REVIEW

Market concentration
  ratio
Antitrust laws
Price discrimination

Tying contract
Rule of reason
Market performance
Market structure

Patent system
Resale price
  maintenance agreements

PART FOUR

DISTRIBUTION OF INCOME

DETERMINANTS OF WAGES

EVERYONE HAS A HEALTHY—indeed, sometimes an unhealthy—interest in income. Organizations as holy as the church and as unholy as the Mob exhibit an interest in this subject. Surely we all need to look carefully at the social mechanisms underlying the distribution of income in our society. Most income is in the form of wages and salaries; that is, it is labor income. What determines the price paid for a particular kind of labor? Why is the wage rate for surgeons frequently in the neighborhood of $100 an hour, while the wage rate for relatively unskilled labor is frequently in the neighborhood of $5 or $6 an hour? Or why is the wage rate of a secretary higher in 1992 than in 1960?

Economists frequently classify inputs into three categories—labor, capital, and land. The disadvantage of this simple classification is that each category contains an enormous variety of inputs. Consider the services of labor, which include the work of a football star like Joe Montana, a salesman like Willy Loman, and a knight like Don Quixote. But it does have the important advantage of distinguishing between different classes of inputs. In this chapter, we are concerned with the determinants of the price of labor. The next chapter will deal with the determinants of the prices of capital and land, as well as profits.

THE LABOR FORCE AND THE PRICE OF LABOR

At the outset it is important to note that, to the economist, labor includes a great deal more than the organized labor that belongs to trade unions. The secretary who works at IBM, the young account executive at Merrill Lynch, the auto mechanic at your local garage, the professor who teaches molecular biology, all put forth labor. About two-thirds of the people employed are white-collar workers (such as salespeople, doctors, secretaries, or managers) and service workers (such as waiters, bartenders, or cooks), while only about one-third are blue-collar workers (such as carpenters, mine workers, or machinists) and farm workers. Moreover, as shown in Table 13.1, many more people work in the service industry and in retail trade than in manufacturing.

Table 13.1
Employment on Nonagricultural Payrolls,
by Major Industry, 1990

INDUSTRY	EMPLOYMENT (MILLIONS)
Mining	1
Construction	5
Manufacturing	19
Transportation and public utilities	6
Wholesale trade	6
Retail trade	20
Finance, insurance, and real estate	7
Services	28
Federal government	3
State and local government	15
Total	110

Source: Economic Report of the President, 1991.

It is also worthwhile to preface our discussion with some data concerning how much people actually get paid. As shown in Table 13.2, average weekly earnings vary considerably from one industry to another. For example, in 1990, workers in manufacturing averaged about $442 a week, while construction workers averaged $524 a week, and workers in retail trade averaged $195 a week. Also, average weekly earnings vary considerably from one period to another. Table 13.2 shows that average weekly earnings in manufacturing in 1965 were only $108, as contrasted with $442 in 1990. In subsequent sections, we shall investigate the reasons for these differences in wages, both among industries and among periods of time.

More broadly, we shall be concerned in subsequent sections with the price of labor, which includes a great many forms of remuneration other than what are commonly regarded as wages. As noted above, economists include as labor the services performed by professional people (such as lawyers, doctors, and professors) and self-employed people (such as electricians, mechanics, and barbers). Thus the amount such people receive per unit of time is included here as a particular sort of price of labor, even though these amounts are often called fees or salaries rather than wages.

Finally, it is important to distinguish between *money* wages and *real* wages. Whereas the money wage is the amount of money received per unit of time, the real wage is the amount of real goods and services that can be bought with the money wage. The real wage depends on the price level for goods and services as well as on the magnitude of the money wage. Particularly during the late 1970s and early 1980s, the inflation we experienced meant that real wages increased less than money wages; thus the increases in earnings in Table 13.2 exaggerate the increase in real wages. In subsequent sections, since we shall assume that product prices are held constant, our discussion will be in terms of real wages.

Table 13.2
Average Weekly Earnings,
Selected Industries,
1955–90 (Dollars)

YEAR	MANUFAC- TURING	CONSTRUC- TION	RETAIL TRADE
1955	76	91	49
1960	90	113	58
1965	108	138	67
1970	134	195	82
1975	190	265	108
1980	289	368	147
1985	386	464	175
1990	442	524	195

THE EQUILIBRIUM WAGE AND EMPLOYMENT UNDER PERFECT COMPETITION

The Firm's Demand Curve for Labor

Let's begin by discussing the determinants of the price of labor under perfect competition. That is, we assume that firms take the prices of their products, as well as the prices of all inputs, as given; and we assume that owners of inputs take input prices as given. Under these circumstances, what determines how much labor an individual firm will hire (at a specified wage rate)? Once we answer this question, we can derive a firm's demand curve for labor. A *firm's demand curve for labor* is the relationship between the price of labor and the amount of labor utilized by the firm. That is, it shows, for each price, the amount of labor that the firm will use.

The Profit-Maximizing Quantity of Labor

Let us assume that we know the firm's production function, and that labor is the only variable input. Given the production function, we can determine the marginal product of labor when various quantities are used. The results of such a calculation are as shown in Table 13.3. If the price of the firm's product is $10, let's determine the value to the firm of each additional worker it hires per day.[1] According to Table 13.3, the firm achieves a daily output of 7 units when it hires the first worker; and since each unit is worth $10, this brings the firm's daily revenues up to $70. By hiring the second worker, the firm increases its daily output by 6 units; and since each unit is worth $10, the resulting increase in the firm's daily revenues is $60. Similarly, the increase in the firm's daily revenues from hiring the third worker is $50, the increase from hiring the fourth worker is $40, and so on.

A firm should hire more workers as long as the extra workers result in at least as great an addition to revenues as they do to costs. While this is a relatively simple idea, when stated this baldly, it nonetheless is very important. Consider the firm in Table 13.3. If the price of a worker is $50 per day, it is profitable for this firm to hire the first worker since this adds $70 to the firm's daily revenues but only $50 to its daily costs. Also, it is profitable to hire the second worker, since this adds $60 to the firm's daily revenues but only $50 to its daily costs. The addition of the third worker does not reduce the firm's profits. But beyond 3 workers per day, it does not pay the firm to hire more labor. (The addition of a fourth worker adds $50 to the firm's daily costs but only $40 to its daily revenues.)

The Value of the Marginal Product of Labor

Thus the optimal number of workers per day for this firm is 3. Table 13.3 shows that this is the number of workers at which the value of the marginal product of labor is equal to the price of labor. What is the *value of the marginal product of labor?* It is the marginal product of labor multiplied by the product's price. In Table 13.3, the value of the marginal

**Table 13.3
The Firm's Demand for Labor under Perfect Competition**

NUMBER OF WORKERS PER DAY	TOTAL OUTPUT PER DAY	MARGINAL PRODUCT OF LABOR	VALUE OF MARGINAL PRODUCT (DOLLARS)
0	0		
1	7	7	70
2	13	6	60
3	18	5	50
4	22	4	40
5	25	3	30

---

[1] For simplicity, we assume that the number of workers that the firm hires per day must be an integer, not a fraction. This assumption is innocuous, and can easily be relaxed.

product of labor is $70 when between 0 and 1 workers are used per day. Why? Because the marginal product of labor is 7 units of output, and the price of a unit of output is $10. Thus this product—7 times $10—equals $70.

To maximize profit, the value of the marginal product of labor must be set equal to the price of labor, because if the value of the marginal product is greater than labor's price, the firm can increase its profit by increasing the quantity used of labor; while if the value of the marginal product is less than labor's price, the firm can increase its profit by reducing the quantity used of labor. Thus *profits must be at a maximum when the value of the marginal product is equal to the price of labor.*

Given the results of this section, it is a simple matter to derive the firm's demand curve for labor. Specifically, its demand curve must be the value-of-marginal-product schedule in the last column of Table 13.3. If the daily wage of a worker is between $51 and $60, the firm will demand 2 workers per day; if the daily wage of a worker is between $41 and $50, the firm will demand 3 workers per day; and so forth. Thus *the firm's demand curve for labor is its value-of-marginal-product curve,* which shows the value of labor's marginal product at each quantity of labor used. This curve is shown in Figure 13.1.[2]

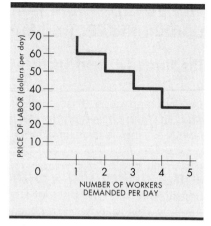

Figure 13.1
The Firm's Demand Curve for Labor under Perfect Competition
The firm's demand curve for labor is the firm's value-of-marginal-product curve, which shows the value of labor's marginal product at each quantity of labor used. The data for this figure come from Table 13.3.

THE MARKET DEMAND CURVE FOR LABOR

In previous sections, we were concerned with the demand curve of a single firm for labor. But many firms, not just one, are part of the labor market, and the price of labor depends on the demands of all of these firms. The situation is analogous to the price of a product, which depends on the demands of all consumers. *The **market demand curve for labor** shows the relationship between the price of labor and the total amount of labor demanded in the market. That is, it shows, for each price, the amount of labor that will be demanded in the entire market.* The market demand curve for labor, like any other input, is quite analogous to the market demand curve for a consumer good, which we discussed in detail in Chapter 4.

But there is at least one important difference. *The demand for labor and other inputs is a **derived demand**, since inputs are demanded to produce other things, not as an end in themselves.* This fact helps to explain why the price elasticity of demand is higher for some inputs than for others. In particular, the larger the price elasticity of demand for the product the input helps produce, the larger the price elasticity of demand for the input. (In addition, the price elasticity of demand for an input is likely to be greater in the long run than in the short run, and greater if other inputs can readily be substituted for the input in question.)

THE MARKET SUPPLY CURVE FOR LABOR

We have already seen that a product's price depends on its market supply curve as well as its market demand curve. This is equally true for labor.

---

[2] Strictly speaking, the firm's demand curve is the same as the curve showing the value of the input's marginal product only if this input is the only variable input. For a discussion of the more general case, see my *Microeconomics: Theory and Applications,* 7th ed., New York: Norton, 1991, Chapter 12.

EXAMPLE 13.1 THE VALUE OF WATER'S MARGINAL PRODUCT: THE IMPORTANT CASE OF CALIFORNIA

In this chapter, we have stressed that, to maximize profit, competitive firms should hire labor up to the point where the value of labor's marginal product is equal to the price of labor. This rule for profit maximization applies to any input, not just to labor. In other words, to maximize profit, competitive firms should hire any input up to the point where the value of the input's marginal product is equal to the input's price.

Water is an important input in California's agricultural industries, particularly during the drought that afflicted the state during 1990 and 1991. The value of the marginal product of an extra acre-foot of water in the production of various California crops has been estimated to be as follows:

Lemons	$62.00	Grain hay	$31.37
Cotton	55.98	Celery	20.77
Onions	51.50	Asparagus	17.40
Oranges	46.86	Peaches	10.59
Tomatoes	32.75	Lima beans	8.83

(a) If an extra acre-foot of water were used to produce lemons, what would be the value of the extra lemons produced? (b) If an extra acre-foot of water were used to produce lima beans, what would be the value of the extra lima beans produced? (c) If a firm produces both lemons and lima beans, would the firm increase its profits if it could transfer (at no cost) an acre-foot of water from its lima bean production to its lemon production? Why or why not? (d) If California's agricultural producers are maximizing profit, is the price of water the same for lemon producers as for lima bean producers? Why or why not?

Solution

(a) $62.00. (b) $8.83. (c) Yes. The extra acre-foot of water would result in an extra $62.00 worth of lemons. By reducing the amount of water devoted to lima beans by one acre-foot, the value of the lima bean production would fall by $8.83. Thus the net effect would be an increase in profit of $62.00 – $8.83 = $53.17. (Note that this assumes that the firm can *costlessly* divert an acre-foot of water from lima bean production to lemon production. This may not be true.

For example, the firm's lemons may be grown in an area far removed from its lima beans.) (d) No. As pointed out above, if firms are maximizing profit (and if they are perfectly competitive), they are purchasing water up to the point where the value of water's marginal product is equal to the price of water. Thus, since the value of water's marginal product differs between lemons and lima beans, one would expect that the price of water to lemon producers is different from the price of water to lima bean producers.[*]

---

[*] For further discussion, see J. Gomez-Ibanez and J. Kalt, eds., *Cases in Microeconomics*, Englewood Cliffs, N.J.: Prentice Hall, 1990. Of course, this brief discussion is highly simplified and abstracts from many institutional and other aspects of California water pricing.

Its **market supply curve** is *the relationship between the price of labor and the total amount of labor supplied in the market.* When individuals supply labor, they are supplying something they themselves can use, since the time that they do not work can be used for leisure activities. (As Charles Lamb, the English essayist, put it, "Who first invented work, and bound the free and holiday-rejoicing spirit down . . . to that dry drudgery at the desk's dead wood?"[3]) Because of this fact, the market supply curve for labor, unlike the supply curve for inputs supplied by business firms, may be **backward bending,** particularly for the economy as a whole. That is, *beyond some point, increases in price may result in smaller amounts of labor being supplied.*

An example of a backward-bending supply curve is provided in Figure 13.2. What factors account for a curve like this? Basically, the reason is that as the price of labor is increased, individuals supplying the labor become richer. And when they become richer, they want to increase their amount of leisure time, which means that they want to work less. Even though the amount of money per hour they give up by not working is greater than when the price of labor was lower, they nonetheless choose to increase their leisure time. This sort of tendency has shown up quite clearly in the last century. As wage rates have increased and living standards have risen, the average work week has tended to decline.

Note that there is no contradiction between the assumption that the supply curve of labor or other inputs *to an individual firm* is horizontal under perfect competition and the fact that the *market* supply curve for the input may not be horizontal. For example, unskilled labor may be available to any firm in a particular area at a given wage rate in as great an amount as it could possibly use. But the total amount of unskilled labor supplied in this area may increase relatively little with increases in the wage rate. The situation is similar to the sale of products. As we saw in Chapter 4, any firm under perfect competition believes that it can sell all it wants at the existing price. Yet the total amount of the product sold in the entire market can ordinarily be increased only by lowering the price.

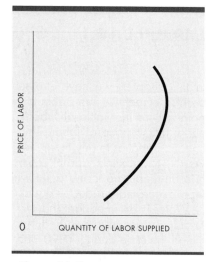

Figure 13.2
Backward-Bending Supply Curve for Labor
Beyond some point, increases in the price of labor may result in smaller amounts of labor being supplied. The reason for a supply curve of this sort is that, as the price of labor increases, the individuals supplying the labor become richer and want to increase their amount of leisure time.

EQUILIBRIUM PRICE AND QUANTITY OF LABOR

Labor's price (or wage rate) is determined under perfect competition in essentially the same way that a product's price is determined—by supply and demand.

The price of labor will tend toward equilibrium at the level where the quantity of labor demanded equals the quantity of labor supplied. Thus, in Figure 13.3, the equilibrium price of labor is *OP.* If the price were higher than *OP,* the quantity supplied would exceed the quantity demanded and there would be downward pressure on the price. If the price were lower than *OP,* the quantity supplied would fall short of the quantity demanded and there would be upward pressure on the price. By the same token, *the equilibrium amount of labor utilized is also given by the intersection of the market supply and demand curves.* In Figure 13.3, *OQ* units of labor will be utilized in equilibrium in the entire market.

---

[3] The answer to Lamb's question is perhaps to be found in Genesis 3:19.

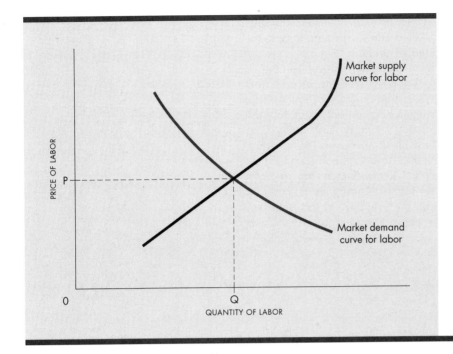

Figure 13.3
Equilibrium Price and Quantity of Labor
The equilibrium price of labor is OP, and the equilibrium quantity of labor used is OQ.

Graphs such as Figure 13.3 are useful, but it is important to look behind the geometry, and to recognize the factors that lie behind the demand and supply curves for labor. Consider the market for surgeons and that for unskilled labor. As shown in Figure 13.4, the demand curve for the services of surgeons is to the right of the demand curve for unskilled labor (particularly at high wage rates). Why is this so? Because an hour of a surgeon's services is worth more to people than an hour of an unskilled laborer's services. In this sense, surgeons are more productive than unskilled laborers. Also, as shown in Figure 13.4, the supply curve for the services of surgeons is far to the left of the supply curve for unskilled

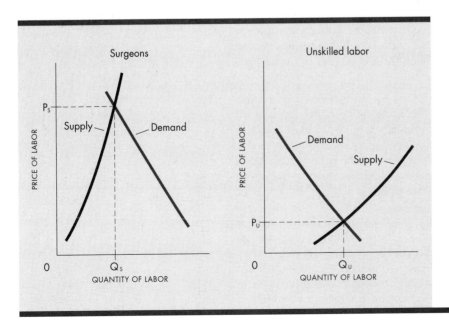

Figure 13.4
The Labor Market for Surgeons and Unskilled Labor
The wage for surgeons is higher than for unskilled labor because the demand curve for surgeons is farther to the right and the supply curve for surgeons is farther to the left than the corresponding curves for unskilled labor.

labor. Why is this so? Because very few people are licensed surgeons, whereas practically everyone can do unskilled labor. In other words, surgeons are much more scarce than unskilled laborers.

For these reasons, surgeons receive a much higher wage rate than do unskilled laborers. As shown in Figure 13.4, the equilibrium price of labor for surgeons is much higher than for unskilled labor. If unskilled laborers could quickly and easily turn themselves into competent surgeons, this difference in wage rates would be eliminated by competition, since unskilled workers would find it profitable to become surgeons. But unskilled workers lack the training and often the ability to become surgeons. Thus surgeons and unskilled labor are examples of **noncompeting groups.** Wage differentials can be expected to persist among noncompeting groups because people cannot move from the low-paid to the high-paid jobs. But this is not the only reason for wage differentials, as we shall see in the next section.

WAGE DIFFERENTIALS

Everyone realizes that, even in the same occupation, some people get paid more than others. Why is this true?

DIFFERENCES IN ABILITY OR SKILL. One reason for such wage differentials is that people differ in productive capacity; thus each worker differs from the next in the value of his or her output. Under these circumstances, the difference in wages paid to workers equals the difference in their marginal products' value. Consider the case of two lathe operators—Roberta and Leo. Roberta works for firm X and Leo works for firm Y. Roberta (together with the appropriate tools and materials) can produce output worth $2,000 per month and Leo (with the same tools and materials) can produce output worth $1,900 per month. In equilibrium, Roberta will earn $100 more per month than Leo. If the difference in wages were less than $100, Leo's employer would find it profitable to replace Leo with Roberta, since this would increase the value of output by $100 and cost less than $100. If the difference were more than $100, Roberta's employer would find it profitable to replace Roberta with Leo; although this would reduce the value of output by $100, it would reduce costs by more than $100.

DIFFERENCES IN TRAINING. Besides differences in productive capacity and ability, there are many more reasons for wage differentials. Even if all workers were of equal ability, these differentials would still exist to offset differences in the characteristics of various occupations and areas. Some occupations require large investments in training, while other occupations require a much smaller investment in training. Chemists must spend about eight years in undergraduate and graduate training. During each year of training, they incur direct expenses for books, tuition, and the like, and they lose the income they could make if they were to work rather than go to school. Clearly, if their net remuneration is to be as high in chemistry as in other jobs they might take, they must make a greater wage when they get through than persons of comparable age, intelligence, and motivation whose job requires no training beyond high school. The difference in wages must be at least sufficient to compensate for their investment in extra training.

OTHER DIFFERENCES. Similarly, members of some occupations must bear larger occupational expenses than others. A psychologist may have to buy testing materials and subscribe to expensive journals. For net compensation to be equalized, such workers must be paid more than others. Also, some jobs are more unstable than others. Some types of construction workers are subject to frequent layoffs and have little job security, whereas many government employees (but not the top ones) are assured stable and secure employment. If the former jobs are to be as attractive as the latter, they must pay more. In addition, other differences among jobs must be offset by wage differentials if the net remuneration is to be equalized. For instance, there are differences among regions and communities in the cost of living. (Living costs are generally lower in small towns than in big cities.)

THE ALL-VOLUNTEER ARMY: A CASE STUDY

In recent years, there has been considerable controversy concerning the advantages and disadvantages of an all-volunteer army, the system used in this country since the early 1970s. Senator Sam Nunn, head of the Armed Services Committee, has advocated a return to the draft; others like former President Reagan have opposed such a step. Many economists have argued that recruiting an all-volunteer army is more efficient and equitable than relying on the draft, which through a complicated system of deferments and exemptions, as well as a lottery system, selected a certain number of young men for military service. Proponents of an all-volunteer army point out (1) that it is more compatible with freedom of choice than the draft, (2) that military personnel are used more effectively because the price of such personnel is a more realistic indicator of its value in alternative uses, and (3) that the cost of military personnel is distributed more equitably among the members of society. Under the draft a small group of draftees bore a large share of the cost, because they received less in wages than would have been required to induce them to volunteer.

Other economists and social observers oppose an all-volunteer army. They argue (1) that the present system can hardly be expected to produce the necessary military personnel in a full-scale war, (2) that an army of "paid mercenaries" might constitute a political danger by attempting to gain improper power, and (3) that an all-volunteer army relies disproportionately on the black population, since young blacks constitute a relatively larger percentage of those without civilian jobs than their white counterparts. In early 1991, whereas blacks were about one-eighth of the adult population, they were about one-fourth of the troops engaged in the war against Iraq in the Persian Gulf.[4]

How did the all-volunteer army come into being? In 1964, President Johnson asked that a study be made to determine whether it would be possible to shift from reliance on the draft to a system in which defense needs would be met entirely by volunteers. A team of economists attempted to learn what it would cost. Essentially they applied the kind of analysis described in this chapter. The basic approach was to estimate the supply curve for labor to the Department of Defense.

[4] *New York Times*, January 25, 1991, p. A12.

Figure 13.5 shows the relationship between the proportion of the male population that enlists and the level of military pay (as a percent of civilian pay), the unemployment rate being held constant at two alternative levels. As would be expected, the number of enlistments increases with the level of military pay and the unemployment rate. Using this supply curve, which was estimated by the economists, one could determine (for given values of the unemployment rate) the level of military pay that was required to bring forth the number of extra enlistments needed to eliminate the draft.

According to the economists, a 60 to 90 percent increase in enlistments was needed to eliminate the draft. To bring forth these extra enlistments, they estimated on the basis of the supply curve that first-term military pay for enlisted personnel had to be increased by about 110 percent (if the unemployment rate were 5.5 percent). Using 1964 military earnings as a base, increases in first-term pay for enlisted personnel had to be about $3,000 to attract enough volunteers to maintain a defense force of 2.65 million. Multiplying 2.65 million volunteers by the average increase in pay, the economists estimated that the increased cost to the Defense Department would be about $5 billion per year.[5] This estimate was very crude, as the economists stressed, since many noneconomic factors influenced the enlistment rate, and the data and underlying assumptions were rough.

By 1973, the draft was no longer being used to obtain military personnel. Whether it will be reactivated in the near future is hard to say. (In 1986, a study for the Joint Chiefs of Staff concluded that a return to the draft would increase costs.) For present purposes, the important point is that economic analysis, based on the fundamental concepts in this chapter, has played a very significant role in the discussion and resolution of this major issue. And in the future as in the past, you can be sure that economists will continue to play a significant role in this area.

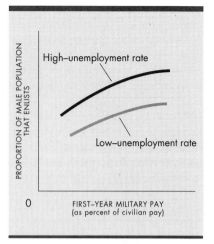

Figure 13.5
Relationship between Military Pay and Number of Enlistments
Holding the unemployment rate constant, the proportion of the male population that enlists is directly related to the level of military pay (as a percent of civilian pay). Using this supply curve, economists determined the level of military pay required to bring forth the extra enlistments needed to eliminate the draft.

SIGNALING IN THE LABOR MARKET

Economists like Stanford's Michael Spence have called attention to the importance of signaling in the labor market. To see what signaling is, suppose for simplicity that there are two distinctly different types of workers (high ability and low ability) that an employer can hire. The marginal product of high-ability workers is greater than that of low-ability workers. However, the employer cannot be sure whether a particular worker is high-ability or low-ability until after the worker has been hired. This is because it takes time on the job for the employer to determine the capabilities and productivity of the worker.

If the employer regards the educational level of a job applicant as a signal, or indicator, of the worker's ability, it may pay workers to invest in their education in order to signal the employer that they in fact are able. Of course, Mary Stuart, in getting an education, may not think of herself

[5] Note that the average increase in pay is less than the average increase in first-term pay. The way S. Altman and A. Fechter, who carried out the study, proceed from the latter to the former is described in their work. Also, note that the costs to the Defense Department, which are estimated here, may be quite different from the social costs of switching to an all-volunteer army.

Michael Spence

as signaling. She will invest in education if there is sufficient return, which will depend on how much more the employer is willing to pay for highly educated than for poorly educated workers.

Assuming that the difficulty (and thus the cost) of attaining a higher educational level is less for high-ability than for low-ability people, it is clear that high-ability people will have more incentive than low-ability people to get high levels of education. Thus the employer's belief that educational level is an effective indicator, or signal, of ability and productivity will be reinforced by experience. Consequently, the employer will continue to find it profitable to offer a higher wage to job applicants with relatively high levels of education, since such applicants are more likely to be high-ability people. Thus high-ability individuals will continue to find it economically worthwhile to invest relatively heavily in their educations.

An important thing to note is that, to the individual, it appears that higher education is a prerequisite to a high-paying job. After all, under these circumstances, the employer pays more for people with more education. Also, to an outside observer, it appears that education enhances the productivity of the worker. This seems to be true because the better-educated people have higher productivity and earn bigger wages than the less-educated people. In fact, however, *even if education has no effect on productivity and is only a signal of a person's ability, there will be a direct relationship between a person's education, on the one hand, and his or her productivity and wages, on the other.* Of course, this is not to say that education doesn't affect productivity; without question, it does enhance a person's productivity. But this doesn't deny that it also serves as a signal.

PRINCIPAL-AGENT PROBLEMS IN THE LABOR MARKET

Frequently, it is difficult for an employer to measure how hard a particular employee is working. For example, sales representatives often spend considerable periods of time traveling from one potential customer to another, and it is not easy for their employers to know whether they are working hard or not. In cases of this sort, there may be a principal-agent problem of the sort discussed in Chapter 6. The worker is, of course, an *agent* who works for the employer, who is the *principal*. What is the principal-agent problem? *The worker may pursue his or her own goals, and neglect the goals of the employer.*

As an illustration, take the case of Richard Ryan, a sales representative for a chemical firm. To keep things simple, suppose that he can generate only three possible levels of monthly receipts for his employer: $20,000, $10,000, or $6,000. If he works hard, he generates $20,000 per month in receipts for his employer if he is lucky, but only $10,000 if he is unlucky. If he does not work hard, he generates $10,000 per month if he is lucky, but only $6,000 if he is unlucky. (Ryan's salary has not been subtracted from these figures; to obtain the net receipts to his employer, it must be subtracted.) Thus, if Mr. Ryan generates receipts of $10,000 in a particular month, there is no way that his employer can tell whether he worked hard and was unlucky, or whether he did not work hard and was lucky. Even if his employer took the trouble to monitor his behavior (which could be prohibitively expensive), there may be no accurate method of gauging how hard he worked.

INCENTIVE SYSTEMS: BONUS PAYMENTS VERSUS A FIXED WAGE

Mr. Ryan's employer would like to establish incentives to get him to work hard because this will increase the firm's profits. One way to do this is to establish a bonus system. Suppose that Ryan receives a fixed monthly wage (say $3,000), regardless of the size of the receipts he generates for his employer. Clearly, this payment scheme will not induce him to work hard, since he will receive no more pay if he works hard than if he doesn't work hard. Thus, unless he likes work for its own sake, he will not work hard. If there is a 50–50 chance that he will be lucky in any month (and a 50–50 chance that he will be unlucky), his employer can expect that he will generate, on the average, 0.5 ($10,000) + 0.5 ($6,000) = $8,000 in receipts per month. Deducting his wage of $3,000 from this gross figure, his employer receives, on the average, net receipts of $5,000 per month. (See Table 13.4.)

On the other hand, suppose that Ryan receives a bonus if he generates a large volume of receipts. To be specific, let's assume that he gets a low wage (say $2,000) if he generates $6,000 or $10,000 in receipts in a particular month, but a much higher wage (say $6,000) if he generates receipts of $20,000 in that month. Since there is a 50–50 chance that he will be lucky in any month (and a 50–50 chance that he will be unlucky), he can expect, on the average, to receive 0.5 ($2,000) + 0.5 ($6,000) = $4,000 per month if he works hard. (Why? Because he will receive $2,000 during those months when he is unlucky and $6,000 during those months when he is lucky.) On the other hand, if he does not work hard, he is certain to receive $2,000 per month. (Why? Because regardless of whether he is lucky or unlucky, he will generate only $6,000 or $10,000 in receipts, which means he will receive $2,000 per month.)

Mr. Ryan now has an incentive to work hard, since his monthly wage is much higher if he works hard than if he doesn't. His employer can expect that Ryan will generate, on the average, 0.5 ($10,000) + 0.5 ($20,000)

Table 13.4
Richard Ryan's Expected Monthly Income and His Employer's Expected Monthly Net Receipts, if He Receives a Fixed Wage and if He Receives Bonus Payments

METHOD OF PAYMENT	IF HE WORKS HARD	IF HE DOES NOT WORK HARD	RYAN'S MAXIMUM EXPECTED INCOME [a]	EMPLOYER'S EXPECTED NET RECEIPTS
Fixed monthly wage of $3,000	$3,000	$3,000	$3,000	$8,000 – $3,000 = $5,000
$6,000 monthly payment if he generates $20,000 in receipts; $2,000 monthly payment otherwise	$4,000	$2,000	$4,000	$15,000 – $4,000 = $11,000

[a] This is his expected income if he works hard or his expected income if he does not work hard, whichever is higher (if they differ).

= $15,000 in receipts per month. Subtracting his average wage of $4,000 per month from this gross figure, his employer receives average net receipts of $11,000 per month, which is greater than if he paid Ryan a fixed monthly wage of $3,000. (See Table 13.4.) Clearly, both Ryan and his employer are better off under this bonus system than if Ryan received the fixed monthly wage.

THE MORAL OF THE TALE

The case of Richard Ryan illustrates an important point: *A bonus payment system can be used by firms to help induce workers to further the aims of the firm when there is no way to measure directly the amount of effort that a worker puts out.* Other incentive systems can be used as well. For example, Mr. Ryan's employer could have instituted a profit-sharing system whereby Ryan would have earned a basic wage plus a certain percentage of the profits in excess of a particular amount. If properly designed, this type of system can also provide an incentive for Ryan to work hard—and to increase the firm's profit.

TEST YOURSELF

1. Suppose that a perfectly competitive firm's production function is as follows:

QUANTITY OF LABOR (YEARS)	OUTPUT PER YEAR (THOUSANDS OF UNITS)
0	0
1	3.0
2	5.0
3	6.8
4	8.0
5	9.0

The firm is a profit maximizer, and the labor market is competitive. Labor must be hired in integer numbers and for a year (no more, no less). If the firm hires 4 years of labor, and if the price of a unit of the firm's product is $3, one can establish a range for what the annual wage prevailing in the labor market must be. What is the maximum amount it can be? What is the minimum amount? Why? Do these numbers seem realistic? Why, or why not?

2. Based on the data in Question 1, plot the marginal product of labor at various utilization rates of labor. Also, plot the value of labor's marginal product at each quantity of labor used.

3. "It is foolish to believe that a bonus payment system can increase a firm's profits. After all, such a system will increase a worker's wage; thus it must increase the firm's costs and reduce its profits." Comment and evaluate.

4. Suppose that the marginal product of skilled labor to a perfectly competitive firm is 2 units and the price of skilled labor is $8 an hour, while the marginal product of unskilled labor is 1 unit and the price of unskilled labor is $5.50 an hour. Is the firm minimizing its costs? Explain. (*Hint:* Regard skilled labor and unskilled labor as two separate inputs, and apply the cost-minimization rule in Chapter 7.)

MONOPSONY

In previous sections, we have assumed that perfect competition exists in the labor market. In some cases, however, **monopsony** exists instead. *A monopsony is a market structure where there is a single buyer.* Thus a single firm may hire all the labor in an isolated "company town," such as exists in the coal-mining regions of West Virginia and Kentucky. What determines the price of labor under monopsony? Suppose the firm's demand curve for labor and the supply curve of labor are as shown in Figure 13.6. Because the firm is the sole buyer of labor, it takes into account the fact that to acquire more labor it must pay a higher wage to *all* workers, not just the extra workers. For example, if the firm wants to increase the number of workers it employs from 5 to 6, it may have to pay the sixth an hourly wage of $9. If the supply curve of labor slopes upward to the right, this wage is more than was required to obtain the first 5 workers. Since the firm must pay all workers the same wage to avoid labor unrest, it must raise the wages of the first 5 workers to the level of the sixth, if it hires the sixth worker. Thus *the cost of hiring the sixth worker exceeds the wage that must be paid this worker.*

The supply curve for labor in Figure 13.6 shows the cost of hiring an additional worker, if workers already employed do *not* have to be paid a higher wage when the additional worker is hired. Thus this supply curve does *not* show the true additional cost to the monopsonist of hiring an additional worker, for the reasons given in the previous paragraph. Instead, curve *A*, which includes wages that must be paid to the workers already employed, shows the true additional cost. For the reasons given above, curve *A* lies above the supply curve.

If profit is maximized, the monopsonistic firm will hire labor up to the point at which the extra cost of adding an additional laborer (shown by curve *A*) equals the extra revenue from adding the additional laborer (shown by the demand curve). Thus the quantity of labor purchased will be *OM* and the price of labor will be *OC* in Figure 13.6. In contrast, under

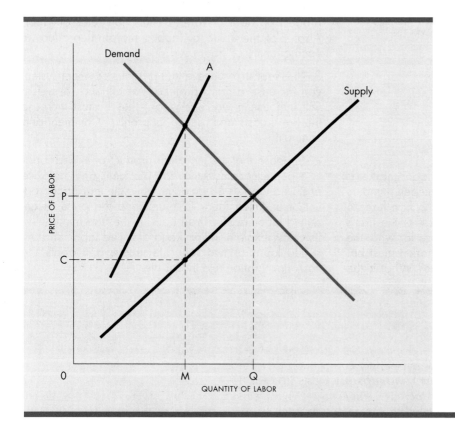

Figure 13.6
Equilibrium Wage and Quantity of Labor under Monopsony
The monopsonistic firm, if it maximizes profit, will hire laborers up to the point where the extra cost of adding an extra laborer, shown by curve A, equals the extra revenue from adding the extra laborer, shown by the demand curve for labor.

perfectly competitive conditions the equilibrium quantity and price would be at the intersection of the demand and supply curves. That is, the quantity of labor purchased would be OQ and the price of labor would be OP.

What is the effect of monopsony on the wage rate and the amount of labor hired? In general, *the wage rate, as well as the quantity hired, is lower under monopsony than under perfect competition.* This is the case in Figure 13.6, and it will generally hold true. This makes sense. One would expect a monopsonist, free from the pressures of competition, to pay workers less than would be required under perfect competition.

LABOR UNIONS

About 1 in 6 nonfarm workers in the United States belongs to a union, and the perfectly competitive model does not apply to these workers any more than it does to monopsonistic labor markets. The biggest unions are the National Education Association, the Teamsters, and the Food and Commercial Workers, each with 1.3 million members or more. Next come the State, County, and Municipal Employees, the United Auto Workers, and the Electrical Workers, each with over a million members.

The **national unions**[6] are of great importance in the American labor movement. The supreme governing body of the national union is the convention, which is held every year or two. The delegates to the convention have the authority to set policy for the union. However, considerable power is exercised by the national union's officers.

A national union is composed of **local unions,** each in a given area or plant. Some local unions have only a few members, but others have thousands. The local union, with its own president and officers, often plays an important role in collective bargaining. The extent to which the local unions maintain their autonomy varies from one national union to another. In industries where markets are localized (like construction and printing), the locals are more autonomous than in industries where markets are national (like steel, automobiles, and coal).

Finally, there is the **AFL-CIO,** a federation of national unions created by the merger of the American Federation of Labor and the Congress of Industrial Organizations in 1955. The AFL-CIO does not include all national unions. The United Mine Workers refused to join the AFL-CIO, and the Auto Workers left it in 1968. (The Teamsters were kicked out in the mid-1950s because of corruption, but in 1987 they were allowed to rejoin.) The AFL-CIO is a very important spokesman for the American labor movement; but because the national unions in the AFL-CIO have given up relatively little of their power to the federation, its authority is limited.

The AFL-CIO is organized along the lines indicated in Figure 13.7. The constitution of the AFL-CIO puts supreme governing power in the hands of a biennial convention. The national unions are represented at these conventions on the basis of their dues-paying membership. Between conventions, the AFL-CIO's business is directed by its president (Lane Kirkland in 1991) and secretary-treasurer, as well as by various committees and councils composed of representatives of various national unions or people elected at the convention. The AFL-CIO contains seven trade and industrial departments, such as building trades, food and beverage trades,

[6] Sometimes they are called international unions because some locals are outside the United States—for example, in Canada.

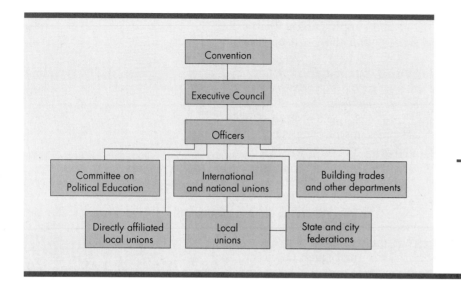

Figure 13.7
Structure of AFL-CIO
The AFL-CIO, which resulted from a merger of the AFL and CIO in 1955, is organized with the governing power in the hands of a biennial convention.

maritime trades, and so forth. Also, as indicated by Figure 13.7, a few local unions are not affiliated with a national union, but are directly affiliated with the AFL-CIO.

RECENT TRENDS IN UNION MEMBERSHIP

In recent decades, union membership has decreased as a percent of the labor force. In 1955, about one-fourth of the labor force belonged to unions; now the proportion is only about one-sixth. To some extent, this has been due to dissension within the labor movement and to a diminution of the zeal that characterized the movement in earlier years. Also, rightly or wrongly, unions have lost a certain amount of public sympathy and respect because of racial discrimination, unpopular strikes, evidence of corruption, and the belief that they are responsible in considerable part for supply-side inflation. But these factors only partly explain this lack of growth. In addition, important changes in the labor force have tended to reduce union membership.

Specifically, the increasing proportion of *white-collar workers* in the labor force seems to have raised important problems for unions. To date, unions have made relatively little progress in organizing white-collar workers. One reason for this lack of progress is that white-collar employees tend to identify with management. Also, the increasing proportion of *women* in the labor force seems to raise important problems for unions. It is sometimes claimed that female workers are harder to organize because they do not stay in the labor force very long and because they are concentrated in jobs—clerical and sales positions—that are difficult to organize. Nonetheless, the majority of the Retail Clerks, the Clothing Workers, and the International Ladies' Garment Workers have been women.

However, even though union membership has not been growing in recent years, it would be a mistake to jump to the conclusion that the American labor movement is of little or no importance. For one thing, membership is not a very good measure of power. A small union can sometimes bring an enormous amount of pressure to bear if it is located strategically in the economy.

EXAMPLE 13.2   CAN A UNION INCREASE EMPLOYMENT?

In many isolated areas, a single firm is the only employer of a certain kind of labor. Suppose that a textile firm is in this position, and that its demand curve for labor, as well as the supply curve for labor, are shown below. Curve A shows the extra cost to the firm of adding an extra laborer.

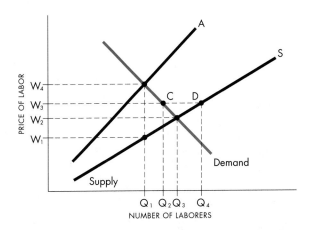

(a) How many laborers will the firm hire, and how much will each be paid? (b) Suppose that a union enters the market and that it sets a wage of OW_3. What now is the supply curve for labor? (c) How many laborers will the firm hire now? Is employment higher than before the union entered? (d) Will there be involuntary unemployment now?

Solution

(a) The firm will hire OQ_1 laborers and pay a wage of OW_1, in accord with our discussion of monopsony. (b) It is W_3DS, because the firm cannot pay a wage below OW_3 under the assumed circumstances. (c) The firm will hire OQ_2 workers, since the extra cost of hiring an extra worker equals OW_3 so long as less than OQ_4 workers are hired. Employment is higher than before the union entered (when it was OQ_1). (d) Yes. At a wage of OW_3, OQ_4 workers will seek employment but only OQ_2 workers will be hired. Thus $(OQ_4 - OQ_2)$ workers will be involuntarily unemployed.

HOW UNIONS INCREASE WAGES

Unions wield considerable power, and economists must include them in their analysis if they want their models of the labor market to reflect conditions in the real world. We shall now see how this is done. Let us begin by supposing that a union wants to increase the wage rate paid its members. How can it accomplish this objective? In other words, how can it alter the market supply curve for labor, or the market demand curve for labor, so that the price of labor—its wage—will increase?

1. *The union may try to shift the supply curve of labor to the left.* It may shift the supply curve, as shown in Figure 13.8, with the result that the price of labor will increase from OP to OP_1. How can the union cause this shift in the supply curve? Craft unions have frequently forced employers to hire only union members, and then restricted union membership by high initiation fees, reduction in new membership, and other devices. In addition, unions have favored legislation to reduce immigration, shorten working hours, and limit the labor supply in other ways.

2. *The union may try to get the employers to pay a higher wage, while allowing some of the supply of labor forthcoming at this higher wage to find no opportunity for work.* In Figure 13.9, the union may exert pressure on the employers to raise the price of labor from OP to OP_1. At OP_1, not all of the available supply of labor can find jobs. The quantity of labor supplied is OQ_2, while the amount of labor demanded is OQ_1. The effect is the same as in Figure 13.8, but in this case the union does not limit the supply directly. It lets the higher wage reduce the opportunity for work.

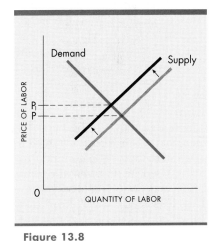

Figure 13.8
Shift of Supply Curve for Labor
A union may shift the supply curve to the left by getting employers to hire only union members and then restricting union membership, or by other techniques.

Strong industrial unions often behave in this fashion. Having organized practically all the relevant workers and controlling the labor supply, the union raises the wage to OP_1. This is a common and important case.

3. *The union may try to shift the demand curve for labor upward and to the right.* If it can bring about the shift described in Figure 13.10, the price of labor will increase from OP to OP_2. To cause this shift in the demand for labor, the union may resort to **featherbedding.** That is, it may try to restrict output per worker in order to increase the amount of labor required to do a certain job. (To cite but one case, the railroad unions have insisted on much unnecessary labor.) Unions also try to shift the demand curve by helping the employers compete against other industries, or by helping to make Congress pass legislation that protects the employers from foreign competition.

COLLECTIVE BARGAINING

Collective bargaining is the process of negotiation between the union and management over wages and working conditions. Representatives of the union and management meet periodically to work out an agreement or contract; this process generally begins a few months before the old labor contract runs out. Typically, each side asks at first for more than it expects to get, and compromises must be made to reach an agreement. The union representatives take the agreement to their members, who must vote to accept or reject it. If they reject it, they may vote to strike or to continue to negotiate.

Collective bargaining agreements vary greatly. Some pertain to only a single plant while others apply to an entire industry. However, an agreement generally contains the following elements. It specifies the extent and kind of recognition that management gives the union, the level of wage rates for particular jobs, the length of the work week, the rate of overtime pay, the extent to which seniority will determine which workers will be first to be laid off, the nature and extent of management's prerogatives, and how grievances between workers and the employer will be handled.

Historically, industries and firms have extended recognition to unions by accepting one of three arrangements—the closed shop, the union shop, or the open shop. In a **closed shop,** workers must be union members before they can be hired. This gives the union more power than if there is a **union shop,** in which the employer can hire nonunion workers who must then become union members in a certain length of time after being hired. In an **open shop,** the employer can hire union or nonunion labor, and nonunion workers need not, once employed, join the union. The closed shop was banned by the Taft-Hartley Act, passed in 1947. The Taft-Hartley Act also says that the union shop is legal unless outlawed by state laws; and in about 20 states there are "right to work" laws that make the union shop illegal. Needless to say, these right-to-work laws are hated by organized labor, which regards them as a threat to its security and effectiveness.

Basic Forces at Work

Collective bargaining is a power struggle. At each point in their negotiations, both the union and the employer must compare the costs (or bene-

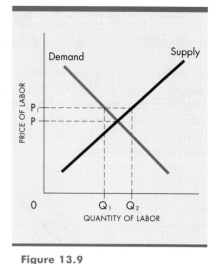

Figure 13.9
Direct Increase in Price of Labor
A union may get the employer to raise the wage from OP to OP_1 and let the higher wage reduce the opportunity for work. This is commonly done by strong industrial unions.

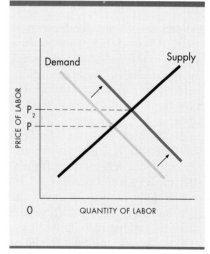

Figure 13.10
Shift in Demand Curve for Labor
A union may shift the demand curve for labor to the right by featherbedding or other devices, thus increasing the wage from OP to OP_2.

fits) of agreeing with the other party with the costs (or benefits) of continuing to disagree. The costs of disagreement are the costs of a ***strike***, while the costs of agreement are the costs of settling on terms other than one's own. These costs are determined by basic market forces. For example, during periods when demand is great, employers are more likely to grant large wage increases because the costs of disagreement seem higher (a strike will prove more costly) than those of settlement. The outcome of the negotiations will depend on the relative strength of the parties. The strength of the employers depends on their ability to withstand a strike. The strength of the unions depends on their ability to keep out nonunion workers and to enlist the support of other unions, as well as on the size of their financial reserves.

UNION CONCESSIONS IN THE 1980S

In the 1980s, many important unions cut back on their wage requests. In the automobile industry, American firms found it difficult to compete with their Japanese rivals, and many experts attributed this partly to the very high wages in the U.S. auto industry. In the trucking industry, unionized firms found it increasingly difficult to compete with nonunion firms. More and more union members in industries like autos, trucking, steel, rubber, and the airlines began to worry about the effects of hefty wage increases on whether or not they would have jobs. The climate for collective bargaining was quite different than in earlier decades.

To illustrate, consider the labor negotiations in the auto industry in 1987. An important issue in these negotiations was the reform in work rules. After seeing productivity increases of 20 percent or more at some plants that adopted Japanese-style manufacturing systems, which organize workers in teams, auto executives pressed for the reduction of rigid union job classifications and work rules. Some union officials agreed, but because work rules are set in local, not national, negotiations, and because

Table 13.5
Workers Accepting Concessions in Labor Settlements as a Percent of Workers Negotiating in the Year, by Union, 1975–88

UNION	1975	1980	1985	1988
United Food and Commercial Workers	—ᵃ	0	46	73
United Auto Workers	6	12	97	100
International Brotherhood of Electrical Workers	0	0	40	60
Service Employees	13	0	26	18
Carpenters and Joiners	0	0	77	—ᵃ
Steelworkers	0	5	91	—ᵃ
Communications Workers of America	0	0	27	—ᵃ
Association of Federal, State, County and Municipal Employees	0	0	22	—ᵃ

ᵃ No contracts negotiated in year.
Source: Linda Bell, "Union Concessions in the 1980s," *Quarterly Review of the Federal Reserve Bank of New York*, Summer 1989.

some union members have strongly resisted such changes, reform has not been easy.

Let's define a union concession as a wage reduction (or no wage increase), a reduction in cost-of-living adjustments in pay, a relaxation of work rules, the adoption of a "two-tier" wage structure (where newly hired workers are paid at a lower rate than existing workers), or the substitution of profit-sharing (and related) plans for a wage increase. In the late 1980s, a majority of workers in unions like the United Auto Workers, Steelworkers, Carpenters, Electrical Workers, and Food and Commercial Workers accepted concessions in their new contracts (Table 13.5). In 1975 or 1980, such concessions were rare.

TEST YOURSELF

1. "The unions should not be exempt from the antitrust laws." Comment and evaluate.

2. Suppose that a perfectly competitive firm suddenly becomes a monopsonist in the market for labor. Do you think that it would pay a lower, higher, or the same wage rate as it did before? Why?

3. Suppose that you were the president of a small firm that hired nonunion labor. How would you go about estimating the marginal product of a certain worker, or of certain types of workers? Would it be easy? If not, does this mean that the theory of wage determination is incorrect or useless?

4. Describe the various ways that labor unions can influence the wage rate. Do you think that they attempt to maximize the wage rate? If not, what do you think their objectives are?

SUMMARY

1. Assuming perfect competition, a firm will employ each type of labor in an amount such that its marginal product times the product's price equals its wage. In other words, the firm will employ enough labor so that the value of the marginal product of labor equals labor's price.

2. The firm's demand curve for labor—which shows, for each price of labor, the amount of labor the firm will use—is the firm's value-of-marginal-product curve (if labor is the only variable input). The market demand curve for labor shows the relationship between its price and the total amount of labor demanded in the market.

3. Labor's price depends on its market supply curve as well as on its market demand curve. Labor's market supply curve is the relationship between the price of labor and the total amount of labor supplied in the market. (Labor's market supply curve may be backward bending.)

4. An input's price is determined under perfect competition in essentially the same way that a product's price is determined—by supply and demand. The price of labor will tend in equilibrium to the level at which the quantity of labor demanded equals the quantity of labor supplied. By the same token, the equilibrium amount of labor utilized is also given by the intersection of the market supply and demand curves.

5. If there are qualitative differences among workers, the differential in their wages will reflect the differential in their marginal products. Also, even if all workers were of equal ability, there would still be differences in wage rates to offset differences among occupations in the cost of training and stability of earnings, and geographical differences in the cost of living.

6. Workers may invest in their own education to signal employers that they are able. Even if education has no effect on productivity and is only a signal of a person's ability, there will be a direct relationship between a person's education, on the one hand, and his or her productivity and wages, on the other. (Of course, this is not to say that education generally has no effect on productivity.)

7. A worker may pursue his or her own interests, and neglect the goals of the employer. To help induce workers to promote the aims of the firm (when it is very hard to measure the amount of effort that a worker puts forth), bonus payment systems are often instituted by employers.

8. There are several ways that unions can increase wages—by shifting the supply curve of labor to the left, by shifting the demand curve for labor to the right, and by influencing the wage directly.

9. Collective bargaining is the process of negotiation between union and management over wages and working conditions. The union's power is based to a considerable extent on its right to strike. In the 1980s, there were many union concessions.

CONCEPTS FOR REVIEW

Firm's demand curve for labor

Value of the marginal product of labor

Market demand curve for labor

Derived demand

Market supply curve for labor

Noncompeting groups

Monopsony

National union

Local union

AFL-CIO

Backward-bending supply curve

Featherbedding

Collective bargaining

Closed shop

Union shop

Open shop

Strike

INTEREST, RENT, AND PROFITS

NOT ALL INCOME is received in the form of wages. The school teacher who has a savings account at the Bank of America receives income in the form of *interest*. The widow who rents out 100 acres of rich Iowa land to a farmer receives income in the form of *rent*. And the engineer who founds and owns a firm that develops a new type of electronic calculator receives income in the form of *profit*. All of these types of income—interest, rent, and profit—are forms of property income. That is, they are incomes received by owners of property. In this chapter, we are concerned with the determinants of interest, rent, and profit. Also, we try to explain the social functions of each of these types of property income.

THE NATURE OF INTEREST

Charles Lamb, the English essayist, said, "The human species, according to the best theory I can form of it, is composed of two distinct races, the men who borrow and the men who lend." Whether or not such a cleavage exists, most of the human species, at one time or another, are borrowers or lenders of money. Thus practically everyone is familiar with **interest,** which is a payment for the use of money. More specifically, *the rate of interest is the amount of money one must pay for the use of a dollar for a year.* Thus, if the interest rate is 8 percent, you must pay 8 cents for the use of a dollar for a year.

Everyone who borrows money pays interest. Consumers pay interest on personal loans taken out to buy appliances, mortgages taken out to buy houses, and many other types of loans. Firms pay interest on bonds issued to purchase equipment and on short-term bank loans taken out to finance inventories. And governments pay interest on bonds issued to finance schools, highways, and other public projects.

Interest rates vary, depending on the nature of the borrower and the type of loan. One of the most important determinants of the rate of interest charged borrowers is the *riskiness* of the loan. If lenders have doubts about their chances of getting their money back, they will charge a higher interest rate than if they are sure of being repaid. Thus small, financially rickety firms have to pay higher interest rates than large blue-chip firms; and the large, well-known firms have to pay higher interest rates than the federal government. Another factor that influences the interest rate is the *cost of bookkeeping and collection*. If a firm makes many small loans and must hound the borrowers to pay up, these costs are a great deal larger than if it makes one large loan. Consequently the interest rate that must be charged for such small loans is often considerably higher than for bigger loans.

Despite the diversity of interest rates encountered at any point in time in the real world, it is analytically useful to speak of the ***pure rate of interest,*** which is the interest rate on a riskless loan. The rate of interest on U.S. government bonds—which are about as safe as one can get in this world—comes close to being a pure rate of interest. Actual interest rates will vary from the pure rate, depending on the riskiness of the loan together with other factors, but the configuration of actual interest rates will tend to move up and down with the pure interest rate.

THE DETERMINATION OF THE INTEREST RATE

The Demand for Loanable Funds

Since the interest rate is the price paid for the use of loanable funds, it—like any price—is determined by demand and supply. The ***demand curve for loanable funds*** shows the quantity of loanable funds demanded at each interest rate. The demand for loanable funds is a demand for what these funds will buy. Money is not wanted for its own sake, since it cannot build factories or equipment. Instead, it can provide command over resources—labor and equipment and materials—to do things like build factories or equipment.

As shown in Figure 14.1, the demand curve slopes downward to the right, indicating that more loanable funds are demanded at a lower rate of interest than at a higher rate of interest. A very large demand for loanable funds stems from firms who want to borrow money to invest in capital goods like machine tools, buildings, and so forth. At a particular point in time a firm has available a variety of possible investments, each with a

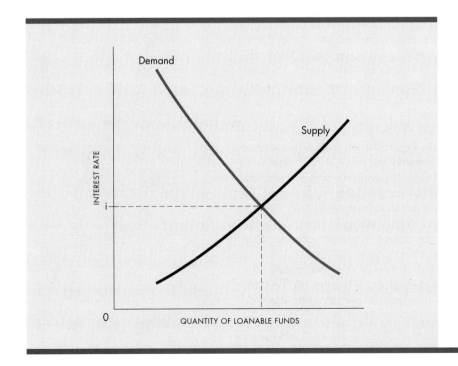

Figure 14.1
Determination of Equilibrium Rate of Interest
The interest rate is determined by the demand and supply of loanable funds, the equilibrium level of the interest rate being *Oi*.

certain rate of return, which indicates its profitability or net productivity. At higher interest rates, a firm will find it profitable to borrow money for fewer of these projects than if interest rates are lower.

To be more specific, *an asset's **rate of return** is the interest rate earned on the investment in the asset.* Suppose that a piece of equipment costs $10,000 and yields a permanent return to its owner of $1,500 per year.[1] (This return allows for the costs of maintaining the machine.) The rate of return on this piece of capital is 15 percent. Why? Because if an investment of $10,000 yields an indefinite annual return of $1,500, the interest rate earned on this investment is 15 percent.

If a firm maximizes profit, it will borrow to carry out investments where the rate of return, adjusted for risk, exceeds the interest rate. For example, it is profitable for a firm to pay 10 percent interest to carry out a project with a 12 percent rate of return, but it is not profitable to pay 15 percent interest for this purpose. (More will be said on this score in a subsequent section.) Consequently, the higher the interest rate, the smaller the amount that firms will be willing to borrow.

Large demands for loanable funds are also made by consumers and the government. Consumers borrow money to buy houses, cars, and many other items. The government borrows money to finance the building of schools, highways, housing, and many other types of public projects. As in the case of firms, the higher the interest rate, the smaller the amount that consumers and governments will be willing to borrow. Adding the demands of firms, consumers, and government together, we find the aggregate relationship at a given point in time between the pure interest rate and the amount of funds demanded—which is the demand curve for loanable funds. For the reasons given above, this demand curve looks like a demand curve should. It is downward-sloping to the right.

The Supply of Loanable Funds

The ***supply curve for loanable funds*** is the relationship between the quantity of loanable funds supplied and the pure interest rate. The supply of loanable funds comes from households and firms that find the available rate of interest sufficiently attractive to get them to save. In addition, the banks play an extremely important role in influencing the supply of loanable funds. Indeed, banks can actually create or destroy loanable funds (but only within limits set by the Federal Reserve System, our central bank.)

The equilibrium value of the pure interest rate is given by the intersection of the demand and supply curves. In Figure 14.1 the equilibrium rate of interest is *Oi.* Factors that shift the demand curve or supply curve for loanable funds tend to alter the interest rate. If people become more willing to postpone consumption to future time periods, the supply curve for loanable funds will shift to the right, and the interest rate will decline. Or if inventions result in very profitable new investment possibilities, the demand curve will shift to the right and the interest rate will increase. (See Figure 14.2.)

However, this is only part of the story. Because of the government's influence on both the demand and supply sides of the market for loanable funds, the interest rate at any point in time is to a considerable extent a

---

[1] It is unrealistic to assume that the yield continues indefinitely, but it makes it easier to understand the principle involved.

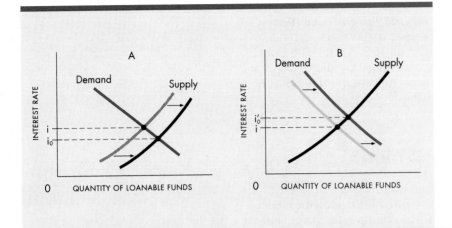

Figure 14.2
Effects on the Equilibrium Interest Rate of Shifts in the Demand or Supply Curves for Loanable Funds
If people become more willing to postpone consumption to future time periods, the supply curve will shift to the right, and the equilibrium interest rate will fall from i to i_0.

If very profitable new investment opportunities are opened up, the demand curve will shift to the right, and the equilibrium interest rate will rise from i to i'_0.

matter of public policy. A nation's monetary policy can have a significant effect on the level of the interest rate. More specifically, when the Federal Reserve pursues a policy of easy money, this generally means that interest rates tend to fall in the short run because the Fed is pushing the supply curve for loanable funds to the right. On the other hand, when the Federal Reserve pursues a policy of tight money, interest rates generally tend to rise in the short run because the Fed is pushing the supply curve for loanable funds to the left. (See Figure 14.3.)

The government is also an important factor on the demand side of the market for loanable funds, because it is a big borrower. During the 1980s and early 1990s, it borrowed huge amounts to finance the mammoth federal deficits. In 1990, total federal debt (excluding the debt of state and local governments) held by the public was about $2 trillion.

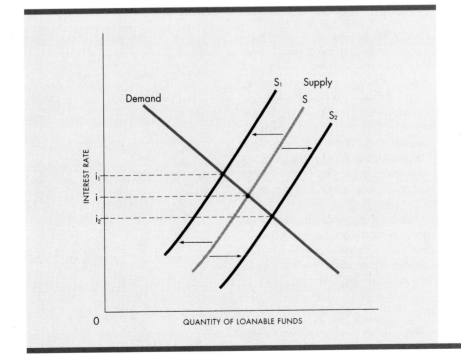

Figure 14.3
Effects on the Equilibrium Interest Rate of Federal Reserve Policies Influencing the Supply Curve for Loanable Funds
When the Federal Reserve pushes the supply curve to the right (from S to S_2), the equilibrium interest rate falls from i to i_2. When the Federal Reserve pushes the supply curve to the left (S to S_1), the equilibrium interest rate increases from i to i_1.

Finally, note that the equilibrium level of the pure interest rate can be determined by John Maynard Keynes's **liquidity preference theory,** as well as by the loanable funds theory described in this section. The liquidity preference theory focuses attention on all money, not just loanable funds, and says that the interest rate is determined by the demand and supply of all money in the economy. The two approaches are not contradictory; rather, they complement one another.

FUNCTIONS OF THE INTEREST RATE

Interest has often been a relatively unpopular and somewhat suspect form of income. Even Aristotle, who was hardly noted for muddle-headedness, felt that money was "barren" and that it was improper to charge interest. And in the Middle Ages, church law outlawed usury, even though interest continued to be charged. In real life and in fiction, the money lender is often the villain, almost never the hero. Yet it is perfectly clear that *interest rates serve a very important function. They allocate the supply of loanable funds.*

At a given point in time, funds that can be used to construct new capital goods are scarce, and society faces the problem of allocating these scarce funds among alternative possible uses. One way to allocate the loanable funds is through freely fluctuating interest rates. When such funds are relatively scarce, the interest rate will rise, with the result that only projects with relatively high rates of return will be carried out since the others will not be profitable. On the other hand, when such funds are relatively plentiful, the interest rate will fall, and less productive projects will be carried out because they now become profitable.

Choosing the Most Productive Projects

The advantage of using the interest rate to allocate funds is that only the most productive projects are funded. To see why, assume that all investments are riskless. *If firms can borrow all the money they want (at the prevailing interest rate), and if they maximize their profits, they will buy all capital goods and accept all investment opportunities where the rate of return on these capital goods or investment opportunities exceeds the interest rate at which they can borrow.*[2] The reason for this is clear enough. If one can borrow money at an interest cost that is less than the rate of return on the borrowed money, clearly one can make money. Thus, if you borrow $1,000 at 3 percent per year interest and buy a $1,000 machine that has a rate of return of 4 percent per year, you receive a return of $40 per year and incur a cost of $30 per year. Since you make a profit of $10 per year, it obviously pays to buy this machine.

At a particular point in time, there is a variety of possible capital goods that can be produced and investment projects that can be carried out. Their rates of return vary a great deal; some goods or projects have much higher rates of return than others. Suppose that we rank the capital goods or projects according to their rates of return, from highest to lowest. If

---

[2] We assume here that the investment opportunities are independent in the sense that the rate of return from each opportunity is not influenced by whether some other opportunity is accepted.

only a few of the goods or projects can be accepted, only those at the top of the list will be chosen. But as more and more can be accepted, society and private investors must go further and further down the list, with the consequence that projects with lower and lower rates of return will be chosen. How many of these capital goods and investment projects will be carried out? As noted above, firms will continue to invest as long as the rate of return on these goods or projects exceeds the interest rate at which they can borrow. Thus it follows that *the most productive projects—all those with rates of return exceeding the interest rate—will be carried out.*

Socialism and the Interest Rate

Although interest is sometimes represented as a product of greedy capitalists, even socialist and Communist economies must use something like an interest rate to help allocate funds. After all, the socialists and Communists face the same sort of allocation problem that capitalists do. And when they try to screen out the less productive projects and to accept only the more productive ones, they must use the equivalent of an interest rate in their calculations, whether they call it that or not. (However, they do not pay interest income.) Prior to the dissolution of the Soviet Union, there were published Soviet acknowledgments that a misallocation of resources resulted from decisions made in earlier years when interest rates—or their equivalent—were ignored. Thus, Soviet decision makers used what amounted to interest rates in their calculations to determine which capital investments should be made and which should not.

Finally, besides its role in allocating the supply of loanable funds, the interest rate plays another important part in our economy: *It influences the level of investment, and thus the level of gross national product.* Increases in the interest rate tend to reduce aggregate investment, thereby reducing total spending, whereas decreases in the interest rate tend to increase aggregate investment, thereby increasing total spending. Through its monetary policies, the government attempts to influence the interest rate (and the quantity of money) so that total spending pushes gross national product toward its full-employment level with reasonably stable prices.

CAPITAL BUDGETING

The principles discussed in the previous section can be applied to individual firms as well as entire societies. In particular, they help to indicate how a firm should make decisions on the choice of investment projects. Suppose that the Bugsbane Music Box Company believes that it will have $10 million from internal sources—primarily retained earnings and depreciation allowances—to invest next year. *To decide which investment projects to accept, it should estimate the rate of return from each one.* Suppose that it finds that it can invest $2 million in projects with rates of return of 30 percent, that it can invest $4 million in projects with rates of return of 25 percent, and so on, as shown in Table 14.1. Applying the principles just discussed, Bugsbane can maximize its profits by allocating the $10 million available from internal sources as follows: All projects yielding rates of return of 20 percent or more should be accepted; and all projects yielding less than 20 percent should not be undertaken. In other words, the projects with the highest rates of return—and with a total cost of $10 million—should be chosen.

This is a very useful step toward solving the firm's problem, but it assumes that the firm is unable or unwilling to borrow. If this is true, then nothing more needs to be said. But, as shown in Table 14.1, the firm has investment opportunities yielding 15 percent per year that it is not undertaking. It would pay the firm to undertake these projects even it it had to pay 10 or 12 percent interest—or anything less than 15 percent, for that matter. If the firm can borrow all the money it wants (within reason), but must pay 12 percent interest, what investment opportunities should it accept? All whose rate of return exceeds 12 percent. Thus, looking at Table 14.1, we see that the firm should invest its $10 million from internal sources and borrow an additional $6 million in order to undertake projects totaling $16 million.

This is an extremely simple case, but it illustrates how the interest rate and the concept of an asset's rate of return are used in practical business situations. *Capital budgeting*—the term applied to this area—has become an extremely important part of a firm's operations, as managers have relied more and more on economic concepts in allocating their firms' resources. Unaided hunch and intuition will no longer do in most major firms. Instead, most big firms insist that the prospective rate of return be estimated for each proposed investment, and that, making allowances for differences in risk, funds be allocated to the projects with the highest rate of return.[3] It is often difficult to make such estimates, but if funds are to be allocated rationally, it is essential that an analysis of this sort be carried out, formally or on the back of an envelope.

CAPITAL AND ROUNDABOUT METHODS OF PRODUCTION

Labor and land are often called the *primary inputs* because they are produced outside the economic system. Labor is created by familiar biological processes (which usually are not economically oriented, one would hope), and land is supplied by nature. *Capital,* on the other hand, *consists of goods that are created for the purpose of producing other goods.* Factory buildings, equipment, raw materials, inventories—all are various types of capital. In contrast to labor and land, capital is an input produced by the economic system itself.[4] A machine tool is capital; so is a boxcar or an electric power plant. These inputs are produced by firms, and they are purchased and used by firms. But they are not final consumption goods; instead, they are used to produce the final goods and services consumed by the public.

Our economy devotes a considerable amount of its productive capacity to the production of capital. The giant electrical equipment industry produces generators used by the electric power industry. The machine tool industry produces the numerically controlled tools used by the automo-

[3] In practice, firms often base their decisions on discounted cash flow rather than rates of return. The present discussion is necessarily simplified. For a more complete treatment, see E. Mansfield, *Managerial Economics*, New York: W. W. Norton, 1990.
[4] Obviously, this distinction requires qualification. After all, land can be improved, and the quality of labor can be enhanced (by training and other means). Thus land and labor have some of the characteristics of capital since to some extent they can be "produced"—or at least enhanced—by the economic system.

Table 14.1
Investment Opportunities for Bugsbane Music Box Company

RATE OF RETURN (PERCENT)	AMOUNT OF MONEY THE FIRM CAN INVEST AT GIVEN RATE OF RETURN (DOLLARS)
30	2 million
25	4 million
20	4 million
15	6 million
10	7 million

bile, aircraft, and hundreds of other industries. The result in many sectors of the economy is a *roundabout method of production*. Consider the stages that lead to the manufacture of an automobile. Workers dig iron ore to be used to make pig iron to be used to make steel to be used to make machine tools to be used to make cylinders to be used to make a motor to be used to make the automobile.

WHY CAPITAL?

Why does the economy bother to produce capital? After all, it may seem unnecessarily circuitous to construct capital to produce the goods and services consumers really want. Why not produce the desired goods and services—and *only* the desired goods and services—directly? Why produce plows to help produce agricultural crops? Why not forget about the plows and just produce the crops the consumers want? The answer is that the other inputs—labor and land—can produce more of the desired consumer goods and services when they are used in combination with capital than when they are used alone. A given amount of labor and land can produce more crops when used in combination with plows than when used alone.

The production and use of lots of capital make the other inputs—labor and land—more productive. But this does not mean that any society would be wise to increase without limit its production and use of capital. After all, the only way a society can produce more capital is to produce less goods and services of direct use to consumers. (For society as a whole, there are no free lunches, if resources are used fully and efficiently.) As the production of capital increases, consumers must cut further and further into their level of consumption at the present time in order to increase their capacity to produce in the future. Beyond a point, the advantage of having more in the future is overbalanced by the disadvantage of having less now. At this point, a society should stop increasing its production of capital goods.

The process by which people give up a claim on present consumption goods in order to receive consumption goods in the future is called **saving.** Just as a child may (infrequently) give up a lollipop today in order to get a lollipop and a candy cane next week, so an entire society may give up the present consumption of automobiles, food, tobacco, clothing, and so forth in order to obtain more of such goods and services later on.[5]

CAPITALIZATION OF ASSETS

In a capitalist economy, each capital good has a market value. How can we determine what this value is? How much money is a capital good worth? To keep things reasonably simple, suppose that you can get 5 per-

[5] In a more poetic vein, this process of saving has been described as follows by William M. Thackeray:

Though small was your allowance,
    You saved a little store;
And those who save a little
    Shall get a plenty more.

If it does nothing else, the foregoing helps explain why Thackeray is better known as a novelist than a poet.

cent on various investments open to you; specifically, you can get 5 percent by investing your money in the stock of a local firm. That is, for every $1,000 you invest, you will receive a permanent return of $50 a year—and this is the highest return available. Now suppose that you have an opportunity to buy a piece of equipment that will yield you a permanent return of $1,000 per year. This piece of equipment is worth $1,000 ÷ .05 = $20,000 to you. Why? Because this is the amount you would have to pay for any other investment open to you that yields an equivalent amount—$1,000—per year. (If you must invest $1,000 for every $50 of annual yield, $20,000 must be invested to obtain an annual yield of $1,000.)

In general, if a particular asset yields a permanent amount—X dollars—each year, how much is this asset worth? In other words, how much should you be willing to pay for it? If you can get a return of $100 \times r$ percent per year from alternative investments, you would have to invest $X \div r$ dollars in order to get the same return as this particular asset yields. Consequently, this asset is worth

$$\frac{\$X}{r}.$$

This process of computing an asset's worth is called **capitalization.**

Thus, if the rate of return on alternative investments had been 3 percent rather than 5 percent in the example above, the worth of the piece of equipment would have been $1,000 ÷ .03 = $33,333 (since X = $1,000 and r = .03). This is the amount you would have to pay for any other investment open to you that yields an equivalent amount—$1,000—per year. To see this, note that, if you must invest $1,000 for every $30 (not $50, as before) of annual yield, $33,333 (not $20,000, as before) must be invested to obtain an annual yield of $1,000.

EFFECTS ON AN ASSET'S VALUE OF CHANGES IN THE RATE OF RETURN ON OTHER INVESTMENTS

Note one important point about an asset's capitalized value. Holding constant an asset's annual returns, the asset's worth is higher the lower the rate of return available on other investments. Thus the piece of equipment discussed above was worth $33,333 when you could get a 3 percent return on alternative investments, but only $20,000 when you could get a 5 percent return on alternative investments. This makes sense. After all, the lower the rate of return on alternative investments, the more you must invest in them in order to obtain annual earnings equivalent to those of the asset in question. Thus the more valuable is the asset in question.

This principle helps to explain why in securities markets bond prices fall when interest rates rise, and rise when interest rates fall. As we saw in Chapter 6, a bond is a piece of paper that states that the borrower will pay the lender a fixed amount of interest each year (and the principal when the bond comes due). Suppose that this annual interest is $100, and that the interest rate equals $100 \times r$ percent per year. Then, applying the results of the previous paragraphs, this bond will be worth $100 ÷ r dollars, if the bond is due a great many years hence. Suppose the interest rate is 5 percent. Then it is worth $2,000. But if the interest rate rises to 10 percent,

WHAT DOES THAT DREAM HOUSE REALLY COST?

The biggest investment you'll probably ever make is in a house. The ordinary procedure is for a house buyer to take out a mortgage, often from a savings and loan association or a bank. A mortgage is a loan; the house itself becomes security (or collateral) for the loan. If you fail to meet the mortgage payments, the lender can foreclose the mortgage, which means that the lender is entitled to take possession of the house.

To figure out how much your payments must be each month, the lender determines how much you must pay so that, when the mortgage terminates, you will have repaid the amount you borrowed and paid the stipulated interest on your debt. The size of the monthly mortgage payment depends on three things—(1) the amount you borrow, (2) how long the mortgage extends, and (3) the interest rate. The more that you borrow, the higher your monthly payment, holding all other things equal. And the higher the interest rate and the shorter the period of the mortgage, the higher your monthly payment.

To be more specific, look at the accompanying table, which shows the monthly payment per $1,000 borrowed. As you can see, the monthly payment is $9.66 per $1,000 borrowed, if the mortgage extends for 20 years and the interest rate is 10 percent. Thus, if you take out a $60,000 mortgage (at 10 percent for 20 years), the monthly payment is 60 times $9.66, or $579.60.

As noted above, much of the monthly payment is used to repay part of the principal of the loan. The rest goes for interest on the portion of the loan that is not yet repaid. Over the lifetime of a mortgage, a very substantial amount is paid by the borrower for interest. If you take out a 20-year, $60,000 mortgage at an interest rate of 10 percent, you will pay $79,104 in interest over the life of the mortgage. And the higher the interest rate, the bigger the amount that you will pay in interest. Thus, if the interest rate is 9 1/2 percent (rather than 10 percent), you will pay $74,352 (rather than $79,104) in interest over the life of a 20-year, $60,000 mortgage. Clearly, *a difference of 1/2 percentage point in the interest rate increases the total interest payments by about $5,000!*

Monthly Mortgage Payments (per $1,000 borrowed)

| INTEREST RATE | LENGTH OF MORTGAGE (YEARS) | | | |
	15	20	25	30
(percent)		(dollars)		
7	8.99	7.76	7.07	6.66
7½	9.28	8.06	7.39	7.00
8	9.56	8.37	7.72	7.34
8½	9.85	8.68	8.06	7.69
9	10.15	9.00	8.40	8.05
9½	10.45	9.33	8.74	8.41
10	10.75	9.66	9.09	8.78

it will be worth only $1,000; and if the interest rate falls to 4 percent, it will be worth $2,500. Securities dealers make these sorts of calculations all the time, for they recognize that the value of the bond will fall when interest rates rise, and rise when interest rates fall.

THE PRESENT VALUE OF FUTURE INCOME

In the previous section, we determined the value of an asset that yields a perpetual stream of earnings. Now let's consider a case where an asset will provide you with a single lump sum at a certain time in the future. Suppose that you are the heir to an estate of $100,000, which you will receive in two years. How much is that estate worth now?

To answer this question, the first thing to note is that a dollar now is worth more than a dollar later. Why? Because one can always invest money that is available now and obtain interest on it. If the interest rate is 6 percent, *a dollar received now is equivalent to $1.06 received a year hence.* Why? Because if you invest the dollar now, you'll get $1.06 in a year. Similarly, *a dollar received now is equivalent to $(1.06)^2$ dollars two years hence.* Why? Because if you invest the dollar now, you'll get 1.06 dollars in a year; and if you reinvest this amount for another year at 6 percent, you'll get $(1.06)^2$ dollars.

With this in mind, let's determine how much an estate of $100,000 (to be received two years hence) is worth now. If the interest rate is 6 percent, each dollar received two years hence is worth $1 \div (1.06)^2$ dollars now. Thus, if the interest rate is 6 percent, the estate is worth $100,000 \div (1.06)^2$ dollars now. Since $(1.06)^2 = 1.1236$, it is worth

$$\frac{\$100,000}{1.1236} = \$89,000.$$

In general, *if the interest rate is $100 \times r$ percent per year, a dollar received now is worth $(1 + r)^2$ dollars two years from now.* Thus, whatever the value of the interest rate may be, the estate is worth

$$\frac{\$100,000}{(1 + r)^2}.$$

Table 14.2
Present Value of a Future Dollar

NUMBER OF YEARS HENCE (THAT DOLLAR IS RECEIVED)	INTEREST RATE (PERCENT)			
	4	6	8	10
		(cents)		
1	96.2	94.3	92.6	90.9
2	92.5	89.0	85.7	82.6
3	89.0	83.9	79.4	75.1
4	85.5	79.2	73.5	68.3
5	82.3	74.7	68.1	62.0
10	67.6	55.8	46.3	38.5
15	55.5	41.7	31.5	23.9
20	45.6	31.1	21.5	14.8

The principle that a dollar now is worth more than a dollar later is of fundamental importance. If you don't understand it, you don't understand a basic precept of the world of finance. Although the example considered in previous paragraphs pertains only to a two-year period, this principle remains valid no matter how long the period of time we consider. Table 14.2 shows the present value of a dollar received at various points of time in the future. As you can see, its present value declines with the length of time before the dollar is received (so long as the interest rate remains constant).

TEST YOURSELF

1. Suppose that the demand curve for loanable funds is as follows:

QUANTITY DEMANDED (BILLIONS OF DOLLARS)	INTEREST RATE (PERCENT)
50	4
40	6
30	8
20	10

Plot the demand curve on a graph. Describe the various kinds of borrowers that are on the demand side of the market for loanable funds.

Suppose that the supply curve for loanable funds is as follows:

QUANTITY SUPPLIED (BILLIONS OF DOLLARS)	INTEREST RATE (PERCENT)
20	4
25	6
30	8
35	10

Plot the supply curve on the same graph you used to plot the demand curve. What is the equilibrium rate of interest? If usury laws do not permit interest rates to exceed 6 percent, what do you think will happen in this market?

2. Describe the social functions of the interest rate. Do you agree with Aristotle that it is improper to charge interest?

3. Suppose that you can get 10 percent per year from alternative investments and that, if you invest in a particular business, you will get $1,000 per year indefinitely. How much is this investment worth to you?

4. If a firm can borrow money at 10 percent per year and will accept only (riskless) investments that yield 12 percent per year or more, is the firm maximizing profit? Explain.

RENT: NATURE AND SIGNIFICANCE

Besides interest, another type of property income is rent. To understand rent, one must understand what economists mean by land. **Land** is defined by economists as *any input that is fixed in supply, its limits established by nature.* Thus, since certain types of minerals and natural resources are in relatively fixed supply, they are included in the economist's definition of land. Suppose that the supply of an input is completely fixed. Increases in its price will not increase its supply and decreases in its price will not decrease its supply. Following the terminology of the classical economists of the nineteenth century, *the price of such an input is* **rent.** Note that rent means something quite different to an economist than to the man in the street, who considers rent the price

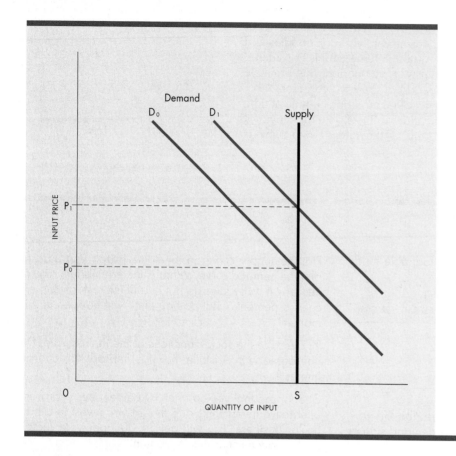

INPUT PRICE

Demand

D_0 D_1 Supply

P_1

P_0

0   S

QUANTITY OF INPUT

Figure 14.4
Rent
Rent is the price of an input in fixed supply. Since its supply curve is vertical, the price of such an input is determined entirely by the demand curve for the input. If the demand curve is D_0, the rent is OP_0; if the demand curve is D_1, the rent is OP_1.

of using an apartment or a car or some other object owned by someone else.

If the supply of an input is fixed, its supply curve is a vertical line, as shown in Figure 14.4. Thus the price of this input, its rent, is determined entirely by the demand curve for the input. If the demand curve is D_0, the rent is OP_0; if the demand curve is D_1, the rent is OP_1. Since the supply of the input is fixed, the price of the input can be lowered without influencing the amount supplied. Thus *a rent is a payment above the minimum necessary to attract this amount of the input*.[6]

Why is it important to know whether a certain payment for inputs is a rent? Because a reduction of the payment will not influence the availability and use of the inputs if the payment is a rent; whereas if it is not a rent, a reduction of the payment is likely to change the allocation of resources. If the government imposes a tax on rents, there will be no effect on the supply of resources to the economy.

[6] In recent years, there has been a tendency among economists to extend the use of the word *rent* to encompass all payments to inputs above the minimum required to make these inputs available to the industry or to the economy. (See Example 14.1.) To a great extent these payments are costs to individual firms; the firms must make such payments to attract and keep these inputs, which are useful to other firms in the industry. But if the inputs have no use in other industries, these payments are not costs to the industry as a whole (or to the economy as a whole) because the inputs would be available to the industry whether or not these payments are made.

The Views of Henry George

In 1879, Henry George (1839–97) published a book, *Progress and Poverty,* in which he argued that rents should be taxed away by the government. In his view, owners of land were receiving substantial rents simply because their land happened to be well situated, not because they were doing anything productive. Since this rent was unearned income and since the supply of land would not be influenced by such a tax, George felt that it was justifiable to tax away such rent. Indeed, he argued that a tax of this sort should be the only tax imposed by the government.

Critics of George's views pointed out that land can be improved, with the result that the supply is not completely price inelastic. Moreover, they argued that if land rents are unearned so are many other kinds of income. In addition, they pointed out that it was unrealistic to expect such a tax to raise the needed revenue. George's single-tax movement gained a number of adherents in the last decades of the nineteenth century, and he even made an unsuccessful bid to become mayor of New York. Arguments in favor of a single tax continue to surface from time to time.

Henry George

Rent: An Example

To make the concept of rent more concrete, consider the following example. There is a lot at the corner of Third Avenue and Winchester Street in a California suburb; this property is on the edge of the town. What will be the rent for this lot? It has various possible uses. It could be the location of a store or restaurant, a small farm, a site for an apartment building, or used for some other purpose. In each possible use, this lot has a certain value as an input.

In a competitive market, this lot will tend to rent for an amount equal to its value in its most productive use. That is, if the value of its marginal product is highest when it is used as the location for a store, a store will be built on it, and the lot will command a rent equal to the value of its marginal product. In this way, the lot will be drawn into the use that seems to yield the highest returns to the renter. From society's point of view, this has much to recommend it, since the use that yields the highest returns is likely to be the one consumers value most highly.

Classical economists viewed rent as a differential that had to be paid for the utilization of better rather than poorer land. They argued as follows. If land becomes scarce, the better lands will receive a nonzero price before the poorer lands. The rent on any acre will rise to the point where it is equal to the difference in productivity between this acre and an acre of no-rent land. Why? Because, as we saw in Chapter 13, the price differential between two inputs will equal the differential in their marginal products.

PROFITS

Besides interest and rent, another important type of property income is profit. Profit is not new to us. In Chapter 6, we discussed at some length the economist's concept of profit and how it varies from the accountant's concept. According to accountants, profit is the amount of money the owner of a firm has left after paying wages, interest, and rent—and after providing proper allowance for the depreciation of buildings and equip-

EXAMPLE 14.1 EXODUS OF SCIENTISTS AND ENGINEERS FROM TEACHING

D. Allan Bromley, President Bush's science adviser, has pointed out that, in mathematics, physics, and engineering, many college teachers have been leaving their jobs to work in industry.

(a) Why do you think that this has been occurring? (b) What might be the effect of such a trend on the size and quality of *future* supplies of scientists and engineers? (c) If society feels that more scientists of a particular type are needed, one way of achieving an increase in supply is to shift the supply curve for this type of scientist to the right, as shown in the graph below. How can the government effect such a shift? (d) Suppose that the supply curve does not shift to the right. If the demand curve for this type of scientist shifts to the right, as shown in the graph, does this result in some scientists of this sort receiving a higher salary than they would be willing to work for? If so, is this a rent?

Solution

(a) Because new Ph.D.'s have been offered higher salaries by industry than by universities. (b) If the quality and number of college teachers were reduced, there might well be an adverse effect on the size and quality of future supplies of scientists and engineers. (c) By scholarship and other programs subsidizing the training of such scientists. (d) If the supply curve does not shift to the right, the equilibrium salary increases from OW_0 to OW_1, and those scientists who were willing to work for a salary of OW_0 receive a windfall of ($OW_1 - OW_0$). Thus it is a rent in the sense that it is a payment above the minimum necessary to attract this amount of this input. But it is not a rent in the sense that the supply curve is vertical. (See footnote 6.)

ment. Economists dissent from this view; their position is that the opportunity costs of the labor, capital, and land contributed by the owner should also be deducted.

Profit Statistics

Available statistics concerning profits are based on the accountant's concept, not the economist's. Before taxes, corporation profits average about 5-10 percent of gross national product. Profits—expressed as a percent of either net worth or sales—vary considerably from industry to industry and from firm to firm. (For example, the drug industry's profits in the postwar period have frequently been about 15-20 percent of net worth—considerably higher than in most other manufacturing industries.) Also, profits vary greatly from year to year, and are much more erratic than wages. They fall more heavily in recessions and rise more rapidly in recoveries than wages do. Table 14.3 shows profit as a percent of stockholders' equity in manufacturing in the United States in 1983–90.

To some extent, the measured differences in profits among firms come about because the profit figures are not corrected for the value of the inputs contributed by the owners. Because they are smarter and more resourceful, some owners provide managerial labor of a much higher quality than other owners do. Profits arising from this fact are, at least in part, wages for superior management. Similarly, some owners put up a lot of the capital and work long hours. Profits arising from these sources are, at least in part, interest on capital and wages for time spent working in the firm.

Innovation, Uncertainty, and Monopoly Power

Why do profits—as economists define them—exist? Three important factors are innovation, uncertainty, and monopoly power. Suppose that an economy was composed of perfectly competitive industries, that entry was completely free, and that no changes in technology—no new processes, no new products, or other innovations—were permitted. Moreover, suppose that everyone could predict the future with perfect accuracy. Under these conditions, there would be no profits, because people would enter industries where profits exist, thus reducing these profits eventually to zero, and leave industries where losses exist, thus reducing these negative profits eventually to zero. This sort of no-profit equilibrium has already been discussed in Chapter 9.

But in the real world, innovations of various kinds are made. For example, Du Pont introduces a new product like nylon, or Henry Ford introduces the assembly line, or Marconi introduces the radio. The people who carry out these bold schemes are the *innovators,* those with vision and the daring to back it up. The innovators are not necessarily the inventors of new techniques or products, although in some cases the innovator and the inventor are the same. Often the innovator takes another's invention, adapts it, and introduces it to the market. According to economists like the late Joseph Schumpeter of Harvard, profits are the rewards earned by innovators. The profits derived from any single innovation eventually erode with competition and imitation, but other innovations replace them, with the result that profits from innovation continue to be made.

In the real world, uncertainty also exists. Indeed, one of the real hazards in attempting to be an innovator is the *risk* involved. According to a theory set forth several decades ago by Frank Knight of the University of Chicago, all economic profit is due to uncertainty. Profit is the reward for risk bearing. Assuming that people would like to avoid risk, they will prefer relatively stable, sure earnings to relatively unstable, uncertain earnings—*if the average level of earnings is the same.* Consequently, to induce people to take the risks involved in owning businesses in various industries, a profit—a premium for risk—must be paid to them. This is similar to the higher wages that, according to the previous chapter, must be paid for jobs where earnings are unstable or uncertain.

Still another reason for the existence of profits is the fact that markets

**Table 14.3
Annual Profit (After Taxes) as a Percentage of Stockholders' Equity, United States, 1983–90**

YEAR	ALL MANU- FACTURING CORPOR- ATIONS	DURABLE GOODS INDUSTRIES	NON- DURABLE GOODS INDUSTRIES
	(percent)		
1983	10.6	8.1	12.7
1984	11.9	11.3	12.4
1985	10.1	9.2	11.0
1986	9.5	7.5	11.5
1987	12.8	11.9	13.7
1988	16.1	14.3	17.9
1989	13.6	11.1	16.2
1990	11.2	7.2	15.0

Source: Economic Report of the President, 1991. The 1990 figures pertain to the third quarter.

Frank Knight

are not perfectly competitive. Under perfect competition, there will be a tendency in the long run for profits to disappear. But, as we have seen, this will not be the case if an industry is a monopoly or oligopoly. Instead, profits may well exist in the long run in such imperfectly competitive industries. And, as we know from Chapter 12, much of our entire economy is composed of imperfectly competitive industries. Monopoly profits are fundamentally the result of "contrived scarcities." Since a firm's demand curve is downward-sloping if competition is imperfect, it pays the firm to take account of the fact that the more it produces, the smaller the price it will receive. In other words, the firm realizes that it will spoil the market if it produces too much. Thus it pays firms to limit their output, and this contrived scarcity is responsible for the existence of the profits they make as a consequence.

THE FUNCTIONS OF PROFITS

To many people, profit seems to be "something for nothing." They do not recognize the innovative or risk-bearing functions of the owners of the firm, and consequently see no reason for the existence of profits. Other people, aware that profits arise because of imperfect competition, ignore the other functions of profit and regard it as entirely the ill-gotten gain of fat monopolists, often smoking big cigars and properly equipped with a rapacious leer. But no group is more hostile to profits than the followers and disciples of Karl Marx. According to Marx, laborers in a capitalist system receive a wage that is barely enough to cover the minimum amount of housing, food, clothing, and other commodities needed for survival. The difference between the amount the employers receive for their products and the amount they pay the laborers that produce them is "surplus value." And, according to Marx, this "surplus value," which includes what we would call profit, is a measure of, and consequence of, exploitation of labor by owners of firms.

Marx's views and those of others who look on profits with suspicion and even distaste are rejected by most economists, who feel that profits play a legitimate and very important role in a capitalistic system. In such a system, consumers, suppliers of inputs, and firms try to advance their own interests. Workers try to maximize their earnings, capitalists look for the highest interest returns, landlords try to get the highest rents, and firm owners seek to maximize their profits. At first glance, this looks like a chaotic, dog-eat-dog situation, but, as we have seen, it actually turns out to be an orderly and efficient system—if competition is present.

PROFITS AND LOSSES: MAINSPRINGS OF A CAPITALISTIC SYSTEM

Profits and losses are mainsprings of any capitalistic system. They signal where resources are needed and where they are too abundant. When there are economic profits in an industry, this is the signal for resources to flow into it; when economic losses exist in an industry, this is the signal for resources to leave it. In addition, profits are very important incentives for innovation, for betting on the future, and for efficiency.

Consider Genentech, a major biotechnology firm. For an entrepreneur like Robert Swanson of Genentech, profits are the bait society dangles be-

DIVERSIFIABLE RISK, NONDIVERSIFIABLE RISK, AND THE CAPITAL ASSET PRICING MODEL

Profit, as we have seen, is a reward for risk bearing. Some kinds of risk can be eliminated by diversification (as we saw on page 111); other kinds cannot. Risk that can be eliminated in this way is called *diversifiable* risk; risk that cannot be eliminated in this way is called *nondiversifiable* risk. Suppose that you are investing in the stock market. *Nondiversifiable risk is the risk that the general level of the stock market will go down because of a recession or for some other reason.* Because the prices of stocks of various companies tend to go up or down together, this kind of risk cannot be eliminated by diversification.

In contrast, *risk due to factors that are specific to a particular company can be eliminated by diversification.* For instance, DuPont's stock may be adversely affected by a new product's being introduced by Union Carbide, or Bethlehem Steel's stock may go down because of a strike. This kind of risk can be eliminated by diversification, because whereas some companies are hurt by new products or strikes during a given period, other companies gain from them. Consequently, if one purchases a considerable number of stocks representing a variety of industries, the effects of such factors are likely to be very small, on the average. Why? Because they will tend to cancel each other out.

In recent decades, the capital asset pricing model developed by economists like William Sharpe of Stanford and John Lintner of Harvard has played an important role on Wall Street, as well as in academic thinking. This theory builds on the long-accepted proposition that investors must receive a higher expected return to induce them to accept higher risk. Thus, if stock in Ford is riskier than stock in General Motors, the expected return from Ford's stock must be greater than that from General Motors' stock. Otherwise, investors would not buy Ford's stock.

In contrast to older doctrine, this theory emphasizes that *not all of the risk in a particular stock must be taken into account in determining how high this stock's expected return must be to compensate the investor for risk bearing.* Surprising as it may seem, *only the nondiversifiable risk is relevant.* Why? Because the diversifiable risk can be eliminated by diversification. Since the diversifiable risk can be avoided so easily, you cannot obtain a higher expected return by assuming this risk. People won't pay you for bearing unnecessary risks.

fore him and his firm to get them to take the risks involved in developing and marketing a new product like Activase, Genentech's gene-spliced heart drug introduced in late 1987. The profits that Genentech earns from this drug will be used to support its new ventures into other areas of biotechnology. The level of profits (or losses) in various fields of biotechnology will signal where more resources are needed and where they would be redundant.

The importance of profits in a free-enterprise economy is clear enough. However, this does not mean that all profits are socially justified or that the system as a whole cannot be improved. Monopoly profits may not be socially justified, and a competitive system, despite its advantages, may produce many socially undesirable effects—for example, an undesirable income distribution. Much more will be said on this score in the next chapter.

THE FUNCTIONAL DISTRIBUTION OF INCOME

In this and the previous chapter, we have been concerned with wages, interest, rent, and profit. How is the total income of the nation as a whole divided among these categories? In other words, what proportion of all income goes to employees? What proportion goes for interest? For rent? For profits? In this section, we take up these questions.

Table 14.4 shows the proportion of national income going for (1) wages and salaries, (2) proprietors' income, (3) corporate profits, (4) interest, and (5) rent.[7] It is clear that wages and salaries are by far the largest of these five income categories. In 1990, about three-fourths of national income went for wages and salaries (including employer contributions to Social Security and pensions). Moreover, this is an understatement of the

Table 14.4
Percentage Shares of National Income, 1900–90

PERIOD	WAGES AND SALARIES	PROPRIETORS' INCOME	CORPORATE PROFITS (PERCENT)	INTEREST	RENT	TOTAL
1900–09	55	24	7	5	9	100
1910–19	54	24	9	5	8	100
1920–29	60	18	8	6	8	100
1930–39	67	15	4	9	5	100
1939–48	65	17	12	3	3	100
1949–58	67	14	13	3	3	100
1963–70	70	12	11	4	3	100
1990	73	9	7	11	—[a]	100

[a] Less than 1 percent.
Source: I. Kravis, "Income Distribution: Functional Share." *International Encyclopedia of the Social Sciences,* New York: Macmillan, 1968, and *Annual Reports of the Council of Economic Advisers.* These figures may not be entirely comparable over time, but they are sufficiently accurate for present purposes.

[7] The concept of rent on which these figures are based is different from the one presented in this chapter, but this does not affect the conclusions presented below.

share of employee compensation in national income, because part of proprietors' income is really wages. As we pointed out in an earlier section, a portion of what the proprietor of the corner drugstore or the local shoe-store makes is compensation for the proprietor's labor, not profit as defined by the economist.

The figures in Table 14.4 indicate a marked reduction over time in the proportion of national income going to proprietors, and a marked increase over time in the proportion going for wages and salaries. Part of this shift is due to the fact that the corporation has become a more dominant organizational form, with the result that many people who would have been individual proprietors owning their own small businesses 50 years ago now work as employed managers for corporations. Another fact that may help to explain this shift is the long-term shift from agriculture (where labor's share of income is low) to manufacturing and services (where labor's share is higher).

Some economists are impressed by the constancy of the share of national income going to labor. Using definitions that are somewhat different than those underlying Table 14.4, they come up with numbers indicating that labor's share has not varied much over time. Other economists, using somewhat different definitions, conclude that labor's share has varied considerably. But one thing is for sure. There is no evidence that a bigger share of the economic pie is going to capitalists in the form of interest, rent, or profits. Perhaps the figures in Table 14.4 exaggerate the extent to which labor's share has increased, but there is certainly no evidence that it has decreased.

TEST YOURSELF

1. Assume that you inherit $1,000, which will be paid to you in two years. If the interest rate is 8 percent, how much is this inheritance worth now? Why?

2. "The supply curve for iron ore is horizontal, so its price is a rent." Comment.

3. "Based on the available data concerning changes over time in labor's share of total income in the United States, it is evident that labor is getting so powerful that it is receiving more and more of the total. This is an important reason for the shortage of capital in the United States." Comment and evaluate.

4. Suppose that a candidate for president proposes that all profits be taxed away. Would you support this proposal? Why, or why not?

SUMMARY

1. Interest is a payment for the use of money. Interest rates vary a great deal, depending on the nature of the borrower and the type and riskiness of the loan. One very important function of interest rates is to allocate the supply of loanable funds.

2. The pure interest rate—the interest rate on riskless loans—is, like any price, determined by the interaction of supply and demand. However, because of the influence of the government on both the demand and supply sides of the market, it is clear that the pure interest rate is to a considerable extent a matter of public policy.

3. Capital is composed of inputs produced by the economic system itself. Our economy uses very roundabout methods of production and devotes a considerable amount of its productive capacity to the production of capital.

4. If more and more capital is produced during a particular period, consumers must cut further and further into their consumption during that period. This process is called saving.

5. In a capitalist system, each capital good has a market value that can be determined by capitalizing its earnings.

Holding constant an asset's annual return, the asset's worth is higher, the lower the rate of return available on other investments.

6. Any piece of capital has a rate of return, which indicates its net productivity. An asset's rate of return is the interest rate earned on the investment in the asset. If firms maximize profits, they must carry out all projects where the rate of return exceeds the interest rate at which they can borrow.

7. Rent is the return derived by inputs that are fixed in supply. Since the supply of the input is fixed, its price can be lowered without influencing the amount supplied. Thus, if the government imposes taxes on rents, there will be no effect on the supply of resources to the economy.

8. Another important type of property income is profits. Available statistics on profits are based on the accountant's concept, not the economist's, with the result that they include the opportunity costs of the labor, capital, and land contributed by the owners of the firm. Profits play a very important and legitimate role in a free enterprise system.

9. Two of the important factors responsible for the existence of profits are innovation and uncertainty. Profits are the rewards earned by innovators and a payment for risk-bearing. Still another reason for the existence of profits is monopoly power; due to contrived scarcity, profits are made by firms in imperfectly competitive markets.

CONCEPTS FOR REVIEW

Interest

Rate of interest

Pure rate of interest

Demand curve for loanable
  funds

Rate of return

Diversifiable risk

Supply curve for loanable funds

Liquidity preference theory

Capital budgeting

Primary inputs

Capital

Saving

Nondiversifiable risk

Capitalization

Land

Rent

Innovator

Risk

Capital asset pricing model

INCOME INEQUALITY AND POVERTY

ON SEPTEMBER 27, 1991 the front-page headline of the *New York Times* was "Poverty Rate Rose Sharply Last Year as Incomes Slipped." The fact is that some Americans are poor—so poor that they suffer from malnutrition—and while poverty may not be a sin, it is no less an inconvenience to the poor. Given the affluence of American society, one is led to ask why poverty exists and whether it cannot be abolished by proper public policies. The purpose of this chapter is to examine these questions.

HOW MUCH INEQUALITY OF INCOME?

We don't have to be very perceptive social observers to recognize that there are great differences in income levels in the United States. But our idea of what the distribution of income looks like depends on the sort of family and community we come from. A child brought up in Lake Forest, a wealthy suburb of Chicago, is unlikely to be as aware of the incidence of poverty as a child brought up on Chicago's poor South Side. For a preliminary glimpse of the extent of ***income inequality*** in the United States, scan Table 15.1, which shows the percentage of all families in the United States that were situated in various income classes in 1989. According to the table, the bottom fifth of the nation's families received an income of less than $16,003 in 1989. On the other hand, the top fifth of the nation's families received an income of $59,550 or more in 1989.

It may come as a surprise to some that so large a percentage of the nation's families made less than $16,003. The image of the affluent society projected in the Sunday supplements and on some television programs is strangely out of tune with these facts. Yet, to put these figures in world perspective, it should be recognized that Americans are very rich relative to other peoples. This fact is shown clearly by Table 15.2, which gives for various countries the 1988 level of income per person, which is the total income of each nation divided by its population. The United States is among the leaders in this table.

WHY INEQUALITY?

Nonetheless, recognizing that our poor are better off than the bulk of the population in many other countries, the fact remains that there is substantial inequality of income in this country. Why is this the case? Based

Table 15.1
Percentage Distribution of Families, by Income, 1989

MONEY INCOME (DOLLARS)	PERCENT OF ALL FAMILIES	PERCENT OF TOTAL INCOME RECEIVED	PERCENT OF FAMILIES WITH THIS AND LOWER INCOMES	PERCENT OF INCOME RECEIVED BY FAMILIES WITH THIS AND LOWER INCOMES
Under 16,003	20	5	20	5
16,003–28,000	20	11	40	16
28,000–40,800	20	17	60	33
40,800–59,550	20	24	80	57
59,550–98,960	15	25[a]	95	82
98,960 and over	5	18	100	100
Total	100	100		

[a] Because of rounding errors, the figures in this column do not sum to 100. To make the total equal 100, this number was changed slightly. For present purposes, this is of no importance.
Source: Department of Commerce.

Table 15.2
Selected Countries Grouped by Approximate Level of Income per Capita, 1988

I. Countries with income per capita exceeding $10,000

United States	Denmark	Sweden
Australia	France	Japan
Canada	Germany	Switzerland

II. Countries with income per capita between $2,500 and $10,000

Uruguay	Greece	Yugoslavia
Ireland	Hong Kong	Thailand
Soviet Union	Spain	Venezuela
Algeria	Iran	Mexico
Brazil	Malaysia	Turkey

III. Countries and regions with income per capita less than $2,500

India	El Salvador	Most of Africa
Indonesia	Haiti	Much of Asia

All figures are expressed in 1988 dollars.
Source: R. Summers and A. Heston, "The Penn World Table (Mark 5): An Expanded Set of International Comparisons," *Quarterly Journal of Economics,* May 1991.

on our discussion of labor and property incomes in previous chapters, this question is not hard to answer. One reason is that some people possess greater abilities than others. Since Mark Davis and Darryl Strawberry have extraordinary skill as baseball players, it is easy to understand why they make a lot of money (over $3.6 million each in 1991 alone).[1] Another reason is differences in the amount of education and training people receive. Thus physicians or lawyers must receive a higher income

[1] *New York Times,* April 10, 1991, p. B8.

than people in occupations requiring little or no training. (Otherwise it would not pay people to undergo medical or legal training.) Still another reason is that some people own large amounts of property. Thus, because of a shrewd choice of ancestry, the Fords, Rockefellers, and Mellons get high incomes from inherited wealth. Still other reasons are that some people have managed to obtain monopoly power, and others have had an extraordinary string of good luck.

A MEASURE OF INCOME INEQUALITY

To what extent has income inequality in the United States changed? Some people say that because of the advent of the "welfare state" the nation has moved rapidly toward greater equality of income. Others say that the rich are getting richer and the poor are getting poorer. Who is right? To answer this question, we need some way to measure the degree of income inequality. The most commonly used technique is the ***Lorenz curve,*** which plots the percentage of people, going from the poorest up, on the horizontal axis, and the percentage of total income they get on the vertical axis.

The Lorenz curve based on the figures in Table 15.1 is shown in Figure 15.1. To see how this diagram was constructed, note that in Table 15.1 families with incomes under $16,003 accounted for 20 percent of all families, but only 5 percent of all income. Thus, plotting 20 percent on the horizontal axis against 5 percent on the vertical axis, we get point A. The table also indicated that families with incomes under $28,000 accounted for 40 percent of all families, but only 16 percent of all income. Plotting these figures in the same way, we get point B. Connecting up all points like A and B, we obtain the Lorenz curve in Figure 15.1.

CASE 1: NO INEQUALITY. Two extreme cases must be understood to see how the Lorenz curve is used. First, suppose that *incomes were the same for all families* (or whatever kinds of recipients are under consideration). Then the Lorenz curve would be a straight line connecting the origin of the diagram with its upper right-hand corner. That is, it would be OP in Figure 15.1. To see this, note that, if incomes are distributed equally, the lowest 10 percent of the families receive 10 percent of the total income, the lowest 20 percent of the families receive 20 percent of the total income, and so forth. Plotting 10 percent on the horizontal axis against 10 percent on the vertical axis, 20 percent on the horizontal axis against 20 percent on the vertical axis, and so forth, one gets a Lorenz curve of OP.

CASE 2: COMPLETE INEQUALITY. Suppose that *incomes were distributed completely unequally*—that is, one person has all of the income and the rest have none. In this case, the Lorenz curve would lie along the horizontal axis from O to M and along the vertical line from M to P. It would be OMP in Figure 15.1. Why? Because the lowest 10 percent of the families have zero percent of the total income, the lowest 20 percent of the families have zero percent of the total income, and so, in fact, do the lowest 99 percent of the families. Plotting 10 percent on the horizontal axis against zero percent on the vertical axis, 20 percent on the horizontal axis against zero percent on the vertical axis, and so on, one gets a Lorenz curve that lies along the horizontal axis from O to M. But since 100 percent of the families must receive 100 percent of the income, the Lorenz curve must then jump up from M to P.

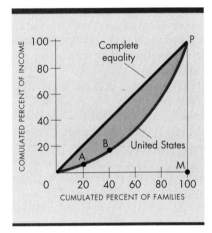

Figure 15.1
Lorenz Curve for Family Income, United States, 1989
OP is the Lorenz curve if income were distributed equally. The shaded area between this hypothetical Lorenz curve and the actual Lorenz curve is a measure of income inequality.

THE IMPORTANCE OF THE SHADED AREA. These two cases make it clear that *the shaded area in Figure 15.1*—the deviation of the actual Lorenz curve from the Lorenz curve corresponding to complete equality of income—*is a measure of income inequality.* The larger this shaded area, the greater the extent of income inequality. Figure 15.2 shows the Lorenz curve for the income distributions in three countries—*D, E,* and *F*. As reflected in the Lorenz curves, income inequality is greater in *F* than in *E,* and greater in *E* than in *D*. Why? Because the area between the actual Lorenz curve and the Lorenz curve corresponding to complete equality is greater in *F* than in *E,* and greater in *E* than in *D*.

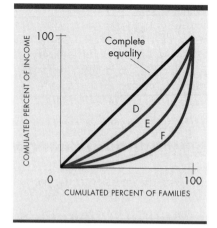

Figure 15.2
Lorenz Curves for Countries D, E, and F
Income inequality is greater in country *F* than in country *E,* and greater in country *E* than in country *D*.

TRENDS IN INCOME INEQUALITY

Let us now return to the question posed at the beginning of the previous section: To what extent has income inequality in the United States changed? Figure 15.3 shows the Lorenz curves for the income distributions in 1929 and 1962. These curves make it clear that there was a considerable reduction in income inequality. The share of income going to the top 20 percent declined by one-fifth between 1929 and 1962. This change, described by some writers as an "income revolution," did not occur gradually throughout the period. Instead, essentially all the reduction in income inequality occurred before the end of World War II. Without question, this was a notable change in the American economic landscape.

One of the reasons for the reduction in income inequality between 1929 and the end of World War II was the increased importance of wages and salaries relative to other sources of income. Wages and salaries are more equally distributed than income from self-employment and property. Also, many public programs were established to provide income for the poor. (The details of these programs are described below.) In addition, the shift from substantial prewar unemployment to the full employment of World War II narrowed wage differentials among various types of workers. Further, the inequality in the distribution of wealth was reduced during this period.

During the 1980s there was an increase in income inequality. The share of total before-tax income received by the 20 percent of American families with highest incomes rose during this period, while the share received by the 20 percent with lowest incomes fell. However, this increase in income inequality was much too small to offset the reduction before and after World War II.

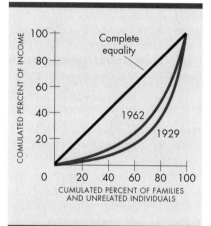

Figure 15.3
Changes over Time in Lorenz Curves for Family Income in the United States
Income inequality in the United States decreased between 1929 and 1962, as indicated by the Lorenz curves.

EFFECTS OF THE TAX STRUCTURE ON INCOME INEQUALITY

So far we have looked at the distribution of before-tax income. But we must also consider the effect of the tax system on income inequality.

A tax is ***progressive*** if the rich pay a higher proportion of their income for the tax than do the poor. A tax is ***regressive*** if the rich pay a smaller proportion of their income for the tax than do the poor.

Needless to say, people who feel that the tax system should promote a redistribution of income from rich to poor favor progressive, not regressive taxes. Obviously, the personal income tax is progressive, since the tax rate is greater for high-income people than for low-income people. Other progressive taxes are inheritance or estate taxes. (The federal government levies a gift tax to prevent wealthy people from circumventing the estate tax by giving their money away before death.) This is applauded by reformers who oppose accumulation and preservation of inherited wealth. But, as in the case of the personal income tax, the portion of an estate subject to taxes can be reduced through clever use of various loopholes, all quite legal. Thus the estate tax is not as progressive as it looks.

Not all taxes are progressive; examples of regressive taxes are not hard to find. General sales taxes of the sort used by most states and some cities are regressive, since high-income people pay a smaller percentage of their income in sales taxes than do low-income people. The Social Security tax is also regressive. It is difficult to tell whether the corporation income tax is progressive or regressive. At first glance, it seems progressive because the owners of corporations—the stockholders—tend to be wealthy people; and to the extent that the corporate income tax is paid from earnings that might otherwise be paid to the stockholders, one might conclude that it is progressive. But this ignores the possibility that the corporation may pass the tax on to the consumer by charging a higher price; in this case the tax may not be progressive.

EXAMPLE 15.1   ECONOMIC EFFECTS OF ILLEGAL ALIENS

During the early 1980s, the number of illegal aliens in the United States was estimated to be between 2 and 12 million. In 1986, Congress, attempting to curb illegal immigration, passed the Immigration Reform and Control Act. Suppose that the value-of-marginal-product curve for labor in the U.S. market is as follows:

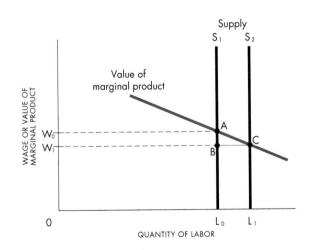

(a) If S_1 is the supply curve for labor *without* immigration of illegal aliens, what would be total labor in-

come under these circumstances? (b) If S_2 is the supply curve for labor *with* immigration of illegal aliens, what would be the total labor income of the native U.S. population under these circumstances? (c) Will the owners of U.S. capital and land benefit from this immigration? Why or why not? (d) Why does La Raza Unidad, a farm labor union representing many Spanish-speaking American citizens, oppose such immigration?

Solution

(a) Total labor income will equal the area of rectangle $OW_0 A L_0$, since it will equal the wage (OW_0) times the quantity of labor employed (OL_0). (b) Since the total supply of native U.S. labor is OL_0, total labor income will equal the area of rectangle $OW_1 BL_0$, since it will equal the wage (OW_1) times OL_0. (c) Yes. The value of the marginal product of the extra ($OL_1 - OL_0$) workers exceeds their wage, OW_1, as can be seen in the graph on the left. Also, the owners of U.S. capital and land benefit from the fact that they can pay native U.S. labor a lower wage. (d) One reason may be that such immigration lowers the wage received by American citizens engaged in farm labor.

Who Pays the Taxes and Receives the Transfer Payments

To get a better picture of the extent to which the government—in terms of both the money it spends and the taxes it levies—takes from the rich and gives to the poor, studies have been carried out to determine how much people in various income brackets pay in taxes and receive in transfer payments (Social Security, welfare payments, food stamps, Medicare, and Medicaid). The results of one important study of this sort are shown in Figure 15.4. As you can see, the effect of taxes (federal, state, and local) and transfers is to reduce income inequality. However, this is due largely to the fact that transfer payments go mainly to the poor. Taken by itself, the tax system is only mildly progressive or slightly regressive, depending on the study's assumptions. Moreover, there is evidence that the tax system was less progressive (or more regressive) in 1985 than in 1966.[2]

Estimates of this sort are interesting, but it is difficult to predict the *incidence* of some taxes—that is, it is difficult to know who *really* pays them. The incidence of certain taxes is relatively easy to determine. For example, it is generally accepted that the personal income tax is paid by the person whose income is taxed. But there are other cases—such as the corporation income taxes we just mentioned—where it is difficult to tell how much of the tax burden the firm shifts to the consumer.[3] For these and other reasons, there is considerable controversy over the extent to which the spending and taxing activities of the government really are progressive or regressive.

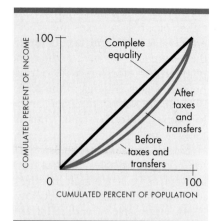

Figure 15.4
Effect of Federal Income Tax and Transfer Payments on Lorenz Curve, United States
In the United States, inequality of income after taxes and transfers is less than inequality of income before taxes and transfers.

INCOME INEQUALITY: THE PROS AND CONS

The Case against Income Inequality

Many distinguished social philosophers have debated the merits and demerits of making the income distribution more equal. We cannot consider all the subtler points, but those who favor greater equality make four main arguments.

1. They say that inequality of income lessens total consumer satisfaction because an extra dollar given to a poor man provides him with more extra satisfaction than the loss of a dollar takes away from a rich man. According to A. C. Pigou, "It is evident that any transference of income from a relatively rich man to a relatively poor man of similar temperament, since it enables more intense wants to be satisfied at the expense of less intense wants, must increase the aggregate sum of satisfactions."[4]

[2] J. Pechman, *Who Paid the Taxes, 1966–85?*, Washington, D.C.: Brookings Institution, 1985. Based on different assumptions about tax incidence, E. Browning and W. Johnson have concluded that the tax system is more progressive than Pechman concludes.

[3] To see how the burden of a tax can be shifted, consider the effects of an *excise* tax—a tax imposed on each unit sold of a particular product. The federal government imposes excise taxes on liquor and tobacco, among many other products. The immediate effect of these taxes is to raise the price of the commodity since the supply curve will be shifted upward and to the left. If demand is price inelastic, most of the burden of the tax is shifted to the consumer. Under these circumstances, firms sell almost as many units of the product as before the tax was imposed, despite the higher price induced by the tax. On the other hand, if supply is relatively inelastic, the burden is borne mainly by the producer. Usually, the aim of excise taxes is to put the burden on consumers. In the case of liquor and tobacco there clearly is a feeling that drinking and smoking smack of sin, and sinners should pay, in this world and the next.

[4] A. C. Pigou, *Economics of Welfare*, 4th ed., London: Macmillan, 1948, p. 89.

EQUAL PAY FOR WORK OF "COMPARABLE WORTH"

Women's earnings tend to be considerably lower than men's, the percentage gap being about 25 percent for persons 25–34 years of age and almost 37 percent for persons 35–44 years of age. A striking fact about female employment is that, although women can be found in virtually all occupations, they predominate overwhelmingly in a few like nursing and secretarial work. In 1986, women constituted 94 percent of registered nurses, 98 percent of secretaries, and 85 percent of waiters and waitresses in the United States.

Some believe that these jobs are underpaid because they tend to be filled by women, and to eliminate what they regard as a major inequity, they argue for "equal pay for work of comparable worth." The idea is to compare the worth of one occupation with that of another occupation, and to press for equal wage rates for them if they are judged to be of equal worth. Thus, if a nurse does work that is of equal worth to that of an accountant, nurses should get the same wage as accountants.

To measure the worth of an occupation, many proponents of "comparable worth" propose the use of a job evaluation point system. In 1983, a federal court found the state of Washington guilty of discrimination because it paid male-dominated occupations more than "comparable" female-dominated occupations. To determine what occupations were comparable, every state job was evaluated in terms of "accountability," "knowledge and skills," "mental demands," and "working conditions." A committee decided how many points to give each occupation on each of these criteria, and two occupations were regarded of comparable worth if they got the same total number of points.

An enormous amount of controversy has engulfed this decision, which said that Washington should raise women's wages and grant restitution for past injuries to them. Although higher courts reversed this

decision, many politicians have supported the idea that an occupation's wage rate should be determined in this way by "comparable worth." In 1989, a law was enacted in Ontario, Canada, that says that employers must assess jobs in which at least 60 percent of the employees are women, and use such a job evaluation system to see how much women should be paid.

Many economists are opposed to the use of such job evaluation systems to set wage rates. In their view, the proper determinants of wage rates are the supply and demand curves discussed in Chapter 13, which together set wage rates in competitive markets. To ignore these supply and demand curves is to run the risk that some occupations will have shortages while others will have too many people. Certainly, job evaluation systems of this sort may reduce economic efficiency. However, proponents of these job evaluation systems emphasize equity, not efficiency; in their view, these systems will promote equity.

A problem in this very appealing argument is its assumption that the rich man and the poor man have the same capacities to gain enjoyment from income. Most economists believe that there is no scientific way to make such comparisons (as emphasized in Appendix C). They deny that the satisfaction one person derives from an extra dollar of income can be measured against the satisfaction another person derives from an extra dollar. Although such comparisons may be drawn, they rest on ethical, not scientific, grounds.

2. It is argued that income inequality is likely to result in unequal opportunities for young people to gain advanced education and training. The children of the rich can get an education, while the children of the poor often cannot. The result is that some able and productive people may be denied an education simply because their parents are poor. This is a waste of resources.

3. It is argued that income inequality is likely to lead to political inequality. The rich may well influence legislation and political decisions more heavily than the poor, and there is likely to be one kind of justice for the rich and another kind for the poor.

4. In the past few years, the arguments for income equality have been carried a step forward by John Rawls, the Harvard philosopher. He says that, *if people were framing a constitution for society without knowing what their class position would be, they would opt for equality.* And he argues that "all social values . . . are to be distributed equally unless an unequal distribution is to the advantage of society's least privileged group." Although Rawls's book, *A Theory of Justice,* has had considerable impact, many economists have pointed out that his prescription for society might not appeal to people who were willing to take risks. Suppose that you were framing a social constitution and that you could establish a society that guaranteed every family $30,000 a year (no more, no less) or one where 99 percent of all families would receive $40,000 and 1 percent would receive $24,000. You might choose the latter kind of society because, although there is a small chance that you would do worse than in the egalitarian case, the chance of doing better seems worth this risk.

The Case for Income Inequality

In general, people who favor income inequality make five arguments.

1. They argue that income inequality is needed to give people an incentive to work and create. After all, if everyone receives the same income, why bother to increase your production, or to try to invent a new process, or to work overtime? Whatever you do, your income will be the same. This is an important point, though it overlooks the fact that nonmonetary incentives like pride in a job well done can be as important as monetary incentives.

2. Advocates of income inequality claim that it permits greater savings, and thus greater capital formation. Although this seems reasonable, it is not hard to cite cases where countries with greater inequality of income invest less, not more, than countries with less inequality of income. Thus some Middle Eastern countries with great income inequality have not had relatively high investment rates.

3. Advocates of income inequality say that the rich have been important patrons of new and high-quality products that benefit the entire society. They argue that there are social advantages in the existence of certain people with the wherewithal to pioneer in consumption and to support art and culture. In their view, a completely egalitarian society would be a rather dull affair.

4. Advocates of income inequality point out that even if everyone received the same income, the poor would not be helped a great deal, because the wealthy are relatively few. If the riches of the rich were transferred to the poor, each person would get only a little, because there are so many poor and so few rich.

5. According to Harvard's Robert Nozick and others, *one must look at the justice of the process leading to the distribution of income and wealth in order to determine whether a certain degree of income inequality is unfair.* For example, suppose that an entertainer carries out a series of shows that are very successful, and that she makes a lot of money. The process by which she makes this money is entirely legitimate. (People voluntarily pay for the tickets to her shows—and enjoy every minute of them!) Thus, according to this view, the resulting inequality of income is not unfair.

The Tradeoff between Equality and Efficiency

Measures taken to reduce inequality are likely to decrease economic efficiency. In other words, if we reduce inequality, we may well cut society's total output. Why? Because, as pointed out in the previous section, people are likely to have less incentive to produce if their incomes are much the same regardless of how much they produce. This does not mean that all measures designed to reduce income inequality are bad. What it does mean is that, if you want to reduce income inequality, you should be sensitive to the effects on output. In particular, you should try to find policies that will attain a given reduction in inequality at a minimum cost in terms of reduced output.

Consider, for example, the effects of very high income tax rates. Although it is sometimes argued that the tax rate for people making several hundred thousand dollars a year should be 80 or 90 percent, one important problem with such proposals is that they might well reduce the amount of work done and output produced. Why put in that extra week of work if Uncle Sam takes 80 or 90 percent of your earnings?

In view of the strong feelings of many advocates and opponents of reduced income inequality, it is not surprising that they sometimes make extreme statements about the nature of the tradeoff between equality and efficiency. Some egalitarians deny that there is any tradeoff at all. They claim that inequality can be reduced without any cut in output. Some opponents of reductions in income inequality assert that there will be a catastrophic fall in output if the existing income distribution is tampered with. Although far too little is known about the quantitative character of this tradeoff, there seems to be general agreement among economists that the truth lies somewhere between these two extremes.

People vary considerably in their evaluation of how much society should pay (in terms of decreased total output) for a particular reduction in income inequality. The late Arthur Okun of the Brookings Institution suggested that, to characterize your own feelings on this score, it is useful to view money as a liquid and to visualize a bucket which carries money from the rich to the poor.[5] The bucket is leaky, so only part of what is

---

[5] Arthur Okun, *Equality and Efficiency,* Washington, D.C.: Brookings Institution, 1975. For an excerpt from this book, see E. Mansfield, *Principles of Microeconomics: Readings, Issues, Cases,* 4th ed., New York: Norton, 1983.

taken from the rich can be given to the poor. If the leak is very small, a dollar taken from the rich may result in 99 cents going to the poor. Many people would accept a loss of this magnitude. If the leak is very large, a dollar taken from the rich may result in only 5 cents going to the poor. Few people would accept this big a loss. How big a loss would you accept? The larger the leak that you would find acceptable, the more willing you are to accept output losses in order to attain decreases in income inequality.

The argument between the advocates and opponents of reduced income inequality involves much more than economics. Whether you favor greater or less income inequality depends on your ethical and political beliefs. It is not a matter economics alone can settle. What economists can do is assess the degree of income inequality in a country and suggest ways to alter the gap between the haves and have-nots in accord with the dictates of the people or their leaders. In recent decades, economists in and out of government have devoted much effort to designing programs aimed at reducing poverty. To understand these programs, we must discuss what poverty is, and who the poor are.

WHAT IS POVERTY?

Some people are fond of saying that everything is relative. Certainly this is true of poverty. Relative to the Mellons or Rockefellers, practically all of us are poor; but relative to the homeless who sleep in railroad and bus terminals, practically all of us are rich. Moreover, poverty is certainly subjective. Consider the average young executive making $50,000 a year. After a bad day at the office or a particularly expensive family shopping spree, he is likely to tell anyone who will listen that he is as poor as a church mouse.

There is no well-defined income level that can be used in all times and places as a touchstone to define poverty. Poverty is partly a matter of how one person's income stacks up against that of others. What most people in America today regard as stark poverty would have seemed like luxury to many Americans of 200 years ago—and would seem like luxury in parts of Asia and Africa today. Consequently, one must be careful not to define poverty in such a way that it cannot be eliminated—and then try to eliminate it. If poverty is defined as being in the bottom 10 percent of the income distribution, how can a war against poverty ever be won? Regardless of what measures are taken, there will always be a bottom 10 percent of the income distribution, unless all income inequality is eliminated (which is highly unlikely).

Perhaps the most widely accepted definition of *poverty* in the United States today is the one developed by the Social Security Administration, which began by determining the cost of a *minimal* nutritionally sound food plan (given by the Department of Agriculture). Then, since low-income families spend about one-third of their incomes on food, this food cost was multiplied by 3 to obtain an income level that was used as a criterion for poverty. Families with less income were regarded as "living below the poverty level."

Based on such computations, a family of four (including two children) needed an income of about $13,359 to make it barely over the Social Security Administration's poverty line in 1990. Although one could quarrel with this figure on various counts, most people probably would agree that families with income below this level are poor.[6]

Two Case Studies

Particular cases of poverty are generally more illuminating and impressive than discussions in the abstract. Consider the following two actual cases in New York City (the names are fictitious).

THE SMITH FAMILY. The Smiths—Christopher, 47, and Irene, 35—opened a small restaurant after years of saving. Within a month, Christopher had a severe heart attack and was laid up in the hospital. The Smiths lost the restaurant, and Irene went to work as a nurse's aide to supplement her husband's small disability benefits. After about a year of working and trying to take care of her husband and two children—John, 13, and Deborah, 12—Irene collapsed from the strain and had to enter a mental hospital. While she was away, a relative took care of Christopher and the children. After getting out of the hospital, Irene learned that her husband had cancer and required expensive surgery. She became so upset that the doctor called in one of the city's charity agencies, which tried to help this troubled and impoverished family as best it could.

THE JONES FAMILY. Jean Jones, 35, is trying to raise seven children. Her husband, an unskilled laborer, never made much money. He drank a lot, terrified Mrs. Jones and the children with his abuse, and was an unfaithful husband. Four years ago, Mrs. Jones separated from him. She gets along as best she can on public assistance, but is having a difficult time. Two of the children have been arrested for theft; two others are in trouble in school; and one daughter is pregnant out of wedlock. Mrs. Jones feels beaten. In recent months, through the help of neighbors, she has consulted a community service bureau where the social workers have given her help and encouragement. But she obviously needs a great deal of aid if she and her family are to get their heads above water.

Neither of these cases is typical. Since they were cited by the *New York Times* as being among New York's 100 neediest cases, it is fair to say that their plight is probably worse than that of the great bulk of America's poor. But they provide some idea of just how bad things can get; and one has to be hardhearted indeed not to feel compassion for people like the Smiths and Mrs. Jones.

INCIDENCE AND CAUSES OF POVERTY

Because college students tend to come from relatively well-off families, they often are unaware of the number of families in the United States whose incomes fall below the Social Security Administration's poverty line. According to estimates made by the federal government in 1990, about 13 percent of the population in the United States was below this line. In absolute terms, this means that over 30 million people were

---

[6] The basic figures come from the Department of Commerce's *Current Population Reports,* which explain in detail the way in which these figures are derived. The method described in the text is crude, but it provides results that are quite close to those of more complicated methods. Since 1969, the poverty line has been calculated on the basis of the Consumer Price Index, not the price of food.

poor—usually not as poor as the Smiths or Mrs. Jones, but poor enough to fall below the criterion described above.

Over the long run, the incidence of poverty (measured by this criterion) generally has been declining in the United States. In 1947, about 30 percent; in 1960, about 20 percent; and in 1990, about 13 percent of the people were poor by this definition. This is what we would expect. As the average level of income rises, the proportion of the population falling below the poverty line (which is defined by a relatively fixed dollar amount of income) will tend to decrease. But the fact that poverty has been declining in the long run does not mean that this process is going on as fast as it should. Many observers feel, as we shall see in subsequent sections, that poverty could and should be eradicated more rapidly.

Naturally, the poor are not confined to any particular demographic group, but some types of families are much more likely than others to be below the poverty line. In particular, *blacks are much more likely to be poor than whites*. In 1989, 31 percent of blacks were poor, whereas 10 percent of whites were poor. Also, *families headed by females are much more likely to be poor than families headed by males*. In addition, very large families—7 persons and over—are much more likely than others to be poor.

To a considerable extent, the reasons why families are poor lie beyond the control of the families themselves. About one-third of the poor adults have suffered a disability of some sort, or the premature death of the family breadwinner, or family dissolution. Some have had to face a smaller demand for their occupation (because of technological or other change) or the decline of their industry or geographical area. Some have simply lived "too long"—their savings have given out before their minds and bodies did. Another instrumental factor in making some families poor is discrimination of various kinds. The most obvious type is racial, but others exist as well—discrimination based on sex, religion, age, residence, education, and seniority. In addition, some people are poor because they have very limited ability or little or no motivation. These factors should not be overlooked.

Finally, there is sometimes a tendency for poverty to be self-perpetuating. Families tend to be poor year after year, and their children tend to be poor. Because the families are poor, the children are poorly educated, poorly fed, and poorly cared for, and poverty is transmitted from one generation to the next. It is a vicious cycle.

TEST YOURSELF

1. Suppose that the following data pertain to the income distribution in the nation of Upper Usher in 1991:

INCOME (DOLLARS)	PERCENT OF FAMILIES WITH INDICATED INCOME
2,000	40
4,000	30
6,000	20
10,000	10

Plot the Lorenz curve for this nation in 1991.

2. In 1992, suppose that the income distribution in Upper Usher is as follows:

INCOME (DOLLARS)	PERCENT OF FAMILIES WITH INDICATED INCOME
2,000	20
4,000	40
6,000	35
10,000	5

Plot the 1992 Lorenz curve, and compare it with the

1991 curve. Did income inequality in this nation increase or decrease between 1991 and 1992?

3. Persons or families are classified as poor on the basis of their current money income. Should the following items also be taken into account? (a) The assets of the person or family; (b) the existence of rich relatives of the person or family; (c) the person's or family's income over a period of years, not a single year.

SOCIAL INSURANCE

Old-Age Insurance

Until about 50 years ago, the federal government played little or no role in helping the poor. Private charity was available in limited amounts, and the state and local governments provided some help, but the general attitude was "sink or swim." Self-reliance and self-support were the watchwords. The Great Depression of the 1930s, which changed so many attitudes, also made a marked change in this area. In 1935, with the passage of the Social Security Act, the federal government established a social insurance system providing compulsory old-age insurance for both workers and self-employed people, as well as unemployment insurance. By 1990, about 40 million Americans were receiving about $20 billion per month in benefits from the resulting system of old-age and survivors' insurance.

Every wage earner covered under the Social Security Act pays a tax, which in 1991 amounted to 7.65 percent of the first $53,400 of his or her annual earnings. The employer also pays a tax, which is equal to that paid by the employee. The amount that one can expect to receive each month in **old-age insurance** benefits depends on one's average monthly earnings. Also, the size of the benefits depends on the number of years one has worked. In 1991, if you retired at 65 and if you had steady lifetime earnings of about $40,000 per year, you would receive about $1,000 per month. If you retire at 65, the monthly benefits are greater than if you retire at 62. These benefits are a retirement annuity. In other words, they are paid to the wage earner from the date of retirement to the time he or she dies. In addition, when a wage earner dies, **Social Security** provides payments to his or her spouse, to dependent parents, and to children until they are about 18 years of age. Further, payments are made to a wage earner (and dependents), if he or she is totally disabled and unable to work.

Controversies over Social Security

There are a number of controversial aspects of the Social Security program.

1. If you work past the retirement age of 65, you can be penalized considerably. For every three dollars in wages that you earn above and beyond $9,720 in 1991, you lose one dollar in Social Security benefits. Thus, since you must pay taxes on your earnings, you get to keep well under two-thirds of every extra dollar that you earn in wages (over $9,720 per year). But you can earn any amount of interest or dividends or pensions without your Social Security benefits being reduced. To some observers, this is unfair discrimination against older people who want to hold down jobs.

2. The Social Security tax is regressive, since those with annual earnings above $53,400 pay a smaller proportion of their income in Social Security taxes than do those with annual earnings below $53,400. For this and other reasons, many observers believe that the system is not as generous to the poor as it should be.

3. Some people are disturbed that the Social Security system is not really an ordinary insurance system at all. An ordinary insurance program must have assets that are sufficient to finance all of the benefits promised to the people in the program. This is not the case for Social Security. But this does not mean that you won't receive your Social Security benefits. What it does mean is that the Social Security system is a means of transferring income each year from the working young and middle-aged to the retired old people. It will be up to future Congresses to determine what these benefits will be. (In 1983, Congress made a number of important changes: for example, up to half of the Social Security benefits of the well-to-do are now taxable under the personal income tax.) Only time will tell how much you will receive.

4. Some people are disturbed that Social Security is mandatory. Milton Friedman is concerned that the government interferes with an individual's freedom to plan for the future by forcing him or her to be a member of the Social Security system. (Workers might be able to obtain larger pensions by investing the money that they contribute to Social Security in investments of their own choosing.) Other observers retort that without a mandatory system, some workers would make inadequate provision for their old age and might become public charges.

5. Some people are concerned that Social Security is an impediment to saving and capital formation. Martin Feldstein, former chairman of President Reagan's Council of Economic Advisers, feels that Americans save relatively little because they depend on Social Security to take care of their old age. This, he believes, tends to depress capital formation in the United States, since savings can be used to build factories, expand old plants, and add in various ways to the nation's stock of capital. He favors a slowdown in the rate of growth of Social Security, and more reliance on private pensions and personal savings.

Medicare, Unemployment Insurance, Other Programs

In 1965, the Congress extended the Social Security program to include **Medicare,** a compulsory hospitalization insurance plan plus a voluntary insurance plan covering doctors' fees for people over 65. The hospitalization insurance pays for practically all the hospital costs of the first 90 days of each spell of illness, as well as some additional costs. The voluntary plan covers about 80 percent of doctors' fees after the first $100. The cost of the compulsory insurance is included in the taxes described above, as well as a 1.45 percent tax on annual earnings between $53,400 and $125,000. In 1992, the federal government paid out about $114 billion for Medicare.

Besides instituting old-age, survivors, and medical insurance, the Social Security Act also encouraged the states to set up systems of **unemployment insurance.** Such systems now exist in all states, financed by taxes on employers. Once an insured worker is unemployed, he can obtain benefits after a short waiting period, generally a week. The average weekly benefits differ from state to state; in December 1990 they ranged from about $220 in Massachusetts and New Jersey to about $115 in Mississippi and Tennessee. In most states, there is a 26-week ceiling on the duration of benefits. Clearly, unemployment insurance is another important device to keep people from falling below the poverty line.[7]

Finally, in 1974, a program was created to replace federal grants to the states to help the aged, the blind, and the disabled. This program, called the **Supplemental Security Income Program,** established a uniform national minimum income for people in these categories who are unable to work. (Also, many states supplement these federal payments.) In 1990, about 5 million people received over $15 billion from this program.

ANTIPOVERTY PROGRAMS

According to the English poet and essayist Samuel Johnson, "A decent provision for the poor is the true test of civilization." There is general agreement that our social insurance programs, although useful in preventing and alleviating poverty, are not an adequate or complete anti-poverty program. For one thing, they focus largely on the elderly, which means that they do not aid many poor people. They do not help the working poor; and even for the unemployed, they provide only limited help for a limited period of time.

Consequently, the government has started a number of additional programs specifically designed to help the poor, although many of them are aimed more at the symptoms of poverty than at its basic causes. There are programs that provide goods and services to the poor. The biggest of these programs is **Medicaid,** which pays for the health care of the poor. The federal government's 1989 disbursements for this program were about $30 billion. In 1990, Congress passed legislation extending Medicaid coverage to more and more children; by 2003, all poor children up to the age of 18 will be covered by Medicaid.

The **food programs,** which have distributed food to needy families, are also of major significance in this regard. (Before 1973, this food generally came from surpluses due to the farm programs described in Chapter 16.) The federal government has given **stamps** that can be used to buy food to local agencies, which have sold them (at less than the equivalent of market prices) or have given them to low-income families. In 1989, the cost of this program to the federal government was about $13 billion.

Not all antipoverty programs give particular commodities to the poor; some programs provide them with cash. These are what people generally have in mind when they refer to **welfare.** There are advantages to cash payments. They allow a family to adapt its purchases to its own needs and circumstances. There are obvious disadvantages too, since the money may be spent on liquor and marijuana rather than on food and milk. The most important single program of cash payments gives **aid to families with dependent children.** In 1988, this program paid out more than $16 billion.

To qualify for this program, a family must contain dependent children who are without the support of a parent (usually the father) through death, disability, or absence (and in some states, through unemployment

---

[7] In 1991, some observers worried that fewer workers were eligible for unemployment insurance than in the past, because states had tightened requirements. For example, workers sometimes had to work longer and earn more to be eligible. Other people felt that the tightening of requirements was justified.

as well). The amount paid to a family under this program varies from state to state, since each state administers its own program and sets it own schedule of payments—as well as contributes part of the cost of the program, with the federal government providing the balance. In 1988, the average monthly payment was about $550 in states like Massachusetts and New York and about $115 in states like Mississippi and Alabama. To determine eligibility, the family's affairs are examined; and while receiving aid the family may be under the surveillance of a social worker who supervises its housekeeping and child care.

In 1988, Congress passed a welfare reform act, which was aimed at increasing the extent to which welfare recipients work or participate in job-training programs. This is called "workfare," the idea being that able-bodied adults should work in order to be eligible for welfare benefits. In general, the 1980s saw a reduced emphasis by the federal government on many welfare programs. The Reagan administration felt that income assistance should be confined to those that were undeniably needy; others would be taken care of by a strong private economy.

The Negative Income Tax

There is widespread dissatisfaction with current antipoverty—or welfare—programs. The cost of these programs has risen alarmingly; the programs themselves are judged by many experts to be inefficient; and, in some people's view, the welfare recipients are subjected to unnecessary meddling and spying. Moreover, there is little incentive for many people to get off welfare. Both Republicans and Democrats seem to agree that current welfare programs need improvement. What changes might be made? One suggestion that has received serious consideration is the negative income tax, an idea proposed by Stanford University's Milton Friedman (an adviser to presidential candidate Barry Goldwater in 1964 and to President Nixon) and Yale's James Tobin (an adviser to President Kennedy).

A **negative income tax** would work as follows: Just as families with reasonably high incomes *pay* taxes, families with low incomes would *receive* a payment. In other words, the poor would pay a *negative* income tax. Figure 15.5 illustrates how a negative income tax might work; it shows the amount a family of four would pay—or receive—in taxes, depending on its income. According to Figure 15.5, $6,000 is the **break-even income**—the income at which a family of four neither pays nor receives income taxes. Above $6,000, a family pays taxes. Thus a family with an income of $9,000 pays $750 in taxes. Below $6,000 a family receives a payment. Thus a family with an income of $1,500 is paid $2,250.

There are several advantages of a negative income tax.

1. It would give people on welfare more incentive to work. As indicated in Figure 15.5, for every extra dollar it earns, the family receives only 50 cents less from the government under this kind of negative income tax. Thus the family gets to keep half of every extra dollar (up to $6,000) it earns, which is a larger portion of this extra dollar than has been true under the present system.

2. There would be no intrusion into the internal affairs of families on welfare and no regulations that cut off welfare payments if the husband remains with his family. In the past, the welfare system has given families an incentive to break up, and encroached on the dignity of poor people.

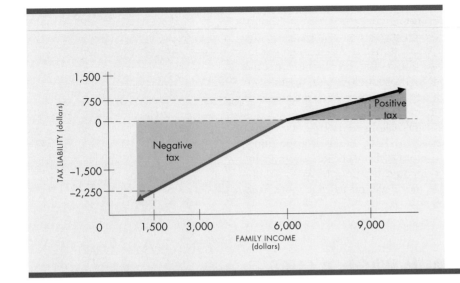

Figure 15.5
Example of Negative
Income Tax
A family with more than $6,000 in income pays taxes. Thus a family with an income of $9,000 pays $750 in taxes. A family with an income less than $6,000 receives a payment. Thus a family with an income of $1,500 is paid $2,250.

3. It might cost less to administer the negative income tax than the present system, and differences among states in benefits might be reduced.

Despite these advantages, many citizens remain skeptical about the negative income tax. For one thing, they are antagonistic to the idea of

EXAMPLE 15.2   WHY NOT CURE POVERTY WITH A CHECK?

If the United States government were to mail checks to all poor families to raise their incomes to the poverty level, these checks would amount to less than 1 percent of our gross national product. Suppose that the government decides to solve the poverty problem in this way.

(a) If the poverty level is $15,000 per year, what is the relationship between a family's income before subsidy and its income after subsidy? (b) Up to $15,000, does a family's earnings influence its income after subsidy? (c) For people whose pre-subsidy earnings are below the poverty level, what would be the effect of this program on the incentive to work? (d) For people whose pre-subsidy earnings are slightly above the poverty level, what would be the effect of this program on the incentive to work? (e) Would the cost of this program be greater than the amount of the checks mailed to the poor?

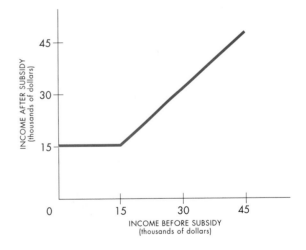

Solution

(a) This relationship is shown in the figure at right. (b) No. (c) Because they can get $15,000 without working, some would be likely to quit working, or to work less hard. (d) Because they can get almost as much as their current income without working, some would be likely to quit working, or to work less hard. (e) Yes. There would be the additional costs due to the diminished incentives to work. For reasons discussed above, people would work less, and fewer goods and services would be produced.

giving people an income without requiring any work in return. They also are unwilling to transfer large amounts from rich to poor. This amount would depend on how high the break-even income was set and on the negative tax rates. In the late 1960s, it was estimated that a negative income tax would have meant that those above the break-even income level would transfer about $25 billion to those below the break-even level. Despite the attractive features of a negative income tax, a transfer of this magnitude proved unacceptable in many quarters.

Also, some economists regard the results of the experiments with a negative income tax in Seattle and Denver to have been disappointing. These experiments, carried out with a sample of households, seem to indicate that under a (generous) negative income tax people work significantly less, apparently because they are more willing to quit work, and less willing to search hard for a new job.

INCREASES IN THE MINIMUM WAGE: A CURE FOR POVERTY?

At first glance, it may appear that the government can eradicate poverty by raising the minimum wage. In the United States, the minimum wage goes back over half a century. In 1938, the Congress passed the Fair Labor Standards Act, which established a minimum wage of 25 cents per hour. With inflation and changes in social attitudes and values, the minimum wage has been increased repeatedly. In 1991, it equaled $4.25 per hour.

Despite occasional claims to the contrary, the truth is that *increases in the minimum wage cannot cure poverty*. The effects of a minimum wage are demonstrated in Figure 15.6, which shows the demand and supply curves for unskilled labor in a competitive labor market. Without the minimum wage, the equilibrium wage rate is $4.00 per hour, and OL_2 hours of labor are hired. If a minimum wage of $5.00 per hour is put into effect,

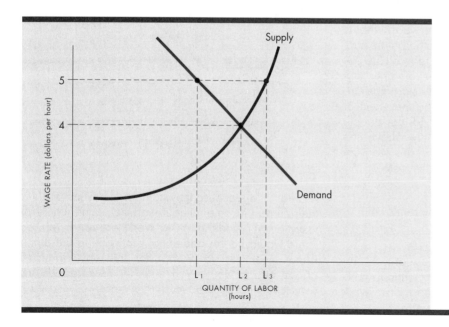

Figure 15.6
Effect of a Minimum Wage
Without the minimum wage, the equilibrium wage is $4 per hour, and OL_2 hours of labor are hired. With a minimum wage of $5 per hour, only OL_1 hours of labor are hired.

employers will cut back on the amount of labor that they hire. Rather than employing OL_2 hours of labor, they will employ only OL_1 hours of labor. Unemployment will be created. Whereas workers would like to work OL_3 hours, they will only be able to work OL_1 hours. Not all of this unemployment will be reflected in the government's unemployment statistics, since some people who are unable to find jobs may give up looking for work (and thus not be counted in the government's figures).

Clearly, the unskilled workers who keep their jobs are better off because of the minimum wage; they get $5 an hour rather than $4 an hour. But those who lose their jobs or are unable to find jobs are worse off. In general, one would expect that *the least skilled and most disadvantaged would be the ones that would be hardest hit by the minimum wage.* In particular, many economists believe that the minimum wage pushes up the unemployment rate among black teenagers. To soften the effect on teenagers, Congress established a training wage of about $3.60 per hour in 1991 for workers from 16 to 19 years old in their first job. (This training wage can be paid to a particular worker for no more than six months.) It is too soon to tell how effective this new training wage will be.

THE WAR ON POVERTY: SOME FINAL VOLLEYS

Before concluding this chapter, it is worthwhile pointing out that there are considerable differences of opinion among politicians and economists concerning the severity of the poverty problem in the United States. The official government statistics concerning the incidence of poverty do not recognize the fact that many people below the official poverty line receive non-cash benefits from the government, such as food stamps, subsidized school lunches, public housing, Medicaid, and Medicare. These benefits accounted in 1980 for more than two out of every three dollars of government assistance. According to the U.S. Bureau of the Census, the percentage of the U.S. population below the poverty line is much smaller than the official statistics indicate, when these government non-cash benefits are taken into account. Specifically, the figure according to official statistics has been about 10 percent. When underreporting of incomes is taken into consideration, some economists conclude that only about 4 percent of the population have fallen below the poverty line in recent years. Based on these statistics, some observers claim that the war on poverty in the United States has been won.

On the other hand, many economists argue that the official poverty line established by the government is too low, the result being that a substantial number of poor people are not classified as poor in the official statistics. In 1990, the House of Representatives voted to give $600,000 to the National Academy of Sciences to study this issue. Whether or not the official statistics underestimate the poverty problem, it seems self-evident that a problem does exist. After all, even if only 4 percent fall below the poverty line, this means that about 10 million people are poor. Moreover, a disproportionately large number of children are being raised in poverty. According to the official statistics, one child in five lives in a family with income below the poverty line. Unquestionably, it is difficult to design and implement effective and efficient policies to alleviate poverty, but our society has no reasonable alternative than to try.

TEST YOURSELF

1. Many people feel that Aid to Families with Dependent Children should be transformed into a vehicle for education, training, and work. In what sense is work the solution to dependency? Can training and job placement enable long-term welfare recipients to break out of poverty and dependency?

2. "The Social Security system is actuarially unsound. The amounts currently collected in Social Security taxes do not equal the amounts currently paid out in benefits. We cannot keep this up!" Comment and evaluate.

3. According to some economists, Social Security should be voluntary, not mandatory. Present the arguments on each side of this issue in as much detail as you can.

4. Do the official government statistics concerning poverty recognize that many people below the poverty line receive non-cash benefits from the government? If not, does this mean that these statistics are useless? Explain.

SUMMARY

1. Lorenz curves are used to measure the extent of income inequality. They make it clear that there was a considerable reduction in income inequality in the United States between the late 1920s and the end of World War II.

2. Many factors are responsible for existing income differentials. Some people are abler, better educated, or luckier than others. Some people have more property, or more monopoly power, than others.

3. Critics of income inequality argue that it lessens total consumer satisfaction because an extra dollar given to the poor provides them with more extra satisfaction than the loss of a dollar taken away from the rich. Also, they argue that income inequality leads to social and political inequality.

4. Defenders of income inequality point out that it is scientifically impossible to make interpersonal comparisons of utility, and argue that income inequality is needed to provide incentives for people to work and create, and that it permits greater capital formation.

5. There is no well-defined income level that can be used in all times and all places to determine poverty. Perhaps the most widely accepted definition of poverty in the United States today is the one developed by the Social Security Administration, according to which about 13 percent of the population in the United States—over 30 million people—fell below the poverty line in recent years.

6. Black families, families headed by a female, and very large families are more likely than others to be poor. To a considerable extent, the reasons for their poverty lie beyond the control of the poor people. About one-third of poor adults have suffered a disability of some sort, or the premature death of the family breadwinner, or family dissolution. Most heads of poor families do not have jobs.

7. Because private charity is judged to be inadequate, the nation has authorized its government to carry out various public programs to aid the poor. There are programs to provide them with goods and services—Medicaid and food-stamp programs, for instance. Other programs, like aid to families with dependent children, give them cash. When these programs are taken into account, the percentage of the population falling below the poverty line is reduced considerably.

8. There is widespread dissatisfaction with existing antipoverty—or welfare—programs. They are judged to be inefficient; their costs have been increasing at an alarming rate; and they provide little incentive for people to get off welfare. One suggestion to remedy these problems is a negative income tax. In most of the forms put forth it involves a transfer of income that seems presently to be beyond the realm of political feasibility.

CONCEPTS FOR REVIEW

Income inequality

Lorenz curve

Progressive tax

Regressive tax

Tax incidence

Poverty

Old-age insurance

Social Security

Medicare

Unemployment insurance

**Supplemental Security Income
   Program**

Food programs

Welfare

**Aid to families with dependent
   children**

Negative income tax

Break-even income

PART FIVE

GOVERNMENT AND THE ECONOMY

THE ECONOMIC ROLE OF THE GOVERNMENT

TO STATE THAT THE UNITED STATES is a mixed capitalist system, in which both government decisions and the price system play important roles, is hardly to provoke a controversy. But going a step beyond takes us into areas where viewpoints often diverge. The proper functions of government and the desirable size and nature of government expenditures and taxes are not matters on which all agree. Indeed, the question of how big government should be, and what its proper functions are, is hotly debated by conservatives and liberals throughout the land.

LIMITATIONS OF THE PRICE SYSTEM

Despite its many advantages, the price system suffers from limitations. Because these limitations are both prominent and well known, no one believes that the price system, left to its own devices, can be trusted to solve all society's basic economic problems. To a considerable extent, the government's role in the economy has developed in response to the limitations of the price system, which are described below.

DISTRIBUTION OF INCOME. There is *no* reason to believe that the distribution of income generated by the price system is *fair* or, in some sense, *best.* Most people feel that the distribution of income generated by the price system should be altered to suit humanitarian needs; in particular, that help should be given to the poor. Both liberals and conservatives tend to agree on this score, although there are arguments over the extent to which the poor should be helped and the conditions under which they should be eligible for help. But the general principle that the government should step in to redistribute income in favor of the poor is generally accepted in the United States today.[1]

PUBLIC GOODS. Some goods and services *cannot be provided through the price system because there is no way to exclude citizens from consuming the goods whether they pay for them or not.* For example, there is no way to prevent citizens from benefiting from national expenditures on defense, whether they pay money toward defense or not. Consequently, the

---

[1] Also, because the wealthy have more "dollar votes" than the poor, the sorts of goods and services that society produces will reflect this fact. Thus luxuries for the rich may be produced in larger amounts and necessities for the poor may be produced in smaller amounts than some critics regard as sensible and equitable. This is another frequently encountered criticism of the price system.

price system cannot be used to provide such goods; no one will pay for them since they will receive them whether they pay or not. Further, these goods, like the quality of the environment and national defense (and others cited below), *can be enjoyed by one person without depriving others of the same enjoyment.* Such goods are called **public goods.** The government provides many public goods. Such goods are consumed collectively, or jointly, and it is inefficient to try to price them in a market. They tend to be indivisible; thus they frequently cannot be split into pieces and be bought and sold in a market.

EXTERNAL ECONOMIES AND DISECONOMIES. In cases where *the production or consumption of a good by one firm or consumer has adverse or beneficial uncompensated effects on other firms or consumers, the price system will not operate effectively.* An **external economy** is said to occur when consumption or production by one person or firm results in uncompensated benefits to another person or firm. A good example of an external economy exists where fundamental research carried out by one firm is used by another firm. (To cite one such case, there were external economies from the Bell Telephone Laboratories' invention of the transistor. Many electronics firms, such as Texas Instruments and Fairchild, benefited considerably from Bell's research.) Where external economies exist, it is generally agreed that the price system will produce too little of the good in question and that the government should supplement the amount produced by private enterprise. This is the basic rationale for much of the government's huge investment in basic science. An **external diseconomy** is said to occur when consumption or production by one person or firm results in uncompensated costs to another person or firm. A good example of an external diseconomy occurs when a firm dumps pollutants into a stream and makes the water unfit for use by firms and people downstream. Where activities result in external diseconomies, it is generally agreed that the price system will tolerate too much of the activity and that the government should curb it. For example, as we shall see in Chapter 17, the government, in keeping with this doctrine, has involved itself in environmental protection and the reduction of air and water pollution.[2]

WHAT FUNCTIONS SHOULD THE GOVERNMENT PERFORM?

There are wide differences of opinion on the proper role of government in economic affairs. Although it is generally agreed that the government should redistribute income in favor of the poor, provide public goods, and offset the effects of external economies and diseconomies, there is considerable disagreement over how far the government should go in these areas, and what additional areas the government should be responsible for. Some people feel that "big government" is already a problem; that government is doing too much. Others believe that the public sector of the economy is being under-nourished and that government should be allowed to do more. This is a fundamental question, and one that involves a great deal more than economics.

---

[2] The effects of external economies and diseconomies can also be taken care of by legal arrangements that assign liabilities for damages and compensate for benefits. However, such arrangements often are impractical or too costly to be used.

CONSERVATIVE VIEW. On the one hand, conservatives, such as Stanford University's Nobel laureate, Milton Friedman, believe that the government's role should be limited severely. They feel that economic and political freedom is likely to be undermined by excessive reliance on the state. Moreover, they tend to be skeptical about the government's ability to solve the social and economic problems at hand. They feel that the prevailing faith in the government's power to make a substantial dent in these problems is unreasonable, and they call for more and better information concerning the sorts of tasks government can reasonably be expected to do—and do well. They point to the slowness of the government bureaucracy, the difficulty in controlling huge government organizations, the inefficiencies political considerations can breed, and the difficulties in telling whether government programs are successful or not. On the basis of these considerations, they argue that the government's role should be carefully circumscribed.

LIBERAL VIEW. To such arguments, liberals like Nobel laureate Paul Samuelson of the Massachusetts Institute of Technology respond with telling salvos of their own. Just as conservatives tend to be skeptical of the government's ability to solve important social and economic problems, so liberals tend to be skeptical about the price system's ability to solve these problems. They point to the limitations of the price system, discussed above, and they assert that the government can do a great deal to overcome these limitations, by regulating private activity and by subsidizing and providing goods and services that the private sector produces too little of. Liberals tend to be less concerned than conservatives about the effects on personal freedom of greater governmental intervention in the economy. They point out that the price system also involves coercion, since the fact that the price system awards the available goods and services to those who can pay their equilibrium price can be viewed as a form of coercion. In their view, people who are awarded only a pittance by the price system are coerced into discomfort and malnutrition.[3]

ESTABLISHING "RULES OF THE GAME"

Although there is considerable disagreement over the proper role of the government, both conservatives and liberals agree that it must do certain things. The first of these is to establish the "rules of the game"—that is, a legal, social, and competitive framework enabling the price system to function as it should. Specifically, *the government must see to it that contracts are enforced, that private ownership is protected, and that fraud is prevented*. Clearly, these matters must be tended to if the price system is to work properly. Also, *the government must maintain order (through the establishment of police and other forces), establish a monetary system (so that money can be used to facilitate trade and exchange), and provide standards for the weight and quality of products.*

As an example of this sort of government intervention, consider the Pure Food and Drug Act. This act, originally passed in 1906 and subsequently amended in various ways, protects the consumer against im-

---

[3] See P. Samuelson, "The Economic Role of Private Activity," and G. Stigler, "The Government of the Economy," in E. Mansfield, *Principles of Microeconomics: Readings, Issues, and Cases,* 4th ed.

proper and fraudulent activities on the part of producers of foods and drugs. It prohibits the merchandising of impure or falsely labeled food or drugs, and it forces producers to specify the quantity and quality of the contents on labels. These requirements strengthen the price system. Without them, the typical consumer would be unable to tell whether food or drugs are pure or properly labeled. Unless consumers can be sure that they are getting what they pay for, the basic logic underlying the price system breaks down. Similar regulation and legislation have been instituted in fields other than food and drugs—and for similar reasons.

FDA inspectors

MAINTAINING A COMPETITIVE FRAMEWORK

Besides establishing a legal and social framework that will enable the price system to do its job, *the government must also see to it that markets remain reasonably competitive.* Only if they are will prices reflect consumer desires properly. If, on the other hand, markets are dominated by a few sellers (or a few buyers), prices may be "rigged" by these sellers (or buyers) to promote their own interests. For example, if a single firm is the sole producer of aluminum, it is a safe bet that this firm will establish a higher price than if there were many aluminum producers competing among themselves.

As previous chapters have indicated, the unfortunate thing about prices determined in noncompetitive markets—rigged prices, if you will—is that they give incorrect signals concerning what consumers want and how scarce resources and commodities are. Producers, responding to these incorrect signals, do not produce the right things in the right quantities. Consumers respond to these incorrect signals by not supplying the right resources in the right amounts, and by not consuming the proper amounts of the goods that are produced. Thus the price system is not permitted to function properly in the absence of reasonable competition.

To try to encourage and preserve competition, the Congress, as we have seen, has enacted a series of **antitrust laws,** such as the Sherman Antitrust Act and the Clayton Act, and it has established the Federal Trade Commission. The antitrust laws make it illegal for firms to collude or to attempt to monopolize the sale of a product. Both conservative and liberal economists, with some notable exceptions, tend to favor the intent and operation of the antitrust laws.

REDISTRIBUTION OF INCOME

We have already noted, particularly in Chapter 15, the general agreement that the government should redistribute income in favor of the poor. In other words, *it is usually felt that help should be given to people who are ill, handicapped, old and infirm, disabled, and unable for other reasons to provide for themselves.* To some extent, the nation has decided that income—or at least a certain minimum income—should be divorced from productive services. Of course, this doesn't mean that people who are too lazy to work should be given a handout. It does mean that people who cannot provide for themselves should be helped. To implement this principle, various payments are made by the government to needy people—including the aged, the handicapped, the unemployed, and pensioners.

SEMATECH: SHOULD THE GOVERNMENT SUBSIDIZE SEMICONDUCTORS?

In 1987, America's semiconductor manufacturers, facing intense competition from the Japanese, set out to establish a program based on Pentagon money and industry collaboration to reestablish their world leadership—or in the case of some firms, their viability—in the production and design of advanced computer chips. The project, known as SEMATECH, called for research on advanced manufacturing techniques. The Pentagon and industry would put up equal amounts of money, and there would be close cooperation between the semiconductor manufacturers and their customers and suppliers.

Semiconductor chips are the hearts of computers and telecommunications devices that play a central role in military guidance systems, as well as other defense-related products. The Defense Science Board Task Force on Semiconductor Dependency regarded the decline in the U.S. semiconductor industry vis-à-vis the Japanese as "an unacceptable threat" that damages the technology base that is important to American national security. Claiming that the U.S. military establishment had become too dependent on Japanese chips, it stated that: "The Japanese cannot be relied upon to transfer leadership semiconductor technology to U.S. systems suppliers for military uses."

In December 1987, Congress appropriated $100 million to SEMATECH, almost half its annual budget. SEMATECH is sponsored by 14 major semiconductor manufacturers including IBM, Intel, and Texas Instruments. It has three primary missions: to do research and development on advanced semiconductor manufacturing techniques, to test them on a demonstration production line, and to transfer the techniques to American producers. The 14 members of the research consortium will have first call on SEMATECH's results. In early 1988, the decision was made to locate SEMATECH in Austin, Texas, but there was some grumbling by Pentagon officials that the operating plan for SEMATECH was too vague. In July 1988, after considerable difficulty in obtaining a chief executive, Robert Noyce, former vice chairman of Intel Corporation, took the position, but died soon afterward. His successor was William Spencer, formerly senior technical officer at Xerox.

SEMATECH headquarters

According to Spencer, new technology is not SEMATECH's major achievement. In his view, "the biggest thing coming out of SEMATECH is the way equipment suppliers, semiconductor manufacturers, and systems houses are working together. . . .[I]f we don't pull together and do business differently, we're going to go out of business."[1]

Although Congress has been persuaded to subsidize semiconductor research and development in this way, many observers wonder whether the government should use taxpayers' money to help bail out industries in trouble. Also, some people question whether firms in so competitive an industry are really willing to cooperate. Each firm might be inclined to get what information it could from its rivals, but disclose as little as possible. Economists and others will look closely at SEMATECH's performance, since many fundamental questions are involved. Certainly, SEMATECH is a far cry from garden-variety free enterprise.

[1] "SEMATECH May Give America's Middleweights a Fighting Chance," *Business Week*, December 10, 1990, p. 186.

These **welfare payments** are to some extent a "depression baby," for they grew substantially during the Great Depression of the 1930s, when relief payments seemed to be a necessity. But they also represent a feeling shared by a large segment of the population that human beings should be assured that, however the wheel of fortune spins and whatever number comes up, they will not starve and their children will not be deprived of a healthy environment and basic schooling. Of course, someone has to pay for this. Welfare payments allow the poor to take more from the nation's output than they produce. In general, the more affluent members of society contribute some of their claims on output to pay for these programs, their contributions being in the form of taxes. By using its expenditures to help certain groups and by taxing other groups to pay for these programs, the government accomplishes each year, without revolt and without bayonets, a substantial redistribution of income.

STABILIZING THE ECONOMY

It is also generally agreed that *the government should promote the maintenance of reasonably full employment with reasonably stable prices.* Capitalist economies have tended to alternate between booms and depressions in the past. The Great Depression of the 1930s hit the American economy—and the world economy—a particularly devastating blow, putting millions of people out of work and in desperate shape. There are important differences of opinion among economists regarding the extent to which the government can stabilize the economy. But it is generally agreed that the government should do what it can to avoid serious recessions and to maintain employment at a high level.

Also, the government must try to maintain a reasonably stable price level. No economy can function well if prices are gyrating wildly. Through its control of the money supply and its decisions regarding expenditures and taxation, the government has considerable impact on the price level, as well as on the level of employment. Unfortunately, during the 1970s in particular, the government was not very successful in maintaining price stability. According to many economists, the government's own policies contributed to this inflation.

PROVIDING PUBLIC GOODS

As we have indicated, the government provides many public goods. Let's consider the nature of public goods in more detail.

WHAT IS A PUBLIC GOOD? One hallmark of a public good is that it can be consumed by one person without diminishing the amount that other people consume of it. Public goods tend to be relatively indivisible; they often come in such large units that they cannot be broken into pieces that can be bought or sold in ordinary markets. *Once such goods are produced, there often is no way to bar certain citizens from consuming them.* Whether or not citizens contribute toward their cost, they benefit from them. As pointed out in a previous section, this means that the price system cannot be used to handle effectively the production and distribution of such goods.

WHY THE TENNESSEE VALLEY AUTHORITY?

TVA dam at Fort Loudon

The Great Mississippi Flood of 1927 left 800,000 homeless and focused national attention on the federal government's responsibility for flood control. Such control had been considered for years on the Tennessee River. Senator Norris of Nebraska campaigned for federal support for river control in the 1920s and 1930s, but his attempts were unsuccessful—largely because local utilities feared that by building dams, the federal government would be providing not only flood control but electric power as well.

The debate continued until in 1933 the Roosevelt administration created the Tennessee Valley Authority (TVA). The TVA was foremost a construction project that would create jobs in a depressed economy, but it was also created for regional development that would yield benefits for many years to come. In addition to its responsibility for flood control and for improving the navigability of the Tennessee's waters, the TVA built housing, worked on agricultural development, and provided electric power to the depressed area. And the local utilities challenged the TVA all the way.

By 1954 the TVA was well established and requested funds from Congress to build a steam-driven electric plant. Congress rejected the proposal because it did not feel that the TVA should be expanded further into a federal power facility not exclusively hydroelectric, nor should it be made into an even larger business.

Why is it proper for the government to provide for flood control, but not proper for it to build steam-driven electric power plants? The rationale for the government to provide a service is a breakdown of the free market—that is, when the private sector will not provide the proper quantity of certain goods and services. Congress accepted the idea that flood control and navigation were public goods, and that, insofar as electrification was a by-product of flood control, it was reasonable for the government to provide this service too. But the proposed steam-driven electrical generators could have been as easily provided by the private sector as by the government.

N.B.

NATIONAL DEFENSE: A PUBLIC GOOD.   National defense is a public good. The benefits of expenditure on national defense extend to the entire nation. Extension of the benefits of national defense to an additional citizen does not mean that any other citizen gets less of these benefits. Also, there is no way of preventing citizens from benefiting from them, whether they contribute to their cost or not. Thus there is no way to use the price system to provide for national defense. Since it is a public good, national defense, if it is to reach an adequate level, must be provided by the government. Similarly with flood control, environmental protection, and a host of other such services.

DECISION MAKING REGARDING PUBLIC GOODS.   Essentially, deciding how much to produce of a public good is a political decision. The citizens of the United States elect senators and members of Congress who decide how much should be spent on national defense, and how it should be spent. These elected representatives are responsive to special-interest groups, as well as to the people as a whole. Many special-interest groups lobby hard for the production of certain public goods. For example, an alliance of military and industrial groups presses for increased defense expenditures, and other interested groups promote expenditures on other functions.

The tax system is used to pay for the production of public goods. In

---

EXAMPLE 16.1   THE ECONOMICS OF URBAN BLIGHT

During the past 40 years, the federal government has promoted and encouraged the redevelopment of the inner core of our major cities. Consider two adjacent urban properties. Suppose that the two owners, Mr. Lombardi and Mr. Moore, are each trying to determine whether to invest $100,000 to redevelop their properties. If they do not invest the $100,000 in redevelopment, each can get a 10 percent return from other forms of investment. The rate of return on the $100,000 investment by each owner (which depends on whether the other owner redevelops his property as well) is shown below:

	OTHER OWNER REDEVELOPS	OTHER OWNER DOES NOT REDEVELOP
	rate of return (percent)	
Redevelop	12	5
Do not redevelop	15	10

(a) If Mr. Lombardi redevelops his property, is Mr. Moore better off by redeveloping his property as well? (b) If Mr. Lombardi does not redevelop his property, is Mr. Moore better off by redeveloping his property? (c) Will either owner redevelop his property? (d) In a situation of this sort, can social gains be achieved by government intervention?

Solution

(a) No, because the rate of return Mr. Moore receives if he redevelops is 12 percent, whereas the rate of return he receives if he does not redevelop is 15 percent (because his property benefits from Mr. Lombardi's investment in redevelopment even though he pays nothing). (b) No, because the rate of return Mr. Moore receives if he redevelops is only 5 percent (because little is accomplished so long as Mr. Lombardi does not redevelop too), whereas the rate of return he receives if he does not redevelop is 10 percent (which is what he can obtain from other investments). (c) No. Consider Mr. Moore. As pointed out in (a) and (b), whether or not Mr. Lombardi redevelops, Mr. Moore receives a higher return if he does not redevelop than if he does. Thus he will not redevelop. Neither will Mr. Lombardi, for the same reasons. (d) Yes. From society's point of view, or from the point of view of the two owners acting together as a unit, redevelopment may be desirable. If carried out properly, government intervention may bring this about.

effect, the government says to each citizen, "Fork over a certain amount of money to pay for the expenses incurred by the government." The amount a particular citizen is assessed may depend on his or her income (as in the income tax), the value of all or specific types of his or her property (as in the property tax), the amount he or she spends on certain types of goods and services (as in the sales tax), or on still other criteria. In the 1990s, the tax system has often been the object of enormous controversy. More will be said about the tax system, and the controversies swirling around it, in a later section of this chapter.

EXTERNALITIES

It is generally agreed that *the government should encourage the production of goods and services that entail external economies and discourage the production of those that entail external diseconomies.* Take the pollution of air and water. When a firm or individual dumps wastes into the water or air, other firms or individuals often must pay all or part of the cost of putting the water or air back into a usable condition. Thus the disposal of these wastes entails external diseconomies. Unless the government prohibits certain kinds of pollution, or enforces air and water quality standards, or charges polluters in accord with the amount of waste they dump into the environment, there will be socially undesirable levels of pollution.

EFFECTS OF EXTERNAL DISECONOMIES. To see how such externalities affect the social desirability of the output of a competitive industry, consider Figure 16.1, where the industry's demand and supply curves are contained in the left-hand panel. As shown there, the equilibrium output of the industry is OQ_0. If the industry results in no external economies or diseconomies, this is likely to be the socially optimal output. But what if the industry results in external diseconomies, such as the pollution described above? Then the industry's supply curve does not fully reflect the true social costs of producing the product. The supply curve that reflects these social costs is S_1, which, as shown in the middle panel of Figure 16.1, lies to the left of the industry's supply curve. The optimal output of the good is OQ_1, which is less than the competitive output, OQ_0.

What can the government do to correct the situation? There are a variety of ways that it can intervene to reduce the industry's output from OQ_0

Figure 16.1
Effect of External Economies and Diseconomies on the Optimal Output of a Competitive Industry
The optimal output is OQ_0 if neither external economies nor diseconomies are present. If there are external diseconomies, curve S_1 reflects the true social costs of producing the product, and OQ_1 is the optimal output. If there are external economies, curve D_1 reflects the true social benefits of producing the product, and OQ_2 is the optimal output.

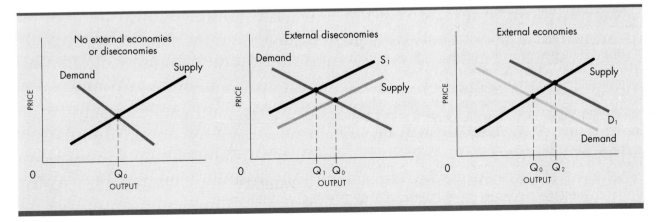

to OQ_1. For example, it can impose taxes on the industry. If these taxes are of the right type and amount, they will result in the desired reduction of output.

EFFECTS OF EXTERNAL ECONOMIES.   What if the industry results in external economies? For example, what if the manufacture of one industrial product makes it cheaper to produce other products? Then the industry's demand curve underestimates the true social benefits of producing the product. The demand curve that reflects these social benefits correctly is D_1, which, as shown in the right-hand panel of Figure 16.1, lies to the right of the industry's demand curve. The optimal output of the good is OQ_2, which is greater than the competitive output, OQ_0.

As in the case where the industry results in external diseconomies, the government can intervene in various ways to change the industry's output. But in this case, the object is to increase, not decrease, its output. To accomplish this, the government can, among other things, grant subsidies to the industry. If they are of the right type and amount, they can be used to increase the industry's output from OQ_0 to OQ_2.

SIZE AND NATURE OF GOVERNMENT ACTIVITIES

How Big Is the Government?

Up to this point, we have been concerned primarily with the reasons why the government must intervene in our economy—and the types of role it should play—but we have made little or no attempt to describe its role in quantitative terms. It is time now to turn to some of the relevant facts. One useful measure of the extent of the government's role in the American economy is the size of government expenditures, both in absolute terms and as a percent of our nation's total output.

The sum total of government expenditures—federal, state, and local—was about $1.8 trillion in 1990. Since the nation's total output was about $5.5 trillion, this means that government expenditures were about one-third of our total output. The ratio of government expenditures to total output in the United States has not always been this large, as Figure 16.2 shows. In 1929, the ratio was about 10 percent, as contrasted with over 30 percent in 1990. (Of course, the ratio of government spending to total output is smaller now than during World War II, but in a wartime economy, one would expect this ratio to be abnormally high.)

There are many reasons why government expenditures have grown so much faster than total output. Three of these are particularly important. First, *the United States did not maintain anything like the kind of military force in pre-World War II days that it does now.* In earlier days, when weapons were relatively simple and cheap, and when we viewed our military and political responsibilities much more narrowly than we do now, our military budget was relatively small. The cost of being a super-power in the days of nuclear weaponry is high by any standards. Second, *there has been a long-term increase in the demand for the services provided by government,* like more and better schooling, more extensive highways, more complete police and fire protection, and so forth. As incomes rise, people want more of these services. Third, ***government transfer payments***—*payments in return for no products or services*—*have grown very substantially.* For example, various types of welfare pay-

MEDICAL CARE: CAN ECONOMIC ANALYSIS BE USED?

One of the most pressing problems facing the American economy is the seemingly inexorable rise in the costs of medical care. Corrected for inflation, per capita personal health care expenditures have risen at over 4 percent per year since 1950. According to official forecasts, the United States will devote about 15 percent of its total output to health care by the year 2000. This is a huge amount, and there are good reasons to think it is excessive, but despite the fact that government agencies (as well as leading corporations and others) have tried in a variety of ways to curb medical costs, they have continued to grow.

The reasons why health costs are likely to be excessive are described very well by Henry Aaron of the Brookings Institution and William Schwartz of Tufts University:

> Standard economic theory suggests that spending on health care is excessive. According to this doctrine, when people pay less than the full cost of what they buy, they will consume more than is socially optimal unless their consumption benefits not only themselves but others. This line of argument suggests that insurance induces excessive health expenditures because people pay for only part of the cost of care.
>
> Patients in 1987 paid, on the average, only about 10 cents of each dollar devoted to hospital care, a share that has changed negligibly for two decades. And they pay about 26 cents of each dollar paid to physicians, a share that has fallen steadily. Although these averages conceal large differences among patients, the fully insured (or those who have exceeded ceilings on patient outlays) and physicians acting in the patients' interests have the incentive to seek any service, however costly, that provides any benefits at all. Because of insurance, these decisions impose large costs on others.[1]

Given these effects of health insurance (for example, Blue Cross, much of it paid for by employers), it is not hard to see why medical costs have risen so greatly. The most important factor is the advance of medical technology, including open-heart surgery, magnetic resonance imaging, organ transplants, anti-ulcer drugs, and a host of others. These new tech-

[1] H. Aaron and W. Schwartz, "Rationing Health Care: The Choice Before Us," *Science*, January 26, 1990.

Henry Aaron

niques are very expensive to develop and apply. Another important factor is that output per hour of labor in hospitals has not risen very rapidly. It is difficult to increase the efficiency of nurses and orderlies. Still another factor is the aging of the population. Obviously, older people tend to require more health care than do younger people.

Confronted with this growth in costs of medical care, the federal government has sought in various ways to slow it down. For example, in 1984, the Health Care Financing Administration (HCFA) started to pay hospitals fixed sums for Medicare patients (patients insured under a government program for the aged described on page 306) based on diagnoses at the time of their admission to the hospital. Formerly, HCFA had reimbursed hospitals for whatever costs (covered by the Medicare program) they incurred. Under the new system, hospitals ordinarily receive the same amount no matter what they spend. Based on preliminary evidence, this new system has slowed the growth of medical costs, although how much of this is due to poorer quality care, rather than increased efficiency, is hard to say.

According to leading experts, the potential savings from cutting out useless medical procedures are huge. Health maintenance organizations (HMO's) say that they lower the costs of medical care through greater efficiency and the elimination of useless services (primarily extra hospital days). For example, one study found that an HMO provided health care for about 25 percent less than did organizations paid on a fee-for-service basis for fully insured patients. (However, for patients that paid a substantial share of the costs, the fee-for-service care was no more costly than the HMO.)

Economists have suggested that more competition among health care providers can help to cut the rate of growth of the costs of health care. There have been proposals that only part of employer-financed health insurance premiums be excluded from an employee's income in computing his or her income tax, thus making the employee more conscious of the costs of medical care. Also, it has been suggested that data be developed and disseminated regarding the quality and cost of care provided by various hospitals and physicians. Such data could help patients and their employers to avoid hospitals and physicians that are high-cost relative to the quality of care they provide.

Economic analysis can be of use, as illustrated by an example given by Louise Russell of Rutgers University.

Suppose that a community's board of health has $300,000 to spend on a new health program and three possible programs on which to spend it. The programs are mutually exclusive and each will use the full $300,000—it is not possible to do a little of all of them. Program A will save 100 years of life, program B 10 years, and program C 1 year. Thus the cost per year of life saved is $3,000 for program A, $30,000 for program B, and $300,000 for program C. In each case the estimates of lifesaving are based on impeccable scientific evidence; there is no doubt that the programs are effective and that they will have the effect estimated. As will be evident later, real and respectable medical interventions vary as much in their cost per year of life saved as do these hypothetical programs.

If the object is to improve health as much as possible with the money, the choice seems obvious—program A, which will save 100 years of life. If program B is chosen, only 10 years will be saved with the same money, and the 100 years that could have been saved with A will be lost. Thus the opportunity cost of choosing program B is the loss of the opportunity to do program A and of the 100 years it could save. More generally, the opportunity cost of using resources in one way is the loss of the benefits they could have achieved had they been put to their next best use. By contrast, the opportunity cost of program A is much

Louise Russell

lower—the 10 years of life that would be saved if the money were spent instead on program B.

It is desirable to keep the opportunity cost of our choices as low as possible. Although the choice that does so is obvious in the example, choices in real life are usually more difficult. First, better health is an important objective, but not the only one, and more objectives make it more difficult to decide which alternative is best. Second, it is harder to give up real opportunities, even for better ones, than hypothetical opportunities. Third, and of critical importance, it is often not easy to determine the true opportunity cost of a decision.[2]

To illustrate how economic analysis can be used, consider Table 1, which shows that, if all women are given a Pap test for cancer every three years (from the age of 20 to the age of 75), the cost per year of life saved (compared with no testing) is about $14,000. On the other hand, if the test is carried out every two years, the cost per year of life saved (compared with no testing) is about $450,000. And if the test is carried out every year, the cost per year of life saved (compared with no testing) is over $1 million. Clearly, society must question whether annual testing of this sort is a good use of its resources, or whether the opportunity costs are too high.

Why does the cost per year of life go up so rapidly for more frequent testing? Because cervical cancer develops slowly and can readily be treated in

[2] L. Russell, "Some of the Tough Decisions Required by a National Health Plan," *Science,* November 17, 1989.

Table 1
Cost per Year of Life Saved by Pap Smear Test Conducted Every 3 Years, Every 2 Years, and Every Year

FREQUENCY OF TEST	COST PER YEAR OF LIFE (1986 DOLLARS)
Every 3 years	$14,300
Every 2 years	451,200
Every year	1,144,000

Source: L. Russell, *op. cit.*

its early stages. Thus there is only a small additional health benefit from testing annually rather than testing every three years. And since testing annually requires tripling the total cost of testing, the cost per year of life saved is a great deal higher if tests are conducted annually rather than every three years.

As shown in Table 2, the United States devotes a larger percentage of its total output to health care

Table 2
Health Care Outlays as a Percentage of Total Output, 1986

COUNTRY	PERCENTAGE
Australia	7.2
Canada	8.5
Denmark	6.1
France	8.5
Germany (West)	8.1
Italy	6.7
Japan	6.7
The Netherlands	8.3
New Zealand	6.9
Norway	6.8
Sweden	9.1
Switzerland	8.0
United Kingdom	6.2
United States	11.1

Source: H. Aaron and W. Schwartz, *op. cit.*

than any other developed country. Yet life expectancies in other industrialized countries typically match or exceed our own. Given the many questions that have been raised concerning the efficiency of health care provision in the United States, and given the good reasons for believing that health costs are excessive, it seems likely that health cost containment will be one of the big domestic economic issues of the 1990s. The government has a major stake in this issue, as illustrated by the fact that federal expenditures on Medicare alone exceeded $100 billion in 1992.

Probing Deeper

1. Why do patients pay only about 10 cents of each dollar spent on hospital care? Who pays the rest?

2. What are the advantages of the government's paying fixed amounts to hospitals for Medicare patients with particular illnesses, rather than reimbursing hospitals for whatever costs they incurred? What are the potential problems?

3. Why do economists tend to favor more competition among health care providers?

4. What problems arise in applying economic analysis in the field of medical care?

5. Suppose that the cost of saving a particular person's life is $1 million. Using economic analysis, should this life be saved?

ments have risen, and Social Security payments increased from about $20 billion in 1965 to about $250 billion in 1990. Since transfer payments do not entail any reallocation of resources from private to public goods, but a transfer of income from one private citizen or group to another, Figure 16.2 is, in some respects, an overstatement of the role of the public sector.

What the Federal, State, and Local Governments Spend Money On

There are three levels of government in the United States—federal, state, and local. The state governments spend the least, while the federal government spends the most. This was not always the case. Before World War I, the local governments spent more than the federal government. In those days, the federal government did not maintain the large military establishment it does now, nor did it engage in the many programs in health, education, welfare, and other areas that it currently does. Figure 16.2 shows that federal spending is now a much larger percentage of the total than it was 60 years ago. Table 16.1 shows how the federal government spends its money. *About one-fourth of the federal expenditures goes for the defense and other items connected with international relations and national security. About one-half goes for Social Security, Medicare, welfare (and other income security) programs, health, and education. The rest goes to support farm, transportation, housing, and other such programs, as well as to pay interest on the federal debt and to run Congress, the courts, and the executive branch of the federal government.*

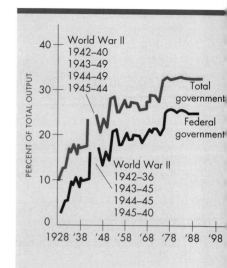

Figure 16.2
Government Spending as a Percent of Total Output, United States
Government expenditures—federal, state, and local—totaled about $1.8 trillion in 1990. These expenditures, which include transfer payments, have grown more rapidly than total output in this period.

Table 16.1
Federal Expenditures, Fiscal 1992

PURPOSE	AMOUNT (BILLIONS OF DOLLARS)	PERCENT OF TOTAL	PURPOSE	AMOUNT (BILLIONS OF DOLLARS)	PERCENT OF TOTAL
National defense	295	20	Transportation	33	2
International affairs	18	1	Community and		
Energy	4	a	regional		
Veterans' benefits	33	2	development	6	a
General science,			Interest	206	14
space, and			General government	13	1
technology	17	1	Income security	185	13
Agriculture	15	1	Administration of		
Education, training,			justice	14	1
employment, and			Medicare	114	8
social services	46	3	Social security	289	20
Health	81	6			
Natural resources			Offsetting receipts	−41	−3
and environment	20	1	Total[b]	1,446	100
Commerce and					
housing credit	93	6			

[a] Less than ½ of 1 percent.
[b] Because of rounding errors, the figures may not sum to totals.
Source: Economic Report of the President. 1991. These are estimates made in 1990.

What about the local and state governments? On what do they spend their money? Table 16.2 shows that *the biggest expenditure of the state and local governments is on schools.* Traditionally, schools in the United States have been a responsibility of local governments—cities and towns. *State governments spend most of their money on education; welfare, old age, and unemployment benefits; and highways.* (Besides supporting education directly, they help localities to cover the cost of schooling.) In addition, the local and state governments support hospitals, redevelopment programs, courts, and police and fire departments.

CHANGES IN VIEW OF GOVERNMENT RESPONSIBILITIES

We have already seen that government expenditures in the United States have grown considerably, both in absolute amount and as a percentage of our total output. Up to about 1975, this growth in government expenditures was part of a general trend in the United States toward a more extensive role of government in the economy. Two hundred years ago, there was considerable suspicion of government interference and meddling, freedom was the watchword, and governments were viewed as potential tyrants. In the nineteenth century, the United States prospered mightily under this *laissez-faire* system, but gradually—and not without considerable protest—the nation began to interpret the role of the government differently.

Increases in Government Role

Responding to the dangers of noncompetitive markets, states were given the power to regulate public utilities and railroads. The Interstate Commerce Commission was established in 1887 to regulate railroads operating across state lines; and the Sherman Antitrust Act was passed in 1890 to curb monopoly and promote competition. To help control recurring business fluctuations and financial panics, banking and finance were regulated. In 1913, the Federal Reserve System was established as a central bank controlling the member commercial banks. In 1933, the Federal Deposit Insurance Corporation was established to insure bank deposits. And in 1934, the Securities and Exchange Commission was established to watch over the financial markets.

In addition, the government's role in the fields of labor and welfare expanded considerably. For example, in the 1930s minimum-wage laws were enacted, old-age pensions and unemployment insurance were established, and the government became an important force in collective bargaining and labor relations. Furthermore, the power of government was used increasingly to ensure that citizens did not fall below a certain economic level. Food-stamp programs and programs to provide aid to dependent children were established. *In general, the broad trend in the United States in the century up to about 1975 or 1980 was for the government to be used to a greater and greater extent to achieve social objectives.*

Recent Changes in Attitude

However, during the 1970s and early 1980s there was a pronounced change in the public's attitude toward the government. People seemed

Table 16.2
Expenditures of State and Local Governments, United States, 1988–89

TYPE OF EXPENDITURE	AMOUNT (BILLIONS OF DOLLARS)	PERCENT OF TOTAL
Education	264	35
Highways	58	8
Public welfare	98	13
Other	342	45
Total[a]	762	100

[a] Because of rounding errors, the figures may not sum to totals.
Source: Economic Report of the President, 1991.

THE SAGA OF THE B-1 BOMBER

About $300 billion of federal spending goes for defense. Decisions concerning how much to spend on what kinds of weapons systems are enormously complex and involve a mixture of military, political, and economic considerations. To illustrate some of these considerations, take the case of the B-1 bomber. As early as 1954, the Air Force began to think about a replacement of the B-52 bomber, but both Presidents Kennedy and Johnson were not impressed with the need for it, since they felt that strategic missiles would be more efficient and accurate than a new manned bomber.

Nonetheless, the Air Force and its contractors did not give up on the idea of the new bomber, and even after President Carter blocked the production of such a bomber in 1977, they continued to push for it. Moreover, the Armed Services Committee of the House of Representatives approved more than $300 million for research and development on this airplane between 1977 and 1980. Within the Pentagon, a group of Air Force officers, led by General Kelly Burke, worked hard to make the bomber a reality. When the Reagan administration was elected in 1980, the political climate was much more favorable, and in January 1982 Congress voted approval of the B-1 program.

To help build political support for the B-1 program, Rockwell, the builder of the B-1, farmed out the airplane's production among thousands of subcontractors. For example, the prototype engines were built in Lynn, Massachusetts; the actuators were built in Kalamazoo, Michigan; and so on. Nearly every member of Congress had a firm in his or her district that had a stake in the B-1 program.

The B-1 program was estimated to cost about $20 billion. But the costs of weapons systems are often underestimated, since this makes it easier to sell them to Congress. For a long time, the B-1 systems program office at Wright-Patterson Air Force Base made two different cost estimates; according to one report, "one [estimate] showed what we'd said the B-1 would cost. The other showed what we really thought it would cost."[1]

Whether the B-1 is an effective weapons system

has been the subject of great controversy. Some argue that it is slow, sluggish, and limited in range. There are problems, which may never be fully corrected, in the plane's electronic defensive systems. According to Congressional critics, these and other problems have resulted from the Air Force's assuming the role of prime contractor. In 1987, the House Armed Services Committee concluded that "the United States Air Force has been a greater threat to the success of the B-1 bomber than has the Soviet Union."[2]

The amount of resources devoted to military programs of this sort is nothing less than mammoth. (In the case of the B-1, the cost of 100 airplanes is about $25 billion!) Few people would question the need for a strong and effective national defense, but there is a widespread feeling that the weapons acquisition process is not as efficient as it might be. In September 1987, one of the first B-1 bombers crashed in southern Colorado, and in December 1987 the Strategic Air Command suspended low-level flights for these new bombers, thus provoking more controversy concerning this already controversial military procurement program. Another crash occurred in 1988. And when war broke out in the Persian Gulf in 1991, critics pointed out that the B-1 was not being used there.

[1] "Is the B-1 a Plane Whose Time Has Come?," *Philadelphia Inquirer,* March 18, 1984.

[2] "Turbulent History Still Buffets B-1 Program," *New York Times,* September 29, 1987, and "Low-Level Flights of B-1 Are Halted," *New York Times,* December 4, 1987. Also, see "The Military's New Myths," *New York Times,* January 30, 1991.

more inclined to question the government's capacity to solve the difficult social problems that confront our nation. In part, this seemed to be due to the apparent failure of large and expensive government programs initiated to solve a variety of social ills, such as poverty. In part, it seemed to reflect a general cynicism concerning government and politicians. One public-opinion poll after another showed that the public was irritated by the payment of what it regarded as excessively high taxes.

In 1978, California's voters supported Proposition 13 by nearly a 2-to-1 margin. Proposition 13 called for a 57 percent cut in the property tax and decreed that no local tax may increase by more than 2 percent per year. Californians were angry at the rapid increase in their property taxes during the 1970s. One Los Angeles family bought a house for $64,000 in 1968 and its property tax then was $1,800. By 1976, it had increased to $3,500, and without Proposition 13, it soon would have gone to $7,000. Californians supported Proposition 13 as a way to offset past increases and limit future increases in the property tax.

In the 1980 elections, Ronald Reagan won the presidency in part by promising to get government "off the backs" of citizens. In his first years in office, he cut back the rate of growth of federal expenditure and reduced many government programs. In 1984, he ran again on a platform that emphasized the reduction of government's role (but an increase in defense expenditure). Again he won. And in 1988, George Bush won with a similar platform. How long this sort of public attitude will persist is hard to say, but while it lasts, conservatives tend to be happy and liberals tend to be concerned.

WHAT THE FEDERAL, STATE, AND LOCAL GOVERNMENTS RECEIVE IN TAXES

To get the money to cover most of the expenditures discussed in previous sections, governments collect taxes from individuals and firms. As Table 16.3 shows, *at the federal level the **personal income tax** is the biggest single money raiser.* It brings in almost one-half of the tax revenue collected by the federal government. The next most important taxes at the federal level are the social insurance (Social Security) taxes. Other noteworthy taxes are the corporation income tax, excise taxes (levied on the sale of tobacco, liquor, imports, and certain other items), and death and gift taxes. (Even when the Grim Reaper shows up, the Tax Man is not far behind.)

*At the local level, on the other hand, the most important form of taxation and source of revenue is the **property tax.*** This is a tax levied primarily on real estate. Other important local taxes—although dwarfed in importance by the property tax—are local sales taxes and local income taxes. Many cities—for example, New York City—levy a sales tax, equal to a certain percent—4 percent in New York City—of the value of each retail sale. The tax is simply added on to the amount charged the customer. Also, many cities—for example, Philadelphia and Pittsburgh—levy an income (or wage) tax on their residents and even on people who work in the city but live outside it. *At the state level, **sales (and excise) taxes** are the biggest money raisers,* followed by income taxes and highway-user taxes. The latter include taxes on gasoline and license fees for vehicles and drivers. Often they exceed the amount spent on roads, and the balance is used for a variety of nonhighway uses. (See Table 16.4.)

Table 16.3
Federal Receipts by Tax, Fiscal 1992

TYPE OF TAX	AMOUNT (BILLIONS OF DOLLARS)	PERCENT OF TOTAL
Personal income tax	530	45
Corporation income tax	102	9
Social insurance taxes	429	37
Excise taxes	48	4
Estate and gift taxes	13	1
Other revenues	43	4
Total[a]	1,165	100

[a] Because of rounding errors, the figures may not sum to totals.
Source: Economic Report of the President, 1991. These are estimates made in 1990.

Table 16.4
State and Local Tax Revenues, by Source, 1988–89

SOURCE	REVENUES (BILLIONS OF DOLLARS)	PERCENT OF TOTAL
General sales tax	166	25
Property tax	143	22
Personal income tax	98	15
Corporate income tax	26	4
Other taxes	228	34
Total[a]	661	100

[a] Because of rounding errors, the figures may not sum to totals.
Source: Economic Report of the President, 1991.

1. "I believe the government should do only that which private citizens cannot do for themselves, or which they cannot do so well for themselves." Interpret and comment. Indicate how one might determine in practice what the legitimate functions of government are, according to this proposition.

2. "The ideal public policy, from the viewpoint of the state, is one with identifiable beneficiaries, each of whom is helped appreciably, at the cost of many unidentifiable persons, none of whom is hurt much." Interpret and comment. Indicate how this proposition might be used to help predict government behavior.

3. Explain why national defense is a public good but a rifle is not a public good.

4. "I cannot get the amount of national defense I want and you, a different amount." Explain. Is this true of all public goods?

5. According to the 1991 *Economic Report of the President,* the federal government will spend about $17 billion on general science, space, and technology in fiscal 1992. Why should the government support each of these activities?

THE ROLE OF GOVERNMENT IN AMERICAN AGRICULTURE

Thus far, we have been discussing the government's role in the American economy in rather general terms. Now we turn to a particular example of the economic programs carried out by our government—the nation's farm programs. It is important to recognize at the outset that these farm programs are not being held up as a representative sample of what the government does. There are a host of other government economic programs—poverty programs, urban programs, defense programs, research programs, education programs, transportation programs, fiscal programs, monetary programs, and many more. Most of these programs are discussed at some point in this book.

Agriculture is an enormously important sector of the American economy. Even though its size has been decreasing steadily—and this contraction has been going on for many decades—agriculture still employs almost 3 million Americans. Its importance, moreover, cannot be measured entirely by its size. You need only think about how difficult it would be to get along without food to see the strategic role agriculture plays in our economic life. Also, when it comes to technological change, agriculture is one of the most progressive parts of the American economy. The efficiency of American agriculture is admired throughout the world.

THE FARM PROBLEM

Nonetheless, it is widely acknowledged that American agriculture has had serious problems. Historically, the clearest indication of these problems has been shown by a comparison of the average income of American farmers with the average income among the rest of the population. Frequently, the average income of farm families has been 20 percent or more below the average income of nonfarm families. Moreover, a substantial proportion of the rural population has been poor. Thus the National Advisory Commission on Rural Poverty found that "rural poverty is so widespread, and so acute, as to be a national disgrace." Of course, this does not mean that all farmers are poor: on the contrary, many do very well indeed. But a substantial percentage of the nation's farmers has been poor by any standard.

This farm problem is nothing new. During the first two decades of the twentieth century, farmers enjoyed relatively high prices and relatively high incomes. But in 1920, the country experienced a sharp depression that jolted agriculture as well as the rest of the economy. Whereas the Roaring Twenties saw a recovery and boom in the nonfarm sector of the economy, agriculture did not recover as completely, and the 1930s were dreadful years; the Great Depression resulted in a sickening decline in farm prices and farm incomes. World War II brought prosperity to agriculture, but in the postwar period, farm incomes continually have been well below nonfarm incomes. In 1973 to 1975, prosperity returned to the farms, but the late 1970s and 1980s saw renewed complaints by farmers about prices and incomes. All in all, agriculture has had difficulties for many decades.

Causes of the Farm Problem

The simple models of market behavior presented in previous chapters—the models involving market demand curves and market supply curves—can be used to explain the basic causes of the problems that have tended to besiege agriculture.

CHARACTERISTICS OF DEMAND AND SUPPLY. Let's start with the market demand curve for farm products. If you think about it for a moment, you will agree that this market demand curve must have two important characteristics. First, *its shape must reflect the fact that food is a necessity and that the quantity demanded will not vary much with the price of food.* Second, *the market demand curve for food is unlikely to shift to the right very much as per capita income rises,* because consumption of food per capita faces natural biological and other limitations.

Next, consider the market supply curve for farm products. Again, you should be aware of two important characteristics of this market supply curve. First, *the quantity of farm products supplied tends to be relatively insensitive to price,* because the farmers have only limited control over their output. (Weather, floods, insects, and other such factors are very important.) Second, because of the rapid technological change emphasized in a previous section, *the market supply curve has been shifting markedly and rapidly to the right.*

DECLINE IN RELATIVE FOOD PRICES. If you understand these simple characteristics of the market demand curve and market supply curve for farm products, it is no trick at all to understand why we have had the sort of farm problem just described. Figure 16.3 shows the market demand and market supply curves for farm products at various points in time. As you would expect, the market demand curve for farm products shifts rather slowly to the right as incomes (and population) grow over time. Specifically, the market demand curve shifted from D in the first period to D_1 in the second period to D_2 in the third period. On the other hand, the mar-

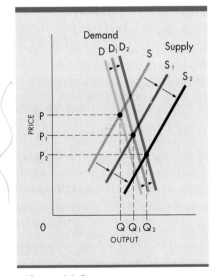

Figure 16.3
Shifts over Time in Market Demand and Supply Curves for Farm Products
The market demand curve has shifted rather slowly to the right (from D to D_1 to D_2), whereas the market supply curve has shifted rapidly to the right (from S to S_1 to S_2), with the result that the equilibrium price has declined (from OP to OP_1 to OP_2).

ket supply curve for farm products shifted rapidly to the right as technology improved over time. Specifically, it shifted from S in the first period to S_1 in the second period to S_2 in the third period.

What was the consequence of these shifts in the market demand and supply curves for food products? Clearly, *the equilibrium price of food products fell (relative to other products)*. Specifically, the equilibrium price fell from OP to OP_1 to OP_2 in Figure 16.3. This price decrease was, of course, a large part of the farm problem. If we correct for changes in the general level of prices (which have tended to rise over time), there was, in general, a declining trend in farm prices. That is, agricultural prices generally fell, relative to other prices, in the last 60 years. Moreover, *given this fall in farm prices, farm incomes tended to fall, because, although lower prices were associated with greater amounts sold, the price reduction was much greater than the increase in quantity sold,* as shown in Figure 16.3.[4]

This simple supply-and-demand model explains the fact that, in real terms, farm prices and farm incomes have tended to fall in the United States. Certainly there is nothing mysterious about these trends. Given the nature and characteristics of the market demand curve and market supply curve for farm products, our simple model shows that these trends are as much to be expected as parades on the Fourth of July.

Slow Exit of Resources

However, one additional fact must be noted to understand the farm problem: *people and nonhuman resources have been relatively slow to move out of agriculture in response to these trends.* As we have pointed out repeatedly in previous chapters, the price system uses such trends—lower prices and lower incomes—to signal producers that they should use their resources elsewhere. Farmers have been loath to move out of agriculture (even though they often could make more money elsewhere)—and this has been a primary cause of the farm problem that has existed over most of the past 50 years. If more people and resources had left farming, agricultural prices and incomes would have risen, and farm incomes would have come closer to nonfarm incomes. (Poor education and race were, of course, significant barriers to migration.)

Nonetheless, even though farmers have been slow to move out of agriculture, they have left the farm in the long run. In 1930 the farm population was about 30 million, or 25 percent of the total population; in 1950, it was about 23 million or 15 percent of the total population; and in 1989, it was about 5 million, or 2 percent of the total population. Thus the price system has had its way. Resources have been moving out of agriculture in response to the signals and pressures of the price system. This movement of people and nonhuman resources unquestionably has contributed to greater efficiency and production for the nation as a whole. But during most of the past 50 years, we have continued to have a "surplus" of farmers—and this has been the root of the farm problem.

[4] The amount farmers receive is the amount they sell times the price. Thus, in Figure 16.3, the amount farmers receive in income is $OP \times OQ$ in the first period, $OP_1 \times OQ_1$ in the second period, and $OP_2 \times OQ_2$ in the third period. Clearly, since the price is decreasing much more rapidly than the quantity is increasing, farm incomes are falling.

GOVERNMENT AID TO AGRICULTURE

Traditionally, farmers have had a disproportionately large influence in Congress; and faced with declining economic fortunes, they appealed to the government for help. They extolled the virtues of rural life, emphasized that agriculture is a competitive industry, and claimed that it was unfair for their prices to fall relative to the prices they have had to pay. In addition, they pointed out that the movement of resources out of agriculture has entailed large human costs, since this movement, although beneficial to the nation as a whole, has been traumatic for the farm population. For reasons of this sort, they argued that the government should help farmers; and in particular, that the government should act to bolster farm prices and farm incomes.

The Concept of Parity

Their voices were heard. In the Agricultural Adjustment Act of 1933, Congress announced the concept of parity as the major objective of American farm policy. This concept acquired great importance—and must be clearly understood. Put in its simplest terms, the concept of *parity* says that a farmer should be able to exchange a given quantity of his or her output for as much in the way of nonfarm goods and services as he or she could at some time in the past. For example, if a farmer could take a bushel of wheat to market in 1912 and get enough money to buy a pair of gloves, today he or she should be able to get enough money for a bushel of wheat to buy a pair of gloves.

To see what the concept of parity implies for farm prices, suppose that the price of gloves triples. Obviously, if parity is to be maintained, the price of wheat must triple too. Thus the concept of parity implies that farm prices must increase at the same rate as the prices of the goods and services farmers buy. Of course, farmers buy lots of things besides gloves, so in actual practice the parity price of wheat or other farm products is determined by the changes over time in the average price of all the goods and services farmers buy.

Two major points should be noted about parity. First, to use this concept, one must agree on some base period, such as 1912 in the example above, during which the relationship of farm to nonfarm prices is regarded as equitable. Obviously, the higher farm prices were relative to nonfarm prices in the base period, the higher farm prices will be in subsequent periods if parity is maintained. It is interesting to note that 1910–14 was used for many years as the base period. Since this was a period of relatively high farm prices and of agricultural prosperity, the farm bloc must have wielded considerable political clout on this issue. Second, note that the concept of parity is an ethical, not a scientific proposition. It states what the relative economic position of a bushel of wheat ought to be—or more precisely, it states one particular view of what the relative economic position of a bushel of wheat should be. Based on purely scientific considerations, there is no way to prove (or disprove) this proposition, since it is based on one's values and political preferences. Using the terminology of Chapter 1, it is a proposition in normative, not positive economics.

PRICE SUPPORTS AND SURPLUS CONTROLS

During the four decades up to the 1970s, the concept of parity was the cornerstone of a system of government price supports. In many cases, the government did not support farm prices at the full 100 percent of parity. For example, Congress may have enacted a bill saying that the secretary of agriculture could establish a price of wheat, corn, cotton, or some other product that is between 65 and 90 percent of parity. But whatever the exact level of the price supports, the idea behind them was perfectly simple: it was to maintain farm prices above the level that would result in a free market.

Using the simple supply-and-demand model developed in previous chapters, we can see more clearly the effects of these price supports. The situation is shown in Figure 16.4. A support price, OP', was set by the government. Since this support price was above the equilibrium price, OP, the public bought *less* of farm products (OQ_2 rather than OQ) and paid a *higher* price for them. Farmers gained from the price supports, since the amount they received for their crop under the price support was equal to $OP' \times OQ_1$, a greater amount than what they would have received in a free market, which was $OP \times OQ$.

Note, however, that since the support price exceeded the equilibrium price, the quantity supplied of the farm product, OQ_1, exceeded the quantity demanded, OQ_2. That is, *there was a surplus of the farm product in question,* which the government had to purchase, since no one else would. These surpluses were an embarrassment, both economically and politically. They showed that society's scarce resources were being utilized to produce products consumers simply did not want at existing prices. Moreover the cost of storing these surpluses was very large indeed: in some years, these storage costs alone hit the $1-billion mark.

Policies to Cut Surpluses

To help reduce these surpluses, the government followed two basic strategies. First, *it tried to restrict output of farm products.* In particular, the government established an acreage allotment program, which said that farmers had to limit the number of acres they planted in order to get price supports on their crops. The Department of Agriculture estimated how much of each product would be demanded by buyers (other than the government) at the support price, and tried to cut back the total acreage planted with this crop to the point where the quantity supplied equaled the quantity demanded. These output restrictions did not eliminate the surpluses, because farmers managed to increase the yields from acreage they were allowed to plant, but undoubtedly they reduced the surpluses. With these restrictions, the situation was as shown in Figure 16.5, where OQ_3 was the total output that could be grown on the acreage that could be planted with the crop. Because of the imposition of this output control, the surplus—which the government had to purchase—was reduced from $(OQ_1 - OQ_2)$ to $(OQ_3 - OQ_2)$. Farmers continued to benefit from price supports because the amount they received for their crop—$OP' \times OQ_3$—was still greater than they would have received in a free market, because the amount demanded of farm products was not very sensitive to their price.

Second, *the government tried to shift the demand curve for farm products to the right.* An effort was made to find new uses for various farm

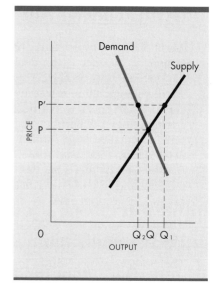

Figure 16.4
Effects of Farm Price-Support Program
The support price, OP', is above the equilibrium price, OP, so the public buys OQ_2, farmers supply OQ_1 units of output, and the government buys the difference $(OQ_1 - OQ_2)$.

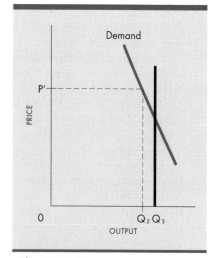

Figure 16.5
Effects of Price Supports and Output Restrictions
The government restricts output to OQ_3, with the result that it buys $(OQ_3 - OQ_2)$ units of output.

products. Also, various antipoverty programs, such as the food-stamp program, used our farm surpluses to help the poor. In addition, the government tried to expand the export markets for American farm products. Western Europe and Japan increased their demand for food, and the Communist countries purchased our farm products to offset their own agricultural deficiencies. Moreover, the less developed countries were permitted by Public Law 480 to buy our farm products with their own currencies, rather than dollars. The result was a reduction in farm surpluses, as shown in Figure 16.6. Since the market demand curve for farm products shifted to the right, the surplus was reduced from $(OQ_3 - OQ_2)$ to $(OQ_3 - OQ_4)$. Because of these demand-augmenting and output-restricting measures, surpluses during the late 1960s and early 1970s were considerably smaller than they were during the late 1950s and early 1960s.

FARM POLICY: THE PAST TWENTY YEARS

In 1973, farm prices increased markedly, due partly to very great increases in foreign demand for American agricultural products. This increase in foreign demand was due to poor harvests in the Soviet Union, Australia, Argentina, and elsewhere, as well as to devaluations of the dollar. (In 1972–73, the Soviet Union alone bought over $1 billion of grain—on terms that provoked considerable controversy in the United States.) As a result, farm incomes reached very high levels, farm surpluses disappeared, and for the first time in 30 years the government was trying to stimulate farm production rather than restrict it.

Taking advantage of this new climate, Congress passed a new farm bill which ended price supports. This bill, the Agriculture and Consumer Protection Act of 1973, aimed at reducing government involvement in agriculture and at a return to freer markets. Specifically, agricultural prices were allowed to fluctuate freely in accord with supply and demand. However, the government made cash payments to farmers if prices fell below certain "target" levels established by the law. These target levels were above the prices that generally prevailed in the past, but they were below the high levels of prices prevailing in 1973.[5] A program of this kind was originally proposed in 1949 by Charles F. Brannan, who was secretary of agriculture under President Harry Truman. (Recall Chapter 4.)

Increases in Government Involvement

During 1976 and 1977 U.S. farmers harvested bumper crops, with the result that prices fell considerably. The price of wheat, which had been about $3.50 per bushel in 1975, fell to about $2.30 per bushel in 1977. Farmers protested, and exerted political pressure for increased government price and income supports. In 1977 Congress passed the Food and Agricultural Act, which contained flexible price-support levels and income supports. No longer was there much talk about a return to freer markets. Instead, the emphasis seemed to be on more support for farm prices and incomes.

The early 1980s were a time of recession, and farmers (with large debts

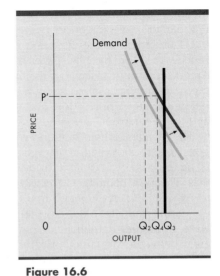

Figure 16.6
Effects of Price Supports, Output Restrictions, and a Shift to the Right in the Demand Curve for Farm Products
By shifting the demand curve to the right, the government reduces the surplus from $(OQ_3 - OQ_2)$ to $(OQ_3 - OQ_4)$ units of output.

---

[5] Actually, the provisions of the law were more complicated than this, but for present purposes, this simplified description is sufficient.

incurred for expansion in the 1970s) were battered by low farm prices and higher costs. Target prices were raised by Congress in the 1981 farm bill. Due in part to the increased value of the dollar relative to other currencies in the early 1980s, which pushed up the price to foreigners of American farm products, our exports of farm products were hurt. In 1984, the price of wheat fell to about $3.50 a bushel, which was about a dollar below the target price. More and more farmers began to default on loans and to go bankrupt.

The Reagan administration, while originally opposed to large-scale government intervention in agriculture, responded with aid. In 1985, Congress passed a farm bill that lowered the price of American farm products in export markets. Government stocks of farm products were given to exporters to be provided free (as bonuses) to foreigners who bought our farm products. Also, target prices were reduced, but farm incomes were supported by deficiency payments (that are based on the discrepancy between the target price and the market price). During the late 1980s, the situation on the nation's farms improved, although 1988 saw a drought in the Corn Belt (and the summer of 1989 was dry in some winter-wheat states).

By the early 1990s, optimism began to spread throughout many parts of American agriculture. According to Gary Benjamin of the Federal Reserve Bank of Chicago, "Land values have recovered, and farm debts have declined 30 percent from the peak of 1983."[6] But many observers are concerned about the government's large role in agriculture. As Mark Drabenstott of the Federal Reserve Bank of Kansas City put it in 1990, "What is very bothersome is that after three years of a strong recovery, agriculture is still so dependent on government payments."[7] In 1988 alone, the federal government spent over $50 billion on agriculture.

At a rally to defend the small farmer from falling prices

EVALUATION OF GOVERNMENT FARM PROGRAMS

It is obviously hard to evaluate the success of the government's farm programs. Farmers will certainly take a different view of price supports and other measures than their city cousins. Nonetheless, from the point of view of the nation as a whole, these farm programs have received considerable criticism. To understand these criticisms, we must hark back to our discussion earlier in this chapter of the proper functions of government, and ask what justification there is for the government's intervening in this way in agriculture. Perhaps the most convincing justification is that the government ought to help the rural poor. As we saw previously, most people agree that the government should redistribute income in this way.

HAVE THE POOR BEEN HELPED? Unfortunately, however, *our farm programs have done little for the farmers most in need of help*, because the amount of money a farmer has gotten from these programs has depended on how much he or she produced. Thus the big farmers have gotten the lion's share of the subsidies—and they, of course, needed help least. (The crown prince of Liechtenstein, as a partner in a Texas rice farm, received a subsidy of more than $2 million.) On the other hand, the small farmers,

[6] *New York Times,* May 18, 1990, p. D16.
[7] Ibid.

the farmers who are mired most deeply in poverty, have received little from these programs. Recognizing this fact, many observers have pointed out that, if these programs are really aimed at helping the rural poor, it would be more sensible to channel the money to them through direct subsidies, than to finance programs where much of the benefits goes to prosperous commercial farmers.

HAS THE FARM PROBLEM BEEN SOLVED? It must also be recognized that *our farm programs have not dealt with the basic causes of the farm problem.* In the past at least, we have had too many people and resources in agriculture. This, as we stressed in previous sections, is why farmers' incomes have tended to be low. Yet the government's farm programs have been directed more toward supporting farm prices and incomes (and stabilizing a sector of the economy that historically has been unstable), rather than toward promoting the needed movement of people and resources out of agriculture. Indeed, some people would say that the government's farm programs have made it more difficult for the necessary adjustments to take place.

Given these defects, many proposals have been made to alter our farm programs. In the view of many observers, agriculture should return to something more closely approximating free markets, and the price system should be allowed to work more freely. The changes that occurred in the early 1970s were a step in that direction, but more recently the government has still been intervening heavily in agriculture.

We began this chapter by stressing the fact that the price system breaks down under some circumstances, and that the government must intervene. It is also worth stressing that the government sometimes intervenes when it shouldn't—and that even when it should intervene, it sometimes does so in a way that wastes resources. *This, of course, doesn't mean that the government should play no part in the American economy. On the contrary, the government must—and does—play an important role. What it does mean is that, just as the price system is no all-purpose cureall, neither is the government.*

TEST YOURSELF

1. Suppose that the demand and supply curves for paper are as shown at right. If paper production results in serious pollution of rivers and streams, is the socially optimal output of paper less than, greater than, or equal to OQ? Does the supply curve reflecting the true social costs of producing paper lie to the right or to the left of the supply curve shown at right? Why?

2. Suppose that paper production results in some important uncompensated benefits to other industries. If there are major external economies of this sort (and if paper production no longer results in any pollution), is the socially optimal output of paper less than, greater than, or equal to OQ in Question 1? Does the demand curve reflecting the true social benefits from paper output lie to the right or to the left of the demand curve shown in Question 1? Why?

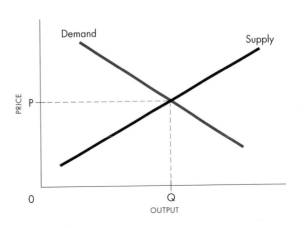

3. Explain the nature of America's farm problem. To what extent have government policies solved the problem?

4. Suppose that the demand curve for corn is as follows:

PRICE (DOLLARS PER BUSHEL)	QUANTITY DEMANDED PER YEAR (MILLIONS OF BUSHELS)
1	70
2	65
3	60
4	55
5	50
6	45

If the government supports the price of corn at $4 per bushel, and if it restricts output to 60 million bushels per year, how much corn will the government have to buy each year? If the government stopped supporting the price of corn, what would its price be?

5. The Council of Economic Advisers, in their 1987 Annual Report, said that "The Food Security Act of 1985 and its predecessors have helped to create many new problems that affect the U.S. agricultural sector, and have failed adequately to solve many old problems. The fundamental flaw is that Federal farm subsidies are linked directly to farm production.... [That is,] farmers are paid subsidies (explicit or implicit) that are proportional to their output...." Why is this a flaw?

6. "The sharp increases in the price of wheat during the mid-1970s were due primarily to shifts in the supply curve for wheat." Comment.

SUMMARY

1. The price system, despite its many virtues, suffers from serious limitations. There is no reason to believe that the distribution of income generated by the price system is equitable or optimal. Also, there is no way for the price system to handle public goods properly, and because of external economies or diseconomies, the price system may result in too little or too much of certain goods being produced.

2. To a considerable extent, the government's role in the economy has developed in response to these limitations of the price system. There is considerable agreement that the government should redistribute income in favor of the poor, provide public goods, and offset the effects of external economies and diseconomies. Also, it is generally felt that the government should establish a proper legal, social and competitive framework for the price system, and that it should promote the maintenance of relatively full employment with reasonably stable prices.

3. Beyond this, however, there are wide differences of opinion on the proper role of government in economic affairs. Conservatives tend to be suspicious of "big government" while liberals are inclined to believe that the government should do more.

4. Government spending is now much larger, both in absolute terms and as a percent of total output, than it was in the early decades of this century. (It is now about one-third of our total output.) To a large extent, this increase has been due to our greater military responsibilities, as well as to the fact that, as their incomes have risen, our citizens have demanded more schools, highways, and other goods and services provided by government. Also, government transfer payments like Social Security and Medicare have grown substantially.

5. To get the money to cover most of these expenditures, governments collect taxes from individuals and firms. At the federal level, the most important form of taxation is the personal income tax; at the local level, the property tax is very important; and at the state level, sales (and excise) taxes are the biggest money raisers.

6. One example of the role of government in the American economy is the farm program. American agriculture has been plagued by relatively low incomes. In general, the demand for farm products has grown slowly, while rapid technological change has meant that the people and resources currently in agriculture could supply more and more farm products. Because people and resources did not move out of agriculture as rapidly as the price system dictated, farm incomes tended to be relatively low.

7. In response to political pressures from the farm blocs, the government set in motion a series of programs to aid farmers. A cornerstone of these programs was the concept of parity, which said that the prices farmers receive should increase at the same rate as the prices of the goods and services farmers buy. The government instituted price supports to keep farm prices above their equilibrium level. But since the support prices exceeded the equilibrium prices, there was a surplus of the commodities that the government had to purchase and store. To help reduce these surpluses, the government tried to restrict the output of farm products and expand the demand for them.

8. These farm programs received considerable criticism. From the point of view of income redistribution, they suffered from the fact that they did little for the farmers most in need of help. As tools of resource allocation, they suffered because they dealt more with the symptoms of the farm

problem than with its basic causes. In 1973, price supports were ended, but the government pledged to make cash payments to farmers if farm prices fall below certain target levels. During the late 1970s, 1980s, and early 1990s, the government continued to intervene heavily in agriculture.

9. The government's farm programs illustrate the fact that government intervention, like the price system, has plenty of limitations. Neither the price system nor government intervention is an all-purpose cure-all.

CONCEPTS FOR REVIEW

Public goods

External economy

External diseconomy

Welfare payments

Government transfer payments

Personal income tax

Property tax

Sales tax

Parity

GOVERNMENT AND THE ENVIRONMENT

IN 1990, SECTIONS OF Long Island Sound were described as "a dead sea, with oxygen-starved waters sometimes fatal to shellfish and devoid of fin fish. Beaches throughout the 600 miles of coastline have been closed for hundreds of days a year, and sewage pollution has wiped out tens of thousands of acres of shellfish beds."[1] Unfortunately, Long Island Sound is not an isolated case. Environmental pollution is an important problem in the United States, and one which the government is trying to help solve.

Without question, the public is genuinely concerned about environmental problems. However, in the effort to clean up the environment, choices are not always clear, nor solutions easy. In this chapter, we consider the economic aspects of environmental decay, the purpose being to indicate the extent of our environmental problems, the factors that are responsible for them, and the sorts of public policies that have been adopted to help deal with them.

OUR ENVIRONMENTAL PROBLEMS

Water Pollution

To see what we mean by environmental pollution, let's begin with one of the most important parts of mankind's environment: our water supplies. As a result of human activities, large amounts of pollutants are discharged into streams, lakes, and the sea. Chemical wastes are released by industrial plants and mines, as well as by farms and homes when fertilizers, pesticides, and detergents run off into waterways. Oil is discharged into the waters by tankers, sewage systems, oil wells, and other sources. Organic compounds enter waterways from industrial plants and farms, as well as from municipal sewage plants; and animal wastes, as well as human wastes, contribute substantially to pollution.

Obviously, we cannot continue to increase the rate at which we dump wastes into our streams, rivers, and oceans. A river or ocean, like everything else, can bear only so much. The people of New Jersey know this well. In the summer of 1987, many New Jersey beaches were closed, when hundreds of dead dolphins, raw sewage, and even used syringes washed ashore. Of course, this is an extreme case, but many of our rivers,

[1] *New York Times*, June 6, 1990.

including the Hudson and the Ohio, are badly polluted. Water pollution is a nuisance and perhaps a threat.

Air Pollution

If clean water is vital to human survival, so too is clean air. Yet the battle being waged against air pollution in most of our major cities has not been won. Particles of various kinds are spewed into the air by factories that utilize combustion processes, grind materials, or produce dust. Motor vehicles release lead compounds from gasoline and rubber particles worn from tires, helping to create that unheavenly condition known as smog. Citizens of Los Angeles are particularly familiar with smog, but few major cities have escaped at least periodic air pollution. No precise measures have been developed to gauge the effects of air pollution on public health and enjoyment, but some rough estimates suggest that perhaps 25 percent of all deaths from respiratory disease could be avoided by a 50 percent reduction in air pollution.[2]

One of the most important contributors to air pollution is the combustion of fossil fuels, particularly coal and oil products: by-products of combustion comprise about 85 percent of the total amount of air pollutants in the United States. Most of these pollutants result from impure fuels or inefficient burning. Among the more serious pollutants are sulphur dioxide, carbon monoxide, and various oxides of nitrogen. The automobile is one of the principal sources of air pollution.

The battle for clean air goes on in cities throughout the United States. During 1983–85, air pollution, as measured by the number of carbon monoxide molecules per million molecules of air, was highest (among cities with 1 million or more inhabitants) in Los Angeles, Denver, Phoenix, Newark (N.J.), New York, Minneapolis, Boston, Baltimore, Washington, and Chicago. Clearly, the pollution problem is not confined to a few regions; it is a national problem.

THE IMPORTANT ROLE OF EXTERNAL DISECONOMIES

The reason why our economic system has tolerated pollution of the environment lies largely in the concept of external diseconomies, which we mentioned in Chapter 16. An ***external diseconomy*** occurs when one person's (or firm's) use of a resource damages other people who cannot obtain proper compensation. When this occurs, a market economy is unlikely to function properly. The price system is based on the supposition that the full cost of using each resource is borne by the person or firm that uses it. If this is not the case and if the user bears only part of the full costs, then the resource is not likely to be directed by the price system into the socially optimal use.

Consider electric power companies, which frequently do not pay the full cost of disposing of wastes in the atmosphere. They charge an artificially low price, and the public is induced to use more electric power than is socially desirable. Similarly, since the owners of automobiles do not pay the full cost of disposing of exhaust and other wastes in the atmosphere,

[2] See L. Lave and E. Seskin, *Air Pollution and Human Health,* Baltimore: published for Resources for the Future by the Johns Hopkins University Press, 1977.

they pay an artificially low price for operating an automobile, and the public is induced to own and use more automobiles than is socially desirable.

To understand why divergences between private and social costs can cause the price system to malfunction, we might begin by reviewing briefly how resources are allocated in a market economy. As we saw in Chapter 3, resources are used in their socially most valuable way because they are allocated to the people and firms who find it worthwhile to bid most for them, assuming that prices reflect true social costs. Under these circumstances, a firm that maximizes its profits will produce the socially desirable output and use the socially desirable amount of labor, capital, and other resources. Under these circumstances, there is no problem.

Suppose, however, that because of the presence of external diseconomies people and firms do not pay the true social costs for resources. For example, suppose that some firms or people can use water and air for nothing, but that other firms or people incur costs as a consequence of this prior use. In this case, the **private costs** of using air and water differ from the **social costs:** *the price paid by the user of water and air is less than the true cost to society.* In a case like this, users of water and air are guided in their decisions by the private cost of water and air—by the prices they pay. Since they pay less than the true social costs, water and air are artificially cheap to them, so that they will use too much of these resources, from society's point of view.

Note that the divergence between private and social cost occurs if, and only if, the use of water or air by one firm or person imposes costs on other firms or persons. Thus, if a paper mill uses water and then treats it to restore its quality, there is no divergence between private and social cost. But when the same mill dumps harmful wastes into streams and rivers (the cheap way to get rid of its by-products), the towns downstream that use the water must incur costs to restore its quality. The same is true of air pollution. If an electric power plant uses the atmosphere as a cheap and convenient place to dispose of wastes, people living and working nearby may incur costs as a result, since the incidence of respiratory and other diseases may increase. In such cases, there may be a divergence between private and social cost.

We said above that pollution-causing activities that result in external diseconomies represent a malfunctioning of the market system. At this point, the nature of this malfunctioning should be clear. *Firms and people dump too much waste material into the water and the atmosphere. The price system does not provide the proper signals because the polluters are induced to use our streams and atmosphere in this socially undesirable way by the artificially low price of disposing of wastes in this manner. Moreover, because the polluters do not pay the true cost of waste disposal, their products are artificially cheap, so that too much is produced of them.*

DIRECT REGULATION BY GOVERNMENT

Pollution is caused by defects in our institutions, not by malicious intent, greed, or corruption. In cases where waste disposal causes significant external diseconomies, economists generally agree that government intervention may be justifiable. But how can the government intervene? Perhaps the simplest way is **direct regulation,** through the issuance of certain enforceable rules for waste disposal. For example, the government can prohibit the burning of trash in furnaces or incinerators, or the dumping of certain materials in the ocean; and make any person or firm that violates these restrictions subject to a fine, or perhaps even imprisonment. Also, the government can ban the use of chemicals like DDT, or require that all automobiles meet certain regulations for the emission of air pollutants. Further, the government can establish quality standards for air and water.

At present, our nation relies heavily on direct regulation to reduce pollution. However, economists agree that direct regulation suffers from some serious disadvantages:

1. Such regulations have generally taken the form of general, across-the-board rules. For example, if two factories located on the same river dump the same amount of waste material into the river, such regulations would probably call for each factory to reduce its waste disposal by the same amount. Unfortunately, although this may appear quite sensible, it may in fact be very inefficient. Suppose that it is much less costly for one factory to reduce its waste disposal than for the other. In such a case, it would be more efficient to ask the factory that could reduce its wastes more cheaply to cut down more on its waste disposal than the other factory. For reasons of this sort, *pollution reductions are likely to be accomplished at more than minimum cost, if they are accomplished by direct regulation.*

2. *To formulate such regulations in a reasonably sensible way, the responsible government agencies must have access to much more information than they are likely to obtain or assimilate.* Unless the government agencies have a detailed and up-to-date familiarity with the technology of hundreds of industries, they are unlikely to make sound rules. Moreover, unless the regulatory agencies have a very wide jurisdiction, their regulations will be evaded by the movement of plants and individuals from localities where regulations are stiff to localities where they are loose. In addition, the regulatory agencies must view the pollution problem as a whole, since piecemeal regulation may simply lead polluters to substitute one form of pollution of another. For example, New York and Philadelphia have attempted to reduce water pollution by more intensive sewage treatment. However, one result has been the production of a lot of biologically active sludge that is being dumped into the ocean—and perhaps causing problems there.

EFFLUENT FEES

The government can also intervene by establishing effluent fees. An *effluent fee* is a fee a polluter must pay to the government for discharging waste. In other words, a price is imposed on the disposal of wastes into the environment; and the more firms or individuals pollute, the more they must pay. The idea behind the imposition of effluent fees is that they can bring the private cost of waste disposal closer to the true social costs. Faced with a closer approximation to the true social costs of their activities, polluters will reduce the extent to which they pollute the environment. Needless to say, many practical difficulties are involved in carrying out this seemingly simple scheme, but many economists believe that this is a better way than direct regulation to deal with the pollution problem.

The use of effluent fees has the following advantages over direct regulation. First, *it obviously is socially desirable to use the cheapest way to*

A wastewater treatment plant

achieve any given reduction in pollution. A system of effluent fees is more likely to accomplish this objective than direct regulation, because the regulatory agency cannot have all the relevant information (as we noted above), *whereas polluters, reacting in their own interest to effluent fees, will tend to use the cheapest means to achieve a given reduction in pollution.*

To see why this is the case, consider a particular polluter. Faced with an effluent fee—that is, a price it must pay for each unit of waste it discharges—the polluter will find it profitable to reduce its discharge of waste so long as the cost of doing so is less than the effluent fee it saves. Thus, if this firm can reduce its discharge of wastes relatively cheaply, it will be induced to make such a reduction by the prospect of increased profits. On the other hand, if it cannot reduce its discharge of wastes at all cheaply, it will not make such a reduction, since the costs will exceed the saving in effluent fees. Thus a system of effluent fees induces firms that can reduce waste disposal more cheaply to cut down more on their waste disposal than firms where such a reduction is more expensive. This means that a given reduction of pollution will occur at a relatively low cost.

Another advantage of effluent fees is that they do not require government agencies to have the detailed technological expertise often required by direct regulation. After all, when effluent fees are used, all the government has to do is meter the amount of pollution a firm or household produces (which admittedly is sometimes not easy) and charge accordingly. It is left to the firms and households to figure out the most ingenious and effective ways to cut down on their pollution and save on effluent fees. This too is a spur to inventive activities aimed at developing more effective ways to reduce pollution. Also economists favor the use of effluent fees because financial incentives are likely to be easier to administer than direct regulation.

While economists tend to favor the use of effluent fees, they are not always against direct regulation. Some ways of disposing of certain types of waste are so dangerous that the only sensible thing to do is to ban them. For example, a ban on the disposal of mercury or arsenic in places where human beings are likely to consume them—and die—seems reasonable enough. In effect, the social cost of such pollution is so high that a very high penalty—imprisonment—is put on it. In addition, of course, economists favor direct regulation when it simply is not feasible to impose effluent fees—for example, in cases where it would be prohibitively expensive to meter the amount of pollutants emitted by various firms or households.

The Ruhr: A Case Study

Let's consider a well-known case of effluent fees in use: the Ruhr valley in Germany. The Ruhr is one of the world's most industrialized areas. It contains about 10 million people and about 4,300 square miles. Water supplies in the Ruhr are quite limited. Five small rivers supply the area. The amazing amount of waste materials these rivers carry is indicated by the fact that the average annual natural low flow is less than the volume of effluent discharged into the rivers. Yet the local water authorities have succeeded in making this small amount of water serve the needs of the firms and households of this tremendous industrial area, and at the same time the streams have been used for recreation. Moreover, all this has been

View of the Ruhr valley, Germany

done at a remarkably low cost. The success of water management in the Ruhr seems to be due in considerable part to institutional arrangements that allowed the German water managers to plan and operate a relatively efficient regional system. Collective water quality improvement measures are used. Water quality is controlled by waste treatment in over 100 plants, regulation of river flow by reservoir, and a number of oxidation lakes in the Ruhr itself.

Effluent fees are an integral part of the institutional arrangements governing water quality. The amount a firm has to pay depends upon how much waste—and what kind—it pumps into the rivers. A formula has been devised to indicate how much a polluter must pay to dispose of a particular type of waste. In simple terms, the formula bases the charge on the amount of clean water needed to dilute the effluent in order to avoid harm to fish. Using this formula, the local authorities can determine, after testing the effluent of any firm, the amount the firm should pay. Specifically, the amount depends on the amount of suspended materials that will settle out of the effluent, the amount of oxygen consumed by bacteria in a sample of effluent, the results of a potassium permanganate test, and the results of a fish toxicity test. You need not understand the nature or specific purposes of these measurements and tests. The important thing is that you understand their general aim—which is to measure roughly the amount of pollution caused by various kinds of wastes. Having made these measurements and tests, the local authorities use their formula to determine how much a firm must pay in effluent fees.

TRANSFERABLE EMISSIONS PERMITS

Another way that the government can reduce pollution is to issue ***transferable emissions permits***. These permits, each of which allows the holder of the permit to generate a certain amount of pollution, are limited in total number. They are sold by the government to the highest bidders. Thus the price of a permit is set by supply and demand, as indicated in Chapter 3. If there is a great demand for such permits, and if the total number is small, the price of a permit will be high. If there is a weak demand for such permits, and if the total number is large, the price of a permit will be low.

One advantage of transferable emissions permits is that the authorities can predict how much pollution there will be. After all, the total amount of pollution cannot exceed the amount authorized by the total number of permits issued. In contrast, if an effluent fee is adopted, it is difficult to predict how much pollution will result, since this depends on how polluters respond to the particular level of the effluent fee that is chosen. For this reason, transferable emissions permits are often preferred over effluent fees.

TAX CREDITS FOR POLLUTION-CONTROL EQUIPMENT

Still another way for the government to intervene is to establish ***tax credits*** for firms that introduce pollution-control equipment. There are, of course, many types of equipment that a plant can introduce to cut down on pollution—for example, "scrubbers" for catching poisonous gases, and electrostatic precipitators for decreasing dust and smoke. But such pollution-control equipment costs money, and firms are naturally reluctant to spend money on purposes where the private rate of return is so low.

To reduce the burden, the government can allow firms to reduce their tax bill by a certain percentage of the amount they spend on pollution-control equipment. A typical suggestion is that the government offer a *tax credit* equal to 20 percent of the cost of pollution-control equipment. In this way, the government would help defray some of the costs of the pollution-control equipment by allowing a firm that installed such equipment to pay less taxes than if no such tax inducements existed.

However, such schemes have a number of disadvantages:

1. Subsidies to promote the purchase of particular types of pollution-control equipment may result in relatively inefficient and costly reductions in pollution. After all, other methods that don't involve special pollution-control equipment—such as substituting one type of fuel for another—may sometimes be a more efficient way to reduce pollution.

2. Subsidies of this sort may not be very effective. Even if the subsidy reduces the cost to the firm of reducing pollution, it may still be cheaper for the firm to continue to pollute. In other words, subsidies of this sort make it a little less painful for polluters to reduce pollution; but unlike effluent fees, they offer no positive incentive.

3. It seems preferable on grounds of equity for the firms and individuals that do the polluting—or their customers—to pay to clean up the mess that results. Effluent fees work this way, but with tax credits for pollution-control equipment, the government picks up part of the tab by allowing the polluter to pay lower taxes. In other words, the general public, which is asked to shoulder the additional tax burden to make up for the polluters' lower taxes, pays part of the cost. But is this a fair allocation of the costs? Why should the general public be saddled with much of the bill?

HOW CLEAN SHOULD THE ENVIRONMENT BE?

One of the most fundamental questions about pollution control is: How clean do we want the air, water, and other parts of our environment to be? At first glance, it may seem that we should restore and maintain a pristine pure environment, but this is not a very sensible goal, since the costs of achieving it would be enormous. The Environmental Protection Agency has estimated that the cost of achieving zero discharge of pollutants would be hundreds of billions of dollars—a truly staggering sum.

Fortunately, however, there is no reason to aim at so stringent a goal. *It seems obvious that, as pollution increases, various costs to society increase as well.* Some of these costs were described at the beginning of this chapter. For example, we pointed out that increases in air pollution result in increased deaths, and that increases in water pollution reduce the recreational value of rivers and streams. Suppose that we could get accurate data on the cost to society of various levels of pollution. Of course, it is extremely difficult to get such data, but if we could, we could determine the relationship between the amount of these costs and the level of pollution. It would look like the hypothetical curve in Figure 17.1. The greater the level of pollution, the higher these costs will be.

But these costs are not the only ones that must be considered. *We must also take into account the costs of controlling pollution.* In other words,

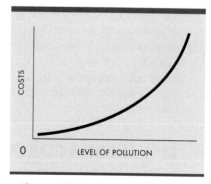

Figure 17.1
Costs to Society of Pollution
The costs to society of pollution increase with the level of pollution.

we must look at the costs to society of maintaining a certain level of environmental quality. These costs are not trivial, as we saw at the beginning of this section. To maintain a very low level of pollution, it is necessary to invest heavily in pollution-control equipment and to make other economic sacrifices.[3] If we could get accurate data on the cost to society of controlling pollution, we could find the relationship between the amount of these costs and the level of pollution. It would look like the hypothetical curve in Figure 17.2; the lower the level of pollution, the higher these costs will be.

A Goal of Zero Pollution?

At this point, it should be obvious why we should not try to achieve a zero level of pollution. *The sensible goal for our society is to minimize the sum of the costs of pollution and the costs of controlling pollution.* In other words, we should construct a graph, as shown in Figure 17.3, to indicate the relationship between the sum of these two types of costs and the level of pollution. Then we should choose the level of pollution at which the sum of these two types of costs is a minimum. Thus, in Figure 17.3, we should aim for a pollution level of *A.* There is no point in trying for a lower level; such a reduction would cost more than it would be worth. For example, the cost of achieving a zero pollution level would be much more than it would be worth. Only when the pollution level exceeds *A* is the extra cost to society of the additional pollution greater than the cost of

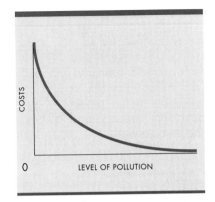

Figure 17.2
Costs to Society of Pollution Control
The more pollution is reduced, the higher are the costs to society of pollution control.

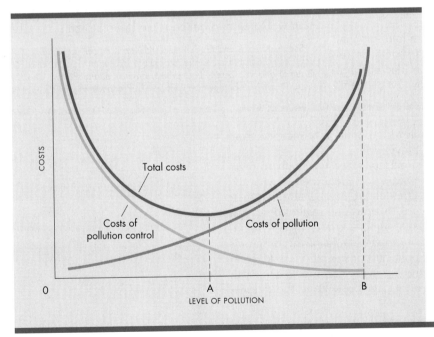

Figure 17.3
Determining Optimal Level of Pollution
The optimal level of pollution is at point *A,* since this is where the total costs are a minimum. Below point *A,* the cost to society of more pollution is less than the cost of preventing it. Above point *A,* the cost to society of more pollution is greater than the cost of preventing it.

---

[3] It is important to recognize that the costs of pollution control extend far beyond the construction of more and better water treatment plants, or the more extensive control of gas emission, or other such steps. A serious pollution-control program can put firms out of business, put people out of work, and bring economic trouble to entire communities. Further, a pollution-control system can result in a redistribution of income. For example, automobiles, electric power, and other goods and services involving considerable pollution are likely to increase in price relative to other goods and services involving little pollution. To the extent that polluting goods and services play a bigger role in the budgets of the poor than of the rich, pollution controls hurt the poor and help the rich.

EXAMPLE 17.1   HOW TO REDUCE THE COSTS OF CLEANING UP

According to estimates made by Allen Kneese and Charles Schultze, the cost of achieving a one-pound reduction in the amount of pollutants emitted at a petroleum refinery and a beet-sugar plant are as shown below:

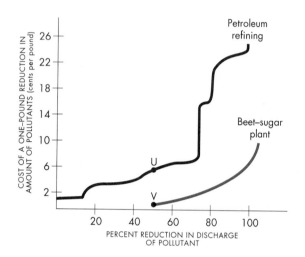

(a) Suppose that it is decided that the total amount of pollutants discharged by both plants should be reduced by 50 percent. If the government decrees that each plant should cut its discharge by 50 percent, what would be the cost of a one-pound reduction at each plant? (b) Can you suggest a way in which this total reduction in pollution can be achieved more efficiently? (c) To achieve this reduction most efficiently, which plant (the petroleum refinery or the beet-sugar plant) should reduce its discharge by the greater percentage? (d) Would an effluent fee achieve this reduction at less cost than the regulation in (a)?

Solution

(a) The petroleum refinery would operate at point U, where the cost of a one-pound reduction in pollution is 6 cents. The beet-sugar plant would operate at point V, where the cost of a one-pound reduction would be 1 cent. (b) Since the beet-sugar plant can reduce pollution at less cost than the petroleum refinery (1 cent per pound rather than 6 cents per pound), it should cut its pollution more and the petroleum refinery should cut its pollution less. (c) The beet-sugar plant, for the reasons given in (b). (d) Yes. If an effluent fee were established, the cost of a one-pound reduction in pollution would tend to be the same at both plants.[*]

[*] See A. Kneese and C. Schultze, *Pollution, Prices, and Public Policy*, Washington, D.C.: The Brookings Institution, 1975; and W. Baumol and W. Oates, *Economics, Environmental Policy, and the Quality of Life*, Englewood Cliffs, N.J.: Prentice-Hall, 1979.

preventing it. For example, the cost of allowing pollution to increase from A to B is much greater than the cost of prevention.

It is easy to draw hypothetical curves, but not so easy actually to measure these curves. Unfortunately, no one has a very clear idea of what the curves in Figure 17.3 really look like—although we can be sure that their general shapes are like those shown there. Thus no one really knows just how clean we should try to make the environment. Under these circumstances, expert opinion differs on the nature and extent of the programs that should be carried out. Moreover, political considerations and pressures enter in. But one thing is for sure: we will continue to live with some pollution—and that, for the reason just given, will be the rational thing to do.

POLLUTION-CONTROL PROGRAMS IN THE UNITED STATES

In recent decades, there has been considerable growth in government programs designed to control pollution. To take but one example, federal expenditures to reduce water pollution increased in the period from the mid-1950s to 1970 from about $1 million to $300 million annually. To curb water pollution, the federal government has for years operated a system of grants-in-aid to state, municipal, or regional agencies to help construct treatment plants; and grants are made for research on new treatment methods. In addition, the 1970 Water Quality Improvement Act authorized grants to demonstrate new methods and techniques and to establish programs to train people in water control management. (The federal government has also regulated the production and use of pesticides.) The states, as well as the federal government, have played an important role in water pollution control. They have set standards for allowable pollution levels, and many state governments have provided matching grants to help municipalities construct treatment plants.

In 1969, the Congress established a new agency—the Council on Environmental Quality—to oversee and plan the nation's pollution control programs. Modeled to some extent on the Council of Economic Advisers, the Council on Environmental Quality, which has three members, is supposed to gather information on considerations and trends in the quality of the environment, review and evaluate the federal government's programs in this area, develop appropriate national policies, and conduct needed surveys and research on environmental quality. The tasks assigned to the council are obviously important ones.

In 1970, the federal government established another new agency, the Environmental Protection Agency (EPA). Working with state and local officials, this agency establishes standards for desirable air and water quality, and devises rules for attaining these goals. The 1970 Clean Air Amendments directed EPA to establish minimum ambient standards for air quality, and it set limits on the emission of carbon monoxide, hydrocarbons, and nitrous oxides from automobiles. But after a number of clashes between EPA and the auto makers, the EPA relaxed the deadlines when these limits were supposed to be met. In 1972 amendments to the Water Pollution Act authorized EPA to set up effluent standards for both privately and publicly owned plants. A stated goal of the amendments was to eliminate the discharge of pollutants into water by 1985, but, for reasons discussed in the previous section, this goal was unrealistically stringent.

DIRECTIONS OF ENVIRONMENTAL POLICY SINCE 1975

In the late seventies and early eighties, policy makers became increasingly concerned that regulatory agencies like EPA had been paying too little attention to the costs involved in reducing pollution. For example, a government study found that a relaxation of EPA's 1977 standard for water-pollution control in the steel industry *with no change in its more stringent 1983 standard* would allow savings in capital costs of $200 million. As President Carter's Council of Economic Advisers pointed out, "In making regulatory decisions on the speed of attaining standards, we should explicitly make a qualitative judgment about whether the gains from earlier attainment are worth the costs." Also, some experts, like Lester Lave of Carnegie-Mellon University and Gilbert Omenn of the Brookings Institution, concluded from their studies that the Clean Air Act was not very effective. In their view, "the application of pollution controls to existing plants and older cars has been limited, and costs have been excessive,

Lester Lave

WHAT SHOULD BE DONE ABOUT GLOBAL WARMING?

According to many world political leaders, there is an urgent need to take action to halt global warming. Scientists have long known that certain gases, notably carbon dioxide, in the atmosphere trap solar energy and heat our planet. (See Figure 1.) Many leading scientists now believe that these gases are being generated faster than the biosphere can neutralize their effects, and that as a consequence the global climate is warming up. Because of this "greenhouse effect," it has been estimated that the earth's global mean temperature could increase by about 5 degrees by the end of the next century, with the result that the sea level may increase by about 2 feet.

Faced with this situation, 68 nations (including the United States, Japan, and the Soviet Union) agreed in late 1989 that carbon dioxide emissions would have to be curbed, and a United Nations report called for a 60 percent cut in "greenhouse" gas emissions. Because fuel combustion is the primary source of carbon dioxide emissions, lower energy consumption would probably be required to curb carbon dioxide resulting from fossil fuel consumption. As pointed out by the Council of Economic Advisers,

A variety of policy tools, including user charges, correction of market failures, regulatory standards, expanded funding for research on and development of substitutes for fossil fuels and other sources of greenhouse emissions, and efforts to reduce and reverse deforestation, could be used to slow the buildup of greenhouse gases in the atmosphere. These approaches are relevant for nearly all greenhouse gases, not just carbon dioxide. While international attention has naturally focused on carbon dioxide as the single largest contributor to the greenhouse effect, control costs must also be considered in the design of any strategy to reduce net emissions of greenhouse gases. A cost-effective strategy may involve a focus on other gases or on sinks that absorb greenhouse emissions. Different approaches may be suitable for different countries.

A fee, charge, or tradable allowances system for greenhouse gas emissions based on an index of the global climate impacts of each greenhouse gas would provide a least-cost reduction in such emissions. A fee or a tradable allowances scheme would lead firms and individuals to consider the social cost of greenhouse emissions in their private decisions. An emission charge or the need to consider the value of allowances would affect decisions ranging from the choice among alternative technologies for generating electricity, to the energy efficiency of cars, buildings, and industrial equipment, to the demand for automobile travel. Because market-based approaches are flexible and provide incentives that affect decisions at all points along the production-consumption chain and across all industries, they automatically focus on those activities where emissions reductions can be achieved at least cost.[1]

Alan Manne of Stanford University and Richard Rickels of the Electric Power Research Institute have carried out a detailed study to estimate the economic costs of constraining carbon dioxide emissions.[2] In particular, they look at what would happen to world output if these emissions were stabilized at current levels, and then gradually reduced by 20 percent by the year 2020. Based on their results, the economic costs would be huge. In particular, gross national

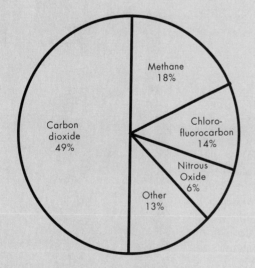

Figure I
Gases Creating the Greenhouse Effect, 1989
Source: New York Times, November 19, 1989.

Carbon dioxide 49%

Methane 18%

Chloro-fluorocarbon 14%

Nitrous Oxide 6%

Other 13%

[1] *Economic Report of the President,* Washington, D.C.: Government Printing Office, 1990, p. 218.
[2] A. Manne and R. Rickels, "CO2 Emission Limits: An Economic Analysis for the U.S.A."

Alan Manne

product would be reduced by about 3 percent in the United States and by about 1 to 2 percent in Europe and Japan. The present value of the cumulative loss over the next century for the United States alone would be about $1 trillion. Because the United States relies relatively heavily on coal as an energy source, the impact would be greater than in Europe or Japan. Moreover, the cost would be great in China, which wants to exploit its rich coal supplies to promote its economic development.

Given that the costs will be greater in some countries than in others, there has been considerable concern over the chances of obtaining a broad, enforceable agreement among countries to limit carbon dioxide emissions. Unless Russia, Eastern Europe, and the less developed countries (like China and India) are willing to commit themselves to such an agreement, there will be only a modest benefit from limitations of this sort in the United States, Western Europe, and Japan. Particularly in the less developed countries, where the rate of growth of energy use is double the world average, it may be difficult to obtain strong enforcement of any agreement. (See Figure 2.)

Confronted by these daunting potential costs and problems, many leading economists have suggested that it would be wise to wait until more is known before adopting strong measures. To support this view, they point out that scientists are sharply split in their views concerning the likelihood of global warming. Some scientists, like Richard Lindzen of Massachusetts Institute of Technology, argue that current forecasts of global warming "are so inaccurate and fraught with uncertainty as to be useless to policy makers."[3] Others argue that if the warming is modest, as they think likely, it could result in benefits such as longer growing seasons in temperate zones and more rain in dry areas.

Given these basic uncertainties, the Council of Economic Advisers concludes as follows:

The highest priority in the near term should be to improve understanding in order to build a foundation for sound policy decisions. Until such a foundation is in place, there is no justification for imposing major costs on the economy to slow the growth of greenhouse gas emissions. Policies that may result in slower growth in greenhouse emissions, but can also be fully justified on other grounds, are the best short-run way to address this potential problem while the uncertainties that exist today are reduced. Being justified on other grounds

[3] "Skeptics Are Challenging Dire 'Greenhouse' Views," *New York Times*, December 13, 1989.

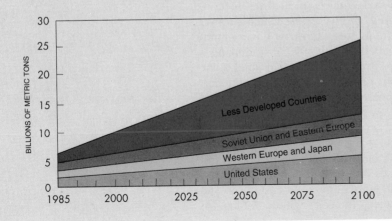

Figure 2
Carbon Dioxide Emissions by Region
The share of carbon dioxide emissions from the less developed countries (like China and India) is projected to grow rapidly. The U.S. share is projected to decline.
Source: Environmental Protection Agency. *Policy Options for Stabilizing Global Climate* (Rapidly Changing World Scenario).

means that a program yields non-greenhouse benefits commensurate with its costs; it cannot mean simply having some non-greenhouse benefits. The adoption of many small programs, each of which would fail a standard cost-benefit test, could significantly slow economic growth and eliminate jobs.

Because the intense research currently underway may reveal that it is desirable to slow the growth of greenhouse gas emissions, it is useful to consider the elements of what would be an economically rational strategy to do so. Any strategy to limit aggregate emissions without worldwide participation would be likely to fail. A cost-effective policy must provide for comprehensive coverage of both sources and sinks of all major greenhouse gases. It must also provide appropriate incentives for emissions reductions and deal directly with market failures. Carbon dioxide emissions, in particular, could be reduced at much lower cost through the use of emissions fees than through government-imposed standards for energy efficiency.[4]

Probing Deeper

1. Why would a fee or tradable allowance system (which involves the use of transferable emissions permits) "provide a least-cost reduction in [greenhouse gas] emissions"?

2. Why could the "adoption of many small programs, each of which would fail a standard cost-benefit test, . . . significantly slow economic growth . . ."?

3. Why would any "strategy to limit aggregate emissions without worldwide participation...be likely to fail"?

4. Why must any effective strategy cover all greenhouse gases?

5. Why could "carbon dioxide emission, in particular, . . . be reduced at much lower cost through the use of emissions fees than through government-imposed standards for energy efficiency"?

[4] *Economic Report of the President, op. cit.*, p. 224. In 1991, the National Academy of Sciences issued a report calling for national energy-efficient building codes, an increase in overall mileage standards for new automobiles to 32.5 miles per gallon from 27.5, more Federal support for reforestation and mass transit, and the development of a new generation of nuclear power plants. This report added further fuel to the controversies in this area.

largely because Congress has failed to confront [many of] the difficult issues . . ."

During the 1980s, environmentalists and others charged that the Reagan administration was dismantling, or at least emasculating, EPA. Anne Gorsuch resigned in 1983 as head of EPA, as criticism of the agency continued to build. James Watt, former Secretary of the Interior, also angered environmentalists. Administration officials retorted to such criticism by claiming that they were trying to promote and restore balance between environmental objectives and economic growth. In 1985, a political battle raged over the superfund, the fund authorized by federal legislation to clean up sites where chemical wastes have been dumped. Environmentalists wanted a fund of $10 billion; the Reagan administration proposed $5 billion. Some observers wanted the oil and chemical firms to contribute more to the fund, while these firms bitterly opposed such a move.

The Bush administration seemed more interested in new environmental initiatives than the Reagan administration. In late 1990, major changes were made in the Clean Air Act. To protect the ozone that shields the earth from harmful ultraviolet radiation, production of chlorofluorocarbons and carbon tetrachloride will be phased out through the 1990s and outlawed by January 1, 2000. Also, the law calls for tighter restrictions on the pollutants causing urban smog and on automobile exhausts (beginning in the 1994 model year), as well as new limits on coal-burning power plants that are aimed at reducing emissions of sulfur dioxide and nitrogen oxide—both regarded as causes of acid rain. Some economists estimated that compliance with this new legislation could cost about $30 billion per year. Whether the benefits exceed the costs will not be known for many years.

Some people believe that public policy is moving too rapidly in this area; others believe that it is moving too slowly. It is not easy to determine how fast or how far we should go in attempting to reduce pollution. Those who will bear the costs of reducing pollution have an understandable tendency to emphasize (and perhaps inflate) the costs and discount the benefits of such projects. Those who are particularly interested in enjoying nature and outdoor recreation—like the Sierra Club—are understandably inclined to emphasize (and perhaps inflate) the benefits and discount the costs of such projects. Politics inevitably plays a major role in the outcome of such cases. The citizens of the United States must indicate, through the ballot box as well as the market place, how much they are willing to pay to reduce pollution. We must also decide at what level of government the relevant rules are to be made. Since many pollution problems are local, it often seems sensible to determine the appropriate level of environmental quality locally. (However, there are obvious dangers in piecemeal regulation, as pointed out above.)

TEST YOURSELF

1. Suppose that the paper industry emits wastes into rivers and streams, and that municipalities or firms downstream must treat the water to make it usable. Do the paper industry's private costs equal the social costs of producing paper? Why, or why not?

2. Suppose that each ton of paper produced results in pollution that costs municipalities and firms downstream $1.00, and that a law is passed that requires the paper industry to reimburse the municipalities and firms downstream for these costs. Prior to this law, the supply curve for paper was:

PRICE OF PAPER (DOLLARS PER TON)	QUANTITY SUPPLIED (MILLION TONS)
1.00	10.0
2.00	15.0
2.50	17.5
3.00	20.0
4.00	25.0

After the law takes effect, what will be the quantity supplied at each price?

3. In Question 2, which output—the one prevailing before the industry has to reimburse others, or the one prevailing afterward—is socially more desirable? Why?

4. If the demand curve for paper is as shown below, what will be the equilibrium output of paper before and after the paper industry has to reimburse the municipalities and firms downstream (as indicated in Question 2)?

PRICE OF PAPER (DOLLARS PER TON)	QUANTITY DEMANDED (MILLION TONS)
1.00	30.0
2.00	25.0
3.00	20.0
3.50	17.5
4.00	15.0

5. Suppose that the social cost (in billions of dollars) due to pollution equals $5P$, where P is the level of pollution, and that the cost (in billions of dollars) of pollution control equals $10-2P$. What is the optimal level of pollution? Is this a typical case?

SUMMARY

1. One of the major social issues of the 1990s is environmental pollution. To a considerable extent, environmental pollution is an economic problem. Waste disposal and other pollution-causing activities result in external diseconomies.

2. Firms and individuals that pollute the water and air (and other facets of the environment) often pay less than the true social costs of disposing of their wastes in this way. Part of the true social cost is borne by other firms and individuals,

who must pay to clean up the water or air, or who must live with the consequences.

3. Because of the divergence of private from social costs, the market system does not result in an optimal allocation of resources. Firms and individuals create too much waste and dispose of it in excessively harmful ways. Because the polluters do not pay the full costs of waste disposal, their products are artificially cheap, with the result that too much is produced of them.

4. The government can intervene in several ways to help remedy the breakdown of the market system in this area. One way is to issue regulations for waste disposal and other activities influencing the environment. Another is to establish effluent fees, charges a polluter must pay to the government for discharging wastes. Still another way is to issue transferable emissions permits. In recent decades, there has been considerable growth in government programs designed to control pollution.

5. It is extremely difficult to determine how clean the environment should be. Of course, the sensible goal for society is to permit the level of pollution that minimizes the sum of the costs of pollution and the costs of controlling pollution; but no one has a very clear idea of what these costs are, and to a large extent the choices must be made through the political process.

CONCEPTS FOR REVIEW

External diseconomy

Private costs

Social costs

Direct regulation

Effluent fees

Transferable emissions permits

Tax credits

PART SIX

INTERNATIONAL TRADE AND ALTERNATIVE ECONOMIC SYSTEMS

INTERNATIONAL TRADE

PRACTICALLY ALL HUMAN beings realize that they are not islands unto themselves, and that they benefit from living with, working with, and trading with other people. Exactly the same is true of nations. They too must interact with one another, and they too benefit from trade with one another. No nation can be an island unto itself—not even the United States. To understand how the world economy functions, you must grasp the basic economic principles of international trade.

This chapter discusses many of the fundamental questions about international trade. What is the nature of American foreign trade? What are the effects of international trade? What determines the sorts of goods a nation will import or export? What are the advantages of free trade and the arguments against it? What are the social costs of tariffs and quotas, and what has been their history in the United States? What are some of the major issues regarding protectionism in the United States today? Some of these questions have occupied the attention of economists for hundreds of years; some are as current as today's newspaper.

AMERICA'S FOREIGN TRADE

America's foreign trade, although small relative to our national product, plays a very important role in our economic life. Many of our industries depend on other countries for markets or for raw materials (like coffee, tea, or tin). Our *exports*—the things we sell to other countries—amount to about 10 percent of our gross national product. In absolute terms, our exports (and imports) are bigger than those of any other nation. Without question, our way of life would have to change considerably if we could not trade with other countries.

When we were a young country, we exported raw materials primarily. During the 1850s about 70 percent of our exports were raw materials and foodstuffs. But the composition of our exports has changed with time. More are now finished manufactured goods and less are raw materials. In the 1960s, about 60 percent of our exports were finished manufactured goods, and only about 20 percent were raw materials and foodstuffs. Table 18.1 shows the importance of machinery and industrial supplies in our merchandise exports. Table 18.2 indicates to whom we sell. Western Europe and Canada take about one-half of our exports, and Latin America takes over 10 percent.

What sorts of goods do we buy from abroad? About 10 percent of our

Table 18.1
U.S. Merchandise Exports, 1990

PRODUCT	AMOUNT (BILLIONS OF DOLLARS)
Food, feed, and beverages	35
Industrial supplies and materials	106
Machinery	120
Automotive vehicles and parts	37
Aircraft	32
Other	59
Total	389

Source: Survey of Current Business, March 1991

Table 18.2
Percent of U.S. Exports, by Area, 1990

COUNTRY	PERCENT
Japan	13
Western Europe	32
Latin America	16
Canada	17
Eastern Europe	1
Other	21
Total	100

Source: See Table 18.1

imports are agricultural commodities like coffee, sugar, bananas, and cocoa. Over 10 percent are petroleum and its products. But a considerable proportion is neither raw materials nor foodstuffs. Over one-half of our imports, as shown in Table 18.3, are manufactured goods like bicycles from England or color TVs from Japan. More than 40 percent of our imports come from Western Europe and Japan (see Table 18.4). But the pattern varies from product to product. Thus Canada is our leading foreign source for wood pulp and nonferrous metals, while Latin America is our leading source of imported coffee and sugar.

ADVANTAGES OF TRADE

We have discussed the extent and nature of our trade with other countries, but not *why* we trade with other countries. Do we—and our trading partners—benefit from this trade? And if so, what determines the sorts of goods we should export and import? These are very important questions, among the most fundamental in economics. The answers are by no means new. They have been well understood for considerably more than a century, due to the work of such great economists as David Hume, David Ricardo, Adam Smith, and John Stuart Mill. Basically, the advantages of trade, both for individuals and for nations, stem from the fact that trade permits specialization, and specialization increases output, as we saw in Chapter 2.

To clarify the benefits of trade, consider the following example. Suppose that the United States can produce 2 computers or 5,000 cases of wine with 1 unit of resources. Suppose that France can produce 1 computer or 10,000 cases of wine with 1 unit of resources. Given the production possibilities in each country, are there any advantages in trade between the countries? And if so, what commodity should each country export, and what commodity should each country import? Should France export wine and import computers, or should it import wine and export computers?

To answer these questions, assume that the United States is producing a certain amount of computers and a certain amount of wine—and that France is producing a certain amount of computers and a certain amount of wine. If the United States shifts 1 unit of its resources from producing wine to producing computers, it will increase its production of computers by 2 computers and reduce its production of wine by 5,000 cases of wine. If France shifts 1 unit of resources from the production of computers to the production of wine, it will increase its production of wine by 10,000 cases and reduce its production of computers by 1 computer.

Table 18.5 shows the *net* effect of this shift in the utilization of resources on *world* output of computers and of wine. World output of computers increases (by 1 computer) and world output of wine increases (by 5,000 cases) as a result of the redeployment of resources in each country. Thus *specialization increases world output.*

Moreover, if world output of each commodity is increased by shifting 1 unit of American resources from wine to computers and shifting 1 unit of French resources from computers to wine, it follows that world output of each commodity will be increased further if each country shifts *more* of its resources in the same direction. This is because the amount of resources required to produce each good is assumed to be constant, regardless of how much is produced.

**Table 18.3
U.S. Merchandise Imports, 1990**

PRODUCT	AMOUNT (BILLIONS OF DOLLARS)
Food, feed, and beverages	27
Petroleum and oil products	62
Other industrial supplies and materials	82
Capital goods	117
Automotive vehicles and parts	86
Consumer goods (excluding autos)	106
Other	18
Total	498

Source: See Table 18.1

**Table 18.4
Percent of U.S. Imports, by Area, 1990**

COUNTRY	PERCENT
Japan	16
Western Europe	30
Latin America	15
Canada	15
Eastern Europe	a
Other	24
Total	100

a Less than one-half of one percent.
Source: See Table 18.1

Thus, in this situation, one country—the United States—should specialize in producing computers, and the other country—France—should specialize in producing wine. This will maximize world output of both wine and computers, permitting a rise in both countries' standards of living. Complete specialization of this sort is somewhat unrealistic, since countries often produce some of both commodities, but this simple example illustrates the basic principles involved.

COMPARATIVE ADVANTAGE

The case just described is a very special one, since one country (France) has an absolute advantage over another (the United States) in the production of one good (wine), whereas the second country (the United States) has an absolute advantage over the first (France) in the production of another good (computers). What do we mean by the term **absolute advantage**? Country A has an **absolute advantage** over Country B in the production of a good when Country A can produce a unit of the good with less resources than can country B. Since the United States can produce a computer with fewer units of resources than France, it has an absolute advantage over France in the production of computers. Since France requires fewer resources than the United States to produce a given amount of wine, France has an absolute advantage over the United States in the production of wine.

But what if one country is more efficient in producing both goods? If the United States is more efficient in producing both computers and wine, is there still any benefit to be derived from specialization and trade? At first glance, you are probably inclined to answer no. But if this is your inclination, you should reconsider—because you are wrong.

A Numerical Example

To see why specialization and trade have advantages even when one country is more efficient than another at producing both goods, consider the following example. Suppose the United States can produce 2 computers or 5,000 cases of wine with 1 unit of resources, and France can produce 1 computer or 4,000 cases of wine with 1 unit of resources. In this case, the United States is a more efficient producer of both computers and wine. Nonetheless, as we shall see, world output of both goods will increase if the United States specializes in the production of computers and France specializes in the production of wine.

Table 18.6 demonstrates this conclusion. If 2 units of American resources are shifted from wine to computer production, 4 additional computers and 10,000 fewer cases of wine are produced. If 3 units of French resources are shifted from computer to wine production, 3 fewer computers and 12,000 additional cases of wine are produced. Thus the combined effect of this redeployment of resources in both countries is to increase world output of computers by 1 computer and to increase world output of wine by 2,000 cases. Even though the United States is more efficient than France in the production of both computers and wine, world output of both goods will be maximized if the United States specializes in computers and France specializes in wine.

Basically, this is so because, although the United States is more efficient than France in the production of both goods, it has a greater ad-

Table 18.5
Case of Absolute Advantage

| | INCREASE OR DECREASE IN OUTPUT OF: | |
	COMPUTERS	WINE (THOUSANDS OF CASES)
Effect of U.S.'s shifting 1 unit of resources from wine to computers	+2	−5
Effect of France's shifting 1 unit of resources from computers to wine	−1	+10
Net Effect	+1	+5

Table 18.6
Case of Comparative Advantage

| | INCREASE OR DECREASE IN OUTPUT OF: | |
	COMPUTERS	WINE (THOUSANDS OF CASES)
Effect of U.S.'s shifting 2 units of resources from wine to computers	+4	−10
Effect of France's shifting 3 units of resources from computers to wine	−3	+12
Net effect	+1	+ 2

vantage in computers than in wine. It is twice as efficient as France in producing computers, but only 25 percent more efficient than France in producing wine. To derive these numbers, recall that 1 unit of resources will produce 2 computers in the United States, but only 1 computer in France. Thus the United States is twice as efficient in computers. On the other hand, 1 unit of resources will produce 5,000 cases of wine in the United States, but only 4,000 cases in France. Thus the United States is 25 percent more efficient in wine.

Trade Depends on Comparative Advantage

Specialization and trade depend on comparative, not absolute, advantage. A nation has a ***comparative advantage*** in those products where its efficiency relative to other nations is highest. So long as a country has a comparative advantage in the production of some commodities and a comparative disadvantage in the production of others, it can benefit from specialization and trade. A country will specialize in products where it has a comparative advantage, and import those where it has a comparative disadvantage.

Consider the case of France and the United States in Table 18.6. The United States has a comparative advantage in the production of computers and a comparative disadvantage in the production of wine. France has a comparative advantage in the production of wine and a comparative disadvantage in the production of computers. Both countries can benefit if France specializes in wine and the United States specializes in computers.

A Geometric Representation of Comparative Advantage

The principle of comparative advantage, like so many important economic concepts, can be displayed diagrammatically. Again, we suppose that in the United States 1 unit of resources will produce 2 computers or 5,000 cases of wine. Consequently, the ***production possibilities curve*** in the United States—the curve that shows the maximum number of computers that can be produced, given various outputs of wine—is the one in panel A of Figure 18.1. The United States must give up 1 computer for every additional 2,500 cases of wine that it produces; thus the slope of the American production possibilities curve is $-\dfrac{1}{2,500}$.[1]

Also, as in the previous section, we suppose that in France 1 unit of resources will produce 1 computer or 4,000 cases of wine. Thus the production possibilities curve in France is as shown in panel B of Figure 18.1. France must give up 1 computer for every additional 4,000 cases of wine it produces; thus the slope of France's production possibilities curve is $-\dfrac{1}{4,000}$.

Now suppose that the United States uses all its resources to produce computers and that France uses all its resources to produce wine. In other words, the United States operates at point A on its production possibilities curve and France operates at point B on its production possibilities curve.

---

[1] As we know from Chapter 2, the production possibilities curve shows the maximum amount of one commodity that can be produced, given various outputs of the other commodity. Since the United States must give up 1/2,500 computer for each additional case of wine that it produces, the slope must be —1/2,500.

Then suppose that the United States trades its computers for France's wine. *AC* in panel **A** of Figure 18.1 shows the various amounts of computers and wine the United States can end up with if it specializes in computers and trades them for French wine. *AC* is called the ***trading possibilities curve*** of the United States. The slope of *AC* is minus 1 times the ratio of the price of a case of wine to the price of a computer, since this ratio equals the number of computers the United States must give up to get a case of French wine. Similarly, the line *BD* in panel B of Figure 18.1 shows France's trading possibilities curve. That is, *BD* represents the various amounts of computers and wine France can wind up with if it specializes in wine and trades it for U.S. computers.

The thing to note about both panels of Figure 18.1 is that each country's trading possibilities curve—*AC* in panel A, *BD* in panel B—lies above its production possibilities curve. This means that *both countries can have more of both commodities by specializing and trading than by trying to be self-sufficient*—even though the United States is more efficient than France at producing both commodities. Thus Figure 18.1 shows what we said in the previous section: If countries specialize in products where they have a comparative advantage and trade with one another, each country can improve its standard of living.

THE TERMS OF TRADE

The ***terms of trade*** are defined as the quantity of imported goods that a country can obtain in exchange for a unit of domestic goods. Thus, in Figure 18.1, the terms of trade are measured by the ratio of the price of a computer to the price of a case of wine—since this ratio shows how many cases of French wine the United States can get in exchange for an American computer. In Figure 18.1, we assume that this ratio equals 3,333:1. It is important to note that this ratio must be somewhere between 2,500:1 and 4,000:1. By diverting its own resources from computer production to wine production, the United States can exchange a computer for 2,500 cases of wine. Since this is possible, it will not pay the United States to trade a computer for less than 2,500 cases of wine. Similarly, since France can exchange a case of wine for 1/4,000 of a computer by diverting its own resources from wine to computers, it clearly will not be willing to trade a case of wine for less than 1/4,000 of a computer.

But where will the price ratio lie between 2,500:1 and 4,000:1? The answer depends on *world supply and demand for the two products.* The stronger the demand for computers (relative to their supply) and the weaker the demand for wine (relative to its supply), the higher the price ratio. On the other hand, the weaker the demand for computers (relative to their supply) and the stronger the demand for wine (relative to its supply), the lower the price ratio.

INCOMPLETE SPECIALIZATION

Figure 18.1 shows that the United States should specialize completely in computers, and that France should specialize completely in wine. This result stems from the assumption that the cost of producing a computer or a case of wine is constant. If, on the other hand, the cost of producing each good increases with the amount produced, the result is likely to be incomplete specialization. In other words, although the United States will

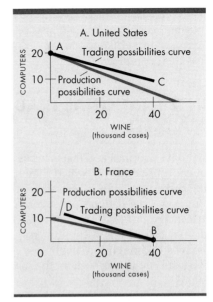

Figure 18.1
Benefits of Specialization and Trade
AC represents the various amounts of computers and wine that the United States can end up with, if it specializes in computers and trades them for French wine. The slope of *AC* equals −1 times the ratio of the price of a case of wine to the price of a computer, assumed to be $\frac{1}{3,333}$. *BD* represents the various amounts of computers and wine that France can wind up with, if it specializes in wine and trades for U.S. computers. *AC* lies above America's production possibilities curve and *BD* lies above France's production possibilities curve. Thus both countries can have more of both commodities by specializing and trading than by attempting to be self-sufficient.

continue to specialize in computers and France will continue to specialize in wine, each country will also produce some of the other good as well. This is a more likely outcome, since specialization generally tends to be less than complete.

INTERNATIONAL TRADE AND INDIVIDUAL MARKETS

We have emphasized that nations can benefit by specializing in the production of goods for which they have a comparative advantage and trading these goods for others where they have a comparative disadvantage.[2] But how do a nation's producers know whether they have a comparative advantage or disadvantage in the production of a given commodity? They do not call up the local university and ask the leading professor of economics (although that might not always be such a bad idea). Instead, as we shall see in this section, the market for the good provides the required signals.

To see how this works, let's consider a new (and rather whimsical) product—bulletproof suspenders. Suppose that the Mob, having run a scientific survey of gunmen and policemen, finds that most of them wear their suspenders over their bulletproof vests. As a consequence, the Mob's gunmen are instructed to render a victim immobile by shooting holes in his suspenders (thus making his trousers fall down and trip him). Naturally, the producers of suspenders will soon find it profitable to produce a new bulletproof variety, an innovation which, it is hoped, will make a solid contribution to law and order. The new suspenders are demanded only in the United States and England, since the rest of the world wears belts. The demand curve in the United States is as shown in panel A of Figure 18.2, and the demand curve in England is as shown in panel B. Suppose further that this product can be manufactured in both the United States and England. The supply curve in the United States is as shown in panel A, and the supply curve in England is as shown in panel B.

Take a closer look at Figure 18.2. Note that prices in England are expressed in pounds (£) and prices in the United States are expressed in dollars ($). This is quite realistic. Each country has its own currency, in which prices in that country are expressed. In early 1991, £1 was equal to about $1.85. In other words, you could exchange a pound note for $1.85—or $1.85 for a £1 note. For this reason, the two panels of Figure 18.2 are lined up so that a price of $3.70 is at the same level as a price of £2, $5.55 is at the same level as £3, and so on.

---

[2] The principle of comparative advantage is useful in explaining and predicting the pattern of world trade, as well as in showing the benefits of trade. For example, consider the exports of Great Britain and the United States. Robert Stern of the University of Michigan compared British and American exports of 39 industries. In 21 of the 24 industries where our labor productivity was more than three times that of the British, our exports exceeded British exports. In 11 of the 15 industries where our labor productivity was less than three times that of the British, our exports were less than British exports. Thus, in 32 out of 39 industries, the principle of comparative advantage, as interpreted by Stern, predicted correctly which country would export more. This is a high batting average, since labor is not the only input and labor productivity is an imperfect measure of true efficiency. Moreover, as we shall see in subsequent sections, countries raise barriers to foreign trade, preventing trade from taking place in accord with the principle of comparative advantage.

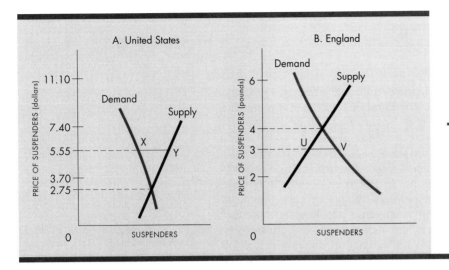

Figure 18.2
Determination of Quantity Imported and Exported under Free Trade
Under free trade, price will equal $5.55 or £3. The United States will export XY units, the English will import UV units, and XY = UV.

No Foreign Trade

To begin with, suppose that bulletproof suspenders cannot be exported or imported, perhaps because of a very high tariff (tax on imports) imposed on them in both the United States and England. (One can readily imagine members of both Congress and Parliament defending such a tariff on the grounds that a capacity to produce plenty of bulletproof suspenders is important for national defense.) If this happens, the price of bulletproof suspenders will be $2.75 in the United States and £4 in England. Why? Because, as shown in Figure 18.2, these are the prices at which each country's demand curve intersects its supply curve.

Foreign Trade Permitted

Next, suppose that international trade in this product is permitted, perhaps because both countries eliminate the tariff. Now what will happen? Since the price is lower in the United States than in England, people can make money by sending this product from the United States to England. After all, they can buy it for $2.75 in this country and sell it for £4 (=$7.40) in England. But they will not be able to do so indefinitely. As more and more suspenders are supplied by the United States for the English market, the price in the United States must go up (to induce producers to produce the additional output) and the price in England must go down (to induce consumers to buy the additional quantity).

When an equilibrium is reached, *the price in the United States must equal the price in England*. If this did not happen, there would be an advantage in increasing American exports (if the price in England were higher) or in decreasing American exports (if the price in the United States were higher). Thus only if the prices are equal can an equilibrium exist.

At what level will this price—which is common in both countries—tend to settle? Obviously, *the price must end up at the level where the amount of the good one country wants to export equals the amount the other country wants to import*. In other words, it must settle at $5.55 or £3. Otherwise, the total amount demanded in both countries would not equal the total amount supplied in both countries. And any reader who has mastered the material in Chapter 3 knows that such a situation cannot be an equilibrium.

The Signal of Market Forces

At this point, we can see how market forces indicate whether a country has a comparative advantage or a comparative disadvantage in the production of a certain commodity. *If a country has a comparative advantage, it turns out — after the price of the good in various countries is equalized and total world output of the good equals total world demand for it — that the country exports the good under free trade and competition.* In Figure 18.2, it turns out—as we've just seen—that the United States is an exporter of bulletproof suspenders under free trade, because the demand and supply curves in the United States and England take the positions they do. The basic reason why the curves take these positions is that the United States has a comparative advantage in the production of this good. Thus, to put things in a nutshell, a nation's producers can tell (under free trade) whether they have a comparative advantage in the production of a certain commodity by seeing whether it is profitable for them to export it. If they can make a profit, they have a comparative advantage.[3]

ECONOMIES OF SCALE AND LEARNING

Specialization and trade may be advantageous even if there is no difference among countries in the efficiency with which they can produce goods and services. In a case like this, although no nation has a technological advantage over any other, specialization and trade may still be of benefit, because there may be economies of scale in producing some commodities. Thus, if one country specializes in one good and another country specializes in another good, firms can serve the *combined* markets of both countries, which will make their costs *lower* than if they could only reach their domestic markets. This is a major argument for forming an international economic association like the European Common Market, discussed later in this chapter. (Also, it is a major argument for the steps taken in the early 1990s to remove trade barriers within the Common Market.)

Another reason for specialization is that it may result in learning. It is well known that the cost of producing many articles goes down as more and more of the articles are produced. In the aircraft and machine tool industries, producers are well aware of the reduction in costs from learning. The unit costs of a new machine tool tend to be reduced by 20 percent for each doubling of cumulated output, due to improved efficiency through individual and organizational learning. If such learning is an important factor in an industry, there are advantages in having one nation's producers specialize in a certain good. Specialization can reduce costs to a lower level than if each nation tries to be self-sufficient. Longer production runs cut costs since *the more a producer makes, the lower the unit costs.*

---

[3] In reality things are not quite so simple. For one thing, high transport costs are often involved in moving goods from one country to another. These costs can impede trade in certain commodities. Also, tariffs or quotas can be enacted by governments to interfere with free trade. Much more will be said on this score in later sections.

INNOVATION AND INTERNATIONAL TRADE

International trade also arises because of technological change. Suppose that a new product is invented in the United States and an American firm begins producing and selling it in the American market. It catches on, and the American innovator decides to export the new product to Europe and other foreign markets. If the new product meets European needs and tastes, the Europeans will import it from the United States; and later, when the market in Europe gets big enough, the American firm may establish a branch plant in Europe. For a time at least, European firms do not have the technological know-how to produce the new product, which is often protected to some extent by patents.

Trade of this sort is based on a *technology gap* between countries. Consider the plastics industry. After the development of a new plastic, there generally has been a period of 15 to 25 years when the innovating country has had a decisive advantage and has been likely to lead in per capita production and exports. It has had a head start, as well as the benefits of patents and commercial secrecy. Production has been licensed to other countries, but often on a limited scale and only after a number of years. Soon after the patents expire, a different phase begins. Imitation is easier, technical know-how spreads more readily, direct technical factors lose importance, and such other factors as materials costs become much more important. Industry from other countries may challenge the innovator in export markets, and sometimes in the innovator's home market as well, although the innovating firm still benefits to some extent from its accumulated knowledge and experience and its ongoing research and development.[4]

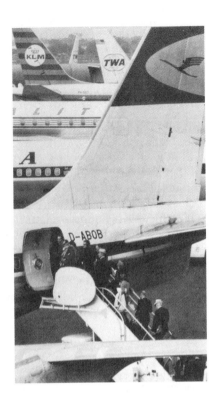

MULTINATIONAL FIRMS

One of the most remarkable economic phenomena of the last 30 years has been the growth of ***multinational firms***—firms that make direct investments in other countries and produce and market their products abroad. For example, Coca-Cola is produced and bottled all over the world. Most multinational firms are American, but companies like Shell in petroleum and Hoffman-La Roche in drugs are examples of foreign-based multinational firms. The available data indicate that the multinational firms have grown by leaps and bounds, and that their shipments have become a bigger proportion of international trade.

The reasons why firms have become multinational are varied. In some cases, firms have established overseas branches to control foreign sources of raw materials. In other cases, they have invested overseas in an effort to defend their competitive position. Very frequently, firms have established foreign branches to exploit a technological lead. After exporting a new product (or a cheaper version of an existing product) to foreign markets, firms have decided to establish plants overseas to supply these markets. Once a foreign market is big enough to accommodate a plant of minimum efficient size, this decision does not conflict with economies of

---

[4] Besides differences in technology, another reason for trade is a difference in national tastes. If Country A likes beef and Country B likes pork, it may pay both countries to produce beef and pork, and Country A may find it advantageous to import beef from Country B and Country B may find it advantageous to import pork from Country A.

scale. Moreover, transport costs often hasten such a decision. Also, in some cases, the only way a firm can introduce its innovation into a foreign market is through the establishment of overseas production facilities.

Effects of Multinational Firms

By carrying its technology overseas, the multinational firm plays a very important role in the international diffusion of innovations. A firm with a technological edge over its competitors often prefers to exploit its technology in foreign markets through wholly owned subsidiaries rather than through licensing or other means. To some extent, this is because of difficulties in using ordinary market mechanisms to buy and sell information. The difficulties of transferring technology across organizational, as well as national, boundaries also contribute to the decision. For these and other reasons, the innovating firm may find it advantageous to transfer its technology to other countries by establishing subsidiaries abroad.

One of the most important effects of the multinational firm has been to integrate the economies of the world more closely into a worldwide system. In other words, multinational firms have tended to break down some of the barriers between nations. Besides speeding the diffusion of new technology, they have linked the capital markets of many countries and promoted the international transfer of important managerial labor.

Particularly in the less developed countries, there has been an impassioned debate over the pros and cons of the multinational firm, which sometimes is viewed with suspicion by the nation-states in which it operates. These nation-states feel that their sovereignty is threatened by the great power of the multinational firm over their national economies. And the tragedy at Bhopal, India, where thousands of people were killed in 1984 by an accident at a plant owned by a major multinational firm—Union Carbide Corporation—has caused further conflict of this sort. (In 1988, an Indian judge ordered Union Carbide to pay about $200 million in compensation to the victims.) Also some observers are wary of multinational firms because of the possibility that they will attain undesirable monopoly power.

TEST YOURSELF

1. Suppose that the United States can produce 3 computers or 3,000 cases of wine with 1 unit of resources, while France can produce 1 computer or 2,000 cases of wine with 1 unit of resources. Will specialization increase world output?

2. Suppose that the United States has 100 units of resources while France has 50 units. Based on the data in Question 1, draw the production possibilities curve in each country. Without international trade, what will be the ratio of the price of a computer to the price of a case of wine in each country?

3. Given the information in Questions 1 and 2, how will firms in France and the United States know whether they should produce wine or computers? Must the government instruct them on this score? Why, or why not?

4. Under the circumstances described in Questions 1 and 2, will each country specialize completely in the production of one or the other good? Why, or why not? What factors result in incomplete specialization in the real world?

TARIFFS AND QUOTAS

What Is a Tariff?

Despite its advantages, not everyone benefits from free trade. On the contrary, the well-being of some firms and workers may be threatened by foreign competition; and they may press for a ***tariff***, a tax the government imposes on imports. The purpose of a tariff is to cut down on imports in order to protect domestic industry and workers from foreign competition. A secondary reason for having tariffs is to produce revenue for the government.

To see how a tariff works, consider the market for wristwatches. Suppose that the demand and supply curves for wristwatches in the United States are as shown in panel A of Figure 18.3, and that the demand and supply curves for wristwatches in Switzerland are as shown in panel B. Clearly, Switzerland has a comparative advantage in the production of wristwatches, and under free trade the price of a wristwatch would tend toward $10 in the United States and toward 14 Swiss francs in Switzerland. (Note that 1.4 Swiss francs are assumed to equal 1 dollar.) Under free trade, the United States would import 10 million wristwatches from Switzerland.

Now if the United States imposes a tariff of $10 on each wristwatch imported from Switzerland, the imports will completely cease. Any importers who buy watches in Switzerland at the price (when there is no foreign trade) of 10 Swiss francs—which equals about $7—must pay a tariff of $10; this makes their total cost about $17 per watch. But this is more than the price of a watch in the United States when there is no foreign trade (which is $15). Consequently, there is no money to be made by importing watches—unless Americans can be persuaded to pay more for a Swiss watch than for an identical American watch.

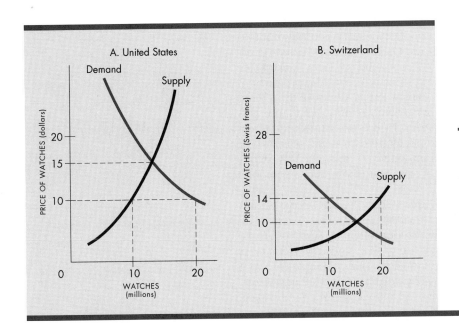

Figure 18.3
Effect of a Tariff on Swiss Watches
Under free trade, price would equal $10, or 14 Swiss francs. If a tariff of $10 is imposed on each watch imported from Switzerland, there will be a complete cessation of imports. Price in the United States will increase to $15, and price in Switzerland will fall to 10 Swiss francs.

The Social Costs of Tariffs

What is the effect of the tariff? The domestic watch industry receives a higher price—$15 rather than $10—than it would without a tariff. And the workers in the domestic watch industry may have more jobs and higher wages than without the tariff. The victim of the tariff is the American consumer, who pays a higher price for wristwatches. Thus the domestic watch industry benefits at the expense of the rest of the nation. But does the general public lose more than the watch industry gains? In general, the answer is yes. The tariff reduces the welfare of the nation as a whole.

The tariff in Figure 18.3 is a ***prohibitive tariff***—a tariff so high that it stops all imports of the good in question. Not all tariffs are prohibitive. (If they were, the government would receive no revenue at all from tariffs.) In many cases, the tariff is high enough to stop some, but not all, imports; and, as you would expect, the detrimental effect of a nonprohibitive tariff on living standards is less than that of a prohibitive tariff. But this does not mean that nonprohibitive tariffs are harmless. On the contrary, they can do lots of harm to domestic consumption and living standards.

The detrimental effects of tariffs have long been recognized, even in detective stories. Thus, in the course of solving the mystery concerning the Hound of the Baskervilles, Sherlock Holmes expressed his enthusiastic approval of a newspaper editorial that read as follows:

> You may be cajoled into imagining that your own special trade or your own industry will be encouraged by a protective tariff, but it stands to reason that such legislation must in the long run . . . lower the general conditions of life on this island.

Of course, Holmes considered this point elementary (my dear Watson) but worth hammering home.

What Is a Quota?

Besides tariffs, other barriers to free trade are ***quotas,*** which many countries impose on the amount of certain commodities that can be imported annually. The United States sets import quotas on sugar and exerts pressure on foreigners to get them to limit the quantity of steel and textiles that they will export to us. To see how a quota affects trade, production, and prices, let's return to the market for wristwatches. Suppose the United States places a quota on the import of wristwatches: no more than 6 million wristwatches can be imported per year. Figure 18.4 shows the effect of the quota. Before it was imposed, the price of wristwatches was $10 (or 14 Swiss francs), and the United States imported 10 million wristwatches from Switzerland. The quota forces the United States to reduce its imports to 6 million.

What will be the effect on the U.S. price? The demand curve shows that, if the price is $12, American demand will exceed American supply by 6 million watches; in other words, we will import 6 million watches. Thus, once the quota is imposed, the price will rise to $12, since *this is the price that will reduce our imports to the amount of the quota.* A quota—like a tariff—increases the price of the good. (Note too that the price in Switzerland will fall to 12 francs. Thus the quota will reduce the price in Switzerland.)

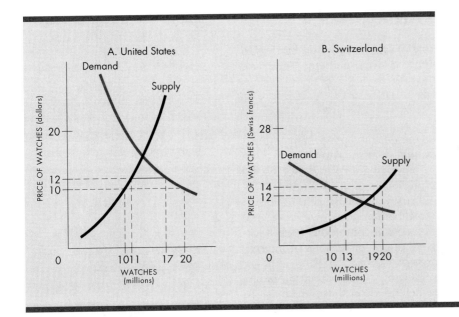

Figure 18.4
Effects of a Quota on Swiss Watches
Before the quota is imposed, the price is $10, or 14 Swiss francs. After a quota of 6 million watches is imposed, the price in the United States rises to $12, and the price in Switzerland falls to 12 Swiss francs.

The Social Costs of Quotas

Both a quota and a tariff reduce trade, raise prices, protect domestic industry from foreign competition, and reduce the standard of living of the nation as a whole. But most economists tend to regard quotas with even less enthusiasm than they do tariffs. Under many circumstances, a quota insulates local industry from foreign competition even more effectively than a tariff does. Foreigners, if their costs are low enough, can surmount a tariff barrier; but if a quota exists, there is no way they can exceed the quota. Moreover, a (nonprohibitive) tariff provides the government with some revenue, while quotas do not even do that. The windfall price increase from a quota accrues to the importer who is lucky enough or influential enough—or sufficiently generous with favors and bribes—to get an import license. (However, if the government auctions off the import licenses, it can obtain revenue from a quota.)

Export Subsidies and Other Nontariff Barriers to Free Trade

Finally, **export subsidies,** another means by which governments try to give their domestic industry an advantage in international competition, are also a major impediment to free trade. Such subsidies may take the form of outright cash disbursements, tax exemptions, preferential financing or insurance arrangements, or other preferential treatment for exports. Export subsidies, and other such measures, frequently lead to countermeasures. Thus, to counter foreign export subsidies, the U.S. government has imposed duties against such subsidies on goods sold here.

Other nontariff barriers to free trade include licensing requirements and unreasonable product quality standards. By granting few licenses (which are required in some countries to import goods) and by imposing unrealistically stringent product quality standards, governments discourage imports.

ARGUMENTS FOR TARIFFS AND QUOTAS

Given the disadvantages to society at large of tariffs and other barriers to free trade, why do governments continue to impose them? There are many reasons, some sensible, some irrational.

The National Defense Argument

One of the most convincing arguments is the desirability of maintaining a domestic industry for purposes of *national defense*. Thus, even if the Swedes had a comparative advantage in producing airplanes, we would not allow free trade to put our domestic producers of aircraft out of business if we felt that a domestic aircraft industry was necessary for national defense. Although the Swedes are by no means unfriendly, we would not want to import our entire supply of such a critical commodity from a foreign country, where the supply might be shut off for reasons of international politics. (Recall the Arab oil embargo of 1973.)

This is a perfectly valid reason for protecting certain domestic industries, and many protective measures are defended on these grounds. To the extent that protective measures are in fact required for national defense, economists go along with them. The restrictions entail social costs (some of which were described in previous sections), but these costs may well be worth paying for enhanced national security. The trouble is that many barriers to free trade are justified on these grounds when in fact they protect domestic industries only tenuously connected with national defense. Moreover, even if there is a legitimate case on defense grounds for protecting a domestic industry, subsidies are likely to be a more straightforward and efficient way to do so than tariffs or quotas.

Other Arguments for Tariffs

Besides national defense, several other arguments for tariffs or quotas can make sense.

1. TARIFFS OR OTHER FORMS OF PROTECTION CAN BE JUSTIFIED TO FOSTER THE GROWTH OR DEVELOPMENT OF YOUNG INDUSTRIES. Suppose that Japan has a comparative advantage in the production of a certain semiconductor, but Japan does not presently produce this item. It may take Japanese firms several years to become proficient in the relevant technology, to engage in the learning described in a previous section and to take advantage of the relevant economies of scale. While this industry is "growing up," Japan may impose a tariff on such semiconductors, thus shielding its young industry from competition it cannot yet handle. This "infant industry" argument for tariffs has a long history; Alexander Hamilton was one of its early exponents. Needless to say, it is *not* an argument for *permanent* tariffs, since infant industries are supposed to grow up—and the sooner the better. (Moreover, a subsidy for the industry would probably be better and easier to remove than a temporary tariff, according to many economists.)

2. TARIFFS SOMETIMES MAY BE IMPOSED TO PROTECT DOMESTIC JOBS AND TO REDUCE UNEMPLOYMENT AT HOME. In the short run the policy may succeed, but we must recognize that other nations are likely to retaliate by enacting or increasing their own tariffs, so that such a policy may not work very well in the long run. A more sensible way to reduce domestic unem-

Paul Krugman

Avinash Dixit

In recent years, an influential band of young economists, led by MIT's Paul Krugman and others, have argued that, in today's world, nations may find it worthwhile to engage in strategic trade policies to secure higher incomes for their residents. Thus, if only two highly profitable firms can exist in a particular industry, it may make sense for countries to use subsidies or tariffs to raise the probability that one of their firms will be one of the fortunate pair. Or if certain high-technology industries result in large technological benefits to the rest of the economy, it may make sense to use subsidies or tariffs to promote and protect these sectors.

Of course, all of this departs from the conventional economic view that nations are best off by promoting free trade. As Krugman indicates,

> The new approaches open up the possibility that there may be 'strategic' sectors after all. Because of the important roles now being given to economies of scale, advantages of experience, and innovation as explanations of trading patterns, it seems more likely that . . . labor or capital will sometimes earn significantly higher returns in some industries than in others. Because of the increased role of technological competition, it has become more plausible to argue that certain sectors yield important [social benefits], so producers are not in fact paid the full social value of their production.

What all this means is that the extreme pro-free-trade position—that markets work so well that they cannot be improved on—has become untenable. In this sense the new approaches to international trade provide a potential rationale for a turn by the United States toward a more activist trade policy.[1]

However, these new approaches raise a great many unanswered questions. How can one identify strategic sectors? It is very difficult to specify the industries where the returns to capital and labor are very high and where public policy could raise GNP by encouraging them to go into the sector. Also, it is very difficult to measure the extent of the social benefits that will result from various kinds of investments. To what extent will these new approaches be used by interest groups to advocate policies that will not benefit the country as a whole? Given the vagueness of the criteria for identifying strategic sectors, many groups could use these ideas to justify protection for themselves and their allies.

Because of such questions, many economists, such as Princeton's Avinash Dixit, are skeptical concerning the usefulness of strategic trade policy. According to Dixit, "The idea that free trade promotes the general interest, and that departures from it are motivated by various special interests, . . . still stands and continues to govern the overwhelming majority of the volume of world trade. . . ."[2] Nonetheless, there can be no doubt that the proponents of strategic trade policy have had a substantial impact on economists and policy makers.

---

[1] Paul Krugman (ed.), *Strategic Trade Policy and the New International Economics,* Cambridge, Mass.: MIT Press, 1986, p. 15.
[2] Ibid., p. 302.

ployment is to use the tools of fiscal and monetary policy rather than tariffs. If workers are laid off by industries that cannot compete with foreign producers, proper monetary and fiscal policy, together with retraining programs, should enable these workers to switch to other industries that can compete.

3. TARIFFS SOMETIMES MAY BE IMPOSED TO PREVENT A COUNTRY FROM BEING TOO DEPENDENT ON ONLY A FEW INDUSTRIES. Consider a Latin American country that is a major producer of bananas. Under free trade, this country might produce bananas and little else, putting its entire economy at the mercy of the banana market. If the price of bananas fell, the country's national income would decrease drastically. To promote industrial diversification, this country may establish tariffs to protect other industries—for example, certain types of light manufacturing. In a case like this, the tariff protects the country from having too many eggs—or bananas (if you want to avoid mixing a metaphor)—in a single basket.

4. TARIFFS MAY SOMETIMES IMPROVE A COUNTRY'S TERMS OF TRADE—THAT IS, THE RATIO OF ITS EXPORT PRICES TO ITS IMPORT PRICES. The United States is a major importer of bananas. If we impose a tariff on bananas, thus cutting down on the domestic demand for them (because the tariff will increase their price), the reduction in our demand is likely to reduce the price of bananas abroad. Consequently, foreign producers of bananas will really pay part of the tariff. However, other countries may retaliate; and if all countries pursue such policies, few, if any, are likely to find themselves better off.

Frequently Encountered Fallacies

Although, as we have just seen, tariffs can be defended under certain circumstances, many of the arguments for them frequently encountered in political oratory and popular discussions are misleading. Although no field of economics is free of popular misconceptions and fallacies, this one is particularly rich in pious inanities and thunderous non sequiturs.

FALLACY 1. One frequently encountered fallacy is that, if foreigners want to trade with us, they must be benefiting from the trade. Consequently, according to this argument, we must be giving them more than we get—and it must be in our interest to reduce trade. This argument is entirely erroneous in its assumption that trade cannot be beneficial to *both* trading partners. On the contrary, as we have seen, the heart of the argument for trade is that it can be mutually beneficial.

FALLACY 2. Another fallacy one often encounters in polite conversation—and not-so-polite political debate—is that a tariff is required to protect our workers from low-wage labor in other countries. According to this argument, since American labor (at $10 an hour) clearly cannot compete with foreign labor (some of which works at extremely low wage levels), we have no choice but to impose tariffs. If we do not, cheap foreign goods will throw our high-priced laborers out of work. This argument is wrong on two counts. First, *high wages do not necessarily mean high unit costs of production.* Because the productivity of American workers is high, unit labor costs in the United States are roughly in line with those in other countries. (Unit labor cost equals the wage rate divided by labor productivity. Thus unit labor cost may be no higher here than abroad, even though the wage rate here is much higher, if labor productivity here is also much higher than abroad.) Second, *if our costs were out of line with those of other countries, there should be a change in exchange rates, which would tend to bring them back into line.*

FALLACY 3. Still another fallacy that makes the rounds is that it is better to "buy American" because then we have both the goods that are bought and the money, whereas if we buy from foreigners we have the goods but they have the money. Like some jokes, this fallacy has an ancient lineage—and one that borders on respectability, since Abraham Lincoln is supposed to have subscribed to it. Basically, the flaw is the implicit assumption that money is somehow valued for its own sake. In reality, all foreigners can do with the money is buy some of our goods, so that really we are just swapping some of our goods for some of theirs. If such a trade is mutually advantageous, fine.

Why So Much Nonsense?

Why do politicians (both Democrats and Republicans) sometimes utter these fallacies? No doubt an important reason is simply ignorance. There is no law that prevents people with little understanding of economics from holding public office. But this may not be the only reason. Special-interest groups—particular industries, unions, and regions—have a lot to gain by getting the government to enact protective tariffs and quotas. And Congress and the executive branch of the government are often sensitive to the pressures of these groups, which wield considerable political power.

Faced with a choice between helping a few powerful, well-organized groups and helping the general public—which is poorly organized and often ignorant of its own interests—politicians frequently tend to favor the special-interest groups. After all, these groups have a lot to gain and will remember their friends, while the general public—each member of which loses only a relatively small amount—will be largely unaware of its losses anyhow. Having decided to help these groups, representatives or senators may not exert themselves unduly to search out or expose the weakness in some of the arguments used to bolster their position. Thus there is the story of a well-known senator who, about to deliver a certain oration, wrote in the margin of one section of his speech: "Weak point here. Holler like hell."

Finally, it is important to recognize once again that, although the majority of citizens benefit from free trade, some are likely to be hurt by it. A reduction in the tariff on shoes is likely to hurt people who own and work in American shoe factories. If our domestic shoe industry cannot compete with foreign producers, workers will be laid off and plants will close. The result will be a considerable loss to domestic shoe producers and workers. Most people believe that society as a whole, which benefits from free trade, should help the minority that is victimized by it. To promote this objective, the United States established "adjustment assistance" for firms or workers who, because of government agreement to reduce barriers to free trade, have suffered idleness or unemployment due to an increase in imports. Workers can enter retraining programs and can obtain allowances to help pay for moving to other jobs. (However, such benefits were reduced substantially in the early 1980s.)

TARIFFS IN THE UNITED STATES

How high are American tariffs, now and in the past? In our early years, we were a very protectionist nation. The argument for protecting our young industry from the competition of European manufacturers was the "infant industry" argument, which, as we saw above, can be perfectly sensible. However, our own industries understandably found it advantageous to prolong their childhood for as long as possible—and to press for continuation of high tariffs. During the nineteenth century and well into the twentieth, the industrial Northeast was particularly strong in its support of tariffs. Furthermore, the Republican party, which generally held sway in American politics between the Civil War and the New Deal, favored a high tariff. Thus, as shown in Figure 18.5, the tariff remained relatively high from about 1870 until the early 1930s. With the exception of the period around World War I, average tariff rates were about 40 to 50 percent. With the enactment of the Smoot-Hawley Tariff of 1930, the tariff reached its peak—about 60 percent. Moreover, these tariff rates understate the extent to which the tariff restricted trade: Some goods were completely shut out of the country by the tariff, and do not show up in the figures.

With the Democratic victory in 1932, a movement began toward freer trade. The Trade Agreements Act of 1934 allowed the president to bargain with other countries to reduce barriers to trade. He was given the power to lower U.S. tariffs by as much as 50 percent. In 1945, he was given the power to make further tariff reductions. Between 1934 and 1948, tariff rates fell substantially, as shown in Figure 18.5. By 1948, the United States was no longer a high-tariff country; the average tariff rate was only about 10 percent.[5]

The Kennedy Round and the European Community

During the 1950s, there were no further decreases in the tariff—but there were no substantial increases either. The movement toward freer trade was continued by President Kennedy in 1962, and during the 1960s, the "Kennedy Round" negotiations took place among about 40 nations in an

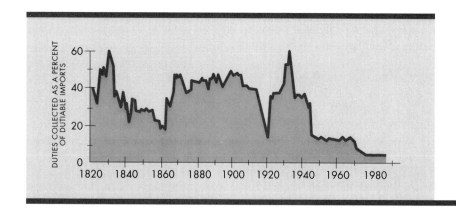

Figure 18.5
Average American Tariff Rates
The tariff generally remained high from about 1870 to the early 1930s; in recent decades it has decreased substantially.

---

[5] In 1947, the United States and 22 other nations signed the *General Agreement on Tariffs and Trade* (GATT), which calls for all participating countries to meet periodically to negotiate bilaterally on tariff cuts. Any tariff cut negotiated in this way will be extended to all participating nations.

attempt to reduce tariffs. In 1967, the United States agreed to cut tariffs by about one-third on a great many items.

The negotiations during the 1960s were prompted by the establishment of the ***European Economic Community*** — or ***"Common Market."*** The EEC was composed originally of Belgium, France, West Germany, Holland, Italy, and Luxembourg; and in the late 1970s, Britain, Denmark, and Ireland joined. When the EEC was formed, the member countries agreed to reduce the tariff barriers against one another's goods — but not against the goods of other nations, including the United States.

The formation and success of the Common Market — and the likelihood that other European countries would join — posed a problem for the United States. The Common Market is a large and rich market, with over 200 million people and a combined gross national product in the trillions of dollars. With the reduction of tariff barriers *within* the Common Market, trade *among* the members of the Common Market increased rapidly, and prices of many items were cut. But American exporters were less than ecstatic about all of this, because the members of the Common Market still maintained their tariff barriers against American goods. While the "Kennedy Round" negotiations succeeded in reducing some of the tariff barriers between the United States and the Common Market, important tariff barriers remained, particularly for agricultural products.

The Tokyo and Uruguay Rounds

In 1973, over 100 nations met in Tokyo to plan a new round of trade negotiations. The aim was to make progress toward the reduction of both tariffs and nontariff barriers to trade. (In recent years, tariffs have been replaced to some extent by nontariff barriers to trade.) After over 5 years of difficult negotiations, an agreement was approved in April 1979. This agreement called for the industrial nations to reduce tariffs on thousands of goods by an average of about 33 percent during an 8-year period. It also tried to reduce export subsidies, phony technical standards for imports (used to keep out foreign goods), and barriers to international bidding for government contracts.

In 1986, a new round of negotiations, called the Uruguay Round, began. An attempt was made to curtail domestic subsidies for farmers, which distort international trade, as well as to reduce nontariff barriers to trade. Also, the industrialized countries like the United States tried to get the poorer countries like India and Brazil to protect intellectual property rights (like patents and copyrights) more effectively. The negotiations did not fulfill these objectives. In December 1990, the trade officials participating in the negotiations gave up, and suspended the talks. But international discussions of these issues continued.

Important trade legislation was passed by the Congress in 1988. Reacting to the huge trade deficits of the 1980s, the U.S. government set out to require "fair" trade. The 1988 Trade Acts empower the government to retaliate against nations that erect substantial and numerous "unfair trade barriers." Also, 60-day notice is required for plant shutdowns, and aid for workers displaced by plant closings is increased.

In Europe, there was an emphasis in the early 1990s on removing barriers to intra-European free trade. For example, European governments have tended to favor firms from their own countries when they have awarded construction or defense contracts. In 1985, the member states of the European Community — or Common Market — undertook to remove such barriers to free trade by 1992. Some American firms fear that, while the removal of such barriers will encourage more intra-European trade, there may be a tendency for the Europeans to maintain barriers against products from outside Europe.

Increased Protectionism

Recent years have seen a marked increase in protectionist feelings in the United States. As Western Europe and Japan have become more formidable competitors abroad and at home, many industries have pressed for quotas and higher tariffs. The automobile, steel, and textile industries have been among the most frequent petitioners for protection. In 1981, the Japanese agreed to limit import of Japanese autos into the United States to 1.68 million per year; by 1988, the quota was increased to 2.3 million per year. The United States stopped asking for the restraints in 1985, but Japan "voluntarily" decided to keep them. (See page 375.)

In the mid-1980s, hundreds of petitions were filed by industry and labor, asking the federal government to protect them from imports. In considerable part, this was due to the very strong dollar. For a variety of reasons, the dollar's value relative to other currencies rose markedly during the early 1980s, the result being that foreign goods became much cheaper to American buyers. Also, in some industries likesemiconductors, the quality of foreign goods sometimes exceeded that of American suppliers. Faced with very stiff competition from imports, American firms asked the government for protection.

EXAMPLE 18.1   THE EFFECTS OF A TARIFF ON SHOES

The quantity of shoes demanded in the United States at each price of a pair of shoes is shown below. In addition, the quantities of shoes supplied by American producers and by foreign producers at each price are shown too.

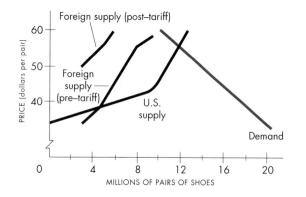

(a) Assuming that the market for shoes is competitive, what is the equilibrium price of a pair of shoes in the United States? (b) What proportion of the U.S. market goes to foreign producers of shoes? (c) Suppose that the United States imposes a tariff of $15 per pair of shoes. How many pairs of shoes will foreign producers now supply if the price is (1) $50, (2) $55, (3) $60? (Note that a $50 price together with a $15 tariff means that the price to the foreign producer is $50 – $15, or $35.) (d) After the imposition of the tariff, what is the equilibrium price? (e) After the imposition of the tariff, what proportion of the U.S. market goes to foreign producers of shoes? (f) How much revenue does the U.S. government get from this tariff?

Solution

(a) $45, since at this price U.S. supply (10 million pairs) plus foreign supply (6 million pairs) equals the quantity demanded (16 million pairs). (b) 6/16. (c) 3 million pairs (since this is what would have been supplied at a price of $35 without the tariff), 5 million pairs (since this is what would have been supplied at a price of $40 without the tariff), 6 million pairs (since this is what would have been supplied at a price of $45 without the tariff). (d) $50, since at this price U.S. supply (11 million pairs) plus foreign supply (3 million pairs) equals the quantity demanded (14 million pairs). (e) 3/14. (f) 3 million x $15, or $45 million.

When the first Japanese cars arrived on the West Coast in the 1970s, no one saw them as a threat to American jobs. Although they were cheaper and more fuel-efficient than American-made cars, most Americans couldn't be bothered; with gasoline at thirty cents a gallon, the difference in cost between a car that got thirty miles per gallon and one that got ten was not very great, even for someone who drove a lot.

But all this changed with the Arab oil embargo of 1973. As gas prices climbed, Americans took another look at small foreign cars. With expensive American labor and outmoded facilities on one side, and Japanese efficiency and management techniques on the other, Japan seemed to be winning the war in the showroom.

Workers rally to fight foreign competition

While imports may create as many jobs as they consume in the long run, in the short run many smokestack industry workers can be left permanently unemployed or underemployed. Worried American workers wanted protection, and they found a strong advocate in Representative John Dingell, one of the leaders of an emerging protectionist movement in Congress. Dingell spoke with President Reagan and Trade Representative William Brock, and urged that if voluntary restrictions on Japanese auto imports weren't adopted, Congress would impose mandatory ones. Faced with this choice, the Japanese agreed in negotiations to voluntary restrictions.

The restrictions worked. As the number of Japanese auto imports dropped between 1981 and 1982, domestic auto industry employment rose. But the cost of saving hundreds of *thousands* of American jobs was restricted choice and higher prices for hundreds of *millions* of American consumers. Hefty dealer markups were imposed on the scarcer but still-popular imports, and as sticker prices rose on Toyotas and Datsuns, General Motors, Ford, and Chrysler found that they could raise prices too.

The combined price paid by consumers for trade restrictions is very high; it has been estimated that each job protected from foreign competition with quotas or tariffs costs consumers about $160,000 in higher prices—more than enough to support the holder of that job. While trade restrictions may save jobs in the short run, they lock inefficiencies into the American economy and merely delay needed efforts to divert people and assets into areas of the economy in which the United States has a competitive advantage—and which therefore offer long-term employment and profit possibilities.

N.B.

In the late 1980s and early 1990s, although the value of the dollar fell substantially, protectionist pressure continued. As indicated in earlier sections of this chapter, the American consumer is the loser when protectionist measures are adopted. Robert Crandall of the Brookings Institution has estimated that auto import quotas have resulted in about a $400 per car increase in the price of U.S. cars and a $1,000 per car increase in the price of Japanese imports, the total annual cost to American consumers being over $4 billion. According to Crandall, "The cost per job saved, therefore, was nearly $160,000 per year. Employment creation at this cost is surely not worth the candle."[6] (Some other industries where the cost per job saved has exceeded $100,000 are book manufacturing, dairy products, and steel.)[7]

Most economists feel that this upsurge in protectionism is an unfortunate development. Although they understand that it will be difficult to beat back the protectionist tide, they hope that this upsurge of protectionist spirit will be short-lived, and that developments here and abroad in the 1990s will enable us and our trading partners to move closer to the realization of the benefits of free trade.

TEST YOURSELF

1. According to Hendrik Houthakker, "Our workers get high real income not because they are protected from foreign competition, but because they are highly productive, at least in certain industries." Do you agree? Why, or why not?

2. According to Richard Cooper, "Technological innovation can undoubtedly strengthen the competitive position of a country in which the innovation takes place, whether it be one which enlarges exports or displaces imports." Give examples of this phenomenon, and discuss various ways that one might measure the effects of technological innovation on a country's competitive position.

3. "The principle of comparative advantage doesn't work. The U.S. exports electronic computers to Japan and imports electronic consumer goods like TV sets from Japan." Comment and evaluate.

4. Would you favor a high tariff on imported steel if you were (a) an automobile worker, (b) a steel worker, (c) an automobile buyer, (d) a plastics worker? Explain your reasoning in each case.

SUMMARY

1. International trade permits specialization, and specialization increases output. This is the advantage of trade, both for individuals and for nations.

2. Country A has an absolute advantage over Country B in the production of a good when Country A can produce a unit of the good with less resources than can Country B. Trade can be mutually beneficial even if one country has an absolute advantage in the production of all goods.

3. Specialization and trade depend on comparative, not absolute, advantage. A nation is said to have a comparative ad-

vantage in those products where its efficiency relative to other nations is highest. Trade can be mutually beneficial if a country specializes in the products where it has a comparative advantage and imports the products where it has a comparative disadvantage.

4. If markets are relatively free and competitive, producers will automatically be led to produce in accord with comparative advantage. If a country has a comparative advantage in the production of a certain good, it will turn out—after the price of the good in various countries is equalized and total

---

[6] R. Crandall, "Import Quotas and the Automobile Industry," *The Brookings Review,* Summer 1984, p. 16.

[7] G. Hufbauer, D. Berliner, and K. Eliot, *Trade Protection in the United States: 31 Case Studies,* Washington, D.C.: Institute for International Economic Studies, 1986.

world output of the good equals total world demand—that this country is an exporter of the good under free trade.

5. Specialization may occur because of economies of scale and learning. Also, some countries develop new products and processes, which they export to other countries until the technology becomes widely available.

6. A tariff is a tax imposed by the government on imports, the purpose being to cut down on imports in order to protect domestic industry and workers from foreign competition. Tariffs benefit the protected industry at the expense of the general public, and, in general, a tariff costs the general public more than the protected industry (and its workers and suppliers) gains.

7. Quotas are another barrier to free trade. They too reduce trade, raise prices, protect domestic industry from foreign competition, and reduce the standard of living of the nation as a whole.

8. Tariffs, quotas, and other barriers to free trade can sometimes be justified on the basis of national security considerations. Moreover, tariffs and other forms of protection can sometimes be justified to protect infant industries, to prevent a country from being too dependent on only a few industries, and to carry out other national objectives. But many arguments for tariffs are fallacious.

9. In our early years, we were a very protectionist country. Our tariffs remained relatively high until the 1930s, when a movement began toward free trade. Between 1934 and 1948, our tariff rates dropped substantially. Again during the 1960s, there was a significant reduction in our tariffs. But more recently, as some of our industries (like steel) have been hit hard by imports, there has been a tendency to push for more protectionist measures. Since 1980, the protectionist tide has been very strong.

10. Although it has equaled only about 10 percent of our gross national product, foreign trade is of very considerable importance to the American economy. Many of our industries rely on foreign countries for raw materials or for markets, and our consumers buy many kinds of imported goods. In absolute terms, our exports and imports are larger than those of any other nation.

CONCEPTS FOR REVIEW

Exports
Imports
Absolute advantage
Comparative advantage
Production possibilities curve

Trading possibilities curve
Terms of trade
Multinational firm
Tariff
Prohibitive tariff

Quota
Export subsidy
European Economic Community
  (Common Market)

THE COMMUNIST COUNTRIES AND MARXISM

IN THE 1990s, countries that have had communist regimes, such as the Soviet Union and China, have been in a state of serious economic turmoil, as some forces push them toward more liberalization and decentralization, and other forces push them in the opposite direction. Due in part to this turmoil, everybody talks and reads about ***communism.*** You hear the word frequently on television and see it frequently in the newspapers, but if you really know what it means, you are in the minority. It is a safe bet that most people have only a vague and distorted idea of what communism is, although about a third of the world's population has lived under Communist rule. The Soviet Union (which broke up in late 1991), China, Cuba, and many other countries have been Communist. You should know something about the nature of communism to understand what has been going on in a large part of the world.

In this chapter we describe and analyze the nature and workings of the economic system in various countries that have had communist governments. After a brief discussion of the doctrines of Karl Marx, the intellectual father of communism, we describe how the Soviet economy worked. Since economic planning played a major role in its functioning, the USSR's planning system is described in some detail. Next, we turn to the economy of China, and to some of the major differences between communism and democratic socialism. Finally, we describe briefly the nature of radical economics, a recent, and still very small, movement in the United States that draws heavily on Marx's views.

THE DOCTRINES OF KARL MARX

The Class Struggle

The name Karl Marx probably makes you think of revolutionaries meeting by candlelight in damp cellars to plot the overthrow of nineteenth-century European governments. If this is the picture you associate with the name, you are quite right! Karl Marx was a revolutionary who wanted the masses to revolt against the existing social order. In 1848, he and Friedrich Engels published the famous *Communist Manifesto,* the spirit of which is given by its closing lines:

> Communists . . . openly declare that their ends can be attained only by the forcible overthrow of all existing social conditions. Let the ruling classes tremble at a Communist revolution. The proletarians have nothing to lose but their chains. They have a world to win. Workers of the world, unite!

This is stirring language, no doubt about it. But why did Marx preach revolution, and what goals do the communists want to achieve?

To understand their aims, it is helpful to look at Marx's famous treatise, *Capital* (the first part of which was published in 1867), which states much of his economic and political thought. According to Marx, the fundamental causes of political and social change are socioeconomic factors. Changes in the ways goods and services are produced and distributed—and in the ways in which people enter into "productive relations" with one another (the feudal lord with the serf under feudalism, or the capitalist with the worker under capitalism)—are responsible for the great political and social movements of history. History can be viewed as a series of class struggles. In ancient times, the struggle was between masters and slaves. In feudal times, it was between lords and serfs. And in modern times, it is between the **capitalists,** who own the means of production, and the workers, or **proletariat.**

According to Marx, every economic system—ancient, feudal, or modern—develops certain defects or internal contradictions, which eventually cause it to give way to a new system. As the old system begins to weaken, the new system gains strength. Thus the feudal system grew out of the ancient system, and the modern system grew out of the feudal system. In Marx's view, *the struggle between the capitalists and the proletariat will eventually result in the defeat of the capitalists. This will set the stage for a new economic system*—**socialism,** *a transitional phase toward communism.* Communism, according to Marx, is the ultimate, perfect form of economic system.

Karl Marx

The Theory of Value and Wages

The reasons for Marx's belief that in modern times there must be a struggle between capitalists and workers lie in his theory of value and wages. *According to Marx, the **value** of any commodity—that is, its price relative to other commodities—is determined by the amount of labor time used in its manufacture.* In other words, if a shirt requires twice as much labor time to produce as a tie, its price is twice that of a tie. By labor time, Marx meant both the amount of labor used in making a commodity and the amount of labor time "congealed" in the machinery used to make the commodity. According to Marx, wages tend to equal the lowest level consistent with the subsistence of the workers, because capitalists, driven by the profit motive, pay the lowest wage they can.

Combining his theory of value and his theory of wages, Marx concluded that workers produce a **surplus value**—a value above and beyond the subsistence wage they receive—which is taken by the capitalists. This surplus value arises because the capitalists make the workers labor for longer hours than are required to produce an amount of output equal to their wage. Consider the worker who may be made to work 10 hours a day, even though her output in 6 hours equals the value of her wage. The output produced in the remaining 4 hours is surplus value.

According to Marx, surplus value is what makes the capitalist world tick. Indeed, the reason why capitalists engage in production is to make this surplus value, which they steal from the workers. Capitalists also use some of it to purchase new capital. Thus capital formation, in Marx's view, comes about as a consequence of surplus value. If the capitalist class is exploiting the workers in the way Marx visualized, it is not difficult to see why he felt that a class struggle between capitalists and workers was inevitable, and even easier to see why he was on the workers' side.

Marx's Vision of the Future

In Marx's view, capitalism would eventually reveal certain fundamental weaknesses that would hasten its demise. As more and more capital is accumulated, Marx felt that the profit rate would be driven down, that unemployment would increase (because of a rise in technological unemployment), that business cycles would become more severe (depressions becoming more devastating), and that monopoly would grow more widespread. As these developments imposed greater and greater hardships on the working class, the chance of revolution would increase. Eventually the workers, recognizing that they "have nothing to lose but their chains," would throw off the yoke of capitalism.

However, Marx did not visualize an immediate progression to communism. Instead, he saw socialism as a way station on the road to communism. *Socialism would be a "dictatorship of the proletariat."* The workers would rule. Specifically, they would control the government, which, according to Marx, is merely a tool of the propertied class under capitalism. Moreover, the socialist government would own the means of production—the factories, mines, and equipment. Under socialism each person would receive an amount of income related to the amount he or she produced.

Finally, after an unspecified length of time, Marx felt that socialism would give way to communism, his ideal system. Communism would be a classless society, everyone working, and no one owning capital or exploiting the other person. Under communism, the state would become obsolete and wither away. The principle of income distribution would be "from each according to his ability, to each according to his needs." Marx was a visionary and a social prophet, and communism was his promised land, the ultimate goal for which he prodded the workers to revolt—and the land into which the forces of history would ultimately propel them.

Criticisms of Marx

Since Marx's doctrines have captured the imagination of huge numbers of people, and hundreds of millions have marched under his banners, it is clear that Marx was a remarkable success as a social philosopher and political activist. But what about Marx the economist? Most economists feel that his economic theories have basic flaws, and that many of his economic predictions have gone badly astray. Although there is almost universal admiration for the power and originality of his mind, few economists in the non-Communist world buy his economic doctrines.

Specifically, there are the following problems with his theories:

1. His labor theory of value simply will not hold water. As we have seen in previous chapters, the price of a commodity depends on non-labor costs as well as labor costs. In particular, capital, land, and entrepreneurship contribute to production. Moreover, the price of a commodity depends on the demand for it as well as on its costs. (You will recall that price is determined by the intersection of the demand curve and the supply curve.)

2. Marx's subsistence theory of wages has long been discredited. It simply isn't true that wages are set at the subsistence level. Far from being barely sufficient to keep the worker alive, wages in the United States are high enough to provide the typical worker with a car, television, travel, and a variety of other conveniences. Further, Marx's prediction that the working class would experience greater and greater misery has not been fulfilled. On the contrary, the standard of living of workers in the West has increased at a remarkable rate in the century since Marx wrote *Capital*.

3. His prediction that the rate of profit would fall has been wrong. Instead, the rate of profit has moved up and down, with no clear trend in either direction. And his prediction of greater warfare between capitalists and workers has not materialized either. On the contrary, workers have tended to buy shares in corporations, thus joining the capitalist class. And the lines of demarcation between the working class and the capitalist class have been blurred, not accentuated, by time.

Nonetheless, despite these and other flaws in his theories, Marx was a very important figure in economics. He recognized some of the most important problems of capitalism—in particular the problems of unemployment, income inequality, and monopoly power—and analyzed these problems forcefully and originally. One need not agree with his ideas, or sympathize with some of his followers, to recognize his remarkable talents.

THE SOVIET ECONOMY

Communism in the USSR

The economy of the Soviet Union provided an important example of the application of Marxian theories. By the beginning of the twentieth century, **Marxism** was an international political force of some significance. In 1917, a Marxist-oriented party established itself in Russia. This was the first time any major country went communist. With V. I. Lenin at its helm, the Communist party overthrew the Russian government in November 1917, and set up the Union of Soviet Socialist Republics several years later. The stated goal of the party was to establish Marxian socialism—and eventually communism—in the USSR. When Lenin died in 1924, his place was taken by Josef Stalin, who ruled until his death in 1953. Since the USSR became by far the most economically advanced and the militarily strongest Communist country, we need to understand how its economy worked.

Two characteristics of the Soviet economy should be stressed at the outset:

1. Although Marx seemed to want the state to wither away, the Soviet government was for many years a remarkably hardy perennial. The Kremlin's influence over Russian life is well known. Power was centralized in the hands of a relatively few top officials who made the big decisions about what was produced, how it was to be produced, and who was to receive how much. This contrasts with capitalist economies like ours, where these decisions are made largely in the marketplace.

2. In accord with Marx's views, most productive resources in the Soviet Union were publicly owned. The government owned the factories, mines, equipment, and so on. This too is quite different from the situation in the United States, where most productive resources are privately owned. Specifically, the Soviet government owned practically all industry, most retail and wholesale stores, and most urban housing. Some farms were government-owned, but most were collective farms. The principal case of private ownership in the Soviet Union was the small strip of land each family on a collective farm was allowed to work for itself. In addition, people were allowed to own furniture, clothing, utensils, and sometimes houses.

SOVIET ECONOMIC PLANNING

The Soviet Union's central planners decided what the country would produce. How did they go about making these decisions, what steps did they follow, and who was involved in this process? Before trying to answer these questions, it is important to recognize that the procedures followed by the central planners changed from time to time as they recognized their mistakes and tried to rectify them. Planning and controlling a vast economy like the Soviet Union's is enormously complicated. In the period immediately after the Russian Revolution of 1917, the Communists made some whopping mistakes, but, as time went on, the planners became better able to carry out their jobs.

This is the general procedure that evolved. First, the principal officials of the Communist party made the fundamental decisions as to how much output would be allocated for consumption and how much for investment, which industries would be expanded and which would be cut back. Once these decisions were made, people at a lower level decided the details concerning how various plants should be operated. Then these decisions were transmitted to and carried out by managers, engineers, and workers. This decision-making process was clearly very centralized. During the 1960s, the Soviets began to experiment with greater decentralization, delegating more of the planning to the individual plants and industries, and doing less of it centrally. But these reforms met with resistance, as we shall see below.

Several groups were involved in planning. The top officials of the Communist party set the overall goals for the economy. These goals generally were enunciated in a ***five-year plan,*** showing where the economy should be in five years. For example, in the Soviet Union's Twelfth Five-Year Plan (for 1986–90), one goal was to increase investment in the energy sector by about 35 percent (about 7 percent per year). When the broad goals were decided, the detailed production plans were drawn up by ***Gosplan,*** the State Planning Commission. Gosplan obtained enormous amounts of data from the ministries responsible for the performance of particular industries. These data described production capacities of various productive units and available productive resources. On this basis, Gosplan made up a tentative production plan.

Once Gosplan's tentative plan was formulated, a host of other groups entered the picture. A number of ministries, each concerned with a particular industry, reported to Gosplan in the Soviet administrative hierarchy. These ministries reviewed Gosplan's tentative plan, as did individual plant managers. The purpose of this evaluation was to make sure that the plan was realistic and feasible. Some plant managers argued that the amount they were asked to produce was too high or that the amount of labor and materials they were allocated was too low. Negotiations took place, and suggestions for revision were sent back to Gosplan. Eventually Gosplan produced the final five-year plan.

Economic Planning: A Simple Illustration

The job faced by the Soviet planners was very difficult and complex. Unless you have some appreciation of how tough it was, you cannot understand the difficulties any planned economy must face. Suppose you are handed the job of planning the performance of a small economy consisting of a chemical industry, a coal industry, and an electric power industry. To produce electric power, one needs coal, chemicals, electric power, and labor as inputs. To produce coal, one needs electric power, coal, and labor as inputs. To produce chemicals, one needs chemicals and labor as inputs. Suppose that the country's political rulers have said that in five years they want the country to consume $100 million of electric power, $50 million of coal, and $50 million of chemicals.

It is not easy to decide what production targets to establish for each industry. For one thing the output set for one industry must depend on the output set for another industry because each industry uses another's output. Thus, if you are not careful, one industry will be unable to achieve its target because another industry has produced too little. Suppose that each industry uses the products of the other industries in the proportions shown in Table 19.1. (The second column of figures, for example, states that every dollar's worth of coal requires $.30 worth of electric power, $.10 worth of coal, and $.60 worth of labor.) Under these circumstances, what should the production targets be? The answer isn't obvious. Try it and see. (It can be shown that the production targets must be as follows. In five years, $144 million of coal, $159 million of electric power, and $818 million of chemicals must be produced. For a proof, see pp. A9-A10.)

This illustration gives you some inkling of the problems faced by the Soviet planners—but only an inkling. Our illustration has only three industries, while in fact the Russians have had to deal with thousands. In the illustration, the input-output coefficients (in Table 19.1) were assumed known. In fact, these coefficients change over time and are not very accurately known. In this simple illustration, we can work out the production target for each industry, using straightforward mathematical techniques. The Soviet planning problem was so much bigger and more complicated that it was impossible, even with the most sophisticated mathematical techniques and the biggest computers, to solve their planning problem the way we could solve it for the three-industry economy.

Table 19.1
Amount of Each Input Used per Dollar of Output

| TYPE OF INPUT | TYPE OF OUTPUT | | |
	ELECTRIC POWER	COAL	CHEMICALS
	(dollars)		
Electric	0.1	0.3	0.0
Coal	0.5	0.1	0.0
Chemicals	0.2	0.0	0.9
Labor	0.2	0.6	0.1
Total	1.0	1.0	1.0

PRIORITIES AND PERFORMANCE

To make the planning problem more tractable, the Soviets set higher priorities for certain production goals than for others. Thus they may have set a goal for the production of houses and a goal for the production of missiles, but the production of missiles may have been given higher priority. If trouble arose in meeting this production goal, the planners took resources away from the housing industry to make sure the higher-priority goal was achieved. This made the planner's job a little easier, but did not guarantee that the economy would be very efficient.

The best-laid plans can go awry. To try to prevent this, the Russians had a number of important organizations to check on the performances of plants and managers. First, there was the **Gosbank,** the state-run banking system. When the plan was published, the Gosbank gave the managers of each plant enough money to buy the resources—labor, materials, and so on—allocated to their plant. If the managers ran out of money, they used more resources than the plan called for. Also, when the managers sold the plant's output, the receipts had to be deposited in the Gosbank. If the deposit was less than the value of output specified in the plan, it was clear that the plant had produced less than the plan called for. In this way, the Gosbank kept close tabs on the performance of various plants. Second, the *State Control Commission* had inspectors who went over the records of the Gosbank. Third, officials of the Communist party were expected to report poor performance to the party bosses.

Soviet Managers and Workers

The Soviet economy was a **command economy**—people were told what to do. The managers of an industrial plant were told that to fulfill the plan, they had to produce a certain amount, their **quota.** Moreover, they were authorized to spend a specific amount on wages (they were free to hire labor in the labor market), and to buy a specified amount of raw materials and equipment. Their job was to carry out these orders, but they were not told *how* to run their plant. That was up to them. The Soviets introduced managerial incentives not too different from those in the West. If managers were resourceful and diligent, they may have been able to exceed their quota. In this case the Soviets—like good capitalists—rewarded them with extra pay, and perhaps a promotion. If they were lazy, foolish, or unlucky, they may have fallen short of their quota, which may have led to a pay cut or disgrace.

However, because managers were generally judged on whether or not they met their quotas, certain problems arose. Managers tried to underestimate what their plants could produce in order to get easy quotas. They tried to hoard and conceal materials and labor so that they would appear to use less resources than they did. And they sometimes allowed the quality of their product to decline in order to meet their quota. Moreover, managers were loath to introduce new methods or other innovations because of the risks involved. If a new method did not pan out, it could mean Siberia for the manager. It was better to play it safe, even though this hurt productivity over the long run.

Soviet workers had considerable freedom to determine where they worked. However, farm workers were not allowed to leave the farms, and personnel were not allowed to leave certain projects of great importance to the government. To get work of the right kind done to fulfill the plan, the planners established wage differentials to induce people to do the needed work. This is quite similar to the incentives that prevail under capitalism. In addition, however, other pressures were used to get people to work hard and in accord with the plan. The government provided awards to workers who did very well. The labor unions, which were really part of the state, pushed for higher productivity. And people who performed poorly were fined. Nonetheless, labor problems of various kinds existed. There were many complaints that Soviet workers were unnecessarily late and absent from their jobs, and that labor turnover was very high.

PRICES IN THE USSR

As we have seen in earlier chapters, prices in a market economy allocate resources to promote the goals and satisfactions of the consumers. Obviously, prices in the Soviet Union did not function like this. On the contrary, they were set by the government to promote the goals of the state. Note that there are two fundamental differences here between the United States and the Soviet Union. Prices are set largely by the market in the United States; they were set by the government in the USSR. And prices should promote the goals of consumers in the United States, but promoted the goals of the government in the USSR.

Prices to Producers

More specifically, how were prices set—and how were they used—in the Soviet Union? The answer varies depending on whether one adopts the point of view of a producer or a consumer. First, consider a producer—a plant producing shoes, say. The government set the price of the shoes, as well as the prices of the labor, materials, and other inputs the producer used. The government tried to set these prices so that a firm of average efficiency would run neither a profit nor a loss. Thus the system of prices was used to see whether a producer was relatively efficient or relatively inefficient. If a plant made a profit, this was evidence that it was efficient; a loss was evidence that it was inefficient.

This is no different from capitalism. But in the USSR, prices of inputs did not reflect the relative scarcity of inputs, as they do in capitalistic economies. Moreover, the price system in the USSR did not determine the output of each commodity, as it does under capitalism. Instead, as we saw in the previous section, government planning determined target output levels.

Prices to Consumers

Next, let's consider the prices consumers must pay. The function performed by these prices was quite different from that performed by the prices that producers must pay. While the prices facing producers were used to gauge the producers' efficiency (and how well they perform according to the plan), the prices facing consumers were used to ration the consumer goods that were produced. Thus the price of a commodity to the producer was likely to be quite different from its price to the consumer. For example, the price of a pair of shoes may have been 10 rubles to the producer and 20 rubles to the consumer. Why 20 rubles to the consumer? Because 20 rubles was the price the government felt would equate the amount demanded with the amount being produced.

Consumer prices were set with an eye toward raising the planned revenue needed for investment. The gap between the price to the consumer and the price to the producer was the ***turnover tax.*** The turnover tax rate—100 percent in the case of the shoes, since the difference between the two prices, 10 rubles, was the same as the price to the producer—varied considerably from commodity to commodity. It provided a good deal of the Soviet government's revenue, and was a way to reduce inflationary pressures and make consumer spending fit in with the government's economic plan.

THE DISTRIBUTION OF INCOME

At this point, recall that one of the fundamental tasks of any economic system is to distribute the society's output among the people. Did citizens in the Soviet Union receive income in accord with their needs, as Marx envisioned? The answer clearly is no. The Soviet planners set incomes in accord with the type of work people did, how hard they worked, and how productive they were. The result was a great deal of income inequality in the Soviet Union. If we look only at income from labor, the extent of income inequality was about as great there as in the United States. However, for all types of income (including interest, dividends, and capital gains, none of which existed in the Soviet Union), there was more income inequality in the United States.

It is important to recognize that about three-fourths of all Soviet industrial workers were paid according to **piece rates.** The amount these workers received was determined by how much output they turned out. Thus, to a much greater extent than in the United States, income was tied directly to a person's production. This was an important reason for the considerable income inequality in the USSR. Moreover, the Soviet labor unions did not play the same role American unions do. Whereas wage differentials in the United States have often been narrowed by union pressures, such pressures were not exerted by unions in the USSR. It is very interesting, and understandable, that the Communists emphasized monetary incentives to coax people to produce more.

Income Differentials

In the Soviet Union, as in the United States, occupations differed greatly in pay and status, Distinguished Soviet scientists and professors, leading ballet and opera stars, and important government officials and industrial managers were at the top of the heap. Their incomes were perhaps 20 times as high as that of an unskilled laborer, and they had the good housing, the plush vacations, the cars, and other luxuries that were scarce in the Soviet Union. The unskilled and semiskilled workers got the lowest incomes in the Soviet Union, as they do elsewhere. This doesn't mean, however, that various occupations could not change their position in the salary scale. On the contrary, the Soviet planners pushed wages for various types of work up or down in order to get the labor required to help fulfill the plan.

To put a floor under the living standards of the poor, the Soviet government provided many free services, including education and health care. Also, the government provided other services at a very low price. For example, very low-rent housing—most of it government owned— was available. These programs reduced income inequality by supplementing the incomes of the poor. The turnover tax, discussed above, was used to finance these programs.

SOVIET ECONOMIC GROWTH

A nation's rate of economic growth is often used as an indicator of its performance. Did the Soviet economy grow more rapidly than the economies of the United States and other non-Communist countries? Before trying to

EXAMPLE 19.1   A PEEK BEHIND SOVIET PRICE TAGS

Consider two goods, X and Y, produced and sold in the Soviet Union. The average production cost, factory profit margin, turnover tax, wholesalers' margin, and retail margin of each good were as follows (in rubles):

	GOOD X	GOOD Y
Average cost of production	100	100
Factory's profit margin	5	5
Factory wholesale price	105	105
Turnover tax	50	15
Wholesaler's margin	5	5
Retail margin	10	10
Retail price	170	135

(a) Did consumers value an extra unit of good X more or less than an extra unit of good Y? (b) Was the cost of producing a unit of good X more or less than that of producing a unit of good Y? (c) Given that the ratio of retail price to cost of production was so much higher for good X than for good Y, would the planners increase the output of good X relative to that of good Y? (d) Why was the turnover tax higher for good X than for good Y?

Solution

(a) They valued an extra unit of good X more than an extra unit of good Y, since they were willing to pay 170 rubles for an extra unit of good X but only 135 rubles for an extra unit of good Y. (b) The cost was 100 rubles for both a unit of good X and a unit of good Y. (c) Not if this was counter to their objectives. Output levels were determined to promote the goals of the state. (d) Because the government felt that it had to be higher for good X in order to equate the amount demanded with the amount being produced.

---

answer this question, it is essential to recognize that the United States was far in front of the Soviet Union economically. Although accurate comparisons are difficult, per capita gross national product in the Soviet Union was only a fraction (less than one-half, according to many estimates) of that in the United States. When comparing the growth rates of the two countries, keep this fact in mind.

THE FIFTIES.   In the 1950s, the Soviet Union achieved a very rapid rate of economic growth. American observers watched with some uneasiness as the Soviet gross national product increased at about 7 percent per year, while our own increased much more slowly. This remarkable Soviet performance was partly responsible for President Kennedy's decision in the early 1960s to attempt to increase our own growth rate. One important reason for the rapid Soviet growth was the heavy investment by the Russians in plant and equipment. Investment constituted about 30 percent of gross national product, in contrast to about 15 percent in the United States. Soviet planners kept a tight lid on consumption. Indeed, consumption per capita grew little, if at all, from the late 1920s to the late 1950s. Soviet consumers were not allowed to increase their standard of living. The increases in production went primarily to build factories and equipment and to build military power. Other reasons for the high Soviet growth rate were the fact that the Soviets could—and did—borrow Western technology, and that the Soviet system did not tolerate unemployment.

THE SIXTIES AND SEVENTIES.   In the 1960s and 1970s, the Soviet growth rate seemed to slump. This, together with the fact that many people began to place somewhat less emphasis on the growth rate as a measure of economic performance, resulted in less concern in the United States over the Soviet growth rate, less pressure for government measures to increase our growth rate, and less talk about "growthmanship." According to leading

Kremlin watchers, an important reason for the decline in the Soviet growth rate was the greater emphasis on consumption in the post-Stalin Soviet Union. The Communist leaders began to allocate more to the consumer, and this increase in consumption goods meant a decrease in the production of investment goods, which in turn lowered the growth rate.

THE EIGHTIES AND NINETIES. According to the best available estimates, the Soviet growth rate remained relatively low during the 1980s, a fact which caused considerable concern among Soviet leaders. In 1990, there actually was a decline in real Soviet GNP, as everyone (including the Soviets) said that the Soviet economy was in trouble. For example, although the Soviet Union is the world's largest oil producer, its oil output fell because of outmoded drilling methods and strikes at equipment plants. Unemployment was up, and inflation hit 10 percent annually. In 1991, Soviet leaders solicited economic aid from the West.

At this point, it should be clear that the social mechanisms determining the rate of economic growth in the Soviet Union were entirely different from those that determine the rate of economic growth in the United States. In the Soviet Union, the central planners attempted to determine the growth rate by their decisions on the rate of investment in various industries, the amount spent on research and development, and the rate of expansion of the educational system. In the United States, on the other hand, decision making is decentralized. The American growth rate is determined largely by countless decisions by consumers and producers attempting to reach their own goals.

Soviet industry in the 1980s

EVALUATION OF THE SOVIET ECONOMY

Soviet Economic Performance

In previous sections, we've described the salient features of the Soviet economy. Now let's try to evaluate its performance. Needless to say, any such evaluation must be incomplete. And since we look at the Soviet economy through American eyes, it is sure to be biased—at least in the eyes of many Russians, Chinese, Cubans, and others. But we cannot avoid trying to make such an evaluation, despite the many formidable problems involved.

FREEDOM. One's evaluation of the Soviet economy must depend fundamentally on the value one places on freedom. The USSR was a command economy; to us, its economy was not free. The planners decided what was produced, how it was produced, and who was to get what. Such an economy may sometimes be able to push industrialization and economic growth at a rapid rate, but at a great cost in economic freedom.

EQUITY. It is difficult to say much about the equity of the income distribution, since there is no scientifically valid way to say that one income distribution is better than another. This is an ethical question, which people must answer for themselves. Perhaps the most interesting aspect of the income distribution in the Soviet Union is that it contained so much inequality. There was less difference between the Soviet Union and the Western industrialized countries in the extent of income inequality than one might expect. Thus those who favor more income equality may find less to say for the Soviet economy than might be expected.

EFFICIENCY. The Soviet economy, while it has worked reasonably well at times in the past, turned in a dreadful performance during the 1990s. Many of its problems are well known. First, incentives for innovation were weak. Managers, fearful of not meeting their quotas, often resisted new techniques. Second, since the planners, not the market, dictated what would be produced, goods consumers did not want sometimes were produced. The link between consumers and producers was not as firm as in the Western economies. Third, the use of production quotas and targets led to inefficiency. Thus, if the quota for a pencil factory was expressed in terms of number of pencils, the manager of the factory might reduce the quality or size of the pencils in order to meet the quota. Fourth, since input prices did not reflect relative scarcities, they often gave improper signals to producers. Fifth, the Soviet Union had many setbacks in agriculture. In 1989 and 1990, it continued to import grain, even in the face of substantial harvests. Soviet agriculture seemed to suffer from the fact that many farms were too big, and that there were too few incentives for efficiency.[1]

GORBACHEV'S 1987 ECONOMIC PROPOSALS

On June 25, 1987, Mikhail Gorbachev, the Soviet leader, called for radical changes in the Soviet economy. In a speech to a meeting of the Communist Party's Central Committee, he said that the economy should be reorganized to eliminate the day-to-day management of the economy by powerful agencies like Gosplan, the central planning agency. Instead, these agencies should only set overall guidelines for the economy and ensure that key institutions, such as the military, would receive adequate resources. Put simply, he asserted that factories should no longer have to produce in accord with the plan handed down by Moscow.

Mikhail Gorbachev

Equally radical was his call for an end to the elaborately controlled and subsidized price system in the Soviet Union. He argued that "the whole of our pricing system, including wholesale, purchasing, and retail prices and tariffs, needs to be rebuilt as a package." Under his proposed reforms, factories would deal with each other and sign contracts based on negotiated prices, rather than prices set at the top. They would be encouraged to compete with one another.

Further, it appeared that job security, a central tenet of Soviet socialism, would be less complete. According to the new plan, unnecessary or lazy employees could be laid off, and inefficient enterprises could be closed. Also, there was talk of the reduction of subsidies for meat, bread, dairy products, and housing. In state stores in Moscow and other cities, meat sold at less than half the cost of production. According to Gorbachev, the Soviet Union devoted more than $115 billion a year to subsidies.

Yet another major proposal was that workers have the chance to get rich. Gorbachev argued that "no limit" should be established on a worker's pay, so long as it really is earned. Needless to say, this was a bold proposal in a society where large disparities in income have been widely resented.

---

[1] Responding to this situation, the United States, as well as Canada, Australia, and other countries, has sold many billions of dollars of grain to the Soviets.

PRESSURES FOR ECONOMIC REFORM

According to knowledgeable observers, the 1987 reforms did not have a major impact on the Soviet economic system. For example, although factories were now free to sign contracts with other industrial enterprises, the state could still place an order with a factory and make sure that its order got top priority—because it kept control of the raw materials. Thus a factory making diesel engines could sell its engines to anyone, but only one customer could pay for the engines with consignments of steel—the state. No other source of steel existed.

In 1988, the Soviet Union legalized cooperatives, small businesses that are as close as the nation came to free enterprise. Between 1988 and 1990, their output grew at a very rapid rate. According to some estimates, by 1990 their output constituted about 5 percent of the Soviet Union's gross national product, and the number of persons working at least part-time in cooperatives reached about 4.5 million. Some cooperative entrepreneurs incurred hostility because of their comparatively flamboyant lifestyles, and there were official attempts to confiscate the profits of these new businesses.

During 1989 and 1990, Gorbachev seemed to come closer to advocating a transition to free markets. In March 1990, the Soviet Parliament passed an ownership law which permitted individuals to own small businesses and also permitted companies to be sold to workers in the form of stock. Another law allowed a family to lease its farm for life and to will it to their children. But Gorbachev was unwilling to accept the idea of private property, as understood in the West, and he repeatedly stated that his people were not willing to accept the amount of unemployment and the extent of income inequality that genuinely free markets would entail. (Recall his statements on page 55.)

Also, the fact that many Soviet households had accumulated very large amounts of Soviet currency (during the long period when they had waited for scarce goods to become available) was a problem because, if prices were freed and if appliances and other desired consumption goods were offered for sale, the demand might be so great that inflation would result. This problem was related to the fact that the Soviet government had run large deficits which were financed by pumping billions of rubles into the economy. In early 1991, the Soviet government confiscated all 50-ruble and 100-ruble notes, thus cutting the currency in circulation by perhaps 20 to 30 percent. Also, retail prices for staple goods were increased; for example, the price of bread tripled.

As the Soviet people came to understand more clearly how much lower their standard of living was than in the West, there was increased pressure for economic reform. But any real acceptance of free markets faced resistance and a lack of comprehension from government ministries that would have no reason for existence in a market economy, as well as from conservatives and some military leaders who feared disorder and reductions in their own budgets and prestige. Western (and some Soviet) economists tended to regard the economic reforms proposed in 1990 as being only limited half-measures.

According to many leading economists, what was required was that factories and apartments be sold by the state to private individuals, that state monopolies be broken up, that the formation of new business enterprises be encouraged, that prices be freed, and that more unemployment and disparity of wealth be tolerated. In late 1991, the Soviet Union disintegrated into a number of independent republics. Major economic changes seemed inevitable, but their precise nature was hard for experts to predict.

TEST YOURSELF

1. Before its collapse, did the Soviet Union's rate of economic growth tend to decline? Did its rate of productivity growth (that is, the rate of growth of output relative to input) tend to decline as well? If so, why?

2. Describe the system of economic planning in the Soviet Union. To what extent was this system to be found in the writings of Karl Marx?

3. Discuss the differences between the United States and the Soviet Union in the way in which prices were determined. What were some of the most important economic effects of these differences?

4. Did the state "wither away" in the Soviet version of communism? Explain. What were some of the problems in Soviet planning?

THE CHINESE ECONOMY

In 1949, another of the world's major powers—China—joined the Communist ranks. With Mao Zedong at its head, the Communist army entered Beijing (then Peking), the capital of a nation containing one-fourth of the world's population. China was a poor country, with little capital, little technology, and little education—a less developed country par excellence, despite its ancient civilization. Further, the Communists inherited an economy marred by many years of war with the Japanese. The country needed as much economic growth as possible, and quickly.

The First Five-Year Plan

The Chinese Communists responded with a ruthless drive toward industrialization. China's Five-Year Plan of 1952–57 emphasized investment in heavy industry like steel and machinery and some expansion of light industry. It also called for a massive reorganization of agriculture, involving collective ownership of some farms and transfer of land from the rich to the poor. To permit the high rate of investment called for by the plan, the Chinese government pared consumption to the bone. The Chinese people were asked to work long and hard—for little return in goods and services.

Most observers agree that the plan achieved its goal of rapid economic growth. Even though China's population increased considerably, output per capita increased by about 4 or 5 percent per year during the 1950s. This was an enormous achievement for a country whose economy had been stagnant for centuries. To accomplish these objectives, China adopted measures that seem stern even when compared with the Soviet Union. (China, like the USSR, operated a command economy, but this did not prevent the development of considerable tension between them. To buttress its own position, each nation claimed that the other had abandoned the true faith of Marxism.)

The Great Leap Forward

Having succeeded in pushing the economy ahead in the Five-Year Plan of 1952–57, in 1958 China's leaders launched a more ambitious plan, called the Great Leap Forward. Its aim was to increase per capita output by 25 percent. The large number of underemployed workers in China were to be swept into the employed labor force, and there was to be a great increase in investment. It all sounded very impressive on paper, but it turned out to be a disaster. Despite all the slogans and propaganda, the plan was unrealistic. Literally millions of people were asked to produce steel in primitive furnaces in their back yards. The result was a lot of unusable scrap metal. Also, poor planning directed millions of workers to produce other goods of little or no value. And too many people were ordered to leave agriculture and enter factories, with the result that far too little food was produced.

By 1960, the Great Leap Forward was obviously a failure of catastrophic proportions, and China's leaders had little choice but to alter their policies. In 1961, they published their new economic plan, which called for more emphasis on agriculture and less on industry. Industries that contributed to agricultural productivity—like the tractor industry—would receive more capital, while less would be devoted to industries that did not affect agriculture. Also, higher priority was given to the production of consumer goods for the peasants. Despite the new emphasis, the gains in agricultural production and efficiency seem to have been modest during the 1960s. Apparently, the Great Leap Forward had wreaked so much havoc that it was difficult to get agriculture moving ahead.

Workers in a farm-equipment factory

The Cultural Revolution

The so-called Cultural Revolution that began in 1968 saw large-scale political disorders in Communist China. Because the data on Chinese economic performance are meager and unreliable, even the experts find it difficult to estimate the effects of this social turmoil on the economy. But by 1971, it seemed likely that the economy had recovered in large part from the economic disorders arising from the Cultural Revolution. According to estimates by Thomas Rawski, Chinese industrial production in 1971 was perhaps double what it had been in 1963.

Movements Toward Decentralization, and Back Again

During the late 1970s and early 1980s, China began to move toward a more decentralized economic system where market forces were allowed to play an important role. In December 1978, China's Central Committee approved a new system of incentives for China's 800 million peasants, under which those that produced more were rewarded. The result was a sharp increase in farm output, and China's communes began to break up as individual households became the basic agricultural unit. According to some estimates, per capita food consumption increased by about 50 percent between 1978 and 1987.

In October 1984, China announced sweeping changes in its urban economy. About a million state-owned enterprises were to be given greater independence—and the necessity to compete to survive. Extensive government subsidies for consumer products like food and clothing were to be phased out, central planning was to be limited, and the prices of many products and services were to be determined by supply and demand. By late 1987, many dramatic changes had occurred, although China remained a Communist country.

In 1988, the Chinese government announced a series of stringent measures intended to reduce sharply the role of the free market in economic affairs, and controls were re-imposed on the prices of many commodities. According to China's Communist party chief, these changes occurred because of three problems: inflation, "unfair" distribution of wealth, and corruption in party and governmental institutions. In 1989, industrial output in China grew by only about 7 percent, as compared with 18 percent in the previous year, and the inflation rate fell to under 10 percent. In June 1989, the Chinese government sent tanks into Tiananmen Square in Beijing to crush a rising democracy movement. This event signaled a further step back from liberalization. In 1990, there were reports of slow economic growth in China, but no indications that China's leaders were interested in putting more emphasis on free markets.

DEMOCRATIC SOCIALISM

We have described two brands of communism—Russian and Chinese. And in previous chapters, we have described capitalism. Now we must stress that there are other types of economic systems besides capitalism and communism. One of the most important of these is **democratic socialism,** which has included France's and Sweden's socialist governments and Britain's Labor government, among others. In many ways, the democratic socialist economies occupy a middle ground between our more capitalist system and the Communist systems. They generally favor government ownership of heavy industry like coal and steel (although the fervor for nationalization of such industries has died down in recent years); heavy taxation of the rich; and extensive welfare programs (social security, medical care, and so on); as well as a certain amount of economic planning, rather than the unfettered play of market forces.

But in contrast to the Communists, the democratic socialists generally do not favor violent revolution. Instead, they believe that democratic means should be used to obtain power. A good example is the British Labor government, which came into office after World War II. During the 1920s and 1930s, the Labor party had worked within the existing political system and gained strength. Finally, after the war it got its hands on the reins. Since then the Labor party has remained a major influence in British politics (although it has been in and out of office). As it has gathered further experience, its goals have changed somewhat. Thus, because government ownership of industry seems to have been inefficient, the socialists are much more tolerant of private property, and less interested in nationalizing industry, than they were 40 years ago.

Changes in the United States

To a considerable extent, the more capitalist countries—like the United States—have taken over many of the socialist programs. The United States has moved a long way toward heavy taxation of the rich and toward extensive welfare programs. If Calvin Coolidge could be retrieved from the Great Beyond—and if Silent Cal could be induced to comment—he surely would be impressed (and perhaps dismayed) by how far the United States has traveled toward socialism since his presidency in the 1920s. Even though *planning* is viewed with suspicion in the United States, the government has become more and more involved in various aspects of our economic life, as we have seen in earlier chapters. The adoption by essentially capitalistic countries of many of their programs has taken some of the appeal—and some of the vitality and direction— from the socialists.

RADICAL ECONOMICS

In the United States in recent decades, a new force in economics has appeared: **radical economics.** The radical economists draw heavily on the views of Karl Marx. Looking at the urban, racial, environmental, and poverty problems of today, they argue that the conventional tools of economics are too biased toward maintaining the *status quo* to analyze many of these problems properly. They challenge the methods and assumptions of conventional economics, criticize conventional economists for neglecting many important social problems, and question the reasonableness of many of our society's economic goals.

The analytical framework underlying radical economics consists largely of the following hypotheses. First, following Marx, the radical economists argue that the structure of any society is determined principally by the society's dominant mode of production, and that the most distinctive features of the mode of production under capitalism is the use of the wage-contract, the dominance of impersonal markets, and the private ownership of capital. Second, according to the radical economists, the pressure under capitalism for capital accumulation and riches tends to create a momentum in and of itself, which creates important contradictions and social problems. Third, according to the radical economists, the United States has reached a state of economic development where class struggles are not necessary or rational, since there is enough productive capacity so that all citizens can share adequately in wealth and leisure. To solve existing social problems, the radicals argue that the basic institutions of our society must change. In their eyes, nothing less will suffice.

The flavor of the radical position is well conveyed by this quotation from David Gordon:

> Radicals criticize capitalist society essentially because it evolves irrationally. Its basic mode of production and the structures of its institutions create conflicts which do not need to exist. In the language of economics, it forces "trade-offs" that are not necessary. Fundamentally, radicals argue, capitalism forces a conflict between the aggregate wealth of society (and obviously the enormous wealth of some individuals) and the freedom of most individuals. In another, truly democratic, humanist and socialist society, radicals argue, conditions could be forged in which increases in aggregate social wealth complemented the personal freedom of all individuals. Edwards and MacEwan mention some of the other unnecessary conflicts created (or sustained) by capitalist societies: "income growth versus a meaningful work environment, employment versus stable prices, private versus social costs, public versus private consumption, and income versus leisure." Other conflicts can be specified, but the criticisms gain force in the context of the radical vision of a "better" society. It should be emphasized in discussing the radical vision that many modern socialist radicals, though socialist, do not view most modern socialist countries with great approval. To many Western radicals, the purposes and the realities of the socialist

revolution in Cuba provide the closest manifest approximation to their ideals. Che Guevara, in many ways a more important ideologue of that revolution than Fidel Castro, has often expressed those ideals most eloquently.[2]

Response to Radical Economics

As you would expect, the economics profession has responded in a variety of ways to the emergence of radical economics, with its relatively small number of followers. Some economists have chosen to ignore them, while others, like Nobel laureate Robert Solow of M.I.T., have responded sharply. In Solow's view,

> Radical economics may conceivably be the wave of the future, but I do not think that it is the wave of the present. In fact, to face the issue head on, I think that radical economics as it is practiced contains more cant, not less cant; more role-playing, not less role-playing; less facing of the facts, not more facing of the facts, than conventional economics. In short, we neglected radical economics because it is negligible. There is little evidence that radical political economics is capable of generating a line of normal science, or even that it wants to.[3]

Since radical economists are still engaged in the work that will tell whether theirs is really a contribution to science, it is premature to attempt to evaluate the accuracy or importance of their efforts. Admittedly, they have attracted considerable attention, despite the smallness of their numbers, but attention and agreement are two different things. The vast majority of the economics profession unquestionably would disagree with their conclusions. Most economists do not believe that capitalism should be replaced. Nor do they agree with the radicals' view of how our society works, or with their indictment of conventional economics.

DOES CAPITALISM HAVE A FUTURE?

Most economists today do not seem to believe that our modern version of capitalism is about to wither on the vine. On the contrary, capitalism seems to be gaining ground, particularly in Eastern Europe, while socialism seems stagnant at best. This is particularly noteworthy, since at the end of World War II, many distinguished non-Marxist economists and social seers, as well as the Marxists, were predicting the demise of capitalism and the rise of socialism. One of the most significant developments of the past 45 years has been the extent to which these prophecies have fallen flat on their faces.

Contrary to Marx's predictions, capitalism does not seem on the wane. The essentially capitalistic economies of the world have shown a tremendous vitality, have grown at a relatively rapid rate, and have avoided any deep depressions (although inflation has proved to be a persistent difficulty). This is a great achievement, and one that should be recognized and appreciated. It does not mean that we do not have many problems. On the contrary, much of this book has been devoted to the discussion of our important social problems. But it does mean that our modern version of capitalism seems to be more than holding its own.

[2] D. Gordon, *Problems in Political Economy: An Urban Perspective.* Boston: Heath, 1971, p. 7.
[3] R. Solow, "The State of Economics," *American Economic Review,* May 1971.

TEST YOURSELF

1. "In a field where controlled experimentation is impossible, the relative performance of India and China gives some idea of whether a Communist or a democratic system results in faster economic development." Comment and evaluate.

2. Several years ago, there were complaints in Chinese newspapers that the centralized system of job allocation was unable to find work for all the entrants into the labor force. According to some estimates, about 20 million people were waiting for job assignments. Does this amount to what would be called unemployment in the West? Explain.

3. According to some critics, like Assar Lindbeck, whereas either markets or centralized power can be used to organize a modern economy, the radical economists are against both. How then can an economy like ours be organized?

4. Compare the economic systems of the Soviet Union (prior to its disintegration) and China. To what extent did they depart from Marx's teachings? To what extent were their economic institutions much the same? What were the major differences in the way economic decisions were made? Which of them seemed to perform better economically?

SUMMARY

1. Karl Marx viewed history as a series of class struggles, the present class struggle being between the capitalists, who own the means of production, and the workers. In Marx's view, capitalists and workers struggle because the workers are exploited. Marx, who subscribed to a labor theory of value, believed that the workers create a surplus value, the difference between the value of what they produce and the subsistence wage they receive. Capital formation, in Marx's view, comes about as a consequence of this surplus value.

2. According to Marx, the lot of the workers would inevitably get worse. Consequently, capitalism would eventually be overthrown and succeeded by socialism, then by communism. Socialism would be a "dictatorship of the proletariat." After an unspecified period of time, Marx felt that socialism would give way to communism, which would be characterized by a classless society, the withering away of the state, and the distribution of income according to the principle: "From each according to his ability, to each according to his needs."

3. The Soviet Union, the first country to embrace Marxian socialism, had a command economy where power was concentrated in the hands of a relatively few Communist officials who made the big decisions on what was to be produced, how it was to be produced, and who was to receive how much. The government owned the factories, mines, equipment, and other means of production—and was the primary focus of power.

4. The top Soviet officials established the overall goals for the economy. The detailed production plans to realize these broad goals were drawn up by Gosplan, the State Planning Commission. In 1991, the Soviet Union disintegrated into independent republics, and there were intense pressures for economic reform.

5. In the Soviet Union, the government, not the market, set prices. Prices facing producers were set in such a way that a firm of average efficiency would make neither a profit nor a loss. Prices facing consumers were set to ration the consumer goods produced and to raise the planned revenue needed for investment. The difference between the price to the consumer and the price to the producer was the turnover tax.

6. Another type of Communist system is found in China, which is a very poor country despite its ancient civilization. China's first Five-Year Plan was an ambitious drive toward industrialization that seemed to achieve its objectives, but Mao's Great Leap Forward was a disaster that set back the country's economic development. During the 1970s and 1980s, China began to move toward a more decentralized economic system where market forces were permitted to play an important role; but more recently, it has reduced sharply the role of the free market in its economy.

7. In the United States, radical economics, which is based largely on Marxism, has entered the scene in recent decades. The radical economists challenge the methods and assumptions of conventional economics, and advocate basic institutional change. Many economists question whether radical economics is a contribution to science at all. At present, it is difficult to say, since radical economics is relatively new.

8. The essentially capitalist economies of the world have shown great vitality in the postwar period. They have grown at a relatively rapid rate, and have managed to avoid any deep depressions. Contrary to many predictions of over 40 years ago by some distinguished social seers, our modern version of capitalism seems to be more than holding its own in the world of today, although it obviously is beset by many serious problems.

CONCEPTS FOR REVIEW

Communism

Capitalist

Proletariat

Socialism

Value

Surplus value

Marxism

Five-Year Plan

Gosplan

Gosbank

Command economy

Quota

Turnover tax

Piece rates

Democratic socialism

Radical economics

APPENDICES: DIGGING DEEPER INTO THE ECONOMIST'S TOOL BOX

APPENDIX A: LINEAR PROGRAMMING[1]

In this Appendix, we look at the firm's production problems from a somewhat different angle—that of ***linear programming.*** Linear programming is the most famous of the mathematical programming methods that have come into existence since World War II. It is a technique that permits decision makers to solve maximization and minimization problems where there are certain constraints on what can be done. First used shortly after World War II to help schedule the procurement activities of the United States Air Force, linear programming has become an extremely important part of economic analysis and a very powerful tool for solving managerial problems. Its remarkable growth has been helped along by the development of computers, which can handle the many computations required to solve large linear programming problems.

There are at least two reasons why it is important to re-examine the theory of the firm in terms of linear programming:

1. The programming analysis is more fundamental in one respect than the conventional analysis presented up to this point. The conventional theory is based on the production function, which assumes that the efficient production processes have been determined and given to economists before they attack the problem. But in the real world, economists are usually confronted with a number of *feasible* production processes, and it is very difficult to tell which ones—or which combinations—are *efficient.* The choice of the optimal combination of production processes is an extremely important decision, and it can be analyzed more fully by linear programming.

2. The programming analysis seems to conform more closely to the way managers view production. The language and concepts of linear programming, though abstract and by no means the same as those of management, seem to be closer to those of managers and engineers than the ones used by conventional theory. This means that often it is easier to apply linear programming to many types of production problems in industry and government.

The Linear-Programming View of the Firm

To economists who use linear programming, *the technology available to a firm consists of a finite number of* ***processes,*** *each of which uses inputs and produces one or more outputs.* IBM can choose among a number of different processes to manufacture a computer, and Bethlehem Steel can use a number of processes to manufacture steel. Typically, a firm can use various alternative processes to do a particular job. An important assump-

---

[1] To understand this Appendix, the reader should have covered Chapter 7 (and its Appendix).

tion in linear programming is that *each process uses inputs in fixed proportions.* Consider the case of an automobile manufacturer that, among other things, assembles truck engines. Suppose that one process it can employ is Process X, which uses 10 hours of labor and 1 hour of machine time to assemble 1 truck engine. If this process uses inputs in fixed proportions—as assumed in linear programming—this 10:1 ratio of labor time to machine time must be maintained. It cannot be altered.

Any process can be operated at various activity levels; the **activity level** of a process is the number of units of output produced with the process. If Process X is used to assemble 3 truck engines, its activity level is 3; if it is used to assemble 100 truck engines, its activity level is 100. If the output of any process is varied, it is assumed that the inputs used by the process vary proportionately with the output of the process. Consequently, the amount of any input used by a process equals the activity level of the process—i.e., the number of units of output produced with the process—times the number of units of input the process requires to produce a unit of output. In our example, the amount of labor used by Process X to assemble 5 truck engines is 50 hours, since the process is operated at an activity level of 5, and Process X requires 10 hours of labor to assemble each truck engine.[2]

Linear programming views the firm's production problem as follows. *The firm has certain fixed amounts of a number of inputs at its disposal. Thus a manufacturing firm has available a limited amount of land, managerial labor, raw materials, and equipment of various kinds.* (These limitations on the amounts of various inputs that the firm can use are called **constraints.**) *Each unit of output resulting from a particular process yields the firm a certain amount of profit. This amount of profit varies in general from process to process. Knowing the profit to be made from a unit of output from each process and bearing in mind the limited amounts of inputs at its disposal, the firm must determine the activity level at which each process should be operated to maximize profit.* This is the firm's problem in a nutshell—a linear-programming nutshell, that is.

Removing Defects from Sheet Metal: An Example

No general description of linear programming can give more than a very incomplete idea of the nature of linear programming and its power to solve real-life problems. We can get a somewhat better idea from a simple case study which concerns a metalworking firm that removes defects from sheet metal. Suppose that there are three processes the firm can use—Processes A, B, and C. Process A requires 2 hours of labor and 1 hour of machine time to remove the defects from 1 square foot of sheet metal, Process B does the same job with 1.5 hours of labor and 1.5 hours of machine time, and Process C requires 1.1 hours of labor and 2.2 hours of machine time. The same kind of machine is used for each process.

Assume that the firm has contracted to remove the defects from 100 square feet of sheet metal per week, and that it will receive a price of $10 a square foot for this service. Also assume that the firm must pay $3 per hour for labor and that the cost of an hour of machine time is $2. (The firm is located in a low-wage country, which explains the low wage rate for labor.) Given these circumstances, the firm must decide which process

[2] It is also assumed that, when two or more processes are used simultaneously, they do not interfere with one another or make each other more productive.

or processes it should use to satisfy this contract. Should it use any single process to remove the defects from all 100 square feet of sheet metal per week? If so, which process should it use? Should it use some combination of processes, such as Process A for 50 square feet and Process B for the rest? Which of the myriad of possibilities will maximize the firm's profits?

Since the firm receives $1,000 a week for the work (100 square feet × $10 per square foot) regardless of which processes it uses, the firm will maximize its profits by minimizing its costs. Thus, in this simple case,[3] the problem boils down to determining which process or processes can do the job at least cost. We begin by assuming that the firm can hire all the labor that it wants and that it has plenty of the necessary machines. (This assumption is contrary to our earlier statement that linear programming views the firm as having limited amounts of certain inputs, but we relax this assumption in a later section.) Letting Q_1 be the number of square feet of sheet metal subjected to Process A, Q_2 be the number of square feet subjected to Process B, and Q_3 be the number of square feet subjected to Process C, *the firm's problem can be regarded as the following simple linear programming problem. Choose the lowest possible value for*

$$\text{total cost} = 8.0\,Q_1 + 7.5Q_2 + 7.7Q_3 \qquad (A.1)$$

subject to the constraints —

$$Q_1 + Q_2 + Q_3 = 100 \qquad (A.2)$$

$$Q_1 \geq 0;\ Q_2 \geq 0;\ Q_3 \geq 0. \qquad (A.3)$$

Why should the firm seek the lowest possible value for the expression in Equation (A.1)? Because this expression equals the firm's total weekly costs of doing the job. The cost of each square foot of sheet metal subjected to Process A is $8.00, since Process A requires 2 hours of labor (at $3 per hour) and 1 hour of machine time (at $2 per hour). Thus the total cost of the sheet metal subjected to Process A is $8.0Q_1$. Similarly, the total cost of the sheet metal subjected to Process B is $7.5Q_2$, since the cost of each square foot of sheet metal subjected to Process B is $7.50. And the total cost of the sheet metal subjected to process C is $7.7Q_3$, since the cost of each square foot subjected to Process C is $7.70. Clearly, the total cost of the job is the sum of whatever costs are incurred using each of the processes, which is the expression in Equation (A.1).

Why must the firm conform to the constraints in Equation (A.2) and Inequality (A.3)? Equation (A.2) must hold if the firm is to meet its contract, since it states that the sum of the amounts of sheet metal subjected to each process must equal 100 square feet. That is, $Q_1 + Q_2 + Q_3$ must equal 100. Also, the inequalities in (A.3) must hold. All they say is that the number of square feet of sheet metal subjected to each process must be either zero or more than zero, which certainly must be true. (If you wonder why such an obvious constraint must be specified, remember that electronic computers won't recognize it as being true unless they are told.)

Solving the Problem: No Constraints on Inputs

It is convenient to begin solving the problem by providing a graphic representation of each of the three processes. Since a process is defined to

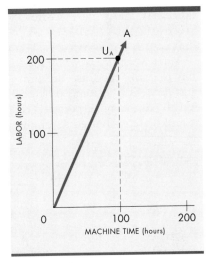

Figure A.1
Graphical Representation of Process A
The ray OA includes all points where labor time is combined with machine time in the ratio of 2:1, since this is the ratio used by Process A. The point U_A corresponds to an output of 100 square feet of sheet metal per week. (Why? Because Process A uses 2 hours of labor and 1 hour of machine time per square foot of sheet metal. Thus 200 hours of labor and 100 hours of machine time are required to produce an output of 100 square feet.)

[3] In general the problem of maximizing profit does not boil down to the minimization of cost because the firm's total revenue is not fixed as it is in this simple case.

have fixed input proportions and since all points where input proportions are unchanged lie along a straight line through the origin, we can represent each process by such a line or **ray**. In Figure A.1, the ray OA represents Process A. Process A uses 2 hours of labor and 1 hour of machine time per square foot of sheet metal—in other words, 2 hours of labor for every hour of machine time. Consequently, the ray OA includes all points where labor time is combined with machine time in the ratio of 2:1.

Two things should be noted about ray OA. First, *each point on this ray implies a certain output level*. For example, Point U_A, where 200 hours of labor and 100 hours of machine time are used, implies an output of 100 square feet of sheet metal per week. Second, *every possible output rate corresponds to some point on this ray*. This is true because all possible points at which labor time is combined with machine time in the ratio of 2:1 are included in the ray OA.

In Figure A.2, we show the rays corresponding to all three processes: OA corresponds to Process A, OB to Process B, and OC to Process C. Each ray is constructed in the same way. Using these rays, we can draw the isoquant corresponding to the output of 100 square feet of sheet metal processed—the curve that includes all input combinations that can produce this amount of output. Focusing first on Processes A and B, point U_A is the point corresponding to an output of 100 square feet of sheet metal with Process A, and Point U_B corresponds to an output of 100 square feet with Process B. Thus *U_A and U_B are points on the isoquant corresponding to an output of 100 square feet of sheet metal*.

Moreover, *any point on the line segment joining U_A and U_B is also on this isoquant*, because the firm can simultaneously use both Process A and Process B to remove defects from a total of 100 square feet of sheet metal. For example, point U_D corresponds to the case in which Processes A and B are each used to remove defects from 50 square feet of the metal;

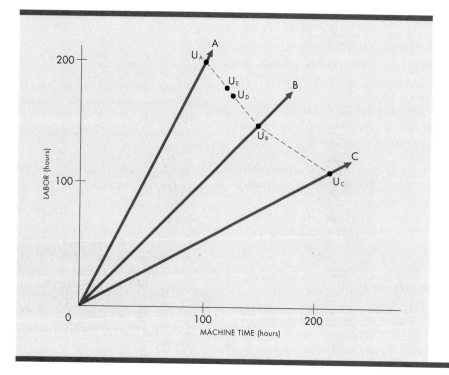

Figure A.2
Graphical Representation of Processes A, B, and C
Ray OA pertains to Process A, ray OB to Process B, and ray OC to Process C. Based on these rays, we derive the isoquant corresponding to an output of 100 square feet per week, $U_A U_B U_C$. (Since Process B uses 1.5 hours of labor and 1.5 hours of machine time per square foot of sheet metal, point U_B is at 150 hours of labor and 150 hours of machine time. Since Process C uses 1.1 hours of labor and 2.2 hours of machine time per square foot of sheet metal, point U_C is at 110 hours of labor and 220 hours of machine time.)

and point U_E corresponds to the case in which Process A is used for 60 square feet and Process B for 40 square feet. By varying the proportion of the total output subjected to each of these two processes, one can obtain all points on the line segment that joins U_A to U_B.

To complete the isoquant, we must recognize the existence of Process C, too. In Figure A.2, U_C is the point corresponding to the use of Process C to remove defects from 100 square feet of sheet metal. Thus U_C *is also a point on this isoquant.* Moreover, *any point on the line segment joining* U_B *and* U_C *is also on this isoquant,* because the firm can simultaneously use both Process B and Process C to remove defects from a total of 100 square feet of sheet metal.[4] Consequently, *the entire isoquant is* $U_A U_B U_C$. Note that this isoquant, like all in linear programming, consists of connected line segments, and, while not smooth, has the same basic shape as the isoquants of conventional theory.

Given the isoquant $U_A U_B U_C$, it is simple to solve the firm's problem. All we have to do is construct Figure A.3, which contains this isoquant as well as some isocost curves, each of which shows all input combinations that cost the firm the same amount. The isocost curves corresponding to $600 and $750 are shown in Figure A.3. To find the input combination that minimizes the cost of removing defects from 100 square feet of sheet metal, we need only follow the procedure recommended in the Appendix to Chapter 7: *find the point on the isoquant that is on the lowest isocost*

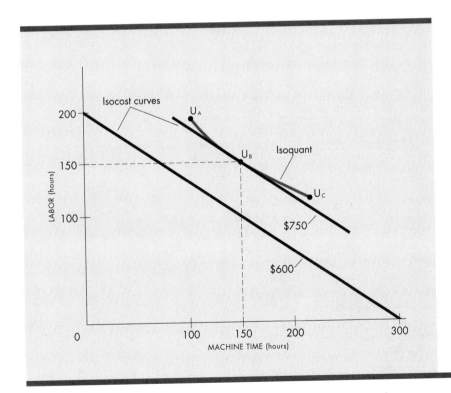

Figure A.3
Isoquant and Isocost Curves
The point on the isoquant $U_A U_B U_C$ that is on the lowest isocost curve is point U_B. (The $600 isocost curve shows all combinations of labor and machine time that can be obtained for $600. The $750 isocost curve shows all combinations of labor and machine time that can be obtained for $750.)

[4] At first glance, one might wonder why the line segment joining U_A to U_C is not part of the isoquant. After all, it too represents various combinations of labor time and machine time that can remove the defects from 100 square feet of sheet metal. This line segment is excluded because the points on it are inefficient. They use as much of one input and more of the other input than some point on $U_A U_B U_C$. Recall from the Appendix to Chapter 7 that an isoquant contains only efficient combinations of inputs.

curve. This is U_B—the point corresponding to the use of Process B alone. Thus the firm should use only Process B, its total costs will be $750, and it will make a profit of $250 per week on the contract, which is the best it can do.

Solving the Problem: Constraint on Machine Time

The foregoing problem is simple—so simple that it can easily be solved outside the framework of linear programming.[5] Let's complicate the problem a bit and make it somewhat more realistic. In the previous section, we assumed that the firm could use all the machine time it wanted—at $2 per hour. But in the short run, the firm is likely to have only a certain number of machines available. It therefore is constrained to use no more than a certain number of machine hours per week. Specifically, suppose that the firm can use no more than 120 hours of machine time per week; this is the maximum capacity of the machines it owns or to which it has access. Now which process or processes should be used to satisfy the contract?

This problem recognizes that the firm has limited amounts of certain inputs in the short run; thus it contains constraints of the sort visualized in the linear-programming view of the firm. The objective is still to minimize the expression in Equation (A.1), and the constraints in Equation (A.2) and Inequality (A.3) must still be met, but there is now a new constraint:

$$Q_1 + 1.5Q_2 + 2.2Q_3 \leq 120. \qquad (A.4)$$

Why? Because the number of hours of machine time per week must be less than (or equal to) 120, and the total number of hours of machine time used per week equals $Q_1 + 1.5Q_2 + 2.2Q_3$.

To see that this is so, recall that the removal of defects from each square foot of sheet metal by Process A requires 1 hour of machine time; thus, since Q_1 is the number of square feet of sheet metal treated per week by Process A, the number of hours of machine time per week used on Process A must also equal Q_1. Similarly, the number of hours of machine time per week used on Process B must equal $1.5Q_2$ since the removal of defects from each square foot of sheet metal by Process B requires 1.5 hours of machine time. Moreover, the number of hours of machine time per week used on Process C must equal $2.2Q_3$ since Process C requires 2.2 hours of machine time per square foot of metal. Thus the *total* amount of machine time used per week on *all* processes must be $Q_1 + 1.5 Q_2 + 2.2 Q_3$.

How can this problem be solved? The constraint in Inequality (A.4) means that many of the points in Figure A.3 are no longer feasible, because they require more than 120 hours per week of machine time. These nonfeasible points are shown in the shaded area of Figure A.4. To solve the problem, we must find that *feasible* point on the isoquant $U_A U_B U_C$ that is on the lowest isocost curve. The feasible points on this isoquant are all on line $U_A U_E$ in Figure A.4. Isocost curves representing costs of $600 and $780 are also shown in Figure A.4. It is evident that the point on $U_A U_E$ that

---

[5] All this problem really entails is a choice among three methods of production, the cost of producing a unit of output being constant for each process and no constraint being placed on the amount that can be produced with a certain process. In such a case, the answer is obvious. Produce the required volume of output with the process with the lowest cost per unit of output. The simplicity of this case does not detract from its usefulness as a first step in the discussion of the nature of linear programming.

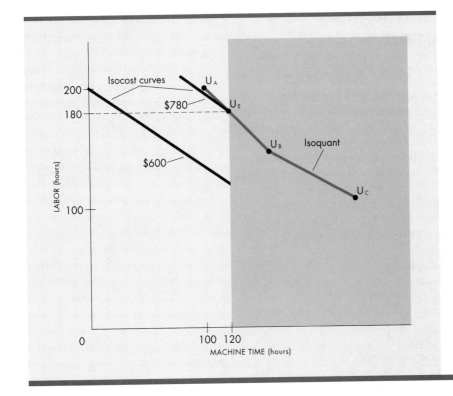

Figure A.4
Isoquant (with Constraint on Machine Time) and Isocost Curves
If the firm cannot use more than 120 hours of machine time per week, the shaded area is no longer feasible, so the feasible point on the isoquant that is on the lowest isocost curve is U_E. (The $780 isocost curve, which is the lowest isocost curve touching the line $U_A U_E$, shows all combinations of labor and machine time that can be obtained for $780.)

is on the lowest isocost curve is U_E. Thus the firm should use 180 hours of labor and 120 machine hours per week—which means that Process A should be used on 60 square feet of sheet metal per week and Process B on 40 square feet.[6] The firm's total cost is $780, and it makes $220 per week—which is the best it can do under these circumstances.

Linear Programming and Management Science

Linear programming is only one of a number of analytical tools that have been developed in the past 40 years to aid decision making in the private and public sectors of the economy. These techniques form the core of **management science** or **operations research,** a very important field that draws on economics and other disciplines. Although management is still very much an art, the development and application of techniques like linear programming are making it more and more a science. Many problems that were "solved" 20 years ago by guesswork and seat-of-the-pants judgment are now being handled by linear programming and other such techniques, with the result that decisions are better, firms are more efficient, and society gets more out of its available resources.

---

[6] Since the total amount of hours of labor used equals 180 hours, $2Q_1 + 1.5Q_2 = 180$. And since the total amount of machine time used equals 120 hours, $Q_1 + 1.5Q_2 = 120$. Solving these two equations simultaneously, $Q_1 = 60$ and $Q_2 = 40$. Thus Process A should be used on 60 square feet and Process B on 40 square feet.

APPENDIX B: GENERAL EQUILIBRIUM ANALYSIS AND INPUT-OUTPUT MODELS[7]

Partial Equilibrium Versus General Equilibrium Analysis

In this book, we looked in detail at the behavior of individual decision-making units and the workings of individual markets. We looked at consumers, at firms, and at various types of product markets and input markets. We almost always viewed each single market in isolation. According to the models we have used, the price and quantity in each such market are determined by supply and demand curves, with these curves drawn on the assumption that other prices are given. Each market is regarded as independent and self-contained for all practical purposes. In particular, it is assumed that *changes in price in the market under consideration do not have serious repercussions on the prices in other markets.* This is *partial equilibrium analysis.*

General equilibrium analysis recognizes that *changes in price may affect other prices, and that the changes in other prices may have an impact on the market under consideration.* No market can adjust to a change in conditions without causing *some* change in other markets, and in some cases this change may be substantial. Suppose that an upward shift occurs in the demand for barley. In previous chapters, it was generally assumed that when the price and output of barley changed in response to this change in conditions, the prices of other products would remain fixed. However, the market for barley is not sealed off from the markets for rye, corn, wheat, and other foodstuffs. (For that matter, it is not completely sealed of from the markets for nonfood products like sewing machines and autos.) Thus the market for barley cannot adjust without disturbing the equilibrium of other markets *and having these disturbances feed back on itself.*

Both partial and general equilibrium analyses are very useful, each in its own way. Partial equilibrium analysis is perfectly adequate when a change in conditions in one market has little repercussion on prices in other markets. Thus, in studying the effects of a proposed excise tax on the production of a certain commodity, we often can assume that prices of other commodities are fixed and remain close to the truth. However, if a change in conditions in one market has important repercussions on other prices, a general equilibrium analysis may be required.

Input-Output Analysis

Input-output analysis, due largely to Nobel laureate Wassily Leontief, puts general equilibrium analysis in a form that is operationally useful to governments and firms faced with a variety of important practical problems. An important feature of input-output analysis is its emphasis on the *interdependence* of the economy. Each industry uses the outputs of other industries as its inputs, and its own output may be used as an input by the same industries whose output it uses. Recognizing this interdependence, input-output analysis attempts to determine the amount each industry must produce so that a specified amount of various final goods will be turned out by the economy. This type of analysis has been used to help predict production requirements to meet estimated demands. Economic planners have applied it to military mobilization, to problems

[7] To understand this Appendix, the reader should have covered Chapter 9.

of economic development in less developed countries, and to many other areas.

To put general equilibrium analysis in a usable form, input-output analysis makes a number of simplifying assumptions. Thus it generally uses as variables the *total* quantity of a particular good demanded or supplied, rather than the quantity demanded by a particular consumer or supplied by a particular firm. This reduces enormously the number of variables and equations in the analysis. Also, in the simpler versions of input-output analysis, it is assumed that consumer demand for all commodities is known. Input-output analysis attempts to find out what can be produced, and the amount of each input and intermediate good that must be employed to produce a given output. It views these questions as largely a matter of technology.

Finally, input-output analysis assumes that inputs are used in *fixed proportions* to produce any product and that there are *constant returns to scale.* This is a key assumption of Leontief's input-output system. In the production of steel, Leontief would assume that, for every ton of steel produced, a certain amount of iron ore, a certain amount of coke, a certain amount of fuel, and so on would be required. The amount of each input required per unit of output is assumed to be the same, whatever the level of output. If a certain amount of iron ore is required to produce 1 million tons of steel, it is assumed that 10 times that amount is required to produce 10 million tons of steel.[8]

A Numerical Example

With some basic algebra, the essentials of input-output analysis are quickly grasped. Suppose that the economy consists of only three industries—coal, chemicals, and electric power. Each industry uses the products of the other industries in the proportions shown in Table B.1. Thus the second column of Table B.1 states that every dollar's worth of coal requires $.30 worth of electric power, $.10 worth of coal, and $.60 worth of labor. (One could just as well carry out the analysis with inputs and outputs measured in physical units—labor-hours or tons per year—as in money.)

This economy has set consumption targets of $100 million of electric power, $50 million of coal, and $50 million of chemicals. Input-output analysis takes up the question: *How much will have to be produced by each industry in order to meet these targets?* Let's begin with coal. If electric power output is E, chemical output is C, and coal output is X ($E, C,$ and X are measured in millions of dollars), it follows from Table B.1 that

$$X = .5E + .1X + 50 \qquad \text{(B.1)}$$

if the target is met. Why? Because the electric power industry needs an amount of coal equal in value to $.5E$, the coal industry needs an amount equal in value to $.1X$ and an amount equal in value to 50 must be produced for consumption. Thus the total output of coal must be equal to the sum of these three terms, as shown in Equation (B.1.)

If we construct similar equations for electric power output and chemi-

Table B.1
Amount of Each Input Used per Dollar of Output (Dollars)

TYPE OF INPUT	TYPE OF OUTPUT		
	ELECTRIC POWER	COAL	CHEMICALS
Electric power	.10	.30	.00
Coal	.50	.10	.00
Chemicals	.20	.00	.90
Labor	.20	.60	.10
Total	1.00	1.00	1.00

[8] In previous chapters, we said that the proportion in which inputs are combined can generally be altered. This is a direct contradiction of the assumption of fixed proportions in input-output analysis. But it often takes a fair amount of time for changes to be made and they are often gradual, with the result that Leontief's assumption of fixed proportions may work reasonably well in the short run.

cal output, we find that

$$E = .1E + .3X + 100 \qquad (B.2)$$
$$C = .2E + .9C + 50 \qquad (B.3)$$

if the targets are to be met. For example, Equation (B.3) must hold because chemical output must equal the amount needed by the electric power industry ($.2E$) plus the amount needed by the chemical industry itself ($.9C$) plus 50 for consumption.

What's the Answer?

Since Equations (B.1) to (B.3) are three equations in three unknowns, X, E, and C, we can solve for the unknowns, which turn out to be $X = 144$, $E = 159$, and $C = 818$. We have answered our question—*$144 million of coal, $159 million of electric power, and $818 million of chemicals must be produced to meet the consumption targets*. We can also find out how much labor will be required to meet these targets, since (according to Table B.1) the total value of labor required equals

$$.2E + .6X + .1C. \qquad (B.4)$$

Substituting the 144, 159, and 818 for X, E, and C, respectively, in Equation (B.4), we find that $200 million of labor is required. If this does not exceed the available labor supply, the solution is feasible; otherwise the targets must be scaled downward.

This simple example illustrates the fundamentals of input-output analysis. It also suggests why the assumption that inputs are used in fixed proportions is so convenient. Without this assumption, the input-output table in Table B.1 would not hold for each output level of the industries. Instead, the numbers in the table would vary depending on how much of each commodity was produced. The added complexity that would arise (without this assumption) is obvious. Even with this assumption, the computational and estimation problems involved in solving large input-output models can be substantial. Government agencies, such as the Departments of Commerce and Labor, have constructed a model of the U.S. economy involving several hundred industries. Usually, however, far fewer industries are included in such models.

Applicability of Input-Output Analysis

Whether input-output analysis can be applied fruitfully in a particular situation depends in part on whether the **production coefficients**—the numbers in Table B.1—remain constant. (See footnote 8.) There are at least two important factors that might cause changes over time in such coefficients. First, changes in technology may change the relative quantities of an input used. For this reason, among others, the amount of coal required to produce many goods decreased considerably in the years since World War II. Second, changes in the relative prices of inputs may result in changes in production coefficients as cheaper inputs are substituted for more expensive ones.

In recent decades, much has been done to implement and extend input-output analysis. Basic research has been conducted by academic economists interested in the quantitative significance of various types of economic interdependence. Applied research has been devoted to formulating techniques that would be useful in decision making in government and business. Other countries have used input-output analysis to determine the relationship of imports and exports to domestic production, as well as to analyze various problems of economic development. Also, business firms have used input-output analysis to forecast their sales.

APPENDIX C: OPTIMAL RESOURCE ALLOCATION AND PERFECT COMPETITION[9]

One of the great goals of economics is to determine how best to allocate society's scarce resources. Questions concerning the optimal allocation of inputs among industries and the optimal distribution of commodities among consumers are general equilibrium problems, since the optimal usage of any input cannot be determined by looking at the market for this input alone, and the optimal output of any commodity cannot be determined by looking at the market for this commodity alone. On the contrary, the optimal allocation of resources between two products depends on the relative strength of the demands for the products and their relative production costs.

The term **welfare economics** covers the branch of economics that studies policy issues concerning the allocation of resources. (Do not confuse welfare economics with the various government "welfare" programs you read about in Chapter 15). It should be stressed from the start that welfare economics, although useful, is certainly no panacea. By itself, welfare economics can seldom provide a clear-cut solution to issues of public policy. But in combination with other disciplines, it can frequently show useful ways to structure and analyze these issues.

Interpersonal Comparisons of Utility

Perhaps the most important limitation of welfare economics stems from the fact that *there is no scientific way to compare the utility level of different individuals*. There is no way to show scientifically that a bottle of Château Haut-Brion will bring you more satisfaction than it will me, or that your backache is worse than mine. This is because there is no scale on which we can measure pleasure or pain so that interpersonal comparisons can be made scientifically. For this reason, the judgment of whether one distribution of income is better than another must be made on ethical, not scientific, grounds. If you receive twice as much income as I do, economists cannot tell us whether this is a better distribution of income than if I receive twice as much income as you do. This is an ethical judgment.

However, most problems of public policy involve changes in the distribution of income. A decision to increase the production of jet aircraft and to reduce the production of railroad locomotives may mean that certain stockholders and workers will gain, while others will lose. Because it is so difficult to tell whether the resulting change in the distribution of income is good or bad, it is correspondingly difficult to conclude whether such a decision is good or bad.

[9] To understand this Appendix the reader should have covered Chapters 4 to 10 of this book.

Faced with this problem, economists have adopted a number of approaches, all of which have significant shortcomings. Some economists have simply paid no attention to the effects of proposed policies on the income distribution. Others have taken the existing income distribution as optimal, while still others have asserted that less unequal income distributions are preferable to more unequal ones. Purists have argued that we really cannot be sure a change is for the better unless it hurts no member of society, while others have suggested that we must accept the judgment of Congress (or the public as a whole) on what is an optimal distribution of income.

For now, the major thing to note is that the conditions for an optimal allocation of resources, described in the following sections, are incomplete, since they say nothing about the optimal income distribution. Whatever the income distribution you or I may consider best on ethical or some other (nonscientific) grounds, the conditions below must be met if resources are to be allocated optimally. Remember, however, that there may be many allocations of resources that meet these conditions, and the choice of which is best will depend on one's feelings about the optimal income distribution.

Optimal Resource Allocation: Condition 1

Fundamentally, there are three necessary conditions for optimal resource allocation. The first pertains to the optimal allocation of commodities among consumers, and states that *the ratio of the marginal utilities of any two goods must be the same for any two consumers who consume both goods.* That is, if the marginal utility of good A is twice that of good B for one consumer, it must also be twice that of good B for any other consumer who consumes both goods. The proof that this condition is necessary to maximize consumer satisfaction is quite simple. We need only note that, if this ratio were unequal for two consumers, both consumers could benefit by trading.

Thus assume that the ratio of the marginal utility of good A to that of good B is 2 for one consumer, but 3 for another consumer. This means that the first consumer regards an additional unit of good A as having the same utility as 2 extra units of good B, whereas the second consumer regards an additional unit of good A as having the same utility as 3 extra units of good B. Then, if the first consumer trades 1 unit of good A for 2.5 units of good B from the second consumer, both are better off. (Why? Because the first consumer receives 2.5 units of good B, which he prefers to 1 unit of good A, and the second consumer receives 1 unit of good A, which she prefers to 2.5 units of good B.)

Optimal Resource Allocation: Condition 2

The second condition, which pertains to the optimal allocation of inputs among producers, states that *the ratio of the marginal products of two inputs must be the same for any pair of producers that use both inputs.* That is, if the marginal product of input 1 is twice that of input 2 in one firm, it must also be twice that of input 2 in any other firm that uses both inputs. If this condition does not hold, total production can be increased merely by reallocating inputs among firms.

To illustrate this, suppose that for the first producer the marginal product of input 1 is twice that of input 2, whereas for the second producer the marginal product of input 1 is three times that of input 2. Then, if the first producer gives 1 unit of input 1 to the second producer in exchange for 2.5 units of input 2, both firms can expand their output. To see this, suppose that the marginal product of input 1 is M_1 for the first producer and M_2 for the second producer. Then the output of the first producer is reduced by M_1 units because of its loss of the unit of input 1, but it is increased by $2.5 \times M_1/2$ units because of its gain of the 2.5 units of input 2, so that on balance its output increases by $M_1/4$ units because of the trade. Similarly, the output of the second producer is increased by M_2 units because it gains the 1 unit of input 1, but it is decreased by $2.5 \times M_2/3$ units because it loses the 2.5 units of input 2, with the consequence that on balance its output increases by $M_2/6$ units because of the trade.

Optimal Resource Allocation: Condition 3

The third condition pertains to the optimal output of a commodity. It states that *any commodity's output level, if it is optimal, must be such that the marginal social benefit from an extra unit of the commodity is equal to its marginal social cost.* If this condition is violated, social welfare can be increased by altering the output level of the commodity. Specifically, if the marginal social benefit from an extra unit of the commodity exceeds its marginal social cost, an increase in the output of the commodity will increase social welfare. (Why? Because the extra social benefit resulting from an extra unit of the commodity outweighs the extra social cost.) And if the marginal social benefit from an extra unit of the commodity is less than marginal social cost, a decrease in the output of the commodity will increase social welfare.

Optimal Resource Allocation: A Case Study

Let's turn now to a case study of how these conditions can be applied to one of our most important commodities—water. If the first condition is to hold, the ratio of the marginal utility of water to that of any other good must be the same for all consumers. To be specific, suppose that the other good is money. Then the ratio of the marginal utility of water to the marginal utility of money must be the same for all consumers. That is, if resources are allocated optimally, *the amount of money a consumer will give up to obtain an extra unit of water must be the same for all consumers.* This follows because the ratio of the marginal utility of good A to the marginal utility of good B equals the number of units of good B that the consumer will give up to get an extra unit of good A.

The common sense underlying this condition has been described well in a study of water resources done at the RAND Corporation:

The RAND Corporation

Suppose that my neighbor and I are both given rights (ration coupons, perhaps) to certain volumes of water, and we wish to consider whether it might be in our mutual interest to trade those water rights between us for other resources—we might as well say for dollars, which we can think of as a generalized claim on other resources like clam chowders, babysitting services, acres of land, or yachts. . . . Now suppose that the last acre-foot of my periodic entitlement is worth $10 at most to me, but my neighbor would be willing to pay anything up to $50 for the right. . . . Eventually, if I transfer the right to him for any compensation between $10 and $50, we will both be better off in terms of our own preferences. . . . But this is not yet the end. Having given up one acre-foot, I will not be inclined to give up another on such easy terms (and) my neighbor is no longer quite so anxious to buy as he was before, since his most urgent need for one more acre-foot has been satisfied. . . . Suppose he is now willing to pay up to $45 (for another acre-foot), while I am willing to sell for anything over $15. Evidently, we should trade again. Obviously, the stopping point is where the last (or marginal) unit of water is valued equally (in terms of the greatest amount of dollars we would be willing to pay) by the two of us . . . . At this point no more mutually advantageous trades are available—and efficiency has been attained.[10]

If people can trade water rights freely—as in this hypothetical case—an efficient allocation of water rights will be achieved. But what if water rights cannot be traded freely, because certain kinds of water uses are given priority over other types of uses, and it is difficult, even impossible, for a low-priority user to purchase water rights from a high-priority user? The effect is to prevent water from being allocated so as to maximize consumer satisfaction. Unfortunately, this question is not merely an academic exercise. It focuses attention on a very practical problem. In fact, there is a wide variety of limitations on the free exchange of water rights in the United States. Thus some legal codes grant certain types of users priority over other types of users, and free exchange of water is limited. Experts believe that these limitations are a serious impediment to the optimal allocation of water resources. (For related material, see Example 13.1 on page 255.)

Perfect Competition and Welfare Maximization

One of the most fundamental findings of economic theory is that a perfectly competitive economy satisfies the three sets of conditions for welfare maximization set forth in previous sections. An argument for competition can be made in various ways. Some people favor it simply because it prevents the undue concentration of power and the exploitation of consumers. But to the economic theorist, the basic argument for a perfectly competitive economy is that such an economy satisfies these three conditions. In this section we prove that this is indeed a fact.

Condition 1—The Ratio of the Marginal Utilities of any Pair of Commodities Must Be the Same for All Consumers Buying Both Commodities. Recall that under perfect competition consumers choose their purchases so that the marginal utility of a commodity is proportional to its price. Since prices, and thus price ratios, are the same for all buyers under perfect competition, it follows that the ratio of the marginal utilities between any pair of commodities must be the same for all consumers. If every consumer can buy bread at $.50 a loaf and butter at $1 a pound, each one will arrange his or her purchases so that the ratio of the marginal utility of butter to that of bread is 2. Thus the ratio will be the same for all consumers—2 for everyone.

To make sure you understand this point, let's consider any two goods, A and B. Based on our discussion in Chapter 5, we know that each consumer will buy amounts of these goods so that

$$\frac{MU_A}{P_A} = \frac{MU_B}{P_B},$$

where MU_A is the marginal utility of good A, MU_B is the marginal utility of good B, P_A is the price of good A, and P_B is the price of good B. Multiply-

[10] J. Hirshleifer, J. Milliman, and J. DeHaven, "The Allocation of Water Supplies," in E. Mansfield (ed.), *Microeconomics: Selected Readings,* 4th ed., New York: Norton, 1982.

ing both sides of this equation by $P_A \div MU_B$, it follows that

$$\frac{MU_A}{MU_B} = \frac{P_A}{P_B}.$$

Since $P_A \div P_B$ is the same for all consumers, $MU_A \div MU_B$ must also be the same for all of them, which means this condition is satisfied.

Condition 2—The Ratio of the Marginal Products of any Pair of Inputs Must Be the Same for All Producers Using Both Inputs. We have already seen in Chapter 7 that under perfect competition producers will choose the quantity of each input so that the ratio of the marginal products of any pair of inputs equals the ratio of the prices of the pair of inputs. Since input prices, and thus price ratios, are the same for all producers under perfect competition, it follows that the ratio of the marginal products must be the same for all producers. If every producer can buy labor services at $8 an hour and machine tool services at $16 an hour, each one will arrange the quantity of its inputs so that the ratio of the marginal product of machine tool service to that of labor is 2. Thus the ratio will be the same for all producers: 2 for each.

To make sure you understand this point, let's consider any two inputs, X and Y. Based on our discussion in Chapter 7, we know that each firm will buy amounts of these inputs so that

$$\frac{MP_X}{P_X} = \frac{MP_Y}{P_Y},$$

where MP_X is the marginal product of input X, MP_Y is the marginal product of input Y, P_X is the price of input X, and P_Y is the price of input Y. Multiplying both sides of this equation by $P_X \div MP_Y$, it follows that

$$\frac{MP_X}{MP_Y} = \frac{P_X}{P_Y}.$$

Since $P_X \div P_Y$ is the same for all firms, $MP_X \div MP_Y$ must also be the same for all of them, which means this condition is satisfied.

Condition 3—The Marginal Social Benefit From an Extra Unit of any Commodity Must Be Equal to Its Marginal Social Cost. Recall from Chapter 9 that under perfect competition firms will choose their outputs so that price equals marginal cost. If a commodity's price is an accurate measure of the marginal social benefit from producing an extra unit of it, and if its marginal cost is an accurate measure of the marginal social cost of producing an extra unit of it, the fact that price is set equal to marginal cost insures that this condition will be met.

Thus, in summary, *all three conditions for optimal resource allocation are satisfied under perfect competition.* This is one principal reason why many economists are so enamored of perfect competition and so wary of monopoly and other market imperfections. If a formerly competitive economy is restructured so that some industries become monopolies, these conditions for optimal resource allocation are no longer met. As we know from Chapter 10, each monopolist produces less than the perfectly competitive industry that it replaces would have produced. Thus too few resources are devoted to the industries that are monopolized, and too many resources are devoted to the industries that remain perfectly competitive. This is one of the economist's chief charges against monopoly. It wastes resources because it results in overallocation of resources to competitive industries and underallocation of resources to monopolistic industries. The result is that society is less well off. Similarly, oligopoly and monopolistic competition are charged with wasting resources, since the conditions for optimal resource allocation are not met there either.

However, in evaluating this result and judging its relevance, one must be careful to note that it stems from a very simple model that ignores such things as technological change and other dynamic considerations, risk and uncertainty, and external economies and diseconomies. Also, there is the so-called *theory of the second-best*, which states that unless *all* of the conditions for optimal resource allocation are met, it may be a mistake to increase the number of such conditions that are fulfilled. Thus piecemeal attempts to preserve or impose competition may do more harm than good.

BRIEF ANSWERS TO ODD-NUMBERED TEST-YOURSELF QUESTIONS*

CHAPTER 1 (P. 8)

1. (a) Iron ore that is still in the ground is included in land. (b) The 747 is capital. (c) These inventories are capital, as explained on p.6. (d) If the University owns the telephone, it is part of the university's capital.

3. Yes, use of the catalyst alters the relationship between inputs of crude oil and the refined oil output. By making the refining process more efficient, the catalyst allows a larger volume of refined oil to be gleaned from a barrel of crude oil. The services of engineers and scientists, as well as research laboratories, were used to obtain the invention.

CHAPTER 1 (P. 16)

1. Preparing the meal costs the family $50.00, assuming that Ms. Harris could see patients during that hour.

3. The $1,000 figure is correct because the remaining cost of room and board must be met whether the student goes to college or works instead.

CHAPTER 2 (P. 23)

1. 2 million bushels generate $2 million; 1 million bushels generates $2 million. No, I would produce 1 million bushels since I can sell it for as much as I can get for 2 million bushels.

3. The demand curve in Figure 2.2 shifts to the right when preferences change in favor of playing tennis.

CHAPTER 2 (P. 36)

1. (a) No. (b) Yes. (c) The combination of 20 million tons of food and 6 million tractors is inside the curve. Possible contributory factors: unemployment, inefficiency, or bad weather.

3. Yes, it is on the new curve. The horizontal intersection is 24 million tons, and the vertical one is 60 million tractors.

---

* The answers provided here are meant only to be brief guides, not complete or exhaustive treatments. Many were contributed by Michael Claudon of Middlebury College, who is responsible for the *Instructor's Manual* accompanying this book.

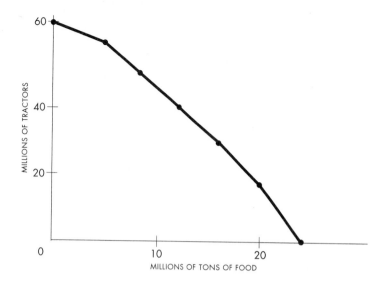

5. This statement is true. Of course, it is also important to note that not all individuals have the same number of votes, because of income inequality.

CHAPTER 3 (P. 46)

1. This is a direct relationship. Supply curves are generally direct relationships.

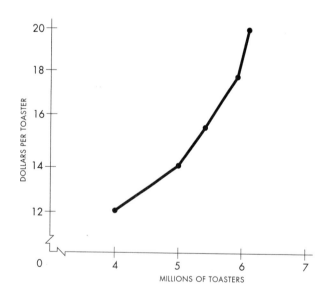

3. No, quantity demanded will exceed quantity supplied. Black markets and queues may arise. If black markets develop, the price may rise above the official price of $14. Such a ceiling might be introduced as part of an anti-inflationary program or to help the poor.

5. Equilibrium price = $3.33, and equilibrium quantity = 6.67 million pounds.

CHAPTER 3 (P. 62)

1. The toaster demand curve shifts: (a) right; (b) right; (c) left; (d) right; (e) no shift.

3. The impact on price is ambiguous. Equilibrium quantity rises.

5. The demand for beets and beet growers' profits rise. The opposite happens for string beans. Bean growers spy beet growers' high profits and plant beets instead of beans. Beet supply rises and string bean supply falls.

CHAPTER 4 (P. 74)

1. About 0.4. About 1.4. Teenagers have lower income than adults.

3. It is price elastic.

CHAPTER 4 (P. 79)

1. (a) not true; (b) not true for some goods; (c) true.

3. Because of changes in tastes and incomes, and greater familiarity with cars, the demand curve may have shifted to the right between 1914 to 1916. Also, the price elasticity of demand may have been different then than in more recent years.

CHAPTER 5 (P. 89)

1. 2 utils. 1 util. Yes.

3. Air is cheap because its marginal utility is quite low. In general, people are willing to pay relatively higher prices for commodities having higher marginal utilities.

CHAPTER 5 (P. 94)

1. The quantity demanded is 26 at a price of $1, 23 at a price of $2, 19 at a price of $3, 14 at a price of $4, and 11 at a price of $5.

3. Bill's consumer's surplus = 6 cents. This number tells us how much more Bill would have been willing to spend on the two apples per day he consumes.

CHAPTER 6 (P. 113)

1. The new olefins plant is not a firm; it is part of Exxon, which is a firm. A proprietorship is unlikely to build such a plant due to a lack of resources.

3. (a) and (b) are false because neither the University of Texas nor Massachusetts General Hospital are run to make profits. (c) is false because many firms are individual proprietorships with only one owner. (d) is false because many stockholders or partners do not participate in the management of the firms of which they are part owners.

5. Bondholders are not owners of the corporation, but stockholders are. Bondholders have lent money to the corporation at an agreed-upon interest rate, whereas stockholders' returns are based upon the profitability of the corporation they own.

CHAPTER 6 (P. 124)

1. All but (h).

3. Column 1: $700,000; Column 2: $1,100,000 and $2,000,000. The owners owe $1,600,000. The owners have contributed $400,000. The difference between current assets and fixed assets is the length of time before they will be converted into cash.

CHAPTER 7 (P. 132)

1.

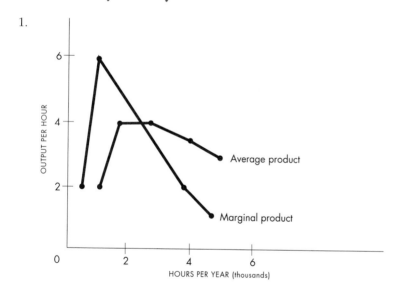

3. Labor is a variable input since the amount of labor is not fixed. Machines are a fixed input; their number cannot be changed during the period.

CHAPTER 7 (P. 137)

1. The price of a unit of capital is $8.00.

3. This does not seem sensible. For one thing, it denies the existence of diminishing marginal returns in the short run.

CHAPTER 8 (P. 151)

1. Total fixed costs = $20,000. The total variable cost of 4 units of output is $500.

3. The average costs are: $20,100, $10,100, $6,767, $5,125, and $4,160.

5. The marginal cost increases with output, since each extra unit of output increases total variable cost by more than the previous one does.

CHAPTER 8 (P. 160)

1. (a) False, the statement describes increasing returns to scale. (b) False, the statement confuses the short run (decreasing marginal returns) with the long run (returns to scale). (c) False, what is important in determining the optimal number of firms in an industry is the shape of the long-run average cost function.

3. No. A linear total cost curve implies constant marginal cost. If the actual marginal costs rise quickly with output, the break-even chart is not likely to be very accurate.

CHAPTER 9 (P. 174)

1. Between 3 and 4 is the optimal output.

3. Marginal cost is unchanged since the total variable cost function is unchanged.

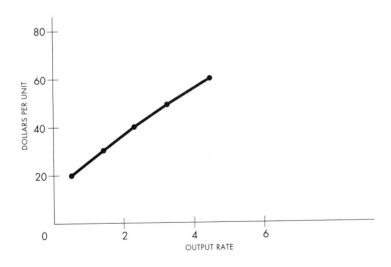

CHAPTER 9 (P. 184)

1. Quantity supplied increases by about 0.1 percent.

3. Price = 1/2. The market period supply curve is vertical.

CHAPTER 10 (P. 198)

1. No, because marginal revenue is negative when demand is price inelastic. Thus a reduction in output will raise total revenue. Since it is also likely to reduce total cost, it will increase profits.

3. Marginal cost equals average variable cost over this range of output. Output will be between 2 and 3 units per year, and price will be between $6,000 and $7,000.

5. Output falls to between 1 and 2 units of output, and price increases to between $7,000 and $8,000.

CHAPTER 10 (P. 205)

1. See the sections in the text on "Perfect Competition and Monopoly: A Comparison" and "The Case Against Monopoly."

3. Perfectly competitive firms can earn high accounting profits if they are more efficient than are other firms. Also, in the short run, they may earn large profits.

CHAPTER 11 (P. 217)

1. Cartel output will be 3,000 units per year.

3. If other members of the cartel hold their prices fixed (in accord with the agreement), each firm has a strong motive for lowering price, expanding sales, and increasing its profits.

CHAPTER 11 (P. 230)

1. Lever Brothers still has a dominant strategy (concentrate on magazines), but Procter and Gamble no longer has a dominant strategy. If Lever Brothers concentrates on TV, Procter and Gamble should concentrate on TV, but if Lever Brothers concentrates on magazines, Procter and Gamble should concentrate on magazines.

3. As the demand curve becomes closer and closer to horizontal, it is tangent to the long-run average cost curve at a point that is closer and closer to the minimum point.

CHAPTER 12 (P. 243)

1. The statement is incorrect. One cannot prove that perfect competition results in an optimal distribution of income. Also, the United States really hasn't opted for perfect competition, which is an abstract model.

3: The four-firm concentration ratio is 90 percent.

CHAPTER 12 (P. 249)

1. The issue is whether firms can escape the discipline of the market. According to this quotation, they can: many (probably most) economists take a different view.

3. The answer should touch on the difficulties of establishing intent and, in some circumstances, its irrelevance.

CHAPTER 13 (P. 263)

1. The maximum is $3,600, since if the wage exceeded this amount, the firm would hire 3, not 4, years of labor. The minimum is $3,000, since if the wage were below this amount, the firm would hire 5, not 4, years of labor. These wage rates seem unrealistically low for the United States at present.

3. If a bonus payment system results in a worker's working harder, thus increasing the firm's sales or productivity, it may increase the firm's profits even though the worker may get paid more because of its existence.

CHAPTER 13 (P. 270)

1. The focus of the answer should be upon whether the unions can be considered as monopolizers of a service.

3. This is not an easy task, as you would need data relating output responses to changes in various types of labor. No, the theory is not useless. Employers must form judgments of some sort on this score.

CHAPTER 14 (P. 283)

1. Borrowers might include: consumers purchasing durable goods, businesses financing inventories, and local, state, and federal governments financing expenditures.

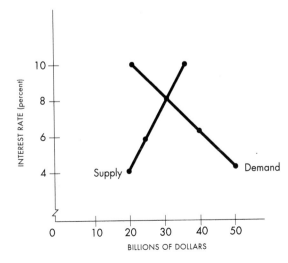

Eight percent is the equilibrium interest rate. If usury laws put a 6 percent ceiling on interest rates, there would be an excess demand for loanable funds.

3. The capitalized value of the asset is $1,000 \div .10 = $10,000.

CHAPTER 14 (P. 291)

1. $1,000 \div (1.08)^2 = $857.34.

3. As indicated in the chapter, much of the apparent increase in labor's share may have little to do with the growth of labor's power. Moreover, in recent years, it is not clear that labor's power has grown. The links to the alleged shortage of capital also are unclear.

CHAPTER 15 (P. 304)

1. The proportion of total income received by families with incomes of $2000 equals $40 \times 2,000 \div (40 \times 2,000 + 30 \times 4,000 + 20 \times 6,000 + 10 \times 10,000) = 19.0$ percent. The proportions received by families with incomes of $4,000, $6,000, and $10,000 are 28.6 percent, 28.6 percent, and 23.8 percent, respectively. Thus the Lorenz curve is as follows:

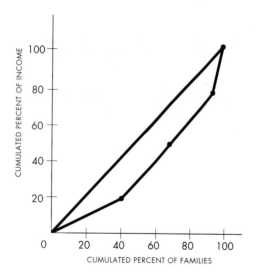

3. (a) Yes, since people can sell assets to maintain consumption. (b) No. (c) Yes.

CHAPTER 15 (P. 312)

1. To be free of dependency, welfare recipients must be able to earn a living. Training and job placement seem to be worthwhile activities, but it may be difficult to train some welfare recipients effectively, since they lack basic education and skills.

3. See p. 305 on "Social Insurance."

CHAPTER 16 (P. 330)

1. It is very difficult in many cases to know whether a certain activity can be performed better by government than private citizens can do for themselves. But the first half of this chapter indicates a number of areas where most economists believe the government has legitimate functions.

3. You can consume the services provided by national defense without depriving another person of also doing so simultaneously. Also, citizens cannot be prevented from benefiting from national expenditures on defense, whether they pay money toward defense or not. A rifle is not a public good; the hallmark of a public good is that it is consumed collectively or jointly.

5. Such activities result in external economies.

CHAPTER 16 (P. 337)

1. The socially optimal output of paper is less than OQ. The supply curve reflecting true social costs lies to the left of the one shown because the latter neglects part of the social cost of paper production.

3. Government programs supported prices of farm products. See pp. 331–37 of the text. Federal government programs have not solved the problem. See the section of the text on "Evaluation of Government Farm Programs."

5. The essential point here is one shared by many government programs, be they protective tariffs or farm subsidies. The benefits of the programs are concentrated on a relatively small and highly organized group of people, while the programs' costs are spread across the population at large.

CHAPTER 17 (P. 353)

1. No, the private costs are less than the social costs because of the required downstream water treatment.

3. The output prevailing after the industry has to reimburse others is more desirable, because it reflects the social costs of paper manufacture.

5. The total cost equals $10 - 2P + 5P = 10 + 3P$. Thus it is minimized when $P = 0$. No.

CHAPTER 18 (P. 364)

1. Yes, since the domestic opportunity cost of a computer is 1,000 cases of wine in the United States and 2,000 cases in France. The United States has a comparative advantage in computers, and France has one in producing wine. The United States is three times as efficient as France in computers, but only 50 percent more efficient in wine production.

3. No, forces of supply and demand will set the price of each good in world markets so that U.S. firms will find it profitable to make and export computers, while French firms will find it profitable to make and export wine.

CHAPTER 18 (P. 376)

1. Yes, protection is likely to reduce, not increase, a country's standard of living. On the other hand, a country's standard of living tends to be directly related to its productivity.

3. The United States may have a comparative advantage in computers, but not in TV sets.

CHAPTER 19 (P. 391)

1. Both declined for reasons given on pp. 388–90.

3. The response should focus on the differences between the price mechanism and planning in solving the basic economic problems (what, how, for whom, and how much growth). See the section on "Prices in the USSR."

CHAPTER 19 (P. 396)

1. Some people have stated this view, but so many factors are not held equal that it is hard to see that very much can be learned from this simple comparison. Nonetheless, comparative studies of this sort, if conducted carefully, can be valuable.

3. For the views of the radical economists on this score, see the section on "Radical Economics."

HOW TO MAKE THE TRANSITION FROM COMMUNISM TO CAPITALISM: THE CASE OF POLAND (PP. 54–56)

1. The central planners must have a great deal of information concerning the technology of each industry, in order to try to determine whether resources should be allocated to one industry or another. Also, the output set for one industry often depends on how much another industry will produce, so the planners must look at the economy as a whole, not just at specific industries in isolation.

2. Because individuals do not own the firms, they often do not receive any substantial reward if they increase the firms' efficiency. Thus, there often is little incentive for their improving resource allocation.

3. If managers receive little reward for innovation or for improved quality of product, they will have little incentive to carry out innovations or to improve quality.

4. Very few people in Poland have sufficient wealth to make a bid, and even if they did, it would be very difficult for them to determine how much to bid since Poland does not have a well-developed price system.

5. Because such subsidies tend to reduce the incentives for managers to reduce costs and to operate efficiently and effectively.

6. If a nation adopts a capitalist system, it must tolerate some bankruptcies and unemployment. Firms that are unsuccessful must be allowed to fail. People who want to leave a particular job must be able to do so. Firms must be able to fire people who cannot succeed at a particular occupation.

"HAS THE UNITED STATES LOST ITS TECHNOLOGICAL EDGE?" (PP. 117–18)

1. If American firms develop and introduce a relatively large proportion of the new products and processes in the industry, take out a relatively large proportion of the significant patents, do a relatively large share of the research and development, and have relatively high levels of productivity, these are signs that the U.S. has a technological lead.

2. It depends to a large extent on how much American industry and government spend (relative to other countries) to advance technology, on the quality of our educational system, the competitiveness of our markets, the alertness of our managers, and a host of other factors.

3. Such an industry may find it difficult to compete with foreign rivals. Jobs may be lost, and profits may decline. Communities where this industry is located may be depressed.

4. In some cases, firms may underinvest in particular types of research and development, because they cannot appropriate the benefits fully. More will be said on this score in Chapter 16.

5. No.

6. Yes. The United States has tried in many ways to promote the eco-

nomic welfare and political stability of its European and Asian allies, as well as other countries. The fact that the technological gap has narrowed is, in many respects, from the point of view of the world as a whole, a healthy sign.

"CAN AMERICAN FIRMS COMPETE?" (PP. 156–58)

1. No. Advertising, styling, finance, and a variety of others.

2. Because it costs money to hold, store, and finance inventories.

3. Because if a worker makes a single item and passes it to the next worker immediately (rather than making a large batch of the items and then passing them on all at once), the first worker will be informed very soon if the next worker finds them defective. Thus the causes of defects tend to be nipped in the bud.

4. Absenteeism raises a firm's costs, because redundant labor must be hired to cover for unexpected absence of workers. Greater incentives can be established to induce workers to reduce absenteeism.

5. Yes. Using Japanese managerial techniques, plants that formerly were relatively inefficient have been transformed into efficient ones without substantial investments in advanced automation.

6. A firm can invest in spotting the causes of product defects, so the problems can be dealt with at the source rather than after the fact.

MEDICAL CARE: CAN ECONOMIC ANALYSIS BE USED? (PP. 323–25)

1. A great many people have health insurance (for example, Blue Cross), much of it paid for by employers.

2. The advantage is that the hospitals have an incentive to reduce costs. One problem is that the hospitals may respond by lowering the quality of health care.

3. Economists feel that more competition would tend to bring down the costs of health care and promote efficiency, as well as reduce the price of health care.

4. It is very difficult to measure the benefits of saving a life or improving the quality of life. Are some lives more valuable than others? Are some extensions of life more beneficial than others?

5. It depends on the valuation one places on this person's life, and while economists can contribute to a discussion of this topic, economics alone cannot provide a full or completely satisfactory answer.

WHAT SHOULD BE DONE ABOUT GLOBAL WARMING? (PP. 350–52)

1. See page 344 for a discussion of why a fee would result in a least-cost reduction in emissions of pollutants. The reasons are essentially the same for a system of transferable emissions permits.

2. Because the costs would outweigh the social benefits, thus reducing the rate of economic growth.

3. Because if some countries limited emissions, but other countries failed to do so, little might be achieved.

4. Because, if only some greenhouse gases are covered, but other greenhouse gases are not covered, little may be achieved.

5. See page 344 for a discussion of why an effluent fee is likely to be less costly than direct government regulation as a means of reducing pollution.

GLOSSARY OF TERMS

Absolute advantage the ability of one country to produce a good or service more cheaply than another country.

Aid to Families with Dependent Children (AFDC) an antipoverty program that provides cash payments to families with children.

Alternative cost the value of what certain resources could have produced had they been used in the best alternative way; also called **opportunity cost.**

American Federation of Labor-Congress of Industrial Organizations (AFL-CIO) a federation of national labor unions formed in 1955 by the merger between the American Federation of Labor (originally a federation of unions organized along craft lines) and the Congress of Industrial Organizations (originally a federation of unions organized along industrial lines).

Antitrust laws legislation (such as the Sherman Act, the Clayton Act, and the Federal Trade Commission Act) intended to promote competition and control monopoly.

Asymmetric information situation where all participants in a market do not have the same information (for example, sellers may know more about the quality of a product than do potential buyers).

Average fixed cost the firm's total fixed cost divided by its output.

Average product of an input total output divided by the amount of input used to produce this amount of output.

Average product of labor total output per unit of labor.

Average total cost the firm's total cost divided by its output; equal to average fixed cost plus average variable cost.

Average variable cost the firm's total variable cost divided by its output.

Backward-bending supply curve for labor a supply curve for labor inputs showing that, beyond some point, increases in price may result in smaller amounts of labor being supplied.

Balance sheet an accounting statement showing the nature of a firm's assets, the claims by creditors on those assets, and the value of the firm's ownership at a certain point in time.

Barometric firm in an oligopolistic industry, any single firm that is the first to make changes in prices, which are then generally accepted by other firms.

Bond a debt (generally long-term) of a firm or government.

Break-even chart a chart that plots a firm's total cost and total revenue, and that shows the output level that must be reached if the firm is to avoid losses.

Budget line a line showing the market baskets that the consumer can purchase, given his or her income and prevailing prices.

Capital resources (such as factory buildings, equipment, raw materials, and inventories) that are created within the economic system for the purpose of producing other goods.

Capitalism an economic system characterized by private ownership of the tools of production; freedom of choice and of enterprise whereby consumers and firms can pursue their own self-interest; competition for sales among producers and resource owners; and reliance on the free market.

Capitalization of assets a method of computing the value of an asset by calculating the present value of the expected future income this asset will produce.

Cartel an open, formal collusive arrangement among firms.

Closed shop a situation where firms can hire only workers who are already union members.

Collective bargaining process of negotiation between the union and management over wages and working conditions.

Collusion a covert arrangement whereby

firms agree on price and output levels in order to decrease competition and increase profits.

Common stock certificate of ownership of a corporation. Holders of common stock are owners of the corporation.

Comparative advantage the law that states that a nation should produce and export goods where its efficiency *relative to other nations* is highest; specialization and trade depend on comparative, not absolute advantage.

Complements commodities that tend to be consumed together, i.e., commodities with a negative cross elasticity of demand such that a decrease in the price of one will result in an increase in the quantity demanded of the other.

Constant returns to scale a long-run situation where, if the firm increases the amount of all inputs by the same proportion, output increases by the same proportion as each of the inputs.

Consumer an individual or household that purchases the goods and services produced by the economic system.

Consumer's surplus the difference between the maximum amount that a consumer would pay for a good or service and what he or she actually pays.

Corporation a fictitious legal person separate and distinct from the stockholders who own it, governed by a board of directors elected by the stockholders.

Cost function the relationship between cost and a firm's level of output, i.e., how much cost a firm will incur at various levels of output.

Council of Economic Advisers a group established by the Employment Act of 1946, whose function is to help the president formulate and assess the economic policies of the government.

Craft union a labor union that includes workers in a particular craft (such as machinists or carpenters).

Cross elasticity of demand the percentage change in the quantity demanded of one commodity resulting from a one percent change in the price of another commodity; may be either positive or negative.

Decreasing returns to scale a long-run situation where, if the firm increases the amount of all inputs by the same proportion, output increases by a smaller proportion than

each of the inputs.

Demand curve for loanable funds a curve showing the quantity of loanable funds that will be demanded at each interest rate.

Depreciation the value of the capital (i.e., plant, equipment, and structures) that is worn out in a year; also called a **capital consumption allowance.**

Derived demand demand for labor and other inputs not as ends in themselves, but as means to produce other things.

Differentiated oligopoly a market structure (such as those for automobiles and machinery) where there are only a few sellers of somewhat different products.

Diffusion process the process by which the use of an innovation spreads from firm to firm and from use to use.

Direct regulation government issue of enforceable rules concerning the conduct of firms.

Diversifiable risk risk that can be avoided by diversification.

Dominant firm in an oligopolistic industry, a single large firm that sets the price for the industry but lets the small firms sell all they want at that price.

Dominant strategy a strategy that is best for a player regardless of what the other player's strategy may be.

Economic profits the excess of a firm's profits over what it could make in other industries.

Economic resources resources that are scarce and thus command a nonzero price.

Economics the study of how resources are allocated among alternative uses to satisfy human wants.

Economies of scale efficiencies that result from carrying out a process (such as production or sales) on a large scale.

Efficiency wage a wage rate that is higher than the perfectly competitive wage. Firms may pay such a wage to reduce shirking and raise worker productivity.

Effluent fee a fee that a polluter must pay to the government for discharging waste.

Equilibrium a situation in which there is no tendency for change.

Equilibrium price a price that shows no tendency for change, because it is the price at which the quantity demanded equals the quantity supplied; the price toward which the actual price of a good always tends to move.

Exchange rate the number of units of one currency that can purchase a unit of another currency.

Excise tax a tax imposed on each unit sold of a particular product, such as cigarettes or liquor.

Explicit cost the cost of resources for which there is an explicit payment.

Exports the goods and services that a nation sells to other nations.

External diseconomy an uncompensated cost to one person or firm resulting from the consumption or output of another person or firm.

External economy an uncompensated benefit to one person or firm resulting from the consumption or output of another person or firm.

Featherbedding a practice whereby a union restricts output per worker in order to increase the amount of labor required to do a certain job.

Firm an organization that produces a good or service for sale in an attempt to make a profit.

Firm's demand curve for labor a curve showing the relationship between the price of labor and the amount of labor demanded by a firm, i.e., the amount of labor that will be demanded by a firm at various wage rates.

Firm's supply curve a curve, usually sloping upward to the right, showing the quantity of output a firm will produce at each price.

Fixed input a resource used in the production process (such as plant and equipment) whose quantity cannot be changed during the particular period under consideration.

Food programs federal antipoverty programs that distribute food to the poor, either directly from surpluses produced by farm programs or indirectly via stamps that can be exchanged for food.

Free resources resources (such as air) that are so abundant that they can be obtained without charge.

Game a competitive situation where two or more players pursue their own interests and no player can dictate the outcome.

Historical cost of assets what a firm actually paid for its assets.

Implicit cost the cost (for which there is no explicit payment) of the resources that are provided by the owner of a firm, measured by what these resources could bring if they were used in their best alternative employment.

Imports the goods and services that a nation buys from other nations.

Income effect the change in the quantity demanded by the consumer of a good due to the change in the consumer's level of utility resulting from a change in the price of the good.

Income elasticity of demand the percentage change in the quantity demanded of a commodity resulting from a one percent increase in total money income (all prices being held constant).

Income statement an accounting statement showing a firm's sales, costs, and profits during a particular period (often a quarter or a year).

Income tax a federal, state, or local tax imposed on personal income and corporate profits.

Increasing returns to scale a long-run situation where, if a firm increases the amount of all inputs by the same proportion, output increases by a larger proportion than each of the inputs.

Indifference curve a curve representing market baskets among which the consumer is indifferent.

Indirect business taxes taxes (such as general sales taxes, excise taxes, and customs duties) that are imposed not directly on the business itself but on its products or services, and hence are treated by firms as costs of production.

Individual demand curve a curve showing the relationship between individual consumer demand and prices, i.e., how much of a good an individual consumer will demand at various prices.

Industrial union a labor union that includes all the workers in a particular plant or industry (such as autos or steel).

Inflation an increase in the general level of prices economy-wide.

Innovation the first commercial application of a new technology.

Innovator a firm that is first to apply a new technology.

Input any resource used in the production process.

Interest the payment of money by borrowers to suppliers of money capital.

Interest rate the annual amount that a borrower must pay for the use of a dollar for a year.

Isocost curve a curve showing the input combinations the firm can obtain for a given expenditure.

Isoquant a curve showing all possible efficient combinations of inputs capable of producing a certain quantity of output.

Labor human effort, both physical and mental, used to produce goods and services.

Labor force the number of people employed plus the number of those unemployed (i.e., actively looking for work and willing to take a job if one were offered).

Labor productivity the average amount of output that can be obtained for every unit of labor.

Land natural resources, including minerals as well as plots of ground, used to produce goods and services.

Law of diminishing marginal returns the principle that if equal increments of a given input are added (the quantities of other inputs being held constant), the resulting increments of product obtained from the extra unit of input (i.e., the marginal product) will begin to decrease beyond some point.

Law of diminishing marginal utility the principle that if a person consumes additional units of a given commodity (the consumption of other commodities being held constant), the resulting increments of utility derived from the extra unit of the commodity (i.e., the commodity's marginal utility) will begin to decrease beyond some point.

Law of increasing cost the principle that as more and more of a good is produced, the production of each additional unit of the good is likely to entail a larger and larger opportunity cost.

Liabilities the debts of a firm.

Local unions labor unions, organized around either craft or industrial lines, that are set up in particular geographical areas or plants, and which may or may not belong to a larger national union.

Long run the period of time during which all of a firm's inputs are variable, i.e., during which the firm could completely change the resources used in the production process.

Long-run average cost function a representation of the minimum average cost of producing various output levels when any desired type or scale of plant can be built.

Lorenz curve a curve that measures income inequality by showing what percentage of the people receive what percentage of total income.

Marginal cost the addition to total cost resulting from the addition of the last unit of output.

Marginal cost pricing a pricing rule whereby the price of a product is set equal to its marginal cost.

Marginal product of an input the addition to total output that results from the addition of an extra unit of input (the quantities of all other inputs being held constant).

Marginal product of labor the additional output resulting from the addition of an extra unit of labor.

Marginal revenue the change in total revenue that results from the addition of one unit to the quantity sold.

Marginal tax rate the proportion of an extra dollar of income that must be paid in taxes.

Marginal utility the additional satisfaction derived from consuming an additional unit of a commodity.

Market a group of firms and individuals that are in touch with each other in order to buy or sell some good or service.

Market demand curve a curve, usually sloping downward to the right, showing the relationship between a product's price and the quantity demanded of the product.

Market demand curve for labor a curve showing the relationship between the price of labor and the total amount of labor demanded in the market.

Market period the relatively short period of time during which the supply of a particular good is fixed and output is unaffected by price.

Market structure the type or organization of a market. Markets differ with regard to the number and size of buyers and sellers in the market, the ease with which new firms can enter, the extent of product differentiation, and other factors.

Market supply curve a curve, usually

sloping upward to the right, showing the relationship between a product's price and the quantity supplied of the product.

Market supply curve for labor a curve showing the relationship between the price of labor and the total amount of labor supplied in the market.

Medicaid a federal program that pays for the health care of the poor.

Medicare a compulsory hospitalization program plus a voluntary insurance plan for doctors' fees for people over 65, included under the Social Security program.

Model a theory composed of assumptions that simplify and abstract from reality, from which conclusions or predictions about the real world are deduced.

Monopolistic competition a market structure in which there are many sellers of somewhat differentiated products, where entry is easy, and where there is no collusion among sellers. Retailing seems to have many of the characteristics of monopolistic competition.

Monopoly a market structure (such as those for public utilities) in which there is only one seller of a product.

Monopsony a market structure (such as that for the single firm that employs all the labor in a company town) in which there is only a single buyer.

Multinational firm a firm that makes direct investments in other countries, and produces and markets its products abroad.

Natural monopoly an industry in which the average costs of producing the product reach a minimum at an output rate large enough to satisfy the entire market, so that competition among firms cannot be sustained and one firm becomes a monopolist.

Negative income tax a system whereby families with incomes below a certain break-even level would receive, rather than make, a government income tax payment.

Nondiversifiable risk risk that cannot be reduced by diversification.

Normative economics economic propositions about what ought to be, or about what a person, organization, or nation ought to do.

Old-age insurance benefits paid under the Social Security program to retired workers, from taxes imposed on both workers and employers.

Oligopoly a market structure (such as those for autos and steel) in which there are only a few sellers of products that can be either identical or differentiated.

Open shop a situation where a firm can hire both union and nonunion workers, with no requirement that nonunion workers ever join a union.

Opportunity cost the value of what certain resources could have produced had they been used in the best alternative way; also called **alternative cost.**

Parity the principle that a farmer should be able to exchange a given quantity of farm output for the same quantity of nonfarm goods and services he would have been able to purchase at some point in the past; in effect, the principle that farm prices should increase at the same rate as the prices of the goods and services that farmers buy.

Partnership a form of business organization whereby two or more people agree to own and conduct a business, with each party contributing some proportion of the capital and/or labor and receiving some proportion of the profit or loss.

Payoff matrix a table showing each player's payoff (often profit) if various strategies are chosen by each player.

Perfect competition a market structure in which there are many sellers of identical products, where no one seller or buyer has control over the price, where entry is easy, and where resources can switch readily from one use to another. Many agricultural markets have many of the characteristics of perfect competition.

Positive economics descriptive statements, propositions, and predictions about the economic world that are generally testable by an appeal to the facts.

Price discrimination the practice whereby one buyer is charged more than another buyer for the same product.

Price elastic the demand for a good if its price elasticity of demand is greater than one.

Price elasticity of demand the percentage change in quantity demanded resulting from a one percent change in price; by convention, always expressed as a positive number.

Price elasticity of supply the percentage change in quantity supplied resulting from a one percent change in price.

Price inelastic the demand for a good if its price elasticity of demand is less than one.

Price leader in an oligopolistic industry, a firm that sets a price that other firms are willing to follow.

Price supports price floors imposed by the government on a certain good.

Price system a system under which every good and service has a price, and which in a purely capitalistic economy carries out the basic functions of an economic system (determining what goods and services will be produced, how the output will be produced, how much of it each person will receive, and what the nation's growth of per capita income will be).

Primary inputs resources (such as labor and land) that are produced outside of the economic system.

Principal-agent problem the problem that arises because managers or workers may pursue their own objectives, even though this reduces the profits of the owners of the firm.

Prisoners' dilemma a situation in which two persons (or firms) would both do better to cooperate than not to cooperate, but where each feels it is in his or her interests not to do so; thus each fares worse than if they cooperated.

Private cost the price paid by the individual user for the use of a resource.

Product differentiation the process by which producers create real or apparent differences between products that perform the same general function.

Product group a group of firms that produce similar products that are fairly close substitutes for one another.

Product market a market where products are bought and sold.

Production function the relationship between the quantities of various inputs used per period of time and the maximum quantity of output that can be produced per period of time, i.e., the most output that existing technology permits the firm to produce from various quantities of inputs.

Production possibilities curve a curve showing the combinations of amounts of various goods that a society can produce with given (fixed) amounts of resources.

Profit the difference between a firm's revenue and its costs.

Progressive tax a tax whereby the rich pay a larger proportion of their income for the tax than do the poor.

Prohibitive tariff a tariff so high that it prevents imports of a good.

Property tax a tax imposed on real estate and/or other property.

Proprietorship a firm owned by a single individual.

Public goods goods and services that can be consumed by one person without diminishing the amount of them that others can consume. Also, there is no way to prevent citizens from consuming public goods whether they pay for them or not.

Public sector the governmental sector of the economy.

Pure rate of interest the interest rate on a riskless loan.

Quota a limit imposed on the amount of a commodity that can be imported annually.

Rate of return the annual profit per dollar invested that business can obtain by building new structures, adding new equipment, or increasing their inventories; the interest rate earned on the investment in a particular asset.

Regressive tax a tax whereby the rich pay a smaller proportion of their income for the tax than do the poor.

Rent in the context of Chapter 14, the return derived from an input that is fixed in supply.

Reproduction cost of assets what the firm would have to pay to replace its assets.

Resource market a market where resources are bought and sold.

Resources inputs used to produce goods and services

Retained earnings the total amount of profit that the stockholders of a corporation have reinvested in the business, rather than withdrawing as dividends.

Rule of reason the idea that not all trusts, but only unreasonable combinations in restraint of trade, require conviction under the antitrust laws.

Sales tax a tax imposed on the goods consumers buy (with the exception, in some states, of food and medical care).

Short run the period of time during which at least one of a firm's inputs (generally its plant and equipment) is fixed.

Social Security a program that imposes taxes on wage earners and employers, and provides old-age, survivors, disability, and medical benefits to workers covered under the Social Security Act.

Substitutes commodities with a positive cross elasticity of demand (that is, a decrease in the price of one commodity will result in a decrease in the quantity demanded of the other commodity).

Substitution effect the change in the quantity demanded (by a consumer) of a commodity resulting from a change in the commodity's price, if the consumer's level of utility is held constant.

Supply curve for loanable funds a curve showing the relationship between the quantity of loanable funds supplied and the pure interest rate.

Tariff a tax imposed by the government on imported goods (designed to cut down on imports and thus protect domestic industry and workers from foreign competition.)

Tax avoidance legal steps taken by taxpayers to reduce their tax bill.

Tax evasion misreporting of income or other illegal steps taken by taxpayers to reduce their tax bill.

Technological change new methods of producing existing products, new designs that make it possible to produce new products, and new techniques of organization, marketing, and management.

Technology society's pool of knowledge concerning how goods and services can be produced from a given amount of resources.

Terms of trade the ratio of an index of export prices to an index of import prices.

Tit-for-tat a strategy in game theory where each player does on this round what the other player did on the previous round.

Total cost the sum of a firm's total fixed cost and total variable cost.

Total fixed cost a firm's total expenditure on fixed inputs per period of time.

Total revenue a firm's total dollar sales volume.

Total variable cost a firm's total expenditure on variable inputs per period of time.

Trading possibilities curve a curve showing the various combinations of products that a nation can get if it specializes in one product and trades that specialty for foreign goods.

Tying contract the practice whereby buyers must purchase other items in order to get the product they want.

Unemployment according to the definition of the Bureau of Labor Statistics, joblessness among people who are actively looking for work and would take a job if one were offered.

Unemployment rate the number of people who are unemployed divided by the number of people in the labor force.

Union shop a situation where firms can hire nonunion workers who must then become union members within a certain length of time after being hired.

Unitary elasticity a price elasticity of demand equal to one.

Utility a number representing the level of satisfaction that a consumer derives from a particular market basket.

Value of the marginal product of labor the marginal product of labor (i.e., the additional output resulting from the addition of an extra unit of labor) multiplied by the product's price.

Variable input a resource used in the production process (such as labor or raw material) whose quantity can be changed during the particular period under consideration.

Wage rate the price of labor.

Photograph Credits

UPI/Bettmann (4, 10, 18, 55, 60, 149, 156, 204, 293, 300, 336, 340); Bureau of Land Management (6); U.S. Department of Labor (6); Sperry New Holland (7); Terry Ashe, *Time Magazine* (12); Courtesy of Princeton University (13, 286); Warder Collection (14, 31, 51, 246, 360, 379, 382, 385); Free-Lance Photo Guild, photo by Kerwin B. Roche (33); Steve Liss, *Time Magazine,* (34); Chris Niedenthal, *Time Magazine* (38); Photo by Amanda Adams (39); United States Department of Agriculture (45, 255, A14); Photo by Jay Bruff (50, 92, 93, 136, 141, 199, 272, 299); Courtesy of Harvard University (54); Photos by Jeremy Townsend (58, 106); Courtesy of Apple Computer, Inc. (65); Ford Archives (72); Courtesy of Crate & Barrel (81); Historical Picture Service (83); Courtesy of Gary Becker (95); Courtesy of IBM (103, 104); Edward C. Topple, NYSE Photographer (108); Wide World Photos (109); Courtesy of the University of Chicago (111, 202); Courtesy of Baruch College/City University of New York (111); Courtesy of William Sharpe (111); Mexican Government Tourism Office (115); Courtesy of AT&T Archives (117, 210, 240); Courtesy of the Philadelphia Phillies (122); Photo by James L. Mairs (123); General Motors (128); Bethlehem Steel Corporation (180); Chicago Mercantile Exchange (165); Courtesy of Charles Plott (178); Iowa Department of Economic Development (181); Washington Apple Commission (182); Federal Energy Regulatory Committee (203); Courtesy of Alfred Kahn (203); United Dairy Industry Association (213); American Honda Motor Company, Inc. (216); Wal-Mart (225); Harvard University Archives (233); Aluminum Corporation of America (238); United States Department of Justice (239); © Pabst Brewing Company, Milwaukee, Wisconsin (244); Courtesy of Michael Spence (260); AFL-CIO News Photo (265); AP/Wide World Photos (266, 389); Courtesy of Jacques E. Levy (281); NYPL Ford Collection (285); Reprinted from the *Journal of Political Economy,* Vol. 81, No. 3, May/June 1973. Copyright © 1973 by the University of Chicago (287); New York Stock Exchange (289); United Nations, S. Potner (303); U. P. Laffont/Sygma (307); Food and Drug Administration (316); Courtesy of SEMATECH (317); Tennessee Valley Authority (319); Courtesy of Henry Aaron (323); Courtesy of Louise Russell (324); © Larry Mulvehill Science Source/Photo Researchers (325); U.S. Air Force Photo (328); Caterpillar Tractor Company (330); National Archives, photo by Joseph Sterling (342); E. I. DuPont de Nemours and Company (343); German Information Center (344); Courtesy of Lester Lave (349); Courtesy of Alan Manne (351); Burt Glinn/Magnum Photos (363); The Picture Group (368, 375); Courtesy of Paul Krugman (369); Courtesy of Avinash Dixit (369); United Nations (380, 388, 392); Rand Corporation (A13).

INDEX

Definitions of terms appear on pages set in **boldface** type.

perfect competition (*continued*)
wage differentials and, 258–59
welfare maximization and, A14–A16
Persian Gulf War, 10, 259, 328
personal income tax, *see* income tax
Philadelphia Inquirer, 328n
piece rates, **386**
Pigou, A. C., 298
players in game theory, **218**
Plaza Accord (1985), 394
Plott, Charles, 178
Poland, capitalism in, 38, 54–56
pollution, 340–53
of air, 277–78, 314, 321, 341–44, 352
direct regulation of, **342**–44
effluent fees and, **343**–45
as external diseconomy, **314,** 321–22,
341–42
public policy toward, 341–46, 349–53
reducing costs of control of, 348
social costs of, 314, 342–44, 345–46,
347–48
U.S. control programs for, 348–49
of water, 314, 321, 340–41, 342–46
zero, 347–48
see also environmental quality
positive economics, normative economics
vs., **15**
poverty, **4**–5, **302**–12
in agricultural sector, 330–31, 336–37
case studies of, 303–4
declining incidence of, 304
"dollar votes" and, 313n
elimination of, 4–5, 308–12
reasons for, 305
war on, 311
see also income inequality; welfare
preferred stock, **107**–9
present value of future income, 280–81
price and output:
of cartels, **211**–12
in long run, 177–80, 195
market period and, **176**
in monopolistic competition, 227–28
in monopoly, 166–77, 192–97, 216–17,
232–33
in perfect competition, 166–71, 176–81,
195–96
in short run, 166–77, 192–97, 216–17,
232–33
price controls (price ceilings), 59–60
price discrimination, **202, 237**
price elasticity of demand, 68–77, **69, 73**–74,
254
calculation of , 69–70
determinants of, 71
farm problem and, 75–76
total money expenditure and, 71–**73**
in U.S., for selected commodities, 71
price elasticity of supply, **175**–76
price floors (price supports), 60, 334–37
price inelastic, 71–**73**
price leadership, **214**
price levels:
changes in market demand curves and,
41–42
changes in market supply curves and,
42–43
exchange rates and, 382–83, 387–89

stability of, as responsibility of government, 316–20
U.S. changes in, 3
see also depression; equilibrium; inflation
prices:
agricultural, 43–48, 60, 66, 68, 74–76,
330–38
equilibrium, *see* equilibrium price
regulation and, 201–5
in Soviet Union, 383, 385
price supports (price floors), 60, 334–37
price system, **32**–35, 38–63
in Broadway theater, 57–59
government regulation vs., 59–62, 313–14,
335–36
limits of, 35–36, 313–16, 337
tasks of economic system and, 32–35,
49–59
see also capitalism
principal-agent problem:
in labor market, 261–63
in profit maximization, 115
prisoner-or-war camp, price system in,
53–57, 176
private costs, 341–**42**
processes in linear programming, **A8**–A9
Procter & Gamble, 218–19, 240
product differentiation, **226,** 230
product group, **227**
production, 49–51
agricultural, 330–35
capital and roundabout methods of,
277–79
production coefficients, **A10**–A11
production function, **116,** 126–28, **127**
average product and, **129**
isoquants and, 138–40
linear programming vs., A1–A3
marginal product and, **129**
production possibilities curve, 23–30, **24,**
358–59
"bowed out" vs. "bowed in" shape of, 26
determination of how goods are produced
and, 26–28
determination of what is produced and,
23–26
economic growth and, 28–30
income distribution and, 28–30
law of increasing cost and, 25–26
productivity, labor, *see* labor productivity
product markets, 60–**61**
products:
circular flows of money and, 60–62
development of, 215–16
market structure and, 163–65
profits, 51, **113**–14, 119–20, 285–86
economic vs. accounting, 122–24
functions of, 53, 288–90
innovation, uncertainty, and monopoly
power and, 53, 287–88
maximization of, 113–14, 115, 167, 170,
179–80, 253, 274
in monopolistic competition, 227–28
in monopoly, 191–96, 287–90
in perfect competition, 163–71, 172–74,
233–34, 253–54
statistics on, 286–87
zero economic, **177**–79
Progress and Poverty (George), 285

prohibitive tariffs, **366**
proletariat, **379,** 380
property taxes, **297,** 324, 329
Proposition 15, 329
proprietorships, **105,** 106
protectionism, 366–67, 370–71, 375–76
public goods, **313**–14, 318–21
public policy, importance of economics in,
13–16
see also government; government expenditures, U.S.
Pure Food and Drug Act (1906), 315
pure rate of interest, **273**

quotas, 362n, 366–67
argument for, 367–68
social costs of, 367
in Soviet Union, **384**–85, 388–89

racial problems, poverty and, 4–5
Radford, R. A., 56n
radical economics, **394**–96
railroads:
government regulation of, 204
market demand curves for, 67–68
RAND Corporation, 95, A13–A14
R and D, *see* research and development
rate of interest, **272**–73
rate of return, **274,** 280–82, 723–24
rational choice, 84–88
Ravenscraft, David, 241
Rawls, John, 300
Rawski, Thomas, 392
Reagan Administration, 259, 308, 328, 329,
352
agricultural aid in, 335–36
antitrust law and, 242
real estate investment, 134
regulation, regulatory agencies, 318
competition reduced by, 189, 203–5,
232–33, 243–49, 314–17
deregulation movement and, 203–5
monopoly and, 188–89, 200–208, 232
price setting by, 201–5
prices increased by, 205
see also specific agencies
regulatory lag, **205**
rent, 283–85
rent control, 60
reproduction costs, 200–201
resale price maintenance, **247**–48
research and development (R and D), 216,
328
see also technological change
resource allocation, 5–6, 342
in monopoly, 196, 198–99, 232
opportunity cost and, **8**–9
in perfect competition, 180–84, 196–97,
A13–A16
Smith's views on, 12
as task of economic sysem, 21–28
welfare economics and, A12–A14
resource markets, 60–**61**
resources, **5**–6, 332
diminishing marginal returns and, **130**–32
economic, **6**–7
efficiency of use of, 53
free, **5**–6
international trade and, 356–57